POLITICAL POWER AND DEMOCRATIC CONTROL IN BRITAIN

Political Power and Democratic Control in Britain sets out an up-to-date and compelling analysis of the huge and flexible powers of the executive in the United Kingdom, and details the absence of effective checks and balances and the inability of Parliament, in particular, to render the executive open and accountable. In doing so, it provides a comprehensive audit of the formal institutions and processes of the British liberal democratic state, including:

- the Prime Minister and cabinet
- the civil service, ministers, bureaucrats and government departments
- executive agencies and the quango state
- elections
- Parliament
- the judiciary and the rule of law.

This study measures democratic practice in the UK specifically against a unique index of democratic criteria, specially constructed by the authors. The index is an important new tool for monitoring the quality of democracy around the world. The book is essential reading for those studying British politics and is equally accessible for the interested general reader.

Stuart Weir is a Senior Research Fellow and Director of the Democratic Audit, University of Essex. He edited the *New Statesman* from 1987 to 1991 and is founder of Charter 88. **David Beetham** is Professor of Politics and Director of the Centre for Democratisation Studies, University of Leeds.

The Democratic Audit is based at the Human Rights Centre, University of Essex. *Political Power and Democratic Control in Britain* is the second of the Audit's two bench-mark studies of democracy and political freedom in the UK. The first volume, *The Three Pillars of Liberty*, on political and civil rights, also published by Routledge, has been widely praised as an outstanding study. The Democratic Audit has also published influential studies of quangos and the British electoral system, and undertakes international consultancy and educational work.

Political Power and Democratic Control in Britain

Stuart Weir and David Beetham

The Democratic Audit of the United Kingdom

ROUTLEDGE

London and New York

First published 1999
by Routledge
11 New Fetter Lane, London EC4P 4EE

Simultaneously published in the USA and Canada
by Routledge
29 West 35th Street, New York, NY 10001

Typeset in Baskerville by
The Florence Group, Stoodleigh, Devon

Printed and bound in Great Britain by
T.J. International Ltd, Padstow, Cornwall

British Library Cataloguing in Publication Data
A catalogue record for this book is available from the British Library

Library of Congress Cataloguing in Publication Data
A catalogue record for this book has been requested

ISBN 0–415–09643–X (hbk)
ISBN 0–415–09644–8 (pbk)

Contents

List of Figures, Tables and Boxes

Figures

Tables

Boxes

Foreword

The election of Tony Blair's Labour government in May 1997 at once raised the public's confidence in the way this country is governed. Public confidence in British government, as measured by opinion polls, had been falling sharply through the late 1980s and 1990s and there was a widespread and persistent sense of unease, both about standards in public life and more widely, about the governing institutions and democratic practice of the state (see the Rowntree Reform Trust *State of the Nation* polls). The incidence of sleaze, unjustifiable patronage, and undemocratic practice under the Thatcher and Major governments was unarguable, and the weakness of the Major government intensified the sense of public disquiet. We were undoubtedly being badly governed. But was the wider concern about the governing system itself justified? Had Britain, which had always been held up to others, rightly or wrongly, as a model of democracy, fallen behind the standards of democratic and effective government of other western nations? In short, how free and democratic were we?

The Democratic Audit of the United Kingdom seeks to provide systematic and robust answers to these questions, using an index of rigorous criteria and standards for assessing the quality of British democracy. These build on internationally accepted criteria for democracy, but go further. Existing criteria tend to regard democracy as a matter of free and fair elections on the one hand, and civil and political liberties on the other. We also measure how responsive and accountable government is between elections, and how much power it is willing to share with ordinary people. In this respect our criteria are, and we think rightly, more rigorous and comprehensive than any others. They are also in tune with the wishes of the British people who feel that they have too little power between elections, as the polling firm ICM have discovered, and would like to have a great deal more.

It may be thought that the election of the Blair government, with a substantial programme of democratic reforms, has made this democratic audit redundant. After all, this is a self-proclaimed 'People's Government', intent on restoring trust between government and the people, and consulting and carrying people with them on major policy changes. Its reform programme acknowledges the legitimacy of public disquiet about the way we are governed, and shows its determination to 'clean up' and 'modernise' British politics. Power is being devolved to the peoples of Scotland, Wales and Northern Ireland, and London is to have its own government again. Doesn't this demonstrate the fabled flexibility of our governing arrangements, and their capacity for self-renewal?

In our view however, the Blair reform agenda makes this audit even more necessary. To begin with, though far-reaching in many respects, the agenda hardly touches on the key problem of British government: the enormous powers concentrated in the hands of the central executive. 'Modernising' the procedures of the House of Commons rather than strengthening its ability to call the executive to account; improving the coordination of government through an 'enforcer' in the Cabinet Office; extending the power of the Treasury over other ministers and departments; sharpening government's public relations machinery; removing hereditary peers from the House of Lords and leaving appointed peers in charge: it is arguable that all these measures tend to increase the powers of the Prime Minister and the executive rather than making British government more open and accountable.

Further, the inheritance that Blair and his colleagues entered into in May 1997 will have a considerable influence on their conduct. British government is shot through with a culture of strong and flexible government, pre-democratic in significant respects, and is very poor at consulting the public and even worse at enabling them to participate in making policies and decisions at all levels. It will take a marked exercise of political will for the government to fulfil its own pledges to consult people to democratise rather than simply 'modernise' the way they govern. Yet the signs are that Blair and his ministers have little interest or belief in the programme of democratic reforms, most of them legacies from the era of the late Labour leader, John Smith; and that Blair himself is more of a populist than pluralist (in the sense that he believes he can identify the popular will rather than perceives the need for checks and balances within the British governing system which allow people to express their own wills directly).

This book describes the inheritance that Labour came into in May 1997 (though partially updated), and thus spells out the governing powers that the government has at its disposal and the prevailing attitudes which will influence how they are used. This historical point of reference is therefore vital to measuring exactly how democratic the Labour government will prove to be, and how Parliament, the judiciary and other agencies respond to the challenge of making the new government open and accountable. It provides benchmarks with which to assess how Labour's reforms work out in practice and offers standards for good democratic practice by the Prime Minister, ministers and bureaucrats, MPs and judges.

This is a companion volume to *The Three Pillars of Liberty*, also published by Routledge, which provided the most systematic assessment so far of the condition of civil and political rights in the United Kingdom. The publication of that volume first reflected our belief that any inquiry into democracy should begin with the citizen, and with the conditions which empower citizens in the political process, public life and the associations of civil society. This volume systematically examines Britain's electoral and governing arrangements from the same perspective. Why should these arrangements matter to anyone outside the political class itself, and the so-called 'chattering classes'? Our conviction is that the democratic character of government matters to ordinary citizens for a variety of reasons. It affects the quality of political decision-making and its responsiveness to people's needs. It determines how people experience their everyday relationship to the agencies of the state, and their trust and confidence in them. More intangibly, but equally important, it affects how we see ourselves as a people, and shapes what kind of people we are.

Stuart Weir
David Beetham

Acknowledgements

This volume owes a great deal to the advice and generosity of a number of scholars and individuals who have been supportive of the Democratic Audit of the United Kingdom from its origins in 1993. Lord Smith of Clifton, Vice-Chancellor of the University of Ulster, had the idea of a 'democratic audit' in the first place and has been a source of advice for the Democratic Audit ever since.

The idea of a Democratic Audit was developed into a fully-fledged enterprise by three of us who remain central to its activities: Professor Kevin Boyle, director of the Human Rights Centre, University of Essex, which is the home of the Audit; Stuart Weir, director of the Audit and a Senior Research Fellow at the Centre; and David Beetham, Professor of Politics at the University of Leeds.

Kevin Boyle, the academic editor of the whole Democratic Audit project, has given unstintingly of his time and expertise in making the Audit into a viable and academically sound institution. We also received valuable advice early on from Professor Dawn Oliver, of the Faculty of Laws, University College, London; from Anthony Barnett, then convenor of Charter 88; and from members of the Law, Government and Politics Departments at the University of Essex; and various ad-hoc advisory groups. Anthony Barnett wrote the original bid to our sponsors, the Joseph Rowntree Charitable Trust, which won us the contract to act as its proactive research arm on democratic matters.

This book is the second of two companion studies of the state of political freedom and democratic practice in the UK. The first, *The Three Pillars of Liberty* (Routledge 1996), by Francesca Klug, Keir Starmer and Stuart Weir, audited the protection of political and civil rights in the UK against an index of international human rights standards. This book audits the conduct of government and Britain's democratic institutions against a set of 'democratic criteria' (see Chapter 1). These two volumes are intended to be 'bench-mark' studies against which we can audit the progress of political freedom and democracy in the UK at regular intervals hereafter.

This volume is very much the product of collaboration, of the two authors themselves, and also of a wide range of academics and others. David Beetham conceived of the democratic criteria around which the book is organised and wrote the first draft of these criteria. They have since been developed in practice by the two authors, both in the writing of this book and through joint teaching sessions with international groups of students on courses run for the British Council by the Human Rights Centre, at Essex, and elsewhere. As for the book itself, Stuart Weir is responsible for organising the material, conducting most of the research, and writing and editing it; David Beetham wrote the first draft of Chapter 1, and kept a vigilant eye on its arguments and the use of the criteria, commenting and drafting passages throughout the book. The Foreword and Conclusions were jointly written.

We are grateful to a number of scholars for their assistance in the preparation of the book. We commissioned working papers from a variety of people on aspects of democratic practice in the United Kingdom and organised a seminar at which they debated the main themes and gave freely of their ideas and advice. These papers and the seminar covered a wider range of issues than this book does or could, but they provided a valuable base from which we were able to construct this audit. Some working papers have also proved valuable in writing the book. We cannot fairly attribute any one chapter neatly to any of these individual contributors because ideas, data and arguments have been organised and positioned to conform to the dictates of the democratic criteria, and working papers have been cut, added to and amended.

However, we owe, in order of chapters, a considerable debt to: historian Stephen Howe, Ruskin College, Oxford, for a brilliant essay on the political history of the United Kingdom, on which much of Chapter 1 is based; Dr Helen Margetts, Birkbeck College, London, and Professor Patrick Dunleavy, London School of Economics, with whom Stuart Weir has worked for six years on electoral systems, for much of the material in Chapter 3, and Patrick Dunleavy and Helen Margetts of LSE Public Policy Group for permission to reproduce Figures 3.1 and 3.2 (any later application by any other party to Routledge to reproduce the figures should be referred to the LSE Public Policy Group, LSE, Houghton Street, London WC2A 2AE); Patrick Dunleavy for a radical background essay on the executive, which underlies much of Part 2; Wendy Hall, the Audit's former research officer, with whom Stuart Weir studied the quango state, for material and data on quangos in Chapters 8 and 9; David Byrne, University of Durham, for a perceptive briefing paper on regional government in England; Dr Martin Smith, Sheffield University, for a background paper on external interests in government, which provides the core of Chapter 10; Kevin Theakston, Leeds University, for a thoughtful and thorough analysis of the civil service, which we have drawn upon for Chapter 7; Richard Norton-Taylor, Whitehall correspondent of the *Guardian*, for a masterly guide to the security services, which appears in truncated form in Chapters 7 and 14; Professor David Judge, University of Strathclyde, for a treasure house of ideas and information on Parliament, on which Chapters 13 and 14 draw heavily; and Maurice Sunkin, Department of Law, Essex, and Professor Dawn Oliver, Faculty of Laws, UCL, respectively, for drafts on judicial review and the rule of law, which frame the whole of Chapter 15. Professor Patrick Birkinshaw, Hull University, and James Cornford, chairman of the Campaign for Freedom of Information, provided detailed advice on freedom of information in Britain.

Tony Barker, of the Department of Government, Essex, has been a true friend to this enterprise. He has read and commented on the whole of Parts 2 and 3, and the Conclusions. His advice has been invaluable, and all the more so for being delivered with wit as well as knowledge. Helen Margetts and David Farrell, University of Manchester, commented knowledgeably on Part 1 on elections. Professor John Stewart, School of Public Policy, Birmingham University, advised the Audit when we began our studies of quangos, and again drew upon his fund of knowledge about local government and quangos to guide us on Chapters 8 and 9. Kevin Theakston gave us the benefit of his experience in commenting on Chapters 7 and 11. Keir Starmer advised on Chapter 15, and Francesca Klug and Lord Smith of Clifton on the Conclusions.

The book draws upon the work of two research officers at the Democratic Audit, Wendy Hall and Iain Byrne. Anjuli Veall has provided last-minute research checks. Jack Kneeshaw, University of Essex, carried out a discrete research project on manifestos for Chapter 5.

All authors must thank the scholars, colleagues and others who have made contributions, direct and indirect, to their work. The Democratic Audit aims to be a collegiate enterprise, and we have been fortunate in working within a close network of scholars, journalists and others. Among those who have given us their time and advice whom we have not credited above are Professors Ian Budge and Francoise Hampson, both of the University of Essex; Professor David Donnison, Glasgow University; Professor Gabriele Ganz, Southampton University; Professor David Held, Open University; Professor Paul Hirst, Birkbeck College, London; Professor David Marsh, University of Birmingham; Professor Elizabeth Meehan, Queen's College, Belfast; James Mitchell, University of Strathclyde; Sir Patrick Nairne, Chancellor of Essex University; John Osmond, Institute for Welsh Studies, Cardiff; Professor Donald Shell, University of Bristol; and Colin Warbrick, Sheffield University. Though our base is at the Human Rights Centre, University of Essex, 27 academics from 16 other universities and academic institutions have contributed to the Audit's activities. Thanks also to John Bird and John Fortune, and Vera Productions Limited, for their permission to let us use copyright material from their sketch on the 1997 general election broadcast on Channel 4 TV.

We must add the usual disclaimer. While several of the above have prevented us from misinterpreting information and making errors, those errors which remain are our responsibility. We should be interested to hear from anyone who would like to comment on this book's contents, as we are committed to a follow-up study after the current Labour government's first term of office.

Kevin Boyle joins us in expressing the thanks we owe to the Joseph Rowntree Charitable Trust and members of its Democratic Panel, past and present, and especially to Grigor McClelland and David Shutt, successive chairmen of the Panel, and Steve Burkeman, secretary of the Trust, an unfailingly supportive presence.

Caroline Wintersgill and Patrick Proctor, our editors at Routledge, have been enthusiastic and very patient. We would also like to acknowledge the administrative support provided by Wendy Fryer, Alison Jolly and Anne Slowgrove, at the Human Rights Centre.

Finally, we must express our appreciation of partners, children and friends who continue to make our lives away from word-processors, seminar rooms, telephone and e-mail far richer than we deserve.

Stuart Weir
David Beetham

List of Abbreviations and Acronyms

ACAS	Advisory, Conciliation and Arbitration Service
AMS	Additional Member System
ANDPB	Advisory Non-Departmental Public Body
ASA	Advertising Standards Authority
ATP	Aid and Trade Provisions
AV	Alternative Vote
BBC	British Broadcasting Commission
BOSS	South African intelligence agency
BOTB	British Overseas Trade Board
BRF	British Road Federation
BSC	British Steel Corporation
BSE	Bovine spongiform encephalopathy
CA	Consumers' Association
C&AG	Comptroller and Auditor General
CBI	Confederation of British Industry
CFI	Campaign for Freedom of Information
CID	Committee of Imperial Defence
CIPFA	Chartered Institute of Public Finance and Accountancy
CJD	Creutzfeldt-Jakob Disease
COT	Committee on the Toxicity of Chemicals in Food, Consumer Products and the Environment
CPA	Commissioner for Public Appointments
CSD	Civil Service Department
CSM	Committee on the Safety of Medicines
DA	Democratic Audit
DAC	Democratic Audit Criterion
DA Papers	Democratic Audit Papers (see bibliography for details)
DA Volume No. 1	*The Three Pillars of Liberty: Political Rights and Freedoms in the UK* by F. Klug, K. Starmer and S. Weir (Routledge, 1996)
DERA	Defence Evaluation Research Agency
DfID	Department for International Development
DH	Department of Health
DIS	Defence Intelligence Staff
DTI	Department of Trade and Industry
DV	Deviation from proportionality

ECHR	European Court of Human Rights
EDH	Cabinet committee on home and social affairs
EDP	Cabinet committee on economic affairs
EEC	European Economic Community
EMU	European Monetary Unit
EOC	Equal Opportunities Commission
ERM	Exchange rate mechanism
FAS	Funding Agency for Schools
FCO	Foreign and Commonwealth Office
FDA	First Division Association
FDF	Food and Drinks Federation
FEFA	Further Education Funding Agency
FEFC	Further Education Funding Council
GCHQ	Government Communications Headquarters
GIS	Government Information Service
HAC	Home Affairs Committee
HC	House of Commons
HC Deb	House of Commons Debates (followed by Hansard reference)
HC Deb (WA)	House of Commons Written Answer (followed by Hansard reference)
HEFC	Higher Education Funding Council
HL Deb	House of Lords Debates (followed by Hansard reference)
HMSO	Her Majesty's Stationery Office
IPCS	Institute of Professional Civil Servants
IPPR	Institute for Public Policy Research
IT	Information technology
ITC	Independent Television Commission
JIC	Joint Intelligence Committee
LEC	Local enterprise company
MAFF	Ministry of Agriculture, Fisheries and Food
MI5	The domestic security services (government agency)
MI6	Secret Intelligence Service
MMC	Monopolies and Mergers Commission
MOD	Ministry of Defence
NAO	National Audit Office
NCC	National Consumer Council
NDPB	Non-departmental public body
NFHA	National Federation of Housing Associations
NFU	National Farmers Union
NHS	National Health Service
NSA	National Security Agency
OCPA	Office of the Commissioner for Public Appointments
ODA	Overseas Development Administration
OPB	Overseas Project Board
OPD	Overseas Policy and Defence Committee (cabinet committee)

PAC	Public Accounts Committee
PCA	Parliamentary Commissioner for Administration (Ombudsman)
PEB	Party election broadcast
PFO	Principal Finance Officer
PII	Public Interest Immunity
PLP	Public Law Project
PPS	Parliamentary private secretary
PQ	Parliamentary Question
PR	Proportional representation
PSC	Public Service Committee
PSIS	Permanent Secretaries Committee on the Intelligence Services
QPM	*Questions of Procedure for Ministers*
RAWMAC	Radioactive Waste Management Advisory Committee (quango)
REPC	Regional economic planning council
RHA	Regional health authority
RIPA	Royal Institute of Public Administration
RRP	Relative reduction in parties
SACHR	Standing Advisory Committee on Human Rights (Northern Ireland)
SASC	Senior Appointments Selection Committee
SEAC	Spongiform Encephalopathy Advisory Committee
SI	Statutory instrument
SRB	Single regeneration budget
SSA	Standard spending assessment
STV	Single Transferable Vote
TCSC	Treasury and Civil Service Committee
TEC	Training and enterprise council
TISC	Trade and Industry Committee
UGC	University Grants Committee
VFM	Value for money
WDA	Welsh Development Agency

INTRODUCTION

1 Auditing Democracy in Britain

Introducing the Democratic Criteria

The reforms I have set out will transform our politics. They will re-draw the boundaries between what is done in the name of the people and what is done by the people themselves. They will create a new relationship between government and the people, based on trust, freedom, choice and responsibility . . . they are deeply political reforms because they are concerned with the essence of our democracy and how people can exercise power in our society.

(Tony Blair in *New Britain – My Vision of a Young Country*, 1996)

In framing a government which is to be administered by men over men the great difficulty lies in this: you must first enable the government to control the governed; and in the next place oblige it to control itself. A dependence on the people is, no doubt, the primary control on government; but experience has taught mankind the necessity of auxiliary precautions.

(James Madison, later a US President, in *Federalist Paper* No. 51, 1788)

The idea of conducting a democratic audit of a country's public life and institutions is a novel one, and fraught with difficulties. Our starting point has been the widespread sense of unease among both the public and political elites about the quality of government and public life in the UK and the deteriorating relationship between the people and their government. This unease is long-standing and cumulative. The public now tend to believe that their country is becoming less democratic; they want more power than they now have between elections; and they have lost confidence and trust in elected politicians (Rowntree Reform Trust 1991–96; Channel 4 1994). There has been a broad gap in the 1990s between people's satisfaction with their own lives and with public life, politics and democracy in Britain (Whiteley *et al.* 1998).

The manner in which the election campaign of 1997 was conducted did nothing to restore faith in British party politics. The public clearly seized the opportunity to vote for a major change in direction and considerable social and democratic reform, but without great enthusiasm. We do not doubt the strength of the government's commitments, as set out in the Prime Minister's speech on the Queen's Speech in May 1997, to reforming and decentralising government in Britain, giving people greater rights to hold government to account, and restoring faith in public life (HC Deb, 11 May 1997, c60–67). Indeed, as we write in early 1998, the government is on the brink of a huge reform programme: devolution in Scotland and Wales; the partial incorporation of the European Convention on Human Rights into British law; public access to official information as of right; reform of the House of Lords; a referendum on electoral reform; and much else besides.

However, these changes are not as far-reaching as they seem at first sight. For example, the Human Rights Bill does not make Convention rights fully part of British law and preserves UK legislation which is inconsistent with the Convention. We also identify other significant problems in this Audit – for example, the huge and flexible powers at the disposal of the executive, and its near complete dominance of Parliament. Will the government's programme seek to redress the balance between government and Parliament? Our overriding goal is to ascertain what are the enduring strengths and failings of our political arrangements that lie beyond the individual character of policy and politician: in sum, to construct a 'balance sheet' of the democratic condition of the UK on the eve of the millennium. But in choosing May 1997 as the bench-mark for this audit, we will also be able to audit the progress the new Labour government has made over this Parliament in democratising this country and empowering its citizens. In this sense, we are setting a marker for further democratic advance.

To help us do this, we have taken over the concept of 'audit' as applied in a variety of institutional settings, and adapted it to assess the condition of public life itself. Basically, an audit is a systematic assessment of institutional performance against agreed criteria and standards, so as to provide a reasonably authoritative judgement as to how satisfactory the procedures and arrangements of the given institution are. How far are the relevant standards met, and where is there most cause for concern? If this idea of an audit is relatively simple, deploying it to measure the quality of democracy and public life raises a number of difficulties.

First, a country's polity or political system is not just a single institution or even a body of interlocking institutions which may be audited separately. The auditor must focus primarily on a set of *relationships* – between the institutions of democracy, between those institutions and citizens, and between the citizens themselves. Identifying these relationships, and assessing their character and adequacy, is necessarily a more complex task than assessing the performance of a single institution. It requires some sense of how a particular element fits into the complex as a whole. In addition, it is not immediately obvious where the boundaries of the political system should be set, and how far it encompasses the relationships of economic and social life as well as the more exclusively 'political'.

This problem of identifying the relevant subjects of assessment is closely bound up with the question of the standpoint from which they are to be audited. Why a *Democratic* Audit? The straightforward answer is that Britain claims to be a democracy, and has in the past, if not the present, seen itself as a model for other countries to emulate. At the same time, it is a member of a family of western countries whose relationship is based upon a shared democratic heritage, and which appeal in part at least to democratic standards to govern their relations with other countries. It is therefore by democratic criteria that the UK's own political institutions and practices should be assessed, and these criteria are the ones that must govern any selection of what is to be assessed.

This conclusion immediately raises a third problem. What concept of democracy are we to work with, as a basis for identifying our subjects of assessment, and the democratic criteria which are to govern their assessment? Is any such concept necessarily subjective and contestable? Answering this question will be the major task of this introductory chapter. For the moment, however, it is sufficient to exclude from consideration one conception that we shall not be adopting. This is the conception which takes the traditions, the norms, the received political culture of the UK as themselves providing the touchstone, or authoritative standard, against which current practice should be assessed. Such a conception is inadequate for several reasons. Not only is there room for considerable disagreement about what these norms actually are. More crucially, to treat them as self-evidently 'democratic' is to presuppose precisely what has to be demonstrated. A moment's reflection will suggest elements of the received political culture that are aristocratic rather than democratic (the monarchy, the House of Lords, the class system more widely); others that are strongly paternalistic (exemplified in the culture of secrecy, the 'we know best' attitude of government); yet others, such as the yearning for 'strong government', which are at best ambiguous in relation to democratic principles. The received political culture has, of course, a place in this audit, and we discuss it thoroughly in Chapter 2. But only a concept of democracy that is independent of the received political culture and institutions can provide us with criteria for assessment that will avoid circularity.

The sheer scale of a democratic audit is another problem. Any audit process involves at least four distinct stages. You must first identify the criteria appropriate for assessment, which help define and select what is to be assessed. The second stage is to determine the standards of good or best practice, which provide a bench-mark for the assessment. Third, and most time-consuming, is to assemble the relevant evidence from both the formal rules of a given institution and its informal practices, to enable a judgement to be made. This will include an analysis of key events or outcomes which can be seen as symptomatic of a more general condition. The final stage is to review the evidence in the light of the audit criteria and defined standards so that a systematic assessment can be reached. To do this across the whole range of a country's political life is a huge undertaking. We have therefore been forced to be selective in what we cover in this volume. That such an 'audit' is in principle possible, however, has already been demonstrated by the publication of the first volume of the Democratic Audit, under the title *The Three Pillars of Liberty: Political Rights and Freedoms in the UK* (henceforth DA Volume No. 1). International human rights instruments – such as the European Convention on Human Rights – and case law were used to define the authoritative criteria and standards against which the protection of civil and political rights in UK law and practice should be assessed. This 'human rights index' formed the key tool for the audit. The volume then assembled evidence about the distinctive system for protecting rights in the UK and how it works in practice, and subjected this evidence to a systematic evaluation in the light of the relevant standards. The conclusion was a discrete set of findings which together formed a 'balance-sheet' of the condition of political rights and freedoms in this country. We believe that this 'audit' method has enabled the Democratic Audit to produce the most systematic and authoritative study of its kind to date.

Principles of democracy

The present volume seeks to provide a similar audit for the central political institutions and processes in this country. Unlike the earlier volume, there is not the same degree of international agreement on the standards governing, for example, parliamentary procedure, executive accountability, electoral process, popular representation, and so on, as there is in the field of civil and political rights. What counts as 'democratic' is less definitive, and more open to legitimate variation in practice between different countries. Yet the relative lack of agreement on standards can be overstated. We are convinced that it is possible to arrive at a defensible and widely acceptable account of democratic principles, and of the audit criteria to be derived from them, even though the institutional arrangements through which these criteria are met may vary from one country to another.

In 1993, we published a consultative paper on democratic principles and criteria for this audit which deals more fully with certain of these issues (DA Paper No. 1). The criteria which we have developed for the UK Democratic Audit are not inscribed in stone and they have already undergone a considerable process of evolution since 1993 as we have discussed them in seminars, both domestically and internationally, debated them with correspondents, and tried to use them in practice. (In addition, we have developed in association with this volume a 'do-it-yourself' Audit Pack, which can be used by groups of citizens in any country to conduct an impressionistic audit of their own level of democracy.) We welcome any feedback from readers about the content or methodology of our own audit and its criteria.

We think that any debate about these criteria will itself be a contribution to the democratic process. This isn't merely an abstract good. Core decisions and policies impact directly and indirectly on the lives of all citizens of the UK; and as the UK is a unitary state, they generally do so without checks or intervention from intermediary bodies, or by regional or local government. These decisions and policies directly determine or at least affect how the state apparatus treats ordinary citizens on issues of vital importance to their daily lives – from pension levels and immigration rules, tax demands and employment prospects, criminal laws and regional disparities, education standards and housing conditions, to the protection of their everyday environment, risks from radiation and pollution, the safety of drugs and food and the very quality of the air they breathe. We have found evidence in research for this volume that suggests that democratic practice in government is likely to provide 'good' and effective government; and hard evidence that its absence contributes to poor and damaging government. The resulting policy mistakes have literally led to disasters, such as the BSE crisis, which affect people's daily lives for the worse, and cost some people their lives. Finally, only democratic government can provide the proper framework for the society of self-confident citizens which is the unspoken aim of public policy in this country.

The basic principles of democracy

The idea of democracy has different, if overlapping, meanings for different people in different places, and at different times. This is because the word 'democracy', which was originally a term of disparagement, has become one of the most generalised words of approval in the political lexicon during the twentieth century. As a result, it has tended to become synonymous with whatever the particular user happens to approve of – whether individual freedom or social equality, majority rule or minority rights, popular participation or elite competition, as the case may be. One way of avoiding these differences, and the underlying tendency to empty the concept of any specific content, is to define democracy descriptively, in terms of the institutional procedures and practices of those countries which are commonly called 'democratic' – legislatures, judiciaries, constitutions, procedures such as multi-party elections, universal suffrage, the separation of powers, the rule of law, and so on. Yet there are major problems with such a purely descriptive or institutional definition. First, no reason can be advanced as to why we should call these institutions 'democratic' rather than, say, 'liberal', 'pluralist', 'polyarchic', or whatever other term we choose. What is it that makes these institutions distinctively *democratic*? Secondly, any definition of democracy in terms of the institutions of government alone makes it impossible to understand why we should also want to call the arrangements of associations in civil society – clubs, work groups, economic institutions, and so on – democratic or undemocratic, as the case might be. Is there no common thread that links these different usages? Finally, and most importantly from the standpoint of a democratic audit, unless we have some point of reference for our concept of democracy which is independent of the institutions and practices of democracy themselves, it will be impossible to assess how democratic they actually are in practice, or how they might become more so. By what criteria might such an assessment be made?

Our solution to these problems is to define democracy in terms of the two basic principles which underlie the implicit contract that representative democracy makes between the state and people. The appeal of democracy comes from the idea that ordinary people 'rule' – the original Greek, δημοκρατία, literally means 'people power'. In a modern democracy people cannot rule directly, and many people will probably not wish to do so. Instead, the idea of the people's power is realised through a representative system in which they have the final say. If that system is to remain broadly faithful to the implicit contract between state and people, it must satisfy our two basic principles – the first is that of *popular control* over the political processes of decision-making within their society; the second is that of *political equality* in the exercise of that control. The two principles are of course most fully realised in small groups or associations where everyone has in effect an equal right to speak and to vote on policy in person. In larger associations, and especially at the level of a whole society, practical considerations of time and space necessitate that collective decisions be taken by representatives, or designated agents, acting on behalf of the rest. Here democracy is realised in the first instance not as direct popular control over decision-making, but as control over the decision-makers who act in the people's stead. How effective that control is, and how equally distributed it is between different citizens, are key criteria for how democratic a system of representative government is. Democracy thus entails a certain kind of *relationship*, on the one hand between government and citizens, and on the other, between citizens themselves.

The two basic principles are both embodied in the familiar institutions and procedures of western democracies, and it is in the terms of these same principles that these institutions and procedures can be described as 'democratic'. By their very nature, they cannot be applied as absolutes, only as measures. That is to say that they can provide us with the criteria against which we can measure how far they are realised in practice by any democracy's institutions and procedures. Democracy is thus always a matter of 'more or less' – it is neither an all-or-nothing affair nor is it capable of final attainment. To put the matter another way, the principles by which we can recognise the arrangements of democracy as *democratic* also indicate the direction in which the two basic principles might be more fully realised. They serve together as instruments for recognising or identifying what is democratic, and as critical standards for assessing how democratic existing arrangements may be.

It is important to locate the democratic idea and these two principles in their proper context: that is, in the sphere of the *political*, where the collectively binding rules and policies for any society, group or association are determined, and where the resolution of disagreement about these rules and policies should take place. Situating democracy in this sphere of the political excludes immediately one misconception about democracy, recurrent in the British culture, that it means the greatest possible individual choice or individual freedom. Democracy certainly entails a variety of individual rights and freedoms – of speech, expression and association, the suffrage and so on. These are important in their own right if people are to possess autonomy and live fulfilling lives. But their point of reference is the process of collective decision-making, which is necessarily prior to their being granted and realised, because it provides the preconditions and boundaries for individual choice and action. Democratic politics, like any politics, presupposes that we are primarily social creatures, living lives that are interdependent, and therefore requiring common rules and policies, as well as procedures for collective action. Thus democracy belongs to the sphere of political decision-making for any association or collectivity, not just at the level of society, the nation-state or association of states. Any system of collective decision-making can be defined as 'democratic' to the extent that it is subject to control by all members of the relevant association considered as equals. Popular control and political equality remain the key democratic principles.

How can we be so sure that these two principles are indeed the basic principles of democracy? It is partly because, whenever and wherever democracy has become a serious issue of political practice and public debate, it is the ideas of popular rule and equal citizenship that have provided its inspiration. Political struggles waged under the banner of democracy have always been struggles to subject government to greater popular control, to restrain arbitrary rule, to make politics more inclusive, and to ensure greater equality between citizens. And if we examine what opponents of democracy throughout the ages have objected to, it has been precisely the idea that ordinary people might be qualified to pass judgement on matters of government, or that everyone should be given equal consideration in public policy, and equal opportunity to influence it. Of course, democracy does not mean always giving the majority what it wants, regardless of the conditions for informed decision, or the impact of any decision on the rights of others. What it means is that the conditions for popular control over government and for political equality should be secured on an ongoing basis.

Popular control and political equality constitute simple but powerful principles which can be used both to assess how democratic a system of collective decision-making is, and as ideals to be realised in practical institutional form. On their own, however, they may be too general to provide us directly with the criteria to audit the democratic character of a representative system of government, without the help of intermediate principles which give greater specificity to the core ideas. Among these mediating principles which enable us to recognise the relation between government and governed as 'democratic' are the following:

- the *authorisation* by the people of key public officials, typically through an electoral process in which there is significant choice between candidates and the corresponding power of removal from office on a regular basis. The idea of authorisation also includes direct popular involvement in and approval of a basic constitution, and revisions to it (through a referendum, for example);
- the idea of the *accountability* of government to the people, both directly to the public and to individuals, and also indirectly, through mediating institutions which ensure the legal, financial and political accountability of all government officials for their policies and actions undertaken in the people's name;
- the idea of the *responsiveness* of government to a full range of public opinion in the formulation and implementation of law and policy, through systematic processes of consultation and dialogue.

In a system of representative government these three concepts are what give substance to the idea of popular control. They cannot be effective, however, without guaranteed rights for citizens to information, to the freedoms of expression, association, and so on, or without the active participation of citizens, individually and collectively, in the political process. Popular participation is what gives life to the institutional arrangements of authorisation, accountability and responsiveness.

The other key democratic principle of political equality is threaded through all the above, requiring a distinctive relationship between citizens at the same time as one between them and their government. This is one of equality in the enjoyment of citizen rights, in the value of their votes, in the effective opportunity to stand for office, regardless of the social group to which a person belongs, in access to and redress from government, and so on. One of the indicators of political equality is to be found in the degree of *representativeness* of political institutions and of public bodies of all kinds, and in the degree to which they reflect the diversity and pluralism of society, not only in respect of political opinions, but of social composition and identities. Equality is thus not incompatible with diversity. In fact, it requires it to be reflected in the representativeness of public bodies.

These, then, are the mediating principles that give substance to the core ideas of popular control and political equality in a representative democracy: popular authorisation, public accountability, governmental responsiveness, the representativeness of public bodies, reflecting and promoting equality of citizenship. Together these principles give us our main criteria for assessing the quality of democracy in the different aspects of a country's democratic processes and institutions.

Representative democracy

The different components of representative democracy

Given these core ideas and principles, how should we divide up the different aspects or components of democracy for audit and assessment? We distinguish four different components that are crucial for any functioning democracy:

1   The electoral process, which is the key site for the popular authorisation and control of government, carrying with it the sanction of removal from office. The democratic criteria here can be summed up in the concept of 'free and fair elections', though this is a somewhat imperfect characterisation.
2   The continuous and open accountability of government institutions and public officials to the electorate, both directly and indirectly through Parliament, the courts, the Ombudsman, tribunals, public audit and other means; and the responsiveness of government to public opinion. We call this 'open, accountable and responsive government'.
3   The guarantee of civil and political rights and freedoms, enabling citizens to associate freely with others, to express divergent or unpopular views, to create an informed public opinion, and to find their own solutions to collective problems.
4   Those elements in people's lives, habits and culture which combine to make up a 'democratic society': richness of associational life, the accountability of economic institutions, social inclusion, attitudes of mind, self-confidence, and a culture of tolerance and civic responsibility.

Together these four aspects or components of democracy can be represented as a pyramid, in which each element is necessary to the whole.

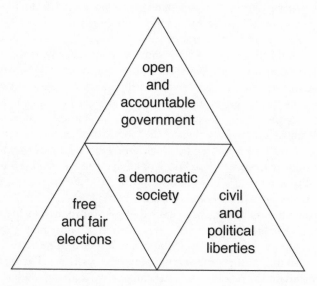

Figure 1.1 The democratic pyramid

For each of the four areas, we have formulated specific indices, the Audit's democratic criteria, for assessing how far the different aspects of this or any other country's governing institutions, practices and life measure up to our basic principles. These are our auditing tools. We have set out these Democratic Audit criteria (**DACs**) in the form of questions posed in relative terms (how much? how far? to what extent?), according to the assumption, already argued, that democracy is a matter of 'more or less' rather than a perfect state of being which may be attained. Some of the questions are much 'bigger' than others, and could well be broken down into a sub-set of further questions. The exact balance between them must be a matter of judgement and emphasis (see DA Paper No. 1).

Free and fair elections

People are the starting point of representative democracy. It is the people who elect a Parliament and a government to represent them. It is thus appropriate that the starting point for a democratic audit should be with an examination of the electoral process. The first five Democratic Audit criteria examine the reach, inclusiveness, independence, integrity and impartiality of elections in Britain, as well as how equally the electoral process treats citizens, how much effective choice it offers them, how far governments actually fulfil the electoral choices made, and how many people in practice exercise the right to vote. A further criterion concerns the right of the electorate in a democracy to vote directly on any measures of change in the governing or constitutional arrangements which significantly alter the relationship between people and government (as, for example, in the 1975 referendum over remaining in the (then) European Community, the 1997 referendums over devolution to Scotland and Wales and the promise of a referendum on changes to the electoral system for Westminster elections).

DAC1. How far is appointment to legislative and governmental office determined by popular election, on the basis of open competition, universal suffrage and secret ballot; and how far is there equal effective opportunity to stand for public office, regardless of which social group a person belongs to?

DAC2. How independent of government and party control and external influences are elections and procedures of voter registration, how accessible are they to voters, and how free are they from all kinds of abuse?

DAC3. How effective a range of choice and information does the electoral and party system allow the voters, and how far is there fair and equal access for all parties and candidates to the media and other means of communication with them?

DAC4. To what extent do the votes of all electors carry equal weight, and how closely does the composition of Parliament and the programme of government reflect the choices actually made by the electorate?

Representative democracy

DAC5. What proportion of the electorate actually votes, and how far are the election results accepted by the main political forces in the country?

DAC6. How far is there systematic opportunity for the electorate to vote directly on measures of basic constitutional change?

Open, accountable and responsive government

Once elected, a government should remain continuously accountable to the people and to the people's representatives. The powers at its disposal to take decisions and make policies are 'public' powers – that is, they are granted by the public to their representatives and should be exercised in accordance with rules which ensure that the public are informed and consulted about their use and which prevent their arbitrary abuse. Accountability is only possible if the public is fully informed about the government's actions and procedures for the systematic and equal consultation of public opinion are in place. This section begins with a question (**DAC7**) about open government, and continues with a series of questions on different aspects of governmental accountability: of non-elected officials to those elected, of the executive to Parliament, and of MPs to the public (**DAC8–10**). The criteria then concern the key issues of the rule of law, the legal accountability of governments and their officials, and the independence of the judiciary (**DAC11–12**); address the direct accountability of government to citizens through procedures for individual redress (**DAC13**); bring the principle of equality to bear upon the internal working of public bodies (**DAC14**); and focus on the procedures for consultation and accessibility necessary to accountable and responsive government (**DAC15–16**). Finally, we apply the principles of openness, accountability and responsiveness to the different levels of government, both above and below the state, and especially to local government, whose vitality is so important to a country's democratic life (**DAC17–18**).

DAC7. How accessible to the public is information about what the government does, and about the effects of its policies, and how independent is it of the government's own information machine?

DAC8. How effective and open to scrutiny is the control exercised by elected politicians over non-elected executive officials, both military and civilian?

DAC9. How extensive are the powers of Parliament to oversee legislation and public expenditure, to scrutinise the executive and hold it accountable, and to secure redress when necessary; and how effectively are they exercised in practice?

DAC10. How publicly accountable are political parties and elected representatives for party and private interests, including sources of income that might affect the conduct of government and public duties and the process of election to public office?

DAC11. How far is the executive subject to the rule of law and transparent rules governing the use of its powers? How far are the courts able to ensure that the executive obeys the rule of law; and how effective are their procedures for ensuring that all public institutions and officials are subject to the rule of law in the performance of their functions?

DAC12. How independent is the judiciary from the executive, and from all forms of interference; and how far is the administration of law subject to effective public scrutiny?

DAC13. How readily can a citizen gain access to the courts, Ombudsman or tribunals for redress in the event of maladministration or the failure of government or public bodies to meet their legal responsibilities; and how effective are the means of redress available?

DAC14. How far are appointments and promotions within public institutions subject to equal opportunities procedures, and how far do conditions of service protect employees' civil rights?

DAC15. How systematic and open to public scrutiny are the procedures for government consultation of public opinion and of relevant interests in the formation and implementation of policy and legislation?

DAC16. How accessible are elected politicians to approach by their electors, and how effectively do they represent constituents' interests?

DAC17. How far do the arrangements for government both above and below the level of the central state meet the above criteria of openness, accountability and responsiveness?

DAC18. To what extent does government below the centre have the powers to carry out its responsibilities in accordance with the wishes of regional or local electorates, and without interference from the centre?

Civil and political rights and liberties

All the features of democracy considered above are anchored in a framework of citizen rights, which are necessary if the people are to play their active roles in political life as the counterpart to those of government. The first of the Audit's criteria in this section on safeguarding civil and political rights raises a very broad question indeed (**DAC19**), and answering it occupied most of the first volume already published. The next three criteria explore the implications of various kinds of social and economic inequality for the exercise of civil and political rights (**DAC20**); and take the existence of strong pressure groups for the defence of such rights (and their freedom from interference) and well-developed rights education as significant indicators of how seriously a society takes the defence of basic rights (**DAC21–22**). Finally, we address the contentious issue of the rights of aliens, acknowledging the right of a democratic country to determine who should be admitted to live in the country, though only on non-arbitrary criteria, and assuming that residence over time itself generates legitimate claims to citizenship (**DAC23**).

DAC19. How clearly does the law define the civil and political rights and liberties of the citizen, and how effectively are they safeguarded?

DAC20. How equal are citizens in the enjoyment of their civil and political rights and liberties, regardless of social, economic or other status?

DAC21. How well developed are voluntary associations for the advancement and monitoring of citizens' rights, and how free from harassment are they?

DAC22. How effective are procedures for informing citizens of their rights, and for educating future citizens in the exercise of them?

DAC23. How free from arbitrary discrimination are the criteria for admission of refugees or immigrants to live within the country, and how readily can those so admitted obtain equal rights of citizenship?

A democratic society

The final set of criteria is premised on the assumption that the quality and vitality of a country's democracy will be revealed in the character of its civil society as well as its political institutions. As already suggested, there is considerable difference of opinion about the precise characteristics needed for a democratic society, and these are also subject to variation according to time and place. However, the idea that there should be some minimum agreement on the political nation, and tolerance of difference within it (**DAC24–25**), is quite standard. So too is the emphasis on a flourishing associational life, whose activities are also democratically accountable; and on a diversity of media of communication, which are accessible to different opinions and sections of society (**DAC26–28**). Finally, there is the important issue of social and economic inclusion, and the significance of education in equipping future citizens for a variety of social and political roles (**DAC29**), and the connected, more general question of the confidence of citizens in their own capacity to influence the collective decisions that matter for their lives (**DAC30**). The ultimate goal of democracy is a society of self-confident citizens.

DAC24. How far is there agreement on nationhood within the established state boundaries, and to what extent does support for political parties cross regional, linguistic, religious or ethnic lines?

DAC25. How tolerant are people of divergent beliefs, cultures, ethnic backgrounds, life-styles, etc., and how free are the latter from discrimination or disadvantage?

DAC26. How strong and independent of government control are the associations of civil society, and how accountable are they to their own members?

DAC27. How publicly accountable are economic institutions for their activities, and how effective is their legal regulation in the public interest?

DAC 28. How pluralistic are the media of communication in terms of ownership and accessibility to different opinions and sections of society; and how effectively do they operate as a balanced forum for political debate?

DAC29. How far are all citizens able to participate in economic, social and cultural, as well as political, life; and how effective is the education to equip them for doing so?

DAC30. To what extent do people have confidence in the ability of the political system to solve the main problems confronting society, and in their own ability to influence it?

Comparison with other indices of democracy

How do these criteria we have developed for democratic audit compare with the indices of democracy employed by other political scientists? The ones most frequently used stem from the work of Robert Dahl, the well-known American theorist (1971). Dahl produced, on the one hand, a list of political rights and freedoms; and, on the other, a list of electoral conditions for 'competition and inclusiveness' – that is, allowing all citizens a choice between various parties at election time with no signifi-cant exclusions. There would be something very odd indeed if there were no significant overlap between our criteria and such widely-used indices of democracy among the political science profession.

However, there are also a number of significant differences. First, our criteria extend beyond the areas of civil and political rights and electoral democracy, to include the two further areas of the accountability of government and a democratic society. To take accountability alone, the sheer range of issues – all very broad in their own terms – that we have had to consider to make an effective audit of this area shows what a serious omission this is. Second, we take the principle of political equality much more seriously than the standard political science indicators. They are usually content to take the inclusiveness of the suffrage – i.e. the proportion of the adult population eligible to vote – as the only criterion for political equality. For us the principle must be operative throughout the political process. Third, we do not believe that the quality of a country's democracy can be adequately assessed simply by aggregating a number of indices into a single score line, as political scientists tend to (Bollen 1991; Hadenius 1992; and others).

Indices of democracy

Two different issues can be distinguished at this point. One is the question of how far it is possible to *quantify* the degree of democracy which any country has in general, or in specific areas. Certainly, some criteria or indices of democracy are much more amenable to quantification than others. This applies particularly to some aspects of electoral democracy, such as how proportional election results are, how large turnout is, how many votes are 'wasted', and which groups may or may not take part. It is then possible to compare the performance of different countries with different electoral systems and measure whether they are *more* or *less* democratic, according to our criteria (as we do in Chapter 3). However, to make judgements of this kind neither requires nor assumes precise quantification. Showing, for example, that government is less open in the UK than the US is a matter of identifying the different respects in which law and practice in one country is inferior in comparison to the other, through a systematic but discursive type of analysis and assessment (see DA Paper No. 3 (1994), which examines how democratic practice in Britain compares with five other nations). Putting a figure to these differences will only give an illusory aura of precision.

This is all the more so when the different dimensions of democracy are then *aggregated* into a single score or league table of democracy or of freedom, in which countries are marked out of 10 or 100 as the case may be. Not only are such aggregations eminently contestable, in view of the arbitrary nature of the numerical values assigned to the different aspects of democracy. From the standpoint of a democratic *audit*, they obscure the necessary complexity of the judgements to be made, especially where the purpose is to identify which particular aspects of a country's democratic life are most in need of strengthening or reform, and which are more satisfactory from a democratic point of view. For such a purpose the method of discursive analysis and assessment using fine-grained criteria is the most suitable. We also take the view that the most appropriate people to act as auditors of a country's democratic condition are its own citizens, rather than outsiders sitting in judgement upon it. Comparison with other democracies is of course an important part of this assessment, but its purpose for us here is to highlight the strengths and weaknesses of the UK rather than to judge the others.

This brings us to the question of the appropriate standards against which a given country's democracy should be audited. *Criteria* serve to define the relevant aspects of democratic life for analysis and assessment, based on an understanding of what democracy involves, and serve as analytical tools for assessing how far a country's arrangements might be said to be more or less democratic. *Standards* define the appropriate level within each of the criteria or indices, against which the assessment should be made. What counts as the appropriate standard or benchmark for audit? Three possibilities suggest themselves. One is comparison with the country's own past, to show whether its performance has improved or declined from a democratic point of view. However, such a comparison tells us little about whether or how far the original condition was itself particularly democratic. And it presupposes that the relevant data are available in appropriate form for a given point in the past. We do not possess sufficient data for such a comparison in respect of the UK. However, we intend that the two volumes of the current Democratic Audit should constitute a significant reference point, located at the end of a long period of Conservative rule, against which any future developments, or lack of them, might be mapped.

A second possible standard could be an ideal one. We could, say, postulate some perfect level of freedom, openness, accountability, responsiveness, political equality, protection of rights, and so on – a condition of democratic perfection – against which the assessment could be made. Here, questions of practicability and attainability, as well as compatibility between the different criteria, clearly intrude. In particular, governments, including democratic governments, have to be able to govern, to keep order, to decide and implement policies, and to do so sometimes with speed and determination. Further, we recognise that public order is a significant pillar of democracy; that the effective delivery of policies is important for electoral confidence, as well as whether those policies accord with people's electoral choices; and that value for money is an important ingredient of democratic policy-making. We have not, however, included these dimensions of performance – 'good', 'orderly' or perhaps 'strong' government – in our explicit criteria, partly because what counts as 'good', 'orderly' or 'strong' government is a contestable political matter, but mainly because it is not *in and of itself* a democratic criterion. Our view is that there is a demonstrable link between democratic and effective government: systematic consultation, openness and accountability contribute to policy decisions which are more likely to be measured and considered and to generate public approval and acceptance. Yet clearly we have to recognise that there may be a point where pushing democratic criteria to their limits may hamper or even undermine 'good' government, let alone the 'orderly' or 'strong' version.

This leaves us with our third possible standard, that of good or best practice, as established either internationally or through comparison with other countries. 'Best practice' suggests a standard that is realistic and attainable, because it has already been attained somewhere, without detriment to governmental performance or effectiveness. Such standards or benchmarks have already been established internationally for some areas of democratic audit, such as the conduct of elections or the defence of civil and political rights. In other areas standards of best practice are in the process of formulation or consolidation, as for example US or Swedish legislation on freedom of information which sets an attainable standard for open government. In yet others comparative analysis can help to establish such standards where these are not yet recognised. Does the acceptance of common standards of best practice, against which a country's democratic condition may be assessed where these are available, tend to assume a uniformity of democratic practice, regardless of a country's history, traditions or institutional practices? Does it, by extension, assume that a given practice, workable in one democracy, can readily be imposed on another, regardless of its suitability or practicability? Not necessarily. There may be very different ways in which criteria for, say, governmental accountability or responsiveness, or the defence of basic rights, might be secured. A democratic audit does not prescribe a particular means for the attainment of a given standard. As we argued in the first volume of the Democratic Audit, the issue is not whether the UK's distinctive system of human rights defence conforms to continental models, but whether its claim to meet international human rights standards, albeit in its own way, can be justified (DA Volume 1 No. 1).

Thus, our criteria must be couched in sufficiently general terms to enable us to distinguish those differences that comprise legitimate variations of practice from those that constitute deviations from a given standard of democracy.

The criteria must also be firm enough to allow us to judge, say, in the absence of good practice elsewhere, whether existing arrangements in the UK fall short of what is desirable from a democratic perspective, and to argue for higher standards in a way which is realistic as opposed to 'idealistic'. It is also important that we are not led to rely wholly on the democratic advances and standards established in other countries. It is arguable, for example, that the European Court of Human Rights tends on balance to be more sympathetic to the interests of states than those of their citizens when establishing the *de facto* standards for particular rights; and such a tendency may grow to accommodate the cruder standards of some developing democracies which have signed the European Convention. Over-reliance on precedents or standards from abroad could inhibit perfectly attainable democratic initiatives which may grow out of existing practices at home. So our criteria have to be couched in sufficiently general terms not only to allow for variation in democratic practice, but also to identify the strengths, weaknesses and potentialities of any system of government, regardless of what is the practice elsewhere.

In practice, we have employed a mix of means of establishing the standards for auditing democratic practice in the UK. It is, however, important to stress that we have found that the analytical process of audit alone, according to appropriately precise and general criteria, does in itself clarify the strengths and expose the weaknesses of any given system of government. It is a valuable and illuminating exercise in its own right and we hope that the first two Audit volumes are proof of that.

How open and accountable is government in Britain?

It is important to set out the full range of the audit criteria here, covering all four components or areas, so that readers may have some overall sense of the potential scope of a democratic audit, and of where the present volume is to be located within it. However, to audit all four component areas of democracy together would be a huge undertaking – an intellectual equivalent of painting the Forth Bridge. It is certainly one that demands more resources than those at the disposal of the Democratic Audit. In this volume we concentrate on the first two components – electoral democracy and open and accountable government. The third component has of course already been audited in *The Three Pillars of Liberty* (DA Volume No.1). The fourth must wait for a later volume, as must important aspects of all four component areas – for example, democratic arrangements within the European Union; the influence of social and economic factors on citizenship and democratic participation; questions of pluralism raised by the structures and ownership of the media; the openness, accountability and responsiveness of local government; the regulation of utilities in the public interest; and so on. In part, our response to such subjects is determined by practical problems, such as the state of flux in which the EU's institutions and arrangements find themselves in the late 1990s; in part by the existence of alternative 'audits', like the huge outpouring of analytical reports on the state of local democracy (from the official

Widdicombe report in 1986 (Widdicombe 1986a) through numerous academic writings to the Joseph Rowntree Foundation canon and the papers and final report of the Commission for Local Democracy from 1994–96 (CLD 1995 and Stoker 1996)). However, we have also been able to carry out smaller audits of critical issues through special reports, as the Democratic Audit has done in respect of executive and advisory quangos, elections in Britain, and democracy in Northern Ireland at the beginning of the peace process (DA Papers No. 2 (1994) on executive quangos; No. 3 (1994) on advisory quangos; No. 5 (1995) on Northern Ireland; No. 7 (1996) on the UK electoral system; and No. 8 (1996) on both executive and advisory quangos).

Even in the two areas on which we focus – elections and open and accountable government – we are obliged to be far more selective than we would wish. Among the prominent omissions at national level, for example, we scarcely deal at all with the opaque workings of what former minister William Waldegrave described as 'the media-political complex . . . by which we are ruled' (Hennessy 1995: 23). We neglect the inner workings of the two major parties at a point when in both, in significantly different ways, difficult questions of intra-party democracy, organisation and funding were raised in the run-up to the 1997 general election and clearly affected the election result. We have left out of the reckoning research we have done on the quality and diversity of representation of the people and minorities in elected politics, Whitehall and the public service, and the judiciary (**DAC1** and **DAC14**). Britain's Ombudsman service, tribunals and to a less developed degree, the Citizen's Charter, are an important source of redress (**DAC13**), which we are only able to touch on. The National Audit Office, the Audit Commission and regulatory agencies have become increasingly significant public bodies. The role of the monarchy is being seriously re-examined. Questions of MPs' interests, bribery, ministers' and senior officials' work opportunities in industries relevant to their time in office, all these and other issues of public morality, have raised their head. Our reasons, as auditors, for leaving all these matters largely (though not all wholly) on one side fall into two categories: the first is one of priority, the second our view that the Parliamentary Commissioner for Standards and parliamentary committees, and other bodies, like the Neill Committee on Standards in Public Life, the National Consumer Council, the Hansard Society, *Private Eye* and other media, are between them monitoring these areas of public life, though not always and certainly not consistently from a democratic perspective. The Parliamentary Commissioner and official disciplinary mechanisms are too recently installed for audit at this stage, and we will look at these issues fully in the follow-up volume.

Our emphasis is thus on the electoral system, the inner workings of the core executive and machinery of state, their openness to Parliament and the public, the ways in which both are (or are not) accountable to Parliament in the political sphere and the judiciary in the legal sphere, and Parliament's ability and willingness to render government accountable. All these processes and institutions are interlinked. The first check on government is the electorate's periodic power of recall and its ability to replace a governing party or coalition with their rivals. But the quality of that periodic check may be blunted by imperfections in the electoral process. Equally, electoral imperfections may wholly undermine the House of Commons' ability or willingness to exercise constant invigilation of government polices and practice at all levels to ensure it conforms to

Parliament's and the electorate's wishes, as may the rules, powers and resources at the House's command. The rule of law is a historic element in Britain's governing arrangements – that is, the idea that government should be limited in its powers and conducted in accordance with laws and procedures that provide safeguards against oppressive, inequitable or arbitrary government. We consider how effectively the rule of law carries out these functions and evaluate how far the legal scrutiny of the courts may be hampered by the unjusticiable discretionary powers of the executive, government's command of the legislative supremacy of Parliament, the absence of a written constitution with defined legal procedures, the non-legal status of the rules governing the conduct of ministers and civil servants (conventions, codes, official 'guidance', the Citizen's Charter, etc.), and the limits on the processes of public audit.

We believe that our inquiries and audit raise questions which stand at the centre of any country's democratic life. However, it is also evident that these matters relate directly to the structural weaknesses which underlie the current crisis of confidence in the way Britain is governed. We sympathise with the Prime Minister's determination to restore the people's trust in Britain's democratic actors and institutions – government ministers, MPs, Parliament and politics in general. 'Trust' is a vital part of our democratic culture and is inextricably linked with our society's ability to make significant progress in other areas of national life. We welcome the firm actions the Prime Minister has already taken to restore public confidence in the standards of public life. However, trust in our governing arrangements is not independent of those arrangements. It depends in part on their ability – through laws and procedures, Parliament, the courts and other agencies – to order the powers and conduct of ministers, politicians and civil servants; to restrain oppressive or arbitrary measures in government; to provide redress in cases of injustice or maladministration; to make government open, accountable and responsive to Parliament and the general public; and to ensure that MPs and other politicians fulfil their representative role. To return to our opening quotations (**p. 3**), there is no doubt about the ability of government in Britain to 'control the governed'. What is in doubt is the reality of the people's 'primary control' of government and their ability to 'oblige it to control itself'. As Madison's words imply, men and women in government and politics are to be trusted only if they are properly accountable, if they act under the law, and if their conduct is open to scrutiny.

Sources and words

A country's politics is a seam rich in principles, practices and personalities, high drama and absurdity, honour and sleaze, triumphs and tragedies, falls from power and from grace, achievement and hubris. In quarrying this seam for the factual evidence to be audited according to the criteria we have described above we have been determined not to lose sight of the human element in democratic politics. We decided early on to call as witnesses politicians, journalists, civil servants, columnists and other practitioners, making use of their memoirs, television appearances, news items and columns, investigative TV and radio programmes and books, personal interviews, and so on, to compile as full a dossier as possible of practical political experience of the way Britain's democratic arrangements work.

We have concentrated largely on the postwar period, but have sought to place current politics in historical perspective, since the past – real and invented – has a particular influence on present constitutional and political practice in the UK. We have also drawn very heavily on the research and knowledge of contemporary political scientists, some of whom have contributed directly to this volume (their contributions are noted in Acknowledgements). We have conducted our own research into areas, like quangos, where information was scarce, collaborating alike with investigative TV journalists and political scientists. In other areas, we have collaborated with academics in developing new critiques, most particularly on the workings of the 'first-past-the-post' electoral system. The aim has been to acknowledge the diversity of knowledge and experience of the complex evidence and to gain as full and rounded a grasp on it as we can.

This is a large volume, as the needs of an audit dictate a comprehensive approach. As with the first volume, we expect people to use it in various ways; some will read it right through, others will choose chapters on particular areas of government, and others will use it as a reference book. So each chapter must to some extent stand on its own as a survey of the current position on, say, the deployment of quangos. Further, we trace a great variety of issues such as ministerial powers from their base in the core executive (Part 2) to consider checks on their use in Parliament and the courts (Part 3). For both reasons, there is therefore an overlap both between individual chapters and between Parts, and an element of repetition. We pull the separate chapter audits together in a final 'Findings' section, which precedes our Conclusions.

Throughout, the intention has been to provide an audit of the position in the UK as a whole. However, we have been obliged to leave out of the reckoning electoral politics and special practice in Northern Ireland (which is the subject of a separate Audit report: DA Paper No. 5) and Scotland's separate judicial system. On occasions, we use the terms 'national', 'British' and 'this country' informally, largely to smooth the narrative, and not as a derogation from our intention to provide a UK audit. However, when we say 'Great Britain', we mean Great Britain. Historically, people have assumed that MPs, civil servants and other political actors are all men and so have used the masculine pronouns in references to them; some people still do. In this volume, we simply quote our witnesses word for word, and see no need to add a superior '(sic)' after such solecisms. Finally, our choice of the pronoun 'we' is democratic, not royal. We have chosen to use the pronoun 'we', partly to reflect the fact that two of us are ultimately responsible for the whole of this volume, partly to reflect the knowledge and experience which our colleagues, who are thanked elsewhere, have contributed to the making of this volume. However, we also decided not to adopt a magisterial impersonal style in order to emphasise that the judgements, although directed by clear and systematic criteria, are necessarily subjective in the final event.

2   Ancient and Modern

The governing culture in Britain

There is quite as much trouble in the reformation of an old constitution as in the establishment of a new one; it is just as hard to unlearn as it is to learn.
                                                    (Aristotle, *The Politics*, c335 BC)

We are dealing with a set of arrangements which (a) is historically rooted and determined, (b) has to be read by practising politicians as a set of rules which are, for the moment, binding and so ought to be coherent, and (c) is unmistakably under a variety of pressures which will lead to further evolution.
(Ferdinand Mount, practical journalist, in *The British Constitution Now*, 1992)

Our existing, unwritten constitution is famously two-faced. Looking backward as well as forwards, it had a brilliant record of preserving itself through partial reform until, under Margaret Thatcher, it was deformed rather than reformed.
                (Anthony Barnett, practical intellectual, in *This Time*, 1997)

Within its own country, the British state is one of the most powerful in the world. Yet it is also probably the most ambiguous and indeterminate. The term, 'the state', is unknown to the law. Executive power is vested in 'the Crown', and the Crown has developed as 'a convenient symbol for the state', and stands in law for central government (Wade and Bradley 1993: 245). Yet while the Queen may reign formally, it is the Prime Minister and other ministers who rule. In the absence of a fully written constitution, the doctrine of parliamentary supremacy in law-making is un-restrained by constitutional limits; no formal separation of powers between the executive and Parliament exists; and the judiciary is subordinate to Parliament. No-one knows exactly what to call the executive – usually we say 'central government' or 'the government of the day'. The state bureaucracy – the civil service – is often known simply as 'Whitehall'.

Thus, the shape and significance of both state and executive is half-hidden. No-one can be sure where ultimate authority lies – with the Queen or 'Crown', the Prime Minister, the cabinet, ministers, the House of Commons, Parliament, the state bureaucracy, the people? No-one likes to talk of the 'governing system' because it is too unsystematic and unknowable; instead we use the looser term, 'governing arrangements'. The executive and Parliament are subject to informal constitutional rules, known as conventions, which are constantly changing. A team of academics who set out simply to map the organisational structures of the central state in the late 1970s found the task frustratingly difficult. The formal rules were 'mystical and elusive, even if they are not actually secret', and much harder to discover than the informal processes of 'what actually goes on'. Thus there was no backdrop against which to assess 'what actually goes on' stories (Hood *et al.* 1978). The task of staking out the fragmented state of the 1990s is even harder.

Much of 'what actually goes on' under the conventions, procedures and under-standings of the 'unwritten constitution' has its roots in its political history. This history, through tradition and culture, continues to exercise a profound influence on current political and democratic practice. In order to audit British democracy, there-fore, it is necessary first to analyse the political tradition and culture which in part shape it. Our constitutional arrangements are, as the constitutional theorist, Graeme C. Moodie once wrote, 'a continuously changing blend of the ancient and modern' (1964: 16). Government in Britain, Parliament, the civil service and the courts are long-standing institutions with a pre-democratic history and culture which still inform their formal processes and informal behaviour. Political scientists thus often refer to 'British exceptionalism'. And history is of particular importance in understanding the exceptional constitutional mixture which places Parliament at the very centre of the British state – in its fusion of legislative and executive powers – yet which simul-taneously places the emphasis firmly upon 'strong' and 'flexible' government rather than the collective decision-making capacities of Parliament, and which makes the judiciary subordinate to both. As will become evident, the executive's strength and flexibility work hand-in-hand, to ensure that it can evade checks and restraints on its exercise of power.

The evolution of democracy in Britain

Generations of British school children have been brought up to believe that Westminster's claim to be the 'Mother of Parliaments' means also that the UK – or rather England – is also the 'home of democracy'. British politicians glory in a tradition which regards the progress of liberty and democracy as an almost seamless development. At Bruges, in 1988 for example, Mrs Thatcher said, 'Since Magna Carta in 1215 we have pioneered and developed representative institutions to stand as bastions of freedom'. Certainly, this country has a long and uninterrupted tradition of at least partially representative government under the law since 1689 and much else to be proud of. In 1940, for example, Britain stood alone in defence of political freedom. But an objective use of history indicates that, long-lived though England's parliamentary institutions are, the idea of 'democracy' was greatly feared from the era of the Napoleonic Wars to the first years of the twentieth century and representative democracy was introduced into parliamentary government here in carefully-judged doses to prevent the adoption of 'mass', or popular, democracy. Parliament, as an institution of gradually widening political elites, pre-dates the modern British state by several centuries.

Universal adult suffrage, the basic component of popular control, came slowly, reluctantly, and relatively late, to Britain, in a series of Reform Acts from 1832 to

1928, when men's and women's voting rights were finally equalised (at 21). But some people could cast more than one vote in parliamentary elections up to 1949. Therefore, the first elections in which men and women voted in accordance with the principle 'one person, one vote' – the basic component of political equality – were those in February 1950, 45 years after proud boasts from constitutional theorists, like A. V. Dicey, that Britain had already become 'something like' a democracy at the turn of the century. Inequities in voting rights persisted in Northern Ireland into the 1970s under sectarian Unionist rule (1922–72) along with gerrymandered electoral boundaries, 'fixed' elections and systematic discrimination against the Roman Catholic minority.

By comparison, Switzerland formally introduced full male suffrage from the 1830s, and achieved it in practice from the 1870s (but female suffrage was delayed until 1971). Australia introduced full adult suffrage in 1903 (subject to some state-level exclusions of Aborigines), New Zealand in 1907 and Canada in 1920 (though recent immigrants were denied the vote). The first great wave of democratisation in Europe was set rolling by the First World War. Denmark and Norway adopted universal adult suffrage in 1915, Sweden and Austria in 1918, Finland, Germany and the Netherlands in 1919. All these nations were well in advance of the three celebrated democracies of modern history: Britain (1928), France (1946), and the United Stated (the 1960s, when voting restrictions on blacks and poor people in various Southern states were finally abolished). Similarly, to talk of 'the British people', or Britain, or the UK, as long-established entities is misleading. Even today, there are significant confusions over 'national' identities, with many contemporary figures echoing the elision of the 'English' and 'British' that Dicey made in 1905. Since the Middle Ages, 'Britain' has been a multi-national state, in which England has been the dominant actor. The defining moments for British constitutional analysis – the Glorious Revolution of 1688–89, the conquest of Ireland in 1691 and the Acts of Union in 1706 and 1707 – were above all an 'English' political settlement, imposing a unitary state upon the British Isles under the rule of the 'Crown in Parliament'. The unitary 'British' state has come under challenge ever since, violently in the case of Scotland and Ireland, by political means recently in Scotland and Wales.

A traditional belief in an 'Anglo-Saxon' aptitude for democratic institutions is buried deep in the English psyche. This belief tends to confuse the two related, but distinct, ideas of individual freedom and democracy. The idea of personal freedom has a long and chequered – and always limited – history in Britain and is often traced back to Magna Carta (DA Volume No. 1: 3–5). For example on its 750th anniversary in 1956, Lord Denning celebrated Magna Carta as 'the foundation of the freedom of the individual against the arbitrary authority of the despot'. The tradition finds more popular expression in the story of Robin Hood and a sturdy Anglo-Saxon resistance to the 'Norman Yoke' (Pocock 1987). It also has strong Conservative roots, laid in the resistance of the Tory country gentry to the Whig oligarchy in the eighteenth century (Colley 1982). This idea of ancient constitutional rights has served two functions; it may be deployed against state power on behalf of the oppressed or excluded, but may equally well be used by those in power against threats from below or outside, as it was in the time of the French Revolution

(Dickinson 1977; Dozier 1983), and in anti-democratic and anti-collectivist argument thereafter. In other words, the defence of liberty – uniquely English or British – was often a defence against democracy. Plainly, there are genuine tensions between the principles of liberty and democracy; as between individual or minority rights and majority decisions, and between principles of constitutionalism and the rule of law and the idea of popular sovereignty. But this historic notion of liberty was (and still is) strongly based on property rights – and was and often remains sharply divorced from the idea of democracy. And popular sovereignty is still not formally established in the UK; we are ruled in the name of the 'Crown', not the people. We are subjects, not citizens.

The tenacious belief in Britain's uniquely democratic past is but one example of long-standing ideas that still shape its democratic politics. The classic texts of English constitutional theory – from Edmund Burke (1790) to Walter Bagehot (1867), Albert Venn Dicey (1885) and Sir W. Ivor Jennings (1933–39) – remain very influential to this day. Yet they are anti-historical tracts, manufacturing a myth of timeless advance, organic continuity and magical quality. In 1790, Burke argued that Britain's governing institutions were not akin to a man-made machine, but to mysterious living organisms. Change must therefore be only slow and organic. The British constitution was 'the disposition of a stupendous wisdom, moulding together the great mysterious incorporation of the human race', or a 'great oak', the proud product of centuries' growth (Burke 1790: 46). High-sounding notions of this kind have become a tradition. In the Granada Guildhall lecture in 1987, for example, Lord Hailsham described cabinet government as 'one of the permanent gifts conferred by British political genius on the science and art of civilised government'. Even the imagery of continuity and organic change still exerts its magic. The Conservative writer, Ferdinand Mount, transforms Burke's oak into a 'ramshackle but pleasant old house', unfortunately situated 'right out on the promontory, at the mercy of wind and tide' (Mount 1992: 218). For Professor Peter Hennessy, a social democrat beguiled by 'that magically flexible constitution of ours', Britain's constitutional system grows 'like coral; the gradual accretion of centuries' (Hennessy 1995).

It is through such attitudes that the continuity and flexibility of the 'unwritten' British constitution continue to be legitimised. Yet the idea of continuity is surely not easily reconciled with the practice of flexibility. Can a polity really, as if by magic, simultaneously provide continuity *and* change, stability *and* fluidity? Ferdinand Mount subjected one of the classic statements of continuity to question in a way which reveals the importance of the paradoxical twinning of the two qualities of British constitutional arrangements (1992: 15–23). He quoted from Sir David Lindsay Keir's *Constitutional History of Modern Britain* to reveal the 'trick', so to speak, inherent in the confidence of the argument:

> Continuity has been the dominant characteristic in the development of English government. Its institutions, though unprotected by the funda-mental or organic laws which safeguard the 'rigid' constitutions of most other states, have preserved the same *general appearance* throughout their

> history, and have been regulated in their workings by principles which *can
> be regarded as constant* . . . [our emphasis]
>
> (Lindsay Keir 1946: 1)

'General appearance' . . . 'can be regarded as constant' . . . The phrases are revealing. The simple fact is that much of the continuity is in appearance alone. The House of Commons, for example, of 1997 is a mere shadow of the self-confident chamber of mid-Victorian times. Modern MPs pre-eminently represent not their constituents but their parties and obey the whips rather than employ their own judgement. Mrs Thatcher changed the ministerial conventions of government to create 'nearly presidential' government (Foster 1997: 1) and now we are informed that Gordon Brown, the Chancellor, is 'Prime Minister' to Tony Blair's 'President'.

Not only can the institutions of government change fundamentally over time; they are also to a real extent unprotected. Take the recent history of local government in the UK. Until 1979, though already seriously weakened, it was regarded as an important counterweight to central government and was supposed by most informed observers to be protected by convention. For Mrs Thatcher's ministers, local authorities held a lesser democratic authority than they themselves held, and they acted accordingly to determine key policy changes from the centre, to remove many of the executive functions and powers of local authorities and almost to destroy their financial autonomy. The *appearance* of local government may seem unchanged. In reality, local government was effectively unprotected, its world was turned upside down and Britain became even more a highly centralised state (Jenkins 1995). After 1983, Conservative governments 'reinvented' central government, introducing free-market principles into the workings of the civil service and devolving most functions and services to executive agencies, quangos and private enterprises. These are revolutionary changes, for which government had no mandate and which did not require it to go through special constitutional procedures encouraging public debate about the changes and highlighting the significance of 'what was actually going on'. The idea of continuity masks even a revolution in Whitehall.

The tradition of strong government

The most dominant of these ideas of unbroken constitutional continuity is that of 'strong government'. This idea is often described in terms of concealment. The two great Victorian constitutional writers, Walter Bagehot and A. V. Dicey, detected the 'secret' of power and efficiency at the centre of the English tradition of government. They both placed in an English setting the ancient idea of Plato's 'noble lie': the adoption of a public discourse which both justifies and conceals a private political culture possessing the widest possible powers of discretion within a set of moral rules of its own. In Victorian England, these were the rules of 'the club' which applied equally within a like-minded elite to public conduct in Westminster, Whitehall and the City. In Parliament, these club rules became dignified as political 'conventions'; within a newly reformed civil service, they were institutionalised as an informal code of conduct for the highly disciplined new body of senior civil servants. Such club rules and conventions still apply today as a major constitutional check on the use or abuse of the flexible powers, unconstrained by legal rules, which remain at the disposal of ministers and civil servants – that is, the state. It is part of our task to determine whether they are effective in the first instance; and whether they work in accordance with the basic democratic principle of popular control and open and accountable government. In other words, how far can the 'magically flexible constitution' really be described as '*ours*'?

In 1867, Walter Bagehot produced a most influential formulation of the myth of unbroken constitutional continuity. Unlike Burke, he saw the glamour of the monarchy and the past not as an emotionally compelling truth, but as a facade which concealed the 'efficient secret' of the constitution. For Bagehot, this secret was the power of the cabinet: 'The interlaced character of human affairs requires a single determining energy . . . . The excellence of the British Constitution is that it has achieved this unity; that in it, the sovereign power is single, possible and good' (Bagehot 1867: 222).

Dicey, a more passionate man, similarly found under the formality and myths of the British constitution 'an element of power which has been the true source of its life and growth. This *secret* [our emphasis] source of strength is the absolute omnipotence, the sovereignty of Parliament' (Dicey 1885: 168). That they both regarded the most important aspects of Britain's constitutional arrangements as 'secrets' revealed an implicit belief in government reserved for superior males. Neither man bothered to conceal his profound contempt for (in Bagehot's terms) the 'clownish mass' or 'lower classes' (1867: 147). The traditions which both men celebrated still substantially weaken the concept of citizenship in the UK, both in its formal status and role in political culture. Adults in this country are still subjects of the Crown, not citizens. Both men insisted on the necessarily unitary nature of power and sovereignty and their insistence has reinforced the realities of centralised power in the UK with a powerful ideological force. In 1885, Dicey wrote that:

> Two features have at all times since the Norman Conquest characterised the political institutions of England. . . . The first of these features is the omnipotence or undisputed supremacy throughout the whole country of the central government. . . . The second, which is closely connected with the first, is the rule or supremacy of law.
>
> (1885: 179)

Dicey's belief in a single omnipotent institution – checked only by the principle of the rule of law, reinforced simply by the ordinary operations of courts with no power over legislation – made him a bitter opponent of Irish and Scottish devolution; his theories inhibited such devolution to this day, as well as confusing the UK's status in the European Union.

However, he did uncover amid all the myths of 'ancient tradition' one real unbroken continuity: that of a strong central power. Medieval English kings probably exerted more effective authority over more of the territories they claimed to rule than any of their European neighbours. From the reign of Edward I (1216–72) onwards, a highly centralised royal executive was matched by a unified aristocratic Parliament, which came to establish the principle of consent not as a challenge to strong, executive government, but in support of it. Consent meant soliciting the views of the 'political nation' – that is, the king's most powerful subjects in Parliament – on important policy matters. The medieval political system rested, then, on the premise that monarchical power was conditional. The basic principles of consent and representation developed also served to clarify the legislative and judicial roles of Parliament itself. Sovereign power was vested in the 'Crown-in-Parliament' and Parliament came therefore to assume a legislative role, not in 'making' statute laws – that remained the king's prerogative – but in assenting to them. This idea of balance between strong government and consent still matters, though it is now nuanced to allow for the advent of universal suffrage. For example, in 1991 John Patten, then a Conservative minister, paid tribute to the 'strong and balanced political culture' which Britain had developed 'over time'. The balance, he said, 'is one between effectiveness – the capacity of government to govern – and consent – maintaining popular support for the political system' (1991: 8).

It is indeed remarkable how much the distinctive pattern of developments in Britain's political framework after 1688 – when recognisable features of the modern state began to take shape – owes to a continuity with medieval and Tudor political forms (Judge 1993: 6–16). None of the upheavals of subsequent centuries, not even the seventeenth century power struggle between the institutions themselves, destroyed the essential continuity of the two central ruling institutions, Crown and Parliament. Over time, their authority was augmented by the creation of a small and efficient state bureaucracy and national systems of taxation. The result was a state machine which wielded more effective power than any other European monarchy. However, when James I and Charles I resorted to arbitrary government, the Commons claimed a traditional right of consultation which was finally upheld in 1688–89 when the fractured unity of 'Crown-in-Parliament' was reconstituted with the emphasis upon Parliament rather than upon the Crown. That the Glorious Revolution and 1689 settlement was a *coup d'état* has not diminished its constitutional potency. The settlement rolled back the frontiers of absolutism, which were triumphing in the rest of Europe. What was asserted and accepted was the principle of parliamentary sovereignty. Legal supremacy was placed in Parliament, rather than in the monarch or courts.

By the eighteenth century, political stability rested on the balance between monarch, Lords and Commons – a balance in which strong central government was maintained by the general recognition of the king's 'right to rule' – that is, to choose his own ministers – and the existence of sufficient Crown patronage to limit parliamentary obstruction. The king, or his ministers, governed, but with the consent of Parliament which became the focus of state decision-making. Only those with an 'interest' in the system, primarily those with property, had the right to influence public policy. This 'political public' remained limited both in size and composition until the early nineteenth century. As the monarch's effective role diminished over this period, the discretionary prerogative powers required for an executive to take day-to-day command of the state passed from the monarch to his (or her) ministers.

(The Prime Minister and ministers apply these monarchical powers to this day, alongside the statutory powers which Parliaments have showered upon them.) And Britain became a constitutional monarchy, in which the king or queen reigned and the Prime Minister and ministers ruled.

Establishing the rule of law

The rule of law in the UK is a largely symbolic presence so far as executive power is concerned. The idea that the executive – then the monarch – was subordinate to some higher law was already established in medieval times; and after the writings of John Locke, came to be associated with doctrines of legality and legitimacy – the idea that government was bound by laws which applied to it as to individuals, and ought not to use its powers arbitrarily, or for individual or factional purposes. In practice, the rule of law evolved largely through the seventeenth century combat against arbitrary government described above. The judges developed principles of constitutionalism, not democracy, and imposed them on monarchs and public bodies under England's unique judge-made 'common law' system ('common' that is to the whole realm) (DA Volume No. 1: 91–104).

In three cases in the seventeenth and eighteenth centuries, English judges used their common-law powers to establish three fundamental principles. In the first, the *Case of the Prohibitions del Roy* (1607), the Chief Justice, Sir Edward Coke, ran the risk of being accused of treason by ruling that 'the King in his own person cannot adjudge any case'. He had to dispense justice through his judges. The case established the separation between the courts and the executive and asserted that the rights of citizens or subjects were governed by laws and not by the whims or interest of the executive. It did not secure a separate and independent judiciary because the monarch still appointed judges, as the executive does to this day (though the 1701 Act of Settlement subsequently protected judges from dismissal, except on an address by both Houses of Parliament; again establishing what is still the current position). In the second case (the 1611 *Case of Proclamations*), Coke established that the king, or executive, could make laws only through Parliament. The judgment imposed a proper procedure on the legislative process and inaugurated the principle of parliamentary consent.

Finally, the idea that government cannot interfere with the liberties of individuals without the consent of Parliament – one of the most central elements of the 'rule of law' in the UK – was secured in what is believed by many to be the most important case in English constitutional legal history (*Entick v Carrington*, 1765). Four 'King's Messengers' had entered Entick's house, arrested him and seized his books and papers on a minister's warrant. They argued that the government's power to issue such warrants was 'essential to government, and the only means of quieting clamours and sedition'. But the Lord Chief Justice, Lord Camden, held that, 'By the laws of England, every invasion of private property, be it ever so minute, is a trespass'. He specifically rejected the 'argument of State necessity', stating that public officials required the authority of 'some positive law' to justify such invasions.

The three strands of the rule of law have persisted, in principle at least, insisting that the executive is subject to the law, just as ordinary citizens are; that the executive must obtain the consent of Parliament for its policies and decisions; and that British citizens are protected by the law against arbitrary arrest. What is missing is a secure foundation for them in law given the executive's power, through Parliament, to re-make the law for its own purposes and the absence of any 'higher law' safeguarding constitutional practice or governing the executive's conduct. For example, Camden's principle has long been eroded by the practices of the security forces and police, and even in recent Home Office guidance. Hitherto unlawful police surveillance was given a dubious legitimacy in recent legislation. The then Conservative government and Labour opposition agreed the terms of the Police Act 1997, creating a statutory class of cases of 'serious crime' in which chief constables could authorise invasions of privacy without obtaining a legal warrant, and only public outcry and the prospect of a rebellion in the House of Lords finally secured a measure of quasi-judicial scrutiny (and that retrospective in 'urgent cases').

The rule of law in the UK is more a set of beliefs than of legal rules and working practices. The failure to develop it legally in the nineteenth century was in part due to the strength of the 'club ethic' – the idea (which we describe above) that politicians and others in public life could be relied upon to police their own behaviour. But legal and constitutional authorities also failed to understand the nature of the executive's power over Parliament and the realities of growing bureaucratic power. Dicey, for example, believed that the courts were capable of applying the common law equally to the state as to individuals and scorned the idea of developing administrative, or public, law to regulate the use and abuse of public powers. As two legal writers suggest:

> Because no crisis of legitimacy occurred, the need to pledge inalienable rights, to set firm limits to the exercise of executive power, or to speak specifically to tailored forms of redress against the state was never felt to be as strong a need in Britain as elsewhere.
>
> (Harden and Lewis 1988: 27)

The courts are largely still bystanders when it comes to executive decision-taking, even though judicial review has expanded hugely since the 1960s in the judiciary's attempts to correct the legal deficit. Yet Dicey's arguments remain the governing ideology, assisted by political ignorance of the proper constitutional role of the judiciary (Loveland 1997: 162–170). As a nation, we pay lip-service to the ideal of the rule of law rather than applying it.

The emergence of parliamentary democracy

The first broad-based demands for universal suffrage and other democratic reforms in the late eighteenth century owed little to celebrated, but ambivalent, figures like Wilkes and Charles James Fox. They feared 'mob rule' as much as they detested aristocratic privilege. The people who formed the reform movements of the 1780s and 1790s were a mix of skilled tradesmen and the lower-paid professions, non-conformists and early trade unionists. The first such movement was dispersed amid the patriotic fervour and intermittent government repression of the Napoleonic Wars, but re-emerged with wider support in the 1820s. Here, for the first time, are the lineaments of a popular democratic campaign, with something approaching a mass base. Despite the varieties of views and aims, core reformers shared a common belief in equality of civil, political and social rights, and pursued a substantial common programme, including universal male suffrage, and rights of association and assembly. Their bible, when it was not the Bible itself, was Thomas Paine's *The Rights of Man* (1791). The most eloquent counter arguments were those of Edmund Burke, who argued that Parliament already contained a proper balance of those whose material stake in the country's well-being guaranteed that they would have it always at heart. Their upbringing and education, 'lofty birth and fortune', imbued them with independent judgement and qualities of leadership, though there was always a place for rare individuals of ability from humbler origins. It was in this context that Burke argued for slow and organic change. Such counter arguments infused much pro-reform sentiment after the 1790s.

The reformers were sober men, never revolutionary, not even in the 1790s. They wanted parliamentary reform and barely challenged the doctrine of parliamentary supremacy. Even when notions of popular sovereignty and republican ideas were expressed, all but a revolutionary fringe assumed that their aims would be expressed through, and safeguarded by, a reformed Parliament. Very few radicals, too, challenged the model of the centralised, unitary state. Even the agitation for universal male suffrage and political reform in 1829–32, and the subsequent Chartist campaigns, emerging as they did out of the previous reform generation, pursued change of and through the existing state structures (Stedman-Jones 1983). In the spirit of Burke, the Great Reform Act 1832, pivotal though it was for the future, was carefully designed to conserve the past. It did not change the political system because it was not intended to (Cannon 1972: 257). No more did it empower the new urban middle classes who finally secured the representation of their interests in Parliament. The franchise was conceded only to a propertied bourgeoisie who joined the system in insufficient numbers to establish an autonomous party of their own. Their interests were channelled through the existing party structures of an aristocratic Parliament.

The most powerful result was to entrench a two-party system in which the Whigs were, as they had anticipated in sponsoring the bill, at least equal contenders for power. The tendency towards two-party politics had long been in the making, a product partly of the electoral system, partly of centralised government which tended to polarise parliamentary groups loosely into a 'Court' faction and 'Country' party. Early in the nineteenth century the waning prestige and patronage of the monarch created both the need, and room, for a new emphasis on stable government by way of party. By the mid-1830s it began to be assumed that each of the two existing parties would seek to form a government through securing an electoral majority in opposition to the other. Parties remained loose coalitions of patron–client networks, but the 1832 Act made inevitable the gradual and uneven development of party organisation, discipline and cohesion, in the interests of 'strong government'. Sir Robert Peel was one of the first politicians deliberately to develop a 'party' majority in the Commons. Sir James Graham, Peel's Home Secretary, wrote that 'the state of Parties and of relative numbers [was] after all . . . the cardinal point: with a majority in the House of Commons, everything is possible; without it, nothing can be done' (quoted in Beattie 1970: 109). In 1855, Lord Derby, refusing office, explained that he had insufficient parliamentary support and could not 'feel any assurance of forming – that which I concur in deeming most desirable and necessary for the country at the present period – a strong government' (*ibid.*: 112). Alongside this emphasis on two-party politics and 'strong government', concern with government stability led at the same time to the developing convention of collective cabinet responsibility.

As party government developed in the 1830s so Parliament began to legislate with considerable vigour to structure and regulate economic and social relations in a rapidly industrialising nation. Within the state itself, governments took on more regulatory responsibilities as a consequence of Parliament's legislative activism. And beyond Parliament, a host of organised sectional and functional representative bodies began to emerge, largely as a result of Parliament's legislative activity. The characteristics of modern British government – the ascendancy of the executive, or government, and a complex system of interest representation – were thus foreshadowed in the golden age of 'parliamentary government', when the House of Commons acted as an electoral college of men of independent judgement, able to make and unmake cabinets and ministers, and the cabinet was simply a 'committee' of the parliamentary majority. Bagehot's portrait of the mid-Victorian Commons is often dismissed as a species of political romanticism. But true or false, it was short-lived.

In a state of panic and fear, respectable working men were at last admitted to the franchise in 1867, doubling the (still very limited) electorate overnight. Radicals and liberals were almost as reluctant as Bagehot to see them join the 'political nation'. The liberal John Stuart Mill, for example, mindful of the 'collective mediocrity' and ignorant intolerance of masses, feared what the tyranny of the majority might bring (Roper 1989). Major changes in British politics did follow – but not of the kind Mill and others feared. Instead, the modern contours of party government were soon established. The Conservative and Liberal parties were restructured as large membership organisations. Electioneering on a national scale began to take shape after 1879, with canvassing, mass meetings, press coverage and, above all, the expectation that every seat would be contested. The two new mass parties were at once subject to dominance by the parliamentary party itself. MPs in the majority party were expected, as elected party representatives, to adhere to party policy and give consistent support to their government. Governments gradually extended their control over the Commons through party majorities and changes in procedure. After 1867, too, party politicians adopted the term 'democracy' in their rhetoric, but not in practice. 'Democracy', in the shape of active citizen participation, was discouraged.

By 1910, both major parties had effectively insulated party leadership in Parliament from extra-parliamentary control; the Conservatives explicitly, the Liberals more circuitously. Within Parliament, MPs were schooled by respected commentators in the necessity of party discipline: 'If party government is to be carried on . . . [t]he first condition of its success is that the Government should have a stable, permanent, disciplined support behind it' (Lecky 1899: 112). As a result, the responsibilities of opposition and critical scrutiny were removed from the Commons as a whole, and handed over to the largest minority opposition party. The House of Commons in effect ceased to be a collective entity, scrutinising and checking the executive, yet the idea that it still retains these responsibilities persists against the evidence to the contrary. The modern British state thus took on its present form early – Parliament remained sovereign in constitutional theory, but 'government' became largely the preserve of an executive which was 'sovereign' in practice (see Griffith 1982). As most political scientists agree, government in Britain is 'through Parliament and not by Parliament', just as it is 'for the people, not of or by the people'. In effect, Edward I's legacy has survived into modern times: representative government in Britain has historically been conceived, and largely works, as a means of legitimising executive power. The 'political nation' has now grown to encompass 'the people', or rather 'the electorate'. But popular participation has been routed through the existing structures of Parliament and the political parties represented there. The continuing strength of this tradition is evident in emphasis given to the word *parliamentary* in the phrase used to describe British democracy – *parliamentary* (i.e. not popular) democracy. The role of Parliament is clearly stated in Hugo Young's distaste for Tony Blair's use of the idea of 'The People':

> The people's Britain, as [Mr Blair] deploys it, runs against the grain of British life and the British constitution. The People is an entity that sits easily with direct democracy, but is out of place in the parliamentary system as hitherto understood. Here the popular will works through the filter of representative democracy. Parliament, not The People, is sovereign: an arrangement that constrains the power of demagogues and protects minorities against coarse majority self-interest.
>
> (*Guardian*, 2 October 1997)

A strong two-party system emerged in late Victorian times as the major framework for strong government, with its own set of club rules and conventions. The need for strong government, in turn, gave birth to a near fundamental belief in the role of the two-party system, and the importance of an electoral system which produces the 'clear result' necessary for either party to provide strong government. Most British politicians and observers since the 1880s have therefore viewed the absence of a two-party situation, or the breakdown of party cohesion, as undesirable, even unnatural. Single-party governments, kept in office by an unearned Commons majority, are always believed to be preferable to a coalition, even today when the three major parties represented in Parliament are all minority parties in the country at large.

The influence of imperialism on rule in Britain

For more than a century from the 1850s onwards, Britain ruled over a substantial empire. During the very period of British history in which the executive came to dominate Parliament and consolidated the creation of the modern civil service (from the 1870s to the 1920s), British governments simultaneously took control of this empire. The domestic polity and empire were run in incompatible ways. While the domestic franchise was reluctantly democratised, the executive ruled hundreds of millions of overseas subjects with a liberal concern to improve their lot, but no respect for democracy. Writing in 1939, George Orwell decried the notion that a Franco-British alliance against Nazi Germany was a coalition of democracies, pointing to 'six hundred million disenfranchised human beings' in their combined empires (Crick 1980: 376–377). The selective lack of awareness about Britain's empire was not accidental. It was carefully inculcated in Britain by a wide range of devices. The administration of the colonies was kept formally separate; colonial taxes and spending were almost wholly ring-fenced; and overseas officials were never counted in the statistics of the British state. To avoid repeating the catastrophic loss of the American colonies, the promise of 'dominion' status – that is, self-government within a nexus of military, financial and trade co-operation – was held out to white-dominated territories and even to non-white colonies in the (much) longer run.

These imperial arrangements defined a whole series of constitutional, political and administrative arrangements in Britain which have endured to the present day. They created a mixed democratic/authoritarian apparatus, governed at the centre by mechanisms of a similarly mixed character. Constitutionally, the British Parliament created a devolved administration in professional hands and lodged overall executive oversight in new Whitehall departments, often quite small in size but holding multiple levels of power. The ministers involved in 'imperial' issues formed a sizeable bloc inside the cabinet of ministers – including the Foreign Office – which exercised 'Crown prerogative' powers, the most unfettered powers of executive action. The insulation of these unaccountable structures of power from the oversight of Parliament was accepted almost universally, with liberals like John Stuart Mill fiercely arguing the case for 'professional' rule (Mill 1861: 348–388). A huge effort went into social-ising administrators (including the police and military) in the values which would keep the empire running smoothly.

The same philosophy was adopted at home. The mid-century Northcote-Trevelyan reforms of the civil service created an uncorrupt and meritocratic bureaucracy and defined the civil service for some 140 years. The reforms are celebrated for bringing 'the flower of our youth' – bright new graduates from the reformed universities, and especially Oxford – into the public service. But as Peter Hennessy notes in *Whitehall*, these wholly beneficial reforms 'were far from revolutionary in a democratic sense'. For their patron in Number 10, W. E. Gladstone, they were intended to 'strengthen and multiply the ties between the higher classes and the possession of administrative power' (Hennessy 1989: 31). Equally significantly, the reforms modelled the new permanent civil service explicitly on the Indian Civil Service and were linked to the challenges of imperial rule. Sir Charles Trevelyan, the leading reformer, wrote to Gladstone in 1854:

> We are apparently on the threshold of a new era pregnant with great events, and England has to maintain in concert with her allies the cause of right

and liberty and truth in every quarter of the world. Our people are few compared with the Multitudes likely to be arrayed against us; & we must prepare for the trial by cultivating to the utmost the superior morality and intelligence which constitute our real strength.

(Hughes 1949: 70)

Both men sought a regeneration of political and administration elites because 'these are the genuine elements of national power'. In the era of imperialist expansion the project succeeded spectacularly, binding much of the aristocracy and the upper middle class into the very considerable, but unrecorded, imperial state apparatus – which became another of the 'efficient secrets' of the British political system.

The mixed character of executive institutions – with the Prime Minister, cabinet, and significant ministers and bureaucrats operating half in and half out of the imperial sphere – meant that the values of an elite and insulated executive infiltrated its dealings with Westminster and domestic issues. In diverse ways, the elitist attitudes of imperial rule not only percolated into domestic political practice, but penetrated internal party politics and much wider political debates (see, for example, Sutherland 1990: 302–303). Scores of critical observers complained about the way in which MPs and party politicians interfered, or sought to interfere, in imperial affairs, greatly limited though their influence was. In 1910, Lord Hugh Cecil denounced even cabinet control as a destabilising influence: 'The highest authority of our immense and unequalled Empire lies alternately in the hands of one or two knots of vehement, uncompromising and unbalanced men' (Gilmour 1978: 89).

But the most permanent legacy of the imperial rule lay in its appeal to Britain's classically trained administrative elite, for it came close, in theory at least, to the model of Plato's *Republic*. In this perfect state, a detached group of honest and disin-terested 'guardians' ruled in the public interest, thus creating a just society in which everyone did what they were best at, confident that its political direction would be stable and uncorrupt. Plato's idea of 'guardianship' was a persuasive ideal for Britain's bureaucratic rulers overseas. But it also provided the unifying philosophy which sustained leading bureaucrats and politicians in Britain. For Trevelyan the new higher civil servants were to be a Platonic elite of guardians, 'occupying a position duly subordinate to ministers . . . yet possessing sufficient independence, character, ability and experience to be able to advise, assist and to some extent influence those who are from time to time set over them' (Mount 1992: 105).

The cumulative impact of this experience over almost a century in the defining 'modern' period of British government made a twofold imprint on their governing practices and their minds. Their practices became deeply ambivalent in terms of accountability to Parliament and the public; and they developed a profound belief in the necessities of state power and strong government and a non-democratic cultural bias, resonant with liberal virtues and assured in the secrets of power. The lure of imperial guardianship ideals long outlasted the framework of tasks they grew up to justify and make intelligible (Hennessy 1989: 214–215).

The power (and ultimately, too, the long-term influence) of imperial over domestic politics also found a narrower, but powerful, expression in the late 1880s with the creation of a powerful new cabinet committee, known first as the Colonial Defence Committee and, after 1902, as the Committee of Imperial Defence (CID). This committee soon became the prototype for others. Its powers were continuously expanded and with the outbreak of the 1914–18 War the CID became:

> a body having almost executive power to advance its own decisions; but it remained, in theory, a committee of the Cabinet . . . supplemented by expert assistance. Its relations to the Cabinet, however, were obscure and not very satisfactory, until the drastic rearrangements which took place in December 1916 once more left it the great expert War Council of the Empire.
>
> (Jenks 1923: 206)

The cabinet reorganisation after 1919 reaffirmed its position, unparalleled in domestic politics, at the leading edge of executive power. The Cabinet Office was developed in peacetime as a cabinet secretariat, on exactly the same lines as those which governed the CID secretariat, absorbing its ethos and procedures and generalising them across the whole run of government business. The Cabinet Office took control of intelligence through a new co-ordinating body, the Joint Intelligence Committee (JIC), whose existence was formally acknowledged only in 1993 (though it is probably most accurately regarded as one of the inefficient secrets of the British constitution). The creation of similarly powerful cabinet committees became an important ingredient of wartime government from 1939–45 and they were consolidated in peacetime Britain after 1945 (see **p. 140**). The postwar Labour government converted CID into the Overseas Policy and Defence (OPD) Committee of the cabinet, in theory bringing it fully under cabinet control. But the decisions to build an independent nuclear deterrent and to join the Korean War rapidly pushed the new committee into the semi-autonomous and secret role of its predecessor (see **pp. 128–9** and Hennessy 1986: Chapter 4).

One of the most remarkable aspects of the postwar period is how the essentials of this governing tradition of a powerful and insulated executive, anchored on an elite state bureaucracy, have imprinted themselves on British government while society at large has become more open and less deferential than in the prewar period. The Welfare State, potentially a democratising process, was cast in a statist, and often authoritarian, mould from the very beginning from 1945–51 and was never 'grounded' in popular experience (see Dunleavy 1989). The revolutionary *Next Steps* programme in the 1980s and 1990s – breaking up the unified civil service and shifting operation and service functions to semi-autonomous agencies (see Chapter 8) – left the core policy-making mandarinate of Whitehall untouched. Britain's entry into the EEC in 1973 and its growing closeness to Europe has had a considerable impact upon British institutions, business and industry, the courts and law, and has intensified the problems of democratic accountability, but the nature of executive control has remained broadly constant; and the machinery of liaison and negotiation with Brussels operates through the royal prerogative powers of ministers.

Conclusions

This, then, is a brief portrait of the makings of the modern British state. It is exceptional in many respects, being now only one of three liberal democracies which does not possess a written constitution (the others being Israel and New Zealand). We have seen that democracy came late to the British state, and that its character was already shaped by its monarchical history and imperial role; and that crucial governing arrangements are remarkable in their ability to absorb and survive major changes, such as the introduction of the welfare state, Mrs Thatcher's revolutionary changes in Whitehall, and even incorporation into the European Union. This resilience may prove a significant obstacle for the new Labour government's already ambiguous ambition of transferring power to the public.

Defenders of the liberal and democratic credentials of the British state argue that the informality of its constitutional arrangements has enabled it to adjust to the requirements of a democratic age more successfully than other countries with a written constitution. In their view, individual liberties have been sufficiently protected by the common law and a vigilant Parliament. The executive is strong and flexible in order that it might govern effectively, but is effectively held accountable to the public by making ministers answerable in Parliament and through the scrutiny of the media; and made subject to the rule of law by the courts. These checks and balances are in turn reinforced by the discipline of the ballot and the presence in Parliament of an official opposition party as an alternative 'government in waiting'. In our previous volume, *The Three Pillars of Liberty* (DA Volume No. 1), we examined the first of these claims about the distinctive quality of the arrangements for protecting civil and political rights in the UK, and found them wanting. In this volume, we examine the claims about the democratic character of the central governing institutions of Whitehall and Westminster and test them systematically against our Audit criteria. We begin with the electoral system and examine how far it meets our criteria of popular control over government and political equality.

PART I

Elections and Mandates

Introduction

Free, fair and regular elections stand at the very heart of representative democracy. They embody the two basic principles of the Democratic Audit – popular control of government and political equality in the exercise of that control. In the first Audit volume, *The Three Pillars of Liberty*, we assessed Britain's arrangements for elections against international human rights standards (DA Volume No. 1: Chapter 14). There is an overlap between those standards and the criteria we have developed for auditing conformity with the two principles of popular control and political equality. Thus, the first volume substantially dealt with some of the questions posed by the first two Democratic Audit criteria:

DAC1. How far is appointment to legislative and governmental office determined by popular election, on the basis of open competition, universal suffrage and secret ballot; and how far is there equal effective opportunity to stand for public office, regardless of which social group a person belongs to?

DAC2. How independent of government and party control and external influences are elections and procedures of voter registration, how accessible are they to voters, and how free are they from all kinds of abuse?

We found that national elections in the UK largely met international human rights standards, being held at regular intervals by almost wholly secret ballot, and being free of bribery, intimidation and other abuses. However, the informal and archaic nature of some of the rules and practices governing British elections means that damaging defects can prejudice fully free and impartial elections. Our first concern is that the ballot at national and local elections alike is not wholly secret, since the authorities have unexamined access to voting papers and counterfoils which identify each voter (**DAC1**); we assess the implications of this lapse in Chapter 4, **pp. 80–1**. Further, the registration system for voters is obsolete. It dates back to 1918 and needs to be adapted to the needs of a more mobile and pluralist society. Between 2 and 3.5 million people eligible to vote are disenfranchised at any one time and progressively fewer eligible people are being registered. Members of certain disadvantaged groups – inner-city residents, especially those in insecure rented accommodation, black people, the homeless – are more likely to be unregistered, which points to structural inequalities in the operation of registration procedures. A report by a Home Office working party in February 1994 dismissed proposals for reform, largely on the grounds of the likely cost (between £4 and £12 million), which might seem a small price to pay for a more inclusive suffrage. Ministers were said to be considering the report in the period before the 1997 election, but failed to come to any conclusions (DA Volume No. 1: 281–287). Most convicted criminals and homeless people are denied the vote and the effect of Home Office guidance deprives compulsorily detained mentally ill patients in hospital of the right to vote, not on grounds of competence but simply for bureaucratic convenience. Defects in arrangements for postal and proxy votes go unremedied, thus denying some elderly, sick and disabled people a full opportunity to vote. The absence of a constitutional right to vote in Britain means that these and other excluded people have no remedy in law. Electoral registration officers are servants of the Crown and are thus formally independent of government, but they depend on the Home Office and local authorities for their funding. To this extent, then, they are not wholly free from 'government or party' interference (though the remedy of judicial review exists in cases of blatant reluctance to promote registration by local authorities) (*ibid.* 286–288).

The informality of the voting system is open to abuse. The most serious problem has been the absence of strict rules governing the descriptions of candidates and parties on ballot papers. In the 1994 Euro-election, an official Liberal Democrat candidate lost to the Conservative candidate in a Devon constituency by 700 votes, while a previously unknown candidate, standing as a 'Literal Democrat', polled over 10,000 votes. But the courts found that there is no requirement in British law that the party description 'be true, fair or not confusing'. So a political party was deprived of a seat in the European Parliament and a majority of voters of their choice of candidate. Britain has no laws requiring political parties standing for election to register and also has no Electoral Commission, as in other European democracies and Commonwealth countries, to resolve such anomalies. Home Office officials were supposed to find a solution in meetings with the 'main political parties' but no proposals emerged before the 1997 election. The same 'Literal Democrat' stood as a candidate in Winchester, making the final result desperately close for the eventual Liberal Democrat victor. The government is legislating to introduce the registration of political parties and to prevent misleading descriptions on ballot papers. But generally the process for considering electoral problems and reforms does not lie in an impartial Electoral Commission, a constitutional court or Parliament, but with the curious Speaker's conference procedure – a private meeting of the leaders of parties represented at Westminster, impartially chaired by the Speaker. The reasons for their recommendations are not usually published and the recommendations are not binding on government (DA Volume No. 1: 281–282). We concluded that UK elections required more certain constitutional protection than a single statute – the Representation of the People Act 1983 – especially as it is silent on significant issues.

In this volume, we concentrate on parliamentary elections, leaving out of the reckoning local and Euro-elections. However, the UK Parliament fails to satisfy our first Audit criterion, since the second chamber, the House of Lords, is not subject to election at all. Its lack of democratic legitimacy prevents it from fulfilling its function as a check on the House of Commons effectively (see Chapter 14). In the absence of any electoral process for the House of Lords, our analysis is confined to elections to the House of Commons. We apply parts of **DAC1** and **DAC2** (above) and the remaining three Audit criteria on the electoral process:

DAC3. How effective a range of choice and information does the electoral and party system allow the voters, and how far is there fair and equal access for all parties and candidates to the media and other means of communication with them?

DAC4. To what extent do the votes of all electors carry equal weight, and how closely does the composition of Parliament and the programme of government reflect the choices actually made by the electorate?

DAC5. What proportion of the electorate actually votes, and how far are the election results accepted by the main political forces in the country?

We give most emphasis to **DAC4**. In Chapter 3, we examine Britain's existing voting system – the plurality-rule (or 'first-past-the-post') system – and assess in detail how far it satisfies the principle that citizens should possess votes of 'equal value'. We also analyse the parties' election strategies and consider how they affect the equality of the ballot, and discuss the range of choice and information which is made available to citizens at election time (**DAC3**). We do not seek to analyse one significant issue in depth – that of the principle of equal opportunities to stand for public office, 'regardless of which social group a person belongs to' (**DAC1**) – since we have decided to leave aside the question of the social composition of public life for another report. However, in Chapter 3, we check briefly on whether women and people from the ethnic minorities have an 'equal effective opportunity' to stand for election to the Commons. In the same chapter we also consider the question of turnout and how far election results are accepted by political forces in the UK (**DAC5**). In Chapter 4, we assess those questions of the independence of elections from government and party control which were not dealt with in the first Democratic Audit volume, in particular the secrecy of the ballot and government influence over electoral boundaries (**DAC4**). In Chapter 5, we consider the idea of the electoral 'mandate' and how far government programmes reflect voters' choices (**DAC4**); and the opportunities afforded to the electorate to vote directly on measures of constitutional change (**DAC6**; see **p. 12**).

We are unable exhaustively to explore all the issues raised by these criteria, several of which demand a book in their own right. Apart from the decision not to analyse how far membership of the House of Commons is effectively open to people from all social groups, the most notable omission is the influence of the media on elections, and the range and choice of information available during elections, which we treat very briefly in Chapter 3. We have sought funding for research into the complex issues raised by the interplay of the state, politics and the media, and media influence upon public opinion and voting intentions. We have left the question of opinion polling during elections to one side, as this was adequately dealt with by the Hansard Society Commission on Election Campaigns (1991).

Finally, we are aware that Britain's plurality-rule, or 'first-past-the-post', election system has caused widespread disquiet over the past 25 years. Before the 1997 election the Labour and Liberal Democrat parties pledged themselves to give the electorate a choice between the existing system and a 'single proportional' alternative in a referendum and an Electoral Commission has been established to choose that alternative. In September 1997, the Democratic Audit published *Making Votes Count* (DA Paper No. 11), an important study of how alternative systems might have worked under British conditions in 1992 and 1997. The study is based on major surveys in which people 'voted' on the appropriate ballot papers for the main alternative systems. We followed this study up by examining how a mixed system – of the alternative (or supplementary) vote, with an additional member top-up – would work in British conditions (*Making Votes Count 2*, DA Paper No. 14). We briefly discuss the implications of change in Chapter 3.

3   The Other National Lottery

The political effects of Westminster elections

We always come up against the problem of the current electoral system in which the gambling, betting and sporting instincts of the nation seem to have found their characteristic political expression.

(Egon Wertheimer, *Portrait of the British Labour Party*, 1929)

If we had voting like last night, there would be a Labour government with a clear majority, able to do what it wished, without let or hindrance.

(John Major, on the Wirral South by-election loss,
Independent, 1 March 1997)

Voting is the only political act most British citizens undertake. More than four out of five people report that they have voted at least once in general elections and some two-thirds in local elections. By contrast, only about one in eight has ever joined an organised group and fewer than one in ten has attended a political rally (Parry, Moyser and Day 1992: 44). In practice and principle, therefore, free, fair and regular elections stand at the very heart of representative democracy in this country. They are the key controlling device which citizens possess over the elected governors of the nation, their legislation and their policies.

This chapter examines how well elections perform their controlling role in the light of the two principles of democracy – political equality and popular control. Ultimately, it is through the ability of citizens to retain or dismiss their elected representatives in regular elections, and the political parties for which they stand, that the principle of *popular control* over government becomes practical politics. In the UK, the role of elections is particularly significant since constitutional accountability is based primarily on the electorate's ability to recall governments and replace them periodically, through Parliament, and on the existence of an opposition party able to pick up the reins of government. The ideas of an equal value for each vote, and an equal right to stand for election, are central to the principle of *political equality*; put at its simplest, this principle requires that every elector's vote should count for one, and none for more than one. But it is also important that electors should have a range of choice at elections which broadly reflects their political preferences and needs – and that those choices are effective. Thus this chapter concentrates on two of the Audit's criteria:

Role of elections

DAC3. How effective a range of choice ... does the electoral and party system allow the voters?

DAC4. To what extent do the votes of all electors carry equal weight, and how closely does the composition of Parliament ... reflect the choices actually made by the electorate?

Yet we also have to bear in mind other objectives and outcomes. In any parliamentary democracy, elections have to accomplish two tasks: to produce an elected assembly which is representative of the people; and a government which is both effective and accountable to the people's representatives in the assembly. As noted above, the upper House of Parliament in the UK is not subject to election at all and is not intended to be representative. In elections to the lower House, there is a pronounced conflict between the two tasks of representation and government formation. The plurality-vote – or 'first-past-the-post' – electoral system in Great Britain, originating in the Middle Ages, has survived in place on the grounds that it achieves strong government, even though it fails to represent the electorate's votes for parties proportionally in the House of Commons. The use of the system is justified on the grounds precisely that it normally over-represents the leading two parties and so both gives the governing party a 'working majority' and establishes a clear alternative opposition party – in effect, a government in waiting.

In theory, Britain's electoral system seeks to reconcile the idea of strong government with the principle that everyone's vote should count equally, though, as we shall see, it gives far more emphasis to the first objective and neglects the second. The House of Commons, like similar assemblies in other liberal democracies, is supposed to represent the electorate in a 'microcosmic' sense – that is, to be representative of them as a smaller body may be representative of a larger one (Birch 1972: 15–21). The crucial question, however, is *what manner* of representativeness is being sought. There are three ways in which the House of Commons could be made representative of the electorate:

- according to geographical distribution;
- according to each party's share of the votes cast; and
- according to its social characteristics.

These three modes of representation are *all* important for the Democratic Audit. The first, because voters should not be privileged or disadvantaged just because they live, say, in the country rather than a city, or in one region than another; nor should Parliament be weighted disproportionately towards one set of geographical interests at the expense of another. The second, because elections nowadays are primarily about choosing a party or parties to form a government: votes should not be more or less effective according to which party people vote for, nor should their relationship to seats in Parliament be decided by arbitrary chance. The third, because a Parliament heavily biased towards one social group, or set of groups, or which excludes certain groups, will be limited in experience and probably more narrowly focused, and is more likely to suffer loss of esteem, trust or even legitimacy – especially among people who are excluded, and who may very well be disadvantaged and feel alienated from society as a result. These three dimensions of representation and political equality are plainly inter-related with each other and with yet another principle – that of 'effective opportunity to stand for public office, regardless of which social group a person belongs to' (**DAC1**). The third aim cannot be realised if this principle is not satisfied. But while we deal briefly with the representation of women and ethnic minorities in Parliament, we do not assess the issues of social composition and equal opportunities to stand for Parliament in this volume (for reasons already discussed; see **p. 19**).

We are therefore dealing with two questions. How does the current electoral system rate on the two dimensions of representation and political equality? And why does it fail where it fails? We begin with the rationale for the existing electoral system, based as it is on the idea of geographical equality – that all votes should count for the same, regardless of where people happen to live. This principle is evident in the work of the Boundary Commissions, four quangos charged with making the size of constituencies throughout Britain as equal as possible, so that all parts of the country get equal representation according to their population; and so that all votes carry equal weight, *as between constituencies*. The result is a House of Commons which is highly proportionate geographically, being intended to mirror the distribution of the electorate across the country (but see **p. 48** further). In the Middle Ages, counties and boroughs were regarded as natural communities. At first, members of medieval parliaments were chosen by common consent: the theory was that the 'unanimous mind' of the county or borough could be discerned. But after 1430 the plurality principle was introduced in the shires: those with 'the greatest number' of supporters were to be returned to Parliament and over time the rule of the bare majority became established (Hart 1992: 5). General elections were – as they remain in their structure – not national contests, but a series of local constituency contests. Thus, the basic system pre-dates the existence of political parties – which still remain only partially recognised in electoral law and practice.

The concept of 'proportional representation' seeks to embody our second dimension of political equality and representation. Put simply, it holds that parties are the principal agents of political choice; that the votes of all electors should count for the same, *regardless of the party they have voted for*; and that the political parties should therefore be allocated seats in an elected assembly in proportion to the number of votes they have obtained in an election. This concept does not necessarily rule out geographical considerations, but it does mean that they cannot be made exclusive. Most liberal democracies in Europe practise some form of proportional representation (PR). Some, like Germany, combine a geographical base with PR. Germany uses a system – the additional member system (AMS) – in which people vote in constituencies for 'local' representatives, as electors in the UK do, but then elect additional MPs regionally to make the overall election result proportional.

The UK is the only European state which uses an unmodified 'first-past-the-post' (plurality) system. In the rest of the world, those countries which do not employ PR systems tend to belong to the older Anglo-Saxon tradition (like the USA, India and

Geographical representation

Zimbabwe), though New Zealand has just switched from plurality voting to a PR system like Germany's and Australia uses the alternative vote (a close cousin to first-past-the-post voting). Neither plurality nor PR voting systems can ever be 'perfect'; some supposedly proportional systems only imperfectly deliver proportionality in practice (Irish Republic), some are manifestly inappropriate for the countries in which they operate (South Africa is a case in point; see Johnson and Schlemmer 1996: 368); some give excessive power to unrepresentative small parties (as in Israel). PR elections in European democracies, however, normally produce highly proportional results and stable governments (Farrell 1997).

Representing 'natural communities' in Britain

> 5. EQUAL CONSTITUENCIES, *securing the same amount of representation for the same number of voters.*
>
> (*The People's Charter*, 1837)

> *As nearly as is practicable, one man's vote in a congressional election is to be worth as much as another's.*
> (The United States Supreme Court, 1964 (*Westberry v Sanders*, 376 US 1)

The plurality electoral system seeks to achieve representation of people according to where they live rather than their political preference. In other words, people are in theory supposed to be voting on behalf of the 'natural community' inherent in constituencies like Haltemprice and Howden and Aldridge-Brownhills, rather than for a political party. It is at once evident that this premise does not reflect social and political realities. Constituency boundaries are legally supposed to take 'local ties' and local authority areas into account, but no-one could argue that they embody 'natural communities'. For example, Haltemprice is a suburb of Hull, Howden a small rural town; Aldridge an expanse of postwar suburban housing, Brownhills an ex-mining town. The one seat was created in 1974, the other in 1995. More broadly, research in 1992–93 by MORI into 'community identity' for the Local Government Commission showed that people attached very low priority to 'sense of local community' and 'historical or traditional boundaries' when they were asked what was important in deciding new structures for local government. Very few members of the public make representations to the Boundary Commissions or attend their inquiries into new parliamentary constituency boundaries. Electors in modern elections are not seeking primarily to determine who will best represent the interests of the locality in Parliament (though the idea of a 'local MP' remains important to people). They choose between national party programmes and national leaders and nowadays they vote in constituencies largely composed of artificial slices of the electorate.

Nevertheless, strictly speaking, it would still be possible to achieve some sort of parity between the vote of a resident of Brighton and another in Newcastle, if constituencies were of an equal and appropriate size. This principle has however never been upheld. The original rules for the Boundary Commissions, the politically neutral, semi-judicial bodies which periodically determine parliamentary boundaries, were fixed in 1944. One of the rules then obliged the Commissions to ensure that electorates should not vary in size by more than 25 per cent either way of an 'electoral quota'. This quota is calculated by dividing the total number of electors by the total number of constituencies. A variance either way of 25 per cent may seem more than broad enough, but within three years, the then Labour Home Secretary removed the 25 per cent limit, announcing that it was 'too restrictive' – 'ancient communities shall not be dismembered and representation placed on a purely numerical basis' (HC Deb, 13 November 1945, c77–79). Thus the current rule on electoral equity – rule 5 – simply requires the Commissioners to make the size of constituency electorates as near a fixed 'electoral quota' as is practicable.

This watered-down rule of equality is utterly compromised however by the fact that the UK has four Boundary Commissions, one for each of the four 'home countries' – England, Northern Ireland, Scotland and Wales – and the electoral quotas they apply differ significantly. This is because Scotland is entitled to a minimum of 71 seats in the House of Commons; Wales to 35 seats; and Northern Ireland to 16–18. For the fourth periodic reviews (1991–95) which produced the boundaries on which the 1997 election was fought, the quota size which would have produced equal constituency electorates in England was 69,281; for Scotland, 54,569; for Wales, 58,525; and for Northern Ireland, 67,852. These quotas are based on electoral registers which are unreliable and, in particular, under-represent urban voters (see DA Volume No. 1: Chapter 14) and were set at differing times. But they already vary considerably – Scotland's quota is more than 20 per cent lower than the English quota. From the moment their work began, therefore, the four sets of Boundary Commissioners were bound to create constituency electorates of vastly varying size.

The goal of equal-sized electorates is further compromised by other rules which contradict rule 5. The Commissioners are asked to fix constituency boundaries which, 'so far as is practicable', do not cross the boundaries of London boroughs or English counties; to 'have regard' to local authority areas in Scotland; and are instructed not to split wards into different Northern Irish constituencies (rule 4(1) (a)–(c)). They may depart from rule 5 to allow for special 'geographical considerations', such as the size, shape and accessibility of a constituency (rule 6). And finally, rule 7 absolves them from fully obeying all previous rules and, in particular, asks them to consider 'local ties' and the inconvenience which boundary changes cause. This contradictory package gives the Commissioners considerable discretion to vary the sizes of constituency electorates. This discretion was reinforced by the Court of Appeal in 1983 when Michael Foot, then the Labour leader, objected to the third periodic report on the grounds that the Commissioners had not given proper weight to the principle of equal representation in rule 5. The Court's judgment held that rule 7 (on taking local ties and inconvenience into account) in effect removed any mandatory element from the first six rules and reduced the rules, 'while remaining very important indeed', to the status of guidelines. The judgment specifically said that the Commission's task was not merely 'an exercise in accountancy', but was a 'more far-reaching and sophisticated undertaking, involving striking a balance between many factors which point in different directions. This calls for judgment, not scientific precision' ([1983] QB 600 at 624 and 631–632).

Geographical representation

By contrast, the overriding criterion in fixing electoral districts in the United States is equality of population. In 1964, the Supreme Court held that, 'as nearly as is practicable, one man's vote in a congressional election is to be worth as much as another's', and in 1969 affirmed that this principle required a state to make a good-faith effort to achieve precise mathematical equality; and that states were obliged to justify any population variance (McLean and Mortimore 1992). The Court of Appeal rejected an attempt by Michael Foot's lawyers to introduce the Supreme Court judgments in the 1983 case.

The greatest pressure on the Boundary Commissions is not to increase the number of seats in the House of Commons. The fourth periodic reviews added eight seats, five of them English. But the reviews did substantially reduce the inequalities in size within the four home countries, though crucially not *between* them. In all, 537 (out of 659) constituencies had electorates within 10 per cent of each country's electoral quota, compared with 328 (out of 651) previously. These differences matter politically. Had these boundaries been in effect in 1992, a team of election experts calculate that John Major's majority would have been larger by six more seats (Rallings, Thrasher and Denver 1996: 173). But the improvements leave considerable disparities in the size of electorates, especially if you assess them on a UK basis by aggregating the four Commissions' quotas (see Table 3.1). Constituencies like Meirionnydd Nant Conwy (32,866) in Wales, and Orkney and Shetland (31,837) and the Western Isles (23,015) in Scotland, deviate by more than 40 per cent from the UK norm. In the south, the Isle of Wight (101,784) has more than four times as many voters as the Western Isles. Plainly, in both cases, geography dictates this grossly unequal outcome, but it would not do so under most proportional systems.

Table 3.1 Deviations from electoral quotas in UK constituencies, 1997

Deviation from quota*:	More than 30%	Between 20–30%	Between 10–20%	Within 10%
England (quota 69,281)	1	3	81	444
Wales (58,525)	1	1	9	29
Scotland (54,569)	2	3	17	50
Northern Ireland (67,852)	—	—	4	14
UK:				
1 On aggregated BC quotas (66,988)	6	46	174	433
2 On the latest electoral statistics (66,610)	6	47	185	427

Source: Adapted from Rallings, Thrasher and Denver (1996)
Notes:
* Quotas are given in brackets.
The UK deviations were calculated by the Democratic Audit as follows:
1 On the basis of an aggregate figure for the four Boundary Commissions' quotas 1991–93, to give an assessment of the overall value of their work at the time their recommendations were published.
2 On the basis of the latest figures for the UK electorate in 1995 (*Electoral Statistics*, OPCS Series EL No. 22).

Overall, four constituencies are either 30 per cent above or below an aggregate electoral quota for the UK as a whole; 52 deviate by 20 per cent or more; and 226 – a third of all constituencies – are adrift by 10 per cent or more. If we update the electoral quota, using the 1995 electoral statistics, 53 constituencies in the UK are either 20 per cent above or below the new electoral quota, and 238 (36 per cent) deviate by 10 per cent or more. These figures will progressively worsen up to the next boundary reviews currently set for 2005–07.

The 1990s redistributions also leave in place a significant electoral bias in favour of Labour, caused by the concentration of the party's vote in smaller constituencies, though it is now smaller than previously. In effect, Labour will continue to get a greater return in seats for any given share of the vote than the Conservatives. If, for example, the two parties had polled 39 per cent of the vote in 1992, the Conservatives would have had 38 fewer seats than Labour – 282 as against 320. In 1997, the gap was only slightly reduced to a 33-seat advantage. But the gap will grow again as shifts in population increase the size of the electorates in Conservative seats and diminish those in safe Labour seats. As a legal review of British elections concludes, 'the edifice of Parliamentary government in Britain appears to rest upon somewhat insubstantial foundations' (Rawlings 1988: 61).

The influence of party on fixing boundaries

The independence of the Boundary Commissions from party political influence is jealously guarded. Their probity and conscientiousness are not in doubt. Further, 'as soon as may be' after the Commissions have submitted their reports, ministers are required by statute to lay the reports before Parliament, together with draft orders giving effect (with or without modification) to their recommendations. By convention, no Home Secretary has ever laid orders modifying the recommendations of the Commissions. However, politics is an insidious business; and for all the diligent independence of the Commissioners, politicians naturally regard boundary-fixing as being too important to be left entirely to them.

In 1969, for example, the then Home Secretary, Jim Callaghan, complying with convention, laid their reports unamended before Parliament, but without the orders and at the same time presented a bill introducing only parts of the boundary changes. His motive was to avoid Labour fighting the 1970 election on disadvantageous new parliamentary boundaries, though he gave impending local government changes as his reason. He withdrew his bill after the House of Lords blocked it and an elector applied to the courts for an order obliging him to lay the orders. Callaghan undertook to lay the orders, but did so with a recommendation to reject them. The 1970 election was fought on the 1954 boundaries (which was worth, according to one estimate, 11 extra seats for Labour; Reeve and Ware 1991). Thus, thanks to its parliamentary majority, a ruling party can delay boundary changes it doesn't like.

The Commissions themselves are not insulated from subtle, but strong, party political manipulation. They are obliged by law to hold local inquiries into their draft proposals for new boundaries and the political parties are the dominant players in initiating and shaping these inquiries. In certain areas, like Colchester and Bedford, there was strong public interest in the Commissions' proposals. But most of the representations and petitions the Commissions receive (at the fourth periodic review, 40,000 representations and petitions bearing 82,820 signatures) and the witness evidence they hear are inspired by the political parties. Naturally, most of the challenges concentrate on rule 7 (local ties and arguments of inconvenience). Outside Scotland, the Commissioners holding the inquiries are lawyers with little or no local knowledge, which gives the political parties a lot of room to manipulate the inquiries, often using local groups, local authorities and individual residents as their proxies. Their aims are obvious – to maximise the number of safe seats for their party throughout the country and to make their opponents' seats electorally vulnerable to them. These aims must be hidden in what they and their proxies say in their representations, and inevitably their arguments will vary in different constituencies and different parts of the country. Generally, the only challenges to one party's arguments come from rival parties, so the ingenuity, quality and apparent diversity of partisan advocacy tends to carry the day. The Commissioners' lack of local knowledge, their imprecise brief and the ambiguous nature of the rules almost guarantees inconsistency in their decisions around the country. There is, for example, no working definition of the crucial 'local ties' provision.

There is no doubt that representations had an effect on the final decisions of the fourth periodic reviews. In England, the provisional recommendations of the Commissioners were revised in 44 out of 64 cases, and often radically. The six public inquiries in Scotland all led to revisions (at least one of which was major) and seven Welsh inquiries brought about two revisions. It is generally agreed that Labour proved to be by far the most organised and effective party in manipulating the process in 1991–95 and were the overall 'winners', though there is considerable debate over exactly how much they gained. David Gardner, Labour's principal organiser, estimated that Labour faced a possible loss of between four and 17 seats, due to boundary changes, and finally gained four winnable seats and effectively neutralised the effect of redistribution (Gardner 1995). Party resources as well as their ingenuity and organisation play a part. The Liberal Democrats, for example, performed poorly. David Rossiter, of the University of Essex, found that in 82 inquiries in Great Britain (three of them 'double inquiries'), the Conservatives played a 'significant role' in 80, Labour in 77, and the Liberal Democrats in only 17. Overall, though the process is formally neutral, it is clearly dominated by the political parties. Gardner concluded his paper to a Nuffield College conference on redistribution as follows:

> Political parties have a vital role to play in the redistribution of constituencies. They influence the statutory criteria in Parliament, are consulted on the ground-rules, generate counter-proposals, marshal their forces for the public inquiries and obviously have an impact on the views of local authorities. So long as this is not at the expense of the wider public interest and that the process and objectiveness of the final decisions are beyond reproach, this is a healthy, beneficial and necessary part of the process.
>
> (Gardner 1995)

The wider public interest, however, surely lies in equalising the sizes of constituency electorates across the whole country. The objectivity of the commissions is unquestioned, but the process hardly merits the same judgement. It is inevitable that the political parties will involve themselves at every stage of fixing constituency boundaries, but their dominant position in the process hardly seems either 'beneficial' or 'necessary'. (Additionally, governments can determine the boundaries of local authorities on a partisan basis which, in turn, has an indirect effect on shaping parliamentary boundaries; see Chapter 4). Iain McLean and Roger Mortimore, who have studied the history of boundary fixing in the UK, concluded one of their studies in starker terms than Gardner:

> This failure to understand (let alone deal with) the issue of fair apportionment is alarming. Disraeli is supposed to have said that England is governed not by logic but by Parliament. Surely only an English politician would be proud of that.
>
> (McLean and Mortimore 1992)

Making votes for political parties equal in their effect

So far we have concentrated on the principle of equality between voters on a geographical basis. We now turn to the question, 'Does the British electoral system treat voters equally according to which party they vote for?' As we shall show, plurality-rule elections fail to do this. They not only treat voters very unequally; they thereby produce Parliaments which are generally highly unrepresentative of the party choices actually made by the electorate. This is a serious failing from a democratic point-of-view, precisely because it is primarily a choice between parties, their leaders and policies, rather than between individual candidates or even local representatives, that is the chief purpose of contemporary elections (**DAC4**). No single party has gained power and ruled on a majority of the popular vote since 1900 (when, in the midst of party turmoil, the Conservatives and Liberal Unionists won 50.3 per cent of the popular vote). It is not even the case that the party which gains the most votes necessarily wins (see Box A).

First-past-the-post elections in more than 650 constituencies also favour parties with geographically-concentrated backing against those whose backing is more evenly spread. It is this characteristic of the voting system which saved Labour's political standing against the Alliance in 1983 and 1987. Labour's votes were simply more concentrated than the Alliance's. Similarly, in 1997, the Liberal Democrats' success in building a regional concentration of votes in the south-west of England finally won them more parliamentary seats on fewer votes than in 1992. By the same token, the Nationalists have generally picked up more seats than the Liberal Democrats in Scotland and Wales; and in 1997, the Conservatives won 17.5 per cent of the vote in Scotland and 20 per cent of the Welsh vote, but received no seats in either country because their votes were too evenly spread.

Further, even the idea of 'geographical representation' is imperfect under plurality-rule elections in Britain. While at least token attempts are made to ensure that a

BOX A   THE QUALITY OF FIRST-PAST-THE-POST ELECTIONS IN POSTWAR BRITAIN

How far is appointment to legislative and government office determined by popular election? *Democratic Audit criterion 1*

How closely does the composition of Parliament reflect the choices actually made by the electorate? *Democratic Audit criterion 4*

- *In 1951*, Labour received the highest share of votes in the postwar period and had 250,000 more votes than the Conservatives. But they won 26 fewer seats and lost the election. Sir Winston Churchill ruled with an overall majority of 17 seats.
- *In February 1974*, the Conservatives gained 225,789 more votes than Labour, but emerged from the election with four fewer seats. Harold Wilson's minority government then ruled on the basis of a 37.1 per cent share of the popular vote.
- *In 1983*, Labour and the Alliance (of Liberals and the SDP) both received a little over a quarter of the vote, but Labour had 209 seats (32 per cent) of the seats in the Commons and the Alliance only 23 (3.5 per cent). The electoral system arguably blocked the Alliance's advance and saved Labour from the consequences of its divisions.
- *In 1987*, the Alliance won 22.5 per cent of the popular vote and received just 3.5 per cent of the seats in the Commons (22 seats).
- *In 1987*, Mrs Thatcher gained 42.3 per cent of the popular vote and had a grand 102-seat majority over all other parties. *In 1992*, John Major gained 41.9 per cent of the popular vote, but was returned with an overall majority of a mere 21 seats. The differences in the size of their majorities had a profound political significance; the difference in their share of the vote was just 0.4 per cent.
- *In 1997*, Tony Blair's New Labour party won 44.4 per cent of the popular vote and gained 418 seats (two thirds of the seats in the Commons). The party's majority over all other parties was 179 seats. *In 1964*, Labour had 44.1 per cent of the popular vote under another energetic leader. But Harold Wilson's Labour took only 317 Commons seats (just half the seats in the chamber) and its overall majority was just four seats. *In 1970*, on just one single percentage point less, Labour lost the election.
- *In 1997*, the Conservatives were reduced to a mere 165 MPs, yet their share of the vote was only one percentage point lower than Labour's in 1987, when Labour were rewarded with 229 seats; and two points lower than Labour's vote in 1983, when Labour had 209 MPs (44 more than the Tories in 1997).
- *In 1997*, Paddy Ashdown's Liberal Democrats secured 17.2 per cent of

the popular vote, slightly less than in 1992 (17.8 per cent), but they more than doubled their representation in Parliament from 20 to 46 seats.

To what extent do the votes of all electors carry equal weight?
Democratic Audit criterion 4

■ *In 1997,* it took 32,370 votes to elect a Labour MP, 58,185 for every Conservative MP, and 113,729 for every Liberal Democrat MP. *In 1992,* the corresponding figures were 41,943 votes for every Conservative MP, 42,656 votes for each Labour MP, and 299,970 for every Liberal Democrat MP. Similar variations have obtained at every election since 1974.

vote in Surrey is worth the same as a vote in Newcastle, a Labour vote in Surrey is not worth the same as a Conservative vote there, and vice versa in Newcastle; Conservative votes in the south count far more than Conservative votes in Scotland; both Conservative and Labour votes in most parts of the country count for far more than Liberal Democrat votes; and Liberal Democrat votes count more than votes for the Greens which, electorally speaking, are worthless. These inequalities clearly contradict the principle that votes should be of equal value (**DAC4**) and, in practice, such trends produce absurd results on the ground. For example, more people voted Labour in Kent in 1992 than in Glasgow, but Labour obtained no seats in Kent and all ten seats in Glasgow. Such phenomena have knock-on effects. Conservative dominance in the south-east of England during the 1980s encouraged the party in government to privilege its voters in that area, and to neglect the interests of voters in traditional Labour areas in the north and north-east.

This chapter is confined to analysis of elections for Westminster, but plurality voting is also used in local elections and hitherto in elections to the European Parliament (the 1999 Euro-elections, will be held under a regional list PR system). Locally, it has tended to create virtual one-party local authorities throughout Britain, removing rival parties almost entirely from council chambers. It has also distorted the UK's representation at Strasbourg: in the 1989 European elections, for example, the British Greens received a higher vote than any other European Green party, but won the fewest seats: none.

These examples do not mean that there is no relationship between votes and seats in British elections. There is, but it is distorted by a variety of factors, the principal one of being the number of parties contesting an election. Our voting system is simple to use, but exceedingly complex and unpredictable in its operations. Even the most skilled psephologists agree that they do not understand how it allocates seats – a point which those who complain about complex PR allocation systems might bear in mind! Generally, the results of general elections in the early post-war period were more proportionate because Labour and the Conservatives were

Deviation from proportionality

politically popular within a 'two-party' system. Few people quarrelled with Labour's 1945 mandate (on 48 per cent of the vote), nor with the Conservatives' right to rule in the 1950s (when they gained over 49 per cent of the vote in 1955 and 1959). The popularity of the two major parties has diminished since the early 1970s, as support for the Liberals (in several forms), the Nationalists and other parties has grown. But the two parties have maintained their grasp on power, even if less convincingly. Since 1974, they have won seven elections in a row on less than 45 per cent of the vote; the average winning vote has been 41.6 per cent. Both Mrs Thatcher's 1980s victories were based on a fraction more than 42 per cent of the vote, but she obtained overall parliamentary majorities of 144 seats in 1983 and 102 seats in 1987. Thus, all the power which accrues to the winning party in Britain in our 'winner-takes-all' elections was won on little more than the support of two-fifths of those who voted (and less of those eligible to vote).

Generally, both the major parties have been over-represented in the Commons throughout the postwar period, and the Liberal Democrats have been seriously under-represented. Government and legislative office has not been the prize of popular election, as it is generally understood (**DAC1**).

Measuring the distortions of British elections

It is possible to reinforce this survey of the party political effects of elections in Britain with more systematic analysis of the quality of representation in Britain, using objective indicators developed by political science – and so to answer more precisely the questions posed by **DAC4**: 'How closely does the composition of Parliament reflect the choices made by the electorate?' and, 'To what extent do the votes of all electors carry equal weight?' Table 3.2 presents the results of the 1997 election in an unusual form – in terms of 'deviation from proportionality' (or DV). We adopted the most widely used formula for calculating DV for the calculations in this chapter.

Table 3.2 Deviation from proportionality in the 1997 general election*

Party	Votes (%)	Seats (%)	Deviations
Conservative	31.4	25.7	−5.7
Labour	44.4	65.4	+21.0
Liberal Democrat	17.2	7.2	−10.0
Scottish National Party	2.0	0.9	−1.1
Plaid Cymru	0.5	0.6	+0.1
Referendum	2.7	0	−2.7
Others	1.7	0.2	−1.5
Overall deviation for 1997 general election			21%
Largest deviation (for Labour)			21%

Source: DA Paper No. 11, 1997: 10
Notes:
* Excluding Northern Ireland.

The higher the figure for deviation from proportionality rises, the more inequality between individual voters rises and the more uncertain the political control exercised by the electorate becomes.

Table 3.2 puts talk of a 'landslide' victory for Labour into perspective. In fact, Labour won a modest 44.4 per cent share of the vote in 1997 and its huge 179-seat majority is the result of massive over-representation rather than its popularity with the voters. For the Democratic Audit report on the 1997 election, *Making Votes Count*, we calculated a DV score for the election result as a whole, by totalling the deviations for all the parties (discarding their plus or minus signs, so that they don't cancel each other out) and dividing by two (DA Paper No. 11, 1997: 10–12). This produces a 21 per cent 'deviation score' for the 1997 general election; and the 'deviation score' measuring Labour's over-representation is also 21 per cent. In effect, the 1997 DV score means that more than one in five MPs in the House of Commons are not entitled to their seats in terms of their party's actual share of the national vote. This is broadly the going rate for all elections since the mid-1970s when substantial Liberal and other third party voting became a feature of British political life.

The gaps between the percentage of seats won and votes cast for the parties is immediately evident in Table 3.2. The Liberal Democrats gain a far lower proportion of seats than their percentage share of the vote, but their new bases in south-west England, the urban south-east and London suburbs have halved the disadvantage under which they suffered in 1992 (when their DV score was minus 14.7 per cent). Their under-representation is their lowest since 1970, and their seats/votes ratio is their highest postwar score. An almost unique feature of the 1997 election is that Labour did not only plunder seats from third parties, but also took seats to which the Conservatives were entitled on their share of the vote. Usually, the second main party is also over-represented. The main cause of this decline was that their vote fell to 31 per cent, and Britain's plurality-rule system severely penalises any party whose vote falls below a 33 per cent threshold. As with Labour in the 1980s, the Conservatives also ceased to be a 'national' party in 1997. They achieved a broad parity between votes cast and seats won in only five out of 18 regions in Britain, and in eight regions they are now badly under-represented.

The national DV scores since 1945 reflect the shifts in popular support for the political parties, rising from a low point of 4 per cent in 1955 in the heyday of two-party politics to high points of 24 per cent in 1983 and 21 per cent in 1987 when three main parties were in contention. The two 1980s scores indicated a significant level of distortion and, thanks to the media interest in the performance of the Alliance, it was hard to ignore their manifest 'unfairness'. So the political classes were relieved in 1992 to be able to congratulate the ability of the voting system to right itself and return towards normality and stability. The national DV score fell to 17.4 per cent. Voters were seen to have reined back the Tories' 'landslide' majorities of the 1980s, and to have rewarded Labour for a return to 'respectability'. The continued under-representation of the Liberal Democrats was glossed over. Now, disproportionality has risen again (though it remains three percentage points below its peak in 1983), but has been masked by the dramatic quality of Labour's win. These national DV scores are among the largest on record among liberal democracies in the past

Deviation from proportionality

25 years. In western Europe, PR systems commonly produce DV scores of 4–8 per cent – a level only briefly achieved in Britain during the two-party era of the 1950s. (Other DV formulas show the first 20 European nations with deviation scores from 0.67 to 4 per cent, while the UK weighs in at No. 32 on a 10.76 DV score; Farrell 1997: Table 7.1). In the USA, the strongly-established two-party system returns a stable DV score of about 7 per cent in Congressional elections. So Britain's first-past-the-post elections are broadly three times worse at translating votes accurately into seats than the countries against which we normally measure our democracy.

But national DV scores for Britain tell only half the story. They are misleadingly low if compared with other countries, because areas of pro-Conservative deviation in southern England are offset by areas of pro-Labour deviation in the north and Scotland. Thus, the national figures conceal the far higher levels of distortion which occur in the English regions and home countries. In 1992, the national DV score was 17.4 per cent, but this figure concealed the very high DV score in south-east England – 43 per cent, which is about as high as you can get in a liberal democracy. On the ground it meant that the Conservatives won 97 per cent of the seats on just 55 per cent of the vote. As Figure 3.1 shows, this high DV score was partly offset by very high deviations towards Labour in central Scotland (43 and 33 per cent) and north England (30 per cent). In 1997, the national DV score was 21.1 per cent and the highest regional score (in Strathclyde) was 42 per cent. Figure 3.2 shows the full range of regional DV scores in the 1997 general election – 12 of which are higher than the national DV figure, and only six are lower. It is possible to calculate a weighted aggregate DV score, averaging out the regional scores and not allowing the scores for the various parties to cancel each other out. The table below sets out the aggregate regional scores for the 1992 and 1997 general elections and compares them with the conventional national figures.

Deviations in recent British general elections, 1992 and 1997

	Conventional national DV score %	Aggregate regional DV score %
1992	17.4	29.2
1997	21.1	23.8

Source: Dunleavy and Margetts 1997: 741

These DV figures are not to be disparaged as mere 'arithmetic'. They prove both that the electoral system fails to ensure that the composition of Parliament reflects voters' party choices; and that it denies people votes of equal value (**DAC4**). They

---

Figure 3.1 Regional deviation from proportionality for the UK, 1992

Source: Data produced by LSE Public Policy Group; map design by Jane Pugh, Drawing Office, Geography Department LSE

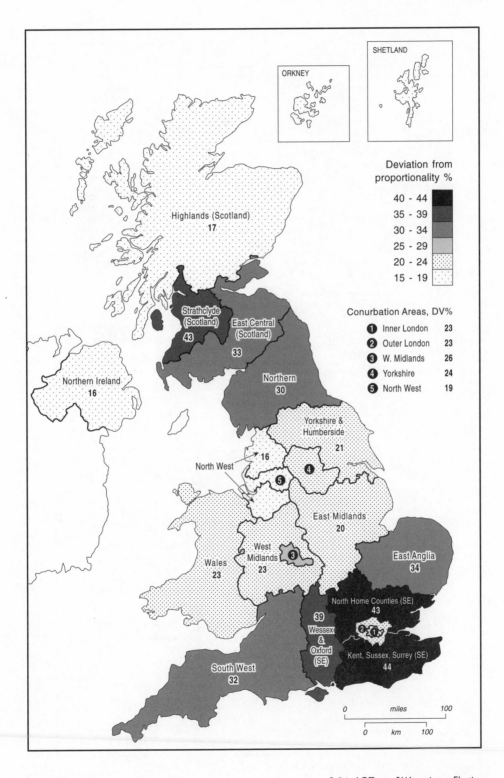

Deviation from
proportionality %

40 - 44
35 - 39
30 - 34
25 - 29
20 - 24
15 - 19

Conurbation Areas, DV%

1 Inner London 23
2 Outer London 23
3 W. Midlands 26
4 Yorkshire 24
5 North West 19

ORKNEY

SHETLAND

Highlands (Scotland)
17

Strathclyde
(Scotland)
43

East Central
(Scotland)
33

Northern
30

Northern Ireland
16

Yorkshire &
Humberside
21

North West
16

East Midlands
20

East Anglia
34

Wales
23

West
Midlands
23

North Home Counties (SE)
43

Wessex
&
Oxford
(SE)
39

Kent, Sussex, Surrey (SE)
44

South West
32

0   miles   100

0   km   100

Deviation from proportionality

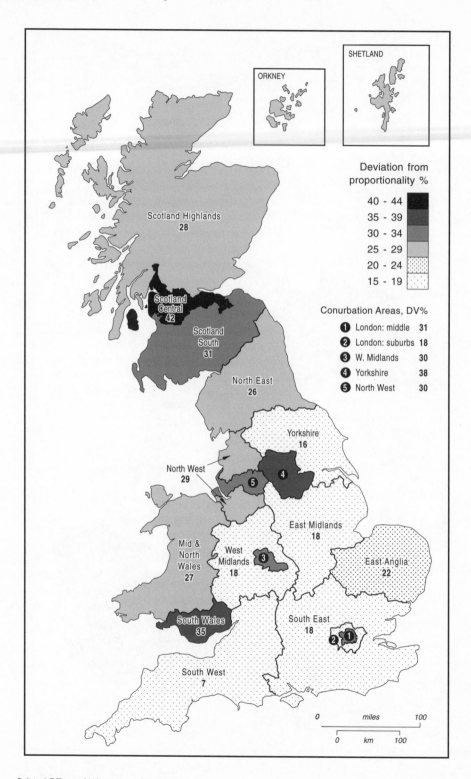

ORKNEY

SHETLAND

Deviation from proportionality %

■	40 - 44
■	35 - 39
■	30 - 34
■	25 - 29
▪	20 - 24
▫	15 - 19

Conurbation Areas, DV%

❶ London: middle   31
❷ London: suburbs 18
❸ W. Midlands   30
❹ Yorkshire   38
❺ North West   30

Scotland Highlands
28

Scotland
Central
42

Scotland
South
31

North East
26

Yorkshire
16

North West
29

❺

❹

East Midlands
18

Mid &
North
Wales
27

West
Midlands
18

❸

East Anglia
22

South Wales
35

South East
18

❷ ❶

South West
7

0   miles   100

0   km   100

also reveal that the current electoral system has an adverse effect on the range of choice that voters have at general elections (**DAC3**). They also throw into relief people's experience of voting at the regional level, which affects the way they define and interpret the value of the ballot (see Dunleavy and Margetts 1993b). Since 1852, people have talked about 'wasted votes'; since the 1970s, people have begun to vote in their constituencies not for their first-choice party, but for other parties which are more likely to beat the party they don't want. In the recent past, for example, Labour sympathisers in the south-east have abandoned their allegiance to Labour to vote for Liberal, Alliance and Liberal Democrat candidates who had more apparent chance of defeating Conservatives. For Liberal Democrat sympathisers in most areas outside south-west England the deterrent to voting for their first-choice party is as strong.

Measuring the electoral squeeze on third parties

It is possible also to measure the effect that the electoral system has on the range of choice voters have at general elections more specifically (**DAC3**). The idea of the electoral 'squeeze' on parties in individual constituencies, especially in by-elections, is familiar. The votes for what are believed to be third parties are reduced, or 'squeezed', as people shift their support to the two parties which seem to be in the lead locally. But it is also possible to measure the overall squeeze on parties which takes place during elections under the influence of the electoral system itself – a phenomenon which clearly affects the range of party choice that electors possess. This measure, formally known as the 'relative reduction in parties' (RRP), computes the proportion of parties voted for by the electorate but not effectively represented in the legislature. Thus, whereas DV measures how representative an assembly is of parties, RRP shows how far the electoral system squeezes third and subsequent parties, protecting established political parties by excluding rival candidates from representation in the popular assembly (Dunleavy and Margetts 1993a: 25). It thus also provides a measure of the real choice between parties for intending voters. This does not necessarily mean that they will only be able to choose between very few parties, but rather that very few parties they may choose between have a real chance of gaining seats in the assembly (for a fuller discussion, see Dunleavy and Margetts 1994).

Briefly, the 'third-party squeeze' is calculated from vote and seats scores for parties and usually has an effective minimum score of zero and a maximum of around 70 per cent. An ideally democratic system would score close to zero, as this would mean that it did not exclude any significantly mobilised political view from representation. The national figure for third-party squeeze in the 1997 general election was 34 per cent – in other words, the system discarded over a third of the parties voted for.

Figure 3.2 Regional deviation from proportionality for the UK, 1997

Source: Data produced by LSE Public Policy Group; map design by Jane Pugh, Drawing Office, Geography Department LSE

Wasted votes

But, as with deviation scores, the national figure conceals higher rates of squeeze across the regions. In 1997, they rose as high as 62 per cent in central Scotland, 57 per cent in the Yorkshire conurbation area, and above or very close to 50 per cent in four other regions. Eleven out of 18 regions had scores of more than the national average. In the United States or any west European nation using PR for its elections the RRP score would be around 10 per cent. Only one region in Great Britain achieved such a low score – south-west England. If we compute the national third-party squeeze as an average of the regional RRP scores (while weighting the regions for their different population sizes), we find that the reduction of choice experienced by British voters as a whole came to 39 per cent in 1997. The score in 1992 was 41 per cent (Dunleavy and Margetts 1997). The table below, showing the aggregate regional RRP scores in elections to the popular assembly in other liberal democracies, demonstrates that the British scores are remarkably high.

Third-party squeeze in liberal democracies 1988-91

Country	Third-party squeeze (%)
Britain	41.1
Australia	34.3
Spain	28.7
Germany	14.1
Sweden	8.9

Source: Dunleavy and Margetts 1993b: 32

Wasted votes

In a perfect democracy, everyone's vote would count. This is of course the aim of the proportional representation systems employed around the world (one of which, the single transferable vote, seeks to count not only voters' first choices, but further preferences too). Thus, one measure of how well any electoral system works is how few votes are 'wasted'. This is, however, a rather crude idea because of course many voters gain satisfaction from making their choice, whether or not they choose the candidate who wins in their constituency. Thus, people who voted Labour in the 165 constituencies which returned Conservative MPs in 1997 may very well still have felt that they had contributed to the Labour win nationally and shared in the post-election euphoria. Further, most countries using PR systems choose not to make every vote possible count, as they try to screen out 'fringe' parties from their popular assemblies with vote thresholds.

However, the traditional idea of the 'wasted vote' does provide another way of analysing Britain's electoral system in terms of political equality. We have already seen the consequences of voting in single-member constituencies for party representation in Parliament. But plurality-rule elections also affect equality between voters at constituency level and between constituencies in respect to the part their votes play in electing MPs. It is in this sense that votes can be described as 'wasted'. In this section we have chosen the 'strong' version of the idea. We distinguish those voters who were efficacious in the highly restricted sense that their vote was absolutely essential to return the MP elected in their local constituency. By definition, these voters cannot have supported defeated candidates. But voters for candidates who won locally but whose votes merely swelled the winners' majorities were also not efficacious on this view. The total of wasted votes therefore includes both votes for losing candidates and surplus votes for winners.

Admittedly, this is a rather abstract view of what voting means to people, as defenders of the status quo argue. Yet other electoral systems are not so wasteful and most votes do count or are recycled; unlike in Britain, where 'losing' votes count for nothing and surplus votes pile up in tens of thousands in some safe seats and may as well be weighed as counted. The result, from the Audit's point of view, is that citizens' votes cannot be regarded as being of equal value. Table 3.3 breaks down wasted votes between 'losing' and 'surplus' votes by region. 'Wasted' votes varied across regions from 66 to 81 per cent and 'losing' votes from 37 to 55 per cent. Overall, the figures in Table 3.3 emphasise the narrow base on which electoral success can be founded under the plurality rule. They also have important links to political practice, notably the way in which the parties campaign. They show why the three main parties concentrated almost exclusively on the 500,000 or so 'swing' voters in marginal seats in the 1997 election – a minority whose voting decisions could have swung a close election one way or the other.

Another anomaly of the existing system is that candidates in local constituencies frequently now win seats in Parliament on less than a majority of the votes cast.

Table 3.3 'Wasted' votes by region in 1997 (%)

Region	Surplus majority votes	Losing votes	Total 'wasted' votes
South Wales	45	37	82
North East	41	37	78
North West conurbation	38	39	77
Scotland (south)	25	50	75
London (middle)	35	41	76
Scottish Highlands	21	52	73
North and mid Wales	21	52	73
Central Scotland	32	45	77
Yorkshire conurbation	33	41	74
Rest of Yorkshire	22	49	71
North West (rest)	22	46	68
East Midlands	19	49	68
East Anglia	13	55	68
South East	14	54	68
West Midlands conurbation	27	44	71
West Midlands (rest)	17	50	67
South West	12	55	67
London suburbs	15	51	66
Great Britain	25	47	72

Source: Democratic Audit research

Marginal seats and tactical votes

The most striking example of this effect in 1997 was in Tweeddale, Ettrick and Lauderdale, won by the Liberal Democrat candidate with 31.2 per cent of the vote. But seats are won with fewer than half the votes cast all over the country, though unevenly between regions. In 1997, under the plurality rule, almost half of MPs elected did not have majority support in their constituency:

MPs returned to parliament on a minority vote

	1997	1992
MPs with majority support	340 (53%)	383 (60%)
MPs with plurality support only	301 (47%)	251 (40%)

Source: DA Paper No. 11, 1997: 13

Modified pluralist systems, such as the alternative vote (AV) used in Australia and France's 'double ballot', ensure that all seats are won on a full majority vote. The trouble with AV, which is favoured by influential New Labour figures, is that it can be as disproportionate and unpredictable as first-past-the-post. In 1997, it would have produced a more distorted result – with a 23.5 per cent DV score – giving Labour an even larger majority and robbing the Conservatives of 55 more seats (DA Paper No. 11: 4–5).

Bootle Man, Worcester Woman and the tactical voter

The plurality-rule electoral system has an increasingly profound effect upon the conduct both of the parties and voters in elections. British elections are won and lost not across the country as a whole, but within the 100 or so 'marginal seats' where the parties are more evenly matched, the majorities are smaller and the seats are therefore the most vulnerable. Thus, as Martin Kettle wrote in the *Guardian* on 19 March 1997, 'the 1997 general election is all about target seats' – and, he might have added, pretty select sets of voters within those seats too. As it turned out, the system's effect on voters also had a marked knock-on effect in 1997. For in this election, early calculations suggest that nearly 1.6 million people voted tactically not for their first-choice Labour or Liberal Democrat candidate, but for the candidate in their constituency who seemed most capable of beating the Conservative (Curtice 1997). Labour's so-called 'landslide' electoral triumph in 1997 was therefore not fought and won on the basis of a national campaign and uniform swing towards the party; the party battle was targeted on marginal constituencies and key voters in them, the decisive edge was supplied by a combination of stay-at-home Conservative voters and tactical voters. These tactical voters overturned Conservative majorities in seats like Michael Portillo's Enfield Southgate which were not even on Labour's marginal target list; and may have delivered eight Tory seats to Labour and 16 to the Liberal Democrats. Both these reactions to the electoral system's operations – targeting seats and tactical voting – diminish the quality of democracy in Britain. All in all, probably three million people – or one in ten of all those who voted – voted not for their first-choice candidate, but tactically. Such figures severely qualify the principle of electoral choice in Britain.

In 1997, the first day of Tony Blair's campaign took him to Gloucester, the pivotal marginal seat which acquired symbolic status as the seat that would give Labour an overall majority in the election. Some 100–150 marginal seats were the key election battle ground: Labour targeted the 90 most marginal Conservative seats; the Conservatives 130 key seats, but largely concentrated on defending the 100 most vulnerable government-held seats. The Liberal Democrats focused on 50 seats where they hoped to break through, while defending 20 of their own seats. Within those seats, refined research techniques had been employed well in advance to identify 'target' voters and the issues which they found important. Both major parties, for example, conducted focus groups among people who had voted Conservative in 1992, but had since defected. Labour wanted to keep them on board, the Conservatives wanted them back. Labour 'floaters', people in particular social groups, like the C2s (semi-skilled and white-collar workers and their families), and 'unde-cideds' were also targeted. The Conservatives did not only test people on political issues, but also invested in in-depth interviewing on people's values – *emotional issues* rather than policy issues.

Perhaps as many as 500,000 people in the marginals became the electorate on which the two larger parties concentrated. Both parties made systematic and concen-trated efforts to identify and contact key swing voters in marginal seats in the run-up to the election and during the campaign. 'Niche marketing' replaced old-fashioned Platonic visions of a national forum at election time. As Kettle wrote:

> The parties are fighting the real election, the one that counts, and unless you are a swing voter in a marginal constituency, you are not part of it at all ... this is where the election will be won and lost and where the parties long ago dug themselves in.
>
> (*Guardian*, 18 March 1997)

As swing voters were, by definition, those people who used to vote Tory and now contemplated voting Labour and other 'undecideds', Kettle continued, their views were generally to the right of Labour's traditional values, and their pre-occupations were self-interested. They mourned Mrs Thatcher and her regime of strong lead-ership; so Blair had to appear strong. As the Conservatives were also seeking to win their votes, the promises and positions of the parties converged at the same time as the effective electorate shrunk. What the election expert, David Butler, described as 'a politics of close marking' ensued.

The one thing these target voters were was not typical. The situation was brilliantly caricatured in the John Bird–John Fortune dialogue in the Channel 4 pre-election show, *Bremner Bird & Fortune: Three Men & a Vote* (27 April 1997). John Bird is seeking to explain the idea of choosing a government through the electoral process to a visitor from Middle Mars (John Fortune in green face):

> BIRD: Well, we have what is called a democracy. That is to say, sort of counting heads. I mean everybody has a vote.
>
> FORTUNE: So everybody decides?

Marginal seats and tactical votes

BIRD: Well . . . in theory everybody decides. But actually in this case it will be a relatively small number of people who will decide the actual outcome.

FORTUNE: People with more heads than other people? Is that right?

BIRD: No, no.

FORTUNE: More intelligent people? Better informed people?

BIRD: No, no, these people are basically the people who can't make up their mind. They are called 'floating voters', and the parties are very desperate for them to vote for them, you see.

FORTUNE: So the people who choose who the government is going to be are the people who can't decide about anything?

BIRD: Yes.

Thus, both parties still counted on their core voters and safe seats, such as Blaenau Gwent and Bootle for Labour and the Conservatives' Kensington and Chelsea. But they did not count for much when it came to framing and propagating the parties' messages. 'Bootle Man' and 'Kensington Lady' no doubt received their election addresses, courtesy of a free mail service, but they were not solicited by direct mail, they were not telephoned six times during the campaign, their views were not sought nor their fears assuaged, they were not invited to an intimate question-and-answer session with a party leader. Such privileged status was reserved for the 'swing voters'. Of course, these swing voters' views and fears were not wholly divorced from those of the rest of the electorate, and they will have reflected at least those of the wider social groups to which they belonged. Nevertheless, they came to be characterised as 'Worcester Woman', a composite focus which was said to be typical of the 2 per cent of the electorate who really mattered, and by definition not of significant elements in the electorate as a whole.

Further, as is well known, the focus of the parties' activities has shifted irrevocably from the public meeting and street to mass media and modern forms of communication. Hi-tech has replaced the 'poor bloody military' of local activists delivering leaflets and canvassing door-to-door in the old hit-and-miss way. The important canvassing is now carried out from banks of telephones, remote from people's homes, and delivering prescribed messages. Election campaigns are now structured primarily to address swing voters through the media by way of concerted speeches, repetitive key phrases, sound-bites, orchestrated photo opportunities, and so on. John Major, harking back to the 'good old days' on his soapbox, was just one more contrived new image. The parties sought to get pre-planned images onto TV screens which are aimed primarily at swing voters, and not at the generality of voters. The media, of course, responded by seeking to shove the politicians off their prepared texts and by introducing ordinary people into the election on a variety of television and radio shows. The BBC reported the election debates thoroughly in the tradition of public-service broadcasting and television as a whole, current affairs radio and the broadsheet press made consistent efforts to review and report the issues, including those the parties deliberately neglected and the nature of their campaigns. But they made little overall impact on campaigns which are now prepared, disciplined and systematic, guided by marketing and media professionals and governed by more and more centralised decision-making. They took place in their own worlds and the media were obliged to report them.

Voters are, of course, not impotent. Over the past 15 years, an unknown quantity of voters has begun a process of tactical voting to avoid wasting or splitting their votes. Consciously and often unconsciously, for example, voters across the south of England began shifting their votes from Labour to the Liberals, Alliance and Liberal Democrats in the face of the apparent impregnability of the Conservatives' electoral hegemony (there is circumstantial evidence for this shift in that the Labour vote in south-east England fell by more than it did nationally in the ten years to 1992). From 1987 onwards, cross-party Labour and Liberal Democrat groups began openly to advocate and organise tactical voting, though on a small scale. In the 1992 and 1997 elections, public campaigns marshalled a country-wide campaign of tactical voting against Conservative candidates; the campaign in 1997 was informed by the experience of tactical voting in local elections and by detailed press reports (for example, in the *Observer, Guardian* and *Daily Mirror*). This process had an obvious impact in 1997, most notably in Scotland where no Tory MP survived, and as we stated above, may have delivered eight Tory seats to Labour and 16 to the Liberal Democrats. There were also signs of Conservatives voting tactically for the Liberal Democrats against Labour candidates they disliked in the big cities and (most obviously) Tony Benn's Chesterfield constituency.

We have already discussed the issue of tactical voting (**p. 64**). However, welcome though it is to discern voters manipulating the power they possess through their votes to mitigate the effects of the electoral system, a high level of tactical voting suggests a higher level of wasted votes than would occur under a system which offers voters the chance directly to express effective preferences. Further, people vote tactically with an imperfect knowledge of how others who may share the same objective are voting rather than with the clarity that a PR system would give them. It is a process which frequently malfunctions at a constituency and personal level. Indeed, it may well be that thousands of those who voted tactically in 1997 would not have wished to present Labour with the scale of victory that the party was given.

The choice between first-past-the-post and proportional representation

This review has demonstrated that first-past-the-post elections seriously distort the party choices that voters make; severely restrict the range of party choices on offer; and fail to achieve the system's own goal of geographical equality. Yet the political classes have long agreed that, 'broadly speaking, the system works'. These were actually the words of Herbert Morrison, then Labour's deputy premier, but they could have been spoken by most major politicians up to the present. Morrison was addressing the House of Commons on the occasion of the last major reform of elections in Britain – the Representation of the People Bill (HC Deb, 17 February 1948, c1111). He agreed that 'mathematical criticisms' of the existing system were correct; and that 'governments do not always represent the majority of the electorate' (as his failed to do), but he argued:

> I would rather have governments with strength and power behind them – even though I do not agree with them – so long as they observe the democratic forms, than a Parliament which can only live by the making and unmaking and re-making of coalitions and bargains of all sorts.

Morrison stood four-square in the robust tradition of 'strong government'. Defenders of the status quo point out rightly that elections must produce governments capable of ruling effectively; and they place this good above the quality of representation. The tradition of strong government is, as we have seen, historically entrenched in British politics, and since the nineteenth century there has been a particular fear that electoral reform would undermine the major parties and weaken government. In an essay, Walter Bagehot foretold inaction if minorities were represented in the Commons (as nineteenth century reformers such as J. S. Mill wanted), arguing that British elections produced strong governments, usually by over-representing in the Commons the party with the most votes. Bagehot's descendants are impatient with ideas of 'fairness' and use words such as 'mathematical' and 'scientific' as derogatory terms which ring false within the 'organic' culture of British politics. As a historian of the debate over voting in Britain has remarked, they have consistently refused to regret even gross misrepresentation of the electorate's opinions in Parliament. They have argued that a strong and consistent government, even if it has bad policies, is better than a weak, more representative government which cannot carry its policies, good or bad, and infinitely better than coalition government (Hart 1992: 266–274).

The idea of the two-party system is so deeply embedded in the political culture that the discrepancies between the votes cast for the parties in general elections and their representation in Parliament are rarely remarked upon. The four great electoral triumphs of this century – that of the Liberals in 1905, Labour in 1945, Mrs Thatcher in 1979 and New Labour in 1997 – have all been hailed as 'landslides', yet all were won on a minority of the popular vote. So dominant is the two-party tradition that, in 1950, *The Times* criticised the Liberals for the 'irresponsible spattering of the electoral map with hundreds of candidates', few of whom had any chance of winning; instead, Liberal voters should be forced to choose between the other two parties. In 1951, the Labour Party won 250,000 more votes than the Conservatives in a close-run election, yet it was the Conservatives – not the leading party – who were returned to power with an exaggerated parliamentary majority (of 17; and 26 more seats than Labour). There were few complaints. *The Times* described the result as 'The Electors' Choice'. Psephologist David Butler concluded that the electoral system's 'capacity for producing decisive and even overwhelming parliamentary majorities from relatively narrow majorities in votes is in no way diminished', without observing that the narrow majority in this case had been reversed (Butler 1952: 277). The Liberals criticised a system which entrusted the fate of the country to the greatest of gambles. Labour made no complaint.

Right up to the 1997 election, the political classes have found it hard to let go of the received idea that British politics operates within a two-party system. The concept of a 'two and a half' party system represents a half-hearted attempt to accommodate the awkwardly persistent Liberal Democrats in the equation (though not the Nationalists), but it doesn't properly reflect their political position in British politics (see Dunleavy and Margetts 1997: 734–739). Generally the Conservatives and Labour are still described as the 'major parties' and the Liberal Democrats as a 'minor party', and the media reflect and perpetuate this perception. There was a great deal of impatience in the broadcast media, for example, with Paddy Ashdown's claim to participate in the aborted 1997 television 'election debate' between the party leaders, which broadcasters envisaged primarily as a Major–Blair confrontation. Yet in any other liberal democracy in Europe, the Liberal Democrat share of the vote in elections since 1974 (ranging from 15 to 26 per cent) and their central position on the left–right spectrum would make them significant political actors – but there of course elections are (with the exception of France) held under PR systems. Here, the Conservatives and Labour are regarded as the 'major parties' largely because they maintain a double monopoly in government, thanks of course to the electoral system. Naturally the determining factor for politicians in the two parties which could effect a change has always been not the actual arguments for and against the various electoral systems, but the concrete benefits of the existing system for their own party (see Bogdanor 1987: 115–121). Tony Blair's vision of a new left-centre domination of British politics, with Labour and Liberal Democrats co-operating, might change his party's calculations.

The benefits of individual representation of constituencies

One of the most frequently quoted advantages of the first-past-the-post system is the close relationship between MPs and their constituents that single-member constituencies create. The socialist writer Harold Laski once defined liberal democracy to include the representation of local constituencies by single-member MPs. It is therefore argued that any move to abandon or enlarge single-member constituencies under PR systems would either remove this invaluable link or increase the number of electors whom each MP represents. Constituencies would probably double in size under the German AMS system for it to produce fully proportional results, but as we write, it seems that the British public may very well be asked to consider a variant of AMS which involves fewer 'top-up' MPs, and so less drastic change at constituency level, in the referendum on electoral reform. STV would require multi-member seats at least five times larger, and returning five MPs (DA Paper No. 11). Larger constituencies, the argument goes, would reduce MPs' ability to represent their constituencies effectively for as their size increases, the MP's knowledge and understanding of local needs and problems would decline. MPs would find it more difficult to deal with their caseloads individually, and would become less accessible and hence less accountable to electors.

But the nature of the relationship between MPs and their constituents requires more careful examination than this. There is no doubt that in recent years MPs

Single-member constituencies

have taken their constituency responsibilities more seriously (partly because it adds to the incumbent's inbuilt advantage at election time). But political analysts warn against adopting overly sentimental visions of the 'sacred trust' and 'indissoluble bond' between MPs and their local constituents (Crewe 1986). MPs have limited resources to service their constituents and are besieged with conflicting duties and interests. Government ministers whose heavy schedule obliges them to delegate constituency work to a proxy are given no extra allowance to encourage them to do so adequately. Relations between MPs and their constituents are conducted within a framework which does not encourage and often actively discourages close ties. Neither MPs nor candidates are obliged legally to live in or anywhere near their constituencies. MPs lack any legal or administrative jurisdiction over the matters on which constituents are likely to contact them; civil servants, local officials and public employees are in no sense individually responsible to them. Though conscientious MPs may develop considerable expertise in certain areas, they are rarely knowledge-able, let alone trained, in the kinds of legal, welfare and planning matters which most constituents bring to their surgeries. A reliable network of well-funded Citizen's Advice Bureaux would give better value. Though both MPs and the public give their local representational role pride of place among MPs' duties, the reality is that they owe their first duty to their party in Parliament. MPs can be effective campaigners on local or regional issues, as home counties Tory MPs were over proposals to widen the M25 motorway, but an MP's expression of a constituency interest at Westminster and in Whitehall is usually greeted more by tolerance than action.

Moreover, the relationship between MPs and constituents is rarely close. Opinion polls suggest that only about half the population can name their MP (and more know the identity of his or her party). Some two out of five electors profess to be satisfied with their local MP, while a third admit they have no view or simply don't know. A survey at the end of the 1970s found that only about one in eight people had ever seen their MP in person and only 18 per cent had ever been in touch with their MP to ask for information or help (Crewe 1986). More recent research suggested that about one in ten people had contacted their MP in the previous five years:

Contacting in past 5 years	At least once (%)	Often, now and then (%)
MP	9.7	3.4
Civil servant	7.3	3.1
Councillor	20.7	10.3
Town hall	17.4	8.9
Media	3.8	1.6

Source: Parry, Moyser and Day 1992

These figures appear to be roughly in line with those for other European countries (which generally use electoral systems with either no or far larger constituencies), although less than in the United States where one in five (22 per cent) American citizens had contacted their representative in Congress in the previous four years. Again, electoral districts in the US are far larger than British constituencies. So the available evidence suggests that the relationship between electors and their elected representatives is not close in the UK and does not necessarily depend on small constituencies. As Ivor Crewe, the political analyst, concluded after his study, 'Parliamentary constituencies as natural communities are a sociological myth and the British MP's electoral dependence on constituents rather than party, is of course, a political myth' (Crewe 1986).

The price paid for the myth of the 'constituency MP', serving a local community, seems unduly high in terms of distorted representation in Parliament. Most voters have a two in three chance of living in a constituency where their vote will be wasted and nearly one in two of them, on average, will be represented by an MP who has not even won a simple majority of the votes in his or her constituency. Nevertheless, opinion polls suggest that people remain attached to the idea of being represented locally by a single MP and reject the idea of being served by several MPs in far larger constituencies (as under STV), let alone losing a constituency link altogether (as under most PR list systems).

Finally, there is the argument that a change to proportional representation would inevitably lead to government by coalition and bring Britain's historic advantage of 'strong government' to an end. This is an argument which we cannot fully air here. The results of the 'replay' of the 1997 election under alternative systems undertaken in the *Making Votes Count* survey show that fully proportional systems – the German additional member system and list PR systems – would have robbed Labour of its overall majority, though under STV (which is only contingently proportional) Labour would have retained a small overall majority of 25 seats (see Table 3.4). The

Table 3.4 The allocation of Commons seats under alternative electoral systems, 1997

	Con	Lab	Lib-Dem	SNP/PC	Others	Largest party	Other parties	Overall majority
First-past-the-post	165	419	46	10	19	Lab–419	240	179
Alternative vote	110	436	84	10	19	Lab–436	223	213
STV	144	342	131	24	18	Lab–342	317	25
Additional member	203	303	115	20	18	Lab–303	356	−53
List PR (1)	212	320	89	19	19	Lab–320	339	−19
List PR (2)	205	295	121	19	19	Lab–295	364	−69
List PR (3)	205	345	72	18	19	Lab–345	314	31
Pure proportionality	202	285	110	16	46	Lab–285	374	−89

Source: Calculated from DA Paper No. 11, 1997
Notes:
List PR counting systems:
1 Largest remainder system with a Droop quota
2 Hare quota
3 d'Hondt system.

alternative vote – which is not proportional – would actually have swelled Labour's majority from 179 to 213 seats. In 1992, the same proportional systems and STV would have removed John Major's majority. In both elections under proportional representation, a Labour–Liberal Democrat coalition would have been the most likely outcome. The composition of the House of Commons would also have more accurately reflected the wishes of the electorate; and an AMS system, modelled on that in Germany with half the MPs being returned as local MPs and the other half as 'top-up' MPs voted for regionally, would have been the most proportional in both elections.

Of course, it remains the case that a party which won an election with more than 50 per cent of the votes cast would be able to form a single-party government, but that outcome is highly unlikely. Therefore the price of introducing proportional representation would indeed be coalition government. Defenders of the status quo assume that this would produce less 'strong' government. This may well be the case, but not necessarily. During the postwar years governments in Germany, say, and Scandinavia have generally been strong, whereas it is possible to identify 'weak' governments returned under first-past-the-post over the same period – John Major's being the most recent. The political scientist Arend Lijphart has devoted an academic lifetime to study of election systems and their political effects. In 1994 he concluded:

> the conventional wisdom is wrong in positing a trade-off between the advantages of plurality [first-past-the-post] and PR systems. The superior performance of PR with regard to political representation is not counterbalanced by an inferior record on governmental effectiveness; if anything, the record of the PR countries on macro-economic management appears to be a bit better than that of the plurality systems – but not to the extent that the differences are statistically significant. The practical conclusion is that PR is to be preferred over plurality since it offers both better representation and at least as effective public policy-making.
>
> (Lijphart 1994: 8)

In our view, the emphasis in the UK ought to be on 'effective', or 'good', government rather than 'strong' government. Certainly, one of the arguments of this volume is that strong single-party government has in practice been less open and accountable than is desirable and less effective in action than it might have been. Further, a House of Commons with a more balanced mix of parties might become more powerful in relation to government; an undesirable development so far as 'strong' government is concerned, but a 'strong' House of Commons might well assist in making government more open, accountable – and effective.

But wouldn't coalition government weaken popular control of government through elections? It is argued that with single-party government electors get what they see. They choose between parties at elections and the winning party then implements its manifesto. But if parties must first agree on the terms of a coalition government, then the effective decisions on the government's programme are decided not by the voters, but after the election in 'smoke-filled rooms' (i.e. hidden from the public gaze). However, experience of coalition government in Europe reveals this to be an insular myth; there are open processes for determining coalition governments which are usually closer to fulfilling party mandates than UK governments (see Budge 1998; Budge and Keman 1993; and Chapter 5). Simple parallels with certain countries, say, like Israel or Italy, which employ or have employed PR for their elections are equally misleading, though it is likely that British elections would reflect those in Germany, where the Free Democrats always hold the balance of power in the Bundestag. The Liberal Democrats, a stronger party, may well generally hold the balance of power in the House of Commons, becoming permanent partners in government, with the ability to extract maximum advantage in post-election negotiations. PR elections might thus privilege one party and one set of voters over others; entrench particular, perhaps minority, political positions in government policies; and give the centre an undue influence in British politics, making radical solutions to problems the more unlikely. We consider these arguments more fully in Chapter 5 and then again in our overall conclusions (Part 4).

The representation of social groups

We briefly consider our third dimension of representation – how well does the make-up of the House of Commons reflect various significant elements in the composition of the population as a whole (**DAC1**)? Clearly, the social composition of the House of Commons gives some measure of how far there is effective opportunity for people from different social groups to stand for public office; and additionally gives some indication of how far Parliament represents the interests of society at large. In this section, we deal only with the representation of women and ethnic minorities in the House of Commons (though naturally we are aware of other significant categories, such as social class, disability, age and so on). After almost glacial progress, the 1992 election proved a 'substantial advance for women' – 336 woman candidates stood for the main parties and 60 became MPs (Norris and Lovenduski 1995). This advance was eclipsed in the 1997 election: nearly one in six of all MPs returned were women – a remarkable advance for this country, if not by international standards.

As Table 3.5 shows, the UK rose from 65th to 24th place in the international league table, but we still perform far worse than Scandinavian nations and other European states, such as Germany and the Netherlands. More sobering still, most of this advance was achieved by the Labour Party, which now has 101 of the 120 women MPs in Parliament (though less than a quarter of all Labour MPs are women) and so depends on the party's electoral fortunes. The key to Labour's achievement was the national policy of all-women shortlists in 'target' (i.e. winnable) seats in all regions. Thus, in Labour's target seats, 43 women were returned and 42 men; and even if Labour had only won its target seats, 90 Labour women MPs would still have entered the Commons. Unfortunately for greater equality, the all-women short-lists provoked controversy in the party and the party abandoned the policy after an industrial tribunal ruled against it (rather than appealing). Neither of the other two main parties increased their representation of women in 1997: the Conservatives

Representation of social groups

Table 3.5 Women's shares of seats in popular chambers, 1995 and 1997

		1997			1995
1	Sweden	40.4		Sweden	40.4
2	Norway	39.4		Norway	39.4
3	Finland	33.5		Finland	33.5
4	Denmark	33.0		Denmark	33.0
5	Netherlands	31.3		Netherlands	31.3
6	New Zealand	29.2		Seychelles	27.3
7	Seychelles	27.3		Germany	26.2
8	Austria	26.8		Iceland	25.4
9	Germany	26.2		Mozambique	25.2
10	Iceland	25.4		South Africa	25.0
(24)	UK	18.2	(65)	UK	9.5

Source: Inter Parliamentary Union

fielded fewer women candidates and now have 13 female and 152 male MPs, and the Liberal Democrats three women and 43 men. The evidence strongly suggests that the under-representation of women is not caused by voter discrimination, but the difficulties women have traditionally faced in being chosen as candidates in winnable seats (see Norris and Lovenduski 1995); and the Fawcett Society, which campaigns for equality for women, has demanded 'positive action' from both other parties, urging them to ensure that women do get chosen as candidates in such seats (*Independent*, 30 June 1997).

Nine MPs from ethnic minority backgrounds were returned in 1997 – an increase of only three over the 1992 election. These MPs make up only 1.4 per cent of the 659 MPs in the House of Commons, while the ethnic minorities form 5.5 per cent of the UK population as a whole. Ethnic minority populations tend to be geographically concentrated, but even where they are most heavily represented, they usually make up about a quarter of the electorate – which is not sufficient for them to determine the result in single-member constituencies. The Boundary Commissions have no mandate to provide for representation for ethnic minorities, unlike in the US, where the peculiar shape of the Seventeenth District of New York reflects an attempt to secure ethnic representation (Reeve and Ware 1991). Some Asian communities have begun to organise within local Labour parties in efforts to get their candidates selected, and have succeeded.

Single-member constituencies are in fact generally perceived to have an adverse effect on the social representativeness of an electoral system (Rose 1974). Although proportional representation is neither a necessary nor a sufficient condition for progress in the representation of women or ethnic minorities, it is worth noting that countries with single-member systems have low proportions of women in their popular assemblies, while, with the exception of Malta, all countries with proportional systems have more. If Parliament were to reflect the social balance in the population, it would include about 336 women and 36 ethnic minority MPs.

AUDIT

All the statistical evidence shows that elections in Britain have failed to ensure that people's votes are of equal value. The plurality-rule electoral system has not operated with any degree of consistency or equity. Elections to the House of Commons have allocated seats in arbitrary ways which do not accord with the voters' preferences; have given an enduring electoral advantage to the two largest parties; and have failed to achieve the equality of geographical representation they are supposed to produce. Up until 1997, they blocked the advance of UK-wide third parties – the Liberals and Social Democrats and (in Europe at least) the Greens – denying them the representation their share of the vote in elections had earned. It may, however, be – though nothing is certain with first-past-the-post – that the Liberal Democrats can establish a stronger presence in the House of Commons on a long-term basis. The winner-takes-all character of the voting system exacerbates its failings: it is possible to win a substantial minority of the popular vote – and even a majority – but be denied any real share in power at national level. Elections in Britain can be another form of national lottery. This is not inevitable. The fact that other countries achieve far lower levels of distortion using proportional representation for elections shows that workable alternatives are available in countries, like Germany and Sweden, which also enjoy the advantages of stable and usually effective government. But would they work well in the UK? More study should be carried out on the likely effects of alternative systems in British conditions.

Meanwhile, the supposed advantages of the first-past-the-post electoral system are open to argument. In the late 1970s, and early 1990s, it is not at all clear that this country enjoyed 'strong government'; nor is it entirely obvious that single-party government in the 'winner-takes-all' tradition of British democracy is effective, orderly or responsive government (a theme we return to in Part 2 of this volume). First-past-the-post elections are justified as having saved this country from being governed by coalition government since the mid-1930s, though it is by no means clear that coalition government is worse than single-party government; those who argue the case for more consensual politics in the UK argue that it is better. The evidence suggests that coalition government in western Europe has been no less effective than single-party government in the UK, and possibly superior in terms of economic policy. Similarly, research suggests that the benefits of the single-member constituency are somewhat illusory and little-used by the electorate, popular though the idea of a 'local' MP remains with the public.

DAC1: Is appointment to legislative and government office determined by popular vote?

Formally, elections to the governing House of Commons are determined by popular vote. But the results of that vote are distorted by the electoral system in use. Parties are generally able to form a government and gain majorities in Parliament on a minority of the popular vote, and may even win more seats than another party which has won a majority of votes. As a consequence, it may be said that appointment to legislative and government office is only imperfectly determined by popular vote. Office in the House of Lords is not determined by popular vote. People become members either through the hereditary principle, which overwhelmingly privileges men over women, and those of white European descent over all other ethnic groups; by government appointment; or (in the case of bishops and the law lords) by virtue of appointed public office. While the influence of the House of Lords is secondary, it constitutes a non-democratic part of the British legislature and fails to meet the basic principle of election.

DAC4: Votes of equal value

The system and the parties combine to create inequalities in voters' capacity to influence the election result. The value of their votes varies according to the party they choose to support; the region and local area in which they live; and the marginality of their local constituency. The flawed system encourages the parties to concentrate their electoral platforms and efforts on a minority of perhaps half a million voters out of an electorate of 43 million in the 100–120 or so marginal seats on which elections in Britain normally turn. They are therefore likely to have more influence on the content of manifestos than other electors.

DAC4: How far does the composition of Parliament reflect the electorate's choices?

As we have seen, elections to the House of Commons reflect the votes of the electorate imperfectly and unpredictably, and at some elections produce perverse results (see panel, **pp. 54–55**). If support for, say, four parties were evenly shared 40/30/20/10 per cent in every constituency in the land then it is theoretically possible for the leading party to secure every seat in the Commons on a minority of the popular vote. Of course, this doesn't happen in practice nationally, though some local elections come close to this worst-case scenario. The composition of the House of Lords is entirely unaffected by the electorate's choices.

DAC1: Equal representation of social groups

We have measured the ability of the existing system to offer members of all social groups an 'equal effective opportunity' to stand for public office, in terms of their gender and ethnic origins. Even though 1997 represented a dramatic advance for women in Parliament, Britain still performs relatively poorly by comparison with similar nations. Moreover, the state of the law on positive discrimination in Britain suggests that the key to the adoption of far more women in winnable seats by the Labour party – all-women shortlists – may no longer be available to Labour or rival parties. The ethnic minorities are also poorly represented in the House of Commons. The evidence from other countries suggests that PR systems are better able to secure more equal representation of all social groups, though such systems also have features which may seem undesirable in the British context (the parties' choice of candidates in PR systems is often highly centralised, for example).

DAC3: The range of choice offered by the electoral and party system

As stated above, the electoral system blocks the advance of third parties into Parliament. There is a standard measure of 'third-party squeeze' – the relative reduction of parties (RRP) – on which the UK scores very badly by comparison with other liberal democracies, especially when the regional levels of squeeze are taken into account. RRP also provides a measure of the real choice between parties for intending voters. The results in Britain do not necessarily mean that voters will only be able to choose between very few parties, but rather that very few parties they may choose between have a real chance of gaining seats in the assembly. Though the Liberal Democrats and third parties are most adversely affected, even voters for the Conservatives and Labour lose out in certain regions.

DAC5: The level of turnout

The proportion of the electorate who actually vote is a rough and ready measure of the public's belief in representative democracy and voting. Turnout in postwar Britain reached a peak of 84 and 82.5 per cent in the elections of 1950 and 1951, but these figures are probably as much a reflection of the intense two-party struggle for power as they are a measure of confidence in the efficacy of the vote. Since then, turnout has varied between 72 and 78.7 per cent, shifting up and down (perhaps according to the month of the election, just as much as the level of public commitment). In 1997, turnout fell to 71.5 per cent, the lowest level since 1935. This means that only 30.9 per cent of the electorate actually voted the Blair government into power – a figure which severely qualifies 'landslide' talk. Since 1945, only the Labour governments narrowly returned to power in the two 1974 election victories did so on lower shares of the popular vote (Curtice and Steed 1997: 295). Broadly, the overall picture is that between 20 and 30 per cent of the registered electorate fail to vote in British elections and a further 5 to 9 per cent of people eligible to vote are not registered. The Institute for Democracy and Electoral Assistance, in Stockholm, places the UK at No. 48 in the global league table of turnout since 1945, and at No. 14 out of 25 for western Europe in the 1990s (Reynolds and Reilly 1997).

DAC5: Acceptance of election results

We have not discussed the question of whether 'the main political forces' in the country accept the results of elections, since throughout postwar Britain all election results – and subsequent governments – have been accepted by the political parties and other forces. Perhaps the defining moment was the election of the first majority Labour government in 1945, pledged to a vast programme of nationalisation of the public utilities and the steel industry, and to healthcare reforms which threatened the autonomy of the medical profession. However, Labour had proved its patriotic and responsible credentials by its participation in the wartime coalition government and, in the event, met no organised extra-parliamentary resistance. In Northern

Ireland, insurrectionary violence, born of the troubled history of England's role in Ireland, is currently forsworn by the major terrorist organisations during the 'peace process'. But Loyalist and Republican paramilitary action has caused thousands of deaths and huge damage, mostly in Northern Ireland since the 1960s, and Republican terrorists on occasion directly and violently confronted the democratic and cere-monial fabric of public life (e.g. the murders of Lord Mountbatten and Airey Neave MP; the bomb placed at the Grand Hotel, Brighton, to kill the Prime Minister and cabinet ministers). The popular Protestant uprising and strike in 1974 brought the Heath government's attempt to introduce a 'power-sharing' assembly to an abrupt end, and more recently, official fears of the power of the Loyalist mob and para-military violence persuaded the authorities to capitulate and allow a controversial Orange Order parade to go ahead. (Though, in 1998, the most controversial parade was halted by firm government action.) There can be little doubt that elements in the Protestant majority would, if the need arose, return to the tradition of Edward Carson's private army of Home Rule days (1912–22). On the mainland in 1981, inner-city riots broke out in protest against worsening conditions and the neglect of the then government and a series of wider protests and riots erupted as the poll tax took effect in 1990. But generally the political culture of Britain eschews extra-parliamentary politics of most kinds, and violent protests in particular.

It is not possible to measure how satisfied the general public is with the electoral system or its results with any degree of confidence. Public opinion surveys suggest that the public is fairly evenly divided when they are asked to choose between the existing system and PR alternatives, though of the alternatives on offer, a system akin to Germany's AMS, which combines local constituencies and overall propor-tionality, seems to be a great deal more popular than the single transferable vote with its far larger, multi-member constituencies (Dunleavy *et al.* 1997; Weir 1992). In May 1997, the ICM survey used to 'replay' the election under alternative systems was also employed to hold a 'mock referendum' between first-past-the-post and AMS. The result was too close to call – AMS won by 44 per cent to 41 (with 14 per cent don't knows). Generally people are sceptical about the ability of a change in voting systems to solve 'Britain's problems' (ICM Research, April 1992).

4   The Independence of Elections

Government and outside influences on elections

Every citizen shall have the right and the opportunity, without unreasonable restrictions, to vote and to be elected at genuine periodic elections which shall be by universal and equal suffrage and shall be held by secret ballot, guaranteeing the free expression of the will of the electors.

(The International Covenant on Civil and Political Rights, article 25, 1966)

It is not possible to consider the fairness of elections without examining the pattern of political funding. This is simply because the money may in some circumstances have a major influence on the outcome of elections. Rich candidates and parties may potentially gain a significant and – arguably – unfair advantage. . . . Money may also be a source of undue influence or corruption.

(Michael Pinto-Duschinsky, expert on political funding, 1993)

IT WAS THE SUN *WOT WON IT!*

(Front-page headline, in the *Sun*, 11 April 1992)

If popular control of elections is to work, elections must be independent of state or party; accessible to voters; and free of intimidation, abuses, bribery, and so on. The Democratic Audit has already examined such questions as voter registration, access, abuse and electoral arrangements, and so on, in the first volume, *The Three Pillars of Liberty* (DA Volume No. 1: Chapter 14). Here we examine other issues of state or party control, notably the secrecy of the ballot. Equally, the two principles of popular control and political equality will be diminished if it turns out that some other actor or group of actors has undue influence over the electoral process. We therefore consider the influence of the media and other political forces and interests on the electoral process. The resourcing of the parties also affects both principles. Historically, big business and particular interests, such as the City of London, brewers and major construction companies, have been ready to fund the Conservative Party, and the trade unions have not only sponsored Labour, but played the leading role in creating the party. How transparent is the funding of political parties and how robust are controls against improper influences? These issues are covered in the following edited Democratic Audit criteria:

Secret ballot

DAC1. How far is appointment to office determined by popular election and secret ballot?

DAC2. How independent of government and party control and external influences are elections and procedures of voter registration?

DAC3. How effective a range of information does the electoral and party system allow the voters, and how far is there fair and equal access for all parties and candidates to the media and other means of communication with them?

DAC10. How publicly accountable are the political parties for party interests and sources of income that might affect the conduct of government and public duties and the process of election to public office?

Official access to the secret ballot

People's votes are secret at the point of voting, but the administration of the ballot allows the authorities to make retrospective checks on how individual people voted – an official provision which may be open to abuse. The registration number of everyone voting is recorded on the counterfoil of their ballot paper. After the local count, the counterfoils and ballot papers, bearing each person's vote, are sealed in parcels and despatched to the care of the Clerk of the Crown in Chancery (a senior official of the Lord Chancellor's Office) and kept at 'a secure location in Greater London', as Angela Rumbold, then a Home Office minister, informed Frank Dobson MP in December 1990. Thus, it is possible for the authorities (or others) to identify who any one individual has voted for and, perhaps more pertinently, which individuals have voted for any particular candidate. This provision was made in the Ballot Act 1892, when 'personation' and other electoral fraud was more common than now and was introduced to make it easier to apprehend, or at least to deter, offenders. If any corrupt or illegal practices are reported, the counterfoils and ballot papers are available for inspection. To guard against improper interference with the sealed parcels, they may only be released and opened at the request of a judge of the Election Court with permission from the Speaker of the House of Commons (Liberty/Electoral Reform Society 1997).

In 1982–83, the Home Affairs Committee considering electoral practice took evidence on the current arrangements and concluded that they provided 'a necessary means of checking on any instances of personation'. However, a recent study by the academic lawyer, Robert Blackburn, found that the number of allegations of voter personation in Britain is negligible; that it has never been necessary to order a fresh parliamentary election on such grounds (though this has been done at local level); and that 'vote-tracing hardly helps in the detection and prevention of any offence in itself' (Blackburn 1995: 107 and 487).

The authorities assert that the sealed parcels are kept securely and deny that the intelligence services have ever tampered with them. However, David Northmore, an expert on freedom of information, has identified the 'secure location' as a warehouse at Hayes and alleges that security there is lax (*Guardian*, 23 March 1992). In 1981, Gordon Winter, a former BOSS agent, alleged in his memoirs that the South African intelligence agency knew the identity of everyone who had voted for the Communist Party of Great Britain via vote-tracing by British intelligence agents (Winter 1981: 419–420). In 1992, a Leeds politics don alleged that a postgraduate student had chanced upon a cupboard full of ballot papers recording voters for Communist candidates in local elections in a Midlands 'steel town'. The town clerk allegedly told him that in the 1960s he used to forward the names of all Communist voters to Special Branch. *Guardian* inquiries identified Scunthorpe as the town he was referring to (*Guardian*, 23 March 1992). Evidently, the intelligence services would have an interest in identifying the voters for certain minority parties, such as the Communists and, say, the British Movement. As Winter's boss allegedly said to him about the store of ballot papers:

> in intelligence terms, that's like knowing where there's several thousand tons of gold which can be stolen without anyone knowing. Can you imagine British Intelligence not scrutinising those voting slips? They'd be stupid if they didn't.
>
> (Winter 1981: 420)

Peter Wright, the former MI5 agent and author of *Spycatcher*, said that in the course of 'bugging and burglaring' across London he broke into a flat to obtain the membership list of the Communist Party (Liberty/Electoral Reform Society 1997: 33). There is no proof that British Intelligence has in fact engaged in illicit vote-tracing. Equally, there is no doubt that the potential for agents to do so exists; that existing safeguards would be no match for their sophisticated powers; and that the use of computers would make illicit vote-tracing a relatively easy task. Given the negligible rate of personation in Britain, it seems to us that precautions against the greater possible evil should take precedence; that alternative methods of preventing voting frauds would be more effective than retaining retrospective records; and that the principle of the secret ballot should be upheld.

The government's influence over elections

There are several ways in which the government of the day has an advantage over the other political parties contesting an election. There must be an election every five years, but the current Prime Minister can choose when it falls within that period. For example, between 1964 and 1966, the Labour premier, Harold Wilson, chose the moment for the election very carefully in order to augment his majority via re-election; in 1997, John Major delayed the election date as the economy slowly improved in the hope that his party would benefit from an electoral 'feel-good' factor. This advantage has assumed an even greater significance with the increase in party political polling and more frequent opinion polls. Further, governments can seek to time the 'political business cycle', raising taxes and deflating immediately after an election in order to create potential for a reflationary boom in time for the next election. While evidence for macro-economic manipulation is hard to prove

Government influence

(partly because it is often unsuccessful) it is generally perceived to exist, although the government's ability to manipulate the economy has been reduced by modern global developments and membership of the European Union. Evidence of micro-level policy changes timed to increase support – such as Nigel Lawson's boost to public spending before the 1987 election – is easier to establish. Virtually all other parliamentary democracies fix the timing of elections in law. The Hansard Society Commission on election campaigns recommended that Britain should follow suit, with early dissolutions permissible only when a government lacks sufficient support to continue in office, and Parliament fails to elect a successor (Hansard Society 1991).

The Prime Minister can also decide the length of the campaign period. The government presumably gains by giving as short notice as possible; though in 1997 Major hoped to gain from an official election campaign of six weeks; and seems also to have prorogued Parliament early to prevent the Parliamentary Commissioner's report on allegations of sleaze and bribes against Neil Hamilton and other former ministers from being published in time to influence the election campaign. Knowledge of the likely election date can be an advantage in other ways. For example, the Conservative Party's advertising agency, Saatchi & Saatchi, booked poster sites three weeks before the 1992 election was declared in the name of American clients, and at once switched them to the Conservative Party's account when the election was called (Linton 1994).

Government influence on electoral boundaries

As we have seen, the fixing of parliamentary boundaries is entrusted to scrupulously impartial Boundary Commissions, though the formally objective processes are heavily influenced by the political parties (**p. 52**). Governments are no longer in a position to instruct the Commissioners on politically sensitive issues arising from settling parliamentary boundaries (as, for example, the Disraeli administration did in 1867, instructing them to draw the new urban boundaries around urban overspills in order to purify the counties of 'alien', and likely non-Conservative, elements; Jenkins 1996).

But executive dominance over Parliament gives governments power to restructure local government as they see fit. This power has significant implications for **DAC18** (local authority independence from 'undue interference' from the centre; see **p. 13**). Governments have used it to re-structure local government and re-draw local boundaries to create local authority areas which reflect partisan party interests and to remove local centres of resistance. Moreover, it raises a major question about the independence from government or party control of electoral process at local and national level (**DAC2**), since the exact configuration of local boundaries can profoundly affect the results not only of local elections, but also indirectly of parliamentary elections, and thus the distribution of local and national political power. The knock-on effect to national elections comes about because, to varying degrees, the Parliamentary Commissions are bound to take local authority boundaries into consideration in drawing parliamentary boundaries.

By convention, governments contemplating major changes at local level were bound to set up an independent commission, and to undertake substantial consultation, seeking to base change at least on the legitimacy of a broad political consensus.

However, the final decision has always been reserved to Parliament, and the majority party there, and has never been given democratic validity locally by way of referendum. Even the customary processes have not entirely excluded partisan considerations. The 1973–74 reorganisation, though preceded by English and Scottish commissions and debated in terms of efficiency and structure, was influenced by the Conservatives' political interests, and other vested interests, as several academic studies have shown (Wood 1976; Alexander 1982; Page and Midwinter 1979; Stoker 1991). In 1986, however, the Conservative government entirely broke with convention to abolish the Greater London Council and six metropolitan counties – strategic upper-tier authorities in England's largest conurbations – and then the Inner London Education Authority in 1990. These authorities were all Labour-held; though, ironically, one of the reasons for establishing the Greater London Council in 1965 was to replace the former Labour-held London County Council of inner London with a larger authority which, with the addition of Conservative outer boroughs, was likely generally to be under Tory rule. Admittedly, the 1983–87 government had the tenuous authority of a manifesto pledge of abolition (but see **p. 109**). But the abolitions were dictated by partisan political spite; ministers overrode official advice warning of the confusions which would ensue; and no analysis of the effects of abolition was made nor was the public consulted. Opinion polls in London showed that the public was overwhelmingly against abolition, and a poll in the six conurbations revealed 'considerable and increased confusion and uncertainty about the allocation of local government responsibilities' (Game 1987; Stoker 1991).

By 1991, the Major government was equally determined to abolish the Strathclyde and Lothian regions, both of them a focus of Labour resistance in Scotland, and embarked upon an unashamed partisan recasting of Scottish local government. The Scottish Secretary, Ian Lang, announced that an independent commission was not 'the best or most appropriate way forward'; but promised that this absence would not mean 'a less thorough consultation process' (HC Deb WA, 29 June 1991, c81). However, the consultation was rushed and ruled out keeping the existing system from the start. In June 1993, the Scottish Office published a brief account of 3,317 responses, but they were not discussed or analysed in detail, nor was it clear how far they agreed with the government's proposals. The 28 new authorities were designed to 're-shape the future' of local politics in Scotland, reducing Labour councils to just 10, taking control of their two councils from the Liberal Democrats and removing the SNP's single foothold in Angus. John Curtice, an elections analyst at the University of Strathclyde, concluded that the 'circumstantial evidence of gerrymandering is compelling' (*Scotland on Sunday*, 11 July 1993). Sir David (now Lord) Steel, a Scottish MP for 28 years, said the government's proposals were 'the most corrupt proposals that have been presented to the House by any government in my time' (HC Deb, 8 July 1993, c481). The Scottish Boundary Commission is bound by law to 'have regard' to local authority boundaries, a weaker duty than in England and Wales which gives the Commission more latitude to cross boundaries (a latitude it used in the last review). Even so, the gerrymandered local authority boundaries (if they survive so long) are likely to affect the next review (2003–07); to what extent will depend on the next Commission.

Media influence

The influence of the media on elections

The media play a dominant part in modern elections, since most voters gain their knowledge of the election issues, of the parties' promises and relative performance, and of their leaders from television, radio and newspapers. In this sense, it may be argued that the media are fulfilling their classic liberal role of ensuring that voters are well informed on the significant policy issues and differences between the parties' platforms and basic aims. But their actual role in elections is more complex. The ownership of the press is heavily concentrated and exhibits a major bias towards the Conservative Party and the interests of large corporations. The tabloid press, in particular, was generally grossly partisan in its support for the Conservatives and hostility towards Labour up to 1997, with only two newspapers, the pro-Labour *Daily Mirror* and the *Record* in Scotland to offset a pro-Tory pack of at least four national pro-Tory tabloids. In 1997, the *Sun* decided to stick to Tony Blair (rather than Labour) and the *News of the World* finally also backed Labour. There was speculation about a possible deal between Blair and Rupert Murdoch, the head of News International. On the other hand, Major's government was widely seen to be 'tired, divided and rudderless' (the *Sun*'s verdict), not least among the rest of the media. Overall, 1997 was the first election in which the majority of the press was not anti-Labour; Labour's lead, in terms of readership, was 10 million (Butler and Kavanagh 1997: 83).

In 1992, the *Sun* notoriously claimed to have won the election for the Conservatives. In 1997, the election was largely over before it began. It is generally agreed that the Conservatives suffered in terms of editorial opinion, but a study by the Communication Research Centre, at Loughborough University, concluded that the Conservatives 'broadly achieved parity with Labour in presenting their views on the issues':

> while the Tories may have received a bad press from many of their previous cheerleaders in 1997, in no way can it be said to have approached the level of vitriol heaped on Labour in 1992. Labour's achievement . . . was in decommissioning the big guns of the Tory press rather than in turning their fire on their previous masters.
>
> (Deacon *et al.* 1997)

Further, while the Conservative Party affiliation of most of the press wavered in 1997, 'Conservative values – individualism, Euro-scepticism, anti-unionism, anti-welfarism – remain engraved on the hearts of many papers' (Deacon *et al.* 1997).

There is no doubt, then, that the media seek to bring a powerful 'external influence' to bear upon the decisions of the electorate (**DAC2**), even if their choices in 1997 had a hollow ring. However, the influence of the media on the results of an election is extremely hard to discern and to measure, partly because media influence dissolves into a plethora of other social influences and factors, and increasingly because political strategies and actions are formed and take place within the media framework and may be directly provoked by the actions of newspapers or journalists. Much of Labour's thinking from 1983 onwards was directed to framing policy positions to satisfy editorial and journalistic opinion (on the grounds that the media framed popular perceptions of the party). The issues arising from the media role in elections are thus very complex and require intense analysis for which we do not have space here. So we largely leave them aside (but see Linton 1994 and Marsh 1993). The tabloids' biased reports on Labour's former leader, Neil Kinnock, in 1992 and the right-wing Euro-sceptic press treatment of John Major from 1992–97 must have damaged their cause. But their ultimate influence must be in doubt. All the poll evidence, for example, corroborates the view that the Major government lost the 1997 election when he lost the faith of the British electorate on 'Black Wednesday', 16 September 1992, when sterling was driven out of the Exchange Rate Mechanism (ERM). It is more certain that they have recently diminished the quality of political debate and understanding, between as well as during elections. Historically, too, they have intimidated Labour's leading figures (**DAC3**) and since May 1997, various commentators have expressed the view that Labour in government has been so sensitive to the hostile attitude of the Murdoch press to the single European currency that it has fudged the decision on this country's membership of EMU.

The concentration of media interests in the hands of fewer large-scale institutions and proprietors, with industrial interests to enhance and political views of their own, raises serious questions about the political role of the press, and especially the tabloid press, whether they are actually able to turn an election result one way or another or not. One aspect of their influence has been measured. The *Guardian* journalist, Martin Linton (now a Labour MP), summarised research by the US company EIT on the political reporting of the national press on two days during the 1992 election. It is hardly surprising that EIT found that the tabloid press were more partisan than the broadsheets, with the *Sun* and *Daily Express* carrying no negative reports about the Conservatives or positive reports about Labour; and the *Daily Mirror* no positive reports about the Conservatives or negative reports on Labour. Linton cautiously extrapolated calculations for the whole election period from EIT's research, suggesting that the Conservatives received the equivalent of 221 pages of positive editorial in the *Sun*, *Daily Express* and *Daily Mail* (worth some £5.3 million in advertising costs) and Labour 60 positive pages in the *Mirror* (£1.6 million). In fact, editorial space is worth more than advertising space and this free publicity for the Conservatives and Labour may well have been worth, say, £16 million and £5 million respectively if we assume that editorial coverage is worth three times as much as equivalent advertising space.

Television and elections in Britain

However, the rules governing television coverage of politics and elections bring about a significant levelling of political advantage at election time. Television (and radio) remain the most influential and trusted media. And rules prohibiting political advertising on television and the provision of free time on television for the political parties creates something like equal access to them at elections. The costs of elections in Britain are rising fast, but these rules have prevented the extravagantly expensive

Television coverage

party campaigns in American elections, thus depriving the wealthier parties of the opportunity to establish a hegemony over television coverage (and incidentally checking the 'dumbing down' of election messages). Instead, the political parties are allocated free party election broadcasts (PEBs) on television and radio. Chris Powell, of BMP DDB, who directed Labour's 1997 advertising campaign, says that the commercial value of the PEBs in the last four weeks of an election campaign is considerably greater than the actual party expenditure on posters and press advertisements (Powell 1997). Labour's five PEBs during the campaign reached an aggregate audience of 50 million people – which would cost £5 million at commercial advertising rates. Posters over the same four weeks cost the Conservatives £3 million and Labour £1.6 million.

Party election broadcasts are supposedly allocated through an informal Committee on Party Political Broadcasting on which representatives of the major parties and broadcasters sit. The committee now never meets and the broadcasters generally negotiate ad-hoc deals through the 'usual channels' (i.e., with the parliamentary whips). The allocations of PEBs are decided by 'rule of thumb' on the following broad basis. The Conservatives and Labour get equal time; other parties receive an allocation broadly in proportion to their vote at the previous election. Any party fielding 50 candidates or more receives a minimum five-minute spot on television. The ratio of free television time between the three main parties has been 5:5:4 (Conservative: Labour: Liberal Democrat) at the last two elections. The ratio of time agreed for the broadcasts is also used broadly to determine the balance of news coverage throughout the election, but the 'stop-watch' approach rigidly allocating time has been abandoned. These arrangements generally work in their discreet way, but in 1983 the broadcasters had to overrule the Conservatives and Labour over the time to be given to the new Social Democratic Party; and in 1992 the Liberal Democrats were bitterly angry over their allocation. Yet the rules mean that the Liberal Democrats are not prevented by their relative poverty from reaching the electors through the single most important means of communication – television – at elections and during the run-up to elections. In 1997, the Referendum Party, which fielded 547 candidates, argued that it was entitled to a larger allocation of free time than its one five-minute PEB, but the broadcasters' refusal to give the party more time was upheld by the courts.

The arrangements for allocating PEBs are typically casual. In effect, they are dominated by the broadcasters and agreed by the three larger parties. It may be said that the arrangements work, and do so reasonably fairly. Wounded parties can always appeal to the courts, as they are increasingly prone to do. But there are wider issues on which the public could properly be consulted and other parties standing for election should have some locus in the negotiations. The Hansard Society Commission in 1991 recommended that the current arrangements should be formalised, with access to the negotiations for all interested parties and clear criteria for the allocation of air time (Hansard Society 1991).

The larger parties are still able to purchase a political advantage over their rivals. Party political broadcasts are a high-cost activity. In 1992 and 1997, Labour and the Conservatives spent huge sums on their broadcasts; indeed, in 1992, the

Conservative investment in PEBs was larger than the whole of the Liberal Democrats' election expenditure (see Table 4.1). The two parties invest hugely in highly professional broadcasts which rank with commercial advertisements and employ well-known cinema and television directors such as John Schlesinger, Hugh Hudson and Molly Dineen. As advertisers know, the quality of a broadcast counts and far more hangs on its style and impact than its length. The rules can impose equality in the time given to political broadcasts, but not their quality. And since the parties must bear the costs of their PEBs, the larger parties are clearly at an advantage.

The major terrestrial television networks – the BBC and ITV – are bound by strict rules of impartiality in all their political coverage as well as at election times. The rules are found in the Broadcasting Acts 1990 and 1996 and were explicitly incorporated in the BBC's new Charter and Agreement which came into force in 1996. Broadcasting authorities and companies are not allowed the freedom to 'editorialise' or express their own views on issues of controversy in the way newspapers are. Similarly, political parties, politically-oriented organisations and individuals are disqualified from running independent television or radio broadcasting companies. The BBC and the Independent Television Commission and Radio Authority are obliged to reinforce the requirement to observe 'due impartiality' by publishing codes of practice for programme-makers. The public service traditions of the BBC, which embody a culture of balanced reporting, have also had a long-term influence on independent television and radio coverage, including satellite and cable broadcasting. Thus, most viewers regard television and radio coverage of elections as balanced and impartial; and television, the most popular and potentially influential medium, generally provides a politically neutral background for elections.

In one respect, the rules inhibit the ability of broadcasters to report elections fairly and accurately. Under section 93 of the Representation of the People Act 1993, the BBC and independent companies are forbidden to broadcast reports from local constituencies in which candidates participate unless the broadcast has the consent of all the candidates. Thus, any candidate can wield an effective ban on meaningful constituency reports. The result is stilted and stage-managed reports from constituencies on which real issues rarely arise. The ban especially affects coverage on regional television. It is hard to see why the general rules demanding impartial coverage cannot apply to local reporting as well. Everyone in broadcasting wants a change in the law; as Stephen Perkins, senior programme officer at the ITC says, it would make coverage 'more local, lively and relevant for voters'. The political parties are against a change which would remove their control over local reports. In 1997, the long and unchanging election campaign made for boring, and probably counter-productive television coverage, with Sky's election broadcasts proving more innovative and lively, notably in its live coverage of the party press conferences. All channels made efforts to introduce the public ('real people', as broadcasters tend to call them) more fully into their programming to raise issues and debate alongside the more tightly-controlled formal party campaigns. In a very real sense, the broadcasters were seeking to open up democratic debate, while the party managers were seeking either to control or to prevent it.

Election expenditure

Election expenditure of the political parties

More broadly, the parties' election campaigns turn on providing information in ways which are designed to increase each party's share of the vote; and to some degree, a party's success in getting its messages across will depend on how much it is able to spend. Thus, richer parties may potentially gain a significant and – arguably – unfair advantage in elections. Research in the United States has, for example, demonstrated that the size of a candidate's campaign budget has a vital effect on the results of elections to the US House of Representatives, and research here on local campaigns has found that 'the more a party spends on the campaign in a constituency, the more votes it wins' (Home Affairs Committee (HAC) 1993: 14, 177–183; Jacobson 1980).

As political parties are not recognised in law, controls on political expenditure during elections apply only to individual candidates in their constituencies. The limits in 1997 were £4,642 plus 5.2p for every elector in a county constituency and 3.9p per urban elector. It is widely believed that these totals were exceeded by the parties in 1997; the Nuffield study, for example, talks of suspicions of 'quite a lot of evasion', especially through national or regional telephone and direct mail costs. The Conservatives and Labour (roughly spending an average £5,600 on their candidates) outspent all other parties (the Liberal Democrats spent just £3,200) (Butler and Kavanagh 1997: 233).

At national level, there are no controls at all and electoral spending is a free-for-all. This apparent inequality is mitigated by the relative cheapness of elections in the UK, largely brought about by the ban on political advertising on television, and by the massive subsidy-in-kind which parties in the election receive in free television time. Powell's estimate (see **p. 86** above), and previous estimates, suggest that the total value of free TV and radio broadcasts in and prior to elections in Britain 'dwarfs' the sums paid by the parties for all other types of campaign advertising put together (HAC 1993: 20). Even so, the room for advantage for the two larger, and comparatively wealthy, parties is obvious and has been growing. The important issues here are whether one party or several consistently spend more than their rivals; what discernible effect this has on the result of an election; whether there should be legal controls on the amount of money spent; and whether the state should fund political parties to remove financial inequalities (**DAC3**).

Until the end of the 1950s, central party expenditure on elections was relatively small, amounting to a fifth of all campaign expenditure. The campaign materials of the period, like small-scale posters and public meetings, were much cheaper than those of today – television broadcasts, private polling, poster site and newspaper advertising, telephone banks targeted on key voters, political data-banks like the Conservative PIKE programme for identifying key electors and Labour's 'Excalibur' rebuttal unit, and so on. Evidence from Dr Michael Pinto-Duschinsky, of Brunel University, to the Home Affairs Committee inquiry into the funding of political parties in May 1993 showed that the Conservatives comfortably outspent Labour at postwar elections in 1959, 1964, 1979, 1983 and 1987 (when the differential, at constant 1992 values, was £12.3 million to £5.9 million) (HAC 1993: 10–13). As

Table 4.1 National party spending in the 1992 general election

	Conservatives £s	Labour £s	Liberal Democrats £s
Advertising:			
Posters	4,000,000	1,760,000	58,000
Press	1,800,000	1,500,000	221,000
Total spent on advertising*	6,360,000	3,340,000	279,000
Other spending:			
Producing political broadcasts	2,250,000	668,000	99,000
Grants to constituencies	57,000	1,500,000	284,000
Opinion research	242,000	595,000	55,000
Publications	730,000	112,000	16,000
Leaders' tours, meetings, etc.	972,000	3,000,000	469,000
Total expenditure	11,200,000	10,600,000	1,800,000

Source: Home Affairs Committee (HAC) 1993b: 33
Note:
* The totals shown include expenditures other than those listed.

Table 4.1 shows, total spending by the two larger parties in 1992 was more or less equal, with the Conservatives spending £11.2 million and Labour £10.6 million (at 1992 prices).

Comparable data for 1997 were not available in early 1998. The 1997 Nuffield election study suggested that the Conservatives spent £20 million in the year up to May 1997; Labour reckoned to have spent £13 million 'from central party funds' (note the potentially evasive phrasing); and the Liberal Democrats £700,000 over the same period. These figures cover spending on press and poster advertising, private polls and research, assistance to constituencies, leaders' tours, fees and staff costs (Butler and Kavanagh 1997: 242). Michael Pinto-Duschinsky, an expert on political funding, has issued preliminary estimates which suggest that the Conservatives spent £25 million over the two years to May 1997 and Labour £22 million; the comparable figure for the Liberal Democrats is £3 million. Thus, the largest inequality nowadays rests between the two largest parties and the Liberal Democrats. In both 1992 and 1996–97, the Conservatives spent more than Labour and other parties on advertising. In 1996–97, the Conservatives spent £13.1 million on advertising – nearly twice as much as Labour (£7.4 million) and the Referendum Party (£7.2 million) (Powell 1997). The Liberal Democrats' expenditure was negligible. The two major parties engaged in a year-long heavyweight poster battle, initiated by the Tories in May 1996, both of them ultimately spending some four-fifths of their advertising budget on posters. Neither poster nor national press advertisements are regulated under election laws and political claims made through them are not subject to the rules of truthful presentation in the British code of advertising practice. This exemption can be justified on pragmatic grounds, but it is not justifiable in democratic terms. (They do not entirely escape regulation, however. In August 1996 public complaints about the Tories' 'Demon Eyes' campaign, featuring a demonic Tony Blair, prompted the Advertising Standards Agency to make its first ruling on a political advertisement. The ASA rejected complaints that the posters were offensive, but ruled against the use of Blair's image on the ground that he had not been asked for his permission.) The benefits of this expenditure are impossible to establish. In 1997, Powell says that the Tories' £13 million expenditure 'made barely a dent' in polls showing a commanding Labour lead, whereas in 1979, the 'Labour isn't working' posters made a significant impact – the point being that all such propaganda has to relate to voters' own perceptions.

Be that as it may, it is generally agreed in the advertising industry that a poster campaign must be widespread – and therefore expensive – if it is to work. Trade sources estimated in 1992 that to have the maximum impact on public opinion, a poster campaign required some 5,000–6,000 sites, costing about £2 million, plus £4 million on design. Lord McAlpine, former treasurer of the Conservative Party, held that a poster campaign could persuade the public to believe virtually anything, given enough money: 'a poster campaign costing £1 or £2 million is a waste of money, but give me £8 million and I will deliver whatever you want' (Linton 1994). Expenditure on the scale of the two parties' poster campaigns in 1996–97, and their advertising campaign generally, is out of reach for the Liberal Democrats and smaller parties like the Greens. Further disparities occur in the booking of sites, as very few sites are still available in the four weeks ahead when an election is called and any advance information (likely to be held by the incumbent party) is a great advantage.

Less attention is paid to the parties' spending at local level, yet it is known that the limits on local expenditure were being circumvented on a large scale prior to the Representation of the People Act 1989, which quadrupled the limits in an effort to curtail abuse. Genuine uncertainties about what counts and does not count as local election expenditure abound. The costs of national poster and advertising campaigns, the visits of party leaders, the increasing use of telephone banks at national level to chase voters in marginal constituencies, all raise unresolved issues of legality. The use of telephones is becoming increasingly significant, and is almost impossible to police. The Home Office and returning officers play no part in enforcing the law on local expenditures – it is left entirely to individual candidates or electors to bring election petitions, a costly procedure. Bearing in mind the uncertainties, the legal costs and the dangers of retaliation, the major parties prefer to let sleeping dogs lie. Not since 1929 have Conservative or Labour candidates brought petitions against each other to challenge breaches of the spending rules. Yet the researches of Professors Johnston and Pattie show that the amount the parties spend in local contests is 'directly related to vote-winning'; and that the parties spend more and unequally on marginal seats (HAC 1993: 177–183). Given the pivotal role of marginal seats in most modern general elections – elections are won and lost in these seats – the case for clearer criteria and rules, and for separating out national, regional and local inputs to electioneering, is of great importance. There is also a need to augment the process of individual petitioning by placing the task of enforcing clearer rules in the hands of a public authority – an independent commission for elections in general (Hansard Society 1976).

The inequalities in spending inevitably affect the range of choice and balance of information which voters receive during an election and create imbalances in the access to the media and other means of communication, such as posters and news-paper advertising, for the Liberal Democrats and smaller parties (**DAC3**). Regardless of the difficulties of measuring the effect on the election result of the parties' expen-diture, Table 4.1 does exhibit huge imbalances in election expenditure between the main parties and the smaller parties and suggests an inequality in the parties' ability to affect the election result via expenditure on campaigning. There is an obvious case for expenditure limits at national level, either a general overall limit (as in Canada) or limits on specific sorts of spending, such as advertising and telephone use. The argu-ment for such a proposal is one of political equity. The arguments against such limits are largely practical. The electoral process might be distorted if the parties' spending was capped, but that of pressure groups, industrial interests and trade unions remained unconstrained; while if other expenditures were also limited, the new rules might be regarded as interfering with freedom of expression. The 1991 Hansard Society Commission on Electoral Campaigns came out against limits on spending broadly on such grounds, arguing that 'the regulation of central election expenditures entails a radical change in our electoral structures' which was both impossible and unnecessary (Hansard Society 1991). However, Home Office consultations with all the political parties in 1991 found that 'all parties with the exception of the Conservative Party, agreed that consideration should be given to a system of controls on national expen-diture' (Linton 1994). The general public agree. In the first of the Rowntree Reform Trust's 'State of the Nation' surveys in 1991, MORI found that 81 per cent of respon-dents agreed that there should be limits on national election spending.

The unequal funding of political parties

The escalating cost of the national election campaigns has brought the question of party fund-raising into closer focus. Controversy arose over the sources of party funding in the 1980s, and more so in the 1990s, as the Conservatives raised substan-tial funds from unknown sources, including foreign businessmen and wealthy individuals. In the 1990s, Labour too began fund-raising from rich individuals. A Home Affairs Committee inquiry into political funding in 1993 split on party lines and failed to produce convincing conclusions. The Labour government is committed to reform of party funding, and in 1997 asked the Committee on Standards in Public Life, under the chairmanship of Lord Neill of Bladen QC, to hold an inquiry, with the aim of publishing a report in the summer of 1998. Among issues the Neill Committee has considered are state funding for political parties, possible links between honours and donations, rules of disclosure, and so on. We write this summary of the issues involved in advance of the Neill Committee's findings, and we recom-mend that it should be read in conjunction with these findings.

The issue of party funding is significant for a variety of reasons. First, since the more that any political party spends before and during elections, the more likely it is to win those elections, then the level and sources of political donations will obviously affect the different parties' ability to win political power. Inequalities in finances and resources necessarily result in political inequalities between the parties. These inequalities matter because of the pivotal role that political parties – though private bodies – play in government, politics and public life in this country. Equally, the sources of the parties' funds and resources matter (**DAC10**). The business interests which have traditionally funded the Conservative Party and the trade unions which established and still contribute to Labour have not acted out of altruism; both expect the parties to pursue their interests in (and out of) government. Further, there is the danger of improper influence or even corruption, especially if the identities of those who make substantial donations are not known. In principle, then, the ability of companies, trade unions, other interests and rich individuals to intervene in the political process by funding political parties or their election campaigns raises significant issues of political equality (**DAC4**). It is not just a question of who wins an election, important though it may be for certain interests to promote one party or block another at election time. The parties' ability to place issues on the political agenda; or to prevent them from reaching that agenda; the breadth and depth of government policy and financial interventions in society and the economy; and even party political control of patronage, are all areas over which wealthy sponsors (individual or corporate) might seek to buy influence through investing in a major political party.

In the 1980s, the danger that individual businessmen or organised interests – either within the UK or foreign-based – might purchase undue influence through funding the Conservative Party provoked concern, particularly since the party did not divulge the identity of donors, or even its total income from donations. On the other side of the political divide, the Conservatives and their allies traditionally expressed concern about trade union funding of the Labour party nationally and trade union sponsorship of individual Labour MPs or constituency parties. They found new causes for concern after the revelation in 1997 that Bernie Ecclestone, the Formula One racing supremo, had donated £1 million to Labour's election campaign – especially after the Labour government exempted cigarette advertising in Formula One from its ban on cigarette advertising and sponsorship.

The case for transparency in the funding of political parties is therefore paramount in the light of two democratic criteria – **DAC4** on political equality and **DAC10** on the parties' accountability for funding associated with their pivotal role in politics and public office. Astonishingly, under the obsolete Victorian legal framework for political parties and election campaigns, the political parties are under no legal obligation to disclose the sources of their funding. The three main parties do now publish annual accounts, though the information given varies from party to party and is not as full as may be expected. In particular, the Conservatives do not reveal the sources of individual donations, while Labour has begun to publish partial information (the precise size of declared donations over £5,000 is not disclosed). This is not the place to rehearse in full recent concerns over the funding of the Conservatives, and now New Labour, or the more traditional debate over the trade unions' financial and policy role within Labour. It is estimated that the Conservative Party received

£71 million 'in unspecified and untraced' donations over an eight-year period to 1993, according to the party's own accounts, of which £31 million came from abroad (*Business Age*, May 1993). After analysing the donations of the top 1,500 companies from 1988 to 1992, the Labour Research Department found that a third to a half of Conservative reported income could not be identified – £16 million in all during the run-up to the 1992 election.

It is known or alleged that a remarkable variety of wealthy individuals – disgraced business figures such as the late Octav Batnor, the former Nissan UK chief, Asil Nadir of Polly Peck, and Nuzmu Virani, who was jailed for his part in the BCCI banking scandal; John Latsis, the Greek ship-owner; Li Ka Shing, a Hong Kong businessman; and perhaps the Sultan of Brunei – made substantial donations to Tory party coffers (Marr 1995: 250–251; Home Affairs Committee (HAC) 1993: 41, 90–91). As the political journalist Andrew Marr observed, 'The Conservative Party has not been terribly lucky in its admirers. . . . These are a few names picked out by the press from a system which is mostly confidential and successful in hiding its secrets' (*ibid*.: 250).

After 1992, the Labour Party felt obliged to match the Conservatives and decided to concentrate upon rich individuals. In 1996, Labour recruited Henry Drucker, formerly fund-raiser for Oxford University, for advice on raising political funds. Drucker had studied Conservative fund-raising and concluded that companies rarely gave more than £25,000; large sums had to come from rich individuals who were not obliged to disclose them. Trade union funding fell as a proportion of Labour's income from about three-quarters in the 1980s to less than half (45 per cent) in 1996. As well as Bernie Ecclestone, other rich individuals who made substantial donations to the party were David (now Lord) Sainsbury, of the supermarket family, publisher Paul Hamlyn, the late Matthew Harding, a property man, and Maurice Hatter, electronics tycoon (*Sunday Times*, 16 November 1997). Even while the Labour government was deciding policy on cigarette advertising, party fund-raisers were preparing another approach to Ecclestone. The government had also to determine planning applications from Sainsbury's. The undesirable conflict of interests inherent in raising funds from companies or individuals whose affairs might become matters of government policy is obvious enough. Lord Neill, asked for advice by the Labour Party, clearly recognised the dangers when he advised the party to return the £1 million Ecclestone donation. Further, the indebtedness of the major parties after elections makes them, on the face of it, more vulnerable to undesirable, and perhaps improper, deals. This is not to say that party managers do succumb to temptation, but simply that it is not desirable that it should be seen to exist.

Henry Drucker identified another temptation in conversation with *Sunday Times* journalists:

> Jonathan Powell [Blair's chief of staff] wanted me to tell him how much Labour could make, who to go to and how to do it. Basically we told them how Americans raise money, which means access to the great man, the implied promises of favours, and in this country, honours. There's no question: in Britain people want honours.
>
> (*Sunday Times*, 16 November 1997)

Party funding

Abuse of the honours system is a long-established tradition in British politics, going back at least to the reign of James I. But David Lloyd George's systematic and flagrant sale of honours (peerages, knighthoods, and so on) in the 1920s for party funds became a public scandal and the Honours (Prevention of Abuses) Act 1925 made it a criminal offence to deal in honours, either as a broker or purchaser. There is scarcely any scrutiny of the award of honours. Formally, the Prime Minister is advised by a Political Honours Scrutiny Committee of three Privy Councillors (i.e., senior politicians) who inquire into the character and antecedents of the people who are to be honoured for political services. This is by no means a watchdog committee.

It is not surprising therefore that allegations of abuse of the honours system arise. The Labour Research Department analysed the award of peerages and knighthoods to industrialists between 1979 and 1993 and found that top executives at eight out of the ten largest corporate donors to the Conservative Party shared seven peerages and eight knighthoods (HAC 1993: 102–103). The press from time to time runs articles on honours. A *Sunday Times* 'Insight' investigation in 1992 quoted an unnamed company secretary whose chairman was knighted after his company gave £160,000 to the Conservative Party; 'it was made perfectly clear beforehand that if he did this [gave a donation] he would get a knighthood'. An unnamed industrialist, knighted after making three donations of £50,000, told the 'Insight' journalists that he believed there was a link between donations and honours (*Sunday Times*, 22 September 1992). Four rich people who gave donations of over £5,000 to the Labour Party in 1996 were made peers by Tony Blair after the 1997 election – the former Michael Montague; Sir David Puttnam; Ruth Rendell; and David Sainsbury (*Daily Telegraph*, 12 November 1997).

Legal rules governing the disclosure of donations affect only companies and trade unions and, as Keith Ewing, Professor of Public Law at King's College, London, pointed out in 1993, the legal position is both unsatisfactory and unfair:

> While trade unions (a major source of Labour Party funds) are subject to extensive and detailed control and regulation of their political donations, there is no comparable regulation of companies or other donors of political money. . . . Companies by contrast are required simply to disclose in their annual reports to shareholders donations in excess of £200.
>
> (HAC 1993: 7)

The case for full disclosure embraces more than the need to make political parties and leaders accountable for the monies they receive. It is necessary to inform the public on the interests a party is likely to promote; to restore public confidence in British politics; and to reduce the public feeling that the political system is out of democratic control. It is true that British politics are almost certainly less corrupt than many similar liberal democracies. But legal rules of disclosure would remove the suspicion that improper influences may be brought to bear on the political parties which direct our national affairs as well as acting to prevent actual corruption. In the words of the US Supreme Court Justice Brandeis, 'sunlight is the best disinfectant'. Disclosure rules may even bring some sunlight to bear on the 'closed world of deals and favours' where, according to Andrew Marr:

> the top people in power, whether commercial or political power, tend to become acquainted and lobby one another in a personal, private way that entirely by-passes the formal constitution. . . . If you wanted to see the most involved and important Tory businessmen chewing the fat, you'd find them chewing it at some sporting or operatic entertainment where, in the words of one cabinet minister, 'You are lobbying and being lobbied, but so effectively that you never have to finish your sentences'.
>
> (Marr 1995: 251)

Just how much improper influence is brought to bear through this or other closed worlds is impossible to judge, for such influence is of its essence secret. In October 1990, Ernest Saunders, the former Guinness chief, said on the BBC1 *Panorama* programme that at the time of the controversial Guinness bid for Distillers senior Conservative Party figures referred to the fact that Guinness were not donors to party funds sufficiently frequently for him to realise that, 'if we were to go on rolling, I would have to put this matter to the board and our policy would have to be rethought'. Labour MPs put such issues to the then Tory party chairman during the 1993 inquiry of the Home Affairs Committee, but he dismissed them, arguing that donations did not buy influence or honours:

> A lot of prominent industrialists in this country have supported the Conservative Party for the very good reason that the kind of policies the party has set out have been the policies one would expect them to be supportive of.
>
> (HAC 1993: 56–61)

Trade union influence on and within the Labour party has always been more open, and never more so than when Prime Minister Harold Wilson and his minister, Barbara Castle, sought to get the *In Place of Strife* trade union reforms through the cabinet and onto the statute book in 1969 – and were defeated. As for their internal influence, detailed studies suggest that in the last resort the party leaders have had the final word on policy issues and that trade union leaders have observed a convention of support for the party's leadership (Minkin 1978 and 1991). Internal trade union power and influence within Labour has diminished sharply since 1987.

Disclosure is not the only democratic concern in this area. It is also important to ensure that political parties in the UK have an adequate level of funding, consistent with their popular support, so that there is a fair rivalry between the parties and their candidates in the competition for political office. Further, the funding of the parties ought not to depend upon inappropriate sources. Clearly, the current largely unregulated system does not satisfy either of these aims. Other countries require disclosure of political funding in various ways; impose controls and limits on party political donations; and provide state funding for parties; or combine all or some of these measures. Measures of this kind all require parties to be recognised in law and usually also to be registered. Australia, Canada, France, Germany and the United States all have rules governing the disclosure of donations. France, Germany and the US impose limits on the size and sources of donations. France and the US ban foreign contributions, Germany most foreign contributions. Several Canadian states impose similar restrictions and Quebec operates possibly the most democratic control of all – only electors may make donations (DA Paper No 3: 11–12 and Tables 9–10; HAC 1993: 6–7)

State funding has become the commonest measure for equalising the resources available to parties since 1945. Liberal democracies around the world have adopted varying regimes for the state funding of political parties, including (in Europe), all the major European Union countries; (in the Americas) Canada, Costa Rica, Mexico, the US and Venezuela; and (elsewhere) Australia, Israel and Japan. Democratic Audit Paper No. 3 (Weir 1994) contains a qualitative breakdown of the funding regimes in Australia, Denmark, France, Germany, the UK and the US. Table 4.2 provides a wider and more general survey. Basically, apart from benefits in kind such as free broadcasting time, free postage at elections, and so on, the UK's only source of political funding is the 'Short money' made available to the opposition parties represented in the House of Commons (the total in 1994 was £9.2 million).

The arguments against disclosure and controls on political contributions, and against state funding of political parties, tend to concentrate on the practical difficulties of preventing evasion rather than on principle. We cannot survey all the arguments for and against such measures here. However, we can observe that while the kinds of problems they identify are not unique to Britain, the absence of any serious attempt to deal with them is.

Table 4.2 State aid for political parties, 1993

	Running costs	Election expenses	Legislative party groups	Regional/local elections
UK	no	no[1]	yes	no
Australia	yes	inc[2]	inc	yes
Canada	no	yes	yes	yes
France	no	yes	yes	yes
Germany	yes	inc	inc	yes
Italy	yes	inc	inc	yes
Spain	yes	yes	yes	yes
Sweden	yes	inc	yes	yes
USA	no	yes[3]	no	yes

Source: Labour Research Department in HAC 1993b: 99
Notes:
1 There are subsidies-in-kind, such as free broadcasting time, free postage, etc.
2 'inc' indicates included in running costs.
3 Plus cumulative costs, primary costs (matching).

AUDIT

For democracy to prosper, elections should be contested on as level a playing field as possible. This objective raises questions of regulation and control which are alien to the British tradition and which have as yet not been tackled. The outstanding strength of the rules governing elections in Britain is that the most popular medium of all is strongly regulated; that political advertising on television is prohibited; that rules of impartiality in reporting party political issues on television are strong and respected; that reportage of elections is given considerable weight both on BBC and ITV; and that free political broadcasts offset inequalities of resources between the parties to even out their communications with the electorate. As the cable, digital and satellite revolutions in communications technology gain force, the proliferation of TV channels and other forms of communication will fracture that strength. The inequalities and absence of transparency and rules for party political funding, and the absence of any national limit or regulation of national spending on elections, are great weaknesses.

DAC1: Secrecy of the ballot

The ballot is secret at the point of voting, but the authorities and intelligence agencies have the means to determine how people have voted and which people have voted for particular candidates.

DAC2: Government and party control of elections

Elections are formally free of government and party control, but the Prime Minister's effective power to call an election at the time of his own choosing within the five years of a Parliament gives the governing party an undue advantage which should – and could – be removed. Similarly, a Prime Minister has the power to decide the length of a campaign period, again to his or her advantage. Through their powers to vary the structures of local government, and to determine the size and boundaries of local authorities, ministers have an indirect influence over parliamentary boundaries (and an undesirable partisan power over local democracy; see **DAC18**). Recent governments have broken the spirit and substance of conventions of consultation in making changes at local level. There is a strong case for placing local government on a constitutional footing and removing government powers to interfere at whim in the structures and business of local government. These questions are considered again in Chapter 10.

DAC2: Freedom of elections from external influences

Corporate businesses and wealthy proprietors control most of the press and have the power and ability to determine their newspapers' editorial positions. Similarly, big business, wealthy individuals and the trade unions provide much of the funding of the two major parties. Two issues of political equality arise. First, the press is demonstrably mobilised to promote particular parties and political policies: in the run-up to the 1992 election, the weight of the Tory tabloid press was committed to a campaign of denigration of Neil Kinnock and his party; similarly, after 1992, the Euro-sceptic cause was heavily promoted in the Conservative press, damaging Major's political position. In 1997, Tony Blair succeeded in neutralising the Murdoch press's hostility to 'old' Labour, but this was at least in part because of his radical repositioning of his party which may very well have been heavily influenced by the views of the press, including Murdoch's titles. The basic problem of a heavily biased press remains in place.

The parties' need for large-scale donations to pay for the rapidly escalating costs of national campaigns raises several issues. First, by definition only private companies, trade unions and rich individuals can make such donations, raising the prospect of such interests 'buying' the election, gaining influence over the parties' agendas, and possibly exercising undue influence on their policy-making and conduct in government (and opposition). It is political leaders – and mainly the Prime Minister – who decide on the distribution of honours, with no effective scrutiny of their decisions. The honours system is therefore in danger of being abused. There is then a general danger that external influences through media ownership, or through large-scale donations, can affect not only election results, but also future government policies.

DAC3: The range and choice of information at elections

The rules governing television and radio coverage of elections, as stated above, provide a framework of impartial reporting of elections and pluralist debate on the issues on the most popular and trusted media in the country. The public service ethos influences not only the conduct and coverage of BBC television and radio, but also that of commercial television (and to a lesser degree) radio. The political parties are given 'fair and equal' access to the broadcast media. Rules on television reports from local constituencies, giving any candidate an effective veto, diminish the quality of television coverage of elections. As for the press, broadsheet newspapers are generally fair and balanced in their reporting, though there is a slight bias towards the Conservatives in their editorial stances. There is also a wide diversity of information and comment in magazines, journals and books of all kinds. However, the tabloid press is heavily biased, more often in favour of the Conservatives than Labour. In 1992, the respected American commentator, Anthony Lewis, denounced the British tabloid press as the most biased in the western world. The political parties do not enjoy 'fair and equal access' to the tabloid press.

DAC10: Political equality and major interests

The funding of political parties remains opaque, unequal and unregulated. The Home Affairs Committee report into political funding (HAC 1993) turned up a considerable amount of information, but the committee inquiry became a partisan and divided process which failed seriously to consider the issues. The Labour government's decision in 1997 to refer the issues which arise to the Neill Committee is therefore welcome, removing recommendations for the future to a politically balanced forum which can consider the issues in a practical way. As with the issue of media ownership, the room for improper influence is large. The casualties are the principles of popular control and political equality, and the quality of democratic debate in the UK.

5   Sticking to the Manifesto

Election mandates in action

In earlier days, manifestos were written in general terms. They tended to be written in what I might call disappearing ink . . . . Now they have tended, over the last 15, 20 years to be written in indelible ink . . . . And they have had rather quaint persons called 'guardians' appointed who tick off the fulfilled pledges.

(Lord Bancroft, former mandarin, in interview for *Channel 4 News*, 1987)

After the election we will only do, and exclusively do, what is in the manifesto. We have asked for trust based on the manifesto. What we say before the election is what we will do after the election.

(Peter Mandelson MP, *World at One*, 27 April 1997)

One of the justifications for plurality-rule elections is that they generally promote single-party governments. Thus, as the political parties each put a manifesto to the public at election time, voters have a clear idea of what the parties will do if elected. The party then elected to power has not merely the authority, but a duty, to carry out the proposals that its manifesto contains. This convention is clearly of potential importance for popular control of government in the UK. It is the practical outcome of British constitutional theory. For example, the constitutional authority, C. S. Emden, argued that 'the principle of the people's mandate has been recognised as operative by statesmen and by constitutional experts for the best part of a century', though its operation 'was at first tentative and experimental' and 'after many years of trial, it is still indeterminate and its scope controvertible' (Emden 1956: 315). In the view of later writers, the mandate helps marry Parliament's legal supremacy with the political sovereignty of the electorate (Harvey and Bather 1972: 529); and, they argue, the fact that the parties achieve power on the basis of their manifesto platforms constitutes the 'essence of representative government' (Rallings 1987: 1).

From the Audit's point of view, the idea of the mandate broadens the basic function of the vote by giving electors a measure of control over the policies to be followed by the winning party, and so expands the boundaries of representative democracy. At its simplest, the idea supposes that elections represent a straight choice between rival party manifestos; at its most ambitious, that the people's views, as measured by the election results, are represented in future government policies. In this chapter we briefly analyse the idea of the mandate and its influence on the parties in postwar Britain, concentrating our attention on a section of **DAC4**:

how closely does ... the programme of government reflect the choices actually made by the public?

But we also question how far the public may be said to make their choices at elections on the basis of the parties' manifestos, and thus how far those manifestos may be said to justify future government actions. We also address the question of the public's involvement in measures of basic constitutional change. In the UK, this question is complicated by the fact that most of the constitution is unwritten and significant rules are expressed through non-legal conventions which ministers can set aside largely without public debate – and certainly without express public approval. Yet the public should clearly have a determining voice in any decision which funda-mentally changes the rules under which any representative democracy works. Thus we also ask **DAC6**:

How far is there systematic opportunity for the electorate to vote directly on measures of basic constitutional reform?

The idea of the electoral mandate

Most studies of the idea of the mandate agree that it is a very imprecise concept (e.g., Emden 1956: 315; Harvey and Bather 1972: 529; Rallings 1987). While, for example, most agree that it relates to a government's authority to implement a legislative programme in the electorate's name, they differ over whether a govern-ment is mandated to carry out all its manifesto programme or simply a part of it. Further, does the voters' choice simply authorise a government to carry out what is in its manifesto, or has the government entered into an implicit 'contract' which obliges it to do so? In other words, does a new government's mandate represent the voters' consent to policies or a government's obligation – or authority – to carry them out? On such questions, the theory is pretty vague. The academic literature suggests that there are at least two types of mandate. A weaker, more broad-based version holds that, once elected, a government may enact the sum total of its election platform, as the whole package was seemingly approved by the electorate (see, for example Royed 1996: 46; Kavanagh 1981: 8). This version is weaker in the sense that the relationship between specific policies and popular approval is not clear-cut since the electorate's verdict is necessarily diffuse. In Britain, this version is further weakened by the fact that every government since 1935 has been elected on a minority of the popular vote. The second type of mandate is stronger and narrower, as it recognises only part of the government's policy intentions as legitimate. Only where a clear link between a specific policy and electoral approval can be shown to exist is a mandate in force. The question is: how is that link to be demonstrated? Most theorists hold a position closer to the former (weaker) definition whilst accepting that a precise definition of the mandate is difficult. Psephologist Colin Rallings expresses the general view in the broadest terms, saying that 'parties clearly feel under some obligation to make promises of action on those matters to which they have given general prominence in their election manifestos' (Rallings 1987: 5).

Electoral mandate

The language used in seeking to define the idea of the mandate is instructive. Governments are *authorised* on the basis of *promises* made and are *obliged* to provide *particular* policies supported by the electorate. The electorate is therefore seen to *endorse* a party platform (or specific policies) and the elected officials are then *bound* to enact their programme. The process can clearly be likened to a legal contract. Two analysts of mandate theory argue:

> The idea of a mandate has two distinct senses. One is *command*: the elected government has been *mandated* by the sovereign people to do certain things. ... The second sense is that of authorisation. By submitting its programme to the electorate and gaining a near-majority of votes, the governing party has acquired a moral *right* and *responsibility* to put its programme into effect.
>
> (Hofferbert and Budge 1992: 152)

But how important are manifestos to the parties? Do parties largely want to win power, and therefore formulate policies in order to win elections rather than win elections in order to carry out their policies? Clearly, this is shifting ground. It may be argued, for example, that the Labour Party originally existed and competed for power in order to change the very nature of British society. After 18 years in opposition the party is now arguably committed largely to governing effectively with a far vaguer concept of the good society in mind. Such considerations bring into question the role that elections play in the notion of a mandate. If the mandate is to possess constitutional significance, elections should surely be fought as a contest between alternative party platforms rather than rival sets of political leaders? For it is the election result that legitimates the party manifesto being turned into government policy. If elections decide something else (e.g., that the Conservatives had lost the trust of the electorate in 1997; that Labour looked more effective or less divided; that Tony Blair was more convincing than John Major), it becomes difficult for the winning party to claim that it is the manifesto (rather than the leader or the party's record, or the weakness of other parties) that has been endorsed by the popular vote.

In modern elections, parties do not in general promote their manifestos and campaign around them. Manifestos are simply one among many campaigning tools. The parties' main aim is to seek to attract a fairly wide cross-section of the electorate and this is more likely to be achieved by projecting an image of effective leadership or economic competence rather than by arguing the case for their manifesto. In recent British elections, the electorate's view of which of the two largest parties is better able to manage the economy, as measured by opinion-poll evidence, has clearly had a major influence on people's voting intentions. Another broad indicator has been public beliefs in the parties' ability to keep order and prevent crime. Moreover, in Britain, incumbent parties have been able to maintain themselves in power by managing the macro-economic cycle in such a way as to co-ordinate a 'feel-good' factor among more affluent voters and the timing of an election. Thus, elections are rarely held to resolve policy differences and turn on the most general of issues, such as 'the economy', 'inflation' or even 'trust', and personalities.

Moreover, the increasing reliance on 'negative' campaigning in election campaigns suggests that parties are not campaigning positively for their manifestos. Such campaigning has long been a feature of British elections, and Conservative manipulation of the 'fear' factor against Labour in 1992 was estimated to have won the election for the government. In 1997, Labour both erected defences against a similar negative onslaught and engaged in negative campaigns of its own (the '22 Tax Rises' poster campaign on the Tory record in government; attacks on Conservative pensions policy etc.). A broad analysis of the two parties' press releases found that Labour's were 60 per cent 'attacking' and 40 per cent 'defensive' and the Conservatives' 65:35 'attacking'. In 1997, therefore, it is fair to say that Tony Blair's personal popularity and the prevailing mood of disillusionment with the Conservatives weakens Labour's claim to have received a mandate for its policies.

The significance of manifestos

The notion that the manifesto might exert an influence over both the election result and future government policy is widely believed to have developed out of Robert Peel's *Tamworth Manifesto* in 1834. In his address to the electorate, Peel stated that public confidence in government could only be sustained if election candidates offered the voters 'frank and explicit declarations of principle'. Most modern political scientists accept that this role of the manifesto within the mandate doctrine is crucial. Dennis Kavanagh states in a study of British election manifestos that 'British parties are programmatic; they fight elections on manifestos and, if elected, they promise to carry them out. For the most part, we think it is a good thing; it lies at the heart of responsible government' (Kavanagh 1981: 7). Another political scientist, Richard Rose, agrees. 'Election manifestos are a hinge turning generalised political values and ideas into statements of particular intentions to act'; continuing:

> A party that carried out its intentions would, by following the Manifesto Model, uphold its 'contract' with the electorate. The results might be displeasing to some voters, but they could not complain that they had not been told what the government was going to do.
>
> (Rose 1980: 52, 64–65)

Put simply, the manifesto can be seen to embody 'the democratic creed' – for as long as governments seek to follow policies set down in their party manifestos, their actions are seen to be mandated and democratically legitimate (Topf 1994: 150).

Despite these endorsements, most theorists also harbour suspicions about the manifesto's place in the democratic process. While acknowledging that the mandate doctrine implies a contract between the governing party and the people – based on the party platform – Richard Rose suggested that the term 'contract' can be misleading for two distinct reasons. First, voters neither instruct nor guide the parties in the preparation of their manifestos (except, nowadays, passively through focus groups and polling exercises). Voters cannot veto particular policy items nor can they propose including others. Secondly, manifestos are not legal documents and 'need not be precise or comprehensive'. They are more like 'political journalism' and their wording may be ambiguous – and even deliberately so – and open to varying interpretations. Indeed, their very terms may represent a political 'fudge', designed to reconcile opposing views among those responsible for drafting or approving them. The final decision on their interpretation, moreover, is left to the parties which have drafted and presented them; 'The power to determine what an election mandate is worth rests with the governing party and not with the voters who give it [their approval]' (Rose 1980: 54, 61). Size matters too. Dennis Kavanagh argued in 1981 that the strength of the mandate for specific proposals is the more questionable in longer documents (Kavanagh 1981: 9). But since then – and more specifically since 1983 (when Labour's manifesto was described as 'the longest suicide note in history') – manifestos have tended to become shorter and more bland, thus putting their value in question on other grounds.

Such problems bring us to an associated question. Do voters actually read and compare the party manifestos, long or short? And if not, do they serve a democratic purpose? S. E. Finer, a leading British political scientist, dismissed the very idea that manifestos played a democratic role as 'moonshine' in 1975, arguing that as very few voters actually read the lists of policy intentions in them, the documents were valueless (*New Society*, 13 May 1975). Even those observers who argue that manifestos *do* influence public policy accept that few electors actually read the documents (Budge 1987: 18). They argue that the significant features of the documents are made clear to the electorate by the media. Thus manifestos help set the campaign agenda by providing 'themes' which the media pick up on and filter through to the voters; indeed, they 'are worded and designed in such a way as to enable their main points to be grasped and reproduced for the voters through the mass media' (Topf 1994: 152). There is even evidence that the public itself agrees with this notion:

The public's attitudes towards manifestos, 1997

Which of these statements best describes your attitude to the party election manifestos?

	%
They are important for everyone to read	36
I wouldn't read them but I would hope to hear about them in the media	46
I think they are a waste of time and wouldn't pay any attention to them	14
None of these/don't know	4

Source: Sunday Mirror/MORI (6 April 1997)

The idea of the mandate in practice

Regardless of the theory, just what do manifestos actually mean to politicians and ministers in the real world, and how far do governments seek to carry them out? Parties may not stick to manifestos after election. The most thorough attempt to measure the correlation between what manifestos say and governments do has been carried out by three political scientists, Hans-Dieter Klingemann, Richard Hofferbert and Ian Budge, under the auspices of the Manifestos Research Project. Broadly, they have employed a model which examines the influence of a winning party's manifesto platform on public spending priorities or budget allocations across a variety of liberal democracies. Their latest report affirms the 'seemingly naïve claim' that the contents of manifestos are actually a good predictor of what governments in fact do after elections (Klingemann, Hofferbert and Budge 1994: 20) and finds that 'the policy priorities of governments in modern democracies reflect the formal programs presented by competing parties during elections' (*ibid.*: 2).

Their findings have attracted a good deal of criticism, however, most of it based on methodological differences of opinion. Two other analysts, Gary King and Michael Laver re-analysed earlier data used by Hofferbert and Budge (1992) to show that parties' manifesto platforms have only small effects on spending. They conclude that there is no clear causal connection between party platforms and government expenditure. Rather other variables – including budget trends that pass from one administration to the next, irrespective of party colour – have a greater influence over government spending than the contents of manifestos (King and Laver 1993). A US analyst, Terry Royed, tested the 'mandate model' and also argued that other significant variables were missing. Different types of leadership, economic and social constraints, the 'decision-making environment' (e.g., the size of the governing majority), and similar factors, all tended to weaken the links between manifesto pledges and government policies (Royed 1996: 47).

In other words, the mandate is a pretty faulty mechanism for transmitting the policy preferences of voters to governments. Elections themselves turn on very general issues of competence on which no party can stake out a unique position, or on a diversity of smaller issues which cloud the very idea of mandate. Though some theorists assume that voters, 'explicitly or implicitly, support the programme when they vote for the party' (Kavanagh 1981: 11), it seems doubtful that in choosing one party over another, they approve of all or even most of the prospective policies put forward by the winning party. Many votes may actually be cast *against* a party, based on people's reaction to what a party has done rather than what it and its rivals promise to do (though, in 1997, popular discontent with the Major government may arguably be said to have arisen from the perception that it had broken its promises in 1992 – and thus deserved to be thrown out of office). Manifesto pledges are anyway often highly ambiguous; a host of other pressures and events colour any government's ability to deliver on them; and finally, it is very hard to know whether a government has actually delivered on a pledge or not. Thus, elections decide who will govern, but not the substance of government policy. Anthony King, the pragmatic political scholar, has put the position most trenchantly:

> The connection between elections and public policy is bound to be complicated partly because the voters in an election are not being asked – or at any rate not being asked explicitly – to determine issues of public policy. They are being asked, rather, to say which person or persons, or which party,

they wish to return to the national legislature . . . . If in choosing people and parties the voters are choosing policies, the connection between the two is, at most, an indirect one. It is only in referendums that citizens are given an opportunity to pronounce directly on policy issues. Elections in the first instance are about electing, neither more nor less.

(King 1981: 300)

Vernon Bogdanor, the constitutional expert, also questions the very basis of mandate theory. In a 1981 study of the referendum in British politics, he agrees that elections cannot in most circumstances yield mandates – and certainly not for a government's whole policy programme. He argues that only a referendum can produce a 'specific mandate' for policy action (Bogdanor 1981: 77). He also argues implicitly that a mandate itself must be *specific*. This brings us back to the notion of the weaker and stronger versions of the mandate that we discussed earlier (**p. 101**). If the public is asked to indicate its views on one particular issue (in a referendum), there is then a clear link between electoral approval and government action. Only in such a case would a government clearly have a mandate to act.

Do British governments stick to their election manifestos?

The idea of the mandate in British democratic politics has twice been tested empirically. Hofferbert and Budge conducted a study of the period 1945–87 that asked, 'How far do the pre-election policy priorities of the major political parties really anticipate what will happen to public policy after the election?' They came to three broad conclusions. First, what governments do is positively linked to either their manifesto or their ideology. Second, governments do undertake policies – mostly social policies – which are not in their manifestos and cannot be explained by their known ideological position. Third, their policy programmes were more important to future policy than party ideology for the Conservatives and vice-versa for Labour (Hofferbert and Budge 1992: 151, 178). Richard Rose analysed the records of the Heath government (1970–74) and the Labour governments which followed (1974–79). The available evidence suggested that the bulk of manifesto commitments were acted on (up to 90 per cent by the Heath government and 73 per cent by Labour) (Rose 1984: 65). But the fact that manifesto commitments are usually enacted does not mean that legislation or policy is always based on such commitments. For example, the Heath government performed a notorious U-turn on incomes policy. More generally, Rose's evidence up to 1984 showed that 'only one-tenth of government legislation is based upon initiatives set out in party manifestos . . . . More than three-quarters of all legislation that a government introduces is derived from the ongoing policy process in Whitehall' (*ibid.*: 71). Furthermore, the weight given to a proposal within a manifesto did not necessarily relate to its priority for an incoming government. Privatisation was briefly mentioned in the Conservative manifesto of 1979, and the high profile it finally took in government could hardly have been predicted by a voter reading the manifesto.

We now conduct a brief review of a number of important postwar elections in Britain, analyse the role of party manifestos in those elections and subsequent

government actions, and seek to assess how seriously ministers and politicians themselves took manifesto pledges. The elections that produced 'landslides', or at least
gave a decisive result, are seemingly the most important to mandate theory. After
all, if an election produces a close result it seems pretty doctrinaire to argue that
one party's electoral programme is favoured to a substantial degree over another's.
For this reason, the classic examples of mandate-giving elections usually involve
either a landslide victory or a 'sea-change' in the political attitudes of the electorate.

The 1945 general election is often described as the classic example of a mandate
being awarded to one party rather than another on the basis of the electorate's
appraisal of two, quite distinct prospective party programmes. The Labour manifesto, *Let Us Face the Future*, in contrast to its Conservative rival which looked to
foreign affairs, was a programme based on social justice and postwar reconstruction
at home (McCallum and Readman 1947: 47). Put simply, *Let Us Face the Future* was
a catalogue of nationalisation and welfare measures, based in part on the Beveridge
Report of 1942 which had mainly been ignored by the out-going wartime coalition
government. Labour's electoral triumph (though won on 48 per cent of the vote)
was widely recognised as providing a clear direction for the incoming government's
election policies. For, according to D. N. Pritt, the independent Labour MP and
barrister, 'Labour and the Tories alike set out to fight the election campaign on the
traditional lines of programmes and promises' (Pritt 1963: 26). And for Dennis
Kavanagh, the 1945 election was a classic example of a general election in which
'one issue has predominated and the main parties have been so clearly differentiated
on the issue – and recognised as such by many voters – that the outcome is widely
regarded as having clear implications for the direction of policy' (Kavanagh 1981:
8). Certainly, Labour's 'programmes and promises' were almost wholly acted upon
in a dynamic legislative programme. The Bank of England, Cable and Wireless, the
coal mines, railways, electricity, gas and the steel industry were all nationalised.
Insurance benefits for sickness, invalidity and industrial injuries, maternity benefits
and family allowance, an income-related national assistance 'safety net', a new
national health service and a large public house-building programme were all pushed
through.

The Conservatives responded by seeking to reconcile the Welfare State and full
employment policies with a role for private enterprise and 'individual effort' in policy
documents like *The Right Road for Britain* in 1949, and they fought the 1950 and 1951
elections on the *Right Road* platform. The 1950–51 elections did not amount to a
sea-change in public opinion, more a turning of the tide among a population weary
of postwar austerity. Foremost among the Conservative promises of a better life was
a pledge to build 300,000 houses a year, adopted almost haphazardly in October
1950. Harold Macmillan was given the onerous task of fulfilling this pledge after
the Tory victory of 1951. There is no doubt about the seriousness with which
he and his colleagues regarded the task. Winston Churchill, on appointing him as
housing minister, warned that it was a gamble which would 'make or mar'
Macmillan's political career. Macmillan was beside himself with frustration and
distress, declaring, 'If he [Churchill] wants to kill me politically, then let him do it,
but not this way' (Horne 1990: 339–341).

Role in British government

Macmillan's houses were built and 13 years of Conservative administration ensued. Labour regained power in 1964 in what was more of a 'sea-change' election, in which Harold Wilson's promise of a New Britain, 'forged in the white heat of a technological revolution' and gritty professional attitude perfectly caught the public mood. The actual 1964 Labour manifesto, *The New Britain* offered detailed interventionist social, economic and industrial polices and Labour's record in government on social reforms, with a Commons majority of only four seats, was impressive – in came redundancy payments, anti-discrimination laws, protection from eviction for private tenants, the Trade Disputes Act, leasehold reform, and more. But the government, which had at once been confronted in 1964 by a balance of payments deficit of £800 million – by a long way the largest in British peacetime history – failed to secure the economic and industrial foundations of the New Britain. In 1966, Labour's *Time for Decision* manifesto and the election slogan, 'You *know* Labour Government Works' in effect asked the electorate to provide a mandate to finish the job (Childs 1992: 175; Sked and Cook 1993). Labour was returned with a 96-seat majority, but was immediately in trouble again on the economic front. The forced devaluation in November 1967 wrecked public confidence in Labour, just as John Major's 'Black Wednesday' in September 1992 brought the Conservatives' reputation for economic competence to an end in the 1990s. In both cases, there seems to have been a wider, more diffuse understanding on the part of the electorate that they had been promised economic gains which never materialised. Wilson later said his government had been 'blown off course'.

Much the same could be said of the governments in the 1970s under Heath and Wilson. Both entered office opposed to a statutory incomes policy. But in the face of industrial unrest and rising inflation, the Heath government reversed its policy and Wilson's proposed to do so, before settling on a compromise with the unions. In each case, the defence for the government – at least according to mandate theory – was the fact that some pledges take precedence over others (Kavanagh 1981). 'Control of inflation' was made the crucial pledge that allowed both governments to renege on 'less important' election promises.

The election result of 1979 was regarded as decisive enough to give the new Conservative government a strong mandate to implement its policy platform. However, the radical programmes enacted by Thatcher governments in the 1980s were not set out in the mild manifesto which Mrs Thatcher laid before the electorate. For political columnist Peter Riddell, it was an unspecific document that appealed more to voters' fears of more Labour government than to a positive Conservative alternative and certainly did not represent 'the deliberate start of an ideological revolution' (Riddell 1991: 8). Mrs Thatcher's biographer, Hugo Young, wrote that her radical pre-election brainstorming settled into a manifesto 'of surprising sogginess . . . tactics dictated a necessary vagueness in the party manifesto'. She deliberately did not confront the orthodoxies of the day. The manifesto included income tax cuts, the sale of council houses, and other popular policies; it talked of lower public spending, but not cuts in public services; and even foresaw continued discussions with employers and trade unions over future policies (Young 1990: 128–131, 139). Privatisation (or 'de-nationalisation' as it was then called) was confined to a single pledge. It is not as though no strategic document existed which set out the dynamic approach Mrs Thatcher's governments were to follow. It did. In 1977, two of her ideological advisers produced just such a document for her and her inner circle; entitled 'Stepping Stones', it enthused Mrs Thatcher and pre-figured the 1980s political revolution. Yet it was never published and was not reflected in the party's 1979 manifesto (*ibid.*: 114–118).

In 1983, Mrs Thatcher accepted the case for another 'tame manifesto' and concentrated instead 'on exposing Labour's wildness' (Thatcher 1993: 285). She did, however, manipulate the idea of mandate by insisting on the insertion of a pledge to abolish the Greater London Council. In no sense can the 1983 electorate be said to have endorsed this highly specific policy choice, which was most unpopular in London and has remained so, yet it gave her the 'mandate' to carry it through. Meanwhile, Labour was locked in a bitter internal struggle in which the left wing was seeking (among other objectives) to give the party's National Executive Committee, on which they held a temporary majority, full control of the party's election manifesto. The Labour left wanted to commit the party to a radical programme, approved by the party conference, which would be binding on an incoming Labour government and Labour MPs in Parliament, once it had won the electorate's approval. For the left, capturing the party's manifesto as a pathway to a popular mandate was seen as a significant gain. However, party leaders managed to retain control of the manifesto's contents, but bowed to left-wing pressures by producing a long and specific manifesto programme in 1983 which was widely believed to have contributed to Labour's heavy defeat.

The two main parties then took divergent paths. In 1987, Labour began its long retreat from traditional policies and deliberately cultivated a more bland and less specific style of manifesto. The 1987 Conservative manifesto – the 'best ever produced by the Conservative Party' (Thatcher 1993: 572) – was a radical crusading document. The Conservatives were also raising the scale of their negative campaigning against Labour which began in 1979 and was to be the substance of its 1992 and 1997 campaigns. The 1987 manifesto introduced the community charge (the poll tax) in tandem with a ferocious party and tabloid assault on 'loony left' Labour councils. Despite its prominent place in the manifesto, the poll tax was a 'non-issue' in the 1987 election, as Labour's strategist, Peter Mandelson, was determined to keep the 'loony left' out of the campaign (Butler *et al.* 1994: 105). Mrs Thatcher won a handsome majority against the divided opposition of Labour and Alliance parties. In so far as a general election can be said to give a mandate for any policy, the poll tax would seem to have been an entirely legitimate policy change. The fact is, however, that it sailed through the election campaign unpromoted and unexamined; most voters were unaware of the implications of the new tax; and Mrs Thatcher did not secure a convincing share of the popular vote. She was also aware that it did not command clear backing from her own backbenchers – her ringing declaration to the 1922 Committee of Tory MPs in July 1987 that it was her 'flagship' policy was an attempt to rally support and scotch doubts (*ibid.*: 107). The poll tax proved, of course, to be her downfall because the public hated it. The paradox for crude mandate theory is that if the voters chose to retain or reject her governments on the basis of manifesto pledges in the 1980s, the poll tax was a far more legitimate policy than privatisation. But they did not.

The 1997 general election was said to be another 'sea-change' election. It might at first glance be said to have given New Labour a clear mandate along with a huge majority, but it would then be hard to say with any confidence what it was *for*. The manifesto was bland and glossy. Yet Labour strategists continually hammered away at the idea of mandate. They did so, however, for reasons of strategy. They were convinced that Labour had lost in 1992 because the Tories' negative campaigning on tax and John Smith's 'shadow Budget' had scared the electorate off voting Labour. The idea of mandate was transformed into a tactical device for nailing the Tories' long-running attempt to run a tax scare in 1997. Thus, Labour's two most prominent and far-reaching promises were defensive: income tax rates would not be raised and the Conservative government's public expenditure plans would be retained for two years. At the same time, Labour accused the Conservatives of breaking their 1992 mandate on tax rises, and specifically the promise not to raise VAT rates. Labour combined sound defence against tax and other scares with five more specific, populist promises which were hammered home in campaign speeches and a major poster campaign. The idea of the mandate was, then, a significant element in Labour's strategy, being used for defensive and offensive purposes. It is impossible to measure the effects of this strategy. Perhaps it did contribute to public disillusion with the Conservative government; perhaps it did make people confident that they could trust Labour on tax. But it would be hard to argue that the voters ultimately gave Labour an across-the-board mandate for change. Certain manifesto pledges – such as the abolition of the 'primary purpose' immigration rule – were not salient issues during the campaign. Analysis of the voting showed that the electorate was primarily concerned to eject a divided Conservative government from office. Tactical voting against Tory ministers and MPs and massive defections among Tory voters were the base of New Labour's electoral victory. The importance of New Labour's new-found respectability was that it enabled the public to vote the Conservatives out without fearing for the consequences.

Public opportunity to vote on constitutional change

Referendums have not generally found favour in Britain's political circles. They have traditionally been held to contradict the very idea of *representative* democracy and the basic constitutional doctrine of parliamentary sovereignty; but behind such arguments a deeper elite fear of popular sovereignty has always lurked. Curiously, A. V. Dicey came to favour referendums as a check on single-party government, based on a House of Commons majority, but that was one Dicey view that never hardened into political orthodoxy. Left and right in British politics combined to rule referendums out. For example, the left-wing Labour academic, Harold Laski, wrote that referendums are 'more likely to rally the conservative rather than the progressive forces of society' (quoted in Marshall 1997: 308). Laski's caution was reflected in the views of many pro-European Labour MPs who argued that the 1975 referendum on remaining in the European Community (EEC) could lead to others on, for example, reintroducing the death penalty.

The year 1975 may prove to be a watershed in the use of referendums. The Labour government took the decision to hold a referendum on continued membership of the EEC out of political expediency – the cabinet and parliamentary party were deeply divided on the issue and the only way Harold Wilson could hold his government together was to allow its members to differ. That referendum was the first and only national referendum in Britain at that date. But it had been preceded by a referendum in Northern Ireland in 1973, after the collapse of the Stormont Parliament in 1972. The Ireland Act 1949 provided a guarantee that the constitutional status of the province would not change without the consent of its parliament, and with the Stormont Parliament prorogued, this was transmuted into a 'consent of the people' test. Electors were asked if they wished to remain part of Britain or to join the Irish Republic. The Nationalist parties advised their community to boycott the poll and of the 58 per cent who voted, 98.9 per cent chose the status quo. In 1979 referendums were held in Scotland and Wales on the Labour government's devolution legislation and led to its rejection in both nations.

The referendum now stands high on the political agenda for issues of a constitutional nature. Labour came into power in 1997 committed to holding at least five referendums on constitutional issues: a double-barrelled referendum on its proposal to establish a Scottish Parliament and its taxation powers; a referendum on the proposal for a Welsh assembly; a referendum in London on proposals for a mayor of London; and a referendum on the voting system for elections to the House of Commons. In the run-up to the 1997 election, the three main parties all came to favour a referendum on whether the UK should join the single European currency and a Referendum Party was actually formed to secure a popular vote on further European integration at large. The Liberal Democrats have at various points been in favour of referendums on monetary union, Maastricht and a written constitution. Political expediency featured quite substantially in the attitudes of Labour and the Conservatives on the single currency, jockeying as both parties were up to 1997 to position themselves advantageously on Europe. For Labour, the double-barrelled referendum on Scottish devolution was designed to reassure English opinion on devolution and to neutralise the Conservatives' 'tartan tax' campaign; while the pledge on a referendum on electoral reform was originally introduced by the late John Smith to avoid a damaging split in his own party.

Even so, the democratic argument for holding referendums on major issues of constitutional change is clear; and it is arguable that issues of the kind that they are being introduced to resolve are basic constitutional questions which ought to be put to the British people – or rather, peoples – as a whole. In a representative democracy, political authority ultimately stems from the people, who entrust legislative, financial and administrative decision-making to representatives acting in their stead. But their representatives ought not to assume the authority to decide the terms on which they hold office, or the powers they should wield, since these are prior questions which properly belong in a written constitution, subject to the approval of the people. This is the rationale for holding referendums on constitutional issues, though not on other issues which touch upon people's lives. Popular support for referendums is running high. The 1995 Rowntree Reform Trust 'State of the Nation' poll, conducted by

Referendums

MORI, found that more than three-quarters of people favoured referendums on certain issues, and recent polls showed strong support for referendums on the single currency and for devolution proposals in Scotland and Wales. It is, however, a moot point whether those referendums should not have been held nationwide, since devolution affects the population as a whole, and not only Scottish and Welsh inhabitants.

It might seem, then, that Britain's political parties have stumbled into a practice of holding referendums on matters of constitutional significance. Perhaps a constitutional convention is being formed before our eyes. Yet the Audit's democratic criterion (**DAC6**) specifically asks whether there is a 'systematic opportunity' for the electorate to vote directly on measures of basic constitutional reform; and this question is to be answered within the perspective of ordered and transparent procedures for executive action in British government (**DAC11**). In the absence of a written constitution, there is no constitutional authority by which to decide what constitutes a 'basic constitutional reform' or to determine what issues, if any, ought to be referred directly to the electorate. Only one of the four referendums held so far was in any sense binding on government, by statute, but all four raised constitutional issues, as do those others thus far proposed. Political expediency has played its part in the decisions to hold these referendums, but the significance of the issues has clearly made those decisions appropriate. However, major constitutional changes have previously been made without the use of a referendum: e.g. the Parliament Acts of 1911 and 1949, the Representation of the People Act 1948, the European Communities Act 1972. The 1911 Act was preceded by two elections in deference to its constitutional significance, but no evidence is available from those days on whether the Lords issue influenced any voters, and particularly Liberal and Labour voters. During the political controversy over acceptance of the Maastricht Treaty in 1992–93, Baroness Thatcher and other opponents of the treaty, along with the Liberal Democrats, argued for a referendum, but John Major and the Labour leadership argued against, ostensibly on constitutional grounds, but in reality because they feared it might lead to rejection of the treaty.

Just what constitutes a basic constitutional issue? Clearly, the 1975 decision to join Europe was originally regarded as an issue to be determined by Parliament, and then as a constitutional issue fit for a referendum. The gradual reduction of the status of local government, by convention supposedly worthy of protection as a counterweight to central government (see Chapters 9 and 10), to mere local administration, and the loss of many powers and functions, during the 1980s, was never fully recognised as a constitutional issue at all. Mrs Thatcher's far-reaching *Next Steps* changes to the civil service were accomplished by executive action (see Chapter 8). There was no Next Steps Act 1988, or thereafter. But was this not a constitutional issue, with a significant potential impact on the principle of ministerial responsibility to Parliament? The official answer is 'No'; ours would be 'potentially'.

The fact is, the questions of if and when any referendum should be held, and what constitutes a basic constitutional issue, are likely to continue to be decided by the government, party managers and Parliament, in the light of political expediency, the salience of the issue, the likely attitude of the public, and intra-party divisions. Moreover, those decisions on whether or not to hold a referendum are and will continue to be taken in a constitutional and legal void. Some countries have constitutional or statutory rules which govern the use, timing and conduct of referendums. But there are no established rules for the fair and efficient conduct of referendums in the UK. At the moment, governments in this country have the power to vary significant elements in the process to suit themselves. In 1975, two umbrella campaign organisations, for and against continued EEC membership, were formed and funded by government; and the government itself entered the campaign separately in favour of staying in. But should government-sponsored organisations have a monopoly over intervention? Should there be limits on campaign expenditures, or rules of disclosure of funding? Should government, having initiated a referendum, actually intervene itself, or leave the electorate to decide for itself? Should there be a threshold for participation or decision, below which the referendum result would be void? How should the wording of the vital referendum questions be decided, and by whom? These and other issues are left open (see Constitution Unit 1996d).

There are other issues too. If we are to enter into a period in which referendums become more common, should there not be a generic Referendum Act, deciding the ways in which referendums might be initiated and providing a code of guidance for their conduct? Should there be an independent statutory commission to oversee referendums? And finally, how should referendums relate to the central doctrine of parliamentary sovereignty? The referendums so far held have been advisory and Parliament has in theory retained the right to reject the results. In practice, however, Parliament can scarcely reject a strong expression of public opinion. Edward Short, leader of the House of Commons in 1975, took charge of the rules for the EEC referendum, which he modelled so far as possible on the processes of a general election. He had a pragmatic answer to the question of a possible clash between the popular decision of a referendum and parliamentary sovereignty: 'The government will be bound by its result, but Parliament, of course, cannot be bound' (HC Deb, 11 March 1975, c293).

AUDIT

The idea of the mandate is clearly important to politicians and, to a lesser degree, to the voting public. However, the nature of the idea is imprecise and its value uncertain. The most that can be said with confidence is that manifestos can help to set the broad themes of elections and assist the public in deciding which of the parties to vote for. At times, as in 1945, there has been a strong link between the public mood, a party's manifesto and ensuing government policies. At others, a party leader may catch the public mood, as Mrs Thatcher did in 1979, but publish a manifesto which is less than frank with the electorate about future policies. No electors have any input into the parties' manifestos and very few actually read them; the media and rival parties often neglect either to promote significant policy pledges of their own or to challenge them in other parties' manifestos (as happened in the case of the poll tax in 1987). Thus, it is clear that an electoral win cannot of itself provide a government with a legitimate mandate to carry out every detail of its election platform. The popular vote is too diffuse. Nor does the size of an election victory necessarily provide a party with a stronger mandate for all or part of its programme, given the vagaries of the electoral system and the distorted relationship between votes cast and seats won (see Chapter 3).

The evidence, such as it is, suggests that most parties do carry out a great deal of the detail in their manifestos – even though the bulk of what they do is not (and could not be) spelt out in advance. Politically, too, parties manipulate the idea of the mandate and will produce bland and unspecific manifestos when it suits them, however specific their intentions may be. Broadly, parties tend to regard their manifestos as giving them popular authority to carry out whatever pledges they choose rather than placing them under a duty to carry out the people's will.

The idea of the mandate is closely associated with the electoral system employed in Britain. Defenders of this system argue that this link between popular choice and a government's programme would be broken if elections under a proportional system were introduced. The argument is that only single-party governments can effectively carry out election pledges; as PR elections almost invariably produce coalition governments, electors cannot make an informed choice as the parties' manifestos could not be carried out as they stood, but would have to be negotiated after the election with partners. Yet this is hardly a convincing argument. Manifestos, as we have seen, are in reality only general guides to what parties do in government, and major changes in policy are often forced onto governing parties which break specific manifesto pledges. Moreover, the relevant Democratic Audit criterion asks whether governments' programmes reflect the *choices* made by the public. Under first-past-the-post, any government's programme reflects only the choices made by the largest minority of the voting public. Coalition partners are likely to seek to include in a government's programme aspects of their manifesto programme which are congruent with their general philosophy and popular with their voters. It is therefore generally likely, though clearly not certain, that in a mature democracy like Britain the eventual programmes adopted by any coalition would probably reflect the choices made by a larger section of the public than those of single-party governments.

Traditional reasoning suggests that 'Westminster-style' democracies which produce single-party governments are more likely to provide the best fits between manifesto promises and government action. However, comparative research on party mandates suggests that governments in liberal democracies in which PR elections produce coalition governments, are just as likely to honour manifesto and policy pledges. For example, Hans-Dieter Klingemann and his colleagues began their statistical study of how well election mandates worked under different governing systems, assuming that single-party governments in the UK, Australia and Canada would score higher than stable coalition governments in Austria and Germany, and Sweden's minority coalition governments, and higher still than the more fluid coalitions common in Belgium and the Netherlands. To their surprise, they found that the European coalition governments as a whole were more likely to be accountable 'in terms of policy response to electoral promise' than the single-party Westminster governments. Britain actually performed rather poorly, coming eighth equal with Belgium out of the ten nations in the study (Klingemann, Hofferbert and Budge 1994: 258–261).

DAC4: Do government programmes reflect the choices of the voting public?

The idea of the electoral mandate is a valuable, but imperfect, component of the democratic process in the UK. It commands at the worst lip-service to the principle of popular control and is generally taken seriously by the public, parties and media. There is evidence that the contents of manifestos do influence future government policies, but governments may also be 'blown off course'. Mandates may very well be abused by parties to justify policies which are incidental to the main themes of election campaigns, or they may conceal their real intentions. However, given that one vital aspect of elections is that they give the public the opportunity to recall and reject governments, to a great extent the value of the idea of mandates depends too upon the electorate's willingness to review a government's performance in terms of its promises. It is arguable that this is what happened with John Major's government in 1997. However, even those governments which do honour their manifestos can by definition be sure of satisfying only the relatively large minority of the public who voted for the governing party, and their policies will not generally reflect the choices of the majority. Thus, under first-past-the-post elections, the mandate system cannot fulfil its democratic promise.

DAC6: A systematic vote on basic constitutional issues

There is a clear trend towards placing constitutional proposals directly in front of the public through referendums. This tendency is far from hardening into convention and has no constitutional nor statutory basis. It is up to individual governments from time to time to decide which proposals should be made subject to a referendum and which should not, and their own political purposes and convenience will be the most important factors. There is also an absence of legal rules or even non-legal guidance for the conduct of referendums, leaving various important questions to the discretion of governments. Thus, governments cannot be said to be governed by the rule of law in their decisions to hold referendums or not, and in the way they organise referendums.

PART 2

The Core Executive

Introduction

The idea of 'cabinet government' is central to the democratic arrangements for governing Britain. The received view goes broadly as follows. After an election, the leader of the majority party forms a cabinet to govern the country, to carry out the policies which the party has placed before the electorate, and generally to administer the country and take charge of events. By convention, the Prime Minister and the great majority of his or her cabinet colleagues are elected members of the House of Commons and thus sit in the 'democratic' House alongside the elected MPs to whom they are ultimately responsible. Generally, senior ministers must be MPs, apart from the Lord Chancellor who sits in the House of Lords and presides over its debates and the Leader of the House of Lords. Thus, ministers are physically present in the Commons, to be lobbied and pressured by MPs, as they enter or leave the chamber, or queue up to vote, or sit in the tea-room.

Cabinet ministers are then supposed, according to the received view, to take charge of their departments of state and the machinery of government with the assistance of junior ministers. They receive impartial advice and information from senior civil servants on their policies and actions; major issues and new or changed policies are discussed with their colleagues in cabinet. The Prime Minister, who is *primus inter pares* ('first among equals'), and the cabinet as a whole are responsible for the overall direction of government policy. Thus, within government itself, there are internal checks and balances: first, through the advice, knowledge and experience of the senior civil service, which ministers are bound by their own rules to respect; and second, through collective discussion in cabinet. Ministers and civil servants alike are obliged to observe constitutional rules of convention and procedure (see Chapter 11).

The major democratic checks, however, are exercised by Parliament. The Prime Minister and ministers render account for their actions and policies and their departments' actions to Parliament – in practice, the elected House of Commons – both collectively as a government and individually as ministers under the principle of *ministerial responsibility*. The cabinet, consisting of leading members of the majority party, assumes overall responsibility for government policies and actions, and individual ministers for their own policies and actions and what happens within their separate departments. In the final event, if a majority of MPs, the people's elected representatives, lose confidence in an individual minister, or government, they can dismiss them by majority vote in the House of Commons.

If this received view were an accurate description of what happens, then the basic principle of popular control would be broadly satisfied in modern Britain, after allowing for the complexity and diversity of government. However, as Part 2 on the workings of British government, or the 'core executive', will demonstrate, it falls far short of a more contested and ambiguous *actualité*. We begin this audit of the received view and what actually happens at the heart of government with a series of inter-connected chapters which examine the key institutions and actors who are responsible for making government policies and taking its decisions: the Prime Minister, the cabinet and its committees, ministers and their higher civil servants in government departments, the heads of quangos and other public bodies, and the prominent corporate and other organised interests which work intimately with officials within departments to formulate policies across the whole range of government. We use the term 'core executive' to describe the mesh of institutions and actors we are analysing. They are 'executive' because they influence, make and carry out government's major decisions; they are 'core' because they lie at the innermost authoritative centre of the state apparatus, and their decisions and policies impact directly and indirectly on the lives of all citizens of the UK. They also determine the environment within which the whole state apparatus – government departments, executive and other public agencies, quangos, regional offices and local government – operates and they influence, sometimes decisively, the administration of justice and the quality of the political freedoms and civil liberties of the population at large (as the first Democratic Audit volume, *The Three Pillars of Liberty* (Klug *et al.* 1996), demonstrated).

Our central hypothesis is that the structure, organisation and operation of this core executive is of crucial importance from a *democratic* point of view, because it determines how far government in Britain can be properly accountable to Parliament and the public, how open government decision-making is to scrutiny and to alter-native points of view, how widely and equally it consults a full range of interests in making policies and laws, how responsive it is to public opinion, how representative it is of a range of political interests and forces, and how far it may be said to be subject to the 'rule of law' in its conduct and use of its wide discretionary powers. In other words, the internal organisation of the core executive is critical for the democratic capacity of the political system as a whole and the rule of law.

Our analysis of the core executive touches on six of the Democratic Audit criteria (**DACs**) set out in Chapter 1, though it does not exhaust them. The criteria which form the backbone of the audit in Part 2 and carry over into Part 3 are:

DAC7. How accessible to the public is information about what the government does, and about the effects of its policies, and how independent is it of the government's own information machine?

DAC8. How effective and open to scrutiny is the control exercised by elected politicians over non-elected executive personnel, both military and civilian?

DAC9. How extensive are the powers of Parliament to oversee legislation and public expenditure, and to scrutinise the executive and hold it accountable; and how effectively are they exercised in practice?

DAC11. How far is the executive subject to the rule of law and transparent rules governing the use of its powers? How far are the courts able to ensure that the executive obeys the rule of law; and how effective are their procedures for ensuring that all public institutions and officials are subject to the rule of law in the performance of their functions?

DAC15. How systematic and open to public scrutiny are the procedures for government consultation of public opinion and of relevant interests in the formation and implementation of policy and legislation?

DAC17. How far do the arrangements for government both above and below the level of the central state meet the above criteria of openness, accountability and responsiveness?

DAC18. To what extent does government below the centre have the powers to carry out its responsibilities in accordance with the wishes of regional or local electorates, and without undue interference from the centre?

What we shall be concerned with is the extent to which the organisation of the core executive measures up to these criteria, and promotes or hinders their realisation for the political system as a whole. In Chapter 6 we examine the roles of the Prime Minister, the cabinet and the unseen committee structure, and assess how far their internal processes of decision-taking set a pattern of governing that corresponds to the democratic, or at least collective, ideas inherent in the idea of 'cabinet government'. In Chapter 7 we assess the relationship between ministers and senior civil servants and analyse the policy-making role of government departments. Are civil servants able to maintain sufficient independence from their ministers to provide effective advice and analysis of policies and to check against constitutional impropriety? Are ministers sufficiently in command of senior officials and departments to be capable of discharging their central constitutional duty to account for their own and their departments' actions and policies to Parliament and the public? In Chapter 8 we focus on the evolution of a more fragmented form of government in the UK, and examine the roles and patterns of accountability of executive agencies, and executive and advisory quangos. Chapter 9 is about subsidiarity in Britain – we assess the democratic nature of government at the regional and local level and central government's more active role in 'low politics'. Chapter 10 describes the neglected area of networking between government departments and organised interests and considers how far networks of officials and interested parties compromise the aim of full and equal consultation. Chapter 11 assesses how far existing rules and conventions for ministers and civil servants govern the conduct of the core executive in ways which are consistent with the rule of law and considers the implications of the absence of a written constitution in the UK for democratic accountability.

In Part 3, we go on to audit how far the doctrine of ministerial responsibility, collective and individual, and existing arrangements for open government, meet the demands of the Audit's criteria; Parliament's ability to hold the core executive to account (**DAC7** and **DAC9**); and then the ability of the courts to ensure that the executive obeys the rule of law (**DAC11** and **DAC12**).

From the Democratic Audit point of view, it is vitally important that decisions and policies are determined according to rules which are consistent with the two basic principles of popular control and political equality. To audit the complex world of the core executive according to our first principle, of popular control, it is necessary first to determine exactly which individuals, groups or institutions within the core executive are responsible for taking decisions and framing policies in government; how far the Prime Minister and ministers, collectively, may be said to have the decisive say on government decisions and policies; just how realistic it is to expect the political heads of government to be able themselves to control the civil service and wider realms of government and to be answerable politically in Parliament for their exercise of this control; how well the rules governing the relationship between senior bureaucrats and ministers work in practice; and how effectively the mechanisms of collective and individual responsibility to Parliament actually deliver the accountability that is required to make a reality of popular control. Our second main principle, that of political equality, also demands that we monitor whether the core executive is scrupulous in giving all citizens and interests in civil society equal opportunities to participate in and influence policy-making; and that government is conducted with a degree of transparency which allows any interested member of the public to be informed and to contribute to policy evaluation.

Our concerns are not mere abstract constructs. Core decisions and policies impact directly and indirectly on the lives of all citizens of the UK; and as the UK is a unitary state, they generally do so without checks or intervention from intermediary bodies, or by regional or local government. These decisions and policies directly determine or at least affect how the state apparatus treats ordinary citizens on issues of vital importance to their daily lives – from pension levels and immigration rules, tax demands and employment prospects, criminal laws and regional disparities, education standards and housing conditions, to the protection of their everyday environment, risks from radiation and pollution, the safety of drugs and food and the very quality of the air they breathe.

6   Does The Cabinet Really Govern?

Cabinet government or quasi-presidential rule?

'The question is,' said Humpty-Dumpty, 'which is to be master – that's all.'
(From *Through the Looking Glass*, Lewis Carroll, 1871)

Now the country is governed by the Prime Minister who leads, co-ordinates and maintains a series of ministers all of whom are advised and backed by the Civil Service.
(John Mackintosh, *The British Cabinet*, 1962)

I accept that cabinet government must always be a cumbrous and complicated affair and that this is a price worth paying for the advantage of shared discussion and shared decision, provided the system can keep up with the demands put upon it.
(Lord Hunt, former Cabinet Secretary, 9 June 1983)

The cabinet is the formal keystone of British government. It is in cabinet that major policy issues and the government's overall strategy are supposed to be decided after collective discussion among equals, and are then defended according to the principle of collective responsibility. Of course, the Prime Minister has a pre-eminent place, as *primus inter pares*, but cabinet ministers each have a voice as heads of their departments and equal members of a collective decision-making body. This at least is the theory of 'cabinet government'. In this chapter we examine how far practice accords with the theory.

A Prime Minister and cabinet ministers are very powerful political figures. They lead a single-party government which commands the legislature through a usually loyal majority. They are not required to share power with members of other parties and can generally exclude opposition parties from any influence over their actions. They command a strong, centralised bureaucracy whose governing principle is loyalty to the government of the day. They have at their disposal wide-ranging political powers of two kinds. Most of these powers derive from statute law and they can add to them through new legislation. But significant governing powers derive from the Crown, or royal, prerogative. Legally, the Prime Minister and cabinet ministers hold office at the pleasure of the Crown, and as ministers of the Crown they exercise the surviving discretionary powers of absolute monarchy, gradually assumed by ministers from 1688 onwards. The authority of a Prime Minister and his or her pre-eminent place in government rests on these 'prerogative powers'; it is by their use that Prime Ministers, for example, form or re-shuffle a government, and appoint or dismiss ministers. But these powers have also survived because they are generally essential to the smooth running of government, and especially for ministers' ability to respond to crises or unexpected events, declare war, agree a treaty, run the civil service and government departments, appoint quangocrats, and so on (see Brazier 1997: 203–217; and Chapter 11 further).

The powers concentrated in the hands of a Prime Minister and ministers make the idea of cabinet government central to the character and quality of British democracy. From the Audit's point of view, if democratic accountability is defective or lacking within the cabinet itself, it is less likely to be realised outside it. First, what happens in the cabinet can be seen as a microcosm of the wider relationship between the government, Parliament and people. Cabinet accountability can thus serve as a barometer for democratic accountability more widely. Secondly, the powers at the disposal of its members are not bound by a written constitution or statutory or common-law rules for the conduct of the executive; even the courts have only limited powers to restrain ministers (see Chapter 15). Thus the task of ensuring that government is subject to the rule of law depends a great deal on the political process, and the cabinet's supposed role in that process. Given the elusive nature of the powers, prerogative and statutory, at the disposal of its members, this aspect of the cabinet's role is significant. The monarchical nature of prerogative powers means that they are still possessed of a pre-democratic half-life – they are not precisely defined, and are governed more by politics and its conventions than by the courts.

The idea of collective cabinet responsibility therefore carries an implicit promise that ministers, acting together, are prepared and able to restrain a Prime Minister, or minister, who might not otherwise observe the rules of the game. Further, the promise of collegiate decision-making and co-ordination in government through the principle of collective responsibility suggests that ministers as a whole are answerable politically to the people's representatives in Parliament. On both counts, if most major decision-making actually takes place elsewhere – say, from a couch in Downing Street, an office in an important department of state, an ad-hoc cabinet committee, or a small group of ministers – so that the cabinet is merely a rubber stamp; and if systematic exclusions and manipulations are at work to silence inconvenient voices or points of view, or to render them impotent; then this will set the tone for the political system as a whole and subvert the central idea that government can be made collectively answerable through the cabinet to Parliament.

One broader reason for the Audit's interest in cabinet government stems from our view of what constitutes the distinctive strength of *democratic* policy-making. Everyone wants policy-making to be coherent and governments to be effective. Yet it is difficult to define in the abstract what exactly is meant by terms such as 'effective' or 'good' government. In this audit, we emphasise the distinctive qualities of democratic policy-making and argue that these are also a source of 'effective' and 'good' government. These qualities are: the willingness to listen to a range of expertise, both within government and outside it; to consult widely with different interests and points of view; to test policies against objections and against alternatives; and to do so openly. These conform to our broader criteria of open, accountable and responsive government (**DACs 7–18**; see Chapter 1). To the extent that these are met, government's policy-making is the more likely to avoid damaging mistakes and 'policy disasters', and will command consent from society. Some of these conditions for open, accountable and responsive policy-making are met through the relations between government and societal interests and expertise; some through the relations between ministers and their civil servants; some through the relations of the Prime Minister and cabinet; and some through the character of cabinet government itself. In this chapter we consider whether, and how far, the cabinet and its committee structure provides an adequate forum to meet the criteria of effective and accountable decision-making in a democracy.

The goal of balanced decision-taking

The idea that the UK is still in reality governed by the cabinet has long come under challenge and is continually reasserted. A variety of politicians and observers, inspired by Richard Crossman, an influential member of Harold Wilson's first cabinets, have argued that the cabinet's pre-eminent role has been usurped by postwar Prime Ministers. They argue that we now live under Prime Ministerial, or quasi-presidential, rule. This argument grew in force during Margaret Thatcher's long premiership (1979–90). Mrs (now Lady) Thatcher dominated her cabinets by the force of her personality and, as a biographer noted, removed 'the most vital aspects of policy-making from Cabinet discussion' (Harris 1990: 122, 133). Those who believe in the primacy of the Prime Minister have pointed out how weak Mrs Thatcher's 'wet' opponents in cabinet proved to be. Defenders of the idea of cabinet government respond that the cabinet was ultimately the instrument of her downfall and that normal service resumed under John Major.

This debate has tended to obscure another important development under recent Conservative governments – the advent of 'can-do' ministers and the questionable ability of cabinets to restrain their enthusiasm for poor or even unworkable legislation and policies. Generally, the see-saw of debate between the various theories provides more fun than illumination and obscures the complex realities of modern government. This is not to say that there is no tension between cabinet government and Prime Ministerial power. But both are simply important parts of a larger executive machine that arguably defies full control by either of them.

The idea of cabinet government perpetuates the mid-Victorian view that a cabinet, in substance only 'a committee of the party majority', has delegated to it, for greater convenience, the day-to-day exercise of the power entrusted to the governing party by the electorate. At the very least, it suggests that a highly visible group of men and women, most of whom are elected, are in charge of the country's affairs. It implies that ministers discuss policies together and come to 'collegial' decisions which are therefore more likely to be fully balanced and representative. As cabinet ministers each represents a major department of state, this collegial setting provides an assurance that most relevant views and interests will have been weighed up and considered. Thus, cabinet government is believed – not unreasonably – to be more likely to produce balanced and rational – as well as 'democratic' – decisions than an autocratic Prime Minister, acting alone, bilaterally with one or more ministers or guided by a small

Balanced decision-taking

clique or informal 'inner cabinet'; or a determined minister, backed by his or her department, or a cabal of ministers; or the bureaucracy acting on its own.

But it is more realistically perceived as an ideal rather than actual practice. It is cherished as a safeguard against the apparently unbalanced and unpredictable nature of government in Britain. Effective executive and legislative power is concentrated, generally for periods of up to at least four or five years at a time or even longer, in the hands of single-party governments. Crises, like the Westland affair – a 'bonfire of conventions', according to Peter Hennessy, the modern historian – and the poll tax reveal, when closely examined, just how fluid and unpredictable the British way of government is (Hennessy 1995: 96; Butler *et al.* 1994). The cabinet is therefore regarded variously as a counterweight to Parliament's inability to control or check government, or 'the executive'; as a restraint on arrogant Prime Ministers and over-zealous ministers; and as a collective substitute at the heart of government for formal checks and balances on the exercise of executive power. Thus, at the height of the Westland crisis in 1986, Douglas Hurd, then Home Secretary, declared on LWT's *Weekend World*, 'I think it is very important that people should see that we are under cabinet government. I think that is what people prefer and want to know about' (26 January).

Much weight is given in informed debate to the value of mutual discussion and power-sharing around the cabinet table and how some element at least of collegial decision-making may be re-created; see, for example, the discussion by Peter Hennessy of contemporary British government in *The Hidden Wiring* (1995: Chapter 4). For Hennessy, the idea of cabinet government is one of certain constitutional bequests which are essential if British government is to be kept 'clean and decent and efficient'. He wrote, 'the Cabinet, not No. 10, *should be* the most powerful single body in the state for both accountability and power-sharing reasons'; and, 'The Cabinet *must* at all times act as a necessary restraint upon a potentially overmighty premiership [our emphases]' (*ibid.*: 96, 115–116). But these are statements of normative aspiration rather than actual reality. Peter Hennessy sets out an 'audit of concern' of the weaknesses of the cabinet in practice – it suffers from 'institutional sclerosis', overload, 'tired minds and untrained minds' and sheer size. But in essence he argues that the principle of collective responsibility still sustains cabinet government – 'it is the superglue, the ultimate bonder of Cabinet government'. A few streamlining reforms are all that is necessary to restore cabinet government to its former glory (*ibid.*: Chapter 4).

Similarly, Ferdinand Mount, who was once Mrs Thatcher's policy adviser, seeks to persuade us that the cabinet remains 'the centre of power' – a major co-ordinating body, which gives government a measure of unity. For Mount, the cabinet is still predominantly in charge:

> Every Minister, in framing his proposals, has to bear in mind what his colleagues will and will not tolerate. True, in the case of the Budget or some major foreign policy decision, he knows he can ram it through. . . . But the Cabinet remains the crystallisation of the government as a collective entity. And while it may often be a slothful, inattentive and forgetful body, it retains

the power to spring into life any Thursday morning and assert its constitutional and actual rights.

(Mount 1992: 133)

But the weight of evidence – much of it his own – is against Mount. The reality of
the modern cabinet does not live up to such expectations. Cabinets now meet too
rarely – for two or three hours once a week – really to take charge of government.
Under Mrs Thatcher, cabinet meetings had dwindled to 45 or fewer a year, half as
many as under her predecessors. Cabinets are too large and unwieldy to take on a
major co-ordinating role. Nigel Lawson actually described cabinet meetings as 'the
least important part of being a member of the Cabinet':

> when I was a minister, I always looked forward to the Cabinet meeting
> immensely because it was, apart from the summer holidays, the only period
> of real rest that I got in what was a very heavy job. Cabinet meetings are
> 90 per cent of the time a dignified [rather than an] efficient part of Cabinet
> government.
>
> (quoted in Hennessy 1995: 97)

Cabinets are now expected largely to approve decisions taken elsewhere within the
machinery of government; to act as the final arbiter of unresolved conflicts between
ministers and departments; and to consider major political crises rather than determine major political decisions or policies. The Prime Minister's rules for ministers
explicitly encourage ministers not to take issues to cabinet. Cabinet debates are anyway
usually brief. Ian Gilmour, a leading 'wet' in Mrs Thatcher's first cabinet, recalled that
'Collective decision-making was severely truncated and with it, inevitably, collective
responsibility'. Even though Mrs Thatcher did not have full freedom of choice in 1979,
because the cabinet 'did not agree with the direction the Prime Minister wished to
go . . . it turned out not to matter very much, as only rarely were the most important
issues permitted to reach the cabinet' (Gilmour 1992: 3–5).

The cabinet's role in strategic decision-making

John Major was credited with 'restoring' cabinet government; according to gossip,
Chris Patten compared his first cabinet meeting to the Prisoners' Chorus from *Fidelio*.
Yet most of the Major cabinet's time was taken up by items for report, legislative
timetabling and an explicit 'Part II' session, devoted to party political matters, in
the absence of the cabinet secretary. Cabinets did discuss strategic questions, but
did not take strategic decisions – though Major constantly consulted the whole cabinet
on European issues, encouraging every member to state their views before summing
up. As Europe was the single most divisive question for his party and had been a
catalyst for Mrs Thatcher's removal, this is not to be wondered at. It was common
prudence for Major to ensure that all his ministers were locked into collective cabinet
decisions on Europe. Even Mrs Thatcher took care to guard her back in cabinet,
especially early on in her premiership. The most notable occasion on which she

secured the backing of the entire cabinet was for the decision to send the task force to recapture the Falklands in April 1982.

Yet consider the major decisions which are not made in cabinet under any Prime Minister. It is standard practice that the cabinet does not decide on the Budget. Cabinet ministers are informed of the Budget's contents only on the morning of the Budget Statement (after the Queen, who is briefed the night before) and do not discuss them collectively. Fear of leaks and profiteering on the markets is simply a 'convenient pretext' for this late notice. 'The prime reason is to prevent effective cabinet intervention', says Mount – 'this iron secrecy . . . ensures the impotence of the cabinet in budgetary matters' (Mount 1992: 121–122). A modern Chancellor has to pay attention to the economic and political instincts of a Prime Minister, but may ignore his other colleagues. Further, decisions which are 'delicate, embarrassing or challenging', or form part of 'a [Prime Minister's] difficult radical strategy', are often kept away from cabinet, at least until they are more or less set in concrete (*ibid.*: 123–124). Such decisions normally relate to economic, foreign or defence policy and less often to social policy. But even here significant policy matters are removed from overall cabinet debate. Take the poll tax fiasco. A thorough study of the politics of the poll tax, by David Butler, Andrew Adonis and Tony Travers, concluded that, 'The insignificance of the full cabinet to decision-taking is well attested by the poll tax'; and that the full story shows 'the cabinet itself, the "efficient secret" of Bagehot's account, to be a purely formal institution, insignificant to the evolution of policy or the taking of decisions' (Butler *et al.* 1994: 187–191).

The cabinet did not discuss the proposal for the poll tax until January 1986, 15 months after the initial studies team had been established and more than seven months after the key decision of principle had been taken by a cabinet committee. The cabinet then merely rubber-stamped the Environment Secretary's draft green paper which had already been endorsed some weeks earlier in committee. Nigel Lawson did not even register his well-known opposition at the cabinet meeting – not simply because it was too late, but also because as the former Chancellor explained to Butler and his colleagues:

> the cabinet is far too public a forum for the Chancellor to announce his disagreement with the Prime Minister on a key policy – unless he wants it to be across the world's press the next day, making his or the prime minister's position untenable.
>
> (*Ibid.*: 191–192)

The fact is that the cabinet is now the creature of its own cabinet committees. The cabinet committee structure is now the real 'engine-house' of government policy-making and decision-taking. It is there if anywhere, and not in cabinet, that long-term strategies and policy changes, such as the poll tax, are developed (see **pp. 140–147**). Take for example the well-documented history of postwar nuclear weapons policy. Prime Ministers from Winston Churchill during the 1939–45 war to Jim Callaghan and Margaret Thatcher in the 1970s kept the cabinet and most ministers in the dark about the development of Britain's nuclear weapons. Clement Attlee, Prime

Minister from 1945–51, excluded most of his Labour cabinet members from the crucial decisions to continue atomic research after 1945 and to construct an atomic bomb in 1947. Attlee took the formal decision to make the bomb to a cabinet subcommittee from which he deliberately excluded two senior ministers who were likely to be opposed, as he wanted the decision to go through on the nod. Neither project was mentioned in cabinet or its defence committee agendas. Parliament was finally informed on 12 May 1948, obliquely in a low-key debate, but only because excessive secrecy was hindering progress. Churchill had no need to keep the decision to construct the hydrogen bomb from cabinet after 1951, and Harold Macmillan's negotiations to purchase the US Skybolt were made public only because the US Senate's agreement to the treaty was required. Wilson after 1974, and Callaghan and Thatcher in the late 1970s, kept the whole cabinet in the dark over decisions on the Chevaline missile system and other developments made in cabinet committees (Hennessy 1986: Chapter 4; 1989: 707–711; Mount 1992: 125).

The cabinet has not only lost its influence and important functions by comparison with its mid-Victorian 'golden age', but has continued to do so in recent history. For example as late as the Labour cabinets of the Wilson years, public spending rounds were ultimately settled annually by cabinet and bitter battles ensued. But the practice has since been for cabinet to accept overall limits on spending as a prelude to a closed political process which takes place in a cabinet committee and is not open to cabinet review or notification. In public, the Chief Secretary of the Treasury is apparently entrusted with thrashing out the details of departmental budgets individually with the spending ministers. In fact, the process is dominated by the Treasury. A recent study of the Treasury revealed, 'most decisions about the allocation of programmes continue to be made as the result of mutually acceptable agreements negotiated between the Treasury and spending departments; a few become the subject of bargaining conducted by Ministers face to face in bilaterals'. The study identifies a 'small, permanent, stable, cohesive and exclusive policy network' of some 200 officials (and ministers), which is focused on the annual expenditure round, with an inner core 'of PFOs [Principal Finance Officers] and senior Treasury officials' and fixed rules of conduct (Thain and Wright 1995: 23, 193–195).

Ministers themselves tend to acquiesce in the demotion of the cabinet. Nigel Lawson, for example, believed that Mrs Thatcher's tendency to settle important issues outside cabinet in 'small and informal groups' in an attempt to gain 'effective decisions' was initially justified; he objected only when her use of ad-hoc groups 'degenerated into increasingly complex attempts to divide and rule' (Lawson 1993: 936). Michael Heseltine's protest against Mrs Thatcher's handling of the Westland affair was not only that cabinet had been denied the opportunity to discuss the issues involved, but that she had manipulated a cabinet committee meeting against his departmental interest.

One of the most important decisions taken by Mrs Thatcher's government was to enter the exchange rate mechanism (ERM) of the European Monetary System in October 1990. A sterling crisis in January 1985 persuaded Nigel Lawson to put a stable pound at the centre of his economic policy and set in motion a long-drawn-out wrangle over Britain's entry to the ERM between Mrs Thatcher and Lawson, and then from 1988, between her, Lawson and Sir Geoffrey Howe, the Foreign Secretary. The first and last serious 'cabinet' discussion of the issue took place in November 1985 at a high-level meeting in No. 10 Downing Street, attended by four senior ministers, including Lawson and Howe, the Chief Whip, Leader of the House, the party chairman, the Governor of the Bank of England, and senior Treasury and Bank officials. William Whitelaw, the Deputy Prime Minister, expressed the view, 'If the Chancellor, the Governor and the Foreign Secretary are all agreed that we should join the EMS, then that should be decisive.' Mrs Thatcher refused to accept this view and abruptly ended the meeting. She argued that the meeting was not a proper cabinet committee – 'it was not a meeting that had any constitutional signifi-cance'. If the ministers and officials present wanted to join the ERM, they would have to find a new Prime Minister (Lawson 1993: 497–500). Lawson nearly resigned after this rebuff, but neither he nor any other minister present seriously considered forcing the issue onto the agenda of the full cabinet, 'to see whether Thatcher would indeed resign rather than give way' (Stephens 1996: 51). Indeed, throughout the dispute, one point of agreement between Mrs Thatcher, Lawson and Howe was that the issue should be kept well away from the cabinet. And the cabinet as a whole was irrelevant to the process by which Mrs Thatcher was finally obliged to give way to entry in 1989 and finally in October 1990 (see also **p. 136**).

The balance of power between Prime Minister and cabinet

Ministers are powerful figures in government (see Chapter 7), but a host of examples from Mrs Thatcher's premiership give the lie to the idea that ministers in cabinet can act as a collective restraint on a powerful Prime Minister. For example, Mrs Thatcher's decision to allow the United States to use British bases for the bombing raid on Libya in April 1986 was a conspicuous flaunting of cabinet opinion. When Reagan asked for Britain's assistance, the Prime Minister consulted the Attorney-General on the legality of the operation, talked to three senior ministers (none of whom favoured the proposal) and granted permission. The cabinet was not informed until the night of the bombing and was 'overwhelmingly hostile to unqualified support' for the action and said that Britain should disassociate itself from the bombing raid. Yet in her Commons statement the next day Mrs Thatcher disregarded the cabinet's views and gave unqualified support to the raid; 'thus even the modest, largely retrospective protest of the Cabinet was swept aside' (Mount 1992: 123).

On issues when it seemed that the cabinet might – and in fact did – restrain the Prime Minister, as over economic policy in her first term, Mrs Thatcher soon learned that it was possible simply to avoid it. Mrs Thatcher's first cabinet disagreed with the direction of economic policy and in July 1981 revolted against a £5 billion package of spending cuts. But, as Ian Gilmour recounted, the cabinet was generally powerless to intervene, partly because the Prime Minister and her Chancellor were firm allies and brought Budgets to cabinet as *faits accomplis*, partly because other 'most important issues' did not reach the cabinet (Gilmour 1992: 3–5). The moder-ates were in a majority but Mrs Thatcher, governing 'by clique and committee', pushed through economic policies and decisions, made in No. 10 rather than

No. 11 Downing Street, to which they were opposed. The handful of 'wets', like Gilmour, who did stand up to Mrs Thatcher, gained the occasional tactical success, but lost the war – and office, as she chose to change her cabinets rather than her policies (*ibid.*: Chapter 3). Thereafter, Mrs Thatcher:

> developed a practice, which she carried through by force of personality, by which *ad hoc* groupings of ministers were frequently used instead [of formal cabinet committees], because they were known to be more favourable to the outcome she wanted.
>
> (Foster 1997: 5)

In June 1981, Mrs Thatcher herself gave cabinet ministers the opportunity to unseat her over a pay offer cabinet members wanted to accept in order to resolve a long-running civil service dispute. She was at this time deeply unpopular in the country. On her instructions, William Whitelaw, her deputy, warned cabinet ministers that she would resign rather than make the offer, adding that, if defeated, she could take the issue to the parliamentary party where she would undoubtedly win the day. A number of ministers would have liked her to go, but not over this issue and not if they had to take on 'the burden of taking concrete action' (Young 1990: 228).

The weakness of the Labour opposition in the early 1980s also had a knock-on effect on the cabinet's ability to restrain the Prime Minister. The absence of a convincing opposition, with a serious chance of replacing Mrs Thatcher at the next election, allowed the Prime Minister and her allies to see her increasingly unpopular policies through without backbench MPs becoming too alarmed. It is hard for cabinet ministers even to meet to discuss a common purpose. If they do so outside the formal structures, they risk being branded disloyal, though Gilmour, Jim Prior and Peter Walker did breakfast to discuss tactics on the morning of Howe's 1981 Budget (Young 1990: 215). (The Crossman, Benn and Castle diaries also record many conspiratorial gatherings among left-leaning Labour ministers in Wilson's cabinets.)

In theory, a minister or ministers who disagree with a Prime Minister's policies or are at odds with the direction of government may resign. But this rarely happens in practice for understandable reasons – the most obvious being that resignation usually ends a minister's career at the highest level. Nigel Lawson was utterly opposed to the poll tax and could have made it a resigning issue. He did not do so for the very good reason that, 'if Cabinet ministers resign whenever they disagree with a policy being pursued, Cabinet Government would be impossible' (Lawson 1993: 583). That proposition was proved broadly correct as Mrs Thatcher's government disintegrated as first Heseltine, then Lawson and Howe, all resigned (after being encouraged on their way by the Prime Minister). But in general very few senior ministers ever resign over government policies from which they dissent. The political wisdom is with Winston Churchill – 'Never resign!' Ian Gilmour regretted later that he had not resigned over the Thatcher–Howe economic strategy, but he too quite reasonably saw it as a 'tactical question' at the time – 'we had reason to think that things would be even worse without us. Just to give up the fight and depart would have been craven' (Gilmour 1992: 41).

Quality of cabinet decisions

The quality of cabinet decision-making

Nevertheless, there surely remains what Lord Hunt described as 'the advantage of shared discussion and shared decision' on most issues which come before a cabinet? No doubt such discussion and decision-making does occur, but it is not realistic to regard cabinet ministers primarily as political colleagues, engaged in collegial discussion and decision-making. In fact, ministers tend to act in cabinet as ambassadors for their departments rather than as colleagues and they are naturally wary about offending the Prime Minister or other colleagues bringing proposals forward, by intervening in affairs which do not directly affect their own department. The collegiate ethos is almost entirely absent from their deliberations. Their political reputation depends far more on their ability to represent their own departmental interests in cabinet and its committees, and in Parliament and the media, than on any contribution they may make to collective decision-making. The cabinet is no longer even the most important of these forums.

In any event, ministers are usually simply too busy with their own affairs to be able to maintain an intelligent grasp of other ministers' activities. Ministers who dissent from agreed policies tend not to argue their case in cabinet, but to appeal over their colleagues' heads to the party in Parliament and the country, by way of well-scripted hints of disagreement which are decoded by the media. But most ministers are too busy to dissent. Recent history is well stocked with the regrets of busy cabinet ministers who failed to intervene to stop policies they believed to be wrong-headed, or even disastrous. In the 1950s, Harold Macmillan came to regret that he was 'too engrossed with the Ministry of Housing to press the European issue'; Lord Carrington 'had his hands full with foreign affairs' and could not intervene in economic policy from 1979–82 (Gilmour 1992: 34–35). Besides, there is the territorial imperative – a Foreign Secretary, or any other minister, who dabbles openly in economic or other policy matters invites the ministers affected to interfere in his or her domain. Lawson took a bluntly pragmatic view of his failure to stop the poll tax in its tracks:

> You can never expect to win every battle. In this case [the poll tax] what was at issue was a proposal that did not lie within my own range of ministerial responsibilities, and which was not a matter of high principle but simply a grotesque political blunder.
>
> (Lawson 1993: 583)

Moreover, the terms on which 'shared discussion and decision' take place militate against the collegiate ideal. As Sir Douglas Wass, a former Permanent Secretary to the Treasury has testified, cabinet discussions on policy issues generally take place on the basis of the departmental briefs provided for ministers. If no other minister has an interest to declare or defend, the cabinet simply hears a possibly partial case, and certainly one from an interested party put in terms which suit the minister and department (Wass 1984: 35). Sir Christopher Foster, an experienced adviser to government, argues that the standard of cabinet decision-making has deteriorated since 1979. Previously, he says, departmental policy papers would pass through various stages of discussion and approval at interdepartmental level (including clearance from the Treasury) and finally at cabinet committee, and then go to cabinet as a cabinet paper for approval. After 1979, this chain of staged scrutiny and discussion was broken. Departmental ministers still generally initiated policies, and required Treasury clearance and cabinet approval, but they might well by-pass cabinet committees (thus depriving affected ministers of an opportunity to comment and perhaps amend or oppose the proposals) and proceed by various other routes to cabinet. Under Major, ministers ceased to present papers on policy to cabinet:

> Cabinet was not meant to discuss policy. Rather it listened to an oral report from ministers on the progress of their business which could include seeking formal approval of a policy, or of a staging post on the way to a policy. A paper might have been put to a cabinet committee or to a more informal meeting. Or a letter between ministers might have been used. Nevertheless, the only account many cabinet ministers may have had of that policy was the oral one then given by the minister. . . . Many cabinet ministers may have had no proper opportunity to comment on or approve policies, even sometimes when they had a clear departmental interest.
>
> (Foster 1997: 6)

As a result, there was even less co-ordination of government policies across Whitehall, less commitment by ministers to a policy process to which they might well not be party, and disagreement and faction among ministers. Plainly such changes undermine the very idea of collective responsibility. In short, 'cabinet government' is not an exact or comprehensive description of the way government works in the UK. The cabinet is neither the supreme executive body, nor the forum for major strategy decisions, or even for systematic review and discussion of all the policies of government as a whole. As Mount states, 'We must not mistake the Cabinet for the engine-room. It is this misperception which has fostered such complacency about the central direction of British government since the war' (Mount 1992: 133).

The fact is that many governing decisions are effectively taken by the Prime Minister and/or Foreign Secretary or Chancellor of the Exchequer, singly or severally; many others are taken in cabinet committees, 'partial governments' (often 'partial' in both senses of the word), or in informal groups summoned by the Prime Minister or even a minister; or by one 'lead' minister, possibly in consultation with the Prime Minister or another minister or ministers, or even by exchange of correspondence; or even by junior ministers in various departments acting jointly (as in the case of defence equipment exported to Iraq after 1988); many others still are taken by officials within ministries.

There are two standard explanations for the cabinet's loss of power and influence. It is *too small*; it is *too large*. Modern government is simply too vast and complex an operation to be encompassed by a *small* group of politicians meeting weekly. At the same time, the cabinet is too *large* and unwieldy a group to be able to take effective decisions. To these explanations, Ferdinand Mount adds another: 'its membership must to some extent reflect the broad coalition of views which makes up the governing party' (1992: 124). In other words, it is too broad-based. Thus, there is a practical paradox at the heart of the case for 'cabinet government'. That case depends on the fact that the cabinet is broadly representative of the political party which has been endorsed by 'the electorate' (in fact, invariably only the largest minority of voters, as we have seen in Chapter 3) and thus brings together a variety of stand-points and views in determining key government policies. Yet, on Mount's testimony, the broad nature of a cabinet in practice precisely disqualifies it for exercising this key 'constitutional' role. The fact that the cabinet is no longer the 'efficient secret' of government means that there is no efficient mechanism for strategic planning and overall control of government, let alone one which can plausibly claim a 'demo-cratic' role.

Do Prime Ministers rule Britain?

On the occasions when I spoke to [Thatcher] in office, she conveyed above all a sense of entrapment. Her egotism was of a woman wanting to exert power, not of actually exerting it. She was perpetually at odds with her political surroundings, like a dog straining at the leash, barking at anybody who came near.

(Simon Jenkins, in *Accountable to None*, 1995)

Do we, then, live under Prime Ministerial, or quasi-presidential, rule? The Prime Minister is leader of the majority party, has the opportunity to build his or her personal popularity with the electorate through the media (and official and party 'spin-doctors') and acts as the major government and party spokesperson, often on the international stage. (Though this can be a double-edged benefit: a Prime Minister will be blamed when things go wrong and can lose face in international or European negotiations.) The Prime Minister's prerogative powers over a cabinet and the majority party in Parliament are formidable. He or she may hire or fire cabinet ministers (usually after consulting the Chief Whip) and is expected to engage in periodic re-shuffles of the cabinet. This exercise of naked political power is unre-strained as it would be in most liberal democracies by the need to consult and satisfy coalition partners; 'first-past-the-post' elections normally deliver single-party majority government.

Freedom from departmental responsibilities allows Prime Ministers to intervene over the full range of government policies. They have the power to summon or fail to summon cabinet or cabinet committee meetings, and to decide how frequently the cabinet should meet and for how long. In Bagehot's time, any member of the cabinet could summon a cabinet meeting, but not today. Indeed, in practice they may not even submit papers to cabinet without the Prime Minister's consent; and as Gilmour wryly noted, 'Mrs Thatcher would not have permitted the flaunting of heresy in a cabinet paper, let alone discussion of it around the cabinet table' (Gilmour 1992: 31). Prime Ministers control the agenda of the cabinet, chair its meetings, sum up the conclusions of cabinet discussions and may choose to oversee the writing up of the minutes. They determine the composition of cabinet committees and the business allocated to them; can create cabinet committees and abolish them, or set up ad-hoc committees of ministers. They consult the whole cabinet, or act alone, or with a single minister or several ministers, and will normally consult the Chief Whip (out of common prudence) on re-shuffles.

No strict rules determine how premiers may use or abuse these powers nor how they organise cabinet committees and their business. The room for manoeuvre is all too obvious. Further, Prime Ministers have huge powers of patronage which allow them to offer members of the majority party (and other parties) cabinet or government office, honours and desirable official positions. They hold pole position in media relations by virtue of their office; and if they have the *chutzpah* to defy convention, as Mrs Thatcher demonstrated, may appoint a chief press secretary whose loyalty belongs not to government or party, but to the Prime Minister personally. (Of course, ministers now use their own press officials to brief the press on their own views, and if need be, against their Prime Minister; Stephens 1996: 60.) Finally, they alone have the power, subject only to formal approval from the Queen, to dissolve Parliament and choose the date of a general election.

We still live under the shadow of Mrs Thatcher's long rule. Her formidable energy, convictions and sheer will-power made her exceptional, but it would be a mistake either to see her as unique or to cast the model of cabinet politics forever in the image of her own battle for supremacy over her cabinet colleagues or the two major departments of state, the Treasury and Foreign Office. Long before her arrival, postwar premiers of all parties actively manipulated a Prime Minister's powers to bend events to their will and convinced observers like John Mackintosh, the academic-turned-politician, that cabinet government no longer existed: 'Now the country is governed by the Prime Minister who leads, co-ordinates and maintains a series of ministers, all of whom are advised and backed by the Civil Service' (Mackintosh 1962: 451). Even earlier, John Morley, biographer of Gladstone and Walpole, wrote that the power of the Prime Minister was 'not inferior to that of a dictator, provided the House of Commons will stand by him' (1889: 158); and both Gladstone and another great Victorian Prime Minister, Lord Salisbury, were described as dictators. They and other premiers, like Disraeli and Asquith, dismissed ministers, dominated the media of their day, and often took important decisions themselves on their own or after consulting only a few colleagues (Butler *et al.* 1994: 188–190; Mackintosh 1962). Nor was Mrs Thatcher unique in exploiting the slippery nature of her powers to out-manoeuvre her cabinet; in her defence, Mount argued, 'In all ministries there have been complaints of the Prime Minister's high-handed and underhand manipulation of Cabinet business on the lines set out in Mr Heseltine's resignation statement' (Mount 1992: 119).

In any event, there is a degree to which what Mackintosh describes above is consistent with the idea of cabinet government. A Prime Minister requires to be *primus inter pares*, and to hold the powers described above, simply to make his or her cabinet work effectively. The classic statement of this case is Sir Kenneth Berrill's. Berrill, once head of the government 'think tank', the now abolished CPRS, argues that ministers inevitably promote their own departments' views and policies in cabinet, but 'the sum of spending departments' interests can be a long way from adding up to a coherent strategy'. The Prime Minister's role is therefore to be the guardian of the overall strategy (Berrill 1985: 246–247). To fulfil this role, the Prime Minister must have the powers necessary to co-ordinate ministers' activities, to remove and promote ministers, to handle the media, and so on, simply to ensure that governments keep to their manifesto pledges and coherent strategies. In brief, to make cabinet government work. Thus it is a mistake to regard the comparative powers of a Prime Minister and cabinet wholly in the adversarial terms which became current during Mrs Thatcher's era. The problem is that the powers which are necessary for a Prime Minister to make cabinet government work also make the cabinet vulnerable to manipulation by a determined premier.

Though Prime Ministers have long since become more than simply the 'first among equals' of Bagehotian legend, their rule still falls short of being 'presidential' in the popular sense. First, they are not directly elected, as presidents are; secondly, directly-elected presidents can often rule without the political support of their legislatures (though in practice a US President, for example, depends on money, legislative and some executive votes in Congress, and especially the Senate). Thus, like Margaret Thatcher and others before her, a Prime Minister can be removed or forced out in exceptional circumstances by cabinet colleagues or by the parliamentary party. Ministers often possess personal support of their own in the party and sometimes the country at large; and, at least in combination, they may have the power to force Prime Ministers to adopt unwelcome policies, as Lawson and Howe made Mrs Thatcher commit the UK more firmly to ERM entry with their *demarche* before the Madrid summit in 1989; and their successors, Douglas Hurd and John Major, finally obliged her to agree to entry (see **p. 130**). Most premiers thus expend a great deal of thought and energy to combating plots, real and imagined. But modern Prime Ministers in either of the major parties can generally rely on the backing of their parliamentary parties, at least during a Parliament. 'Whether the direction is right or wrong, the Conservative Party usually follows its leaders, until it gets rid of them,' as Ian Gilmour notes; 'Even after Munich, the Edenite group amounted to only 25 out of over 400 Conservative MPs and Winston Churchill's "party" consisted of three' (1992: 37). Labour's MPs are more loyal still.

The presidential parallel is also misleading in a significant sense. In liberal democracies, the powers of presidents are formally limited by the rules of the constitution. There are scarcely any constitutional limits on the powers of a British Prime Minister; as the political writer Simon Jenkins observed, Mrs Thatcher observed 'few constraints beyond the rudiments of parliamentary procedure and the Parliament Acts governing elections' (Jenkins 1995: 9). Formally, presidents can take far more decisions on their own authority than a British premier, who must generally pursue decisions through others. On the other hand, under normal circumstances, a Prime Minister in command of a parliamentary majority generally exercises considerably more *de facto* power to rule over his or her own domain than a French or US President. The Prime Minister exercises that power within the loose constraints of what cabinet colleagues and the parliamentary party will tolerate; an American president's power to rule is limited by the doctrine of the separation of powers between president, Congress and the Supreme Court. And though not directly elected, leading a party to electoral victory gives any Prime Minister a measure of democratic legitimacy which most are ready to exaggerate.

Richard Crossman maintained that as the machinery of government increased in size, the Prime Minister must become more powerful, being at 'at the apex' of a highly centralised political machine and an equally centralised and vastly more powerful administrative machine (Bagehot 1993: 51). However, the sheer size and complexity of this machinery actually eclipses the Prime Minister's own resources. It is common-place to argue that the development of the Prime Minister's Office and the Cabinet Office have increased the premier's powers within the government machine. But they are no substitute for a dedicated department for the Prime Minister alone, such as those which serve prime ministers in Australia and Canada. Advisers to Mrs Thatcher and John Major – Ferdinand Mount, Sarah Hogg and Jonathan Hill – insist that a Prime Minister's own staff is 'tiny' by comparison with the rest of government (let alone political leaders elsewhere in the world). Under John Major, Hogg and Hill counted about 100 people working in the Prime Minister's office, of whom about 30 were senior officials and advisers. Six private secretaries in a crowded Private Office handled the daily flow of business from departments, fixed meetings, took minutes, provided briefings, and transmitted Major's 'wishes around Whitehall' (Hogg and Hill 1995: 22). Hogg was head of a Policy Unit which contained three civil service 'insiders' and three special advisers ('outsiders'). One of these outsiders, the Political Secretary, acted as a link to Conservative Central Office and as secretary for the 'political' sessions in cabinet, and generally took charge of the party political side of the Prime Minister's work. Major also had a backbench MP as his Private Parliamentary Secretary and a press officer and other miscellaneous officials, such as the Appointments Secretary, and their staff. The cabinet secretary, also now the head of the home civil service, was often in the Cabinet Room or Private Office, but his own office was on the other side of the back door to No. 10 in the Cabinet Office.

The Policy Unit's job was to keep the Prime Minister in touch with outside thinking, to work on his own ideas and to act as a sounding board for ministers, advising on the flow of proposals and counter-proposals that poured in continuously from all around Whitehall. The Prime Minister could use his unit as 'storm troops invading the complacent hinterland of Whitehall; or as peacemakers building bridges between warring departments and Ministers' (Hogg and Hill 1995: 24). The two advisers concluded that:

> At the rough end of the business, dealing with high policy, low politics or the real-life mixture of the two, the heart of government is small. Compared with any Whitehall department, or the offices of heads of government anywhere else in the western world it is tiny. The sheer size of ministerial departments, compared with the Prime Minister's office, creates a healthy pluralism at the centre, but it puts tremendous pressure on Number Ten staff.
>
> (*Ibid.*: 24)

There is of course a much larger corps of advisers in the Cabinet Office. The Cabinet Office has steadily grown in size and influence and taken on more functions since the abolition of the Civil Service Commission in 1991. The Joint Intelligence Committee, the body which co-ordinates the activities of the state intelligence agencies, analyses their data and 'tasks' the agencies, is housed there. The Cabinet Office has also increasingly taken a central role in the 'reinvention of government' and the bureaucracy, taking on the Citizen's Charter exercise, competitiveness policy, and moves towards freedom of information under Major and Blair, among other civil service responsibilities. Its substantive role is as the nerve-centre for co-ordinating and 'reinventing' government at the centre, servicing the critical cabinet committee system and liaising with the governing party machine. Under Mrs Thatcher, Mount maintains, its officials possessed a 'glacial determination to preserve the [Civil] Service's independence and lack of political commitment'; and its separate briefs for the Prime Minister and ministers 'exhale[d] a studied neutrality. . . . Its business [was] to serve the whole of the Cabinet' (Mount 1992: 138). Further, almost every official working in it is seconded by other Whitehall departments; and it is reluctant to assume a policy-making rather than a co-ordinating role since it does not wish to second-guess departments. Of course, the Cabinet Office can always be mobilised to provide a 'Prime Minister's Department' function on any issue which the Prime Minister signals; its intelligence operations are at his or her command; and its co-ordinating role can often serve a premier's interests at the centre. The Cabinet Secretary invariably works closely with a Prime Minister, acts as his or her close adviser, and often as a guardian (see Chapter 11). Even so, Prime Ministers generally lack the resources, expertise and advice to intervene across the board in the complex world of departmental policy-making. Not surprisingly, then, at Downing Street, 'reduced to the tiny staff Britain provides for its Prime Minister, John Major sometimes clearly missed the Treasury corps' (Hogg and Hill 1995: 5).

Part of this weakness of Prime Ministers is that they possess only limited executive resources of their own. They can take most significant decisions, often through their ill-defined royal prerogative powers, and especially so in matters of foreign policy. Through the No. 10 staff and the Cabinet Office they can develop and progress policy initiatives, but they must rely ultimately on departmental resources to carry out the polices in practice. All Prime Ministers, even the strongest, therefore find that proposals dear to their heart may very well be blocked, by either ministers or departments, or both. Harold Wilson's enthusiasm for council house sales could not overcome the hostility of his Environment Secretary and his advisers; James Callaghan wished to follow up his Ruskin speech, responding to parents' concern about standards of education in state schools, with government action, but his Education Secretary was displeased and departmental officials 'made it clear that they were not enthusiastic' about issuing a green paper (Donoughue 1987: 112). Mrs Thatcher had little influence over Peter Walker at Agriculture or Energy and could not overcome his resistance, for example, to privatising the electricity industry; and whatever she and senior ministers might think, 'the gas industry could be denationalised only as a monopolistic single company, because of the influence of its then chairman, Sir Denis Rooke, over Mr Walker. Mrs Thatcher could not by herself compel [Mr Walker] to follow her own preferences; nor did she consider mobilising the will of the Cabinet to coerce him into doing so' (Mount 1992: 140). Mrs Thatcher's ability to press her policies through depended in part on her longevity in office, and in part on her appointments later on of more compliant ministers. Earlier on, Jim Prior insisted on going his own way on trade union reform, and so too did Norman Tebbit later; Tom King proved reluctant to privatise water; Francis Pym protected the defence budget so tenaciously that Mrs Thatcher had to move him to another office; she failed to persuade successive Chancellors significantly to raise the ceiling on mortgage tax relief (the house-owners' subsidy); and the abolition of the rates took her 10 years to achieve.

In other words, cabinet ministers may well be unable generally to impose their collective views on a Prime Minister (though, on occasion, they do; see **p. 136**); but even the most determined Prime Minister cannot readily coerce cabinet colleagues, short of sacking or moving them. Mrs Thatcher was prepared to do both; and her own longevity in office allowed her to gain most of the objectives above, save for a substantial increase in mortgage tax relief. However, her 'handbagging' image is misleading in certain respects; she employed the carrot more frequently than the stick in her dealings with ministers, holding one-day seminars for example at No. 10 or Chequers to consider broad policy matters (e.g. the future of the NHS; agricultural subsidies) to provide ministers with information and ideas in the hope that they would return to their departments 'infused with renewed zeal for reform', or to mobilise a collective will on an issue for several departments (Mount 1992: 142).

The pressure of events and paper batters all Prime Ministers. Harold Macmillan identified 'events' as the great enemy; Harold Wilson confessed after 1970 that his government had been 'blown off course'; Ted Heath's government was torn off course by the miners; Mrs Thatcher was not always able to rise above the turmoil of events; the Falklands War made her more powerful, but it might well have been fatal too. Major's advisers complained about 'the relentless pressure of the timetable in Number 10' (Hogg and Hill 1995: 43). In 1990 and early 1991, for example, the Gulf crisis and war left Major 'very short of time for any domestic issues', but he had also simultaneously to handle five months' intense negotiations over replacing the poll tax – mediating between the Environment Secretary and the Treasury, and chairing the lead cabinet committee, GEN 8, which was split on the issues which arose. By March 1991 the need to resolve the funding of the change from poll tax to council tax in the Budget became acute, and Major had to juggle visits to Moscow and the Gulf with the final decisive meetings in Whitehall. Major was exhausted and under 'the cumulative impact of general tiredness, things began to go wrong. The Prime Minister's schedule had become impossibly overloaded' (*ibid.*: 63–66). It is not to be wondered at that most Prime Ministers succumb 'to the dangers of not pushing hard enough or long enough'; enormous powers are available to a Prime Minister, 'but only if he has the will or the understanding or the support from his fellow members to use those powers effectively' (Mount 1992: 117).

The fact is that there are strong Prime Ministers and there are weak Prime Ministers. The strong dominate their cabinets, the weak rely heavily on the support of senior colleagues. Both types are subject to external pressures over which they have no control, such as trends in the world economy, which may bless them with economic buoyancy or plunge their government into crisis. The vagaries of an unpredictable electoral system might deliver a parliamentary majority of 102 seats over

Cabinet committees

all other parties on 42.3 per cent of the vote (Mrs Thatcher, 1987) or of 21 seats on 41.9 per cent of the vote (John Major, 1992) – differences which have a profound influence on the strength of a Prime Minister's position in the House of Commons. Personalities matter; so does ideology. Major questions, such as Europe, can split a party in government. In short, the loose-knit, unco-ordinated and shifting patterns of power between Prime Ministers, their cabinets and parliamentary parties fluctuate wildly, frequently at the whim of external events. Neither the substance of the office of Prime Minister nor the formal status of the cabinet is defined or established by law. Thus the actual position is left almost entirely fluid by the absence of hard and fast rules about what decisions must be approved by cabinet and what may be settled by the Prime Minister alone or with others. Nevertheless, three conclusions may be reached with certainty:

- A British Prime Minister is a more powerful leader than a mere *primus inter pares*.
- Senior ministers can combine to force Prime Ministers to adopt or abandon policies against their wishes.
- Britain is not governed through a stable and representative system of cabinet government.

The unseen sinews of the body politic

> *A decision by a Cabinet Committee, unless referred to the Cabinet, engages the collective responsibility of all Ministers and has exactly the same authority as a decision by the Cabinet itself.*
>
> (Jim Callaghan, 'A Prime Minister's Minute', February 1978, quoted in Hennessy 1995: 105)

Untangling the balance of power between a British Prime Minister and cabinet is complicated by the existence of a half-hidden cabinet committee structure, below the cabinet, which seeks to co-ordinate government legislation, decision-making and other significant executive activity. Cabinet committees have grown in significance in the shadow of the cabinet to subvert the reality and very idea of government by the cabinet itself. The daily round of the Prime Minister, cabinet ministers and senior bureaucrats, the security services and other state agencies, revolves around the intense round of cabinet committees rather than the actual cabinet. The cabinet committees are formally part of the cabinet, and decisions taken in the committees are as binding on all members of the government as those taken in cabinet itself. And it is within these committees, not cabinet itself, that most of the formal power-broking in the British state occurs; and here the cabinet secretary, Cabinet Office and No. 10 Downing Street also come into the reckoning – linking departmental interests and inputs, preparing agendas and recording decisions, as the central co-ordinating mechanism of the state.

John Major's former advisers describe cabinet committees as 'the unseen sinews of the body politic' (Hogg and Hill 1995: 61). Below the cabinet, this interlocking and highly-developed structure of committees, of varying status and powers, has long been in place to carry out the task which cabinets have failed to perform – dealing in detail with policies, co-ordinating departmental views and holding government together at the centre. The system handles the vast majority of 'government business' and is, in effect, the 'efficient secret' of postwar government in Britain. The current system was developed during the 1939–45 war by the huge wartime expansion of government intervention in all areas of national life (though the first such committee was established in the 1880s; see Chapter 2). Clement Attlee, Labour's peacetime Prime Minister after 1945, retained the committee system set up for the peace-time task of transforming British society and the economy. Attlee employed an 'engine room' of more than 300 committees (Hennessy and Arends 1983). Committees began to divide formally between standing and ad-hoc groups; 244 ad-hoc committees met during the 1945–51 period, only 11 of them more than 10 times.

The key cabinet committees are powerful decision and policy-making bodies in their own right. First, cabinet committees relieve the pressure on the cabinet by settling as much business as possible at a lower level; or failing that, they at least clarify the issues and define points of disagreement. Secondly, and significantly, as John Major's ministerial rule-book, *Questions of Procedure for Ministers*, put it:

> they support the principle of collective responsibility by ensuring that, even though all important questions may never reach the Cabinet itself, the decision will be fully considered and the final judgement will be sufficiently authoritative to ensure that the Government as a whole can be properly expected to accept responsibility for it.
>
> (Cabinet Office 1992: para. 4)

Under Tony Blair the committees play the same role; his *Ministerial Code* emphasises that decisions reached in committees are binding of all members of the government (Cabinet Office 1997: para. 16). In brief, certain cabinet committees at least share parity of authority with full cabinet and possess autonomy in policy-making, even though none of them, by definition, is as broadly based and representative. Cabinet committees nominally report to cabinet, but in practice rarely refer decisions upwards, even though ministers are bound by them. These committees are 'partial govern-ments', often in both senses of the word 'partial', and the decisions they take are as binding on the whole cabinet as any decision taken around the cabinet table itself.

Until May 1992, their very existence – even their titles – was a state secret, as they were regarded as being 'essentially a domestic matter' for ministers, in which neither Parliament nor the public had any legitimate interest. As late as 1978 Jim Callaghan, the Labour premier, argued that this blanket insider's secrecy should be maintained against a growing select committee interest in the system and possible attempts to 'evade the present convention [of secrecy]'. Given that committee decisions often had the same authority as a cabinet decision, he said that 'Disclosure that a particular Committee had dealt with a matter might lead to argument about the status of the decision or demands that it should be endorsed by the whole Cabinet' (Hennessy 1995: 103–105).

Cabinet committees

In other words, he wished to protect the idea of 'cabinet government' and the full collective decision-making process against the reality – which is that many cabinet decisions are taken by 'partial governments' and do not come to full cabinet for decision, or even approval. To his credit, John Major finally dispensed with generations of Whitehall secrecy by releasing basic details of the permanent cabinet committee structure in May 1992. But, as we shall see, his openness was only partial and preserved the essence of Callaghan's concern. The actual operations of all the committees, the sites of decisions, the roles and even the existence of ad-hoc or special committees, remained a closely guarded secret. Major's own version of *QPM* ruled that:

> The internal process through which a decision has been made, or the level of Committee by which it was taken, should not be disclosed. . . . Decisions reached by . . . Ministerial Committees are . . . normally announced and explained as the decision of the Minister concerned. . . . Collective responsibility requires that . . . the privacy of opinions expressed in . . . Ministerial Committees should be maintained.
>
> (Cabinet Office 1992: para. 17)

Blair's code concurs. To all intents and purposes, then, the cabinet committee system is an invisible layer of government.

Officially, there are only two levels of committee, full ministerial committees and sub-committees (which all report to full committees, and hence do not have the 'last word' on issues). However, a more realistic analysis of the cabinet committee structure under John Major revealed four different types of cabinet committee included in the Cabinet Office's listing, and two significant pointers to how powerful committees are. First, small committees are more powerful than big ones; and secondly, cabinet committees consisting wholly of cabinet ministers are the most powerful. The political scientist, Patrick Dunleavy, ranked committees in the following order according to an 'influence score':

- First, the small full OPD committees and the Intelligence Services Committee, all chaired by John Major; the larger economic and domestic policy and its sub-committees; and home affairs.
- A second rank of the full committees handling domestic policy, mostly chaired by non-departmental ministers; and the committee which handles legislation.
- Third, the three sub-committees of the OPD (covering Europe, Eastern Europe and Terrrorism) and two more important domestic sub-committees which have multiple cabinet members.
- The fourth rank consists of the remaining domestic policy sub-committees which include only a single cabinet member. These sub-committees have generally been set up for symbolic purposes, to demonstrate that government takes a given set of issues seriously, rather than to handle politically important business.

Anecdotal comment suggests that overseas and defence (OPD), economic affairs (EDP) and home and social affairs (EDH) are the most important standing committees, through which the major decisions of government are taken (with the legislation committee an important outsider). Ministers in the Thatcher era were especially keen to sit on the economic committee or one of its principal sub-committees; 'if they did not, then they feared they might be considered not to be in the mainstream of political life' (Seldon 1995: 139). We have already discussed the relative powers of the Prime Minister and cabinet ministers. Cabinet committees form the nexus of all major decision-making and cabinet ministers spend at least a day a week working on the committees which matter to them. They are therefore the site of intense ministerial activity, especially on the heavyweight committees:

> Ministers . . . appreciated that, in trying to win the key arguments, timing, the support of the appropriate chair, the position of items on the agenda, and prior lobbying of attenders, were critical. Clever ministers cultivated the important relationships, which could include the chief Cabinet Office civil servant responsible for the committee.
>
> (Seldon 1995: 139)

One purpose of Dunleavy's influence score was to measure the degree of influence of the Prime Minister and ministers within this all-important arena. Dunleavy shared out the influence scores for committees shown above among committee members, with a bonus for chairing committees, in recognition of the chair's power to set agendas and influence committee discussions. (Dunleavy's formula for assessing the influence of the different committees and his methodology are set out in Rhodes and Dunleavy 1995: 304–309.) Here we record the 'influence score' of the four heavyweights of any cabinet, as it stood in 1992, and the total score for other ministers combined:

Minister	Committee influence		Committee status	
	Weighted score	*% of total scores*	*Places*	*Chairs*
Prime Minister	256	14.9	9 + 0	9 + 0
Foreign Secretary	155	9.0	10 + 2	0 + 2
Defence Secretary	138	8.0	9 + 2	0 + 0
Chancellor of the Exchequer	110	6.4	9 + 4	0 + 0
Total: top four	659	38.3		
All other ministers	1060	61.7		
Total	1719	100.0		

Source: Adapted from Dunleavy 1995a: Table 13.2
Notes:
In 'places' (column 3) the first figure shows committee memberships, the second sub-committee memberships. Column 4 ('chairs') follows a similar format for chairs of committees or sub-committees.

The table demonstrates the high level of influence a Prime Minister has within government, owing to his or her chairing role on the most powerful committees.

Manipulation of committees

The Prime Minister had more than 100 points more than his three most influential rivals, the Foreign Secretary, Defence Secretary, and the Chancellor of the Exchequer. In turn, the four cabinet heavyweights ranked considerably higher than any other ministers – the Home Secretary, their nearest rival, had 82 points. There is clearly an arbitrary element to Dunleavy's calculations, but they do provide a relatively transparent counter-balance to the subjective assessments of the balance of power between Prime Ministers and ministers of the politicians themselves, academics, and journalists on which we generally rely. At the least, they throw analytical light on the cabinet-committee system and the real power which lies within it, and add an extra dimension to understanding ministers' powers to influence government decision-making.

Unpicking the cabinet committee structure

As we have seen, cabinet committees 'support' the principle of collective responsibility. Clearly this is the case at least in so far as they reflect the general balance of power between ministers and their departments on certain key strategic policies, and allow ministers to thrash out agreed policies in areas in which their departments have a legitimate interest. However, they are not necessarily even broadly representative of the weight of opinion within a cabinet, and their composition can readily be manipulated by the Prime Minister. As in the early years of Mrs Thatcher's premiership, they can be used as instruments to keep significant policy areas – in this case, macro-economic policy – out of cabinet. Prime Ministers can pack a committee with allies, or exclude cabinet colleagues who are not, to obtain the results they desire. Senior ministers, too, can avoid discussion of their policies. For example, Lord Carrington, as Foreign Secretary, disliked bringing foreign affairs business to the cabinet's Overseas and Defence Committee (and as a result the Falklands issue scarcely figured on the OPD agenda before the Argentinian invasion of the islands in 1982) (Hennessy 1989: 313).

Further, Prime Ministers can always establish ad-hoc committees which may be used to pursue their own policy objectives within a sympathetic arena, or to becalm proposals they do not like, or simply to defuse a potentially difficult issue. Their existence remains a state secret and other cabinet ministers can be kept as much in the dark as the public. Every government employs such committees to deal with crises, new policy proposals and other current business. Clement Attlee used 244 ad-hoc committees, all bearing the designation GEN, during his premiership; and they often conducted highly-significant business, separately from the cabinet, as GEN75 (set up in 1945) and GEN163 (1947) did in developing Britain's atomic capacity and the atom bomb. Mrs Thatcher tackled a 'swathe of high-level business in ad-hoc groups' which fell outside the Cabinet Committee Book (Hennessy 1989: 313). She employed nearly 300 ad-hoc committees, designated MISC, including committees to find ways to free industrial enterprise (MISC14), to defeat a coal strike (MISC57) and develop government policy on AIDS (Hennessy 1997). One such ad-hoc committee was set up in June 1982 to consider the vexed questions of the rates, local government spending and structure, which led to the abolition of the Greater

London Council and exercises in rates limitation. Two MISC committee meetings in 1985 took the decisions which effectively committed her government to the poll tax. In the case of the poll tax, the committee proposals did come to cabinet for approval, but far too late for them to be altered by open and collective discussion (see below). But often the whole cabinet is kept ignorant of what these ad-hoc bodies decide, let alone Parliament and the public. Decision-making in secret committees also means that major policies may be developed and confirmed, either confining consultation to specified outside interests (see Chapter 10), or without consulting outside interests which may have valuable experience or knowledge to contribute.

In 1986, there was a rare exception to the rule of secrecy. The existence of an ad-hoc cabinet committee on AIDS was first disclosed in an *Independent* scoop, but ministers decided that it was in the public interest (as well as their own) to inform the public what measures were being taken and shortly afterwards the Social Services Secretary briefed the media on the outcome of a committee meeting even before the cabinet secretariat had time to type up the minutes (Hennessy 1989: 359). It is not entirely coincidental that the poll tax was a 'policy disaster' whereas the government's AIDS policies may be adjudged a success.

Mrs Thatcher's innovatory style of command subverted important permanent committees with secret ad-hoc groups. For example, she established an ad-hoc economic committee on market-sensitive issues, such as exchange rate policy, which was kept confidential from members of the permanent economic committee. This caused an embarrassing incident in her first term. One cabinet minister, rather slow to collect his papers after an economic affairs committee had ended, heard Sir Geoffrey Howe, then Chancellor, launch into a paper on the abolition of exchange controls. 'Oh, are we going to do that?' the minister asked. Embarrassed silence. Then Howe said, 'X, I'm afraid you should not be here' (Hennessy 1989: 313).

Mrs Thatcher also flanked the committee structure with other ad-hoc groupings, multi-lateral committee meetings and seminars, sometimes with senior officials present, which allowed her to clarify her mind and often to prepare a caucus ahead of full meetings of cabinet committees and cabinet itself (Seldon 1995: 140). These could take the form of lunch or a full day at Chequers; and it was at a full-day seminar at Chequers in March 1985, attended by nearly half the cabinet, that (in Mrs Thatcher's words) 'the community charge was born' (Thatcher 1993: 648). Or they may be very small ministerial meetings, like the one she employed to dish Michael Heseltine's proposals for inner-city investment following the riots of July 1981. In other words, a privileged shanty town of policy bodies was thrown up around the walls of the formal cabinet committee structure.

Other routes of policy-making which tend to bypass the committee structure have grown since 1979. 'Can-do' ministers have asked the Prime Minister, or Deputy Prime minister, to set up ad-hoc groupings of ministers, or have established them themselves. Ministers have decided that it is enough to persuade the Prime Minister of the value of a policy initiative, with little consultation of other affected ministers. This is part of the phenomenon of 'can-do' ministerial politics (discussed more fully at **pp. 166–167**). Christopher Foster states that 'These routes might be followed with varying degrees of formality: for example, civil servants might or might not be present to take minutes. When minutes are not taken different participants may have different recollections of what was agreed, a recipe for further muddle' (Foster 1997: 5). Under Major, the apparatus Mrs Thatcher modified to fast forward conviction policies was used to get through quickly and poorly conceived policy initiatives – 'conviction politics . . . turned all too often into spur-of-the-moment politics' (*ibid.*: 3). There has also been a vast increase in correspondence on policy issues between ministers and their civil servants.

Cabinet committee meetings used to be shadowed by regular interdepartmental meetings of officials, which prepared and clarified the issues and co-ordinated departmental interests and views. But these shadow committees fell victim to Mrs Thatcher's impatience with the civil service and most were left in limbo. Very few now meet, though the official committee on Europe – a key body – remains active. As a result, the co-ordination of government policies through cabinet committees has become weaker and the Treasury, as the single department with which almost all policy proposals must be cleared, is almost solely responsible for co-ordinating government policies – albeit largely from a spending perspective. As officials maintain a looser co-ordination, and recording of decisions is weaker, ministers are freer to interpret decisions and present them publicly in their own way. The aims both of effective and accountable government are undermined. Reviewing these changes in governing practice, Sir Christopher Foster comments, 'Confusion over what policy is adversely affects the executive operations of Government and its agencies' (*ibid.*: 9). Further, collective policy-making becomes more uncertain and the idea of collective responsibility more remote.

A democratic appraisal of the cabinet committee system

There was clearly a need to shift cabinet business to committees as government became increasingly large and complex. Government business must be efficiently processed and dealt with. From a democratic perspective, however, decision-making in cabinet committees has pushed government in Britain towards the creation of more 'partial governments' in two senses: first, the real power to decide issues is invested in more restricted groups of decision-makers than the cabinet; and second, these decision-makers are (potentially) more biased – because they will be more selective in what they take into account, and less broadly 'typical' of government as a whole in their values or experiences. On occasions, ministers have been deliberately chosen, or excluded, by a Prime Minister simply because their views correspond, or do not, with what he or she wants out of a committee. Some cabinet committees have been set up solely for the purpose of securing the 'right' outcome.

It is significant that no-one has publicly justified cabinet committee government in terms of *improving* the quality of decision-making. For to do so would breach the consensus view that collegiate cabinet government is the highest form of democratic decision-making; and that we in Britain still benefit from (to quote Lord Hailsham) 'one of the permanent gifts conferred by British political genius on the science and art of civilised government' (Hennessy 1995: 98). The growth of the extended committee system is perversely justified, therefore, simply as the means of ensuring that full cabinet discussions are reserved for the most 'important' or strategic decisions. There are two major problems with this argument. First, 'important' and strategic decisions are exactly those decisions where the pre-structuring of options and outcomes, already introduced by multiple layers of committee work, means that a full cabinet is highly unlikely to be able to countermand the impetus already built up for a particular decision.

The most spectacular recent example of this is the poll tax, on which Mrs Thatcher, as Nigel Lawson confirmed, 'observed the proprieties of Cabinet Government throughout' (1993: 561). This scrupulous attention to proprieties finally ensured that the full cabinet discussed the poll tax only after 15 months of work and more than seven months after the key decision of principle had been taken by a key committee. It was too late for re-thinking or dissent; and the cabinet 'merely rubber-stamped' a draft green paper which had actually been endorsed by a cabinet committee (Butler *et al.*: 1994: 191–192). Further, as we have seen, 'important' or strategic issues are very rarely settled in full cabinet; and tend to go there only in special cases – e.g. when a Prime Minister needs to bind the whole cabinet to a politically sensitive decision. They are actually decided in cabinet committees – and increasingly, outside them too.

There is a second reason why the existence and importance of the committee system is rarely articulated. It would imply that an appropriate apparatus for making the committees publicly accountable for their decisions and policies should be in place. No mechanisms for public evaluation of the committee process currently exist. Cabinet committee work lies within the government's policy core, which is protected by a steel ring of secrecy (see **p. 368**). A cabinet committee's role in decision-making is kept strictly secret and most decisions are ascribed to the relevant departmental minister. Commons select committees investigating a policy decision must always then ask the departmental minister who is formally responsible to give evidence; and committee members must then make guesses at the extent to which what the minister enunciates as 'policy' has been decided within the department, or was agreed by a cabinet committee, or was settled elsewhere. Neither select committees nor MPs in general debate can question the chair of the relevant cabinet committee about the logic of their final decision, the arguments considered, or the other options available.

The argument that the secrecy surrounding the role of cabinet committees in policy-making protects the free ebb and flow of internal government discussions has little contemporary force. Official secrecy does not prevent elite 'insiders' with political or administrative access or working with officials within 'policy communities' from closely following and seeking to influence legislative proposals and official decision-making (see Chapter 10). Instead it excludes the opposition and political 'outsiders', including almost all MPs (usually including ministers not directly involved) and the general public, from being able to scrutinise or influence what is going on. Thus a core executive dominated by cabinet committee decision-making compounds the imbalances of British constitutional arrangements.

AUDIT

The cabinet is not the centre of the policy-making and decision-taking in the British state. Nor is it even the forum in which the major strategic decisions of government are taken. Prime Ministers have usurped the position of the cabinet, but though they possess considerable powers, they cannot realistically be said to act as presidents. As Mrs Thatcher's experience in office showed, even the strongest Prime Ministers are not necessarily free of all restraint by cabinet or at least the most powerful cabinet ministers, nor are they necessarily able to impose their will on cabinet ministers. Yet the parallel with presidents does throw into relief the paradoxical fact that the power of most presidents is limited by constitutional rules, whereas scarcely any legal rules constrain British premiers. At the same time, cabinet ministers and their departments remain powerful policy-making actors in British government which, as we shall see in detail in the next chapter, remains essentially a federation of departments in its structures of power.

The implicit promise of the idea of 'cabinet government' – that it provides the political base for orderly, reasoned and non-arbitrary government in the absence of constitutional rules governing executive conduct – is not realised in practice. It is, however, strongly argued that cabinet committees represent the continuation of cabinet government by other means. In such arguments, the committees are regarded as an integral part of the cabinet – and thus of 'cabinet government' – which support the principle and practice of collective responsibility. Peter Hennessy celebrates the principle of 'collectivity' as 'the superglue' which bonds full cabinet and cabinet committees together under 'the daily sanction of constitutional impeccability bequeathed by history or the "*cake* of custom", as Bagehot would have put it' (Hennessy 1995: Chapter 4). But it is only in a purely formal sense that cabinet government could be said to remain in place. It plainly does not exist in the practical or 'representative' substance of the idea of collective responsibility – cabinet simply isn't the governing, nor even the coordinating body in modern British government.

We discuss the idea of collective ministerial responsibility fully later (Chapter 12). Suffice it to say here, Hennessy's superglue only imperfectly binds cabinet and its committees together under the reassuring rubric of 'cabinet government'. The potential value of cabinet government lies in a process of deliberation and decision-making by a body of people who are broadly representative of the majority party elected into the House of Commons by the public. Partial governments through formal committees (and other informal bodies and routes), open to manipulation by a Prime Minister and individual ministers and binding unseen on a full cabinet, fail to live up to that broader aim. The umbrella of cabinet government is cast over more than formal cabinet committees. As we have seen, Lawson stated that Mrs Thatcher 'observed the proprieties of cabinet government' throughout the process of adopting the poll tax; yet, as David Butler and his colleagues observe:

> a parallel set of informal forums played a critical role in the evolution of the policy ... all were outside the regular cabinet structure, often dovetailing awkwardly with the formal structure. ... It is often observed that the power

of the Prime Minister lies in his or her ability to control the agenda of meetings. An equally considerable power is his or her ability to control the forum
in which decisions are taken.

(Butler *et al.* 1994: 191–195)

This scepticism seems rather distant from the ideal of Lord Hunt's representative
'shared discussion and shared decision' and suggests that cabinet government has
proved a less permanent gift to civilised government than Lord Hailsham realised.

The idea of cabinet government, secured by collective responsibility, does however
remain important to governments in a lesser sense – implicit in John Wakeham's
assertion in 1993 of the cabinet's importance 'as the cement which binds the government together'. This is a tribute not to any higher representative or constitutional
role for the cabinet and collective responsibility, but to the simple political need to
keep a body of cabinet ministers together, through all the differing views, ambitions
and aims which a body like the cabinet contains and which continually put government under strain from within. The cabinet does hold government together; and
collective responsibility is indeed the superglue or cement which makes that possible.
But it is largely a political mechanism by which, in practice, a cabinet can sustain
its capacity to command the support of its majority in the House of Commons. As
the Major government's local difficulties over the single European currency displayed,
a cabinet at odds with itself over policies will generate or at least intensify divisions
in the parliamentary party. But collective responsibility, as currently defined, does
not provide either broadly representative deliberation in full cabinet on critical
government policy issues or decisions, nor does it ensure that policy decisions are
fully considered, effective in their results, or made with 'constitutional impeccability'.

In terms of the Audit's criteria, the failure of government in Britain to live up to
the ideas implicit in the idea of cabinet government and collective responsibility has
the following consequences.

DAC7: Openness of government

Government policy-making up to 1997 has remained essentially closed from public
view within the government's own code of access to official information. The secrecy
attached to the cabinet committee structure, and even less accessible ad-hoc and
other policy-making arenas, compounds the general refusal to make key policy options
and advice public (though certain corporate interests are made privy to policy
decisions within these structures, at the executive's discretion).

DAC9: Parliament's powers of scrutiny

The complexity of policy-making within the core executive, divided as it is between
formal and informal 'partial governments', and the secrecy within which policies are
prepared, severely constrains the ability of cabinet, let alone Parliament, its members,
select committees and agencies (e.g., the National Audit Office) to keep the executive
under effective scrutiny.

DAC11: Arbitrary government

While most of the powers ministers possess are statutory, and are thus limited to varying degrees, the Prime Minister and ministers also exercise prerogative powers which are not strictly defined. All governments require an element of discretionary power to govern effectively, but they are usually defined in a constitution. We demonstrate that, in the absence of formal and transparent rules of conduct for Prime Ministers, ministers and cabinet business generally, the political constraints within the executive are not sufficient to prevent arbitrary conduct by a determined Prime Minister or ministers. Those rules which exist are neither transparent nor effective. Foster, indeed, argues that Mrs Thatcher's manoeuvres to prevent her cabinets or the civil service from obstructing her policies 'amount to a change in the constitution, if that is judged to embrace the rules by which the Executive operates' (Foster 1997: 2). But changes of this kind are scarcely observable; may be made at the whim of a Prime Minister; and do not require public approval (**DAC6**). The principle of collective responsibility fails to ensure that there are internal limits on the conduct of Prime Ministers and their cabinet colleagues and that they are governed by transparent procedures that provide safeguards against arbitrary government.

DAC15: Public consultation

Policy-making through committees means that certain interests and the public generally are not consulted on proposals until it is too late to have any effective influence on them. It is true that some interests will not only be consulted, but will be well-briefed by departmental officials on what is going on in committees; but others, like the local authorities and their associations during the progress of the poll tax through committees, are deliberately kept in the dark, generally with Parliament, MPs and the general public.

7   Ministers and Mandarins

The powers of ministers, bureaucrats and their departments

Ministers are Kings in this country.
(Nevile Johnson, *In Search of the Constitution*, 1977)

By the mid-1990s the Treasury's patronage and culture permeated government as never before.
(Simon Jenkins, journalist and author, 1995)

Paradoxically, one of the elements of government which subverts any hope of holistic cabinet control are the ministers who stroll like chums before the TV cameras along Downing Street and come together within the Cabinet Room. Traditionally, they co-ordinate the government's policies and decisions and act as a final court of appeal on disputes. In practice, they represent their departments' and their own agendas, policies and needs, which do not necessarily coincide with those of the government as a whole, still less with those of other (often rival) ministers and departments. Ministers work more closely with their own permanent secretaries, private office, advisers and officials than with their cabinet colleagues.

Moreover, ministers' departments may be compared to icebergs of power. Below the surface of ministers, mandarins and high politics, as it were, lie departments with their own powers, resources and interests, and the paraphernalia of 'partial governments' within their spheres of power and influence – executive agencies, quangos, advisory bodies, regulatory agencies, public corporations and other semi-official organisations, plus the networks of organised interests, professional associations, and pressure groups. The significance of departments in British government is often overlooked. The fact is that central government in this country is 'a federation of departments'; and departments are the key policy-making institutions for most government policies (see below); and the powers, resources and policy-making role of departments all lie within the domain of ministers.

In Chapter 6, we reviewed the capacity of ministers to act collectively as a body, to assert the principle of collective cabinet government, and to check or block a Prime Minister or departmental minister from a democratic perspective. We concentrate in this chapter on the flexible and informal nature of governing arrangements at the centre and the significance of key institutions of power – most obviously, the Treasury, but also the Cabinet Office and No. 10 Downing Street. We consider also the role of the security and intelligence services – a significant player in the political life of the country. We analyse the powers and influence of ministers and senior civil servants in relation to each other, their own departments and other ministers and departments. We examine in particular the phenomenon of 'can-do' ministers in recent cabinets; issues of political control of the bureaucracy; the idea that senior civil servants act as Platonic guardians of the decencies of government; allegations that senior bureaucrats obstruct ministers and policies endorsed by the electorate; and, in turn, that ministers have 'politicised' the higher civil service; have required civil servants to perform political tasks; or have bullied bureaucrats into not giving honest advice, or have simply ignored advice, contrary to their own code of conduct. Thus, this chapter continues the scrutiny of accountability within cabinet government, extending it to the link between cabinet ministers and the senior bureaucracy. We do so on the same basis as in Chapter 6: if democratic accountability is defective or lacking within central government, it is less likely to be realised outside it. We examine the efficacy of the conventional rules of conduct more fully in Chapter 11. Here we deal with political realities using the rules as guidelines which complement our own democratic criteria.

Our main concern here is with the actual political processes within government, since in the absence of a written constitution and statutory or common-law rules for conduct in government, the task of ensuring that government is not arbitrary, oppressive or politically (or personally) biased depends a great deal on the part that ministers, senior bureaucrats and departments play in those processes. In brief, then, this chapter considers the democratic implications of an informal, powerful and highly centralised way of governing, applying the following Democratic Audit criteria:

DAC7. Public access to independent information on government policies and their effects.

DAC8. Ministerial control over the non-elected executive.

DAC9. Subjecting the executive to parliamentary scrutiny.

DAC11. Subjecting the executive to the rule of law and transparent rules of conduct.

We go on in Chapter 8 to consider the creation of new executive agencies within government; the deployment of appointed public bodies, known as quangos, their role in government and accountability; and the need to give certain public bodies a measure of 'arm's-length' independence from the executive.

The power of government ministers

Ministers in Britain possess considerable powers in their own right. The cabinet, as such, hardly exists as a legally constituted executive body. Departmental ministers, as Ministers of the Crown, hold almost all the legal authority of government in their hands. Ministers possess prerogative powers in varying degrees, and it is to ministers, not the cabinet or even 'the government', that Parliament gives the far wider-ranging statutory powers of action. They possess countless statutory authorities to act and virtually every new Act they pass gives them more powers to add to their traditional non-statutory prerogative powers of action (see **pp. 389–393**). A single Act, such as the Education Act 1988, can give a minister as many as 400 new powers. Most of these powers are in fact deployed by officials on behalf of departmental ministers (who also specifically delegate certain powers and responsibilities to junior ministers; Theakston 1987). In practice, the exercise of these powers may never involve the individual attention of any minister, and legally, the courts regard the individual decisions by officials using these powers as decisions of the minister (the 'Caltrona doctrine'; from *Caltrona Ltd v Commissioners of Works*, 1943). However, it is important to understand that officials derive their legal powers of action from and through their ministers, not the other way round.

The powers of departmental ministers outside their departments are enhanced by the resources of their departments; within their departments, they are constitutionally sovereign. In both spheres they can count on the backing and advice of Whitehall's 'mandarins' – the departments' senior officials. These experienced senior civil servants are as conscious of their ministers' political needs as they are of their departments' longer-term interests and they devote their considerable gifts and resources to smoothing their ministers' progress. The power of ministers is further enhanced by the fact that their departmental civil servants, from the mandarins at the top down-wards, are directly accountable to them, and only indirectly to Parliament through them (though, in the role of accounting officer, a permanent secretary or agency chief executive is directly responsible to Parliament; see **pp. 323–324**). Thus, minis-ters can control what senior civil servants say in Parliament or in public, and can time or withhold the release of information to suit their own needs. In crises like that over the leaked report on unhygienic slaughterhouses in February 1997, minis-ters may even order their officials to brief the mass media against fellow ministers (as the Scottish Secretary Michael Forsyth did). This sort of practice has survived the change of government.

Senior ministers, then, possess formidable powers of autonomy. Formally, Prime Ministers and cabinets can only encourage or discourage ministers in their course, and their senior bureaucrats can only advise them. None can instruct a minister. As we know, a Prime Minister can dismiss or move a defiant minister, but must usually await a reshuffle. A Prime Minister can try to browbeat a minister face-to-face, but even Mrs Thatcher rarely drew her handbag on a recalcitrant colleague. The characteristic method of communication between a Prime Minister and ministers is routinely *indirect* – through private secretaries and in correspondence – so that he or she should not seem to order a colleague about. The pressure is there however – Nigel Lawson described it as 'creeping bilateralism' (Lawson and Armstrong 1994: 443). But strong-minded ministers can act with real independence. They enjoy considerable room for manoeuvre and command considerably more resources within their domain – and thus, as Mrs Thatcher's former adviser, Ferdinand Mount, says, 'proportionate advan-tages in argument' – over the Prime Minister and cabinet. Ministers also benefit from the informality which has never given the cabinet a legal role. There are no set rules about what decisions must be approved by the full cabinet or in committee, and what may be settled by individual ministers, singly or after consulting other ministers who may be affected. It is true that ministers must bargain with their colleagues over the priority to be given rival pieces of legislation, but they possess almost full control over the contents of their departmental legislation.

Ministers, of course, vary greatly in their exercise of power and influence, which normally reflects the comparative weight of their department in the Whitehall hierarchy (see below). The autonomy of senior ministers in charge of powerful departments, like the Chancellor or Foreign Secretary, is potentially very great, but varies with their ability, their standing in the parliamentary party, and so on. On the other hand, a Prime Minister almost invariably takes a close interest in strategic economic policy and foreign affairs. Thus, Mrs Thatcher was regarded as the true architect of economic policy while Sir Geoffrey Howe was Chancellor. But not so when Lawson took command at the Treasury and developed an economic strategy for three years after 1985 which utterly contradicted Mrs Thatcher's prevailing beliefs. When Mrs Thatcher finally found the right occasion on which to bring him to heel in March 1988, two irreconcilable policies were run in harness, her priority being largely to follow the market and keep interest rates down, his (while publicly accepting hers) to maintain the stability of sterling. Politically, Lawson was too weak, even after his immensely popular 1987 Budget, to get his own way; and she could not sack the Chancellor who had contributed so much to electoral victory in the same year. An acrimonious – and public – gridlock ensued. Finally, Lawson resigned and set out his view of the proper relationship between a Prime Minister and cabinet minister in his resignation speech:

> For our system of cabinet government to work effectively, the Prime Minister of the day must appoint ministers whom he or she trusts and then leave them to carry out the policy. Whenever differences of view emerge, as they are bound to do from time to time, they should be resolved privately; and, whenever appropriate, collectively.
>
> (HC Deb, 31 October 1989, c208)

For all the element of special pleading here, Lawson's is the classic view: politically as well as legally, ministers should possess a high degree of autonomy, to be tempered in the final event collectively. Thus, the political culture too reinforces the position of ministers.

Ministers are not created equal. Within Whitehall, for example, the Chancellor's power over cabinet colleagues, bolstered as it is by the Treasury's pre-eminence among departments, is considerable. Any policy initiative of an Education Secretary, Health Secretary, or most other ministers usually has resources at the heart of it, and here the Treasury's writ runs. The Treasury's agreement is vital to getting the policy off the ground. When Chris Patten inherited the 'poisoned chalice' that was the poll tax from Nicholas Ridley in July 1989, he at once saw that the £33 billion grant for local government for 1990–91, the first year of the poll tax, was too low to cushion the blow. Immediately he asked Mrs Thatcher for an extra £2 billion in that year. The then Chancellor, Nigel Lawson, was furious and 'summoned Patten to a dressing-down at No. 11'. After an ill-tempered meeting of a cabinet committee, Patten received only a £345 million relief package over three years, most of the relief falling in the second and third years. A bitter Patten told a friend at a party afterwards: 'I've been screwed: until I came to this job, I had no idea what a bastard Nigel Lawson was, nor how powerful the Treasury is' (Butler *et al.* 1994: 143).

Michael Howard emerged as one of the most powerful members of John Major's cabinet and probably as the most powerful Home Secretary of recent times. He skilfully rode popular fears of crime and his powers of initiative were redoubled by the credible political challenge from the Labour opposition in the 1990s. Yet any Home Secretary has an inherent power of autonomy, according to Hugo Young:

> Uniquely among ministers, the Home Secretary is lord of his terrain. He has political licence no other minister can match, if he wants to use it. What tethers most other governmental work is either economy or diplomacy – or both. . . . The Home Office lives in a different world . . . policy often costs nothing up front and can be declared by a bold minister after little or no consultation. This is what happened with the 27-point manifesto with which Mr Howard announced himself a crime-buster at the 1992 Conservative Party conference. The first that John Major heard of most of that was when he listened to it on the platform, yet it committed the collective to new policies based on nothing more persuasive than Mr Howard's own prejudices.
>
> (*Guardian*, 29 October 1996)

Whether Young's analysis is right or wrong, and whether Howard's ascendancy depended more on Major's political weakness than the inherent autonomy of a Home Secretary, Howard's four-year reign at the Home Office did display an independence of action which can lie within reach for senior ministers in certain circumstances. Howard, by internal accounts, had his own policy views and pressed them through against the 'departmental view' of the Home Office and the advice of his civil servants:

> Expertise and experience is what they [civil servants] are paid to deliver. But Mr Howard soon showed his disdain for what they had to offer . . . within six months of going to the Home Office, he was the subject of an unprecedented complaint by under- and assistant-secretaries in the policy field, who notified their head of department that they were being ignored and humiliated. Stories of ministerial contempt were legion, and if the stream has now abated, it is only because officials have long given up expecting anything better.
>
> (Hugo Young, *Guardian*, 29 October 1996)

It was not only cabinet colleagues who were unprepared for Howard's 'crime-busting' conference speech. The proposals had been drawn up by Home Office officials and costs discussed with the Treasury without the Prison Service being informed at all;

as Brian Landers, the service's financial chief recalls, 'The biggest prison building programme in modern history was proposed, costed, planned and decided upon without any consultation with the agency'. The policy package arrived at the agency only after the speech was delivered. At once agency officials found that the figures were not robust (one being simply wrong) and that a deviation by Howard from his brief could very easily add substantially to the costs, though 'nobody yet knew precisely what he [Howard] meant' (Landers forthcoming).

The arbitrary nature of a minister's powers is, however, perhaps most vividly illustrated by the allegation that Howard was ready to press his wife's views on officials too. This may or may not have been the case. What is certain is that Derek Lewis, the former prisons director, wrote in his political memoir and informed the ITV programme *World in Action* that he was taken aside in early 1994 by Howard's political adviser and shown a 'his and hers' list of proposals for a code of conduct for prisons. Mrs Howard's were 'housekeeping suggestions', querying 'too generous' standards proposed for hygiene, laundry and nutrition in meals for prisoners. Lewis said that he accepted some changes on hygiene and laundry standards, but refused to cut the nutrition code (*Observer*, 23 February 1997; see also Lewis 1997: 117–118). Howard issued a 'limited denial', but his former adviser refused to deny the allegations. Of course, Howard could be and was overridden over policy issues, as for example on Dunblane and the Cullen report, where Howard's (and the Home Office's) attention to the gun lobby lost out to the Scottish Secretary's concern for public opinion – and his parliamentary seat – and Howard was obliged to ban some 80 per cent of handguns.

Icebergs of power in Whitehall

It would be a great mistake to regard government departments and their senior officials solely as resources at the disposal of ministers. The main government departments have established views and interests of their own, and senior officials naturally seek to defend them. As the former Labour minister, Shirley Williams once put it:

> they have banners to defend on which the departmental traditions and ortho-
> doxy are emblazoned like fading regimental colours in a cathedral – and
> these are defended against all-comers whether they be pressure-groups, select
> committees, international organisations, or other ministries.
>
> (Cited in Hennessy 1989: 380)

She ought also to have said, 'against ministers', as Robin Cook has, for example, been discovering at the Foreign Office since May 1997 after promulgating ideas of 'ethical' foreign policy which ran against the established departmental view. Departments are the key policy-making bodies in central government, its front-line administrative units, and the focus of most of the policy process (see Smith *et al.* 1995: 38–60). As Sir William (later Lord) Armstrong, the former head of the civil service, explained, 'The first thing to be noted about the central government of this country is that it is a federation of departments' (Armstrong 1970: 63–79). This remains true, even after the shock treatment of the Thatcher revolution (see Chapter 8). This uneven federation holds much of the real power of government, as senior departmental civil servants, and their executive agency chiefs, are actually responsible for the great majority of ministers' policy-making activities and have delegated to them a vast range of discretionary ministerial powers. Departments are also, of course, the main channels through which the policies of the core executive as a whole, and departmental ministers individually, are carried out. Thus they both initiate and maintain their own policies and implement those of their political masters. They are the buckle between politics and administration.

Taken as a whole, departments and their satellites form the formidable machinery of central government. As the UK is a unitary state, no lesser democratic authorities interpose themselves between the central state and citizens of the home countries and regions of the UK. In the localities, local government exists, but it has no separate constitutional authority or protection, and may be made or re-made as central government wills it. Central government thus not only makes the major policies and decisions within the core executive, but also makes hosts of other policies and decisions throughout the departments, executive agencies, quangos and other public bodies. The policy-making and decision-taking powers of departments and their associated public bodies are not bound by a constitution nor by a body of general administrative law. Their authority and activities are in fact fuelled by the wide-ranging discretionary and statutory powers of ministers, and thus benefit from the celebrated flexibility of the British governing system. It is true that the courts have limited powers to prevent the unlawful use of these powers (see Chapter 15); and the Ombudsman service protects citizens from 'maladministration' – a shadowy notion which falls far short of a developed canon of principles for open and accountable administration (Lewis and Birkinshaw 1993; see also Chapter 14). Some 73 administrative tribunals also exist to hear appeals against specific administrative decisions, in the public and private sectors. But generally the highly centralised, informal and flexible nature of government in Britain means that no intermediary bodies exist to cushion the impact of the powerful machinery of central government on communities, industries, localities, professions and services, and so on, and on the lives of ordinary citizens. It is therefore vitally important that this machinery should be under open and accountable democratic control.

Government departments at the centre of power

Even during the hectic years of the Thatcher governments, under an interventionist Prime Minister and (some) 'can-do' ministers, departments remained the central units of policy-making, as they do now. While Prime Ministers, ministers and the core executive settle 'heroic' policies and decisions, the great majority of routine policies and decisions are made by officials in central departments, agencies and quangos (see Chapter 8). These decisions may or may not have the express approval of ministers, but even when they do, it is normally at a purely formal level. They do not engage the attention of cabinet ministers, unless they are suddenly sucked into the vortex of political controversy for one reason or another. As the Scott Report showed, officials made most of the running on interpreting the 'Howe guidelines' and the licensing of arms and arms-related equipment for export to Iraq and Iran in the 1980s, generally involving only junior departmental ministers even when critical decisions were made necessary by the Iran–Iraq ceasefire; on occasion officials took decisions on which they kept ministers in the dark (Scott 1996: paras D3.1–3.65). The regulation of hygiene standards in abattoirs in the 1990s and the official investigation of 'Gulf War Syndrome' among those who had served in the 1990–91 war were routine departmental business – but then, the BSE and *E Coli* crises, and the campaigning activities of veterans' organisations, revealed the significance for ordinary people of the officials' decisions and thrust the departments' handling of such issues ingloriously into the adversarial political arena.

So routine departmental business matters. It can at times be literally a matter of life and death. But for most people most of the time most of the government decisions which shape their working, economic and social lives are taken by officials working within government departments, and the executive agencies, quangos and other state agencies which cluster in their shade. These unheroic, but important, 'partial governments' in the government machine remain within the core executive's empire, but usually carry on their business outside its attention, though at any point they may attract it.

It is an untidy empire. The structure of central government in the UK is informal and unsystematic – a historical patchwork continuously adapted and re-adapted to meet new political fashions and expediencies. Departments and ministries are born, named and re-named, merged and unmerged, and occasionally die. Public bodies, quangos and agencies may be established by 'a mere answer in the House, a memorandum from the minister to himself, a wave of the hand, or whatever else may signify a decision to establish a new body' (Barker 1982: 7). In the flexible tradition of Britain's governing arrangements, governments can make up 'central government' as they go along and leave it in a state of flux and inconsistency. One academic observer, Grant Jordan, wrote to the Cabinet Office in 1993 for guidance through the confusion. An unnamed official confirmed for him the 'pragmatic' nature of British arrangements in the following terms:

> Sir Ivor Jennings once wrote that, in the absence of general provisions regulating administration, 'there is, in law, only a heterogeneous collection of ministers, officers, and authorities, exercising a mass of apparently unrelated functions'. Confronted by this situation, Jennings concluded that it would be wrong to assume that there is a specific number of homogeneous entities called Departments of State. . . . It is a complex area where there is, in law, no generally applicable definition of the term 'government department' *nor is its use standardised for everyday purposes.*
>
> (Jordan 1994: 13)

A similar 'pragmatism' is visible even in the staffing of the civil service. It is neither necessary nor sufficient to work in a 'department' to be a 'civil servant' – central government is equally unclear about the basic definitions of either term. Being

pragmatic ourselves, we have identified a central core of some 20 major departments which could be readily found on any list for central government since the
war – though they did change from one administration to another. Under John
Major, there were 19 core departments – 17 of them headed by cabinet ministers,
plus the Law Officers' Department under the Attorney-General (who was not a
cabinet minister in 1997) and the Lord Advocate's Office. The Treasury's pre-
eminence was reflected in the fact that it had two cabinet ministers and the growing
significance of the Cabinet Office's co-ordinating role earned it three cabinet ministers, including Michael Heseltine, the deputy prime minister. (The Prime Minister
had a place in both – the Treasury, as First Lord of the Treasury and the Cabinet
Office, as minister for the civil service.)

It is important to stress at this point just how powerful certain core departments
are within the core executive and government as a whole. As we saw above, the
Treasury stands at the centre of policy-making and public spending decisions in
Britain. It exercises a continuing influence over the policy-making of the core departments through its hegemonic role in the government's public spending reviews. It
has an effective veto over plans which seem to it to be too expensive and its support
for other policy initiatives can be vital. Treasury officials deny that they have policy
priorities of their own, but they certainly have an input into the policy formation
of departments and play just as significant a co-ordinating role in Whitehall as
officials from the department which is there to co-ordinate, the Cabinet Office
(Dowding 1995a: 118–122). If there is an overall corporate presence in Whitehall,
pulling government together, it is the Treasury. The Foreign Office has taken on a
new lease of life, as the department responsible for co-ordinating the government's
– and all departments' – relations with and within the European Union; and the
Cabinet Office has a corporatist and reforming role, seeking to create a more open,
responsive and coherent civil service within the traditional constraints of ministerial
responsibility, executive flexibility and policy secrecy.

The Labour Prime Minister, Harold Wilson, used to complain that the one institution he should have nationalised was the Treasury, but that no Prime Minister
had been able to. 'Mrs Thatcher tried hardest and came nearest to success', Simon
Jenkins records, because she needed it; only through the Treasury could she trans-
mit her power directly through the organs of government (Jenkins 1995: 17).
Mrs Thatcher notoriously appointed her own advisers to give her advice independent of the Treasury and her Chancellors, but at the same time she required its
co-operation to gain her overall objectives. Similarly, she struggled to counteract the
independent views and policy-making of the Foreign Office, especially over Europe,
appointing the official Charles Powell to provide counter-arguments and advise on
her policy responses and speeches.

Jenkins's study of centralisation in government under Mrs Thatcher identifies
the core 'institutions of governing power' which became the principal agents of the
further centralisation of power after 1979 – No. 10 Downing Street, the Treasury,
the Cabinet Office and Whips' Office. They all increased their influence over the
government machine in the 1980s, and that process has continued. Indeed, the signs
are that a further concentration of power among these core institutions has been

taking place under the ambivalent duopoly of Tony Blair and his Chancellor, Gordon Brown, and their key aides, ministerial and otherwise, in the current Labour government. Both Jenkins and Leo Pliatsky, a former mandarin, regarded the Treasury as the principal enabling agent of the Thatcher revolution and of the greater grasp of power at the centre which took place under her regime (Jenkins 1995: 17–18 and Chapter 12). The principal beneficiary was the Treasury itself, which imposed a stringent 'cash-limit' regime over not only Whitehall spending, but also policy-making. The first years of the Blair and Brown regime have been notable for the Treasury's continuing hegemony over both.

The intelligence and security agencies

One powerful set of agencies usually escapes attention, largely because they are rarely publicly involved in policy-making.[1] These are the security and intelligence agencies which exist to serve the 'core executive':

- *MI5*, which is responsible for countering espionage, terrorism, subversion and 'serious crime', and protecting public utilities (air, rail, gas, etc.) and key industries (defence contractors, civil nuclear power, oil, etc.) in the UK;
- the police *Special Branch*, often known as MI5's 'foot soldiers', who assist MI5 and seek to safeguard 'public order';
- the *Government Communications Headquarters (GCHQ)*, which listens in to long-distance telephone, telex, fax and radio communications on selected targets. Its product is intelligence;
- the *Secret Intelligence Service (MI6)*, which provides foreign intelligence and seeks to safeguard and enhance British foreign policy and defence objectives, security and economic and major commercial interests;
- the *Defence Intelligence Staff (DIS)*, which works closely with MI6, concentrating on analysis of the military capabilities of foreign powers and their capacity for nuclear, chemical and biological war;
- the *Special Air Service (SAS)*, which is responsible for special operations in wartime, but also has a peacetime role as the military arm of MI5. The SAS has been deployed in Northern Ireland and Gibraltar, and in both deployments has been accused of 'shoot-to-kill' operations;
- the *armed forces*, which are traditionally used to provide essential services during strikes and may be drafted into action by government to deal with 'urgent work of national importance'. One of the achievements of the British political tradition has been the integration of the armed forces into the machinery of civilian government; and we generally leave aside questions of their accountability in this book. Historically, the record has been superior to those of other European states, but there have also been disturbing aspects of conduct and attitude in their domestic deployment and fatal incidents – e.g. the discriminatory attitudes

[1] Information in this section is based on a briefing paper for the Democratic Audit by Richard Norton-Taylor, Security Editor of the *Guardian*.

rife among troops in Northern Ireland and the fatal shootings of 14 unarmed men on 'Bloody Sunday', 30 January 1972.

The Joint Intelligence Committee (JIC), an arm of the Cabinet Office, is responsible for assessing and analysing the information the agencies collect, notably MI6 and GCHQ, and for distributing reports to Whitehall departments, the Bank of England, large private banks and corporations. The JIC draws up 'wizards', weekly assessments of significant intelligence, for the Prime Minister and ministers and also sets specific 'tasks' and priorities for the agencies. Its members include the heads of MI5, MI6, GCHQ, DIS, senior officials from the Treasury, Foreign Office, Ministry of Defence and Home Office, and the government's intelligence co-ordinator (who produces annual reviews of intelligence requirements and allocates resources). JIC is backed up by some 50 assessment officials and intelligence groups of officials, sometimes seconded from other Whitehall departments. Its activities largely focus on foreign threats to British interests, foreign policy and major international issues of all kinds, including organised crime. But it is also in charge of liaison with foreign intelligence services, notably in the US. JIC is part of the Cabinet Secretary's key responsibilities; both Sir Robert Armstrong and Sir Robin Butler took a 'hands-on', and protective, interest in its work and the activities of the agencies. The Cabinet Secretary chairs the Permanent Secretaries Committee on the Intelligence Services (PSIS) which fixes the expenditure of the agencies, subject to ministerial approval. The senior bureaucrats of the Treasury, Foreign Office, Home Office and Ministry of Defence sit on this influential committee. Thus, although JIC and the agencies are of course ultimately responsible to the Prime Minister, for all practical purposes the security and intelligence network is a powerful and unaccountable arm of the permanent government.

Between them, the agencies employ some 10,000 staff at home and abroad (not counting the Special Branch in Northern Ireland). These agencies have at their disposal the most sophisticated and intrusive technology and discretionary powers of operation wider than those of any other organ of the state, including the police. The scope of their activities is loosely defined by undefined terms, such as 'national security', 'subversion', 'serious crime', and the statutory controls are designed to leave them with wide discretion. MI5 officers are 'self-tasking' and may covertly target individuals and organisations, like trade unions or civil liberties bodies such as Liberty, which are engaged in lawful activities in search of 'subversion', outside any independent control or accountability. MI5 at least probably has access to computer data throughout central government (it advises Whitehall on IT security). GCHQ also targets British citizens, as the Intelligence Services Commissioner revealed in 1996 after repeated government denials; has a capacity to intercept communications greater than that of MI5 and the special branches combined; and evades domestic law and guidelines designed to protect people's privacy through a deal with the US NSA agency, which has listening posts in the UK. Dennis Mitchell, a senior GCHQ official who resigned in protest against the 1984 trade union ban there, described it as 'an industrial complex' whose product was 'intelligence': 'Intelligence is power. Intelligence shared is power shared; intelligence withheld confers power over the unaware. GCHQ provides power to the British government and governments with which it is allied.'

After expressing his concern about the dangers to civil liberties in GCHQ's activities to the then Cabinet Secretary, Sir Robert Armstrong, Mitchell was served with a court injunction to prevent him from disclosing anything about the agency's work.

Until recently, the security and intelligence agencies operated with utmost secrecy within the realm of the royal prerogative, for (as Lord Hailsham admitted) they were, 'by common accounts, commonly doing which can't be justified in law', and so could not be given statutory or parliamentary approval. But a series of scandals forced governments into action. The revelations of the former MI5 officer, Peter Wright, in *Spycatcher* gave inside information on the attempted subversion by MI5 officers of the elected Labour government under Harold Wilson and other political malfeasance. Wright's account also included vivid accounts of how he and fellow agents 'bugged and burgled our way across London at the state's behest, while pompous bowler-hatted civil servants in Whitehall pretended to look the other way' (1987). Further, the flagrant absence of legal and political controls and redress in law, condemned in two judgments by the European Court of Human Rights (ECHR), finally obliged governments over the period 1985 to 1996 to place MI5, MI6 and GCHQ on a statutory footing, define their functions and provide for rudimentary rights of appeal. (For a fuller account, see DA Volume No. 1, Chapter 12; for analysis of the new arrangements, see Chapter 14.) The governments acted partly out of fear of further embarrassing ECHR rulings against the British government. But the facade of legality was also erected as a shield against demands for a full independent inquiry into MI5's past activities and a more open and accountable framework for the future.

As is well known, Mrs Thatcher's government went to extraordinary lengths to seek to suppress *Spycatcher*, but crucially failed in the more open nations of Australia and the US. However, no independent inquiry was held into these and other equally serious allegations which raised the prospect of officers in the state's own security agencies seeking to subvert democratically elected governments and the lawful political activities of trade unions and other organisations in civil society. Ministers have consistently refused to hold such an inquiry: Douglas Hurd, a former Home and Foreign Secretary, for example blandly rejected the idea, saying 'The past is another country'. But, in effect, the security and intelligence services themselves continue to be 'another country', which even Prime Ministers and ministers cannot, will not, or dare not penetrate. They are, of course, formally accountable to ministers: MI5 and the Metropolitan Police's Special Branch to the Home Secretary, other police special branches to chief constables and police authorities, and thereafter to the Home Secretary, and Northern Ireland, Scottish and Welsh Secretaries; GCHQ and MI6 to the Foreign Secretary; DIS and the SAS to the Defence Secretary, JIC and ultimately the Prime Minister. Ministers take formal responsibility for the agencies' operations, signing the warrants which legitimate continued 'bugging and burgling', but they are almost as much in the dark about the agencies' actual activities as anyone else. Like Wright's 'pompous civil servants', they prefer to look the other way. Other western democracies – the United States, Canada, Australia, Norway

– held inquiries into the activities of their security and intelligence agencies after revelations about their irregular conduct, and then enacted vigorous democratic controls upon their future activities. In Britain, ministers endorsed a glossy MI5 charm offensive in the media, finally allowed Parliament strictly limited oversight and erected statutory defence works which legalised executive control and approval of the agencies' activities within a quasi-judicial framework designed to satisfy the ECHR and to prevent the British courts from interfering (see Chapter 12).

Finally, a point about 'effective' government. Our concern about the security and intelligence services derives principally from the fact that this network is an arm of the executive which is barely accountable to the executive and open to none. In the past, files have been marked, 'Not for Ministers' eyes' or 'Not for National Audit eyes'. But there is also the question of its effectiveness. Friendly ministers argue that its successes cannot by their nature be publicised. But what is on the record is not encouraging. For example, the Franks report on the Falklands crisis found that press reports of Argentina's intentions were more accurate than intelligence reports and criticised the lack of awareness of DIS and JIC officials (Franks 1983). The Scott Report revealed that crucial MI6 and GCHQ intelligence reports were withheld from ministers, on occasions deliberately, lost, left lying in cupboards, or just forgotten. Both William Waldegrave, a Foreign Office minister at the time, and Lady Thatcher gave evidence that they had not received critical intelligence reports. Other ministers, including Alan Clark, did not mind missing reports because they did not contain significant or illuminating material, and a senior diplomat said tartly, 'Intelligence is a very imprecise art'. Finally, MI6's goals ran counter to publicly declared government policies on Iraq and Iran (Scott Report 1996: paras D8.4–15).

The loose federation of government departments and agencies

Outside the powerful core of the state bureaucracy, a great variety of government departments and agencies exist. Official and authoritative sources publish for their own purposes differing versions of just how many there are; and even where they broadly agree on a total, they do not necessarily list the same ones. We can briefly give a flavour of the confusion and size of central government. For the Ombudsman, in 1996, there were 31 departments, for the Table Office in the House of Commons, 22 (including the Royal Household). The *Civil Service Yearbook* gave details of 64 departments, ministerial and non-ministerial, and listed in its index 412 'Departments, Next Steps Executive Agencies and Other Organisations'. On the finance side, some 520 accounts were examined by the Comptroller and Auditor General. We found 67 'government departments' which were listed as such in two or more standard sources in 1996. Some of the 67 'departments' amounted to little more than a letter heading. Overall, they form a significant and heterogeneous group of executive bodies with discretionary powers and policies of their own, such as for example the Advisory, Conciliation and Arbitration Service (ACAS), HM Customs and Excise, the Export Credits Guarantee Department, the Forestry Commission, the Registry of Friendly Societies, HM Inland Revenue, the Office of Passenger Rail Franchising, and the Serious Fraud Office. Other similarly powerful bodies, like the British Waterways

Board and Civil Aviation Authority, are nationalised industries and yet others, like the Commons Commissioners, are classed as tribunals.

The range, varying status and complexity of 'departments' raises obvious problems for the principle of ministerial responsibility. Research in the 1970s showed that departments in British government were 'far from perfectly "ministerialised"', and in the official list of ministerial responsibilities in 1977, only 24 of 60 'departments' listed were said to be directly under ministerial control. All the rest were either under ministerial control at a remove, or were in practice relatively autonomous bodies (Hood *et al.* 1978: 25). In 1995, the official list named 23 cabinet ministers, and identified 21 ministerial departments and a further 22 non-ministerial departments. One of the reasons that the Treasury was initially opposed to the *Next Steps* devolutionary process (see Chapter 8) was that its senior bureaucrats feared that they would lose financial control over their spending, especially capital expenditure, and staff pay and conditions. But an early agreement, negotiated by the Cabinet Secretary, kept Treasury controls in place (Jenkins 1995: 232–241). Thus, there is one core institution which maintains a real degree of control, almost certainly damagingly so – the Treasury.

Otherwise, in the absence of across-the-board rules, central government in Britain exhibits what is often described as 'mad empiricism', governed by considerations of political expediency, 'where just knowing how to "work the system" is an esoteric skill, a badge of belonging, and a political asset'. Formal conventions, governing say what constitutes a white paper, how consultation exercises should be organised, or precisely what areas of government ministers are publicly responsible for, are as various observers have found, very hard to discover and may even be secret. One set of observers complained:

> It is a common sentiment that 'informal' rules and practices are more interesting and significant in administration than the formal rules – whatever *they* are. But in British central government . . . the formal rules often seem to be much harder to discover than the informal process of 'what actually goes on', so that one has no real foil or backdrop for 'what actually goes on' stories. Some people . . . see the confusion as a conspiracy, a process by which the bureaucracy cunningly covers its tracks.
>
> (Hood *et al.* 1978: 20–21)

The informal structures of government, the absence of clear rules and the autonomous nature of many public bodies raise other unresolved issues of accountability. The decisions that such bodies take independently often raise important and controversial issues of public policy. In the case of the prosecution role of Customs and Excise, quite properly independent of government ministers, serious abuses have taken place, as in the Matrix Churchill and other criminal cases which arose out of the sale of defence equipment to Iraq (Scott Report 1996: paras K4.6–4.15). But such also are the flexible powers of ministers that, if they choose to intervene, they can erode the institutional independence of public bodies or sanction activities which are quite outside any genuine scrutiny and unbound by transparent rules governing their conduct, interests, and so on. For example, under recent Conservative govern-ments, chairmen were appointed to nationalised industries with an explicit brief to privatise them and were expected to carry on as chairmen of the privatised com-panies, often with a substantial rise in salary and financial benefits. The British Steel Corporation (BSC) acted as the government's agency in restructuring the steel industry, undertaking negotiations in which the role and interests of ministers, the BSC board and private interests could not be distinguished (Harden and Lewis 1988: 171–172).

Overall, then, the machinery of central government has no written rules of oper-ation or conduct, as in most continental administrative-rule countries like Germany. Further, unlike local government, it has no 'easily-defined formal-legal categories of agency' to use as a starting point for information or analysis, or on which to base structures of accountability and openness (see Hood *et al.* 1978: 22). This is largely because the 'federal' model of Whitehall triumphs still over efforts to create a centrally directed or 'corporate' Whitehall. Departmental autonomy reflects the legal fact that it is to ministers, and not to 'the government', that Parliament gives statutory powers and votes funds; and government departments organise their internal structures and public bodies as they or their ministers see fit. It may of course be argued that the traditional federalism of Whitehall is in itself a check on central governmental power, by preventing the accumulation of all powers at a central organising point!

One extraordinary example of the degree of autonomy of departments is the way in which departments were found in early 1997 to be paying private consultants up to £500 an hour to teach them to set up legal tax avoidance schemes, costing the Treasury an estimated £3,000 million a year in lost tax revenues (equivalent to 2p in the pound off income tax). Kenneth Clarke, the then Chancellor, officially wrote to the Lord Chancellor, copying his protest to all spending ministers, complaining that the tax avoidance schemes subverted the government's public expenditure review and a key anti-tax avoidance strategy in his Budget:

> It cannot be right to spend public money on reducing departments' tax liabil-ities where there are not sufficient real-world efficiency gains to justify such activity. Tax advice should not be used simply to increase departmental resources by the back door, circumventing the normal public expenditure survey process, and reducing the Exchequer's tax receipts at the cost to the Public Sector Borrowing Requirement. . . . As you know, the fight against tax avoidance and evasion was a key Budget theme. . . . Increased aggres-sive tax management sits badly with this.
>
> (*Guardian*, 15 February 1997)

Ministers and mandarins – rivals in government?

I don't regard myself as one of the most important chaps in the country, or anything of that sort, because we work subject to the views of ministers of the day.

(Sir Ian (now Lord) Bancroft, then head of the home civil service, on BBC2's *No Minister* series, 14 June 1981)

Ministers and civil servants

The conventions governing the relationship between ministers and mandarins were set out up to our cut-off date, May 1997, in John Major's ministerial code of conduct, *Questions of Procedure for Ministers (QPM)* (Cabinet Office 1992) and the Civil Service Code (see Chapter 11 further). These rules are essentially unchanged by Tony Blair's *Ministerial Code*. The rule-books provide that ministers are ultimately accountable to Parliament for the policies, actions and operations of their departments and agencies; and that:

- Ministers must give due weight to the informed advice of civil servants in reaching policy decisions.
- Ministers must not instruct civil servants to behave improperly or to carry out party political tasks.
- Ministers must uphold the political impartiality of the civil service.
- Senior civil servants must give honest and impartial advice to ministers, even if it isn't what ministers want to hear.
- Senior civil servants must act in such a way as to deserve and retain the confidence of ministers.

These rules protect the traditional relationship between political ministers and the politically neutral officials and departments which serve them. The rules are essential to the proper working of the unique British type of state bureaucracy, which is not structured on a legally-defined basis as on the continent. Mandarins are constitutionally subordinate to ministers, but are supposed to possess sufficient independence, character, ability and experience to be able to advise, warn, assist and influence the politicians who are for a period set over them. Ever since the founding Northcote-Trevelyan report of 1853, civil servants have been encouraged to think of themselves as Platonic guardians of the public interest, say, or as guardians of 'good government'. The advisory role of mandarins has been regarded as a quasi-constitutional buffer, subtly protecting the public from ill-conceived or arbitrary party manifesto commitments or ministerial enthusiasms alike.

It is often argued, then, that there is a built-in tension between ministers, representing the majority party in Parliament, and senior civil servants, unelected representatives of the continuities of the public service. Another more concrete tension can also arise between the manifesto commitments a minister brings with him or her to a department, or the government's general objectives, or the minister's own wishes, and the established policies and interests of the department. Civil servants are ultimately responsible to ministers who, in turn, are accountable for their own and their departments' policies and actions in Parliament (**DAC9**), but not all ministers are able to impose their will upon a department.

After 1979, Mrs Thatcher urged her ministers to challenge attempts by civil servants to restrain them. Some ministers were able to take advantage of the powers inherent in their position and her governments produced 'can-do' ministers a great deal more readily than 'can-do' civil servants. Michael Howard's exercise of ministerial power under John Major (see **pp. 155–156**) was an extreme example of this shift in power from senior civil servants to ministers. Mrs Thatcher had come to power convinced that the civil service was a powerful obstacle to change. This was a common view at that time, and several former Labour cabinet ministers' memoirs testified to civil service attempts to thwart their plans or subject them to the department's policy views (see **pp. 168–169**; and Theakston 1992). She wanted to reduce the influence of the civil service's 'permanent politicians' – the senior bureaucrats – and she encouraged her ministers (as Sir Christopher Foster and Francis Plowden, two colleagues at Coopers and Lybrand, explain) to disregard civil service advice and hurry conviction policies into legislation, however imperfect – 'even if early attempts were sometimes botched and one had to try again' (Foster and Plowden 1996: viii–ix). A senior official complained at the time to Peter Hennessy, then reporting Whitehall for *The Times*, that ministers were telling his colleagues, 'We don't want whingeing, analysis or integrity, that we [i.e., senior civil servants] must do as we are told' (Hennessy 1989: 628). Such conduct upset the traditional partnership of ministers and their senior civil servants, set out in the ministerial rule-book, *Questions of Procedure for Ministers*, under which ministers listened to the advice of their senior bureaucrats before acting. Foster and Plowden say that once the urgency which animated the Thatcher regime had gone, this 'conviction approach' was unnecessary, but Conservative ministers continued to dominate the bureaucracy:

> tending to treat civil servants as mere implementers of their policies rather than, as in the old way, partners; and as a result failing to consult widely before legislation; and in so far as they consulted, failing to reflect those consultations in their policy-making.
>
> (1996: ix)

It is too soon to say what approach Labour ministers since 1997 have adopted, but it is certainly open to them also to choose political conviction over the departmental view, and some have already distinguished themselves by openly choosing to prefer the advice of their own political advisers to that of officials.

The influence of the mandarins

The roles of ministers and senior civil servants are generally analysed in terms of their relative power over each other – who actually has the upper hand? But such an analysis tends to distort understanding of the real relationship. Even 'can-do' ministers depend on their departments. Of course, ministers exercise legal authority over their departments and are charged with giving them political direction. Their departments expect this of them. But how effective is their control of their departments, not only over high-profile matters but over departmental policy and practice in general (**DAC8**)? In practice, ministers rely almost wholly on their departments, senior bureaucrats and private offices, and the resources and advice they can provide. Much of a minister's time is devoted to conducting routine departmental business, guided by officials; arguing the departmental 'view' or cause in cabinet committees, Parliament and the media; and protecting departmental interests and resources. Thus departments exert real influence over ministers, who are judged within their department (and to an extent by fellow ministers) on their ability to represent depart-mental policies and interests within Whitehall.

One of the primary roles of permanent secretaries and senior officials is, as stated, to give their ministers impartial and objective advice. This advice will be politically neutral, but it is not necessarily independent of other influences. Generally it rep-resents the policy views which have developed over time in the department and are under the influence of a department's consultations with its network of organised interests, of professional groups, and the other bodies and individuals which all departments regularly consult. Thus the advice ministers tend to receive will be impartial in a party political sense, but normally reflects a department's common wisdom and its distillation of outside interests. In 1964, Labour's new housing minister, Richard Crossman, vividly recorded the subtle pressures inherent in the service and advice civil servants gave:

> The moment I enter [the department] my bag is taken out of my hand. I'm pushed in, shepherded, nursed, and above all cut off, alone. . . . Whitehall envelops me . . . I am somehow alone even at home, because they have begun to insulate me from real life with the papers and the red boxes that I bring home. . . . I feel like somebody floating on the most comfortable support. The whole Department is there to support the Minister. Everything is done to sus-tain him in the line which *officials think he should he should take* [our emphasis].
> (Crossman 1975: 30–31)

In those days, 'advice' could amount to an attempt to check ministers and govern-ments. Crossman, other ministers and insiders in the Labour governments of the 1960s and 1970s all recounted incidents in which senior bureaucrats attempted to block their policies (Haines 1977; Castle 1980 and 1984; Falkender 1983). The civil service was also capable of blocking other initiatives, such as reforms of the service itself after the 1968 Fulton report (Fulton 1968; Kellner and Crowther-Hunt 1980: Chapters 4 and 5). By the late 1970s, Whitehall was widely regarded as an obstacle to radical change rather than a counterweight to passing partisan fancies, and as a major defender of the postwar status quo. Critics of the left and right argued that Whitehall's role and power could undermine or thwart, rather than serve, the purposes of elected governments. On the left, the career bureaucracy became regarded as a 'negative machine'. The abrasive relationship between Sir Antony Part, the permanent secretary at the DTI, and his minister, Tony Benn, figured prominently in the demonising of Whitehall. Benn's diaries express his interpretation of several hard encounters in which Part took issue with his minister's radical policies, often in defence of industrial and other established interests, and also with Benn's concept of acting 'as an educator and spokesman – speaking for people' (see, for example, Benn 1990: 296–298). On one occasion, Part warned Benn that he was acting in breach of his obligations under the ministerial rule-book, *QPM* (for being involved in a trade union report on aircraft nationalisation). Benn's diaries also record an television exchange between Part and Vincent Hanna in which Part seems to glorify Whitehall's tactics of obstruction:

HANNA: Another quotation which has been made about permanent secretaries is they cannot make an unlikely policy become certain, but they can
certainly make an unlikely policy become impossible.

PART: Yes, I think a *number of my colleagues* [our emphasis] have had considerable skills at blocking tackles and leg-byes, and I suppose it is always possible
to put things in the way to the extent that the policy becomes unworkable.
(Benn 1990: 186–187 and 503)

From Part's viewpoint, he and his colleagues were acting in defence of government
policy, which Benn was seeking to shift, sometimes strong-arming other ministers in
the attempt. Benn's real problem was not merely that he did not have the backing
of his permanent secretary, but that he had no backing from the Prime Minister
and cabinet either. Benn's policies ran counter not only to government policies, but
also to the DTI's existing 'departmental point of view'. Benn wished to subvert the
industrial interests on which that departmental view was founded and questioned
long-established policy positions. Part's defence of such interests was strengthened
by Benn's isolation in the cabinet. On the right, the mandarins were also viewed as
adversaries rather than allies. A former adviser to Mrs Thatcher, Sir John Hoskyns,
argued that the civil service could not in its current form implement the policies of
a radical government (Hoskyns 1983).

Of course, ministers have always found it difficult to translate their formal authority
into real power over the bureaucracy: the sheer size of the civil service is a problem;
ministers often move between portfolios much as unsuccessful football managers do
between clubs; as amateurs in government, ministers need the expertise of the professionals (the civil servants). As stated above, well-established 'departmental views'
often shape the advice ministers receive and the policies they are asked to follow.
As Crossman wrote in his minister's diaries, 'One has to be pretty strong-minded
and curious not to be got down by this astonishing Whitehall hierarchy' and, 'There
is constant debate [between the civil servants below] as to how the Minister should
be advised or, shall we say, directed and pushed and cajoled into the line required
by the Ministry' (1975: 26, 31). A later observer, Ferdinand Mount, listed the tactics
of resistance to a radical minister or a policy which the department disliked:

> A little delay, a modicum of obfuscation, a plea for more time to complete
> the research or the consultation or the drafting, and there is a good chance
> that the over-demanding Minister and/or his headstrong government will be
> gone, and the department will be able to breathe a sigh of relief and reflect
> that its delaying tactics were wholly justified in the interests of the smooth
> continuities of good government.
>
> (1992: 147)

Mount's emphasis here is surely correct: the civil service has not employed its obstructive capacities in the cause of overt political views or out of distaste for radical
party political policies, but rather from a more generally sceptical attachment to the

'continuities' not only of good government, but of the status quo in general and of established interests close to departments (see Chapter 10).

Mrs Thatcher changed all that. Her brusque disregard for cautious advice and her insistence on 'can-do' managerial civil servants made them, as the political scientist Keith Dowding put it, 'more manageable by making them more managerial' (Dowding 1995a: 60).

By 1987, the political writer Hugo Young was warning that the senior civil service was in danger of becoming 'a thoroughly Thatcherised satrapy' (*Guardian*, 21 July 1987). His fears proved exaggerated, but it is true that Mrs Thatcher's ministers brought their officials to heel. They were assisted in this success by the impact of three electoral victories in a row, which in part gave ministers the power and time in which to enforce their will; but also, from an official point of view, suggested that they had an electoral mandate for their conviction politics. Equally, the great election victories of 1905 or 1945 both led to active and radical governments, able to insist on major changes in policy, and 1997 has perhaps done so too. In other words, it seems that the senior bureaucracy will accept that politicians possess a genuine mandate for change, even if that mandate was in fact won (as it was on all these occasions) on a minority of the popular vote.

It would, however, be a mistake to suppose that the 'can-do' Thatcher era has reversed the balance of power irrecoverably away from mandarins to politicians. Just as departments themselves remained the prime site of most policy-making during the long period of Conservative rule up to May 1997, so the policy-makers in the higher reaches of the civil service remained in command of their departments' resources and retained the power and influence which flowed from those resources (Dowding 1995a: 15–16). The most important of these resources remains their control of virtually all the information which reaches ministers, especially through ministers' red boxes. Ministers who are likely to be taking up to 50 'decisions' a day are not in a position to query any but a few of the background briefings which accompany their civil servants' recommendations.

Further, the huge range of decisions, taken under ministers' powers but delegated to officials, remains the domain of the mandarins at the top. Thus, away from the spotlight of controversy, permanent secretaries and their senior colleagues possess a day-to-day edge of advantage over ministers. While the most determined and energetic ministers do have a big impact, even they can generally only set broad objectives. The detailed work of policy-making – forecasting the impact of policies, assessing what is possible, costing the various options, conducting negotiations with interested parties, assessing the external constraints, and so on – is something ministers must rely on civil servants to produce. A Prime Minister can be powerful, the electorate may have endorsed the party's broad political aspirations, and ministers may be ambitious to realise them. But it is the officials who draft the papers ministers see, who filter the information they receive, who define many of the problems, who suggest most of the solutions, who draft the legislation and who ultimately take the great majority of decisions (**DAC8**).

A growing practice which attempts to overcome the imbalance – and the comparative isolation in office which Richard Crossman described – is for ministers to appoint political advisers of their own choosing. This practice is one way of affirming the principle of a civil service independent of political affiliations while strengthening a minister's political grasp of his or her department. From a comparative perspective, the British civil service is a special case. 'The line which separates the politically committed and publicly responsible minister from the politically neutral civil servant is drawn at a particularly high level in Britain,' says former mandarin Sir Douglas Wass. 'In practically no other country is there so little change in the administrative apparatus when a new government takes office' (Wass 1984: 45). Whitehall has nothing like the 3,000 political appointees found at the top of the US federal bureaucracy, or the German 'political officials' who carry party cards and are re-shuffled on a change of government, or the well-developed French system of ministerial *cabinets*. From the 1970s onwards, ministers have increasingly brought in politically appointed special advisers, but these are few in number. The Labour government's decision in 1997 to appoint 38 political advisers – a handful more than under the Major government – and to expand the Prime Minister's Policy Unit caused a short-lived fuss, but they were few in comparison with the corps of 626 permanent senior civil service policy advisers and makers.

Moreover, political advisers rarely participate in the administrative chain of command which implements decisions. The impact of political advisers on 'the extremely fragile structure' (in the words of a practising civil servant) at the top where politics meets administration within Whitehall naturally causes concern to officials, but for many outsiders so does the role of senior bureaucrats practising their 'apolitical loyalty' or 'partisan neutrality' in the same zone. But if the aim of democratic control of the state bureaucracy is to be realised, ministers must be given political advice and research facilities to counteract their departments' near monopoly of policy advice and information. The fact is that the 38 political advisers who accompanied Labour ministers into government in 1997 were too few to right the balance.

The relative permanence of senior bureaucrats contributes to the imbalance. Since 1945, ministers in certain significant departments have on average held their portfolios for about two and a half years, not much more than half the tenure of permanent secretaries (see Table 7.1). Further, most permanent secretaries take over departments in which they have already had experience, sometimes substantial, and they all come into the post with considerable all-round civil service grounding. However, it is important not to exaggerate the advantage they gain. Quite a few permanent secretaries have had scarcely any experience in their department and soon move on. Further, cabinet ministers may well have had previous experience of their departments; and the departmental experience of ministers is often underestimated. For example, a third of Mrs Thatcher's cabinet ministers were either promoted from junior posts in their departments or returned to their previous departments. Thus Peter Barberis, author of a study of permanent secretaries, warns that it would be foolish uncritically to attribute 'any decisive explanatory power' to the mandarins' greater continuity in office in assessing the balance of advantage between them and ministers (Barberis 1996: 191–196). Further, while the overall experience of senior civil servants in the bureaucracy generally does give them an advantage

Table 7.1 Turnover of cabinet ministers and permanent secretaries, 1945–94*

Office or Department of State	Secretaries of State, etc.	Permanent secretaries
Chancellor of the Exchequer	19	10
Home Secretary	19	9
Foreign Secretary	20	14
Defence (from 1947)	23	12
Agriculture	17	9
Education	24	10
Employment	24	10
DTI (exc Industry)	28	14
Scotland	17	7

Source: Adapted from Barberis 1996: 196, Table 10.4.
Notes:
* This table is confined to certain significant departments only.
The figures include permanent secretaries already in post in 1945; and where there were joint permanent secretaries, the longer (or longest) serving is counted. Ministers are counted twice when they returned to the same portfolio.

over ministers, it is not necessarily an advantage that they can or wish to press home: hence the loss of institutionalised scepticism in the 1980s and 1990s under the pressure of 'can-do' government.

At the higher levels of policy-making, there are few enough mandarins in Whitehall to make personal linkages practicable so that they are able to agree and formulate common views and policies across departments. In this sense, though central government is basically an uneven federation of departments, a corporate 'Whitehall' view does emerge, especially where the interests of mandarins or the service as a whole are affected. Insiders talk of the 'civil service village' or 'club' (Dowding 1995a: 22; Heclo and Wildavsky 1974; Ponting 1986: Chapter 1). In 1995, there were 48 senior officials at permanent secretary level, 122 at grade 2, and 466 at grade 3. Thus senior bureaucrats are few enough in number to form manageable networks, able to handle collective problems and initiatives, large and small. They may do so in their own narrow interests. For example, in 1985, senior officials smuggled large increases in top salaries through the system by giving the papers a national security classification and keeping them out of sight of Mrs Thatcher's Policy Unit (Fry 1985: 12). But this elite undoubtedly did come to be dominated by ministers during the long period of Conservative hegemony in Whitehall; as the former Prime Minister Lord Callaghan observed, by the early 1990s the senior civil service had become part of a ministerial 'private fiefdom' (TCSC 1993: Q586).

Ministers and mandarins: partners in government

Civil servants are accountable to ministers who are accountable to Parliament, and civil servants support their ministers in their adversarial role in Parliament. They do not prepare them for a reasoned debate on whether the policies are actually right or wrong; they see their job as making sure that ministers are not embarrassed and can answer the attacks on them. People don't realise that you have to regard ministers and senior civil servants together, as a unity.

(Senior civil servant at Democratic Audit seminar, 1995)

This brings us to a crucial point of this chapter from a democratic point of view. The debate over the relative power of ministers and mandarins obscures the most important feature of their relationship. For they are rarely in conflict. Ministers and mandarins are partners in government. Certainly, ministers depend on the experience and resources of the senior bureaucracy, but they can also count on it. For the most part, a reciprocity is at work within a very close relationship. The democratic questions are: does the closeness of the relationship make it more difficult to ensure that either ministers or mandarins obey transparent rules of conduct (**DAC11**); and does it undermine the ability of Parliament to subject the executive to scrutiny (**DAC9**)?

Within the partnership of ministers and mandarins, the mandarin's role is some parts manipulative *Yes Minister* (as in the popular TV series), some parts straight 'Yes minister'. The exact mix depends on the circumstances, the people and the spirit of the times. On occasion, the senior bureaucracy will make policy, ostensibly but not really under the rule of ministers. But Britain's mandarins do not generally seek to direct policy-making, and in the turbulent early 1970s senior ministers, like Douglas Hurd, were bitterly critical of the civil service for its reticence at moments of crisis (Hennessy 1989: 238). Meritocrats they may be, but they are a special kind of meritocrat. They are schooled in analysing and presenting information, in finding forms of words, and so on. But above all they are negotiators, synthesising views and gaining the confidence of their colleagues, outsiders and above all ministers. As one former mandarin explained to us:

> At the very top, you have to build up an atmosphere of trust between you and your minister. To gain the trust of ministers, civil servants become the sort of people, if they are not already, that ministers like to have around them – which means that they are politically and otherwise sophisticated people, with a metropolitan outlook. Working together as a team with ministers, a degree of socialisation is inevitable in the system. What's wrong with that?

Ministers receive a remarkable degree of loyalty and protection from their senior officials. Officials perform very much as medieval squires once did for knights, serving them with ostentatious servility over minor matters, such as ensuring a minister gets the biscuits he or she prefers with coffee, preparing them for battle, buckling on their political armour and arming them with facts, arguments and political calculations for their appearances in arenas like cabinet committee, cabinet, Parliament and the television studio. Officials remain 'neutral' as between parties, but what they give ministers (and what ministers expect) is partiality – advice and information which fits and defends ministers' policy choices. Thus, they in fact perform a *political* function. They seek to protect ministers, to avoid embarrassment, to spot potential trouble, to draft speeches and answers to parliamentary questions which disguise weaknesses or mistakes. It may well be that this tendency is intensifying. Some civil servants believe (as one former mandarin explained) that the mass media have placed ministers under additional pressures to which they should respond:

> partly because of the development of the media, and particularly the electronic media, they are having to answer any question off the cuff immediately. That puts them in a very exposed position. And there are all the difficulties in terms of partisanship, and all that. But it also means they expect a sort of closeness from the civil service which is of a different order from that which ministers have had in the past. That is leading to a cultural change, and may in the end lead to quite significant changes in the civil service.

Former Labour minister Edmund Dell recently complained on BBC Radio 4 about the degree of 'political sensitivity' of senior bureaucrats. In his view, for example, Treasury officials have 'always been far too understanding of political constraints' and the Treasury was therefore often 'very weak' in the advice it gave to ministers, Conservative and Labour:

> PETER RIDDELL (interviewer): Are civil servants trying to be politicians *manques*?
>
> DELL: I myself found repeatedly when I was a minister that the advice I was given was far more politically sensitive than I wanted it to be. My wish often was to take a rather strong line and my civil servants would say, 'Oh, well, that won't go down very well in cabinet!' So civil servants in this country are trained to be politically sensitive and I think they should stick to their last and give ministers strong advice.
>
> (*Week in Westminster*, 30 November 1996)

This is not a *party* political issue. For example, under the minority Labour government of the late 1970s, the head of the civil service believed that 'the officials' job was really to help the Government survive'; under Mrs Thatcher and John Major, they served the cause of Conservative 'conviction' politics; and they will now perform in much the same way for Labour ministers as they did for their Conservative predecessors before May 1997. As the textbooks tell us, Whitehall will loyally serve whichever party wins power. But the civil service is not neutral as between the government and the opposition. Loyalty to the government and ministers in power is the central organising principle, to such a degree as to be partisan, especially in respect of opposition parties in the House of Commons and MPs generally. The civil service back-up – made manifest in the sight of senior officials sitting near ministers in the House – gives the Prime Minister and ministers a huge political advantage over MPs and their opposition counterparts in Parliament (**DAC9**). The civil service is in fact a political prize in the struggle for power between the parties in Britain's 'winner-takes-all' elections. When one party is in power for a prolonged period, the civil service cannot in the long run remain *impartial*, even if it is able to maintain a formal *neutrality*.

It is not simply that civil servants are socialised to serve ministers. As we have pointed out above, they are themselves part of government and are committed to the central imperative, 'Her Majesty's government must be carried on'. William Plowden, a former senior civil servant, has pointed out that civil servants share with ministers a strong commitment to the view that 'one of the main tests of good government is that the will of the executive shall prevail'. The higher civil service, he maintains, 'believes strongly in the right of government to govern'. This 'executive mentality', as he calls it, derives from and reinforces the inadequate day-to-day external accountability of civil servants and their ministers:

> There is a circular relationship between constraints on the powers of Parliament, the courts, the media and other inquisitive institutions, and the Whitehall (ministers *and* civil servants) view of them as nuisances unfit to express an authoritative view about public policies.

Thus Plowden and Tessa (now Lady) Blackstone, his former colleague, conclude that the civil service would not 'necessarily resist actions which the rest of us might regard as arbitrary, unconstitutional or threatening to the rights of individuals' (Blackstone and Plowden 1988: 191–193).

Certainly, the reciprocity and trust between ministers and mandarins is one of mutual interest: ministers and their senior bureaucrats stand or fall together; ministers' own interests and those of the departments, the interests of the state and of the government of the day, all merge into one. Ministers and mandarins have a shared interest in the secrecy which envelops their close relationship; the protection of civil service advice to ministers insulates and protects both government and the senior civil service from informed outside scrutiny. Further, ministers, advised by civil servants, are able readily to manipulate the public release of all official information, including even regular statistical information. Between them, they decide what official information ought to be disclosed and what should not, and when and how, forming 'an unbreakable ring of self-justification' (in the words of Labour MP Jim Cousins). The much-hyped 'can-do' mentality, encouraged by Mrs Thatcher, was not supposed to produce genuinely entrepreneurial bureaucrats, but rather bureaucrats who did not emphasise problems and said 'can-do' to ministers, and above all to Mrs Thatcher. It was this mentality which lay at the heart of the introduction of the poll tax (Butler *et al.* 1994: 209–218).

Servants of the government of the day

This close relationship of ministers and mandarins reflects constitutional theory. In 1985, Sir Robert Armstrong, then the Head of the Civil Service, stated the standard constitutional doctrine on the role of civil servants in his memorandum, *The Duties and Responsibilities of Civil Servants in Relation to Ministers*:

Loyalty to government of the day

> Civil Servants are servants of the Crown. For all practical purposes the Crown in this context means and is represented by the Government of the day. . . . The civil service as such has no constitutional personality or responsibility separate from the duly elected Government of the day. It is there to provide the Government of the day with advice on the formulation of the policies of the Government, to assist in carrying out the decisions of the Government, and to manage and deliver the services for which the Government is responsible.
>
> (HC Deb WA, 26 February 1985, c128–130)

Armstrong went on to spell out the virtually absolute and unconditional duty placed on civil servants to serve ministers loyally, to carry out their decisions zealously, whether they agree with them or not, and not to disclose information in breach of their obligation of confidence. Furthermore, civil servants officially have no identity in public other than their ministers'. Whatever they do publicly is in their minister's name; whatever they say is on his or her behalf.

The immediate context of Armstrong's code was the controversy surrounding the trial and acquittal on official secrets charges in 1985 of the senior defence official, Clive Ponting, after he had leaked information about the sinking of the Argentinian battle-cruiser, the *General Belgrano*, during the Falklands War to Labour MP Tam Dalyell. Thus Whitehall's most senior official was, in effect, ruling out any suggestion that civil servants had a wider responsibility than that owed to government ministers – one to the public, 'the public interest', or even to Parliament. Armstrong's statement inspired public alarm about the implications of equating the interests of the state with those of the government of the day, largely because there was already substantial concern that Mrs Thatcher and her ministers, after two election victories in a row, were hijacking the civil service for their own ideological purposes. In fact, Armstrong was simply re-stating long-standing principles that have always stood at the heart of the civil service's constitutional position. It is a position popularised in the metaphor of the Rolls-Royce, a quiet and efficient machine waiting to be driven by duly elected ministers wherever they wish to go.

The judiciary has always taken the same view. In the Ponting trial, the judge also held that the 'interest of the state' meant 'the policies of the state', and those policies were those of the government (Ponting 1986: 190–191). This long-standing convention of government remains in force today, and creates deep-seated problems for the efficacy of democratic control of government in this country – problems which are reinforced by the steel ring of secrecy around policy advice and the dealings of ministers and bureaucrats. These long-term problems transcend the fears, current in the 1980s, that the Thatcher governments appeared to be turning Whitehall into an instrument of ministers in ways that went beyond or subverted the traditional practices.

The culture of the civil service mirrors its constitutional position. In terms of its own self-understanding and behaviour, the civil service is the creature of the government of the day. It is most definitely *not* part of the apparatus of democratic checks upon the executive. A strong sense of the interests and claims of the state seems almost to be part of the genetic make-up of the higher mandarinate. In the 1950s, Sir Edward Bridges could take for granted officials' concern with 'the continued well-being of the state'. Sir William Armstrong, head of the service from 1968–74, gave it a dual role as 'the permanent service of the state and also the servant of the administration which is for the time being in power'. In the 1980s, Sir Robert Armstrong liked to quote Queen Elizabeth I's injunction to William Cecil to 'be faithful to the state'. The spirit of the former Civil Service Pay and Conditions of Service Code lives on, stipulating that 'the first duty of a civil servant is to give his undivided allegiance to the State at all times and on all occasions when the State has a claim on his services'. Whitehall's equation of the interests of the state with the interests and policies of the government of the day and the secrecy within which it operates strengthens the government's executive power immeasurably against formal constitutional checks from Parliament, opposition parties, or the courts, and against investigation by the mass media. A serving official explains:

> if you want a politically independent civil service that retains the trust of ministers it must be one that, in relationship to the outside world, in Parliament, in dealings with the media, operates very discreetly indeed. The prime object must be never to embarrass the minister. This is the prime distinction between responsibility and accountability. The civil servant can be accountable to no-one except his own conscience and the minister.

By contrast, senior bureaucrats have been said to exhibit a profound contempt for the House of Commons, its adversarial politics and its weakness. Ferdinand Mount, Mrs Thatcher's head of policy, found that, for most civil servants, Parliament was 'an uncongenial place, full of loud-mouthed and frequently drunken ignoramuses, who understand little and care less about the intricacies of administration' (Mount 1992: 106). 'The MP is often seen [by civil servants] as an actual or potential adversary, to be helped as little as possible', according to Peter Kellner and Lord Crowther-Hunt (1980). The fault-seeking attitude of most MPs challenges – and at the same time – reinforces the blame-avoiding culture of Whitehall. Yet, at the heart of government, this long-standing emphasis on serving ministers rather than any wider concept of 'public service' combines with the absence of direct accountability to Parliament and disdain for MPs to create an almost symbiotic relationship between ministers and the senior civil service which evades democratic checks. Nearly 30 years ago, the political scientist A. H. Birch portrayed Whitehall's view of life in a classic essay as a top-down, government-centred perspective – 'the view of the constitution held by those in power'. Civil servants shared a language, or governing code, with ministers (Birch 1964: 165–166). That a former permanent secretary at a Democratic Audit seminar could recoil from the concept of 'popular control' and declare, 'I'm unhappy about this idea', after an explanation of the Audit's key principles, suggests that Birch's portrait remains a genuine likeness.

'Politicising' the senior civil service

Once the borderlines have been destroyed, why would a successor government, with its own wholly essential project, be in any hurry to restore them?

(Hugo Young in the *Guardian*, November 1996)

Politicisation

Given the close nature of relationships between ministers and senior bureaucrats, there will inevitably be worries that partisan trust and loyalty to ministers can slip into politically partisan behaviour which strengthens the government's political powers and makes it harder for Parliament to act as a watchdog on its policies and decisions (**DAC9**). Accusations of improper loyalty and political involvement on the part of senior civil servants have surfaced from time to time in modern Britain. The classic case is that of Sir Horace Wilson, an arch-appeaser, who ultimately became head of the civil service under the pre-war premier, Neville Chamberlain. Wilson went on a personal mission on Chamberlain's behalf to Hitler, accompanied Chamberlain to Munich, and was accused of 'silencing the civil service'. William Armstrong, head of the home civil service under Edward Heath, became known as 'the deputy prime minister' because he was so closely identified with Heath's policies, especially the statutory prices and incomes freeze of 1972. Armstrong believed personally in the policy and finally admitted that he 'must have put a foot wrong' (Hennessy 1989: 85, 238–241). Sir Robert Armstrong, who held the post under Mrs Thatcher, was described by the former Liberal leader, Sir David (now Lord) Steel as 'damaged goods' after his involvement in the GCHQ, Westland and Wright affairs (Chapters 11 and 12), and David (now Lord) Owen condemned him as 'a civil servant who's very much seen as a supporter of the government' (Hennessy 1989: 668).

Mrs Thatcher greatly sharpened the fear that a Prime Minister could politicise the senior bureaucracy – a fear which could even be described as 'the Thatcher syndrome'. Any incumbent Prime Minister has an opportunity to influence – and perhaps politicise – the higher civil service through her or his power ultimately to choose the two top ranks of civil servant – permanent and deputy secretaries. Mrs Thatcher came into office in 1979 convinced that the civil service belonged to the postwar consensus that she was determined to eradicate. In 1981, she abolished the Civil Service Department (CSD) and enforced the early retirement of Sir Ian (now Lord) Bancroft, head of the home civil service who was second only to the cabinet secretary in the civil service hierarchy. Bancroft had seen himself as the custodian of the public service tradition and differed from Mrs Thatcher on several occasions. The immediate effect of abolition was to place control over top civil service jobs in No. 10 Downing Street and the Cabinet Office, since the cabinet secretary, who comes close to being the Prime Minister's own permanent secretary, acquired the parallel role of head of the civil service as well. However, the standard appointments procedure remained in place, as it still does. A Senior Appointments Selection Committee (SASC), consisting of the head of the civil service, half a dozen mandarins and now a token 'outsider', draw up a short list of candidates for all vacant permanent and deputy secretary posts and present it to the Prime Minister, with their recommendations. The ultimate power to decide who should be chosen lies with the Prime Minister.

Mrs Thatcher played a more active role in making such appointments than previous prime ministers who by and large accepted the nominations of the civil service machine. But all the evidence indicates that she did not apply a party political litmus test (Theakston 1995: 29). Instead she looked for dynamic, managerial, 'can-do' types and made personal choices based on her own knowledge of the candidates; and of course her choice was restricted to the candidates chosen by SASC. As head of government for 11 years, she had a tremendous cumulative impact on the Whitehall elite: by 1990 all of the permanent secretaries had been promoted by her to that rank. Formally, the prime minister's powers over the filling of Whitehall's top jobs date back to 1919–20, so there can be no question of Mrs Thatcher acting unconstitutionally. But in the mid-1980s there was an elite fear that she was packing the senior service with Thatcherite sympathisers, and that Mrs Thatcher's test, 'Is he one of us?' was becoming the key criterion for appointment. Sir Robert Armstrong, who sat on the SASC for nearly four years, unequivocally dismissed the idea in a public lecture in June 1985:

> There is no question of political considerations entering into the choice. The Prime Minister ... takes a keen interest in [appointments]. She attaches much importance, as I do ... to skill and effectiveness in management as well as in the traditional role of policy advice. She is not concerned with, and I can vouch for the fact that she does not seek to ascertain, the political views or sympathies (if any) of those who are recommended. ... She wants, as I do, to have the best person for the job.
>
> (Hennessy 1989: 632)

Finally, a special committee convened by the Royal Institute of Public Administration in 1985 sat for two years and cleared Mrs Thatcher on the charge of politicising the higher civil service, but also noted her unprecedented level of interest in top appointments which had become 'more personalised' in the sense that the impression higher civil servants catching her eye made on the Prime Minister – 'in a favourable or unfavourable manner' – had become more important than in the past (RIPA 1987). In the end, all appointments are subjective, but at this level they ought to be made on the basis of clear and consistent rules. There are grounds for objection to appointments being made almost wholly by a group of the most senior civil servants, for that would give them too much power over new generations of civil servants, may channel or narrow the criteria for success at the top, and may over time ossify the service and inhibit change. To give the ultimate power over appointments to a single individual, the Prime Minister, is equally undesirable: he or she may exercise it in a 'personal' or arbitrary fashion and can act neither as an authoritative nor democratic counterweight to the power of the SASC oligarchy (no more than can the single token outsider who now sits on the SASC). Final oversight of the process of appointments ought to rest in the public domain.

Once again, the emphasis which Britain's political culture places on *party political* issues obscures the significance of Mrs Thatcher's conduct. The point is that a subtler and more insidious process was at work, which was made the more dangerous by her longevity in office. In effect, a channelling of the criteria for success in the civil service was taking place. It seemed that civil servants who adopted a 'can-do' approach, either because it came naturally to them or for more opportunistic reasons, were being preferred over more cautious and sceptical colleagues. If such an approach – or any other – becomes institutionalised by politicians, civil servants will tend to trim. As Lord Bancroft put it on television:

the dangers are of the younger people, seeing that advice which ministers want to hear falls with a joyous note on their ears, and advice which they need to hear falls on their ear with a rather dismal note, will tend to make officials trim, make their advice what ministers want to hear rather than what they need to know.

(*All the Prime Minister's Men*, 10 April 1986)

Many contemporary observers believed that this happened under Mrs Thatcher and her ministers. Mrs Thatcher's governments overturned established departmental views across Whitehall and brought about significant and valuable changes in the organisation of government. But they were also marked by ill-conceived and unworkable legislation and it was fitting that the poll tax should in a sense prove to be Mrs Thatcher's nemesis. For not only did civil servants fail to warn ministers of the dangers of their course; instead senior Environment Department bureaucrats appeared to the authors of an authoritative study of the poll 'to have been enthusiasts for the poll tax, and to have under-estimated its effects almost as seriously as did ministers'. For David Butler and his co-authors, the main question arising from their study was:

whether 'activist' civil servants were too closely involved in the evolution – as distinct from implementation – of a highly contentious policy, and whether they should have done more to alert ministers to the repercussions likely to follow from such a hazardous initiative.

(Butler *et al.* 1994: 208–209)

In other words, there is good reason for inculcating values of scepticism and caution in the advice which civil servants owe to ministers. It makes for more effective government.

In reply to fears about the civil service being politicised during the Conservative years in power, Sir Robin Butler, the cabinet secretary and head of the home civil service, insisted that the civil service would be able to serve another government with equal commitment. He demonstrated the official willingness to work under a Labour administration by organising briefings for shadow Labour ministers in the run-up to both the 1992 and 1997 elections. Plainly, it would damage one of the basic features of British democracy should Whitehall have become imbued with a Conservative, or a 'free-market', mindset and thus find it difficult to work with an incoming Labour government. The very idea that this might happen was damaging in itself. But Butler's reassurances meet only part of the concern about the thin line between proper assistance to ministers and party political assistance. The fact is, as we have shown, the relationship between ministers and mandarins is symbiotic and partisan. Given the additional protection of official secrecy, the relationship presents opposition parties, the media, interested parties and the public with a formidable political alliance which is generally unbreakable (though it is sometimes breached by internal dissensions and leaks).

Between them, ministers and mandarins possess powers, resources and information which are inaccessible to opposition spokespersons, select committees and individual

MPs. So Butler's reassurances, important though they were, do not begin to meet the concern about the partisan nature of the relationship between ministers and civil servants and the various calls for clear standards of conduct in government, rules setting out ministers' and civil servants' roles and responsibilities, protection for officials who seek to resist the identification of a party's interest with the national interest and provision for 'whistle-blowing' in cases of improper conduct (see Chapter 11 further).

The boundary between proper and improper political assistance

Mrs Thatcher's long period in office and Michael Heseltine's behaviour as deputy Prime Minister from 1995–97 provoked alarm that the boundary between proper political assistance to ministers and improper party political assistance was being breached. The controversial nature of Mrs Thatcher's policies, her close interest in senior appointments (see above), and ministers' preference for 'can-do' officials raised fears that she, ministers and mandarins were all crossing the boundaries of constitutional conduct. The retiring mandarin, Sir Ian Bancroft, commented wryly that the 'grovel count' among some civil servants was much higher than normal in the 1980s. The top civil servants' union, the First Division Association (FDA), among others, on several occasions expressed alarm that rules of conduct were not being strictly observed.

Alarm of this kind remained a live issue up to the dying days of Major's administration. This is not surprising. The FDA rightly stated that political neutrality in the civil service is in practice 'a very grey area'. Officials are obliged to carry out activities which in effect help the government against opposition parties in Parliament. For example, they prepare ministers' speeches, research the opposition's positions, warn of possible hazards, even cost an opposition's proposals, and so on. Under John Major's government, civil servants complained to the FDA about being asked to prepare briefings for Conservative Party events and responses to speeches by Tony Blair. A civil servant at the Department of the Environment was given 12 hours' notice to check for accuracy a pamphlet issued for the Conservative Party conference in October 1996. In July 1996, the FDA issued a survey which found that more than 20 members out of the few hundred who worked in day-to-day contact with ministers in 11 departments complained that they had been asked to prepare material for manifestos, alter official reports to provide a party bias, and brief on political responses to opposition speeches. Officials were also asked to supply material subsequently used in party broadcasts and to write political speeches when ministers' political advisers were absent. Elizabeth (now Baroness) Symons, general secretary of the FDA, said the results suggested a 'widespread problem' (*Daily Telegraph*, 11 July 1996).

Under the Conservatives, and Mrs Thatcher in particular, one or two career civil servants close to the Prime Minister made their political preferences quite clear. Charles Powell, Private Secretary to Mrs Thatcher and John Major (1984–91), was very closely associated with Conservative policies on Europe and Mrs Thatcher's wishes generally. In October 1991, Duncan Nicholl, chief executive of the NHS

Management Executive – and a grade 1A civil servant – publicly criticised Labour's policy on the NHS; far from being rebuked, he was praised by ministers for 'telling the truth'.

The most notoriously partisan career civil servant, however, was Bernard Ingham, Mrs Thatcher's chief information officer and later also head of the official Government Information Service (GIS). His conduct in government raised questions not only of improper political conduct, but of the independence and impartiality of government information (**DAC7**). Ingham served his mistress in an intensely personal and politically-charged way, which was clearly incompatible with his neutral status as a senior civil servant (Harris 1994). He crossed the boundary into party political territory, for example playing a key role on Mrs Thatcher's pre-election liaison committee, set up in September 1986 to co-ordinate Conservative Party and government strategy and activities. Five ministers and three senior party officials sat on the committee alongside Ingham. Under his regime as head of the government press corps, an information officer at the Department of Employment complained to his union, the Institute of Professional Civil Servants (IPCS), that he and colleagues had been 'put under increasing pressure from ministers to work on projects which at best can be described as favourably disposed towards the government and at worst as blatantly party political'; had been required to write 'articles of a party political nature on behalf of their ministers for insertion in the press'; and had been asked to participate in dubious campaigns, such as Action for Jobs, 'which said little about the Department of Employment services, but much about the Conservative Party's views on unemployment and the unemployed' (Harris 1994: 816–817). The IPCS drew up a draft code of ethics in April 1989 which Ingham refused even to discuss with the union. A civil service mandarin, Sir Frank Cooper, categorised Ingham's concept of public relations as 'biased information' and suggested that his post was 'a political job in a party sense and is not a job which it is proper for a civil servant to fill' (Harris 1994: 721).

Michael Heseltine argued, more generally, that government information officers are in a 'marginally different' position from civil servants as a whole in evidence to the Public Service Committee in 1994. He said that civil servants, in presenting government policies, ought not to 'cross over the frontier that could be concerned with party politics'. However:

> Information officers have, under both parties, been in the position of articulating government policy in perhaps a more committed way than you would expect from the rest of the Civil Service. That they have always done . . . information officers constantly are defending government policy which might be considered political. It is not their job to avoid controversy.

Heseltine added that he would resist the politicisation of the civil service as a whole 'with every strength I possess' (PSC 1996b: paras 65–71). Again, the narrow view of what constitutes 'political' obscures the undemocratic nature of practice. The public require information about public policies and decisions which is independent of the 'government of the day' (**DAC7**); but under both Conservative and Labour governments, it seems, the role of information officers has been to 'articulate' and 'defend' government policies in a 'committed way'. So much so that Tony Blair's press officer, Alastair Campbell, was critical of the inability of existing information officers to 'sell' government policies after 1997 and several ministers replaced their information officers, and Campbell, too, has been accused of being too partisan for a civil servant.

The line between properly partisan and politically partisan conduct is clearly not merely a fine one. It is also very confused and slippery, and very hard to draw with any confidence. Many observers, for example, believe that it is improper for ministers to ask civil servants to cost opposition policies, but it is officially held to be a legitimate activity. What view then should be taken of the attempt by Michael Heseltine, then Defence Secretary, to enlist the aid of MI5 agent Cathy Massiter in the collection of evidence linking the Labour Party to CND before the 1983 election? Should Scottish Office officials have been asked to use the term 'tartan tax' in government briefing documents designed to undermine Labour's devolution plans? During the arms to Iraq affair, civil servants advised ministers on how to get round the guidelines on the sale of defence-related equipment and how best to present policy so as to keep MPs, journalists and the public in the dark; a DTI official wrote a minute, stating, 'There seems to be considerable merit in keeping as quiet as possible about this politically sensitive issue' (*Independent* 23 November 1992). On what side of the boundary does this official sit? During the Scott inquiry, officials assisted ministers in charting the progress of the inquiry, MI5 officers were diverted to discovering what Sir Richard Scott's judgments on the affair would be, and press officials participated in drawing up misleading press packs (see below). Were they legitimately presenting the views of 'the government of the day' or improperly protecting Conservative ministers? Whatever the rights or wrongs of these cases may be, they all show the government machine working normally.

It is because they are taken for granted that political activities which are not directly party political often ring alarm bells. They throw the weight of the powerful government machine in a partisan way behind the political projects of government ministers and obstruct legitimate attempts by Parliament, the media and civil society to render them accountable (**DAC9**). Let us look in more detail at the way in which Whitehall responded to the inquiries of Sir Richard Scott into the 'arms for Iraq' affair and how Michael Heseltine, Major's deputy prime minister in charge of presenting government policies, and Ian Lang, President of the Board of Trade, mobilised the government's response to the Scott Report itself. The report raised issues of an intensely partisan nature for government, the conduct of the civil service, Conservative ministers and their party. The fate of at least two ministers and the good name of the government and Whitehall hung in the balance. Yet the weight of the civil service machine was directed to serve the interests of the government along with those of executive custom.

This battle of Britain between the many (Whitehall) and the few (the inquiry team) began in March 1993 when Scott said that he, and he alone, would decide which evidence would be taken in public and which in camera. The Whitehall fightback, chronicled by *Guardian* writer Richard Norton-Taylor, began as a:

whispering campaign, with smears discreetly dropped into the ears of chosen journalists, mainly from the Parliamentary lobby. Articles began to appear in the press hinting that Scott was hopelessly naïve and that he lacked understanding of the real world of government decision-making.

There were even articles mocking his personal life and habits (Norton-Taylor *et al.* 1996: 32). A team of some 18 civil servants worked for three years in the 'Scott units' of government departments, tracking the progress and conclusions of the inquiry into irregularities and breaches of government policy in the export of defence-related equipment to Iraq and Iran and seeking to penetrate the secrecy that Scott had imposed on draft extracts. On one occasion, a fax from M15 intended for the Cabinet Office, arrived by mistake at the Scott inquiry offices. Headed 'Piecing together the Scott report', the fax made it clear that intelligence agents, officially employed to counter terrorism and espionage, had been spending their time assembling information about the judge's report (*ibid*.: 30). Behind-the-scenes rows ensued over the way in which the report was to be published and a senior bureaucrat sought to intimidate Christopher Muttukamaru, the inquiry secretary, warning him that his 'career in the civil service might suffer from the assistance he gave', as Scott later informed MPs on the Public Service Committee (PSC 1996c: vol. 3: para. 795).

Ministers withheld copies of the actual report from opposition politicians and the mass media until the last moment. In contrast, Ian Lang and a backroom team of officials worked on the government's response for a week. The government released the results of their labours in an interdepartmental press pack of 13 brief press releases summarising the government's case 'in bite-sized, quotable chunks'. The Treasury's press release was a prime example of how selective quotation can become distortion. An example is Scott's conclusion that 'the overriding and determinative reason' for ministers' misleading answers to parliamentary questions was 'a fear of strong public opposition to the loosening of restrictions on the supply of defence equipment to Iraq and a consequential fear that the pressure of the opposition might be detrimental to British trading interests'. In the release, Scott's conclusion was reduced to ' "The overriding and determinative reason" for answering the Parliamentary Questions and letters in the terms chosen was to protect "British trading interests"'. The Cabinet Office release was also notably disingenuous (see **p. 320**).

Ministers and officials had a common purpose: they defended each other's conduct because they were defending the customary conduct of government in this country. Ironically, they did so by way of a manipulation of the truth quite as dishonest as the government's original behaviour (Norton-Taylor *et al.* 1996: 170–179). Mr Justice Sedley, writing in his personal capacity, commented:

> The experience of Sir Richard Scott, who found that every step he took in an endeavour to be as open as possible in completing and presenting his report became the source of pre-emptive counter-claims designed to undermine it, illustrates how far we have travelled from received notions of public probity.
>
> (*London Review of Books*, 8 May 1997)

Heseltine's conduct as chairman of the cabinet's Co-ordination and Presentation of Government Policy Committee from 1994–97 also raised questions about the impartiality of government information (**DAC7**). This committee met every weekday and was attended by both civil servants and staff from Conservative Central Office. Heseltine's role in charge of the co-ordination and presentation of policy was bound, especially as the election approached, to raise questions about the difference between the presentation of government policies and party propaganda. Heseltine, quizzed by Public Service Committee, conceded there were few rules that categorically determined where the line should be drawn. It relied on an experienced hand like himself, instinctively knowing the 'club rules' of what was proper and what improper:

> I just have to have a feel, based upon some experience of our profession, as to what I can ask civil servants to do and what I cannot ask them to do. I have a feel for the point at which the conversation [on the committee] might be moving into a party-political dimension at which it would be embarrassing for them to be expected to be even present, let alone participate in.
>
> (PSC 1996b: para. 63)

In July 1996, Heseltine chaired ministerial meetings ostensibly on improving standards in the public services, but there was no sign that the meetings actually re-examined policies. It seems that the real motive was to find ways of selling the policies to a sceptical public. A candid Heseltine memo was leaked, stating in essence that the public did not believe politicians, but would believe the people who worked in public services. Ministers decided to set up 'panels of people associated with the public services who could be vigorous and attractive proponents of our policies' and expected civil servants to organise the cheerleader panels. The Cabinet Secretary, Sir Robin Butler, was once again called in and had a meeting with Heseltine, at which they agreed that special advisers were the 'correct route by which this should happen' (*Guardian*, 12 November 1996). This, said Hugo Young, was 'a picayune distinction. Political advisers are invariably designated civil servants and always work hand-in-glove with the departmental apparatus. The result will be the same' (*Guardian*, 14 November 1996).

For Young, Butler's response was part of a process that had gone on for more than a decade: not the formal 'politicisation' of the civil service but its 'de-objectivising' – that is, the retreat from the giving of objective civil service advice to ministers and the joint duty of ministers and civil servants to 'give Parliament and the public as full information as possible'; and the extension of the tradition of 'being economical with the truth' into the deceitful manipulation of government information. An 'objective' civil service is of far greater value to democratic government than the 'impartial' Whitehall model. For Whitehall, impartiality means being partial to whomsoever happens to be in power. Yet it is desirable from a democratic viewpoint for the bureaucracy to give those in power objective information, no matter what party they belong to or how long they have been in government, and then let them take decisions or frame legislation, according to their own partial judgement.

'De-objectivising' has also affected the quality and independence of information given to the public (**DAC7**). As we have shown, the government's 'presentation' of its response to the Scott Report was deliberately misleading. Sir Robin Butler was questioned – too briefly – about the media packs on the Scott Report by MPs on the Public Service Committee (see **p. 320**). He maintained that the press releases did not purport to summarise the Scott report, but rather to present the government's views on Scott's conclusions. This is not an explanation which stands up to scrutiny of the actual documents (we quote one example of a misleading quotation from Scott on **p. 184**). It seems that the symbiotic relationship between ministers and mandarins degenerated into misconduct on both sides. To protect the customary deceits of the state uncovered by the Scott Report they combined to perpetrate further deceits. Senior officials gave their traditional loyalty to ministers and their political projects on a near unconditional basis. Will a Blair government, committed to renewing 'trust' between government and the governed, reverse this decline? It would not be wise to count on it.

AUDIT

In Chapter 6, we found that the idea of collective cabinet government was more myth than reality; but so too was the idea that Prime Ministers had ascended onto a presidential plane of government. In this chapter we have seen that ministers are powerful figures in their own right; that they bring to their departments the authority of prerogative and statutory powers which drives the real engines of government. Ministers and mandarins interact in a complex dance of initiative and restraint, advice and action, but ultimately fuse together in partnerships from which both benefit – ministers can count on the resources of their departments in cabinet, Parliament and the media, mandarins can advance and safeguard their own and their departments' interests. Central government is a federation of departments which take care of the great majority of government decisions, either directly or through agencies of various kinds (see Chapter 8). The governing arrangements of this federation are flexible and informal, but the Treasury's financial *fiat* runs strongly through the whole of government, affecting not only spending decisions but policies as well. The Treasury has thus had a centralising as well as co-ordinating function in government, alongside the Cabinet Office and No. 10 Downing Street. Through the Joint Intelligence Committee in the Cabinet Office, the Cabinet Secretary and key Whitehall officials supervise the state's network of security and intelligence agencies.

In the introduction to Part 2, we argued that governments, ministers and state bureaucrats should be limited in their powers, and that they should act in accordance with transparent procedures that provide safeguards against arbitrary or oppressive government. The assumption is that members of the executive and 'democratic' mechanisms of accountability are both fallible; and that ministers and bureaucrats may be tempted, either individually or in combination, to put other interests – be they interests of state or of the government of the day, as well as party political or personal – before the wider public interest and to mislead Parliament and the public. The mere fact of being a member of an elected party majority in the House of Commons, or of having qualified for high office in the civil service, does not mean that ministers or mandarins will not misbehave. Nor do either occupy their office on a fully democratic basis: in the first instance, though it is common to talk about 'elected ministers', ministers need not themselves have been elected and none of the parties they have represented in Parliament since 1945 have won a simple majority of the popular vote (see Chapter 3). Thus, it is hard to maintain that they hold office with a 'democratic mandate' which ought not to be limited. Civil servants are, of course, appointed officials who owe allegiance to the Crown, or state, or 'government of the day', not to the people.

This chapter finds that rather than ministers and mandarins acting together as checks on each other's conduct of affairs, ultimately neither may be said clearly to govern the conduct of the other. Instead, they act together in a complementary way within a closed and symbiotic relationship. This relationship is almost entirely divorced from wider democratic constraints, transparent rules or practical account-ability to Parliament. On **pp. 307–311** and **320–323**, we set out the principal conventions governing the relationship from the ministerial rule-book, *Questions of Procedure for Ministers* and the Civil Service Code. The practical assumption lying behind these rules is that ministers and mandarins should form a partnership, in which ministers establish broad objectives and mandarins advise them on how best to achieve those objectives. There is supposed to be a built-in tension in this part-nership, possibly even an apolitical check exercisable by senior bureaucrats on the political enthusiasms of ministers. Mandarins should give honest advice to ministers on their intended policies, however unpalatable it might prove, and ministers should give due weight to that advice. The quality of civil service advice and action depends on its objectivity and political neutrality, which both ministers and senior bureau-crats should uphold at all times. Table 7.2 sets out the findings of this chapter.

The evidence of the recent past shows that these conventions, governing the critical relationship between government and the bureaucracy, are in practice fragile. They are capable of being overridden by a determined government or minister; and the traditional selflessness of civil servants can degenerate into political weakness. Yet these conventions are crucial to maintaining the balance between ministers and mandarins, in the British tradition. They create the conditions for considered policy-making and, in the absence of constitutional rules of conduct and effective parliamentary scrutiny, they serve as essential – if partial – safeguards against arbi-trary and even oppressive government.

But there is an inherent flaw in this traditional view of the relationship, which is reinforced by the rule that senior civil servants must act in such a way as to deserve and retain the confidence of ministers. The emphasis on trust is one of the elements which has created a symbiotic relationship between ministers and mandarins, founded on a fusion of interests on both sides, the 'executive mentality' of the civil service, and mutual advantage. The dangers here are evident. While remaining strictly neutral in a party political sense, the civil service acts as a strongly partisan force on behalf of the 'government of the day', even to the point of supplying misleading information in its cause. The advantage to ministers is obvious enough, especially in the govern-ment's dealings with Parliament. The element of tension in the relationship between

Table 7.2 Ministers and civil servants: rules of conduct and recent actual practice

Rules	Recent practice
Ministers must give due weight to informed advice of civil servants	In recent years, 'can-do' ministers have ignored and even disparaged civil service advice, the most notorious example being Michael Howard at the Home Office (**p. 155**)
Ministers must not instruct civil servants to behave improperly	Ministers have obliged civil servants to engage in party political activity and to carry out party political tasks (**pp. 181–185**)
Ministers must uphold the political impartiality of the civil service	The charge against Mrs Thatcher of 'politicising' the senior bureaucracy was unfounded (**p. 179**), but both her and John Major's governments failed to uphold the political impartiality of the service (**pp. 181–185**)
Senior civil servants must give honest and impartial advice to ministers, even if it proves unpalatable	Unfathomable. There is Lord Bancroft's celebrated aside that the 'grovel count' became higher than normal among some civil servants in the 1980s. What is evident is that 'can-do' civil servants received preference in Whitehall after 1979; and that the duty to give objective advice was less scrupulously observed than it might have been

ministers and the civil service – the curious, almost unspoken, idea of an apolitical check on politicians in office – is greatly reduced.

In the culture of Whitehall, the need to gain and keep the trust of ministers has become the paramount consideration of senior civil servants. The case for a relationship of trust hardly needs arguing. But it has developed over time at the expense of a wider democratic accountability and the conventional rules which have defined it more closely have collapsed. Ministers and mandarins thus inhabit a closed and secretive world of policy-making and political calculation of their own making. While civil servants remain for the most part politically neutral, they play a powerfully partisan role in support of the government of the day; their advice may be politically impartial in a party sense, but it is not necessarily objective and is given in the context of the government's political advantage. This fusion makes the government of the day vastly more powerful in its dealings with Parliament, the media, other interests, and the public. For missing from the rules governing the conduct of ministers and mandarins in their inevitably close relationship is any practical concept of accountability wider than their immediate dealings, other than a general exhortation to be open and honest in their dealings with Parliament and the public.

For civil servants, this wider responsibility is exercised only through and with ministers and is infused by the culture of service and trust to ministers and their 'executive ethic'. The release of information is kept under strict control, and is rationed and manipulated to present the government's policies and decisions in the best possible light; and government information officers are expected to 'articulate' and 'defend' those policies and decisions. Further, civil servants are not directly responsible to Parliament, but only through ministers; and the available evidence suggests that they tend to hold the House of Commons and MPs in contempt. For ministers, the symbiotic nature of their relationship undermines the idea that they can be readily accountable in Parliament for their officials' actions and policies. For the most significant of these policies, it is hard to distinguish what civil servants have contributed separately from themselves; and generally ministers are too close to their civil servants to act as custodians of their conduct, actions and policies (as ministerial comment to Scott on improprieties in civil service conduct shows). This, in turn, makes higher civil servants generally unaccountable, since no other mechanism of surveillance or accountability exists. We now turn to our democratic criteria.

DAC8: Ministerial control of the higher civil service

It is evident that ministers are able to exercise control over senior officials, but largely only in the limited areas where they take a direct interest. The process of political control, however, cannot be said to be effective, as it is largely confined to ministers asserting, and if need be, imposing their own broad aspirations and policy aspirations. In so far as the huge majority of departmental actions and policies is concerned, ministers are too dependent on senior officials, especially in terms of information, to act as an effective check. Thus, 'the departmental view' generally rules unchecked by ministers and departments are able to put departmental views into everyday oper-ation in their dealings with industry, local government, civil society and individual citizens. Ministers generally exercise their control out of sight of the public within the closed world of 'policy advice'. Departments are powerful institutions within their spheres of responsibility and a few core departments, notably the Treasury, are dominant forces throughout government as well. It is hard to distinguish between 'departmental' and 'ministerial' policies, but the departmental view is generally the significant element in everyday policy-making; and the Treasury's hegemonic role in government has remained significantly unchanged by changes in government and between Chancellors.

DAC9: Accountability to Parliament

The rules governing the relationship between ministers and mandarins almost wholly remove civil servants from any wider duty of accountability to Parliament or the public for their conduct at the heart of government, other than a general obligation to be open and honest in their dealings with both. Ministers are responsible to Parliament for the conduct of officials, as well as departmental policies and decisions, but their close relations with officials create an identity of interests between them and a shared vision of the interests of the state which is easily confused with their own joint interests. Thus, their ability to take responsibility publicly for their officials and departments in Parliament is undermined. Civil servants have no separate formal identity from their ministers; and as they can act only through and with ministers, they possess no separate locus for a wider democratic responsibility. Further, they act as a partisan arm of the executive, thus greatly strengthening the government of the day and reducing the ability of Parliament to subject it to effective scrutiny.

DAC7: The independence of government policy information

Not only does policy advice and formation take place in a closed world, ministers control the timing and extent of any release of information from that world on any issues of political significance to them. This control extends to the release and timing of research findings and regular government statistics as well as more sensitive policy information. Government information officers are more liable to be partial in their work than other civil servants and, indeed, the former deputy premier, Michael Heseltine, argued that this has been the case under both Labour and Conservative governments. Thus, while government in Britain now divulges a great deal of information, it is always liable to be manipulated when it is in the government's interests. Part of the advice which civil servants give ministers under terms of strict secrecy is precisely on how to handle the release of information to their advantage. Thus, citizens cannot be said to receive open and independent information on government policies. Further, modern methods of public relations being adopted in government, based as they are on tight control of information and promotional techniques, or 'spin', are not appropriate for handling public information and are inimical to democracy.

DAC11: How far is the executive subject to the rule of law?

Chapter 11 examines the scope and efficacy of the rules governing ministers and senior officials in more detail. However, this survey of the *actualité* demonstrates that the main rules governing the relationship between ministers and officials have been broken to varying degrees by ministers in recent governments; and that the constitutional practice and culture of Whitehall, focused as they are on loyalty to the government of the day and its ministers, do not provide civil servants with a firm base for a more independent and impartial relationship with ministers. Further, the fusion of interests between ministers and mandarins, the flexibility within which they work, and the secrecy which surrounds their dealings, undermines the very idea of applying transparent rules of conduct to the core executive's decision-taking and policy-making processes.

8   Agents of Power

The role of agencies and quangos in government

Ministers have discovered that the system can be used for shedding personal responsibility, rewarding friends, expanding the corporate state, diminishing the authority of Parliament, and enabling themselves to retain a measure of control over the interpretation of their own statutes.

(Philip Holland, Conservative MP, 1976)

Appointed bodies are not very public – far from it. Appointment is usually a private affair, secret even. The appointed do not have to tell the public who they are or what they have done. They are not exposed to public questioning or criticism before they are appointed. . . . People find it hard to lobby or influence them. They can't be held to account.
(Labour policy document, *Renewing Democracy, Rebuilding Communities*, 1995)

Mrs Thatcher carried out a revolution in British government which may prove to be more or less permanent. It was continued under the Major government and looks likely to survive under a new Labour government. Mrs Thatcher aimed to break up the civil service and local government, as they stood in 1979, regarding them as inefficient and wasteful bulwarks of big government and the Welfare State. She wanted to make government and the public services cheaper, more efficient and more entrepreneurial.

The revolution had two main strands: the first structural, the second managerial and internal. Structurally, the revolution depended on large-scale 'contracting out' and privatisation programmes and savings reviews which, in turn, brought about a more profound shift of public functions and services from central and local government to executive agencies and quangos, national and local. These structural changes reflected the attempt to 'privatise' the ethos of the civil service. The new bodies were supposed to embody a more efficient managerial approach and gave government the opportunity to recruit private-sector managers (as well as its allies) into the public service. The structural and internal changes were targeted on the '3Es' of economy, efficiency and effectiveness, and the key phrase was 'value for money'. Within the civil service, the old certainties of status, pay and conditions were replaced by performance-related pay, productivity agreements, and the import of private-sector ideas and managers. The most far-reaching changes came largely in Mrs Thatcher's second and third terms, though the momentum of change carried over into the Major years. She succeeded in transforming the civil service from the straight hierarchical and uniform structure, basically unchanged since it became one of the bedrocks of the British state in the 1850s, into a more diverse and complex form.

This chapter examines the structural changes which brought about a proliferation of executive agencies and executive quangos, especially at local level. Executive agencies were carved out of government departments to perform public functions and deliver services which had previously been the direct responsibility of central government. Executive quangos moved under the Conservatives from the 'arm's-length' margins of government to become major agents of government policy and action: large national quangos and hosts of local bodies were pressed into action specifically to accomplish the government's policy goals. Alongside executive quangos there was yet another almost invisible layer of the quango state, made up of 674 advisory committees and bodies. Altogether, there were some 5,681 executive and advisory quangos in British government.

These changes have had profound consequences for openness, accountability and local governance in British government, though to some extent they simply dramatised existing problems by bringing into the open deficiencies in the principle of ministerial responsibility to Parliament, the basic mechanism of accountability in the state, which were concealed within the formal machinery of government by department.

Formally, executive agencies remain part of their original departments, and their accountability is anchored in their ministers' responsibility to Parliament. Executive quangos, national and local, are also supposed to be accountable to Parliament – either directly through statutory provisions, or through their sponsoring departments and ministers – as well as to sponsoring departments, funding bodies or regulators. We deal in detail with the effectiveness of upwards accountability through ministerial responsibility in Part 3. Here we examine the adequacy of other mechanisms for securing the accountability of executive agencies and quangos – asking, for example, whether they fall within the jurisdiction of the Ombudsman, or were made subject to the Code of Practice for Access to Government Information. We apply the following Democratic Audit criteria:

DAC8. Ministerial control over the non-elected executive.

DAC9. Parliamentary scrutiny of government.

DAC11. The rule of law and transparent rules of conduct.

DAC17. Openness and accountability at regional and local level.

DAC18. The independence of governing arrangements at regional and local level.

The birth of executive agencies

The idea for executive agencies was born in the 1988 *Next Steps* report by a former head of the Whitehall think-tank, Sir Robin Ibbs (Ibbs Report 1988). The *Next Steps* report proposed dividing the civil service into two – a central core of policy-making civil servants in Whitehall and its national and regional outposts; and a range of executive agencies (sometimes known as Next Steps agencies) to carry out service delivery and operational tasks. These agencies would have their own chief executives and were to be granted semi-autonomous status, but legally would remain part of their original departments. They would also be subject to quasi-legal contracts and guidance by ministers and civil servants in Whitehall.

The Next Steps plan was rapidly put into action and rescued the then faltering reform programme. The first executive agency was established in August 1988. In the next three years, more than half the civil service had moved into agencies. By the end of 1996, there were 129 executive agencies and two departments – HM Customs and Excise and the Inland Revenue – operating as agencies. Between them, they employed 386,225 civil servants (74 per cent of the home civil service) and over 30,000 members of the armed forces. Another 28 centres, agencies and services were then being prepared or considered for executive agency status.

The Whitehall view is that the Next Steps process has established a politically neutral framework for increasing management efficiency. However, many important questions about the efficacy and future of Whitehall are raised by the process and associated initiatives: recruitment, pay, and career systems; management methods; the ethics and practice of the public service idea; the accountability of the civil service to Parliament; and the coordination of a more fragmented machine. One major study of the changes by the political scientist, R. A. W. Rhodes, argues that the fragmentation makes both 'strategic management' and ministerial responsibility far harder to achieve: 'sheer institutional complexity obscures who is accountable to whom for what'. Moreover, the narrow focus on efficiency has led to neglect of broader ideas of public accountability and service. As the former minister William Waldegrave, one of the begetters of the managerial reforms, once warned, 'It just bears saying straight out: the NHS is not a business; it is a public service and a great one' (Rhodes 1994).

The emphasis on private-sector expertise within the service, and on closer and stronger links with business, has also raised fears that the advice senior civil servants give and the decisions they take may be improperly influenced by private-sector interests, perhaps in return for a lucrative post on retirement in a company with which they have had dealings while in office. The practice of business executives coming into the civil service and then returning to the private sector – 'the revolving door' syndrome – has also aroused alarm about the potential for fraud, corruption and conflicts of interest. (See Scott 1996 for examples: D2.360–395 and D6.29–54.) There are legitimate worries about the confidentiality of personal information about individuals in contracted-out areas. Companies bidding to run state services have not been bound by the equal opportunities policies and commitments that apply to the civil service (though civil service bids are), putting at risk the progress made in this field in recent years.

Sir Robin Butler, head of the home civil service, claimed that the radical changes introduced under the Conservatives would create a civil service 'unified but not uniform' – a claim which John Garrett MP, an experienced management consultant, dismissed as 'mandarinese' (TCSC 1990b: para. 178) and Keith Dowding, author of *The Civil Service*, as 'a typical example of old-fashioned civil service aphoristic nonsense' (1995a: 73). The fact is that the large-scale 'hiving off' and contracting-out of Whitehall functions represents the writing on the wall for a unified civil service of known grades, uniform pay and conditions, and a shared public service ethic. The long-term consequences of the changes are not yet clear. There have clearly been gains in clarity and the provision of information, especially through the shift to executive agencies. The introduction of targets and performance review, the pragmatic audit exercises carried out by the Audit Commission (which began work in 1983), the 1994 code of practice for access to government information and the increasingly influential Citizen's Charter programme, in different ways brought more effective scrutiny and encouraged more openness and higher standards in the public service.

But the programme was not thought through as a whole by the government, and the concerns above were only partially addressed, if at all. The reforms were pushed through with limited public debate and scrutiny – though the Treasury and Civil Service Committee (TCSC) in the Commons did its best to monitor progress. The FDA, the senior officials' trade union, was disturbed by the absence of parliamentary scrutiny over decisions to contract services out and wanted all tenders to be referred to the Comptroller and Auditor General, the official public spending watchdog. That did not happen. In fact, the improvisatory nature of the changes and adaptations remained evident to the last days of the Conservative regime.

The role, status and powers of executive agencies

Executive agencies now form three-quarters of central government and run most of its everyday business in Britain. They vary greatly in size and power, but the largest are major enterprises: the Benefits Agency (with 71,593 staff in April 1996); the Inland Revenue (59,000), now run as an agency; HM Prison Service (38,009); and the Employment Service (34,912). The Benefits Agency dwarfs its controlling department (Social Security) which had 2,750 permanent civil servants in its headquarters and 88,766 in agencies in 1996 (*Civil Service Year Book 1997*). These agencies daily perform functions and take decisions which intimately affect the lives of millions of citizens.

Their accountability is therefore a question of the utmost importance. As the agencies remain part of their originating civil service departments, they are formally accountable to Parliament via ministers. As Sir Peter Kemp, the former project manager for agencies, told MPs on the Treasury and Civil Service Committee early on in their genesis, 'The [civil service] is directly accountable, through Ministers, to Parliament; and I think that will remain for as long as we have agencies within the Civil Service' (TCSC 1991: 102–103). In practice, agency chiefs are also accountable to officials in their parent departments and the Treasury and negotiations within Whitehall – say, with the National Audit Office – are overseen by senior departmental officials. Their chief executives, even if appointed from outside, are civil servants, working within the policy parameters of 'framework agreements' with ministers.

These quasi-contracts, establishing their current and future objectives and operating goals, are drawn up by ministers and senior bureaucrats, who between them remain responsible for making and developing policies. The framework agreements specify the executive and managerial functions and objectives for which the chief executives and agencies are responsible – and which put the government's policies into action.

There is thus, in theory at least, a clear division between policy and administration. The framework agreements are tightly drawn and are supposed to ensure that the agency chiefs 'are operating under discipline', as Kemp told the select committee. The chief executives could argue in private with ministers and departmental officials, but where they disagreed with their targets or policies, they had two options: 'They can buckle down and do what the Minister has asked them to do; or they can resign' (TCSC 1991: 102–103, 106). It is therefore no surprise that the main complaint of chief executives is of interference from parent departments and excessive monitoring. Inevitably this creates additional confusion as to where responsibility lies – the distinction between policy and operations is by no means clear and becomes less clear when ministers intervene, as they do in more politically sensitive agencies. The most notorious example of confusion and conflict occurred between Home Secretary Michael Howard and his officials and Derek Lewis, the short-lived chief executive of the Prison Service (see **p. 348**).

Roger Freeman, then the minister responsible for the public service, argued in 1997 that executive agencies had enhanced the exercise of accountability, 'through clearer public definition of roles in published Framework Documents and the provision of more useful and accessible information' (Cabinet Office 1997a: v). But contrary to the former minister's enthusiasm, government-by-contract is not problem-free, and the dangers it poses (summarised above) are at least as much to do with the democratic accountability of the new-style government machine as they are to do with its efficiency. We go to consider issues of accountability raised by executive agencies in more detail in Part 3. But here it is important to stress that the Next Steps revolution never even began in two of its most fundamental goals: real devolution of power to executive agencies; and the ending of the fiction of ministerial responsibility for all departmental activity.

The original *Next Steps* report was delivered to Mrs Thatcher in May 1987. It was far more radical than the published version and the government's response in February 1988. The original report's main argument was that ministers were grossly overloaded by the governing system in Britain to a point at which they were incapable of managing their departments in any but the most nominal way. The report recommended a major constitutional change, by law if necessary, to end the fiction that ministers could be genuinely responsible for everything done in their name within their departments. At the same time, Ibbs aimed to release civil service energy and long-term capital projects 'from the bondage of Treasury short-termism' with proposals for real devolution of power to the executive agencies over their budgets, manpower, pay, hiring, and so on (Hennessy 1989: 620–621; Jenkins 1995: Chapter 12). The Treasury reacted fast and Nigel Lawson persuaded Mrs Thatcher to suppress the report. The government's final response was to initiate the form of change, but with less substance. At the government's press conference on *Next Steps* in February

Executive quangos

1988, it was made clear that constitutional changes to the doctrine of ministerial responsibility were not on the agenda; that the Osmotherly rules embodying that doctrine and restricting what civil servants could say in Parliament would also apply to the chief executives of agencies; and that Treasury control of the financial and managerial affairs of the new agencies was to remain intact. The two great givens of the British system of government were kept in place and executive agencies in their place.

Thus the chief executives of politically sensitive agencies are vulnerable to interference by ministers and officials. This has been so especially in the case of the Prisons Agency, where Home Office officials have kept command even of some basic functions and the demands of the Home Secretary have bordered on harassment (Lewis 1997; Landers' forthcoming book). In practice, agency chief executives are somewhat freer in giving evidence to Parliament than the conventional rules stipulate, but they remain bound to give information on their ministers' behalf, not to comment on policy issues or discuss disagreements with ministers and their departments. In certain respects, executive agencies are more accountable than quangos. They have, for example, been subject to the code of practice on access to official information; they fall within the jurisdiction of the Ombudsman; they publish annual reports and accounts as a matter of course; their performance is rigorously examined by their parent departments; their chief executives are subject to written questioning directly by MPs and their replies are recorded in Hansard; and they are more likely to come under the surveillance of a select committee. The question that remains is – can they be truly accountable solely through ministers and Parliament?

Executive quangos – government's flexible friends

Executive quangos form an integral and largely unaccountable layer of government in Britain. As early as 1973, the Royal Commission on the Constitution expressed concern about the absence of 'adequate democratic control' of quangos, but the profound questions of accountability which arise have so far been addressed only very crudely. It was not until their apparently sudden rise to influence from the 1970s onwards that such concern became widespread. They are of course neither new nor unique to this country. Governments in all liberal democracies employ such quasi-public bodies, regulatory agencies, tribunals and other extra-governmental agencies and arrangements to assist them in the conduct of public business, to manage the mixed economy and to undertake and regulate all manner of public functions and private activity. As government has expanded, so has quasi-government; and its expansion has raised problems of accountability and transparency in all countries.

The recent radical changes in the business of government made quangos in Britain more common and diverse than they previously were. Conservative governments from 1979 encouraged a 'pluralism' in the forms quangos took, showing a 'sustained willingness to think in flexible – and often in radical – terms about how, and by whom, public services should be delivered', according to the official government progress report, *The Governance of Public Bodies* (Cabinet Office/Treasury 1997: 5). Ministers argued not only that the new diversity of quangos added to the flexibility of government, allowing it to mix public and private activities under public control; but also that the delivery of services through 'smaller, more dedicated, organisations' at local level was more responsive and efficient than, say, services provided by local authorities or a highly-centralised health service.

Clearly, there is a lot to be said for this argument. Quangos can be efficient and focused bodies. They often attract specialist members who would be unlikely to be involved in policy-making through party political channels. They can place a variety of sensitive and specialist issues – from broadcasting to equal opportunities, from the safety of processed foods to nuclear sites – at an arm's length from partisan politics. However, in other democratic polities, quasi-public bodies are usually subject to a legal framework of government which makes them accountable in a variety of ways. By contrast, as we saw in Chapter 7, governing arrangements in the UK are informal and ministers' powers are astonishingly flexible. A minister can, for example, establish a new body by 'a mere Answer in the House, a memorandum from the minister to himself, a wave of the hand, or whatever else may signify a decision to establish a new body' (Barker 1982: 7); and although some executive quangos progress to statutory form, Parliament need not be, and usually is not, involved in their creation (just as it played no part in the creation of executive agencies).

This constitutional spontaneity makes for a less certain and coherent framework of accountability for quangos, which their very diversity has accentuated. The growth in the size and variety of the 'quango state' has taken place within a simplistic and mainly symbolic structure of accountability which depends almost wholly on the idea of individual ministerial responsibility to Parliament. But, in contrast to executive agencies, quangos have not uniformly been made subject to accompanying safe-guards, such as the Ombudsman's writ. At the same time, quangos have tended to reflect the closed and centralised traditions of British government without necessarily being required to observe the code of conduct for access to official information. Quangos operate in the shadow of government, but need to be brought out into the open and become accountable. For they perform significant roles in delivering public services, performing public functions and regulating and negotiating with major private industries. They provide social housing; run schools and further education colleges; rule on the safety of drugs and foods; advise on human rights in Northern Ireland; provide a national network for training young people; and take on a huge variety of roles which are vital to ordinary citizens and their families.

The variety of public bodies in Britain confuses even the civil service itself, let alone outsiders. A diverse host of public bodies exists outside Whitehall which take a variety of forms, from executive agencies (see above), regulators and public corporations, all of which remain part of government, to executive quangos and advisory committees, training and enterprise councils (TECs) and housing associations, 'City Challenge' partnerships, and even on the fringes, say, MOT garages. We generally use the popular term, 'quango' in this chapter to describe quasi-public bodies which are officially at least partially independent of government, but which receive public funds to carry out public functions, or to deliver public services (Barker 1982; Flinders and Smith 1998). Thus, the actual frontiers of the 'quango state' are uncertain and no satisfactory, nor universally agreed, definition of quangos exists. In 1980, the

Executive quangos

government adopted the term 'non-departmental public bodies' (NDPBs) to describe existing executive and advisory bodies, mostly at national level – a term which is still used. But it is far too confined a category to pin down the range and diversity of non-governmental bodies, as the 1994 Democratic Audit report, *EGO-TRIP*, showed (DA Paper No. 2). The report published a full register of some 5,521 quasi-public bodies with executive functions, 4,723 of them not recognised in the government's official register. Of these 'non-recognised' bodies, 4,370 were at local level. Extraordinarily, the government has still not published its own gazeteer to the whole quango state.

The *EGO-TRIP* report criticised the informality of arrangements for establishing executive quangos, the absence of cross-Whitehall rules for their governance, evidence of partisan bias and imbalance in appointments to quangos, the arbitrary nature of the appointments procedures, and the inadequacy of measures to secure the openness and accountability of quangos. The report contributed to growing public concern about the growth of the 'quango state' and a wider unease about 'sleaze' in public life to which the conduct of quangos contributed. For example, there were serious financial irregularities in quangos such as the Welsh Development Agency and the West Midland and Wessex health authorities; examples of quango members holding down several appointments which, between them, took up more than seven days in the week; and blatantly political appointments, sometimes of business people connected to companies which made donations to the Conservative Party. Further, a 'new magistracy' of appointed, but largely unknowable, members of the proliferating local NHS bodies and local quangos in the 1980s and 1990s seemed to be usurping the role of elected local council members and local government in general; and there was a deliberate bias in this local magistracy towards businessmen and Conservative sympathisers (Stewart, Lewis and Longley 1992; DA Paper No. 2: 16–21; Weir and Hall 1995a and 1995b).

The pressure of these concerns about 'sleaze' in public life led the government to establish the Committee on Standards in Public Life, first chaired by the judge, Lord Nolan, in 1994. The first Nolan report in 1995 contained 26 recommendations on the governance, accountability and openness of officially-recognised executive NDPBs and NHS bodies; a follow-up report in May 1996 on local quangos, now officially recognised by the Committee as 'local public spending bodies', made a further 50 recommendations for grant-maintained schools, registered housing associations, and further and higher education bodies, including universities, training and enterprise councils (TECs), and local enterprise companies (LECs). The second report on local quangos commented that 'the public sector is becoming increasingly diverse and the divide from the private sector less clear' (Nolan 1996: 22), and argued that 'The principles of good practice on appointments, training, openness, codes of conduct and conflicts of interest, set out here and in our first report, should be adopted with suitable modifications across the sectors covered in this report (Nolan 1996: 2)'. The Nolan Reports triggered a major reform programme within government and the official 1997 progress report, *The Governance of Public Bodies* (Cabinet Office/Treasury 1997), charted a thoroughgoing attempt to tackle the Committee's recommendations.

BOX B   THE NOLAN COMMITTEE'S REFORM AGENDA

The seven principles of public life

SELFLESSNESS: Holders of public office should take decisions solely in terms of the public interest. They should not do so in order to gain financial or other material benefits for themselves, their family, or their friends.

INTEGRITY: Holders of public office should not place themselves under any financial or other obligation to outside individuals or organisations that might influence them in the performance of their official duties.

OBJECTIVITY: In carrying out public business, including making public appointments, awarding contracts, or recommending individuals for rewards and benefits, holders of public office should make choices on merit.

ACCOUNTABILITY: Holders of public office are accountable for their decisions and actions to the public and must submit themselves to whatever scrutiny is appropriate to their office.

OPENNESS: Holders of public office should be as open as possible about all the decisions and actions that they take. They should give reasons for their decisions and restrict information only when the wider public interest clearly demands.

HONESTY: Holders of public office have a duty to declare any private interests relating to their public duties and to take steps to resolve any conflicts arising in a way that protects the public interest.

LEADERSHIP: Holders of public office should promote and support these principles by leadership and example.

Nolan recommendations and best practice

This is a digest of recommendations on principles, procedures and practice from the first two Nolan reports and other developments.

Appointments

All appointments should be governed by the overriding principle of merit.

The overall composition of boards should represent 'an appropriate mix of relevant skills and background'.

Formal and impartial assessment of candidates with independent appraisal is essential.

Transparency in appointments should be encouraged by, wherever appropriate, advertising posts, consulting interested organisations, and encouraging nominations (including self-nominations).

TECs and LECs should have a formal procedure of identifying potential board members, ideally overseen by a nominations committee, which takes account of the need to produce a balanced board.

Terms of office, which should be renewable, should not normally exceed four years, and re-appointments for third or subsequent terms should be the exception rather than the rule.

Candidates for appointment should be required to declare any significant political activity they have undertaken in the past five years.

Openness

The agendas and minutes of meetings of governing bodies should be widely available, together with board papers where this will not inhibit frankness and clarity.

Boards should hold an open annual meeting at which board members can be questioned by the public and press.

Executive NDPBs should develop and publicise their own codes of openness.

Local quangos should publish annual reports with information on their role and remit, plans or strategies, board members and where further information can be obtained.

Good practice on the limits of commercial confidentiality should be drawn up for higher and further education bodies and they should be encouraged to be as open as possible within those limits.

Codes of conduct

All quangos should have a code of conduct for board members and staff and a statement of the aims and values of the body.

TECs and LECs should make available annual statements of their policies in relation to local accountability, propriety, governance and openness.

Local quangos should publish statements of their obligations towards their customers, staff, community, and other interested parties, their approach to openness, and procedures for handling inquiries and complaints (including independent adjudication).

Staff of higher and further education bodies should be able to speak freely about academic standards and issues without being victimised or disciplined as long as they do so without malice and in the public interest.

Whistle-blowing

Bodies should adopt a clear statement that malpractice is taken seriously in the organisation.

Staff should be able to make complaints or raise concerns without going through the normal management structure and should be guaranteed anonymity.

Staff should be informed of the proper way in which concerns may be raised outside the organisation if necessary.

It is important not to exaggerate the failings of quangos. They can, as the government's report argues, offer 'very effective and economical means of providing essential public services', as they are able to concentrate upon their core business, mostly unencumbered by bureaucracy of their own (*ibid.*: 65) – though not unencumbered by demands from the government's bureaucrats. The Nolan Committee paid tribute to the integrity and commitment to the principles and values of the public service of board members on executive quangos and NHS bodies (Nolan 1995: para. 74) and found that best practice in local quangos conformed to its own principles for public service (Nolan 1996: para. 8). Our concern is not with the effectiveness of quangos in itself, nor with the probity and ethos of quango members, but with the democratic implications of the large quango state and the structures of accountability and openness within which quangos and their board members operate.

The government's 1997 progress report stated its own aims in response to public concerns and the Nolan recommendations: 'Public services need to be *upwardly* [our emphasis] accountable, to be open and transparent, to have fair and accessible complaints mechanisms and, where appropriate, to have consultative arrangements' (Cabinet Office/Treasury 1997: 7).

These were limited aims. First, the report ruled out elections – the primary democratic mechanism – for any local quangos. Secondly, the narrow emphasis on making them *upwardly* accountable rules out other forms of accountability. Local quangos ought, for example, to be *horizontally* accountable to local communities and councils; advisory bodies to, say, consumers, 'peer-group' organisations and specialist communities. But local quangos were required only to be *responsive* to local communities and 'customers' (*ibid.:* 21–22). Secondly, the openness of quangos was based on the existing code of practice for access to government information – a fairly restricted code, and especially so for quangos. We deal in detail with the effectiveness of upwards accountability and the code in general in Chapter 12; here we deal with specific aspects of both in so far as they bear upon the accountability and openness of the quango state, as well as other mechanisms of accountability.

The role of executive quangos

Executive quangos may be large high-spending bodies, or small local agencies. They may be government agencies, primarily charged with carrying out government policies, or 'arm's-length' authorities for whom a measure of independence from government is essential to their role. At the beginning of 1997, there were 5,681 executive quangos within the government machinery in the UK. Of these, 309 were executive non-departmental public bodies at national, regional and local level; nine were executive NDPBs in Northern Ireland (not counted in official statistics); 681 were NHS bodies, mostly district authorities and NHS trusts; and 4,682 were 'local public spending bodies', as shown in Table 8.1.

This quango count includes the major national executive NDPBs, such as the Housing Corporation and Funding Agency for Schools, as well as the most local NDPBs, such as development corporations and housing action trusts on public housing estates. The 'local public spending bodies', or local quangos, are a diverse

Table 8.1 Executive quangos in Britain, 1994 and 1997

	1994	*1997*[1]
Executive NDPBs	350	309
NI executive NDPBs	8	9[2]
NHS authorities and trusts*	629	681
'Local public spending bodies'	4,534	4,682
Local bodies		
Career service companies*	–	91
City technology colleges	15	15
Further education corporations* **	557	560
Grant-maintained schools* **	1,025	1,103
Higher education corporations* **	164	175
Housing associations* **	2,668	2,594
Local enterprise companies (LECs) (Scotland) **	23	22
Training and enterprise councils (TECs) **	82	81
Police authorities*	(52)[3]	41
The total executive quango count	5,573	5,681

Sources: DA Papers Nos 2 and 8, 1994 and 1996; Parliamentary Questions March 1997; specific Democratic Audit inquiries

Notes:

* In the case of these bodies there has been a full or partial loss of local authority control or representation.

** Classified as 'local public spending bodies' by the Nolan Committee (1996).

1 As of 1 January 1997.

2 These bodies are not counted in official government statistics for NDPBs as they are said to perform local government functions.

3 In 1994, the status of police authorities was undergoing a hotly contested legislative meta-morphosis, but they are counted in this table for sake of comparison over time.

set of bodies which operate under appointed or self-appointing boards, even though they may be private bodies (like the TECs and career service companies), or voluntary or charitable bodies (like registered housing associations), or former local authority bodies, like the further education corporations and grant-maintained schools, which remain in the public sector. In its response to the second Nolan Report, the government accepted that these local bodies play a public role which demands a broad measure of government responsibility for their activities.

The list does not include other public bodies which are often described as quangos or perform analogous functions, including:

● the NHS Management Board and its eight regional offices;
● the public regulators (OFSTED, OFFER, OFT, OFGAS, OFLOT, Office of Passenger Rail Franchising, Office of the Rail Regulator, OFTEL, OFWAT), their three Northern Ireland equivalents, and other regulatory bodies, such as the Office of the Data Protection Registrar;

- 10 Office of Water Services executive NDPBs;
- nine executive NDPBs of the Office of the Rail Regulator;
- 15 OFFER (electricity), six OFTEL (telephone) and four other regulatory advisory bodies;
- public corporations, like the Bank of England, the BBC, the Commonwealth Development Corporation, the Covent Garden Market Authority, the ITC, the Radio Authority;
- 14 remaining nationalised industries; and
- 136 boards of visitors and 75 tribunals of all types.

Executive quangos were originally characterised by their 'arm's-length' relationship with government. The first Nolan report described their role as follows: 'They perform functions at arm's length from the day-to-day running of central government, their members often contributing unique specialist knowledge and wider experience to public life' (Nolan 1995: 66).

In this sense, quangos contribute a valuable degree of pluralism, specialist knowledge and 'wider experience' to the conduct of government and public affairs; and certain bodies like the Commission for Racial Equality and Health and Safety Commission are given 'arm's-length' NDPB status, in theory at least, to allow them a measure of freedom from the government of the day to pursue and enhance a wider public interest in racial equality, safety at work, and so on. However, governments have often created or adapted quangos, and increasingly so since the mid-1970s, as agents to pursue particular government objectives and policies (e.g., the National Enterprise Board in the mid-1970s; the Funding Agency for Schools in the 1990s), or to control the policies and budgets of public services (DA Paper No. 2: 12–14). The regimes under which many national executive quangos operate is now almost indistinguishable in practice from that of executive agencies (see above), and they play almost interchangeable roles. The unsystematic nature of Whitehall's ways of creating, defining and categorising quangos makes any reliable division between 'arm's-length' and agency-type quangos, or even an overall quango count, near impossible.

Major national quangos, like the Environment Agency, the Funding Agency for Schools (FAS), the Further Education Funding Agency (FEFA), the Health and Safety Commission and Executive, the Higher Education Funding Council, the Housing Corporation, the Monopolies and Mergers Commission, Scottish Enterprise and the Welsh Development Agency (WDA) perform diverse and significant public roles and are often powerful bodies in their own right. Many more executive quangos perform more specialist and narrowly-drawn tasks, such as the governing bodies of museums, research councils, industrial training boards, the Equal Opportunities Commission, the Horticultural Development Council, the Occupational Pensions Board, the National Blood Authority, the National Consumer Council, and so on.

As they are by definition adaptable and easily established, quangos allow central government fairly easily to set up mechanisms outside existing structures and relatively free from political opposition and formal checks in order to meet its political needs and carry out its policies. They are in this sense flexible friends of central government. The creation of the new hierarchies of control in school and further education shows how quickly this political scaffolding can be rigged up. In both cases, a new 'strategic' quango was established to take control of newly-created local quangos, further education colleges and schools, which had previously performed their public roles under local authority control. The two new strategic quangos – the Funding Agency for Schools (FAS) in 1994 and the Further Education Funding Council (FEFC) in 1992 – were given considerable powers and budgets to direct and fund the new local quangos and carry out government policies. They were in effect government agencies – there was no pretence of an 'arm's-length' relationship with government. The FAS took charge of all grant-maintained schools (1,103 in 1996) from local authorities and was given the powers finally over time to take charge of all state school education in place of local education authorities. The FEFC was set up to oversee local further education corporations (now 444) into which former education colleges, sixth-form colleges and adult education institutes were merged. In a similarly flexible way, government erected networks of quangos in Scotland and Wales as alternative structures of power for carrying out its policies in the two nations whose people were politically opposed to its policies.

Naturally ministers appointed chairpersons and board members they trusted to these 'strategic' national quangos. Quango boards could – and did – become blatantly biased. For example, the Funding Agency for Schools was chaired in 1995 by Sir Christopher Benson, a businessman whose companies had given donations to Conservative Party funds. Benson had previously chaired two other executive quangos performing key roles in government policies under Mrs Thatcher and Major – the Housing Corporation and the London Docklands Development Corporation. Of the 13 members of the FAS board, Benson and four others had links with the Conservative Party; six of the nine members for whom relevant information was available when we checked the membership were actively involved in the grant-maintained school movement (and another in the associated city technology college initiative); and all five of the members with direct experience in schools were on the staff or a governing body of a grant-maintained school. One member, Sir Robert Balchin, chairman of the Grant Maintained School Foundation and a long-serving senior Conservative Party official, informed the *Independent* in 1993 that John Patten, the then Education Secretary, had informed him that 'the first criterion for membership of the board was that you must be supportive of the concept of grant-maintained schools' (Weir and Hall 1995a: 16–18). It is argued that political reliability is a legitimate aim for ministers, particularly while a new government policy is being established, but the absence of balance gravely reduces the representative quality of such bodies; is incompatible with ideas of 'arm's-length' or devolved status; and is likely to lead to poorer decision-making.

Similarly, the Housing Corporation, originally set up to encourage voluntary housing, was made the main channel for public investment in social housing as Conservative governments switched resources away from local authorities. Its former semi-independence was soon lost. David Edmonds, a former chief executive, observed that 'its role is perhaps too important for the DOE fully to respect the original statutory functions'. In evidence to the Environment Select Committee, the Corporation described itself as an executive carrying out government policies and its senior officials described it as 'a government agency'. Board members, according to Edmonds, 'often queried their role when all the main decisions are taken by ministers, civil servants and Corporation staff'; and 'the DOE and its regional structure duplicates and double-checks much of the Corporation's work'. Active members of housing association boards complained about the absence of consultation downwards (one wrote, 'Take-it-or-leave it is the implicit attitude') (Weir 1995: 306–322).

The existence of these hierarchies of power has profound consequences for the quality of democracy in the UK. Thus, in 1996, the Housing Corporation sat at the apex of a social housing hierarchy consisting of its nine regional offices and 2,565 registered housing associations. It exercised substantial powers over the provision of social housing in local areas and decided how virtually all the government's investment in public rented homes (£1.75 billion in 1995–96), as well as substantial private finance, should be allocated. In such cases, it is democracy at regional and local level which suffers. For example, the Corporation employed complex distribution rules to partition its annual budget between different priorities and needs and then to allocate the funding of housing associations in different local authority areas across the country. But the technically-derived 'housing needs indicators' used could be varied by as much as 20 per cent either way by the Corporation's officials in any local authority area. This discretionary provision gave officials strong powers of influence over local authority policies. The whole apparatus came under the scrutiny only of officials in the Department of the Environment and the government's regional offices. Neither local authorities nor local communities had any place in the process; they had no status in seeking information or data, nor in questioning it; and no practicable chance of being able to subject it to public debate.

Thus it is not simply that quango boards – 'strategic' or local – are unelected. In effect, they can take whole areas of public services and functions out of politics, at all levels of government, leaving the public only limited influence as individual consumers. The hierarchies of power also took a geographic dimension. In Wales, the Welsh Secretary was responsible for 1,400 appointments to quangos during the 1990s. Over time, networks of Conservative sympathisers and businessmen, entirely unrepresentative of Welsh society as a whole, were set in power in Wales's quangos (Morgan and Osmond 1995). At local level, the phenomenal increase in appointed and self-appointing quangos gave rise in the 1980s and 1990s to a new political class at local level, the 'new magistracy'. This almost wholly unelected body of people remains in charge of a new system of local administration which has replaced much of local government and stripped it of powers, functions and services (see Chapter 9).

The accountability of executive quangos

The rise of the quango state raises profound questions of accountability, which were originally glossed over, but have now been addressed in a more systematic way. This is largely due to the Nolan process which was not, however, allowed to consider the issue of whether quangos should be subject to elections. The basic assumption was – and remains – that the host of national, regional and local executive quangos are basically made accountable only upwards through ministerial responsibility to Parliament. This is a heavily overcrowded and congested route to accountability, and is generally impassable for affected people trying to ascend it. As we have seen above (**p. 195**), the first *Next Steps* report recognised that ministers cannot realistically answer for their departments' policies and actions; and as we shall see, the mechanisms of ministerial responsibility are flawed (Chapter 12). In the case of executive quangos, a Cabinet Office review found, 'neither Ministers collectively, nor Parliament, currently have the information needed to judge how executive NDPBs overall are performing'. In suitably neutral language, the report identified weak departmental controls of their quangos, neglect by busy ministers of the quangos' objectives, and 'softer' and unfocused targeting and poor information collection on the part of the quangos themselves. In some cases, the relationship between departments and quangos was 'effectively non-existent'. The review recommended that ministers should be personally involved in 'strategic aspects of objective setting and monitoring' as a 'key' element in achieving departments' aims for their quangos (Cabinet Office 1996a: 1–2, 8–9, 15). Clearly, ministers and officials do keep a close eye on the more sensitive quangos – the Arts Council, say, or the lottery commissioners. But, all in all, the idea that ministers are genuinely responsible for such bodies to Parliament is largely unrealistic.

There is the further question of how desirable it is for quangos as a whole to be made accountable in this way. The employment of some major quangos recently as prime agents of government policies does not remove the basic justification for most quangos – that they perform functions which ought to be exercised at arm's length from departmental and ministerial control. It therefore seems obvious that a separate regime of accountability, outside government, is called for. In most European democracies, there is a corpus of public law, creating a distance between government and such bodies, and also making demands which the exceedingly tenuous filament of ministerial responsibility cannot bear. The Cabinet Office acknowledges the need for a measure of independence in its 1996 review of quangos, and then simply declares that it is allowed for under current arrangements: 'By definition, the powers [of ministers in relation to objective setting and monitoring] will reflect the arm's length nature of executive NDPBs'. Having said that, the document fails to show exactly how these powers 'reflect' the arm's-length nature of NDPBs, and argues the need for ministers to 'be involved in some way on a personal basis in strategic aspects of objective setting and monitoring' of executive quangos, given that many provide very significant contributions to the achievement of their 'wider policy aims', and all quangos contribute to these in one way or another (Cabinet Office 1996a: 15). In short, ministers ought not to let go. Ministerial responsibility for quangos operating at national level may well be justifiable in principle, however inadequate it may prove to be in practice. But can it be justified, either in principle or practice, at local level? We seek to answer that question in Chapter 9.

In May 1997, the subsequent *Governance* progress report proposed a 'practical' set of proposals for accountability for national and local quangos:

- accountability upwards, as necessary, to a 'high-level' body – a regulator, funding body, sponsor organisation;
- responsiveness to local communities and 'customers';
- openness, including codes of access to information based on the government's code of practice, publication of key data, annual reports, holding (usually annual) public meetings;
- 'accountability through redress' – i.e. fair and accessible complaints mechanisms, plus access to the Secretary of State, a regulator or independent office holder (e.g., the Ombudsman or another adjudicator); and
- (for local public spending bodies) appropriate consultative arrangements with local authorities, voluntary bodies and other service providers (Cabinet Office/ Treasury 1997: 21–22).

No one doubts the value of these measures of accountability. 'Responsiveness' is important. An immediate response to a complaint, and even perhaps some sort of redress, is clearly more satisfactory than, say, delayed retribution at the ballot box.

But the measures are narrowly defined. Such bodies are responsive only within their national and local policies and are not structured to allow local citizens to set or alter those policies. Nor do we yet know whether as a class of bodies they actually meet the government's aim of immediate and sensitive response to complaints. Can the Funding Agency for Schools or local grant-maintained schools necessarily respond better than elected bodies or local authorities to local communities? According to Tory MP Sir Teddy Taylor, certainly not always. He gave a riveting account to Parliament of how four grant-maintained schools in his constituency combined to agree a radical plan for re-structuring secondary education in his constituency and overrode the view of parents who voted against the plan at consultative meetings (DA Paper No. 2: 37). Need their qualities – especially the managerial focus on a particular service – be obtained at the expense of traditional means of political accountability, rather than adding to their force?

The arrangements among executive quangos for openness and accountability have improved since the first Democratic Audit analysis in 1993 (see Table 8.2). As the table shows, the indifference to openness and accountability in 1993 was breathtaking. On 11 basic measures, only the provision for publishing annual accounts came close to being universally required (90 per cent). No other measure was required of more than half of all the existing executive bodies. Official figures suggested that a public right to inspect a register of members' interests was available for nearly half the bodies (49 per cent). But these figures were artificially raised by being said to be in force for the 2,638 housing associations. Inspection of the actual registers of board members at the Housing Corporation's HQ revealed them to be voluntary, inadequate and out-of-date (DA Paper No. 2: 28). Hardly any executive quangos were obliged to observe the government's code of practice for access to official information (just 2 per cent); and while all NHS bodies came under the jurisdiction of the Health Service Ombudsman, only a third of executive NDPBs and no local quangos were subject either to the parliamentary or local government Ombudsman. Only a third of the executive quangos were subject to public audit by the National

Table 8.2 The openness and accountability of executive quangos, 1993 and 1997*

	Executive NDPBs 1993		Executive NDPBs 1997		NHS bodies 1993		NHS bodies 1997		Local public bodies 1993		Local public bodies 1997		Grand totals 1993		Grand totals 1997*	
	No.	%	No.	%	No.	%	No.	%	No.	%	No.	%	No.	%	No.	%
Required to publish annual reports	201	56	220	69	248	39	681	100	1,866	100	4,094	87	2,315	42	4,995	88
Required to publish annual accounts	191	53	215	67	248	39	681	100	4,534	100	4,659	99	4,973	90	5,555	98
Subject to full public audit[1]	191	53	258	81	629	100	681	100	1,025	22	2,066[2]	44	1,845	33	3,005	47
Under the jurisdiction of the Ombudsman	124	35	156	49	629	100	681	100	0	0	41	1	753	14	878	14
Required to observe the official openness code	124	35	217	68	0	0	681	100	0	0	213	5	124	2	1,111	20
Public right to inspect a register of members' interests	6	2	65	20	0	0	681	100	50	1	3,994	83	56	0	4,740	74
Public right to attend board or committee meetings	6	2	37	12	289	46	125	18	0	0	41	1	295	5	203	3
Public right to inspect agendas of meetings	0	–	–	–	156	20	132	19	1,879	40	1,879	40	2,035	35	2,011	31
Public right to see policy documents for meetings	0	0	–	–	0	0	–	–	0	0	–	–	0	0	–	–
Public right to inspect minutes of meetings	5	1	–	–	289	46	9	1	1,701	38	1,879	40	1,995	36	1,888	30
Required to hold public meetings	2	0.5	24	7	314	50	530	78	105	2	144	3	421	7	698	11

Sources: Parliamentary Questions June–July and November–December 1993, and March 1997; *Public Bodies 1993* and *1996* Cabinet Office/Office of Public Service 1993 and 1996; *Civil Service Yearbook* 1993 and 1997; DA Paper No. 2, 1994: 23, 27; Cabinet Office/Treasury, 1997; original Democratic Audit research

This table is based on departmental replies to PQs. The figures it contains are as far as possible for statutory requirements, but departmental replies sometimes include formal agreements and voluntary arrangements. The column for 'Local public spending bodies' includes universities (higher education authorities) in line with the Nolan definition. As Tables 9.1 and 9.2 omit universities, their figures differ from those shown here.

Notes:

* All figures in this table refer to statutory or mandatory provisions under regulations, codes of practice, etc. These are often augmented by voluntary arrangements which are not included in this table (see text). Most changes shown between 1993 and 1997 show genuine improvements; others may be due to departments reinterpreting the PQs tabled between 1993 and 1997. The total number of quangos for 1993 and 1997 respectively are 5,573 and 5,681.

1 'Public audit' for these purposes means audit under the direction or by the National Audit Office or Audit Commission.

2 In 1997, 2,498 registered housing associations were subject to partial public audit.

Audit Office or Audit Commission – most of these, again, being NHS bodies. In other words, so far as openness and accountability were concerned, the quango state was built on sand.

In 1997, the overall record remained poor. More than four-fifths (88 per cent) of quangos had now to publish an annual report, but what is extraordinary is that this is still not a universal requirement. It is after all the most basic form of openness. Nearly all (98 per cent) had to publish annual accounts. About one in five (1,111) were subject to the code of practice for open government; only 878 (14 per cent) came under the Ombudsman's jurisdiction; and nearly half were still not subject to full public audit. The NHS showed the most marked improvement, with its bodies all subject to at least six basic tests of accountability, but their meetings remained more or less closed to public scrutiny. (From May 1997, however, all NHS trusts were required to hold their meetings in public.) The position on executive NDPBs had improved since 1993, but was still patchy. Many more (80 per cent) were subject to public audit, and the National Audit Office was given 'inspection rights' over the rest. However, only two-thirds were required to observe the openness code, only half were subject to the Ombudsman's writ, and only one in five was obliged to keep a public register of members' interests. Overall, the public still has very few rights of access to the boards of any executive quangos (see Chapter 9 for further analysis of the record of local public bodies).

In 1997, the Conservative government was seeking to improve this position. Its 1997 progress report described a series of measures and goals to unify practice and raise standards of openness and accountability, though not public access, for executive quangos. In future, 'all self-accounting NDPBs should aim to produce an Annual Report and Accounts as a single document and should give it publicly'. The functions, control arrangements and financial management of every NDPB – as well as the continuing need for the body – came under review every five years under a rolling programme, and financial memoranda, framed under Treasury guidelines, set out the terms and conditions on which they received public funds. The National Audit Office's audits of government departments and 'value-for-money' checks examined the financial controls of quangos; and the NAO was encouraged to undertake comparative 'value-for-money' audits for these bodies. There were also annual performance reviews of the strategies and financial plans of the 60 or so largest NDPBs (Cabinet Office/Treasury 1997: 22–25, 59–63). As for local quangos, the government was opposed to a uniform audit regime, but gave the Audit Commission oversight of audit arrangements on a trial basis. Otherwise, the major funding quangos, like the Funding Agency for Schools, oversaw the audit arrangements for the local quangos they funded. Finally, the Citizen's Charter and performance indicators apply to all public services, including those delivered by executive NDPBs, albeit unevenly (*ibid.*: 25, 59–63).

Every executive NDPB not within the Ombudsman's jurisdiction was being reviewed with a view to including the body – and making it subject also to the openness code – 'unless there are valid reasons, specific to its particular circumstances, for excluding it'. A new simple complaints procedure was introduced into the NHS in 1996, and is being monitored, and the Health Service Ombudsman's remit was extended to investigate complaints arising from clinical judgements. Finally, the code of practice for access to government information was to become the 'common reference point' for quangos' approach to openness and the Conservative government asked executive NDPBs outside the Ombudsman's jurisdiction voluntarily to adopt codes based on it (*ibid.*: 52).

The government appears to have been very diligent about this exercise. However we studied 12 key high-level executive quangos to check just how open and accountable they were in 1997, according to our basic measures. As Table 8.3 shows, the government failed to ensure that key bodies were subject to either the Ombudsman's jurisdiction or the openness code. In 1998, of course, the government is publishing

Table 8.3 Twelve key executive quangos: accountability and openness, 1997

	Criteria used:						Public access to:				
	Annual report	Annual accounts	Public audit	Ombudsman	Openness code	Publish register of members' interests	Board/committee meetings	Agendas of meetings	Policy papers	Minutes of meetings	Hold public meetings
Arts Council	❖	❖	✔	✔	✔	❖	✗	✗	✗	✗	✗
Audit Commission	▲	▲	✔	✗	✔	❖	✗	✗	✗	✗	✗
Environment Agency	▲	▲	✔	✔	✔	❖	✗	✗	✗	✗	✗
Funding Agency for Schools	❖	▲	✔	✗	✗	❖	✗	✗	✗	✗	❖
Further Education Funding Council	❖	▲	✔	✗	✗	❖	✗	✗	✗	✗	❖
Higher Education Funding Council	❖	▲	✔	✗	✗	❖	✗	✗	✗	✗	✗
Housing Corporation	▲	▲	✔	✔	✔	❖	✗	✗	✗	✗	✗
Human Fertilisation & Embryology Authority	▲	▲	✔	✔	✔	✗	✗	✗	✗	✗	✗
Northern Ireland Housing Executive	▲	▲	✔	✔	✔	✗	✗	✗	✗	✗	❖
Public Health Laboratory Services Board	❖	▲	✔	✗	✗	✗	✗	✗	✗	✗	✗
Scottish Enterprise	▲	▲	✗	✗	✗	❖	✗	✗	✗	✗	✗
Welsh Development Agency	▲	▲	✔	✗	✔	❖	✗	✗	✗	✗	✗

Sources: Parliamentary Questions, March 1997; Cabinet Office/Treasury, 1997; original Democratic Audit research

Note:

This table is based on departmental replies to PQs. The figures it contains are as far as possible for statutory requirements, but departmental replies sometimes include formal agreements and voluntary arrangements.

Key

❖ voluntary

▲ required under statute, regulations, framework or other controlling document etc.

✔ yes

✗ no

a Freedom of Information Bill. But this fitful coverage raised questions about the past government's 'valid reasons' for excluding bodies. Public access was predictably minimal, though nine of the 12 quangos at least voluntarily publish a register of members' interests.

Overall, there is a single notable feature of the regime of openness and accountability that was emerging up to May 1997. All the measures taken largely excluded any genuine involvement or participation by the public in framing or monitoring policies set either by government, funding quangos and NDPBs, or local quangos. Public services delivered by quangos have been made more responsive to users' needs through information and complaints procedures and, in some cases, independent adjudication. This process has been uneven, but inevitably so. However, the public are recognised as consumers, not as citizens, and the policies and service standards – even when described as 'publicly-approved standards' – are set not by the public, but by the government and the services themselves, within a strong cost-cutting perspective. They have not reflected a real degree of consultation with ordinary citizens, let alone their participation; and the magistracy which rules them is protected from the public's verdict by way of elections. The measures to secure accountability are complementary to the processes of democratic accountability, and are not a satisfactory substitute for them. They have not yet established a basic regime of horizontal openness and accountability for most local quangos, which generally remain both secretive and remote (see Chapter 9). In fact, by May 1997 there remained no uniform and adequate structure for accountability for quangos large or small, national or local, though the vast expansion of activities by these unelected bodies in the shadow of government still requires it.

Measures to patrol patronage on quangos

The Nolan Committee considered the largely unfettered powers of ministers (and government officials) to make appointments to executive quangos in its first report in May 1995. The Committee heard evidence from witnesses who argued that ministerial powers of patronage – they make up to 10,000 appointments a year, including over 2,000 to executive NDPBs and NHS authorities and trusts – represented 'an unhealthy concentration of power', particularly given the limited checks on the exercise of those powers. The Committee found the evidence of bias in appointments 'circumstantial and inconclusive';[1] decided that the partisan character of the House

---

[1] Evidence of patronage was necessarily 'circumstantial' and 'inconclusive', given the secrecy within which government operates and the paucity of reliable official information on the composition of the quangocracy. Yet the 'circumstantial' evidence from official documents, newspaper reports, television programmes, and ministers' own statements up to 1995 was strong enough to demonstrate political bias, and 'caprice and whim', in the making of appointments, and the creation of unbalanced quango boards, under both Labour government in the 1970s and Conservative government in the 1980s and 1990s. In the Democratic Audit report *EGO-TRIP* and research specifically commissioned on behalf of the Nolan Committee, we summarised ample evidence of political bias in appointments to major executive quangos and NHS trusts (which were also dominated by business and professional *men*), as well as the absence of balance on boards and arbitrary ministerial

of Commons rendered proposals for an independent appointing body or democratic scrutiny of the uses of patronage impractical; and in essence decided to bow to the principle of ministerial responsibility, though modestly distanced. Thus the Committee recommended that ministers should continue to exercise 'ultimate responsibility' for appointments and agreed that they should be able to appoint board members committed to working within the policy and resources frameworks they set. 'Appointed bodies should not be able to thwart or undermine the intentions of Ministers and Parliament.' However, the Committee recommended that a Public Appointments Commissioner should be created to scrutinise, regulate and audit appointments. Nolan also suggested that not all quango board members need be personally committed to a particular policy or share a minister's political thinking: 'reasoned scepticism within the board may add to the quality of decision-making and can sometimes be essential to protect the public interest'. The report stressed the need for appointments to be made primarily on merit, and recommended that quango boards should contain 'a balance of relevant skills, interests and backgrounds' (Nolan 1995).

In November 1995, the Major government appointed an independent Commissioner for Public Appointments (CPA), Sir Leonard Peach, to monitor appointments to executive NDPBs and NHS bodies (about 2,000 annually and 8,300 in all). But this Commissioner is weaker than Nolan intended. He is part-time only and lacks the executive resource of the Public Appointments Unit, which Nolan unsuccessfully proposed should transfer from the Cabinet Office to his domain. To put the Nolan reform agenda into practice, the Commissioner has issued a mandatory code of practice for public appointments procedures, guidance on appointments to executive NDPBs and NHS bodies, and reports for 1995–96 and 1996–97 (Office of the Commissioner for Public Appointments (OCPA) 1997: Annex 3 and 1996a; 1996b; and 1997). He declared that his overall objective was 'to create an efficient and transparent process of public appointments which will produce results based on merit and in which the candidates and the general public can have confidence' (press release, April 1996). The code contains seven principles for public appointments, introducing an emphasis on independent scrutiny, openness and transparency, reinforcing previous commitments to appointments on merit, equal opportunities and the importance of probity, and re-stating the principle of ministerial responsibility (OCPA 1997: Annex 3). The key elements are, first, the 'overriding principle of selection based on merit'; and secondly, the mandatory requirement that 'no appointment will take place without first being scrutinised by a panel with independent membership or by a group including membership independent of the department filling the post' (*ibid.*: Annex 3 para. 3.35). The Commissioner has also set up a well-publicised and accessible complaints procedure.

The Commissioner's second report covers the first nine months (July 1996–March 1997) of the new procedures for public appointments in action. Departments, he

appointments (DA Paper No. 2: 16–22; Weir and Hall 1995a). Nor was there much room for balance or Nolan's 'reasoned criticism' in the Funding Agency for Schools, which was deliberately stacked with members committed to the idea of grant-maintained schools (see p. 204).

reported, have been careful to apply the principle of merit and a variety of processes to establish scrutiny of appointments by panels of or including independent members are 'well established' in departments which make a lot of appointments. He found no breaches of his code and stated that 'On a very few occasions, when it appeared that [a breach of the Code] might arise if a Minister pursued a particular course of action, I found it necessary to intervene before the appointment was confirmed' (*ibid.*: 3).

Ministers are of course 'ultimately responsible' for most public appointments (not all – most local bodies are self-appointing). Peach also takes the view that it is perfectly proper for a minister to nominate a candidate for a post for which he is the appointer, since that candidate 'has to be approved by the panel of independent members' (PSC 1997: 17). Overall, however, it seems that the role of ministers has been distanced from the actual process of appointments.

The OCPA auditors, Ernst & Young, audited the procedures in all departments making appointments to executive NDPBs and NHS bodies and will now audit all departments at least once over a three-yearly cycle (plus spot checks) and busier departments more frequently. Ernst & Young's first audit found that departments were seeking to follow the code and guidance; and while there was 'room for improvement', they discovered no evidence of 'malfeasance'. They checked 243 actual appointments (14 per cent of the 1,753 made during the period). Of the 87 people newly appointed (rather than re-appointed) in this sample, nearly a third (28) had replied to advertisements, 15 came from official pools of candidates and 44 were nominated (none by ministers). The Commissioner's report fails to disclose which bodies or individuals provided the nominations or how people's names came to be held on the central or departmental pools.

The report also contains the first statistical analysis of the records which departments are now obliged to keep of their appointments. A series of tables contains and cross-tabulates data on chairpersons, their deputies and board members; full-time and part-time posts; paid and unpaid posts and rates of remuneration; the ratios of men, women and people from ethnic minorities appointed; numbers of appointments and re-appointments; chairpersons and their deputies; the age distribution; multiple appointments; and 'declared political activity'. Political activity for this purpose consists of having been an office holder in a political party (or affiliated body) which fields candidates in local, general or European elections, having spoken publicly for such a party or having stood in elections for the party (OCPA 1996a: para. 3.10). On this test, the survey found that 10.3 per cent of the 1,753 people appointed had been politically active, mostly on behalf of the two main parties (5.9 per cent Conservative; 3.3 per cent Labour). However, the official records thus miss people who belong to pressure groups, professional organisations, trade unions, etc., which might have a particular interest in a quango's work, and also those who have made a political donation or belong to an organisation which has. These omissions are justified on grounds of privacy: 'candidates are not expected to divulge private membership of or association with (including donations to) a political party or trade union, or their voting habits. Their right to privacy in these matters must be respected' (OCPA 1997: Annex 3, para. 3.12).

The Commissioner will therefore accept complaints about appointments which might have been influenced by a political donation, but 'would need to consider an appointee's right to privacy when faced with [such] a claim. . . . Should appointees not wish to comment, the Commissioner cannot oblige them to do so' (OCPA 1996b: 9). Given that people are volunteering for public service, it seems reasonable to take the view that their right to privacy should be qualified to allow for the declaration of information material to their suitability for public office and performance of public duties. The Commissioner has unduly restricted his ability to fulfil his responsibilities in this regard.

Further, the guidance on appointments says nothing specific about questioning candidates on potential conflicts of interest which might arise from other affiliations and interests, let alone declaring them publicly on registers. In 1996, the Public Service Committee questioned Peach about this issue. He replied that the chairperson or independent member of any panel ought to ask questions about possible conflicts of interest. The PSC finally decided that Peach should make it clear in revised guidance that conflicts of interest must be declared and seriously considered, and that he should monitor the practice of bodies in considering such conflicts (PSC 1997: ix, 16).

Several unresolved issues arise which are yet to be tested in action. The CPA's powers of sanction are, according to some critics, confined to 'a slap on the wrist' in the annual report. However, the Commissioner states that 'this under-estimates the power of the threat of uncomplimentary publicity, a sanction for which those in government have a healthy respect' (OCPA 1996b: 3). He is also free to make an adverse judgement known at any time and is not confined to the annual report. However, how willing will Peach be to publicise faults? In evidence to the PSC he made plain his view that publicising violations of his code and guidance might damage his working relationship with departments. Then, there is the question of the independent members. They are appointed by departments or supplied by 'outservice' organisations and nothing is known publicly about them. Yet they surely are, as Peach describes them, 'guardians' of his code who could safeguard the new principles of appointments? Ought they not therefore to be publicly known – and perhaps trained for the role? Moreover, they are appointees of the departments, not of the OCPA, though Peach is already considering whether he should create a list of his own independent scrutineers of the most important quango posts. Had the Public Appointments Unit been incorporated in the Commissioner's Office, as Nolan recommended, then he would have had the resources to appoint all such officers and also to stipulate a clearer set of arrangements for independent scrutiny than now exist.

The absence of resources also has a bearing on the scope of the Commissioner's scrutiny of appointments. He has no responsibility for the appointments to advisory NDPBs – an area in which there is great concern both about individual appointments and the balance of committees (see below), nor for those to boards of visitors, tribunals, nationalised industries, and regulators – some 800 bodies in all with nearly 30,000 board members. Nor does his remit extend to local quangos – 4,480 bodies with some 70,000 board members responsible for spending about £15,000 million of public funds each year. As Tony Wright MP comments, 'the fact that they mostly appoint, and re-appoint themselves, is not a reason for excluding them but for ensuring by their inclusion that they adhere to good practice' (Wright 1998). Peach has argued against extending his responsibilities on the grounds that he lacks the resources to meet new demands.

Finally, there is the question of the public register of public appointments on the Internet. The provision of a web-site with full information on all board members is a prerequisite of genuinely independent scrutiny and analysis of the chosen thousands who run the quango state. However, a Democratic Audit study of the web-site in 1997 found that it was seriously deficient – some departments did not even supply information on their own quangos – including, astonishingly, the Cabinet Office, which is responsible for organising the site. Departments mostly listed only executive quangos, but far from all of them; and the details on members were incomplete, inconsistent and valueless for the purposes of external analysis (DA Paper No. 13). On receiving the report, ministers immediately promised unspecified reforms and appointed a web-master to oversee the government's web-site development. If the Public Appointments Unit were to be transferred to the OCPA, the machinery for accomplishing comprehensive scrutiny of public positions and publishing relevant information would be in place.

Respect for the 'arm's-length' principle

Bodies like the Arts Council, Health and Safety Commission and Executive, the Higher Education Funding Council, the Monopolies and Mergers Commission (MMC), the Commission for Racial Equality, the Equal Opportunities Commission and others, all perform public functions which require a measure of 'arm's-length' independence from government. Policing health and safety at work; regulating monopolies and mergers; investigating and reporting on consumer issues; distributing grants to universities or funding economic and social research; encouraging and enforcing racial equality and equal opportunities, are all public functions which need to be carried out in a wider public interest, which will not necessarily be easily defined or agreed upon, and which certainly cannot be identified precisely with the interests or priorities of the government of the day. For quasi-judicial or for social and cultural reasons, current ministers of the day ought to hold back from executive control and carefully weigh the case for intervention.

Such quangos must be free to act semi-independently of the state, carrying a culture of public service and pluralistic ideas of the 'higher' interests of all citizens such as, say, the need for consumer protection, for artistic innovation or investigative journalism, for safe and healthy working conditions, for academic and artistic freedoms, for equal protection before and in the law, and so on. The commitment to a wider and more pluralist idea of the public interest must allow for room for legitimate differences in view between 'arm's-length' quangos and ministers and departmental officials, and may involve quangos in informed and responsible criticism of government policies or legislation, or even legal or regulatory action against government departments or other public bodies.

Arm's length principle

Even though the duties of all these bodies are set out in their founding statutes or royal charters – which may offer some protection against arbitrary command from above, but may also sanction it – their NDPB status renders them vulnerable to government interference. They rely ultimately for protection on ministers and civil servants observing conventions of respect for their 'arm's-length' status; but, as we point out elsewhere, the ethics of convention in politics are crumbling (see **p. 305**). The Higher Education Funding Council (HEFC) provides an example of central government taking more power over a formerly 'arm's-length' process – the funding of universities – to impose its own priorities. For over 60 years until the early 1980s, the University Grants Committee (UGC), formally an advisory NDPB, allocated grants to universities from a total sum decided by government. Universities had substantial representation on the UGC which traditionally followed broad government policy while exercising its own discretion. Through a series of decisions and statutes, Conservative governments gradually took more control over university funding and policies, first replacing the UGC with an executive quango and taking 'reserve powers' to direct its work, then merging the new quango with the more compliant body in charge of funding polytechnics (when they were raised to university status). University representation on the quango was progressively reduced and the role of industrialists and business people raised in line with government aims to bring universities 'closer to the world of business'. In 1995, the HEFC for England, besides having seven members out of 13 with business experience (two of them also academics), also had two known Conservatives on its governing council, one a former MP and minister, and no member with a known Labour or Liberal Democrat background to provide political balance (Weir and Hall 1995a: 18–20). Academic freedom is vital to a pluralist and open society. The growth of government power over universities, their priorities and policies, channelled through the HEFCs in England, Wales and Scotland, compromises that freedom.

It remains to be seen whether the new arrangements for public appointments will restrict ministers' ability to re-shape the composition of the boards of 'arm's-length' bodies to ensure that they correspond with the minister's own or the government's prevailing pre-occupations. In 1993–94, ministers re-shuffled the membership of such a body, the Equal Opportunities Commission, appointing Ms Kamlesh Bahl, a solicitor and (according to a *Guardian* report which was not denied) 'former Tory activist' with parliamentary ambitions as chairwoman; the wife of former Conservative cabinet minister Sir Leon Brittan as her deputy; and finally two businessmen, both of whom were members of the Institute of Directors, a free-market organisation hostile to the kinds of interventions which the EOC was charged to make in appropriate circumstances. As the EOC board is a 'hands-on' body, closely involved in the organisation's activities, its composition is of particular significance. The EOC case illustrates another aspect of a minister's power over such bodies. According to leaked minutes of a meeting in November 1994 between Michael Portillo, the then Employment Secretary, and Bahl, Portillo had sought assurances from her and the chief executive that the EOC would not turn into a hostile 'rent-a-quote' organisation, holding over their heads the threat of merger with the Commission for Racial Equality. Staff complained that the two were 'keen to comply' with Portillo's demands. On the other hand, Bahl had declared her own backing for a minimum wage (a policy the government opposed) and issued a press release regretting Portillo's decision to veto EU legislation protecting part-time women workers, ignoring a House of Lords ruling won by the EOC (Weir and Hall 1995a: 14–15). The point is that ministers were evidently seeking to nobble the EOC and were in a strong position to do so. It was – and remains – very difficult for the EOC and any other quango with a sensitive and potentially controversial brief to campaign without inhibition over issues which run counter to government policies or ministers' views.

Ministers and senior civil servants can also use their powers of patronage to reward quangocrats who conform to their wishes. It was common up to May 1997 for individuals to be appointed to more than one public body, once they had, so to speak, proved their credentials, or to be re-appointed as a matter of course. This was a natural, but unhealthy, tendency. More generally it tended to encourage a conformity of view on public bodies and to create a class of quango members who were preferred for their amenability and 'good behaviour' – and thus to restrict the pluralism and diversity of experience and talent on which a thriving public life should draw. The Nolan Committee strongly emphasised the need for diversity and a mix of skills and backgrounds in its reports and recommended that people should usually be re-appointed once only. The Commissioner for Public Appointments has taken a strong line against re-appointments. But he has not drawn up effective proposals for the promotion of balanced quango boards, or for monitoring the mix on boards.

Control over funding is another weapon in a minister's, or departmental official's locker. Plainly, ministerial control over the public funding of such bodies can be deployed as another check on activities of which ministers or departments disapprove. The National Consumer Council (NCC), first set up under a Labour government as a consumer watchdog, had a brief which then ran counter to the prevailing view of its sponsoring department, the DTI, under Conservative governments. Officials were especially hostile to the NCC's critical surveillance of newly privatised public utilities and suggested that it 'duplicated' work done elsewhere. This surveillance work was, however, vindicated by an independent managerial review. Staff at the NCC felt inhibited by its financial dependence on the DTI, but relied for protection on the responsible nature of the Council's reports. Ministers received early copies of the Council's reports and press releases. The chairwoman, Lady Wilcox, who later, as Baroness Wilcox, became a Conservative peer, received telephone calls from ministers and officials and often insisted on alterations to reports and press releases. However, the NCC remained largely independent-minded, continuing its work on public utilities and regulators, taking a strong stance against tobacco advertising, and twice supporting Private Members' bills which the government did not like. After a hike in the 1980s, the DTI sharply reduced the Council's grant by nearly a third over three years in the 1990s. Whether political disapproval was a factor in this conspicuous frugality cannot be determined one way or the other. But it might well be that the NCC paid a price for maintaining its ethos.

More generally, the informality of government and the discretionary powers of ministers mean that ministers (and thus their senior officials) can at will intervene and erode the institutional independence even of statutorily defined quangos – and, indeed, statutory public bodies of all kinds. In fact, discretionary powers over such bodies are normally written in to the statutes establishing them. Two academic lawyers, Ian Harden and Norman Lewis, have pointed out the consequences of such informality to which the political classes, conditioned by usual practice, have become blind. For example, Conservative governments appointed chairmen to nationalised industries who were explicitly committed to privatisation, and who were expected to carry on as chairmen of the new privatised corporations, often with a substantial increase in salaries and other benefits. Public and private policy-making are frequently inter-linked and the boundaries between public and private are unclear and opaque. In the 1980s, the British Steel Corporation acted as the government's agency – or as a quasi-government – in re-constructing the steel industry, and administering government assistance to private steel companies. The BSC undertook complex and confidential negotiations with the private sector; 'Pheonix' companies, jointly owned by the BSC and 'independent' steel producers were created. The dangers inherent in such mixed activities is clear enough; but they all took place outside any constitutional rules of conduct and safe from the public or parliamentary gaze (Harden and Lewis 1988: 171–172).

Or take the informality within which ministers and the Monopolies and Mergers Commission, an executive quango, operate. No clear criteria exist for deciding when a proposed merger should be referred to the MMC. The official government position is that decisions on merger references are taken on a case-by-case basis, rather than by applying a 'rigid' set of rules. There are not even general guidelines for judging whether a merger is likely to be approved or not. Ministers often overturn the advice of the Office of Fair Trading. Companies have naturally complained that decisions have been arbitrary and inconsistent, complaints with which the Director-General of Fair Trading has had some sympathy.

In certain cases, there have been allegations that governments have determined cases on the basis of their own political advantage. The most notorious of these was the acquisition in 1980 of Times Newspapers by Rupert Murdoch. The legal position was that the change of ownership should automatically have been referred to the MMC, unless the government was satisfied that the papers were losing money (which they were); and that the delay of some three months might prove fatal to their future. Thomson Newspapers set an arbitrarily brief timetable for the sale, possibly to deter a reference to the MMC, and Murdoch made it known that he might also withdraw if there were a reference. The issues in this case were complex and the journalists and trade unions involved disagreed among themselves on the right course. Murdoch felt that the government owed him a favour in return for his enthusiastic backing for Mrs Thatcher and he and she met. The then minister, John Biffen, decided not to refer the take-over to the commission and the *Sunday Times* journalists soon abandoned their attempt to obtain judicial review of his decision. The Murdoch press remained faithful to Mrs Thatcher to the end. The discretionary powers of ministers, the absence of clearly defined criteria for references, of a need to give reasons for ministers' decisions, and of any public forum in which such decisions can be discussed point to serious failures in British processes for sorting out decisions which involve a public interest wider than the political and commercial interests which are involved in such cases. It is hardly acceptable that the only check which existed in this case was judicial review which depended on an unaccountable private decision to carry on or quit (Harden and Lewis 1988: 176–177; Leapman 1983: 230–236).

Advisory quangos: a near invisible layer of government

The secrecy in which advisory bodies work is based on a wish to protect themselves from informed and perhaps critical scrutiny from outside. In the case of the Medicines Commission, both the department [of Health] and the pharmaceutical industry have a common interest in not being exposed to too much scrutiny. It means they don't have to satisfy consumer groups, expert outside medical opinion, and public pressure.

(Maurice Frankel, Campaign for Freedom of Information, 1995)

Advisory quangos form a near invisible layer of government which is at least as important, and possibly more so, than that of the executive quangos. They tend to be seen as 'fringe bodies'. But at the heart of government, a significant network of these advisory committees – officially classified as advisory non-departmental public bodies (ANDPBs) – helps shape government decisions of vital importance to people's everyday lives. Almost invariably closeted in secret, important advisory committees advise government on, for example:

- the risks attached to medicines and drugs;
- the safety of the chemical compounds and additives which manufacturers add to processed foods and drinks;
- the long-term dangers to British cattle herds and the public from bovine spongiform encephalopathy (BSE);
- the dangers from nuclear activities and installations, hazardous substances and releases of genetic materials into the air;
- cancer risks from chemicals in food, consumer products and the environment, their toxicity and mutagenicity;
- the quality of the air British citizens breathe and environmental pollution of all kinds; and
- the transport, storage and disposal of radioactive waste.

In other words, a key two dozen or so advisory quangos actually perform important monitoring, scrutiny, licensing and regulating roles for government ministers on issues which involve specialist knowledge and potentially high risks to the public. In effect, they perform a vital 'judicial' role in government. From a specialist perspective, they *judge* the safety of medicines, processed foodstuffs, scientific releases into the environment, the nuclear industry, pesticides, and so on, and their judgements directly affect the safety and quality of the daily lives of ordinary people in these vital areas. Mistakes can lead to human tragedies and commercial disaster. The most tragic example of their significance is the bovine spongiform encephalopathy (BSE) crisis in British cattle herds; some two dozen young people have died after contracting the human form of the cattle disease through eating BSE-infected beef products and the beef industry has been brought to its knees (see **pp. 282–289**). But there are other cases where the judgement of these advisory committees is literally a matter of life and death. For example, some dozen people at least have suffered fatal heart attacks after taking the drug Triludan to combat hay fever. In 1997, the US Food and Drug Administration was withdrawing approval for Triludan's active ingredient in the USA, but advisory committees here have decided not to act and the drug remains on sale over chemists' counters in the UK. Drugs taken for therapeutic purposes cause between 3 and 5 per cent of all hospital admissions annually; and one informed estimate of the harm drugs can do suggests that they may cause some 47,000 to 240,000 serious 'adverse reactions' and up to 2,500 deaths a year (Medawar 1992).

But the committees which advise on the safety of drugs, processed foods and other risks, are not forums of open, expert and disinterested inquiry. Rather they are secretive negotiating bodies, in which specialist assessments of risk and damage are balanced against the government's broad policy aims and the interests of affected industries as well as the wider public interest. In recent years, the government's overriding concern to reduce public expenditure has been a significant brake on the advice options of some committees. Another of the government's main aims has been to protect industry's interests. The £2.1 billion British pharmaceutical industry is, for example, the third largest in the world and generated the second largest trade surplus for the UK in 1995, second only to North Sea oil. The Committee on the Safety of Medicines and the Medicines Commission (which regulates and licenses drugs in the UK), are heavily weighted with representatives of the pharmaceutical industry – with a dual, closely linked role both to provide practical experience and knowledge and to protect the industry's interests. Other advisory committees similarly contain representatives of relevant interests.

As well as the 'judicial' bodies described above, other advisory bodies perform important public functions. A powerful network of business-oriented advisory bodies has exerted significant influence over the allocation of overseas aid funds, major government contracts and privatisation policy. Advisory quangos like the DTI's high-prestige British Overseas Trade Board (BOTB), run by an inner circle of ministers and high-ranking civil servants, City figures and industrialists, should be seen as governing institutions. The BOTB co-ordinates a set of high-powered advisory groups, like the Overseas Projects Board, and issues advice to government which has been almost invariably followed on expenditure on soft loans and other financial assistance on major overseas contracts. Similarly influential advisory quangos are the Review Board for Government Contracts, a body established by agreement between the Treasury and the CBI in the early 1960s, and the shadowy Private Sector Forum, another high-level group of City and business figures, which advised Conservative governments on privatisation, 'market-testing', and other civil service reforms. Such advisory bodies are quite as important as the executive quangos which hogged the headlines in the 1990s.

Advisory quangos also assess the effects of industrial injuries and the availability of legal aid and employment opportunities for people with disabilities; advise on industrial development, de-regulation, parliamentary boundaries, top people's salaries, the public lending right, and preserving ancient monuments; monitor government policies on social security benefits and breast cancer screening; scrutinise human rights policies and abuses in Northern Ireland; and oversee political honours, the government's art collections, the export of works of art, sport and recreation. (There are also short-lived advisory groups; departmental or interdepartmental committees; task forces, consultants and special advisers, like Mrs Thatcher's Derek Rayner, from Marks & Spencers, on civil service reform, and the host of ad-hoc bodies set up by Labour ministers after May 1997. Important though they are, we do not check on their activities here.)

Advisory bodies can simply be established under ministers' wide-ranging prerogative powers to seek advice from whomsoever and wherever they see fit, or by Act of Parliament. Of the 674 existing advisory quangos, about half are statutory bodies whose role is set out in law. Executive quangos may also appoint advisory bodies (the Health and Safety Executive and Commission, for example, have 22 advisory bodies).

There is no general statute establishing rules for the conduct, openness or accountability of advisory quangos. They tend therefore to be monitored within the undefined realm of ministerial discretion and policy advice; they are generally accountable only to officials in the departments to which they are attached – which inevitably gives those officials powerful leverage, if required, over the advice they proffer. The official advisory document, *Non-Departmental Public Bodies: a Guide for Departments* (Cabinet Office/Treasury 1992), advises ministers to tell Parliament when they are establishing a new advisory quango. But they are not obliged to do so. For example, DOE ministers set up an Expert Panel on Air Quality Standards in 1991. Its existence was not revealed to Parliament and it did not figure in the official government lists in *Public Bodies*. It finally entered the public domain – onto the full glare of the House of Commons Library shelves – only when it published three reports in 1994. Ministers have also kept the membership of advisory quangos secret. In 1994, the Ministry of Defence resisted requests for the identities of members of its advisory bodies from Labour MP Peter Kilfoyle (now a minister in the Cabinet Office) for three months, and only reluctantly released the names after he protested to the Speaker. The MOD kept the composition of three committees secret – the Nuclear Powered Warships Safety Committee, the Nuclear Weapons Safety Committee and (to protect members from being lobbied!) the Polar Medal Assessment Committee.

Ministers and the civil servants, who in practice generally decide who should join the committees, are not held accountable in law for whom they appoint to them, or for the balance of their memberships. The Committee for Standards in Public Life (now the Neill Committee) has so far failed to consider the special issues which arise in determining the balance between organised interests and consumer and public representation on such committees, and the personal and professional interests of their 'independent' members. The Commissioner for Public Appointments did not in 1997 keep watch over appointments to advisory quangos (see **p. 214**), though this is now to happen; nor are ministers obliged to take advice from the CPA's semi-independent panels on their composition. Ministers are usually constitutionally free to refer issues to these advisory bodies, and to accept or reject their advice, without explaining why to the quangos themselves, let alone to the public.

Advisory quangos

In theory, ministers remain directly responsible to Parliament for all the policies and decisions which emanate from their departments, including those taken on advice from such bodies. Yet they are often used to deflect responsibility. On occasions, ministers and senior officials use advisory bodies as 'stalking horses' for potentially unpopular policies which they are considering, or make them the repositories for tricky policy decisions for which they would rather avoid blame. Throughout the BSE policy disaster, ministers continually deflected any direct responsibility by stressing that they had acted at all times on specialist advice from the Spongiform Encephalopathy Advisory Committee (SEAC), the special advisory body set up to advise on the BSE crisis, even though that advice was influenced by their officials (see **pp. 282–289**).

The important 'judicial' and business-oriented advisory quangos are sometimes formal elements in closed 'policy communities' of civil servants and organised interests; and thus they play a significant role in influencing government policies at a formative stage, almost entirely outside either parliamentary or public scrutiny (see Chapter 10). While the participation on such committees of representatives of the major interests which are affected by their scrutiny, judgement and advice is valuable, not least in the provision of expert knowledge, experience and relevant information – often the *only* information available – the composition of the committees is often unbalanced by their presence; and it must be asked whether what they provide could be passed on in other ways, allowing the advisory bodies to perform a more judicial and disinterested role.

The apparent imbalance of advisory committees in significant policy areas is made more serious by the prevailing ethos of these bodies. The civil servants generally choose to sit on them 'independent members' and specialists who are willing to adopt a 'consensual' approach to the complex issues they address. This should not occasion surprise; as Lady Howe once observed, 'Ministers are not risk-takers. They want people who see the world in the same way as they do, so the same type of guys get appointed' (*Guardian*, 10 April 1991). Moreover, a Democratic Audit survey found in 1994 that members were often recruited through professional networks of contacts and previous service on other quangos – 'the old white lab coat' rather than the 'old school tie'. The survey identified a total of 213 appointed members who sat on 17 key advisory bodies in 1995. Twenty of them held multiple appointments – 44 places in all – on 13 of the quangos. The same five experts sat on both the twin committees on carcinogenicity and mutagenicity (DA Paper No. 4, 1995). There are usually also government assessors and occasionally (and increasingly) a few token consumer representatives on these bodies. However, consumer representatives are bound by rules of secrecy and consensus and are strongly discouraged from acting directly as representatives of consumer organisations or even consulting them. Thus, advisory quangos are often specialist forums within which policy communities of officials and outside interests negotiate and resolve particular or continuing issues; and frequently legitimate the resolution through their 'specialist' advice to ministers.

These tendencies result in advisory committees which are on the face of it close to 'capture' by the industries or interests they are supposed to be watching and regulating in the public interest. This danger is intensified by the fact that specialist or 'independent' members may also have substantial personal or professional interests in the industries on which they are sitting in judgement. It is not possible to quantify the full extent of commercial penetration of advisory quangos, because the individual members are not obliged by law to disclose their interests to the public and few departments list the members of advisory quangos on the official quango web-site, let alone their interests. Only 21 committees (just 3 per cent) choose to disclose this information voluntarily; and even then, they publish only the barest details (the nature of the interests and the companies involved). Yet the information available shows that expert members of the network of advisory bodies looking at the safety of medicines and food, for example, have had an alarmingly high level of personal and professional interests in major pharmaceutical and chemical companies. For example, disclosure of interests in 1995 revealed that:

- On the Committee on the Safety of Medicines, 15 of the 22 members held between them 24 consultancies, five shareholdings, two directorships, and two further posts with drug companies. Major companies provided a cornucopia of financial backing for the academic departments of 18 members.
- On the Medicines Commission – the appeal body (set up for the benefit of the companies) – 14 of 22 members held consultancies and shareholdings in ICI, Glaxo, Ares Serona, Cynanamid and other drug companies. One was a director and shareholder in Wellcome plc and several held shares in drug companies.
- On the Committee on the Toxicity of Chemicals in Food, Consumer Products and the Environment (COT), nine of the 13 members had personal interests in Britain's largest chemical and pharmaceutical companies. Six listed consultancies in 26 companies and four had 11 shareholdings between them. Members of COT with interests in companies whose products are under scrutiny are known to have been allowed to participate in the committee's discussions (DA Paper No. 4: 15–16).

There is no doubt about the scientific and technical competence, the dedication and probity of appointed members on the 17 key advisory quangos we sampled. The Democratic Audit survey revealed that most members serve out of a sense of public duty, their main reward being the professional recognition their membership confers. Some 86 per cent of members serve on an expenses-only basis and make up for the deficiencies in official back-up out of their own resources. Several committees command a world-wide reputation for the quality of their work. It is the framework within which they work that we question. It is impossible to rule out the possibility that the representatives of the affected industries on the committees, and the apparently wide scale of personal interests in those industries among specialist members, ultimately give those industries an undue influence on their decisions. This danger is further compounded by the power that officials, who usually work closely with the major interests involved within policy networks, possess over the committees. These 'government minders' (as one committee member described them) set the committees' agendas, provide much of the data on which they act, work closely with

the chairpersons, and usually draft the minutes and even their reports and conclusions. The consensual ethos of the committees and strong pressures on committee
members 'not to rock the boat' reinforce industry and government influences over
their recommendations. Officials can enforce such pressures through their powers
to replace members, if they so wish, when their terms of office end. Moreover, the
close links between members and industries inevitably leads to a culture of 'shared
assumptions' which may not be shared by excluded experts or the public at large.
In practice, this means that the specialists appointed are generally more open to
compromise with the representatives of the major industries who sit on the committees, with the policies of the sponsoring departments and with the views of the civil
servants who manage the committees.

Thus, it is not so much the danger of individual corruption, but a more subtle,
though discernible, process of accommodation to the needs of industry – often, as
in the case of pharmaceuticals and processed foods, vital to the UK economy – and
of government that is to be feared. The point is that there is ultimately no clear
boundary between the scientific, industrial and public policy aspects of a committee's
findings. They rarely deliver purely scientific, or 'technical', judgements. They are
seeking instead to strike a balance between risks and interests – as a member of the
Food Advisory Committee said, 'to balance purely scientific arguments on toxicology
and nutrition with legitimate industrial needs and pressures and wider issues of
customer acceptability' (DA Paper No. 4: 16).

This is not a function which should be performed in secrecy; it is as much a *political* task as a *scientific* one and thus belongs in the public domain.

In striking this balance, the committees are strongly influenced by two 'poles' –
the interests of industries which they often serve and the views of government departments which they are also serving. These industrial interests and official views
frequently coincide as they have been developed and defined within policy networks.
It is often hard to find the right balance. For example, though some members of
the advisory quango on managing radioactive waste (RAWMAC) felt that it was
'fiercely independent', gave 'balanced advice' and obliged the representatives of
British Nuclear Fuels plc, the government-owned firm, and the nuclear industry
body, Nirex, charged with finding a long-term disposal site for highly radioactive
waste, to explain and justify their proposals 'to a group of people who collectively
have the knowledge, experience and intelligence to make judgments', three others
complained:

> [T]he [nuclear] industry is well represented on RAWMAC and influences
> its work arguably to too great an extent.

> The nuclear industry has privileged access.

> [T]he committee find great difficulty in balancing the views of the industry
> and the public.

In fact, there is no formal balancing 'pole' labelled the 'public interest'. Advisory committees exist not to define and serve a wider public interest, but to advise government.

They consider the issues in the terms laid down for them by senior civil servants. These terms include an attitude towards measuring risks which is out of line with other European thinking. In the 1980s, Germany developed the 'principle of precaution' (*Vorsorgeprinzip*) which holds that policy-makers have a duty to transcend existing limits of scientific knowledge and evidence when making decisions where the consequences of alternative policy options are not determinable on the basis of scientific evidence alone and where potentially high costs may be incurred in taking or not taking action. The UK came into conflict over nitrate levels in drinking water with the European Commission and environmental groups in the 1980s. The British government consistently argued that suggested links between stomach cancer and nitrates in water were not supported by the existing evidence, while the Commission and others argued the need for precaution in case such links did actually exist. In the same way, the Ministry of Agriculture and the BSE advisory committee ignored the 'precautionary principle' in the analysis and handling of the BSE crisis (Professor Brian Wynne in *The Times Higher Education Supplement*, 12 April 1996; and see Chapter 10).

Professor Wynne, who is research director at the Centre for the Study of Environmental Change, University of Lancaster, told us that rather than adopting such a principle, committees often came under strong pressures from both industry and government to come to 'acceptable conclusions' for ministers within existing policy guidelines:

> Against such pressures, it is very hard, with the best will in the world, to establish and defend objectivity. There are intense pressures of severe lobbying from industrial interests to licence products in which a colossal amount of research and development investment has been made.

Further, the bodies often operate under serious pressures of time and resources. Our survey found that members generally felt that their research and administrative back-up was inadequate and they often depended on manufacturers' own data and evidence (on at least one occasion we found that a committee's report was closely based on an industry's own memorandum). Usually, a committee's secretariat writes a draft report which is then collectively amended. Decisions are taken by consensus, not a vote. This process clearly makes a committee's recommendations vulnerable to a subtle steer from officials, who may insert or alter key recommendations or comments (see **p. 286**), or a strong chairperson's wishes, or indeed both. There have been allegations that some reports have been steamrollered through.

The network of major advisory quangos on overseas trade also raises serious questions about the interests of participating companies. Five major building and engineering companies, represented on two of the (then) DTI advisory NDPBs – the British Overseas Trade Board (BOTB) and the Overseas Projects Board (OPB) – took nearly 40 per cent of the government's £1.37 billion Aid and Trade Provision (ATP) between 1978 and 1996. These companies were Trafalgar House (including Davy and John Brown Engineering); GEC; Balfour Beatty, joint contractor on the Pergau dam project in Malaysia (see **p. 323–324**); Biwater; and AMEC. Four of the companies were donors to the Conservative Party, contributing nearly

£1 million from 1979 to 1996. In addition, in the 1980s BICC, the parent company of the fifth, Balfour Beatty, gave £90,000 to Aims of Industry, British United Industrialists and the Economic League – all bodies associated with the Conservative Party. The companies are, of course, specialists in big construction and engineering projects and have proven records. They also enjoyed a close relationship with government and, between them, the boards on which their representatives served had a high degree of influence on Britain's exports and aid and trade policies, and especially on policy on large construction projects. The BOTB was chaired by ministers, but the vice-chairman, the Duke of Kent, was a director of BICC; and below BOTB, the head of AMEC chaired OPB, on which also sat representatives of GEC, Davy and Biwater, with officials from the DTI, the Export Credit Guarantee Board and the Overseas Development Administration (ODA, now DfID). The projects board's role was officially described as follows:

> To provide a means of achieving closer communication between industry and government in respect of major project business; to give industry a voice in the formulation of government policy in relation to major overseas projects; to advise the projects and export policy division of the DTI on the provision of assistance under . . . the Aid and Trade Provision.

The ATP scheme was actually part of Britain's overseas aid budget. ATP funds were diverted to fund part of the Pergau dam project in Malaysia in a link with arms deals worth £1.3 billion (a course of action which the High Court found to be unlawful in 1994). Analysis of overseas aid payments during this period showed that countries like Malaysia and Indonesia, which bought British arms, were far more likely to be beneficiaries than the poorest nations in need of the aid. Andrew Lees, of Friends of the Earth, complained that the boards operated 'like a cosy cartel, or private club, whose members benefit from taxpayers' subsidies which, while lucrative to those companies, are actually of questionable aid and economic benefit (*Independent on Sunday*, 13 February 1993). For example, the Pergau dam project was initially allocated aid funds totalling as much as Britain gave to Somalia, Ethiopia and Tanzania combined in 1992. The gross national product per capita in those countries was £70–£85, compared with £1,775 in Malaysia.

The OPB board members took a close interest in the government's confidential review in 1992–93 of the ATP's budget and workings, prompted by problems with administering the aid. The Pergau dam was not the only controversial project. In January 1985, the DTI had forced through a £14.4 million aid grant for a dam in Sri Lanka, to be built by Balfour Beatty, against objections from the ODA and the Treasury. The company was already constructing two other dams and the National Audit Office reported that the ODA and the Treasury therefore questioned what additional advantage could be gained from further aid assistance. Other trade-related projects provoked objections from the ODA and the Treasury, as well as from aid pressure groups. The OPB was the only organisation which was 'invited' to give evidence to the review of the ATP. No aid groups were consulted. The results of the review – but not any findings – were made public in June 1993. ATP funds were to be switched to 'credit-worthy, low-income ... developing countries' and 'more systematic appraisal' of the ATP's commercial and industrial benefits was promised. But Malaysia, Indonesia, Chile, Morocco and Thailand were all awarded ATP contracts after 1993.

Openness and accountability of advisory quangos

Advisory quangos are secretive bodies. There is no officially recognised principle of public access to their activities. The data and evidence they examine are only rarely disclosed in full, even to other specialists. Their discussions are kept secret, their agendas and minutes are scarcely ever published – only 14 (out of 674 bodies) are required by law to make them available, and another 32 have done so voluntarily (see Table 8.4). The public, specialist observers and members of interest groups which do not have representatives on the committees are excluded from dialogue with them and consultation is generally minimal. No advisory body is governed by the code of access to official information; only five advisory bodies are required to consult the public, and just four must consult relevant outside interests. The government's own guidance on quangos for departments states that annual reports and accounts represent 'the primary method of openness to Parliament and the public'. But even at this most basic level, very few advisory quangos (39) are required to publish annual reports and fewer still (33) to lay them before Parliament. None are required to make a register of their members' interests available to the public. None fall within the jurisdiction of the Ombudsman.

As for their dealings with government, only 12 advisory quangos are under a duty to publish their advice and the government need publish its response to just half of them in return. This includes the Boundary Commissions, whose recommendations

Table 8.4 The openness and accountability of advisory quangos, 1997

| | Required to | | Voluntary arrangement | |
	No.	%	No.	%
Publish an annual report	39	6	64	9
Lay report before Parliament	33	5	23	3
Publish a register of members' interests	0	0	21	3
Publish agendas of meetings	14	2	32	5
Publish minutes of meetings	14	2	32	5
Hold public meetings	14	2	39	6
Observe government's openness code	0	0	–	–
Consult outside interests	4	1	33	5
Consult the general public	5	1	39	6
Publish advice to government	12	2	42	6
Relations with Government				
Government must consult prior to legislating	29	4	3	0.4
Government must respond publicly to advice	6	1	–	–

Source: Parliamentary Questions, March 1997; Democratic Audit research

inevitably belong in the public domain. The government is required to consult just 29 advisory quangos (4 per cent) before legislating in their subject areas, of which two involve substantial policy questions – the Social Security Advisory Committee and the Northern Ireland Standing Advisory Commission on Human Rights (SACHR) (see DA Paper No. 4 further). Again, some quangos act voluntarily – for example, 42 have decided to publish their advice to government. Overall, these obligations mean less in practice than they seem to promise. For example, Conservative governments generally ran roughshod over advice from the Social Security Advisory Committee. In the 1990s, 250 organisations made submissions to the advisory committee on the government's proposals for asylum seekers. They were universally against the asylum proposals, as was the committee's own advice. But Peter Lilley, the Social Security Secretary, ignored their representations and introduced his proposals in regulations which came into force in February 1996 (*Statewatch*, September/October 1996). The government also several times neglected its elementary legal duty to consult SACHR (e.g., over the restriction of the 'right to silence' in criminal trials in Northern Ireland).

Even where advisory bodies are under a statutory duty, it is by no means certain that they follow it. We found in 1995, for example, that some departments did not even know that some of their advisory bodies were under such a duty to publish annual reports. In fact, annual reports were often difficult, or impossible, to obtain (even with the assistance of MPs); and some quangos produced them, but not for public consumption! On an Index of Openness, the average information score for reports we did obtain was a poor 4.5 out of ten (DA Paper No. 4: 10–12).

It is true that quite a few advisory quangos do voluntarily make up for the absence of statutory accountability and openness; our necessarily incomplete figures show for example that, on a voluntary basis, 64 (9 per cent) publish annual reports, 39 (6 per cent) consult the public, and 21 (3 per cent) make a register of members' interests public (see Table 8.4 for more details). Some MAFF advisory bodies publish digests and other material for the public; the advice of the Advisory Committee on Hazardous Substances is said to be 'available for public scrutiny'; RAWMAC says its advice is 'normally published', but at the same time some members complain that its publicity is self-interested public relations which disguises a 'tendency to unnecessary secrecy'. RAWMAC also tried to suppress information which was statutorily available under environmental information regulations, arguing that they did not apply to the committee (DA Paper No. 4: 11) – an attempt which illustrates the obvious point that voluntary action is an inadequate substitute for legal rules. Table 8.5 makes this point forcibly, listing as it does 20 key advisory quangos for which enforceable rules of accountability, openness and public access are very important. Yet statutory rules are as rare as hawks.

In February 1997 the then government promised to consider making 'selected' advisory NDPBs accountable to the Ombudsman, thus making them subject to the openness code at the same time; and now, of course, the Labour government is committed to making all quangos subject to a statutory Freedom of Information (FOI) regime. The promise of statutory openness could mean the opening up of this opaque layer of government. But there will be obstacles. Much of the work of the

Table 8.5 Twenty key advisory quangos: openness and accountability, 1997

	Publish an annual report	Lay report before Parliament	Publish a register of members' interests	Publish agendas of meetings	Publish minutes of meetings	Hold public meetings	Observe openness code	Consult outside interests	Consult the general public	Publish advice to government	Government consults before legislating	Government responds publicly to advice
Advisory Committee on Hazardous Substances	❖	✗	❖	✗	✗	✗	✗	✗	✗	✗	▲	✗
Advisory Committee on the Micro-biological Safety of Food	❖	❖	❖	✗	✗	✗	✗	❖	❖	❖	✗	✗
Advisory Committee on NHS Drugs	✗	✗	✗	✗	✗	✗	✗	✗	✗	✗	✗	✗
Advisory Committee on Novel Foods and Processes	❖	✗	❖	✗	✗	✗	✗	❖	❖	❖	✗	✗
Advisory Committee on Pesticides	❖	✗	❖	✗	✗	✗	✗	✗	✗	✗	▲	✗
Advisory Committee on Releases to the Environment	❖	✗	❖	✗	✗	✗	✗	✗	✗	✗	▲	✗
Committee on Carcinogenicity of Chemicals in Food, Consumer Products and the Environment	❖	✗	❖	✗	✗	✗	✗	✗	✗	✗	✗	✗
Committee on Medical Aspects of Food Policy	❖	✗	❖	✗	✗	✗	✗	✗	❖	❖	✗	✗
Committee for Monitoring Agreements on Tobacco Advertising and Sponsorship	❖	✗	❖	✗	✗	✗	✗	✗	✗	✗	✗	✗
Committee on Medical Aspects of Radiation in the Environment	✗	✗	❖	✗	✗	✗	✗	✗	✗	✗	✗	✗
Committee on Mutagenicity of Chemicals in Food, Consumer Products and the Environment	❖	✗	❖	✗	✗	✗	✗	✗	✗	✗	✗	✗
Committee on the Safety of Medicines	▲	▲	✗	✗	✗	✗	✗	✗	✗	✗	▲	✗
Committee on Toxicity of Chemicals in Food, Consumer Products and the Environment	❖	✗	❖	✗	✗	✗	✗	✗	✗	❖	✗	✗
Food Advisory Committee	❖	✗	❖	✗	✗	✗	✗	❖	❖	❖	✗	✗
Medicines Commission	▲	▲	❖	✗	✗	✗	✗	✗	✗	✗	▲	✗
Nuclear Powered Warships Safety Committee	✗	✗	✗	✗	✗	✗	✗	✗	✗	✗	✗	✗
Nuclear Weapons Safety Committee	✗	✗	✗	✗	✗	✗	✗	✗	✗	✗	✗	✗
RAWMAC (Radioactive Waste Management AC)	✗	✗	✗	✗	✗	✗	✗	✗	✗	✗	✗	✗
Royal Commission on Environmental Pollution	✗	✗	✗	✗	✗	✗	✗	❖	❖	❖	✗	✗
Spongiform Encephalopathy Advisory (BSE) Committee	✗	✗	✗	✗	✗	✗	✗	✗	✗	✗	✗	✗

Source: Parliamentary Questions, March 1997

Key
❖ voluntary
▲ statutory
✗ no

most sensitive advisory quangos may well remain behind closed doors. The documents and advice produced by the 20 'key' advisory bodies in Table 8.5, and other significant bodies such as the British Overseas Trade Board (BOTB) and its satellites, may very well remain secret. Their activities and advice all fall within the categories of 'policy advice', national security and defence, and 'commercial confidentiality', in each of which there will be either a 'simple' or 'substantial' harm test before information will be disclosed under the new FOI regime (Cabinet Office 1997c: Chapter 3). The ethos of responsible 'discretion' imposed on board members by departments will have to be eradicated if a new culture of openness is to take root. Finally, there are also statutory bars on disclosure from certain committees, like the Committee on the Safety of Medicines (CSM) and the Medicines Commission. Members of both bodies commit a criminal offence if they pass on information (under the Medicines Act 1968). Labour's FOI white paper promises to repeal or amend such bars 'where appropriate' (*ibid.*: para. 3.20).

However, no-one should under-estimate the influence which industries affected by the activities of advisory bodies have on government, and especially the senior bureaucrats with whom they may well have formed closed 'policy communities' of mutual value (see Chapter10); such communities often form around advisory bodies, as a pharmaceutical community does around the CSM and Medicines Commission. On past performance, industries and the communities to which they belong are likely to seek to retain statutory bars on disclosure and to protect the secrecy within which advisory quangos now operate. Take, for example, Labour MP Giles Radice's attempt in 1993 to make a limited amount of information on the safety of medicines publicly available. His private member's bill was carefully negotiated with drug companies to make it acceptable to them. As William Ascher, former chairman of the CSM, informed us:

> The Radice bill would not in any way have interfered with commercial confidentiality. It would have enabled people such as myself to explain why a drug is approved or withdrawn, something which I think would have been helpful to the population, and doctors above all, to know.

The government did not openly oppose the bill. But the pharmaceutical industry, which objected to the merest chink of light being cast on the production and safety of drugs, was wholly opposed to its modest proposals. The pharmaceutical community swung into action. Government ministers and civil servants combined with backbench government MPs (one of them a consultant to the pharmaceutical industry) to kill the bill. Drug companies and civil servants provided briefs for the MPs who talked the bill out.

AUDIT

As we have seen, executive agencies and quangos can act as flexible and efficient agents for a wide range of public functions. They form a significant, but largely unaccountable and secretive, layer of government in the UK. A reform agenda is now under way, mostly centred upon executive quangos, and is likely to continue. But in late 1997 quangos remained only fitfully subject to a series of basic measures of accountability, openness and public access, partially offset by voluntary measures in some cases. They are formally accountable upwards to ministers and departments, but at a significant remove from ministers. Executive agencies are, by contrast, formally more accountable and certainly more open than their parent departments, but their accountability rests almost entirely upon the unworkable principle of ministerial responsibility (see Chapter 12).

The informal nature of governing arrangements in Britain means that executive agencies and quangos alike can readily be created by ministers or departments, without being checked by constitutional rules or coming under the scrutiny of a constitutional watch-dog, such as the *Conseil d'État* in France. The issue of public access is important across the board of executive and advisory quangos, and here the contrast with the United States is significant. There postwar 'access' laws require most public agencies to make their meetings open to the public and papers available; insist upon balance in the membership of their boards; and provide legal safeguards against conflicts of interest. The President is also bound to report annually on their activities, status and changes in the composition of their boards.

DAC8: Ministerial responsibility for quangos

We go on in Chapter 12 to examine the principle of ministerial responsibility in full. Clearly, however, the idea that ministers can be responsible for the huge and diverse company of executive agencies, executive and advisory quangos – some 6,450 in all – is absurd. In the case of executive NDPBs alone, the Cabinet Office has admitted that neither ministers nor Parliament had the information needed to judge how they were performing, and noted weak departmental controls and ministerial neglect, stating that in some cases, the relationship between departments and NDPBs was 'effectively non-existent'. We have emphasised the government's deployment of quangos as instruments of its policies. But at the same time the proliferation of 'partial governments' has created a host of potentially independent sources of power and patronage, unchecked both by political mechanisms and a coherent regime of public law.

In the case of 'arm's-length' quangos, the idea that ministers should exercise direct control is questionable. Such bodies are caught in a contradictory trap. On the one hand, they need to be protected from partisan politics and direct government control; on the other, the unchecked exercise of independent powers by unelected bodies is contrary to basic principles of representative democracy. The traditional idea that governments would observe conventions safeguarding the independence of such bodies from political interference might well have provided a reasonable compromise between the two democratic goods in the past, but it no longer does so now. The treatment of the BBC, for example, under Mrs Thatcher's governments is eloquent enough testimony of that (see Barnett and Curry 1994). Bodies such as the National Consumer Council, Equal Opportunities Commission and others are in need of formal arrangements which allow for government's ultimate responsibility for such bodies, but also provide some means to protect their independence.

DAC11: The rule of law and transparent rules of conduct

We consider in Chapter 15 how effectively the courts are able to enforce the rule of law in so far as the conduct of the executive, including quangos, is concerned. However, as we have shown above, quangos are not governed by a regime of constitutional or public law sufficient to render them accountable and open, and to give the public adequate access to their business. The Nolan Committee recommended that the government should undertake a full and co-ordinated review with a view to producing a more consistent legal framework, governing propriety and accountability in public bodies. The government's response was largely confined to audit and financial and administrative controls, and failed to measure up to the need for comprehensive review. Nolan's principles for public life, the new appointments process, the spread of codes of conduct, and so on, represent a significant, but piecemeal, advance in the governance of executive NDPBs. But the need for a full regime of public law is unmet (see Chapter 15).

DAC9: Parliamentary scrutiny of government

There is a sense in which quasi-government diminishes the role and authority of Parliament as well as its more obvious erosion of local government. In practice, the quango state removes layers and areas of policy-making and action from the parliamentary – and public – gaze. The absence of a constitutional framework and the informal and secretive nature of its policy processes blocks scrutiny and parliamentary and public debate about policy goals and outcomes. The government can co-opt and mobilise all manner of bodies, including private companies, consultants and advisers within the domain of quasi-government to carry out major tasks, such as industrial re-structuring, training and employment policies. Parliament has no oversight over the government's creatures, their interests and processes, as they operate under cover of ministerial discretion. Indeed, even the government itself often has no direct control over them.

DAC17: Openness and accountability at local level

DAC18: The independence of local and regional governing arrangements

We deal in detail with the effect of quangos on the arrangements for local and regional governance in the next chapter. Here we briefly review the implications of the hierarchies of national, regional and local quangos which have been erected to remove public functions and services from local government. National and regional quangos are accountable upwards to central government; local quangos are accountable upwards to central government and national quangos, thus usurping the role of locally elected government. Neither national, regional nor local quangos are directly accountable to local communities for the policies they frame for local communities, the resources they make available, the functions they perform or the services they deliver. The current situation is manifestly imperfect and does not possess the potential for local democracy which local government, for all its failings, still does.

9 Government Below the Centre

Government at regional and local level

In the ideally-sized unit, a dissatisfied farmer anywhere within its boundaries ought to be able to travel by public transport to the administrative capital, horse-whip the responsible official, and get home again by public transport, all in the same day.

(Quoted in the Report of the Royal Commission
on the Constitution, 1973)

Local government is government by local communities rather than of local communities. It is a means by which local communities may take decisions affecting the delivery of public services in their areas. It is not a necessary element of local government that it should itself deliver services. . . . Nor is it necessary that it should have the sole power of decision over those services. . . . But it is necessary that local government should allow a local view to be expressed through the taking of decisions.

(The Widdicombe Report on the Conduct of Local
Authority Business, 1986)

The UK is made up of three countries and part of a fourth (England, Wales, Scotland and Northern Ireland) and contains three legal systems. Yet its essential governing structure is unitary. There is a single Parliament and a single executive, or 'government', and the machinery of government reflects this unitary character. Though devolution in Scotland, Wales and Northern Ireland is now on the agenda, in 1997, the UK denied its constituent countries and regions any formally elected democratic expression at regional or 'national' level, and was the only major nation-state in western Europe which did not have elected regional assemblies (and the smaller European states are only the size of UK regions). This chapter considers the democratic implications of this informal, powerful and highly centralised way of governing. Chapter 8 has dealt with central government's deployment of quangos at different levels within Britain, and the analysis of their impact on local government overlaps considerably with this chapter. The two chapters are best read in conjunction. Here, we concentrate on the relationship between central and local government; the centre's presence at regional level; its inroads at local level, including controls over local authority policies and spending, and the shift in local policy-making and service delivery to local quangos. We largely apply two Audit criteria:

DAC17. Openness and accountability at regional and local level.

DAC18. The independence of governing arrangements at regional and local level.

233

Devolution

We also measure regional and local democracy using other Audit criteria, including

DAC1. Popular election at regional and local level.

DAC8. Control of bureaucrats by elected politicians.

DAC16. Access to elected politicians who are able to provide effective representation.

Regional arrangements within Britain

Referendums in Scotland and Wales in September 1997 have endorsed the Labour government's proposals for a Scottish Parliament and Welsh Assembly. This chapter is being written before those proposals reach fruition, and our audit is largely based on existing arrangements, as of mid-1997. The arrangements set in place by the Labour government will be subjected to scrutiny in the next audit of democracy in the UK at the end of the government's current term in office. The central state currently has recognised the existence of two distinct nations within the UK, largely through establishing its outposts – the Scottish and Welsh Offices – in Edinburgh and Cardiff. However, London's senior civil service was always quite clear that both offices belonged to 'Whitehall' rather than Scotland or Wales. Northern Ireland – a special case – did possess a devolved assembly at Stormont, but it was pro-rogued in 1972 as a result of 'the troubles' and Northern Ireland has since been firmly ruled from Whitehall. However, again, peace negotiations within the province have brought about a carefully balanced scheme for devolution and a power-sharing Assembly.

Technically, Scotland did not enter a unitary state in the 1707 Act of Union, but into an 'incorporating union'. Scotland retained its own law and legal system, its local government structure, a distinctive education system, and its own established religion. The Scottish Office was set up in 1885 and the post of Secretary of State for Scotland created. The Prime Minister, Lord Salisbury, said that 'the whole object of the move is to redress the wounded dignities of the Scotch people', and the first Scottish Secretary feared that he would have nothing to do. The first Scottish Office was actually established in London and was very much a token gesture; however, over time, the Scottish Office has achieved a considerable degree of autonomy and it became the primary focus of government in Scotland after 1945. The result was a governing system which was both 'dependent and independent within the British system' (Kellas 1989); Scottish legislation passed through the UK Parliament and a Scottish Grand Committee existed. In all manner of institutions and realms – the law, churches, schools and universities, party politics, the media, poetry, the novel, song and cinema – a sense of Scottish identity has grown during the same period. Nearly two-thirds of Scots people give priority to being Scottish rather than British (Rowntree Reform Trust/ICM 1992). Scotland has thus long been ripe for some degree of devolution. The Scottish Nationalist Party has gradually grown in force.

From 1989–95, a Scottish Constitutional Convention prepared for devolution, uniting Labour, the Liberal Democrats, trade unions, churches, and other bodies and groups, behind proposals for a devolved Scottish Parliament, elected by proportional representation and holding tax-raising and spending powers. These proposals form the basis of the Labour government's devolution legislation.

Wales has no such tradition of autonomy, having been administered by England for more than 400 years. Its nationalist movement has been vexed by divisions, largely between South and North Wales, and has historically been as concerned with the Welsh language as with distinctive politics. Wales only obtained its first designated minister in 1957 (until then, the Home Secretary was responsible for Welsh affairs); the Welsh Office was established only in 1964, when the first Secretary of State, with a seat in the cabinet, was also appointed. The first Plaid Cymru MP – for Carmarthen – was elected in 1996. Under the Conservative government, Wales was ruled by a series of Secretaries of State of English (not Welsh) origin, some of them very able and committed to regeneration of the Welsh economy, often through a new network of quangos (see Chapter 8). In 1993, a Welsh Language Act tackled grievances over the neglect of the language.

Within England, regional identities are generally weak. In 1946, the Treasury established nine 'standard regions' in England for the purposes of central government administration, but in a typically piecemeal way central functions were decentralised over time to create a bewildering variety of regional offices, bodies and boundaries, even within departments. When the Department of the Environment was set up in 1971, to integrate the work of three existing departments (housing and local government, transport and works), it found itself with no fewer than 13 separate regional organisations (Constitution Unit 1996a: 16–17). The 1964–70 Labour government established eight 'top-down' appointed regional economic planning councils (REPCs). These were abolished in 1979 by the new Conservative government, but in 1994, the Conservatives established the existing pattern of 10 'integrated' government offices for the regions to co-ordinate and deliver most central government services and functions in the regions. They brought together the regional offices of the departments for the Environment, Trade and Industry, Transport and the training and enterprise division of Employment. But this initiative has not been wholly absorbed within government and conflicts between their boundaries and those of other government agencies and quangos still exist. For example, while the Housing Corporation has adjusted its regional offices to fit regional office boundaries, both the Highways and Benefits Agencies have retained quite different boundaries.

The main task of the regional offices was initially to administer a single regeneration budget (SRB) and to integrate their other departmental programmes. The SRB brought together some 20 separate existing (largely inner-city) schemes into a single £1.4 billion programme for regional regeneration and economic development. In 1997, they also took on responsibility for co-ordinating the 'welfare to work' programme in the regions and localities. At the same time, the new Labour government announced plans for nine powerful new quangos, regional development agencies, but regional assemblies are to be introduced, if at all, in a piecemeal fashion thereafter.

These are significant moves towards regionalism, but they do not represent the kind of democratic advance hinted at by John Selwyn Gummer, the Environment Secretary, at the launch of regional offices in 1994. 'We are devolving responsibility away from Whitehall', he said, promising that local needs would determine the priorities of the integrated government offices. But the new government offices are simply regional arms of central government. They are 'top-down' organisations which are focused on improving central government's activities in the regions rather than representing regional interests and views to central government (though they are officially recognised as government's 'eyes and ears' in the regions). They involve no devolution of powers or responsibilities and remain firmly within the central hierarchy of ministerial responsibility to Parliament. They play a significant role in usurping the functions of local authorities, conducting auctions of bids by local authorities for funding for local developments on criteria of their own, and working closely with networks of local quangos, agencies and businesses which transfer functions and services away from elected councils.

Local authorities therefore play a subordinate role, largely confined to bidding for funds for projects designed by regional officials. Some observers have expressed worries that these officials operate at a distance from ministers, thus weakening the practice of ministerial responsibility to Parliament (Bogdanor 1997: 44). The offices do prepare annual 'regeneration statements', but these are largely for the guidance of business, local authorities, and so on.

The contrast with the progress towards regional democracy in other major European states is striking. Postwar Germany was established as a federal republic, but in Italy, France and Spain the development of effective regionalism has happened since the 1970s. There was undoubtedly a strong technocratic impulse, but regionalism has gradually taken democratic form. In Italy, the regions first acquired administrative functions, but then took on narrowly defined, but real, legislative powers for the exercise of those functions. The French regional assemblies were initially mere co-ordinating bodies, but were given a range of direct powers in France's mid-1980s decentralisation programme. Under a kind of 'de-colonisation' process in Spain, the regions each negotiate powers and a level of autonomy with central government, drawing on a menu of available powers specified by the national constitution.

Britain's flirtations with regionalism have long been inspired by recognition of the key role that regions play in economic progress rather than any desire to devolve democratic powers. Up to 1997, the government offices managed a mix of regeneration and economic programmes under the supervision of a cabinet committee (on competitiveness) chaired by the deputy premier, Michael Heseltine; a cross-departmental management board in Whitehall; and 17 'sponsor' ministers for particular cities and smaller regions. The government offices also had a co-ordinating role over sub-regional and local quangos, such as the training and enterprise councils and career service companies, which were active in training, employment and regeneration activities. The offices themselves have greatly improved the co-ordination of government's regional policies and programmes and the presence of a single regional director in each region has made central government's presence and influence in the regions more visible. Their handling of the single regeneration budget and local authority bids won praise from MPs on the Environment Committee in 1996. They have been able to co-ordinate regional responses to inward investment and packages of remedial measures when major industries close. They have contributed to more integrated transport strategies. But the local authority associations and trade unions have both complained about their lack of consultation with local authorities and communities, and argue that the regional offices have not provided an effective mechanism for enabling local authorities to work in partnership with central government at the regional level (see AMA 1992). In particular, thus far there seems to have been little discretion, tailored to regional differences, over funding economic and industrial initiatives. Local authorities are also frustrated by the scepticism of the government offices about 'Europe of the Regions' and the limited backing they give to local authorities seeking to benefit from EU regional funds (Constitution Unit 1996a).

The 1964–70 Labour government set up two royal commissions to consider sub-national tiers of government. The first, the Redcliffe–Maud Commission on Local Government in England, recommended eight provincial councils, indirectly elected from local government, to co-ordinate the activities of the REPCs. The second, the Royal Commission on the Constitution, was asked to examine the regional dimensions of government in the UK in the light of a revival in Scottish and Welsh nationalism. The Commission was split several ways and issued a majority and minority report in 1973: bare majorities recommended devolution for Scotland and Wales, while the minority report came out strongly for devolution to five English regions. The Labour government of 1974–79 passed Acts creating weak devolved assemblies in Scotland and Wales, but the Scottish proposal for a chamber with no tax-raising powers failed to gain sufficient support in the Scottish referendum which followed; and the Welsh people voted heavily against an assembly. So neither was established. But the demand for devolution continued, strongly in Scotland, less so in Wales. In 1997, the Labour and Liberal Democrat parties agreed jointly on the plans for a Scottish Parliament and Welsh Assembly which are now to be legislated for. They are to be established on a devolved basis – that is, the plans do not envisage a 'federal' UK, but confer a measure of 'home rule' on both nations. Whitehall and Westminster will retain residual authority and certain policy areas, like overall taxation, social security, defence and foreign policy, remain their property. The Scottish Parliament will possess legislative powers in devolved areas of government and limited tax-varying powers; the Welsh Assembly will be able only to pass secondary legislation (see Chapter 13) under UK statutes, and will have no powers over taxation. The role and powers of both chambers in relation to central government would therefore not be determined by a constitution and in theory at least both assemblies could be revoked by the UK Parliament.

There is no corresponding pressure for regional democracy in England, except in London, the north and to some extent in the south-west. Both Labour and the Liberal Democrats have proposed a gradual approach to introducing regional assemblies in England, though their actual proposals differ significantly. The Labour government has prepared proposals for a Mayor for London, who will possess executive powers and will be checked by a small new elected assembly. But these

Regional corporatism

proposals, which were endorsed by a referendum in London in May 1998, are for a local, not regional, authority. Labour's other proposals for the English regions envisage first indirectly elected regional chambers of local authority representatives in the regions (plus a 'corporate' element of business, trade union and community interests). These assemblies could become directly elected where there is demand, subject to a referendum.

State governance at regional level

There has long been a tradition of 'regional corporatism' in the UK, which has incorporated local government (as well as central government), commerce and industry, and traditional land owners. This corporatist regime focused largely on economic development, regional infrastructure, transport and planning issues. After 1979, Conservative governments were supposed to have reversed the 'corporatist tendency' in Britain (Middlemas 1979), but this oversimplifies what has happened at national and regional level. Corporatism has continued in the regions, but it has been a 'select corporatism', with a relative (but not absolute) exclusion of trade unions and local government, and an emphasis on wider business interests and land development capital. This sort of corporatism diminishes democratic practice because the government privileges and negotiates with interest groups in conditions of near secrecy; and the representatives of those groups act with no clear public account-ability, even to the constituencies they represent.

Corporatism became general in the regions under wartime planning systems and flourished again in the 1960s and early 1970s, especially in the north where 'regions' were places suffering from economic decline and required 'regional policies' to solve their problems. The key formal agencies were Labour's regional economic planning councils, on which industrialists, trade unionists and independent experts sat. The crucial role of local authorities as controllers of land development required their presence, and this added a degree of democratic legitimacy by connecting regional activities to democratic structures below. Development capital was also represented, signifying the importance of control over land in shaping regional and city planning processes. It is not yet clear exactly how the new Labour government's regional development agencies are to be constituted, but they look like linear descendants of the 1964–70 government's REPCs (though probably with stronger business representation).

This kind of corporatism was – and may be – more representative than post-1979 'select corporatism', but the REPCs were appointed bodies. There was no popular control over the activities of these secretive bodies. Indeed, initiatives originating at this level and carried out by local authorities or new town agencies made planning unpopular through major and insensitive reconstruction of urban centres, inner-city road schemes and the deportation of communities to 'outer estates'. The local authority members of these corporatist regional bodies were as likely to act as the agents of REPCs at local level as the other way around, but mostly acted 'off their own bat'. The danger therefore is that Labour will thus be re-introducing in the late 1990s a similarly remote corporatist strand of regional governance with the new business-led RDAs, unless a dynamic of elected regional authorities can be established. Under current plans, the RDAs will have local authority representatives on their boards, and will be obliged to consult 'voluntary' regional chambers, but this is only a partial democratic check.

Meanwhile, networks of quangos directing national and regional enterprise, training, employment and urban development policies, remain in place in 1997. Among them are English Partnerships, the Rural Development Commission, Scottish Enterprise, Highlands and Islands Enterprise, the Scottish Economic Council, the Council for Scottish Industrial Development, the Welsh Development Agency, the Development Board for Rural Wales, Enterprise Ulster, the Local Enterprise Development Unit and Industrial Development Board in Northern Ireland, as well as local training and enterprise councils (TECs) in England and Wales, and local enterprise companies (LECs) in Scotland, new town commissions, further education corporations, career service companies, and several advisory panels, though the activities of such bodies as survive in Scotland and Wales will be brought under the democratic surveillance of the new Parliament and Assembly. In general, business people have been appointed to these bodies – some of which are formally constituted as private companies – and dominate them on the New Right principle that choices and efficiency are maximised through the market, and not politics. We dealt in detail with the role of quangos in Chapter 8. Here we briefly consider aspects of their role and operations at varying regional levels and at local level.

The most active bodies are the 105 TECs and LECs which take the form of private companies and generally cover 'journey to work' lower regional areas. At least two-thirds of members must by law be senior private sector managers. Thus the TECs are lead agencies of a new select corporatism, empowering new local business elites to take over a range of responsibilities from local and national government (see Shaw 1990). In 1993, John Selwyn Gummer officially recognised the TECs as 'the key private-sector partners' of the newly established government regional offices, 'for the full range of regeneration and economic development activities in their localities' (HC Deb, 4 November 1993, c516). A government press release the same day asserted that, 'The priorities in each area will be different. The best people to judge that are the people who live there.' However, those people were clearly the 'business leaders on TEC boards', rather than citizens in general or local authorities. Much is made of the responsibility of TECs to the communities which are their 'customers', and various mechanisms have been devised to provide a surrogate accountability. But they are not required to make a reality of even this limited goal and official encouragement of 'openness' clashes with private sector canons of confidentiality. Crucial information has been concealed from public view on the grounds that it is the commercially confidential property of private companies.

The TEC National Council published a framework of local accountability in 1995 and it has been adopted by all TECs. Thus, they are now enjoined to publish their directors' interests and to make public information on their financial operations. Well-publicised public meetings, 'clarity of mission' and 'extensive consultation' are officially regarded as evidence of their commitment to local communities. Moves are being made to restore and enhance links with local authorities. But their very composition makes them closed and elite bodies, dealing with elite partners, outside any democratic structures. Even the most progressive TEC board members resist the idea that members of the public might be given rights of access to meetings and documents and assert that their colleagues would choose not to continue were such requirements to be imposed. As the Nolan report on local public spending bodies pointed out, local publicity, and even consultation, are not the same thing as local accountability, as many TEC board members seem to believe.

The TECs have already played a big role in second-level regional and local governance and seem likely to figure prominently in the new Labour government's employment and training programme (Graham 1998). Just how broad are their responsibilities? From the beginning, each TEC was urged to adopt a broad vision for 'constructive change within its community' because:

> As important as training is, it is not by itself enough to attract and sustain the interest of top chief executives. These men and women will be concerned with the central issues that affect the quality of life in the place where they live and work and where their children go to school. They will be concerned with the education system, with training, with employment and economic development: because they will understand that these are *all* strands that affect local economic growth and community regeneration.
>
> (Stratton 1990: 71)

This statement betrays the weakness of the argument that bodies like TECs simply perform a 'technical' and 'professional' function which can properly be accomplished outside popular control. For this is indeed a 'broad' agenda which may very well 'sustain the interest of top chief executives'. It also sustains a much wider circle of interest. Other citizens are concerned with the 'quality of life in the place where they live and work and where their children go to school', and with schools, employment opportunities, and so on. Thus, it is an agenda which demands democratic participation, preferably under the ultimate control of the vote, and certainly with mechanisms which make the guiding figures popularly accountable. But these are missing under current arrangements.

There are other areas in which quangos have filled in for the absence of a regional tier of government in England, Scotland and Wales, and act as governing institutions in Northern Ireland under the direction of the Northern Ireland Office. Large national quangos, at the head of flotillas of local quangos, are set to continue doing so in England. We have described in detail the role the Housing Corporation and its regional offices play in determining public housing priorities and distributing funds, independently of local authority or local community control (see **p. 205**). The Funding Agency for Schools, which is in charge of grant-maintained schools, and the Further Education Funding Council, which takes responsibility for further education colleges, head two other hierarchies which play a significant role in local education policies.

The National Health Service was from its beginning a highly centralised and non-democratic institution, with appointed members on all its boards. Aneurin Bevan, its founder, soon came to regret this 'defect', admitting that 'election is a better principle than selection' (Bevan 1978: 114). The modern NHS is tightly run by a chief executive and the NHS Executive, which directs local health services through district health authorities, NHS trusts, and other bodies. However, the Scottish and Welsh Offices have taken responsibility for NHS bodies in the two countries, and the NHS in Northern Ireland is separately organised under Health and Social Services boards and councils, responsible to the Northern Ireland Health and Social Services Department. A public element of democracy at regional level was lost in the 1990s 'internal market' reforms when the 14 English regional health authorities (RHAs) were abolished, and along with them the public galleries which opened most of their meetings to public scrutiny, comment and even 'factious interference' (as Sir Peter Baldwin, a former RHA chairman, put it). Also lost, according to Baldwin, were the RHA chairmen's 'NHS cabinet meetings' with the Secretary of State which intensified 'the infusion of policy with practicability, and even with equity' and brought concerns from lower down the scale to ministerial attention; the absorption of RHAs into the departmental machinery has 'spread the fabric of direct answerability between the territorial authorities and department both more widely and more thinly, at the same time as the authorities' public galleries have been closed' (Baldwin 1998).

The argument, as ever, returns to the principle of ministerial responsibility. It is argued that there is a democratic element in these arrangements as the regional offices and quangos are ultimately responsible to a Secretary of State who is answerable in Parliament for their activities; and that they can come under parliamentary scrutiny through select committees, Parliamentary Questions, public audit, and so on. We have already discussed the thinness of this argument. Inadequate as the idea of responsibility at national level for national quangos may be, it is nonsense to suggest that regional quangos could possibly be made accountable on the same basis. In the first place, it is quite impossible. Secondly, it is utterly inappropriate. Arrangements so far removed from the regional levels at which these quangos make policies and take decisions cannot meet the Audit's criteria of 'openness, accountability and responsiveness'. We go on to analyse the parliamentary aspects of ministerial responsibility in Chapter 12. Here we observe simply that ministers are answerable in reality, through Parliament, to the governing party to which they belong. In the 1990s, this party was not in the majority in Scotland or Wales, nor in many of the English regions, and there were no compensating arrangements to make the activities of the offices and quangos open or answerable at regional level. In Wales, networks of Conservative sympathisers and businessmen, unrepresentative of Welsh society as a whole, were set in power in Welsh quangos (Morgan and Osmond 1995). So, finally, at neither of the two levels of governance which can be described as regional, was there any real presence of democracy in the UK in 1997. Most activity was under the control of ministerially-appointed elites or ministerially-controlled civil servants. Labour's devolution proposals may change this position in Scotland and Wales, but not in England.

Local government

The tension between central and local government

Local government is more than the sum of the particular services it provides. It is an essential part of English democratic government.

(The Royal Commission on Local Government in England
(the Redcliffe–Maud Report), 1969)

Local government is an important element in democracies throughout the world. It is especially important to democracy in Britain, as it is the only part of government below Whitehall that possesses the democratic legitimacy of the vote. Historically, too, local government has long embodied a tradition of pluralism. As a result, the importance of local democracy in this country is often argued in a defensive way as a counterpart to the powers of central government; for example, the official Widdicombe report in 1986 declared that local government provides 'political checks and balances, and a restraint on arbitrary government and absolutism' (Widdicombe 1986a: 48, para. 3.13). This argument often takes on a measure of pluralism. Another official report – the Layfield report in 1976 – argued that, 'By providing a large number of points where decisions are taken by people of different political persuasions ... it acts as a counterweight to the uniformity inherent in government decisions. It spreads political power' (Layfield 1976: 53, ch. 4, para. 14).

Layfield does not go far enough. The pluralist expression of views, at local as at regional and national level, is important to democracy in its own right. In the UK, it is even more important at local level given the exclusive nature of the exercise of power nationally. Under recent Conservative governments, the voices of Labour, the official opposition, and other parties counted for nothing; thus it was more important than ever that a diversity of expression and decision should exist at local level.

There is of course a case for local democracy on its own terms (Phillips 1994). Put simply, people in localities are better placed than national politicians and officials to know the issues, problems and conditions in those localities; and, by definition, are the only ones who can know their own concerns, preferences and priorities. Conditions vary significantly from one locality to another and affect the scale of priorities and range of considerations that should be brought to bear on decision-making. The European principle of subsidiarity sums up such arguments: decisions should be made as closely as possible to the people who are affected by them.

In certain fields – like closing streets to through traffic or choosing between an orthodox or 'leisure' pool in a new sports centre – decisions can be readily taken at local level. But there is a genuine tension between local and national or regional decisions in other areas, like education, health, housing, social security, road and public transport policies. Some policies have to be made nationally; yet in most cases, local conditions can justify modifying national or regional policies in the localities and appeal and redress are best dealt with locally. There is also the issue of equality. Public housing policies, for example, must reflect local needs, but those needs must be balanced against the needs of other localities; and there might well be a need to counter local patronage or discrimination in allocation policies. On the other hand, housing, education and other local services can only be effectively established and managed locally, albeit within a national framework. Dealing with complaints and giving redress also has to be undertaken at local level, at least in the first instance. In most cases, for example, schools should deal with parents' needs and complaints. But education authorities deal with queries or complaints from almost two million individuals a year, through officials and elected members, half of which are in writing. Could central government and national quangos actually take on this burden? Yet the more they determine local education policies, the stronger the case is for them to do so, and the less able local education authorities are to deal with them. Finally, local democracy allows people to participate collectively as citizens in decisions which affect them as individuals and neighbours. It makes it possible for them to express their aspirations and views. Such opportunities are normally available for most people only at local level and the only national study of participation shows conclusively that most people participate locally (Parry *et al.* 1992). Local participation does more than create self-confident citizens, and share out political power; it also contributes to a culture of democracy throughout society.

It is important to stress that local democracy and local government are not one and the same thing. In this chapter we primarily assess the degree of autonomy from the centre which local government possesses in the UK. Of course, this affects the degree of democracy which citizens possess in their localities, but that depends also on the quality of local government itself, which we are not auditing in this volume (see **pp. 18–19**). Nor do we address the worrying problem of low turnout in local elections. In this section, we concentrate upon two questions raised by **DAC18**: 'Do local authorities have adequate protection against interference from the centre?'; and, 'Are they politically effective bodies, able to carry out their responsibilities according to the needs and wishes of their electorates?' We also take the opportunity to compare British practice with the standards set out for the protection and democratic freedom of local government in the Council of Europe's European Charter of Local Self-Government 1985 (Treaty Series No. 122). The Charter stipulates that:

- Local authorities must have adequate financial resources of their own (Article 9).
- Financial equalisation processes are not to be used to diminish the decision-making powers of local authorities (Article 9).
- Central government must not undermine local authority powers by administrative action (Articles 4 and 8).
- Local authorities should have powers of general competence (Article 4).
- Local authorities should have freedom of choice as to the way in which services are provided and in their internal organisation (Article 6).
- Local authorities must be able to determine the rate of their own taxes (Article 9).

The absence of constitutional protection of local government

Central government in Britain has the power of life or death over local government. In 1986, the Widdicombe inquiry, charged by the government with finding ways of strengthening local democracy, warned ministers that central government, or 'centralism', was squeezing the democratic life out of local government. After

No constitutional protection

referring to our opening quotation from the Redcliffe–Maud report (above), the Widdicombe committee commented:

> It might be argued now that the local government itself has become, or is in danger of becoming, *less* than the sum of its parts – in that it lacks sufficient financial and political discretion to reflect local choice, even in the basic statutory services which it delivers.
>
> (Widdicombe 1986a)

Given the inevitable tension between the centre and local government, it is vital that there is a balance between the two which enables local government to function as local *government* rather than as local *administration*. Otherwise, local people will cease to vote and participate, fewer able people will come forward to act as council members, and the vitality of local democratic society will diminish. The right to self-government is guaranteed by the constitutions of other west European states; uniquely, British local authorities have no independent status nor even a constitutional right to exist. Parliament is sovereign. All existing local authorities are the statutory creations of Parliament and local government as a whole could lawfully be abolished by a single Act of Parliament. In theory, the powers of central government may be circumscribed by Parliament just as much as those of local government. In practice, the two political parties which have shared power through Parliament have displayed no desire to restrict the powers which they inherit when they win an election. Rather the reverse. But they are generally willing to deploy these powers to control local government.

Local government's powers are further constrained by the legal doctrine of *ultra vires*, which in effect means that they may only do what Parliament, or rather central government, specifically empowers them to do. Apart from this 'negative' limit on their competence, central government may also positively direct them to act, in great detail, if need be against their own assessment of local interests; remove existing functions; or press new ones upon them. There is another contrast here with constitutional practice elsewhere. Local authority structures and powers vary immensely between, and even within, other European countries. But local authorities possess either a constitutional power of 'general competence' (as in Scandinavia), which sets wider limits than the *ultra vires* restraints on British local authorities and does not confine their activities to areas where government has legislated; or they have 'entrenched' legal rights to perform defined functions (as in France, Germany and Italy) which cannot be removed by a simple parliamentary majority. Historically, British local government has 'done more' than local authorities in many other European countries (with the exception of Scandinavia). But whereas during the 1980s, local initiative was severely constrained in Britain, if from a higher base, other European countries have experienced a strengthening of local democracy and experiments in citizen and user participation in local decisions and services.

The absence of constitutional protection does not mean that the summary abolition of local authorities is constitutionally 'acceptable'. They supposedly have the protection of 'a corpus of custom and convention' (as the Widdicombe report described it), as to the manner in which parliamentary sovereignty over local government should be exercised. But this protection does not amount to a 'natural right for local government to exist'. Widdicombe, for example, defined it as a conditional protection, 'based on, and subject to, the contribution that local government can bring to good government' (Widdicombe 1986a). It also depends on central government's willingness to be governed by 'custom and convention' and to respect the constitutional importance of a balance between its priorities and local diversity of need and opinion, and the willingness of a majority party in Parliament to protect local authorities from overweening interference from the centre. In the early 1990s, in fact, ministers and government MPs seriously argued the case for taking over, or 'nationalising', local government, or reducing it to parish pump status, providing for refuse collection, street lighting, and other services out of funds which councils could raise themselves (Hogg and Hill 1995: 58–59). Even though the Prime Minister ruled this drastic option out, it is arguable that the experience of the past 20 years has shown that central government can by increment reduce local government to a mere administrative shadow of local democracy.

Central interference in local government

It is taken for granted that central government has clear responsibilities at the local level; and that the centre will be concerned to set standards and seek value for money. But is this necessarily so? Is it not equally arguable that local electorates should be the prime agencies which control local authorities, and ensure that they deliver effective and responsive services, and are neither wasteful nor corrupt? The services that local government traditionally supplies are of paramount importance to local people's everyday lives, and are they not therefore best placed to take ultimate charge of decisions on their quality and the resources which are devoted to them? If this were the case, then ministers' responsibilities for local government could be confined, say, to strengthening the democratic process locally; keeping in place structures that make local government open and responsive to local opinion; distributing central funding to ensure that all authorities can deliver reasonably uniform service levels across the country; and monitoring services on a comparative national basis.

Yet since 1975, the pressures of centralism have intensified, as the Labour, and then Conservative governments perceived retrenchment at the local level to be necessary in the national interest. The reason lies largely in the financial weakness of British local government. For example, Nigel Lawson complained that while he was Chancellor, local authority spending accounted for a quarter of total public spending, of which roughly half was funded by the Treasury (1993: 562). Under both Labour and Conservative governments it has been axiomatic that retrenchment could only be achieved from the centre and was bound to involve some diminution of local authority discretion to act in what local councils perceived to be the interests of their areas.

On the other hand, local authorities must be politically effective if they are to meet central government's own demands for responsive and effective services. Only

Central interference

elected local government – rather than local administration – can properly be responsive to local needs. For only a local democratic process can involve local people and communities, both in the expression of community views, the assessment of particular local needs and the actual delivery of services. People are able to elect their representatives as councillors and to make them accountable through the ballot, and may continue to influence their authorities collectively through consultation, co-option, and local lobbying. Local councillors and officials are more accessible than MPs and government officials, and infinitely more so than ministers or the 'new magistracy' in charge of local quangos. The only major recent study of political participation in the UK found that the public is twice as likely to contact local councillors and officials as MPs and government officials:

Contacting:	At least once (%)	Often, now and then (%)
MP	9.7	3.4
Civil servant	7.3	3.1
Councillor	20.7	10.3
Town hall	17.4	8.9
Media	3.8	1.6

Source: Parry, Moyser, and Day 1992

Here, the argument of John Stewart, an academic specialist, that local government can provide an integration of local services is of vital importance (Stewart 1995). Local authorities have traditionally provided a variety of services and fulfilled related public functions which can plainly be more readily co-ordinated if they are all run from a single local authority, and those in charge of them work together as colleagues. But the 'town hall' or 'county hall' can also offer local citizens a focal point for the resolution of complaints, proposals for changed or new policies, and so on. The new order of command from on high, mediated through a variety of different agencies run by unknown appointed and self-appointing local 'magistracies' (see Chapter 8 and **pp. 252–260**), fragments coordination and confuses and frustrates local accountability. Local authorities find it hard even to identify local agencies working in their areas, let alone monitor or contribute to their policies and priorities (see, for example, Peet 1998).

Under the Conservatives from 1979–97, local governance was 'reinvented' in a non-democratic direction. The central assumption of Conservative policies was that choice is maximised through the market, not through politics, and it was locally that this assumption found its fullest expression. The quasi-markets of a reformed public sector were to provide a realm of efficient and responsive services for local 'consumers' in contrast to the rule of 'domination and manipulation' in local government, where popular control, 'exercisable in theory, was routinely subverted in practice by producer interests' (Waldegrave 1993). There is no doubt that the management of public services prior to 1979, both nationally and locally, was in urgent need of reform. The system created obvious inefficiencies and the public became fed up with a public sector which was unresponsive to their needs. However, the need for reform locally took second place to the successive Tory governments' overriding objective: to reduce public spending and the public sphere generally. Strict financial disciplines were enforced to 'squeeze' savings out of local authorities and services were removed compulsorily to private contractors and local quangos which were more sympathetic to central objectives, such as reducing costs and shedding staff, than local councils. Other major goals were to make service delivery more responsive and accessible, and in 1991 John Major introduced the Citizen's Charter programme to inform and 'empower' the customers of public services nationally as well as locally. Some local quangos were designed also to give people with a direct interest in services, as parents or council tenants, a real say in the way they were run; and local government was reformed to make it more open, accessible and financially accountable.

The Conservatives' legislative programmes showed just how vulnerable local government is to the centre. From 1979 to 1997, Britain's local authorities were affected by over 200 Acts of Parliament. Of these, 49 were specifically targeted on local government and its services, and at least 16 imposed central control over local authority finances; reduced their independent powers; amputated or privatised major services; created non-elected quangos to take over and deliver services, or extended the role of existing bodies in place of local authorities; or enforced the market-oriented operation of remaining functions. In these Acts, ministers took literally thousands of direct powers over local authorities, powers which were generally at the disposal of officials and major executive quangos (see Chapter 8).

Change after change fell upon local government: for example, the 'right to buy' for council tenants which removed the most desirable public housing from local authority control and allocation for social purposes; the compulsory tendering of council services; the creation in 1983 of the Audit Commission to carry out 'value-for-money' audits of local authorities; acts limiting council powers to subsidise or regulate local transport; a prohibition on US-style 'contract compliance' policies requiring contractors for privatised services to have equal opportunities or 'fair wages' policies; the abolition of the Greater London Council and the six metropolitan county councils; a 1990 act placing local authorities under a duty to design care programmes and manage a 'mixed economy' of community care; the gradual tightening of a noose of central control of local spending, culminating in the 'capping' regime; the introduction of the poll tax in Scotland in 1989, and in England and Wales in 1990, together with the removal of local business rates to a nationally run and distributed uniform business rate; the introduction of the national curriculum and compulsory testing of state school pupils; significant series of changes in the rules governing local authority housing finances; the loss of general powers to inspect local authority schools; the Education Secretary's decision to take personal responsibility for overseeing education, and powers to impose 'education associations', independent of local authorities, to run failing schools; and so on.

The desirability or otherwise of individual changes is not the issue: the weight and diversity of the changes which rained down on local government during a period of intense and continual reduction in services and staff was demoralising for local government and put its existence in question. A permanent revolution was imposed, from above, on local authorities. In 1986, the Widdicombe committee of inquiry

Financial controls

into the state of local government, established to justify the government's onslaught, instead gave it a generally clean bill of health. Indeed, its report warned that 'centralising pressures' might erode or negate the democratic attributes of local government 'to such an extent that it has no obvious advantage over a system of local administration'. Its members were moved to add a plea:

> If there are perceived to be solutions which are more acceptable than a continued drift towards centralism, then central government needs to impose upon itself the same restraint in dealing with local government that a written constitution would provide. The price of that restraint may often be short-term political inconvenience, but that price must be accepted.
> (Widdicombe 1986a: 54–55, para. 3.42)

Yet the legislative blitz intensified after 1986.

The problem as Conservative governments saw it was that local electorates, which benefited from local services, were unwilling to impose economy on their local authorities. The low level of turnout in local elections accentuated the 'lack of financial accountability'. Thus, Tory governments felt compelled to impose on local government the disciplines local electorates could not, or did not wish to, supply. The centre had also to remove local services from elected local government because councils were often too political and subject to the 'excessive influence of producer interests', especially where public-sector trade unions were closely involved in local political power structures (HC Deb, 24 February 1994, c492). The complaint about excessive trade-union influence at least was valid under many inner-city Labour councils; and the rigours of Conservative policies had a beneficial effect in such areas. But the Conservatives were also determined to take central control of local spending decisions and were intolerant of dissent from local authorities – a few of which, in the 1980s, displayed a partisan opposition to central government policies.

The problem for the Democratic Audit is that while Conservative governments undertook valuable 'access' reforms to improve the openness and accountability of local authorities, the major thrust of their changes was openly to marginalise local government, democratic practice and representative politics locally. In their place, the government took central control over local authority policies and resources, and promoted alternatives to council services based on the workings of the market – purchaser/provider splits, privatisation, compulsory tendering of services, contracting them out and buying them in, auditing, market-testing, removing services to local quangos. Local electoral politics was allowed to remain, but a new consumer-based form of accountability, the Citizen's Charter, and stronger financial audits, directed by the new Audit Commission, were introduced to compensate for the perceived weaknesses of local elections and public provision.

Controlling the purse strings

The centre's drive over the same period to impose financial controls and to overcome the strategies by which local authorities strove to evade them – grant-related spending assessments, targets, penalties, the abolition of supplementary rates, the poll tax and the centre's capture of the business rate – culminated in 1992–93 in a universal 'rate-capping' regime. In effect, this regime gave the government direct control over the maximum level of local taxes and the power to 'cap', or limit, capital and current spending in every local authority in Britain. The reality of this control was acknowledged by local authority leaders of all political persuasions. Robin Wendt, of the then Conservative-controlled Association of County Councils, complained that 'the only control local authorities can have is how to cut the cake, not how big the cake can be. The government, in effect, has total control of the system' ('Running out of control', *Guardian*, 23 June 1993).

Rate capping was presented to Parliament as a 'transitional power' when first introduced in the Rates Act 1984; as a 'reserve power' while poll tax legislation was going through (HC Deb, 25 April 1988, vol. 132 c51–52), and as 'transitional' again for council tax purposes in 1991. But from 1990 capping became unashamedly permanent and universal; and the Labour government after 1997 has not, as we write, dismantled this powerful weapon of central control. Capping under the Conservatives provided a democratically dubious example of the subtleties of ministerial power. Any local authority in Great Britain might be designated for capping if, in the opinion of the relevant Secretary of State, its budget was 'excessive'. In order to cap an authority, the government had to make a statutory instrument, which had to be debated and approved by the Commons. However, ministers began to issue 'provisional' non-statutory capping criteria before local authorities set their budgets. This allowed authorities to avoid the cost and disruption of re-setting budgets that might exceed the minister's limits; in this way the minister led most councils to 'cap themselves' to avoid uncertainty without the need for an a statutory instrument or parliamentary approval of any kind. The final criteria were published shortly after authorities had set their budgets. The minister could then designate authorities which exceeded the limits and might finally agree a limit with an authority or impose a cap by order in the House of Commons.

In 1990–91, 21 authorities were capped; by 1996–97 just six were designated. These figures do not represent growing consent, but rather the inexorable logic of a system that effectively forced local authorities to cap themselves, or ultimately have a lower budget set by a government minister who would not disclose how his figure was calculated, or what factors were taken into account. Some local authorities looked to the courts to rescue them from what was in effect partisan dictation from on high, but the judges generally refused to intervene in such a sensitive political issue.

Capping decisions were effectively based on the government's Standard Spending Assessments (SSAs) of 'the appropriate amount of revenue expenditure' which would allow all authorities to provide a standard level of service within the confines of the government's annual decisions on the level of local government expenditure. In other words, SSAs did not provide an absolute definition of local needs. The government decided the size of the cake, or of the national grant, according to its overall economic strategy and not what might have been required locally; SSAs determined how the cake should be divided. Given its definitive role in determining service levels in all local authorities, the SSA system should have been transparent and impartial. It achieved transparency, but not impartiality. It has been widely criticised for using too few 'indicators', employing some of limited relevance or even specially chosen to favour particular authorities, and excluding others of great importance (mortality ratios, long-term unemployment, population density, etc.). A detailed study by geographers at Salford University concluded that:

> large residuals lead to significant shifts in finance at the expense of some very needy authorities. . . . If the SSAs are to achieve their aim of stabilising local authority expenditure at realistic and responsible levels, they must themselves become a stable and fair means of distributing central government resources.
>
> (*Standard Spending Assessment*, Department of Geography, University of Salford, July 1992)

The *Observer* made much the same criticism more pointedly, complaining that 'as long as [the system] survives, the government will be open to the charge of manipulating statistics to direct cash away from poor Labour authorities to more affluent Tory areas' ('Losers' league', 7 January 1993).

The government's Audit Commission drew attention to several technical deficiencies and commented that 'consultation, though extensive, is unsatisfactory'; and that the use of SSAs 'to limit council expenditure has confused accountability for local services between central and local government' (Audit Commission, May 1993). An earlier draft, leaked to the *Guardian* and *Local Government Chronicle* before the final report was published, stated that central controls were now so severe that the powers of local authorities to manage their own finances were 'largely cosmetic'. The logic of the government's position was openly to take local services under central control, but this option was unlikely to be adopted because:

> central government would not welcome a more explicit trail of accountability for local service delivery reaching its door and is content to be shielded by the SSA process. But this obfuscation of accountability is inimical to responsible management. SSAs have a future role, not as a substitute for political accountability, but as an aid to it. It must be clear where the buck stops.
>
> (Leak to *Local Government Chronicle*, 19 March 1993)

Capping has not only confused accountability. It has also removed much of the point of local elections since parties cannot legitimately campaign for higher expenditure on policies.

The fact that Conservative governments reduced the value of the central grant in real terms, while limiting local tax rises, intensified the severity of central controls. For 'very needy' authorities, disadvantaged by their SSA score, the impact was still more severe. In effect, central government continually forced local authorities to reduce services and shed workers, leaving to them only the painful discretion of where to wield the axe. Capping brought to an end local discretion to compensate for loss of grant by raising local taxes. Even if capping did not exist, a council's power to meet local demands for services, over and above those which central government was prepared to fund, was gravely eroded by other government changes which decisively reduced local government's capacity to pay its way – such as the removal of business rates from local control. By 1997, local government raised only 28 per cent of the funds it spent locally through council tax – which meant that it would take a proportionately very large increase in council tax to produce a modest increase in spending power. Even if rate capping were abolished this weakness would remain.

The shift to the local quango state

> *Grant-maintained schools are pursuing programmes of openness which reflect their own particular need to consult parents and ensure the greatest transparency in providing information about both educational and financial performance. . . . Each one also holds an annual open meeting, at which parents may question the governors about the annual report and any other issues they wish.*
>
> (*The Governance of Public Bodies*, Cm 3557, 1997)

> *Somebody was telling me the other day of a meeting at a rather troubled GM school. There was, indeed, the annual parents' meeting and apparently it was very well attended because there were troubles at the school, and some of the parents were very vociferous and when the temperature got to a sufficient height, the Chairman of the governors in effect told the parents present to 'sod off' because the standing of the parents' meeting was zero.*
>
> (Professor Anthony King, member of the Nolan Committee,
> at a committee hearing, 1996)

Britain's 4,500 local quangos, officially recognised as 'local public spending bodies', are self-appointing and appointed bodies, remote from local communities, and they have profoundly changed the face of local governance. They have moved from the periphery of local policy-making to become major agencies with which elected local authorities must share strategic decision-making and service provision (Stoker 1998). But as we have seen (Chapter 8), this is only half the story. Local authorities also share these responsibilities in a subordinate role with regional government officials and major strategic quangos, like the Housing Corporation, the Funding Agency for Schools (FAS), and the Further Education Funding Council (FEFC). The very role of these unelected quango boards – 'strategic' and local – has been to take whole areas of public services and functions out of politics. The Housing Corporation, the FAS and the FEFC have direct powers over their local quangos – housing associations, grant-maintained schools, and further education colleges – and control their resources. Local authorities must bargain at both levels. Moreover, the major quango boards can be blatantly biased, as the FAS undoubtedly has been (see **p. 204**); and they are primarily accountable upwards, to central government.

The local quango state is now extensive and has taken over or usurped the role of local authorities in providing many services. In social housing, the Housing Corporation has taken control of most new housing investment from local authorities.

Local quangos

It also oversees the local housing associations which have become the main channel for investment in new social housing programmes locally (see Chapter 8). Neither local authorities nor local communities have had an influential place in its activities. A handful of housing action trusts have replaced local housing department management on some public housing estates. In education, grant-maintained schools have been removed from local authority control and answer to the FAS; 15 independent city technology colleges have been set up; all further education colleges, formerly run by local authorities, have been merged and transformed into quangos; polytechnics have moved from local authority control to become universities within the province of the Higher Education Funding Council; the school careers service has been taken out of local government and passed on to private companies. In planning, 12 urban development councils were created in England to take over planning in inner-city areas, including the London Docklands, and one in Wales (Cardiff Bay). Employment services were developed outside local authority control, through TECs and their Scottish equivalents, local enterprise companies (LECs), together with national-level and regional enterprise bodies in Scotland, Wales and Northern Ireland. Health has always been a central government service, but local authorities lost their representatives on health authority boards; and their role on the new police authorities was further diminished.

The arrangements for making the local quango state accountable are quite inadequate. It is palpably unrealistic to suggest that the formal accountability of these 4,500 bodies primarily through ministers to Parliament can be justified in principle, let alone work in practice. The idea is both inappropriate and impossible. Arrangements so far removed from the local level at which these quangos make policies and take decisions cannot meet the Audit's criteria of 'openness, accountability and responsiveness' so far as the local communities affected are concerned. Bodies discharging local functions and running local services must be made accountable at local level – 'low accountability', as the former Conservative minister for the Citizen's Charter, Robert Jackson, described it (HC Deb, 24 February 1994, c493–494). Local quangos were said by Conservative ministers to 'empower' people locally, but they empower only the self-appointing or appointed elites who sit on their boards. Local people are not genuinely 'empowered'. Housing action trusts, though appointed bodies, do work closely with the tenants; but while they are generally responsible to them in practice, they remain wholly independent of the tenants. Parents are elected to the boards of grant-maintained schools, but they are in a minority on those boards; parents who don't have children in the schools, but who live in their catchment areas, and the wider community are not represented at all, even though the schools may very well take decisions which affect their children's lives, or the neighbourhood.

It is argued that local quangos need not be accountable locally as they are not initiating policies of their own, but simply carrying out central government's policies. After all, one of the purposes of creating networks of local quangos was to centralise decision-making in the UK even more strongly than before. Governments wanted to be able to impose their policies on bodies which were not as likely as local authorities to insist on local needs and argue back. They ran the argument that they exercised strategic control of policy while local quangos were simply responsible for 'implementation'. But this argument does not stand up. Implementation is not a uniform process. Local elements in national policies require local decisions; local conditions demand different responses within national frameworks; and the distribution of resources, even if determined nationally, will vary accordingly; and hard decisions, mistakes, injustices, and so on, which will affect local people need to be adjudicated locally. As two authors in a major new study of the quango state point out, the government's distinction doesn't bear close examination, 'for policy has to be made at every level of management' (Flinders and McConnel 1998). Yet this argument has borne fruit on some quango boards at least. Two quangocrats argued passionately against measures of local accountability on BBC Radio 4's *In the Dock* programme (30 August 1996) on the grounds that quangos were simply agents of the central state:

> We [the board of an NHS trust] cannot be held responsible for the level of government expenditure on health or the number of beds that are provided. The trust is part of a *national* health service, and the policies and strategy, the standards and the requirements while it remains *national* come from the centre and the local agencies have to operate within what one might regard as this straitjacket.

and:

> A lot of what's talked about in terms of local control has, I suspect, more to do with wanting to make different policies locally rather than control of the implementation of policy that is set out nationally. And that really isn't realistic, it can't be done in that way.

Such views are probably not uncommon among the 'new magistracy' which sits on local quango boards.

The new magistracy in charge of local quangos

One measure of the significance of the local quango state is the sheer size of the 'new magistracy' – the appointed and self-appointing body of people in charge of the new system of local administration. The government's own figures suggest that it runs to more than 64,000[1] members. This figure is broadly three times greater than the total of locally elected councillors in England, Scotland and Wales – just 23,747. The way in which the members of the 'new magistracy' are chosen and its character raise other democratic issues. Appointments to local quangos – other than NHS bodies – do not fall under the scrutiny of the Commissioner for Public

[1] This figure is for housing associations, grant-maintained schools, further education institutions, TECs and LECs. It excludes universities, police authorities, career service companies and local NDPBs.

The new magistracy

Appointments and, with very few exceptions, are not made by ministers and are not generally subject to departmental oversight. Most of the local quangos are wholly or largely self-appointing. All that the official 1997 review of the governance of quangos has to say is that their appointments should be 'made on merit' and be 'capable of public justification'; and that boards should 'contain an appropriate mix of skills and backgrounds'. But there are no mechanisms in place to secure such laudable aims and, indeed, the then government clearly believed that the voluntary and part-time status of appointments does not merit too much attention (Cabinet Office/Treasury 1997: para. 53).

Most of what is known about the way new magistrates are chosen and how they behave derives from a major survey in 1994 of the members of eight types of local quango, undertaken at the University of Birmingham (Skelcher and Davis 1995). Some 1,500 members of TECs, NHS bodies, further education corporations, housing action trusts, urban development corporations, prototype career service companies, and City Challenge boards returned questionnaires (a 37 per cent response rate). On appointments, the two academics who conducted the 1994 survey concluded:

> The process by which members of local quangos are appointed has normally been a 'word-of-mouth' affair, with a consequent lack of transparency about the criteria for selection. The main appointment route is the recommendation of existing board members and senior managers.
>
> (Skelcher and Davis 1996: 14)

Two-thirds of members also strongly prefer 'recruitment by personal contact'. The survey found that members of quango boards 'have a lower level of correspondence to the population as a whole' than elected councillors, though women – the main users of local services – formed only about one in four members both of local councils and quangos. The most striking difference was that only 70 per cent of the new magistracy actually lived in the area of the bodies on which they served (as against all local council members), and only 76 per cent worked in the area. One group was over-represented on local quangos – members of the business community – in line with the wishes of the Conservative government. Board members were inspired by a sense of public duty and a wish for personal development. They saw themselves as individuals, wholly independent from party politics, but as Skelcher and Davis comment, 'The articulation of "independence" can conceal a real set of political interests whose existence is clouded by the lack of openness and local accountability of the membership of these local appointed bodies' (1996: 20).

Accountability was not an issue to which they gave a great deal of attention. The very question often obliged local quango chiefs to think seriously about the issue for the first time. Typical responses were:

> I was there as an individual ensuring that good governance occurred. I suppose I was doing that on behalf of the local community and the Further Education Funding Council – and the staff.
>
> (Further education college governor)

Ah! [Pause] No, no sense of accountability. I suppose accountable to my conscience. [Long pause] I see myself as acting on behalf of patients. [Pause] Yes, if I have an accountability it's to people I've never met.

(NHS trust board member)

[Long pause] I've never actually been asked who I'm responsible to. [Long pause] It's an interesting question. [Pause] The community probably. [Pause] The people of the area. I do feel I'm trying to do something for them. Also, of course, I represent my company.

(City Challenge director)

They seem to be saying that they are serving some unfocused wider community, but through their own personal qualities, not as representatives. This interpretation may be confirmed by the fact that they rarely, if ever, meet members of the public, and certainly not as frequently as elected local councillors do:

Hours in the week spent on:	Contacts with public	Meetings with managers
Local quango chairs	4	11
Leading councillors	17	8
Ordinary quango members	3	4
Ordinary councillors	15	4

Sources: Young, and Rao 1994: Table 3.3; Skelcher and Davis 1995; adapted from compilation in Skelcher and Davis 1996

Most quango board members are unknown and nearly unknowable, as their names and addresses are not published as are those of local councillors. Nor do they hold surgeries as many local councillors do. This remoteness is damaging in itself if you accept our view that local people and communities are better judges of their own needs and views than the most open-minded of administrators or appointees. Moreover, while it is by no means proven that appointees run efficient services anyway, the involvement of the public is far more likely to produce services that are 'effective' rather than simply 'efficient' – that is, services that accurately meet local needs as well as being efficiently run.

The fragmented governance of local affairs makes such involvement impossible across the board. This is all the more disappointing for local services are largely personal services and the qualities of effective democracy – responsiveness, openness, accountability and accessible redress – are most important. This is not to say that local government in practice has managed to achieve such ideals. The postwar experience of mass public housing alone has, for example, provided abundant evidence of local housing authorities riding roughshod over community wishes and personal needs. On the other hand, polls have shown, first, that most people prefer to deal with local authorities rather than central government; and secondly, that they are broadly satisfied with the quality of local authority services they receive.

Openness and accountability

The point is that only local democracy can produce the conditions within which ideals of accountability and openness for local government and its services can be realised.

Public access, openness and accountability in the local quango state

Conservative ministers like William Waldegrave justified the switch of services from local authority control to private contractors and local quangos by arguing that the 'quasi-markets' of the 'reinvented' public sector were creating a realm of efficient and responsive services which were not subverted by political dogma or trade-union pressures. Waldegrave argued:

> The key point is not whether those who run our public services are elected, but whether they are producer-responsive or consumer-responsive. Services are not necessarily made to respond to the public by giving our citizens a democratic voice, and a distant and diffuse one at that, in their make-up. They can be made responsive by giving the public choices, or by instituting mechanisms which build in publicly-approved standards and redress when they are not attained.
>
> (Waldegrave 1993)

However, the remoteness of the new magistracy which directs quangos locally was made worse by government's neglect in the 1980s and early 1990s of formal measures of openness, accountability and public access in the new local quango state.

In response to the detailed critique of the low level of openness and accountability of local quangos, set out in the Democratic Audit paper *EGO-TRIP* (DA Paper No. 2 1994), and subsequent recommendations in the second Nolan Report (1996), the Major governments did gradually introduce such measures, alongside the developing Citizen's Charter programme. But progress was slow, as Tables 9.1 to 9.3 clearly show. The two key requirements are that public bodies should be obliged to observe the government's official code of practice for access to information and come under the writ of the Ombudsman (who can then investigate refusals to give information). Up to mid-1997, only the 41 police authorities among the body of 4,635 'local public spending bodies' were subject to the code and to the official government Ombudsman, the Parliamentary Commissioner for Administration (see Tables 9.1 and 9.2). In 1997, however, registered housing associations, or 'social landlords', in England were statutorily required to join an approved independent Ombudsman scheme for housing associations, and a similar scheme exists for Scottish housing associations. (Welsh associations were due to join an Ombudsman scheme in 1998.) In February 1997, the then government was consulting grant-maintained schools and others on a proposal to bring them under the official local government Ombudsman service. Fewer than half the local public spending bodies were subject to public audit in 1997. Almost all were obliged to publish annual reports and accounts.

Registers of members' interests were said by government departments to be near universally available, but as Table 9.1 shows, if this is so, it is only on an unquantifiable

Table 9.1 Local public spending bodies:* public access and openness to the public, 1997

	Number	Are they subject to the Code of Practice for Open Government?	Are they required to: admit the public to committee meetings?	hold public meetings?	the agendas of meetings?	the minutes of meetings?	Are they required to publish: papers or documents for meetings?	registers of members' interests?
Grant maintained schools	1,103	✗[1]	✗	✔	▲	▲	✔[1]	▲ 'many',❖
City technology colleges	15	✗	✗	❖	✗	✗	✗	'most',❖
Further education corporations	560	'some'❖	'some'❖	'some'❖[4]	▲	▲	✗	'some',❖
Housing associations	2,594	✔	▲	'some',❖	'some',❖	'some'	✗	✗
Police authorities	41	✗	✗	▲	▲	▲	✗	▲
Career service companies	91	✗[2]	✗	✗	✗	✗	✗	▲
Training and enterprise councils	81	✗	✗	▲	✗	✗	✗	❖
Local enterprise companies	22	❖[3]	✗	▲	✗	✗	✗	
TOTAL	4,507*	41▲ (0.9%)	41▲ (0.9%)	1,247▲ (27%)	1,704▲ (38%)	1,704▲ (38%)	1,103✔ (24%)	1,225▲ (27%)

Sources: Parliamentary Questions, March 1997; Cabinet Office/Treasury, 1997; original Democratic Audit research

Notes:

This table is mainly based on departmental replies to PQs and inquiries to government departments, funding bodies and executive NDPBs. It is not possible to guarantee all the figures, however, owing to differing interpretations by government departments and others. Total figures are, wherever possible, for statutory requirements, but we also seek to distinguish between statutory, formal and voluntary arrangements in the columns. These figures too are dependent upon official interpretation and we cannot quantify voluntary arrangements.

* The total figure of 4,507 bodies excludes 175 universities, or higher education corporations, because though the Nolan Committee defined them as 'local public spending bodies', they are not truly local bodies for our purposes here. Local executive NDPBs are also excluded.

1 Grant-maintained schools are not subject to the code. However, the Instrument for Government for grant-maintained schools states that a governing body should ensure that a copy of any report or document considered by the governing body is available at the school for anyone who wishes to inspect it. The governors can exclude any document which it considers to be confidential.

2 But DfEE contracts with TECs stipulate that they comply with the code.

3 Scottish Enterprise expects its LECs to comply with the code.

4 'Most' in England; 'none' in Scotland and Wales.

Key: ✔ yes ❖ voluntary ▲ statutory ✗ no

Table 9.2 Local public spending bodies:* scrutiny and accountability, 1997

	Number	Subject to:		Required to publish:		Subject to:	
		Ombudsman?	Public audit?	Annual reports?	Annual accounts?	Citizen's Charter?	Performance indicators?
Grant maintained schools	1,103	✗	✔	▲	▲	✗	✗
City technology colleges	15	✗	✔	14 ▲	14 ▲	✗	✔
Further education corporations	560	✗	✔	'many'	▲	✔	✔
Housing associations	2,594	✔ 2,499[1]	✗	'some' ❖	▲	✔	✔
Police authorities	41	✔	✔	▲	▲	✔	✔
Career service companies	91	✗	✔	▲	▲	✔	✔
Training and enterprise councils	81	✗	✔	▲	▲	✔	✔
Local enterprise companies	22	✗	✗[2]	❖	✔[3]	✔	✔
TOTAL	4,507	✔ 2,540 (56%)	▲ 1,891 (42%)	3,895 ▲ (87%)	4,506 ▲ (99.9%)	3,389 (75%)	3,404 (75.5%)

Sources: Parliamentary Questions, March 1997; Cabinet Office/Treasury, 1997; original Democratic Audit research

Notes:

This table is mainly based on departmental replies to PQs and inquiries to government departments, funding bodies and executive NDPBs. It is not possible to guarantee all the figures, however, owing to differing interpretations by government departments and others. Total figures are, wherever possible, for statutory requirements, but we also seek to distinguish between statutory, formal and voluntary arrangements in the columns. These figures too are dependent upon official interpretation and we cannot quantify voluntary arrangements.

* The total figure of 4,507 bodies excludes 175 universities, or higher education corporations, because though the Nolan Committee defined them as 'local public spending bodies', they are not truly local bodies for our purposes here. Local executive NDPBs are also excluded.

1 Registered housing associations (or social landlords) in England were bound by statute to enter into an independent Ombudsman scheme in 1997. A similar arrangement applies in Scotland. Registered associations in Wales were bound by law to join an Ombudsman scheme this year.

2 Scottish Enterprise and Highlands & Islands Enterprise now prepare group accounts, including those for LECs. As the NAO is the statutory auditor of the group accounts, it may require to see LECs' accounts.

3 As part of their contracts.

Key: ✔ yes ❖ voluntary ▲ statutory ✗ no

voluntary basis. Only one in four local quangos are statutorily bound to make such registers publicly available. The Housing Corporation maintains a national register of the interests of board members of registered housing associations, and copies are available on a voluntary basis at the offices of individual associations. Whether the standards of voluntary registers would stand up to scrutiny is open to doubt. In Chapter 8, we noted that inspection of the actual registers of interests of board members on housing associations in 1993 revealed them to be voluntary, inadequate and out-of-date (DA Paper No. 2: 28). The position on public access to the policy-making and decision-taking processes of local quangos is poor. Only police authorities are obliged to allow the public to attend their board meetings. The agendas and minutes of meetings are available for the meetings of police authorities, grant-maintained schools and further education corporations (38 per cent of all local public spending bodies), but background papers for meetings are only available to the public from grant-maintained schools. Their governing bodies, however, have the discretion to withhold documents if they consider them to be 'confidential'.

On openness, the Major government began to encourage local quangos to adopt codes of access to information based on the government's own code of practice, together with the publication of key data and annual reports; holding (usually annual) public meetings; and more consultation with local authorities, voluntary bodies and other service providers (Cabinet Office/Treasury 1997: 21–22). But the diverse nature of such bodies made it impossible uniformly to apply public mechanisms, such as the government's Ombudsman service or the official code of practice on openness, or even to create across-the-board provisions, throughout the local quango state. Further, governments have not wished to place explicit requirements on local quangos, and prefer to proceed by way of self-regulation through the representative bodies of quangos. Thus, for housing associations, the government relied on the National Federation of Housing Association's Code of Governance to secure openness, even though the NFHA is not national (it is an English body), and its provisions on openness are very general. For TECs, government negotiated progress through the TEC National Council, which undertook a review of the TEC Framework for Local Accountability after the second Nolan Report.

TECs and LECs are of course private companies. The government's 1997 progress report, *The Governance of Public Bodies* (Cabinet Office/Treasury 1997), states that government contracts with TECs specify that they must comply with the official openness code and that Scottish Enterprise insists on compliance among its LECs. But the report also owns up to an 'inevitable variation in the range of openness' among local quangos, recognising, for example, tension between the wish of 'some' TEC and LEC directors for privacy (which they might expect as board members of a private company) and the need for openness and accountability demanded of bodies spending public money. Openness could not come about overnight, the report continues, and would demand a cultural shift in attitudes over the years; it must be 'tailored to particular needs'; and measures to achieve it 'will necessarily vary according to the differing demands of serving [their] distinct audiences'. Moreover, the code allowed government to keep documents secret on the basis of 'commercial confidentiality', a category which will survive under the Labour government's new freedom of information (FOI) regime.

Right of redress

This provision gives TECs and LECs a large measure of discretion, which is not capable of being investigated under current arrangements by an independent public official, such as the Ombudsman or the new FOI Commissioner. Given their reluctance to embrace openness, we are sceptical about the degree of compliance with official rules for disclosure of information or documents that the public can expect from TECs and LECs. Finally, for all the emphasis on openness, all these bodies exclude the public and their 'customers' from board meetings (except for GM schools and housing associations with tenants' representatives on their boards).

NHS district authorities and NHS trusts are more uniformly open and accountable (Table 9.3). All are subject to the NHS Ombudsman, an official code of openness, and public audit; all are subject to the Citizen's Charter; all publish registers of board members' interests; most (78 per cent) hold public meetings; all publish annual reports and accounts (though 12 NHS bodies in Northern Ireland do so voluntarily, not under statute law). The position on public access is, however, again poor, though some trusts do allow the public into meetings, and make agendas, non-confidential papers and minutes of meetings available, on a voluntary basis. Again, there is no public right to documents and papers for meetings.

The contrast between the measures in force for local quangos and local authorities is marked. Local authorities are, of course, subject to popular control through regular elections. The names and addresses of councillors are on the public record. Local authorities are subject both to a Local Government Ombudsman and to a statutory regime of openness and public access. All council meetings and committee meetings are open to the public (with exemptions for specified confidential business); and the public have rights of access to relevant council agendas, minutes and background papers. Local authorities are subject to public audit via the Audit Commission, and are obliged to publish auditor's criticisms and sets of performance indicators on their services. Further, local authorities are bound to keep public registers of councillors' interests. In brief, local quangos fitfully, and often only voluntarily, observe measures of openness, accountability and public access, which are standard in local government. A third of the local quangos run services which have been wrested from local government – so there has been a direct loss in electoral control, openness and accountability.

The Citizen's Charter, redress and 'practical' reforms

In these circumstances, it is not surprising that the government's 1997 progress report – presented to Parliament jointly by ministers from the Cabinet Office and Treasury – put more emphasis on 'practical' means of accountability than formal or statutory measures for local and national quangos alike. The two ministers, Roger Freeman and Michael Jack, argued forcibly against any idea of direct elections to local public bodies, arguing that it may be:

> an excessively impractical and cumbersome mechanism, requiring local electors to vote frequently on large slates of candidates . . . a possible and very undesirable consequence of this would be to polarise membership of [public]

Table 9.3 NHS authorities and trusts: public access, openness and accountability, 1997

No. of NHS bodies which	England No.	%	Northern Ireland No.	%	Scotland No.	%	Wales No.	%	Total No.	%
observe the openness code	543	100	33	100	68	100	37	100	681	100
admit the public to board or committee meetings	110▲ 'some'❖	18	1▲	3	17▲	25	7▲ 'many'❖	19	135▲	20
hold public meetings	429▲	79	24▲	73	47▲	69	30▲	81	530▲	78
publish agendas of meetings	100▲	18	9▲	27	16▲	24	7▲	19	132▲	19
publish minutes of meetings	'some publish voluntarily'		9▲	27	'many publish voluntarily'		'many publish voluntarily'		9▲	1
publish a register of members' interests	543	100	33	100	68	100	37	100	681	100
are subject to the Ombudsman	543	100	33	100	68	100	37	100	681	100
are subject to full public audit	543	100	33	100	68	100	37	100	681	100
must publish annual reports	543▲	100	33▲	100	68▲	100	37▲	100	681▲	100
must publish annual accounts	543▲	100	29▲	88	68▲	100	37▲	100	677▲	99
are subject to the Citizen's Charter	543	100	4❖	12	68	100	37	100	4❖	1
are subject to the Citizen's Charter									681	100
Total no. of bodies	543		33		68		37		681	

Sources: Parliamentary Questions, March 1997; Cabinet Office/Treasury, 1997; original Democratic Audit research
Key: ▲ under the requirements of statute, regulations, or framework or other controlling documents   ❖ voluntary

bodies on Party political lines. This also risks decisions being made that are not in the interests of the body and those it was established to serve.

(Cabinet Office/Treasury 1997: 21)

Instead, they stuck firmly to the idea of accountability upwards to 'high-level' quangos, funding bodies, regulators and government departments, coupled with 'responsiveness' to local communities and 'customers'.

However, the Major government took very seriously a key recommendation of the second Nolan Report on the need for 'external adjudication' for local quangos (Nolan 1996: 8). The *Governance* report (Cabinet Office/Treasury 1997) introduced a new emphasis on 'accountability through redress' – i.e., fair and accessible complaints mechanisms, plus access to the Secretary of State, a regulator or independent office holder (e.g., the Ombudsman or another adjudicator). The report claimed that redress mechanisms had undergone 'a sustained and systematic improvement' since the mid-1980s, though the increase in redress has come late and measures – for example, the move by Scottish Enterprise and Highlands and Islands Enterprise to set up an external adjudicator – were still being established when the ministers reported in February 1997. In that year, statutory redress mechanisms still covered only about half (56 per cent) of the local public spending bodies. This commitment to effective redress was encouraging, but to some degree it was regarded as a substitute for wider democratic arrangements. Redress, the two ministers argued:

is a key form of accountability, while there may be limits to the extent to which members of the public are prepared or wish to be involved in consultative exercises and the planning of public services, the crucial test of a public body is the quality of the service it provides.

(Cabinet Office/Treasury 1997: 30).

Redress is, of course, a strong element in the concept of the Citizen's Charter. The Democratic Audit has not conducted its own analysis of this reform programme, but we have reviewed the government's own reports (Cabinet Office 1996b), and other 'audits' conducted by *Which?*, the National Consumer Council, The Institute for Public Policy Research, the *Financial Times*, and other observers like Stephen Byers MP (Hall and Weir 1997; Prior *et al.* 1993; Leadbeater and Mulcahy 1996; Bynoe 1996). The consensus is that the Charter has generally made a positive contribution to improving both local and national services. The main gains have been in the areas of consumer information, customer relations, complaints and redress. The non-legal nature of the programme has made it flexible and versatile in practice, and easy for people complaining to use.

But the Charter has also created an ambiguity over the 'rights' of people using services and managers' responsibilities. Many 'rights', or the standards set for services, have been anodyne or undemanding, and are set not by the public, but by the government and the services themselves. They do not reflect a real degree of consultation with the public, let alone their participation, and naturally have often not reflected public priorities. The information that is made available tends to be of an administrative nature and has not dealt with major public concerns. 'Choice' is rarely a real option in services such as meals-on-wheels, public housing or secondary education; this implies a need for 'voice' as well. Redress has been low-level and narrowly-focused, and is only gradually being backed up by independent review. Finally, the Charter has not yet provided a governing framework for most local quangos, which generally remain both secretive and remote bodies. Most 'auditors' of the Charter have been nagged by doubts, but have given the programme provisional approval. The new Labour government has decided that it constitutes a valuable base for further reform.

Redress and 'responsiveness' are important. An immediate response to a complaint, and even perhaps some sort of redress, is clearly more satisfactory than, say, doubtful and delayed retribution at the ballot box. But most of the Conservative measures are voluntary, not statutory, in nature; and they are very narrowly defined. Local quangos are responsive only within the limits of nationally determined policies and resource allocations; and as we have seen above, they are neither structured, nor inclined, to allow local citizens to set or alter those policies. Nor do we yet know whether as a class of bodies they actually meet the government's aim of immediate and sensitive response to complaints. Further, need their qualities – especially the managerial focus on a particular service – be obtained at the expense of traditional means of political accountability, rather than adding to their force?

Nevertheless, government measures up to 1997, and particularly the Citizen's Charter, undoubtedly did improve qualities of responsiveness, redress, and so on, within public services; and these qualities are democratic goods. The Conservatives' changes form an important strand in the new Labour government's 'best value' initiatives in local government, within a more open and democratic agenda. The basic question is: are they necessarily an alternative to democratic accountability? Do Waldegrave's arguments against electoral politics in local government offer an unreal and unnecessary choice? Our view is that, far from being incompatible, immediate (if limited) consumer rights under Citizen's Charters and accountable and accessible local authorities are complementary. The Conservative reforms could just as well have been introduced on the 'solid basis of normality' that their own Widdicombe report found in local government (1986a: 15). They should have left local authorities with the ability to choose, rather than imposing decisions upon them. As it is, they fragmented local governance and created a confused and confusing public–private divide at local level, frustrating any real chance for local citizens to determine who should take responsibility for policy success or failures.

This is not to say that local authorities should again be the sole providers of most local services, or even have sole power of decision over services. But it is necessary that public bodies providing services or performing local functions should be open and accountable so that local views can be expressed in the decision-making process; that the public should have local representatives, who are both accessible and accountable, to whom they can express their views; and that local people should have a continuing influence in assessing and modifying services. Local authorities themselves could be made more democratic structures, most valuably by replacing the existing first-past-the-post elections with proportional representation. Abuse of

Central government incursions

power in local government has mostly arisen within authorities where one party or another holds an unchallenged dominance, created by an electoral system which tends systematically to under-represent opposition parties, and in extreme cases even to exclude them wholly from council chambers.

High politics in the local arena

One of the key distinctions of British politics was that which existed between 'high politics' (defence, foreign and colonial policy, the economy) and 'low politics' (domestic matters). But since the 1970s onwards, Britain's post-imperial governing structure, created to manage the grand accumulation of high political questions, has been gradually eating into the fabric of low politics – local government, public services, planning and micro-economic issues. Denied the greater freedom of manoeuvre for political action and strategic economic policy-making as a mere 'member state' of the European Union, Britain's political leaders and bureaucrats have entered new domains in which to deploy their 'flexible' powers and desires for decisive outcomes. This remains the case under the new Labour government, just as it was under previous administrations; the deployment by ministers of 'hit squads' against 'failing' schools and hospitals is simply a more dramatic illustration of a continuing tendency to assume that the men and women of Whitehall and Westminster know best.

The institutions of the Welfare State and 'mixed economy' developed in Britain by 1970 were heavily statist; and the role of local government within the Welfare State had simply enlarged with little conscious thought being given to choosing or creating appropriate institutional forms, and mechanisms of control and account-ability. Public housing, for example, frequently outgrew the capacity of local authorities to administer an efficient and responsive service; by 1970, Glasgow owned and managed some 170,000 rented flats and houses, Birmingham 120,000 (Dunleavy 1981). Crucially, the postwar Welfare State was 'ungrounded'. Its institutions and arrangements did not rest on secure constitutional, political or social bases. Its public institutions were the creatures of central government, and could be sold off, broken up, abolished or re-organised centrally, unchecked by any other bodies. As we have seen, local authorities did not possess any independent constitutional status within the unwritten constitution. What central government gave, central government could take away. Services provided by local authorities and other public bodies were often low-cost and rationed through long and bureaucratic queuing systems. The whole structure was tightly controlled by professionals and bureaucrats, with no element of popular participation. Thus, when economic weakness focused concern on public expenditure in the 1970s and broke the political consensus on the Welfare State between the Labour and Conservative parties, its institutions were not secured by a broader popular consensus, as in Scandinavia and Germany.

It was in fact the Heath government from 1970–74 which began the centre's first decisive shift into 'low politics'; in the mid-1970s, Labour began to try and restrain local government expenditure. But it was, as we have seen, the Thatcher governments which turned the full weight of the resources of 'high politics' onto local authorities (as well as other area of 'low politics'). The nature of this process is perhaps still not fully appreciated. The kind of freedom of manoeuvre which ministers required for imperial purposes was available to them in their domestic colonisation. Let us take as an example the way ministers invaded schools education. In the 1988 Education Act alone, Kenneth Baker, the then Education Secretary, adopted 415 new powers of central control (HC Deb, 18 July 1988, c793–794) while severely reducing the role of local education authorities. Five years later, John Patten's 1993 Act, which with 308 clauses, or sections, was the longest ever, gave him yet another 50 central powers over local authorities, including unprecedented personal responsibility for oversight of national education policy. The Act also put another device of central control, the Funding Agency for Schools, at his disposal. The House of Lords introduced 570 amendments to the bill, some of which were designed specifically to restore certain strategic planning powers to local education authorities and to clarify the confused division of responsibilities. The government guillotined their rejection through the Commons in just over eight hours. An editorial in the *Times Educational Supplement* commented, 'The government remains determined not to give an inch in the direction of local government power' (*TES*, 23 July 1993).

Among the formidable arsenal of powers ministers assumed in these Acts were powers to change the law made by Parliament as a whole through their own ministerial orders which usually slide unchecked through Parliament. These powers are assumed by way of 'Henry VIII' clauses in bills (see Chapter 13). Baker took Henry VIII powers in the 1988 Act to change fundamental parts of his reforms – specifying the foundation subjects and 'key stages' for pupils in the national curriculum; conferring 'such additional functions as he sees fit' on higher education quangos (funding bodies); and making changes in any Employment Act – and in particular any Act conferring rights on employees – as he considered necessary or expedient when he came to delegate to school governors and university boards powers to appoint and dismiss staff. There were no restrictions on these powers and no explanation of the need for them appeared in the Financial and Explanatory Memoranda which accompanied Baker's bill when it was introduced. Baker's clearly personal (though short-lived) addition to the national curriculum – to require seven-year-olds to learn and recite a piece of verse – was a sign of just how arbitrarily those powers could be exercised.

In another conspicuous measure in 1988 – the Local Government Finance Act which introduced the poll tax – Environment Secretary Nicholas Ridley empowered himself to issue orders to 'make such supplementary, incidental, consequential or transitional provisions as appear to him to be necessary or expedient for the general purposes or any particular purpose of the Act' – and provided that any such order might amend, repeal or revoke any provision of any Act of the same or any earlier session. Such powers were also included in other legislation affecting local government, such as the Local Government and Housing Act of the following year. They are in fact now an accepted part of government action. And yet as Professor Patrick McAuslan, Professor of Public Law at the LSE, pointed out when Baker's bill was being driven through Parliament:

Central government incursions

> A dangerous precedent is being set if matters as important as these, which go to the roots of the reforms being introduced by the bill, can be removed from the full parliamentary scrutiny which accompanies amending Acts of Parliament and is relegated instead to orders which receive to all intents and purposes no parliamentary scrutiny when placed before Parliament.
>
> (McAuslan 1988)

It is not new for central government to be ranged against local authorities on major educational issues – in the 1960s and 1970s, ministers and local authorities battled over the enforced introduction of comprehensive secondary education. Nor is it unusual for a government to control the school curriculum (in countries noted for their liberal and democratic traditions, such as Sweden, the government is fully in control). Nor, in fact, was Baker seizing control of the curriculum from local authorities, which had never had much influence on the curriculum, but rather from the educational establishment and teachers. In the name of 'parental choice' he denied choice. He and later colleagues, such as John Patten, set out to establish a centrally run national schools system in which they and their officials possessed extra-ordinarily wide-ranging discretionary powers. The scale of powers which has become concentrated in the hands of education ministers is overwhelming. In 1993, Patten assumed as Education Secretary the sole duty to 'promote' education and to exercise his powers to that end. The departmental press release 59/93 (25 February 1993) made no mention at all of the role of local education authorities, historically central government's partners in school education.

Education Secretaries have powers over the curriculum, the level of funding for schools, the ability to impose cash limits, the training and number of teachers, surplus school places, admissions policies and 'failing schools'. These powers, as we have already seen, have commended themselves to Labour ministers who were committed in 1997 to legislating for even more direct powers to intervene in local authority education (though the Funding Agency for Schools, a powerful tool for central government control, is to be abolished). As education remains by far the largest local government service, eroded as it has been, the accumulation of powers at the centre shifts the overall balance of power between central and local government still further towards the centre. There are few effective safeguards on these powers. Where consultation is required before an Education Secretary or his officials exercise any of them, the period is usually short. Ministerial responsibility to Parliament provides no extra safeguards because modern governments are adept at using the idea to avoid rather than to accept real responsibility (see Chapter 12).

Patten argued that the government's changes promoted the role of 'active citizens' in school education and trumpeted a 'new constitutional settlement' giving parents and citizens 'real rather than paper rights'. Certain reforms did to some degree empower parents, but the advances were limited. For example, the parents' 'right to choose' the schools their children attend is severely circumscribed in reality and the new admissions policies empowered head teachers to choose parents rather than parents choosing schools. Patten claimed that the changes pushed 'as much power as possible to the community'. But the newly empowered community of active citizens he reckoned to liberate is a fragmented body, in so far as it exists. It has no organising locus; no strategic local control over education policies as a whole; no place for prospective parents as well as incumbent parents; and no role for the wider community, except favoured business people; and as stated above, parent governors on school governing bodies are in a minority.

Only local authorities can exercise the local strategic role and be in a position to offer immediate redress to dissatisfied parents or pupils in local schools. Where do the parents or pupils in grant-maintained schools go if they want to complain? Neither the Funding Agency for Schools nor the Education Secretary are organised to provide redress and any national tribunal system would be remote and expensive, as compared with the casework processes of today's local education authorities. Finally, neither Patten's 'active' nor 'municipal' citizens have any effective control over their new governors at national or local level. Many public decisions cannot be made by rational calculation; they belong in an indefinable zone of values and preferences. The Education Secretaries who stand like national colossi over local education, as Labour's David Blunkett now does, have of course an electoral mandate, but it is exercised remotely from local electors; is largely unconstrained by Parliament or the courts; and leaves them generally unaccountable either to active or municipal citizens.

Let us spell out the implications. Ministerial orders have the same force of law as Acts of Parliament and must be obeyed as such; but they are essentially unchecked by Parliament as a whole and may not be checked by any other public institutions (unless ministers exercise them in such a way as to run foul of the courts; but see Chapter 15). Certainly, local authorities in a unitary state organised on the principle of parliamentary sovereignty possess no countervailing rights or safeguards. The principle of the separation of powers – that is, the idea that the powers of government as a whole should be dispersed among different government institutions and levels of government so that they can act as a check on each other – has scarcely any place in British arrangements. Thus, we are not able to avoid concentrations of uncheckable powers in the hands of central government. Such concentrations of power tend to be abused.

Take, as a last example, central government's power to restructure local government as it sees fit. As we saw in Chapter 4, this power can readily be abused by a government intent on removing local centres of resistance, as Mrs Thatcher and her ministers did in the case of the Greater London Council, the metropolitan authorities, and the Inner London Education Authority, and as Ian Lang, as Scottish Secretary, did with the Strathclyde and other Scottish regional authorities. The boundaries may then be set so as to benefit the party in government – as Chapter 4 showed, this was flagrantly the case in the reorganisation of Scottish local government which followed on the decision to abolish the regional authorities which were under Labour control.

Here, again, are examples of where governments have ignored conventions designed to prevent arbitrary government. It used to be customary for a government contemplating major changes to set up an independent commission, and to undertake substantial consultation, seeking to base change at least on the legitimacy of a broad political consensus. Historically, even these safeguards have not entirely excluded partisan considerations (see Chapter 4). But the Major government set them aside and drove its own proposals through. Mrs Thatcher's government had the limited democratic mandate of an election pledge in the 1983 manifesto for the abolition of the GLC and metropolitan authorities, though not that of the ILEA which was defended by a considerable body of organised parents and other interests. Department of the Environment officials had repeatedly warned against the 'nightmare' of endless problems that abolition would cause. No cost–benefit analysis of abolition nor any public consultation were undertaken. Post-abolition, Greater London and the metropolitan conurbations came under the jurisdiction of complex systems of joint working committees and quangos, some especially created. London was administered by between 70 and 80 public bodies, including a government regional office and a cabinet committee (Stoker 1991; King 1993). A MORI opinion poll in the six conurbations revealed 'considerable and increased confusion and uncertainty about the allocation of local government responsibilities' (Game 1987; Stoker 1991).

AUDIT

The arrangements for regional and local government in the UK entirely fail to meet the criteria by which we measure them. We have not examined the quality of democracy at local or regional level in and of itself, as this has been done exhaustively in recent literature, most directly by the Commission for Local Democracy (CLD 1995; see also Stewart and Stoker 1995). Our main concern has been to evaluate the independence of democratic government at regional and local level from interference by central government (**DAC18**); the effects of central government actions and policies on elected politics (**DAC1**); and openness and accountability (**DAC17**) at these levels. We have also adopted the basic principles of the Council of Europe's European Charter of Local Self-Government, which the Labour government has signed, as an additional guide to best practice.

DAC18: Regional and local freedom from central government interference

Arrangements for regional and local democracy are severely deficient in the UK. At regional level, no elected layer of government existed in 1997, though a devolved Parliament in Scotland, a Welsh Assembly and a power-sharing Assembly in Northern Ireland are being established. Regionally, the country was ruled through departments of state for Scotland, Wales and Northern Ireland; regional government offices in England; and quangos of varying status. None of these directly represented national or regional electorates and they relied upon the national mandate of central government for their democratic legitimacy. In strict terms, the new Scottish Parliament and Welsh Assembly will remain creatures of statute and their independence and powers will be unprotected by constitutional safeguards.

Local government is utterly vulnerable to central government. It was in theory protected by constitutional convention – 'The corpus of custom and convention', of which the Widdicombe Report spoke. This chapter has shown that this convention has failed to restrain central government since 1979. Though they came close to doing so, Conservative governments have not abolished local government, only bits of it. But they have taken such severe and continuing powers over finances and services, and removed so many functions and powers from local government, that the idea of politically effective local authorities, as defined by **DAC17**, is a dead letter. As we have seen, governments with a secure parliamentary majority can impose their will on local authorities and override any local democratic mandate or views. Hierarchies of national and local quangos now run significant local services in place of local authorities, but not 'in accordance with the wishes of . . . local electorates', since they are appointed, not elected bodies. Since 1979, the weight of central government increasingly bore down directly on local affairs throughout the land, leaving no space between powerful ministers and officials, armed with wide discretionary powers, and local communities and individual citizens in which local authorities, or any public bodies, could act as constitutional or political counterweights. Everywhere, the writ of single-party government at the centre ran and local accountability was frustrated.

The Labour government has recently signed up to the Council of Europe's Charter for Local Self-Government. We have already quoted the Charter's guiding principles:

- Local authorities must have adequate financial resources of their own (Article 9).
- Financial equalisation processes are not to be used to diminish the decision-making powers of local authorities (Article 9).
- Central government must not undermine local authority powers by administrative action (Articles 4 and 8).
- Local authorities should have powers of general competence (Article 4).
- Local authorities should have freedom of choice as to the way in which services are provided and in their internal organisation (Article 6).
- Local authorities must be able to determine the rate of their own taxes (Article 9).

The Labour government is pledged to implement the Charter. For the time being, as we have shown, arrangements in the UK fail to achieve any of these goals. They also cause concern on various matters which the Democratic Audit criteria raise. The complexity of national and regional controls over local authorities and quangos, and the diversity of local service providers, now obscure transparency and confuse accountability at local level (**DAC17: openness and accountability**). As budgets and many policies are determined centrally, they do not allow for adequate scrutiny and control by elected local politicians (**DAC8: elective control of bureaucracy; DAC17**). Those who effectively take or limit decisions of local authorities are not accessible to local communities and undermine the principle of representation by local politicians (**DAC16: access to decision-makers**). The existence of local quangos with appointed boards, exercising their powers over a wide range of services, sets aside basic principles of popular control. The governing magistracy is not elected and is not subject to popular recall, its members do not represent local communities or interests, and are not accountable locally (**DAC1: the role of popular**

election); and its presence, size, powers and fragmented nature undermine local representation (**DAC17**). The quangos obscure transparency and confuse account-ability; their budgets and policies are largely determined centrally; and they escape scrutiny and control by elected local politicians.

What the centre can take away, it can restore. The future of local government depends in the first place on the willingness of the new Labour government to give it a secure financial base of its own. Central government's interference in local affairs was tenuously justified on the grounds that 53 per cent of the public money spent by local authorities came from national taxpayers, for which ministers were legally and politically responsible. Freedom from central command depends ultimately on giving local councils powers to raise a higher proportion of their funding locally, and making them directly responsible to local taxpayers. Equally, it is necessary to reform the structures of local governance, giving local authorities strategic powers over local public spending bodies; making use of new means of encouraging popular and user participation; widening the former government's access and redress pro-visions; introducing proportional representation into local elections to create more pluralist local politics; and strengthening the Citizen's Charter. The final require-ment is formal recognition of local government as an integral part of the constitution in the UK, which leaves it flexible and capable of change and reform from above, subject to adequate safeguards.

Only local authorities are equipped to encourage and organise collective decision-making at local level, bringing together all the relevant 'publics' and interests involved in a process of debate and decision and resolving problems in a way that satisfies our two basic principles of popular control and political equality. Neither central government, local administration nor centrally directed or self-governing agencies can replicate this process. It is not simply local democracy which is lost if local authorities continue to be distrusted and downgraded. In present circumstances, more imaginative authorities are unable to take initiatives on major problems or needs that may not be perceived nationally or by narrowly based local agencies.

10   Networks in Power

External influences working within government

> *The great mass of government today is the work of an able and honest but secretive bureau-cracy, tempered by the ever-present apprehension of the revolt of powerful sectional interests, and mitigated by the spasmodic interventions of imperfectly comprehending Ministers.*
>
> (Sidney and Beatrice Webb, practical socialist intellectuals, 1920)

> *To supply 'expertise', or to control its employment in the conduct of rule, does not seem a job Parliament can adequately do. Instead, the job falls mainly to the professional civil service, which enlists the support of research institutes, planning units, and consultative bodies, manned chiefly by the 'scientific estate' and by spokesmen for the larger corpora-tions and other interest groups. As a result, administrative decisions are increasingly articulated in a language that effectively screens them from parliamentary criticism and public debate, and that frequently provides a convenient cover for the interests actually dictating those decisions.*
>
> (Gianfranco Poggi, political sociologist at Edinburgh, 1978)

Major organised interests and professional groups play a significant and often domi-nating role in government policy-making in most significant areas of business and national affairs. The pharmaceutical, car, processed foods, aerospace and arms indus-tries, major brewers, farmers, local government associations, oil companies, British Airways and other airlines, major construction companies seeking work at home and abroad, the privatised utilities, trade associations of many types, trade unions, pressure groups of all colours, doctors, lawyers, and other professions, are among those interests which are consulted regularly by government departments and constantly lobby those departments in their own interests. The relationship between organised interests and departmental officials varies across policy domains, but many interest groups perform an intimate role in the way policies are formulated and are often vital to policies being carried through in practice.

Interest groups are undoubtedly important to the democratic process. Most are self-interested – they represent an industry, say, or a profession. But they may also ensure that minority or marginal interests are represented (e.g. Shelter, MIND), or raise issues that have not previously appeared on the party political agenda (e.g. the 'Black Book' education campaign, or Charter 88's pressure for constitutional reform), or scrutinise, check and report on the activities of government (e.g. Liberty, the Institute of Fiscal Studies). They bring specialist knowledge and experience to bear upon the policy process and introduce an element of pluralism. Informality is an important – and helpful – ingredient of the process. But this informality also means that the boundaries between the public domain and interest and private interests are left undefined.

The emphasis of official accounts of British government centre upon its formal and parliamentary aspects. Yet the whole machinery of government turns upon the daily assumption that officials and departments will be advised, assisted, lobbied and criticised by organised interests; their specialist knowledge and often their active consent is vital to much of the policy-making process, including major public decisions. However, the involvement of interest groups in policy-making through policy communities and networks attached to government departments is ungoverned by any framework of rules to ensure that the public – and ministers for that matter – know what is going on, the policy options agreed and discarded, the arguments for and against decisions, the interests which are protected and those which aren't. The bargaining is secretive as well as being informal, and has been kept secret by governments because it falls within the domains of policy advice and commercial confidentiality.

Thus the role of influential interest groups is often a parallel, and more decisive, system of representation to that of the people through Parliament. For the authors of a contemporary study of government in Britain, 'the major locus of public power in Britain is focused around a federation of the great departments of state and their client groups' (Harden and Lewis 1988: 70). Interest groups have a great deal to gain from being involved in policy communities or networks. It is not merely influence on decision-making which is on offer. Their representations can mobilise government's power to legislate and deploy its administrative authority in their interest, allocate resources and even determine taxes to their advantage. There is no doubt that certain interests, or 'client groups', do exert a sectional influence, as we shall show, and almost always in conditions of secrecy. Their power is not confined to what government does; they may also exert a 'power to veto and at least substantially amend public policies' (*ibid.*: 60) and act as agencies for government, through (for example) carrying out the research and development of arms equipment or contracted-out programmes. In turn, government can become an agency for outside interests. We have already seen that the formal notion that ministers decide and dispose and civil servants simply advise and obey grossly over-simplifies what actually happens in British government; that government departments play a decisive role in most of government's policy-making; and that most of the major decisions on government policy are made within departments.

In this chapter we analyse the way such decisions are often shaped through 'policy communities' and networks of officials, organised outside interests and ministers; the role advisory quangos (see Chapter 8) play within such networks; and the way in which government departments consult interest groups and the public. Officials can often incorporate outside interests as allies in the cause of developed departmental views. But there is also the danger that departments may be captured by their 'client' groups or that the interests of such groups might fuse with perceived departmental interests. There are obvious defences against such tendencies: a strong independent sense of the 'public interest', or the interests of the state; giving clear priority to the mandate of elected ministers; the active encouragement of wider group participation; and, above all, making all consultative processes open to the public. To Whitehall, 'democracy' seems to involve looking mainly to ministers and to established 'insider' groups, just as Sidney and Beatrice Webb saw over 70 years ago.

We measure the processes of government consultation against the principles of popular control and political equality, which demand that:

- government should be required to consider the representation of all relevant external interests;
- consultation of external interests should be conducted in a transparent and open process;
- the House of Commons, on behalf of the electorate, should have the opportunity to examine and check policies and decisions taken as a result of consultation.

It is important openly to recognise the difficulties of holding a proper balance between different categories of interests – e.g. between individual and group or corporate interests; between those who are deeply affected and those with more diffuse concerns; between industrial and financial interests and environmental effects or impacts upon communities. No single interest of this kind can always be paramount – in other words, a tendency to privilege, say, industrial or trade interests over all other considerations would not be appropriate. These difficulties make the need for openness all the more important.

In particular, we audit the processes of consultation as a whole against **DAC15**:

How systematic and open to public scrutiny are the procedures for government consultation of public opinion and of relevant interests in the formation and implementation of policy and legislation?

Other Audit criteria also have a bearing on the issues which arise:

DAC7. Public access to information on government policies and their effects.

DAC8. Ministerial control over non-elected personnel.

DAC9. Parliamentary scrutiny of the executive.

DAC11. Transparent rules governing executive behaviour.

The role of interest groups in policy-making

The significant role that interest groups play in government's policy-making is a long-established phenomenon. During the period in which the modern 'ministerial state' was being formed (1870–1930), organised interests, if recognised at all, were regarded as being part of civil society rather than government. But the state was forever expanding – especially after 1939 – into areas which were previously governed by the market, or by voluntary arrangements. Governments took powers to promote or regulate industrial, economic and social objectives, often intervening in detail and creating explicit or understood partnerships with private business and professional bodies. Increasingly, therefore, civil servants in the expanded state bureaucracy became involved in discussing, bargaining over and carrying out policies with industrialists, business people, professionals, and their interest groups, but the old Victorian model within which the civil service worked had no structured place nor rules for such dealings with outside interests (Beattie 1995). It still does not. The existence of such negotiations became acknowledged at a political level during the postwar period as 'corporatism', a tripartite bargaining process in which ministers bargained with industry and trade unions over the direction of economic, industrial and social policies.

But below the corporatist surface, civil servants in individual departments across Whitehall and external actors were busily engaged in continuing dialogue and negotiation over making and implementing government policies. This less visible corporatism is divided into two sorts of corporate groupings by political scientists: 'policy communities', which are closed to other outsiders and even other government departments, and the more numerous 'policy networks', which are more open consultative and negotiating forums (like the state education networks of the 1950s and 1960s were, including as they did teachers' organisations, local authority associations, and so on). Both sets of arrangements are a significant element in government policy-making, though they vary in influence and intensity. In policy communities, officials and groups meet regularly to discuss policy issues and exchange information on an exclusive footing.

Mrs Thatcher came to power in 1979 intending to reduce the role of corporatism in decision-making. But Conservative governments proved to be very selective in weeding out interest groups; trade union influences were sharply reduced, and often one interest group simply replaced another. They also failed to appreciate that interest groups outside government are often vital to making policies work. Interest groups or agencies which were not consulted made it hard actually to carry out policies by failing to co-operate or comply with them (Marsh and Rhodes 1992: 181). Further, while rejecting old-style corporate negotiations with trade unions and business, Conservative governments were generally committed to consulting business interests and involving them more closely in the processes of government over a wide range of public affairs, services and policies. Compromise, particularly over privatisation policies, was extensive (Marsh 1991). The enhanced role of business interests on executive and advisory quangos increased their practical influence over government decision-making; businessmen flooded onto NHS bodies and took over local training initiatives. Indeed, one observer stated, 'the power of the business lobby and the close links between ministers, senior civil servants and businessmen gives increasing cause for concern' (Dowding 1995a: 113). Certain professional and trade associations also act as agents for government, enforcing non-statutory codes of guidance or professional discipline, or even delivering public services.

Departments and officials are actively engaged on a continuous basis in creating policy communities and deciding which interest groups should be given access. But they have no published rules for recognising which interest groups should be dealt with, for listing publicly which are involved, for defining the terms on which negotiations take place, or for making them transparent. Further, pressure groups are far from equal in their eyes. Certain interests – most especially those of big business generally – have more finance, expertise, information, status and access to Whitehall. A body such as, for example, the Confederation of British Industry is a well-organised professional organisation which has an impeccably 'respectable' reputation in Whitehall. The CBI possesses near automatic access to civil servants and ministers on any issue that affects its members' interests.

The reason why major organised interests of this kind seek to influence government officials is obvious. Government has the power to legislate and make regulations, to acquire political powers and administrative authority, to set taxes and to allocate resources. Major interests thus negotiate with government officials, pass on specialist knowledge and ensure their members co-operate with the legislation and policies which emerge from policy communities in order to advance and protect their interests. They naturally achieve their objectives more readily than poorer pressure groups which do not represent powerful sectional interests whose co-operation government departments require; and which cannot afford professional presentational techniques nor lobbyists. Such groups are often dismissed by officials as 'unreliable' because of the views and arguments they adopt, often simply because these contradict existing departmental views (Grant 1989).

Disregarded groups can, of course, adopt other tactics to gain influence. After some 30 years of presenting disregarded argument and evidence on roads policy to the Department of Transport and losing out in the pro-department public inquiry procedure, a significant minority of environmentalists turned from argument to direct action – first disrupting public inquiries, more recently intervening directly at the construction stage. In the 1990s, the fierce protests coincided with the growing recognition of the financial and environmental costs of the roads programme at government level. Yet the environmentalists' criticisms of policy were arguably right in the first place and ought to have been openly and properly considered.

Policy communities inevitably reinforce this inequality, operating as they do as closed policy-making groups at departmental level, sometimes as smaller communities around internal sub-departments or specialist issues, sometimes crossing departmental boundaries (Jordan and Richardson 1987; Marsh and Rhodes 1992). The influence and power of outside interests within departments clearly vary considerably, and policy networks are fairly open to other external influence and lobbying (Marsh and Rhodes 1992). Clearly, too, the policy views and preferences of the departments and officials involved shape the degree of influence which outside interests, both within and outside these groupings, will have on policies. Departments and their senior officials have views and interests of their own and are quite able to carry out policy regardless of what outside interests tell them. So too are ministers. It is arguable, for example, that the roads lobby only seemed to dominate the Department of Transport's postwar roads policies because its pressures fitted pre-existing departmental plans (Dowding 1995a: 117).

Role in policy-making

Policy communities work out of sight of the public and Parliament and are therefore difficult to detect. Only a few have been identified and analysed in depth in the academic literature (see, for example, Marsh and Rhodes 1992; Smith 1993: Dowding 1995a). Fewer still are known to parliamentarians and the media. Yet within these communities, some groups enjoy privileged access to Whitehall for long periods, often on a day-to-day basis, and have the potential to have a large, and sectional, impact on policy outcomes. The influence of the defence industry on the Ministry of Defence – and even on the supposed parliamentary watchdog, the Defence Select Committee – is profound. The impact of such links is usually unseen as government practice at least up to 1997 has excluded the policy process and commercial information from disclosure – and, in the case of defence, 'national security' considerations are advanced to justify near blanket secrecy (see **p. 362**). These links are inevitably partial: the first concern of members of policy communities is to protect or enhance their own interests and those of the community rather than public interests. The operations of these policy communities are part of a wider process of consultation. Thus when formulating options for new initiatives or reviewing existing policies, civil servants and ministers may well consult widely with the public and a full range of pressure groups, but make decisions based on negotiations within closed policy communities largely consisting of 'respectable' interest groups (see below). A senior civil servant said to one group of researchers:

> Better to consult too many than too few. . . . There are no rules against joining a list. Any discrimination is at the comment stage. Now those determined to interpret the process to suit their prior prejudice will claim that this means that consultation is meaningless.
>
> (Jordan et al. 1992: 23)

A few general rules determine who is in and who is out. Interest groups representing business and key professions come first, often for good practical reasons. Industries and professions can provide government with information the departments need to formulate policy options and their co-operation is usually vital to making policies work in practice. On the other hand, consumer groups and users of services are often ignored because they have little to offer government. Doctors, for example, are more important to making health policies work than patients or their representatives. Moreover, consumer and user organisations are more likely to be critical of government policy. Likewise groups that press views which run counter to ministers' or departmental views, or which represent alternative interests, will often find it difficult to obtain access. Take, for example, the recent experience of the Howard League for Penal Reform. The Howard League enjoyed almost continuous contact with Home Office officials over penal policy while Radical Alternatives to Prisons found access difficult (Ryan 1983). But when Michael Howard became Home Secretary in 1993, the Howard League's influence too waned. But ministers are also often obliged to consult and negotiate with key groups, even when they are hostile to government policies; for example, ministers continued to consult the National Union of Teachers on the education changes of the 1980s, even though the union was determined to defeat their policies.

The danger for specialist groups, such as the Howard League – and for diversity of public debate – is that public criticism of government ministers or policies transgresses the 'rules of the game'. Civil servants prefer to work in a consensual fashion, broadly directed along the lines of existing government policy or practice. The various actors within a policy community clearly do not always agree with each other or with government policy. There are often serious conflicts, but so far as possible, they are contained within the inner circle. There is also consensus on the sort of political behaviour that is acceptable and, to a large degree, on the issues which can be discussed and the policy options which can be considered. This has important implications for the democratic process and the political agenda. Groups which 'rock the boat' by their behaviour – for example, by organising a lobby of Parliament or media coverage for the ideas they propose – are likely to be excluded. Consequently, the political agenda is controlled by the vested interests within the policy process, while specialist interest groups and individuals are forever walking a tightrope between the 'consensual' and 'confrontational'. Sir Douglas Wass, former Treasury permanent secretary and joint head of the home civil service, has described how ministers, officials and interests are mixed together and 'political decisions, at every level of government, are reached with a view, at least in part, to satisfying these pressure groups and interests' (Wass 1984: 105).

Departments can accommodate these outside pressures because the evolution of policy within is subject to little external review or public scrutiny. Circles of satisfaction are generated. Satisfied interest groups do not embarrass ministers; they assist departments to maintain their programmes; they may orchestrate apparent 'pressure' to convince the Treasury and other departments, or manipulate a positive media response; and they get all or most of what they want (Harden and Lewis 1988: 147).

Ministers generally enter the policy process towards the end. Weekly, their civil servants ask them to take some 50 or so decisions, often in areas of policy where they may be entirely unschooled. A former Home Office official estimated that a Home Secretary may be asked to take up to 200 decisions weekly. Many policy areas are so complex that decisions are frequently not shaped by civil servants, individually or severally, but rather by civil servants in discussion with specialists and interests in particular areas. This process may well be made formal through one of the 674 advisory quangos, generally established under prerogative powers formally to advise ministers, but in practice usually to advise and negotiate with senior departmental officials (see Chapter 8). Consequently, public policy is often fragmented into discrete specialist areas. Making and implementing policy in these areas is devolved to networks which inevitably involve interested parties in what may well be highly significant decisions about, say, the safety of drugs or public investment in major construction contracts. Only a limited number of civil servants, interest groups and specialists participate and the specialists may well have links with the interest groups taking part. The civil servants have a broad grasp of the issues and the government's objectives, but they may well not have the specialist knowledge to challenge or interpret the advice and information they are given. The closed and secretive nature of the process removes any element of 'peer review' or public scrutiny. Formally, the public is represented by the minister who actually takes the legal decision; but the decision itself will have been shaped by the processes described above and presented to the minister in the ministerial box, filled to the brim with policy options prepared by the minister's private office.

The existence of closed communities, within which civil servants act as arbiters of policy, strengthens the role of officials within government and enhances their power in relation both to ministers and outside interests. At the same time, officials may come to see the groups they are continually dealing with as surrogates for the 'public interest'. They may be able to incorporate outside interests as allies in the cause of developed departmental views, but their departments equally may be captured by these interests. As we pointed out above, the obvious defences against such tendencies – a strong countervailing idea of the 'public interest' or wider and more open participation – do not exist under current arrangements. Instead, the sheer weight of decision-making and the existence of policy communities undermine and distort the principle of ministerial responsibility to Parliament because they oblige ministers to take decisions in bulk over a wide range of issues; and they introduce key external actors into the policy process (who are not publicly acknowledged; who have interests of their own; who work in the inner track; and who cannot be held to account). Moreover, they often partially usurp Parliament's ultimate role of scrutiny of legislation, primary and secondary, presented in the House of Commons. Ministers often prevent Parliament from amending or rejecting such legislation because it is the result of negotiation and compromise between civil servants and interests which cannot then be readily unpicked. The secrecy of the process does not safeguard only government policy from scrutiny, but also the industries involved in these policy communities. For example, there is evidence of waste, fraud and negligent financial controls in the MOD's dealings with the defence industry which is also safeguarded by secrecy (see **p. 365**).

Closed policy communities in action

Closed networks are most likely to exist where major business interests or professional issues on which government policies have a significant influence are involved. Of those which exist, we take three notorious examples. The first is the major roads lobby which grew up around the Department of Transport, involving formidable interest groups like the British Road Federation (BRF), the AA, RAC, the Road Haulage Association, the Society of Motor Manufacturers and highway engineers. The BRF pulled together a range of big business interests – major construction industries, road caterers (Trust House Forte), car dealers, freight companies, and the AA and RAC – and established a close working relationship with departmental officials. The department became effectively closed to other interest groups, and even other government departments. Departmental officials failed to negotiate on an equal footing with other interested parties, like the Transport Reform Group, Transport 2000 and railway and environmental groups, even though, for example, the environmental effects of road building and traffic were clearly significant (Marr 1995).

The roads lobby dominated all aspects of transport policy, with its arguments that new and wider roads were a key to economic growth. Government policies created huge imbalances between the use of cars and all other modes of transport. Roads were expanded at the expense of rail and unrestricted car use in cities squeezed out reliable bus services and polluted the atmosphere. From the 1960s to 1980s, public spending on what Mrs Thatcher called the Great Car Economy rose inexorably; as late as 1989, the cabinet agreed to raise spending on road building from £5 billion to £12 billion. With the powerful backing of the roads lobby, the Roads Construction Unit within the Ministry of Transport, comprising of ministry officials and road engineers and working closely with local authority highways officials, was able to build roads with continuous ministerial approval and no significant opposition (Dudley and Richardson 1996). As the journalist Andrew Marr wrote:

> the Transport Department became essentially a roads department and, more than that, a road-building robot which operated almost outside the rest of government . . . within the department, the Highways Directorate was a law unto itself, described by an official from a rival department as 'a roads machine' cut off from the rest of Whitehall – unaccountable, unmonitored, unchecked.
>
> (1995: 305–6)

The policy community of officials and lobbyists managed to isolate the roads programme from Treasury control, using the supposed scientific evidence of engineers to convince Treasury officials that extra roads were necessary to relieve traffic congestion and would provide substantial economic benefits (Marr 1995: 306). At the same time, its monopoly hold on policy excluded relevant environmental and other interests from being considered by government and prevented full analysis of the road engineers' data. Thus, instead of open and equal debate on a vital issue, a key policy was actually determined by a handful of officials and vested interests, largely in secret negotiations conducted in Whitehall. In 1995, the then Environment Secretary, John Gummer, finally organised enough political pressure to cut the roads programme back and in 1996 he produced a UK Air Quality Strategy which bore the scars of prolonged intradepartmental battle, not least between Environment and Transport officials. The strategy document was short on urgency and funding and came out eight months late.

The Ministry of Agriculture (MAFF) and the National Farmers Union have formed a similar 'closed' policy community, dominating agricultural policy in postwar Britain, largely free from Treasury or cabinet interference until the 1980s. The NFU has had privileged access to the ministry and a guarantee of generous state funding for farming that was unavailable to most other industries. Farming is extensively represented on the ministry's executive and advisory quangos, often through NFU nominees. In general, consumer interests were formally represented by the Ministry of Agriculture, Fisheries and Food, and took second place to farming interests (see Body 1984). Agriculture officials took the view that they took full account of the interests of consumers – though one told a select committee, 'We do not specifically consult consumer associations'. As for environmental groups, the MAFF–NFU axis argued that farmers were the natural custodians of the countryside, capable of balancing farming interests with those of flora and fauna habitats, wildlife, and so on. Environmental and green groups only rarely gained access to the ministry and when they did so, a 1983 survey found that it was largely token and in return for moderating their demands (Lowe and Goyder 1983: 63–65). Usually the ministry took agricultural decisions affecting the environment, consulting two executive quangos, the Nature Conservancy Council and the Countryside Commission (see Chapter 8). Consultation with these two official bodies, answerable to ministers, blocked direct access to the ministry for the wide range of independent environmental and countryside lobbies (Lowe and Goyder 1983). This closed policy-making greatly distorted the food market and heavily subsidised intensive farming had radical effects on the countryside. The results were neither democratic nor effective government. Agriculture was removed from the democratic parliamentary and public arenas.

Some of the most powerful policy communities in Britain – and possibly the most disastrous – have been centred around food production. The overlapping agricultural and food policy communities have exerted great power over the diet of the whole population, with long-term implications for the nation's health. MAFF has been at the centre of both communities, being formally charged with responsibility for agriculture and food since 1955 (though this position is likely to change under the Labour government). The agricultural community played a visible role in the salmonella in eggs health scare in the 1980s as well as in the longer-running BSE – or 'mad cow disease' – crisis. Salmonella in Britain's egg production became a significant issue when cases of salmonella poisoning rose above 13,000 in 1988. However, the link between eggs and the rise in cases was first raised in 1985 in the USA and MAFF was certainly aware of this link in 1987. The policy community's initial view was that the onus for preventing poisoning lay with consumers rather than the government or farmers, and the options of destroying flocks or even preventing re-infection through a ban on recycling slaughterhouse waste were rejected (Druce 1988: 57).

As the crisis grew, officials played for time. Sir Donald Acheson, then chief medical officer, stated in evidence to the Agriculture Committee, 'the evidence was not sufficiently clear for any firm conclusions to be drawn' (Druce 1988: 37). As in the case of BSE, the policy community was unwilling to act or inform the public until 'firm evidence' was available. By July 1988, the Department of Health's public health laboratory had produced firm evidence of the risk from raw eggs, but still the agriculture community – MAFF officials, the British Egg Industry Council and the British Poultry Federation – wanted to maintain secrecy. Finally, the rivalry between the Agriculture and Health departments erupted. Mrs Edwina Currie announced the danger in dramatic terms in November 1988 and the bottom fell out of the egg market. The NFU forced the government to sack Mrs Currie and introduce an expensive compensation scheme. The government also set up a new advisory committee on the microbiological safety of food and MAFF established a consumer council. But, as the BSE crisis was soon to show (see below), the basic problems remained unchanged.

Britain's huge food production industry has also safeguarded its interests from within the ministry's food network. The Department of Health (DH) maintains an apparently open network of health professionals and specialist advisers around issues of nutrition and food safety, yet the network is dominated by the food industry whose interests have come first. Among the core members are the National Farmers Union and bodies like the Food and Drinks Federation (FDF), the Butter Information Council, the Sugar Bureau and their specialist advisers. In 1997, such interests were fully represented on the advisory quangos which serve the two departments – the Committee on Medical Aspects of Food Policy (DH), the Advisory Committee on the Microbiological Safety of Food (DH), the Advisory Committee on Novel Foods and Processes (MAFF) and the Food Advisory Committee (MAFF). The small network of such advisory committees handles issues of food safety, nutrition and hygiene, reporting to departmental officials. Many committee members have links with the food industry – some being their formal representatives, others 'independent' specialists who are often in receipt of research grants from the industry. (See also Chapter 8.) Until the 1980s, consumer groups' representatives were excluded. The cheap food policy was believed to serve the interests of consumers, so why consult them? In response to mounting criticism of their composition, the department did then begin to place representatives of consumer bodies on these quangos; but they, food retailers, like Tesco and Sainsbury's, the British Medical Association, and quangos like the Health Education Authority and National Consumer Council, were allowed only a peripheral role. More radical critics and groups, some university-based, advocating more interventionist government food and health promotion policies, were excluded and ministers specifically banned Tim Lang, an early campaigner for safe food, from quango membership.

The government's 'hands-off' approach to issues of food, diet and health, which now looks likely to be abandoned, developed in the 1950s. As long as food was 'safe' – in the limited sense that it could not be shown to cause any direct harm – governments left the choice of foods to the market (see Mills 1993). Agricultural and food production became highly industrialised and centred around food that could be bought cheaply and easily processed in order to add value. Cheap potatoes can, for example, be transformed into crisps or frozen chips, both of which have much greater profit margins. Big food producers encourage certain types of consumption through marketing and advertising. Their industry is not concerned with nutritional issues or the potential dangers of additives. It wants to buy basic foodstuffs cheap and sell on profitable highly processed products to the public. It is therefore hostile, for example, to any restrictions – even informative labelling is regarded as a hazard to its profits and the industry uses its influence to reduce it to an uninformative minimum. The industry spends heavily on lobbying government, especially through industry-wide organisations like the FDF, and more specific bodies, such as the Butter Information Council and the Sugar Bureau, which play a significant role in food policy communities and maintain strong day-to-day contacts with Whitehall and MPs (Cannon 1988). The Labour government's powerful new Food Standards Agency, independent of the policy community, has already had to weather intense lobbying from the food industry, and will come under continual pressure once it is in action.

In a whole range of areas, such as the three outlined above, policy is made in relatively closed policy communities which involve departments and select interest groups – for example, between the Ministry of Defence, the armed forces and the major defence contractors; in medicine, between the Ministry of Health and the pharmaceutical giants; in healthcare, between the Ministry of Health, the NHS and the doctors (until broken by Mrs Thatcher's – equally 'closed' – policy review in 1989). These closed groups distort the democratic process, denying popular control of policy-making and political equality in its processes. They often have great influence in the media, influencing the way the public perceives the issues and shielding big interests from critical scrutiny. They can also produce outcomes that are arguably not in the general interest and which may on occasion, as we have seen, amount to human tragedies or 'policy disasters'. The BSE crisis, for example, has already cost some two dozen young lives, devastated the beef and associated industries and, according to official estimates, will finally cost the Exchequer £4.2 billion (*The Times*, 2 June 1997). By March 1996, perhaps some 6,000 jobs in farming and food-related industries had been lost (*Guardian*, 30 March 1996).

It is important to point out that policy communities and networks can be challenged from outside. For example, the increased activity of 'new social movements' in recent years has subjected the policies of a whole range of policy communities to severe criticism and reform. The anti-roads lobby initiated a process of expert criticism and direct action which effectively brought the unbroken official cycle of new road proposals, public inquiry procedures and continuing road building to an end (Young 1994). Public and official concerns about air pollution and other consequences of heavy traffic have also played a part; and the projected doubling or trebling of traffic throughout the UK finally brought more traditional environmental lobbies, such as the Council for the Protection of Rural England, into the line-up. As in food policy, where splits between the Departments of Health and Agriculture helped to open up debate, divisions between Transport and Environment allowed alternative groups to gain influence on roads policies. Consumer groups changed the terms of debate on food policy and the incoming Labour government is pledged to end MAFF's dominion over food issues and to create a powerful new regulatory body under the direction of the Department of Health.

However, the impact of such groups is erratic and may take generations to achieve. Much depends on purely contingent factors, such as whether the media take up the issue, its salience and the degree of inter-departmental conflict. On roads policy, change has begun not least because the Treasury found environmental arguments a convenient way of justifying cuts in public expenditure; on nuclear power, it was the refusal of the private sector to take on the industry which removed the blinkers from government's eyes. Depending on the energy and wit of pressure groups and the Treasury's need for public spending cuts is not a reliable, or democratic, way of checking interest-group policies of this kind. Besides, it may be that the public interest requires additional expenditure, not less, as in the BSE crisis.

BSE: a case study in closed policy-making

Bovine spongiform encephalopathy (BSE) was first discovered in cows on St George's Day (23 April) 1985. This is another case in which the defensive reactions of the policy community delayed effective action and ensured that government placed the interests of producers over those of the general public. It took 11 years for the government officially to recognise the existence of a *possible* link between BSE and the new-strain human brain disease, Creutzfeldt-Jakob Disease (CJD), by which time eight young people had died from exposure to infected meat. From the outset, government ministers and officials denied that such a link was possible and constantly reassured the public that 'British beef is safe'. The most celebrated assurances came from Agriculture Minister John Selwyn Gummer who, in May 1990, attempted to make his young daughter eat a beefburger in front of the television cameras. She sensibly declined to open her mouth, as Gummer said, 'my children, my family and myself eat beef and we are certainly safe because it's British beef. . . . My job is *first and foremost* to make sure the public knows that it is perfectly safe to eat British beef' [our emphasis] . . . 'if I've got the slightest doubt, I will take action'. But other ministers and officials maintained the refrain, including:

- Keith Meldrum, the Agriculture Ministry's Chief Veterinary Officer: 'We don't believe that there are any implications for humans at this time' (November 1988); and on the risk from eating offal, 'we don't believe that there is any risk from the consumption of this type of material because there is no known association between the animal encephalopathis and the encephalopathis in man' (January 1989).
- David Maclean, Agriculture Minister: 'We have so many safety belts and braces on this operation, it's untrue' (January 1990); and 'the safety net we have is foolproof' (May 1990).
- Donald Acheson, Chief Medical Officer: 'There is no risk associated with eating British beef' (May 1990).
- Meldrum: 'I am quite convinced on the basis of the scientific evidence, from experts who know about these diseases, that beef is totally safe to eat' (January 1994).
- Stephen Dorrell on LWT: there was 'no conceivable risk' from eating British beef (3 December 1995).

In September 1994, the impossible began to happen. Stephen Churchill in Wiltshire was the first to die, at the age of 18, from new-strain CJD. The cause of his death was confirmed in 1995. After years of official denial, Stephen Dorrell was obliged to announce in a Commons statement on 20 March 1996 that 10 cases, including Churchill's, of a new variant of CJD had been discovered in people aged under 42 and that, 'The most likely explanation at present is that these cases are linked to exposure to BSE before the introduction of the specified bovine offal ban in 1989' (HC Deb, 20 March 1996, c375–377, 387). The government's advisory body, the Spongiform Encephalopathy Advisory Committee (SEAC) – recently strengthened by the inclusion of five new members, including a public health specialist – had decided that evidence of the link between BSE and CJD was firm enough to act on, and asked for their conclusion to be made public. Their views could scarcely be gainsaid. Yet resistance to revelation continued in the cabinet. According to the *Observer*:

> At an emergency meeting early last week, Deputy Prime Minister Michael
> Heseltine and Conservative Party Chairman Brian Mawhinney led a group
> of Ministers arguing strongly against going public about the suspected link
> between BSE infected meat and a new strain of the human brain affliction
> CJD.
>
> (*Observer*, 24 March 1996)

Even though Dorrell stressed that the 10 people had been exposed to infected meat products *before* an offal ban had been introduced in 1989, the advisory committee was careful not to say that beef was now safe, only that the risk was 'likely to be extremely small' if all the existing controls were rigorously enforced – a significant qualification, given that they were not. Yet the Prime Minister, John Major, again took up the official refrain in the House of Commons on 23 April 1996, 'I'm happy to confirm . . . that it [British beef] is entirely safe and this has been confirmed by British scientists'.

The government's use of scientific advice was central to the crisis from the beginning. For example, Gummer informed the Agriculture Select Committee that:

> I have taken . . . the view that you have the scientists that you have the most
> respect for, and you give them the remit that they must look at things from
> the worst possible angle . . . and I think you then have to stick rigidly to
> what they ask.
>
> (Agriculture Committee 1990: 9)

This statement was simply not true. The first BSE working party, set up by MAFF in 1988 under Sir Richard Southwood, Linacre Professor of Zoology at Oxford, had three other expert members (and three civil servants attached to it). Neither Southwood nor his three colleagues had active research experience of spongiform diseases (such as, say, researchers at Edinburgh's Neuropathogenesis Group) and they simply assessed the available evidence, 'with perhaps the strongest guidance coming from Wilesmith [a veterinary epidemiologist with MAFF] rather than drawing on extensive first-hand evidence' (Winter 1996: 562). The expert SEAC members did not adopt either the 'precautionary principle' for assessing risks (see **p. 225**) or a 'worst-case scenario' (as Professor Robert Lacey did in evidence to the Agriculture Committee, and was scorned by its members). The first BSE working party confined itself to looking for actual evidence of a link (then non-existent) and assessing the likelihood of BSE crossing the species barrier from cattle to human beings. Its report in February 1989 insisted on the absence of evidence of harm. Its members did not rule out the possibility that BSE could cross the species barrier, but said that it was 'highly improbable', adding the *caveat* that if they were mistaken, the implications could potentially be very serious. On this basis, the ministry, the NFU and government officials, the key actors within the policy community, and to a degree also the Department of Health, were able to maintain that 'no scientific evidence whatsoever exists of a risk to man'. Right up to the 1996 SEAC report, they all firmly rejected the idea that BSE could be transmitted to humans, and derided scientists who argued otherwise. Dr Gordon Hunter, of the Institute for Animal Heath (1972–96), has commented:

> It was probably wrong to keep the public in the dark ... it should not have been said, for instance, that there was no evidence for a relationship between BSE and CJD because from the nature of things there couldn't be any direct evidence ... we know that different 'prion' diseases go across species barriers, so it was always possible that this new disease might have had a smaller dose threshold for passing from cow to man ... so I think it was quite wrong to say that there was no risk there.
>
> (BBC1 *Panorama*, 17 June 1996)

The trouble was that the scientific case on which ministers and officials relied was as much a political as a scientific construct. Although government continually emphasised the importance of relying on scientific evidence and scientific evidence alone, their own scientific assessments were based on criteria which were inevitably political in the simple sense that the scientists on the committee worked under the guidance of the civil servants and were sensitive to political realities (see Winter 1996: 562–563). Professor Brian Wynne put it more pointedly, complaining that 'ministers [claimed] innocently to be following scientific advice when it is clear that this advice has been selectively garnered and shepherded' (Wynne 1996).

The Southwood working party did persuade ministers that they had to destroy all 'mad cows', but MAFF and Treasury officials blocked their proposal that farmers should be fully compensated. The government fixed the compensation rate at half market value. Lord Walton, a working party member, said on *Panorama*, 'I believe that if we had been in charge, or given a free hand, that we would have wished to see full compensation', to avoid the danger that farmers would sell infected cattle at market value rather than have them destroyed and receive only half their value (17 June 1996). Yet the working party's report said, 'the evidence does not support this view' (Southwood Report 1989: para. 7.2.3). Who wrote that? asked Gerry Northam, the *Panorama* reporter. Walton replied: 'I think it would have been the secretary to the committee who was a civil servant'. However, he said, it was up to members of the draft report to read it with care. Dr W. B. (Bill) Martin, formerly Director of the Moredun Research Institute, Edinburgh was one of two members who said that, in retrospect, he would rather not have let the issue go:

> GN: How did it get into the report, if it wasn't your view?
>
> BILL MARTIN: I'm not sure. Obviously, we have to rely on the people who are writing these reports, based on our deliberations and recommendations.
>
> GN: Would it be fair to suggest that this has been slipped in?
>
> BM: Well ... we should have looked perhaps more closely at the very point.

It took 18 months for the government to decide to pay full compensation, by which time the evidence of cheating by farmers was overwhelming (and reported cases at once leapt by 75 per cent; Greger 1994). Why didn't the working party also recommend a ban on suspect offal at that time? The members discussed the issue, knew that this was where the greatest risk of infection for humans lay and agreed that it would be 'sensible not to allow brain and spinal cord into the human food chain' Lord Walton was unable to explain to *Panorama* why their view did not find its way into the report. But Southwood revealed that he thought an offal ban would stand little chance at MAFF; 'We felt it was a no-goer ... They already thought our proposals were pretty revolutionary' (see Wynne 1996). This impasse is typical of the position which all such advisory bodies face where hard or costly decisions are involved. It allowed the politicians to claim, on scientific grounds, that a ban was not necessary whereas the scientists only came to this conclusion because they perceived a ban would be politically unacceptable.

Outside the official committee, some scientists made the obvious point that the lack of 'firm' evidence did not mean that there was no link between BSE and CJD. But they were outside the ministry's chosen policy community. Their views were ignored and their work scorned. Critics such as Professor Robert Lacey, Dr Stephen Dealler and others, who were liable 'to rock the boat', were not considered to be suitable members of SEAC. It was alleged that the government withheld co-operation from some outside experts, eminent though they were, and even sought to block their access to research funds. According to Sarah Boseley writing in the *Guardian*:

> These experts are not dangerous radicals but did not accept the MAFF line that BSE could not jump species to infect humans. Nor were they prepared to keep quiet. Soon they were vilified as cranks.... Doors began to shut. Their research funding dried up.
>
> (*Guardian*, 23 March 1996)

Such exclusion is typical of a closed policy community. Views that vary from the consensus within the network are identified as extreme and then 'justifiably' excluded.

Studies by two scientific critics, Dealler and Lacey, both make grave allegations that MAFF and the Agriculture and Food Research Council knowingly blocked BSE research (Dealler 1996; Lacey 1994). Harash Narang, a recognised authority on BSE, suggested that the agent might be a virus rather than a prion, implying that BSE would be found throughout the beef and not just in spinal tissue. This would have had a devastating impact on the beef industry. On raising this question, Narang was deprived of official co-operation by MAFF, and lost his funding and access to the animal brains he required for his research. Giving evidence to the Agriculture Committee in June 1990, Lacey said not enough was known about the causes of BSE, and the evidence suggested that cattle were a 'dead-end host'; but if it was wrong, then the consequences for the public could be grave. In the 'worst case' scenario, thousands of people could die from CJD. Therefore, rather than reassure the public, the aim should be to remove any risk by creating a BSE-free cattle population, even if that required mass slaughter (Agriculture

Committee 1990). It was not so much Lacey's scientific *views* that the ministry (and committee) found 'extreme', but the policy recommendations which logically followed. The select committee questioned his sanity for suggesting that thousands of people might die if BSE could jump the species barrier (Agriculture Committee, 1990: xxi). As the EC Commission later discovered, the policy community (which in effect included the select committee; see **pp. 414–415**) was utterly opposed to mass slaughter of cattle.

Throughout, ministers, civil servants and interest groups were willing to suppress and manipulate evidence and mislead the public. When Colin Whitaker, the vet who diagnosed the first 'mad cow' was due to present his discovery to a professional meeting in 1987, MAFF officials asked him to remove the phrase 'scrapie-like syndrome' from his slide (clearly because if it became known that the disease might have jumped species into cows, it would harm the beef industry). When BBC TV broadcast *Natural Lies* in May 1992 about the dangers of keeping mad cow disease secret, Meldrum said: 'The BBC is very unwise, if not stupid, to put this on. It isn't possible for BSE to enter the human food chain' (*Radio Times*, 31 May 1992). Dr Hugh Fraser, a senior researcher at the Institute for Animal Health, said in May 1989 on BBC Radio 4's *Face the Facts* that it would be 'prudent to remove suspect tissues from certain categories of cattle from human consumption' and that he did not eat beef products himself. 'After that, I and senior colleagues were told we were not to discuss these matters with the media and that if media questions arose, they should be diverted elsewhere.' MAFF officials were aware of the issues, but 'they preferred to manage the way in which this was presented and dealt with' (*Panorama*, 17 June 1996). The ministry was reluctant to publish the official Tyrrell Committee's review of existing research on BSE and it finally emerged, seven months late, in January 1990. After the BSE 'scare' in December 1995, a senior MAFF official leaked a report, scheduled for publication in *Nature* by John Collinge, head of the prion diseases group at St Mary's Medical School, London, on experiments with mice which found no extra incidence of the CJD equivalent in mice after injecting them with BSE. Collinge suggested that BSE might not cross the barrier to humans either. As the official leaked the research findings to reassure the public and restore the Ministry's credit, he set aside Collinge's 'severe qualifications' on his conclusions.

In a curious footnote to fears of BSE's ability to jump species, government experts continued to reassure the public as antelopes in zoos, then cats, then a pig in MAFF's own laboratory tests, developed forms of BSE (October 1992: 'We are concerned that other animals have succumbed, but that doesn't mean that that's any risk to man . . . as far as the public is concerned').

Other scientists were increasingly alarmed, but for four more years the government issued no public alert. The Ministry's attitude still did not reflect scientists' doubts, because as Professor Jeff Almond, a SEAC member said, 'obviously it had the interests of the beef industry at the back of its mind' (*Panorama*, 17 June 1996). Yet, as we have observed, throughout the growing crisis the Ministry did exhibit signs of doubt in practice. While denying that a risk to people existed, it did make BSE a notifiable disease; introduced a policy of slaughter for infected cattle; and banned the sale of beef thymus, spleen, tonsils, spinal cords and brains. But throughout, its reluctant precautions were marred by delays and equivocation – which in the end proved deadly:

- For over two years, until June 1988, the Ministry refused to make BSE a notifiable disease on the grounds that it could not spread to humans. A month later, the Ministry banned the feeding of animal protein to cattle – the most likely cause of the disease.
- In August 1988, it ordered the compulsory slaughter of infected cattle, but (in deference to the Treasury) only half compensated dairy farmers (ensuring further spread of the disease as farmers sold cattle that showed any signs of illness).
- Only in 1990 were farmers given full compensation:
- In 1989, the Ministry banned offal – the most likely transmission agent – from the food chain; but even then, the ban was ineffectively policed and was continuously breached in abattoirs for years.
- In February 1990, environmental health officers warned MAFF in detail of failings that they had observed in abbatoirs, but received no reply.
- In October 1992, Meldrum said, 'I am totally confident that we have the . . . right measures in place to ensure that any possible risk to man is eliminated'. An anonymous meat inspector confirmed to *Panorama* that breaches were still occurring, and said, 'We're all covered by the Official Secrets Act, it's very difficult for us to actually put over our views, we could end up in jail'.
- At last, in 1995, surprise ministry checks on abattoirs found that almost half of them were failing to enforce the offal ban completely – six years after the ban was first introduced!

Despite the contradictory evidence and uncertainties about BSE and CJD and the alarming vistas of human sacrifice and financial loss that loomed over their heads, the policy community maintained a rigid policy of certainty: beef was safe and the government's precautions were fully satisfactory. The lives of thousands of people were put at risk to prevent financial harm to a powerful lobby, the farming industry. The main reason for the refusal to take seriously the welter of scientific doubts that surrounded its chosen course, and the delays and weaknesses in precautionary policies, lay in the policy community's desire to protect dairy farming and the government's concern about the public spending consequences. To some extent, policy-makers were in the Treasury's stranglehold. Even after the link between BSE and CJD became public, the government still tried to protect the farming industry against the EU's demands for the slaughter of all cattle over 30 months. Both Dorrell and the Agriculture Minister, Douglas Hogg, continued to insist that 'British beef is safe to eat'.

Not that the EU itself behaved well. Leaked EU minutes showed that the Commission's veterinary advisory committee decided to take a low-key approach to the BSE crisis in order to avoid unsettling the meat market and asked the British government in 1990 not to publish research on BSE for the same reason. The director-general of the Agricultural Commission wrote in a report, 'Every decision around BSE inevitably causes problems in the meat market. The best thing in order to maintain public calm is that we do not reopen the debate' (*Libération*, 2 September 1996). A report in *El Pais* (3 September 1996) revealed that a member of the veterinary committee who wanted to take a more radical approach was put under pressure from on high to accept the policy of secrecy.

The whole saga of official dishonesty and manipulation was based ultimately on distrust of the public. As in almost every similar area – the safety of medicines, the use of pesticides, the disposal of nuclear waste – government officials and their advisers adopt a patronising and undemocratic attitude towards the public's own understanding of risk. Such an attitude has been well-established throughout Britain's postwar history, and for example, coloured the Macmillan government's refusal to tell the truth to the public about the accidental release of nuclear materials from Windscale (now Sellafield) in 1957. The official view is that the public will be unreasonably prone to panic – and in the case of BSE, will thus be frightened to buy British beef. This attitude is not only unjustifiable by democratic standards (see **DAC7**), but profoundly alienating for the public. Some three-quarters of the British people state that they do not trust the government, or advisory bodies, to tell them the truth about the safety of British beef, food or nuclear installations (ICM poll for the Rowntree Reform Trust, September 1996). As Wynne notes, 'the public is more mature about risk and uncertainty than anyone is willing to admit', and he also comments on:

> the patronisation of public responses as irrational and even hysterical, assuming them to be based on misunderstanding of the risks as perceived by the experts when they are, perfectly reasonably, based on an assessment of whether the controlling actors (including the official experts) can be trusted.
>
> (Wynne 1996)

In fact, the public has good grounds for distrusting official risk assessments and reassurances which have too often proved dishonest. British governments reject the 'principle of precaution' which enjoins policy-makers to recognise the open-ended nature of scientific knowledge when considering policy options where potentially high costs may be incurred (see **p. 225**). Instead, our official culture tends to demand verifiable proof of risk or damage, as recently shown in the BSE crisis and Gulf War syndrome; places the burden of proof on victims to gather evidence; chooses its own experts selectively; seeks to discredit scientists holding different opinions; through the secrecy of the process, denies the public the possibility of expert 'peer review' of official conclusions; and finally refuses to give them the opportunity to make up their own minds on the risks they and their families run. As Frances Hall, the mother of a BSE victim, said, 'The signs were all there for a lot of years that there was something wrong and we were badly informed about it. We weren't allowed to make decisions for ourselves.'

Public consultation

Formal arrangements for public consultation

The essence of consultation is the communication of a genuine invitation to give advice and a genuine consideration of that advice ... to achieve consultation sufficient information must be supplied to the consulted party to enable it to tender helpful advice ... and sufficient time must be available for such advice to be considered by the consulting party.

(Mr Justice Webster, in *R. v Secretary of State for Social Services, ex parte the Association of Municipal Authorities*, 1986)

Two factors – one political, one cultural – have vitiated the British state's formal processes of consultation on government policies, decisions and legislation. First, the prevalence of policy communities and use of advisory quangos, both operating largely in secret, has pre-empted public consultation in many significant policy areas. Secondly, Whitehall is traditionally grudging about simply informing the public about its activities, let alone consulting them or encouraging them to participate in the policy process. The formal nature of the process, and the absence of publicity or any positive efforts to encourage participation from outside the ranks of those who are already familiar with official procedures, discourages the general public from being involved at any level other than the local.

In principle, however, any group or individual can join a departmental consultation list. Most departments keep large lists of groups and individuals to whom they send green papers and consultation documents and from whom they receive responses. However, there is a world of difference between groups being 'consulted' and being involved in day-to-day policy-making; and there is an equally large difference in the attention paid to the contributions of the different groups. For example, the submissions of Liberty on civil liberties issues got short shrift at the Home Office up to 1997. The groups that officials choose to consult on a regular basis are those which matter. Some groups, of course, which are known to be critical of existing policies may be consulted so that officials can argue that they have been properly catholic in their trawl of opinion, or even so that they can advise ministers of likely lines of attack. The pecking order of most government consultation processes can thus be split into four main groups of actors:

- The relevant department or division within a department.
- The core interest groups, usually representatives of major industrial or economic interests, professionals, specialists.
- Groups which are not involved in day-to-day policy advice and negotiations but are consulted on particular issues, even if simply for form's sake.
- Interested parties which are generally excluded from day-to-day policy-making – and from consultation.

There is no developed principle nor practice for consultation – let alone participation – in the government's processes for making decisions or policies, or preparing legislation. John Major's ministerial rule-book, *Questions of Procedure for Ministers*, laid no duty whatever on ministers to consult the public in preparing their proposals for government action, nor did consultation figure on the legislative checklist (which was dominated by financial and legal implications, 'value-for-money' and 'presentational' questions). The three paragraphs devoted to white and green papers, the main formal vehicles for consultation, were concerned only with their 'presentational' and administrative aspects; clearance with the Cabinet Office, cabinet, cabinet committees and the No. 10 Press Office; and avoiding infringing parliamentary privilege (Cabinet Office 1992: paras. 83–85). No duty or exhortation to consult finds a place in the Civil Service Code. *Guidance on Guidance*, the Cabinet Office's guide largely for lower-ranking civil servants, states that 'public consultation plays an important part in the development of policy and in the preparation of legislation', but sets out no overall code for consultation. It suggests that it should be assumed that responses 'will be made available to others'; that consultation papers should be listed in the Commons' Weekly Information Bulletin; that the results of consultation exercises should normally be made publicly available at the time when a decision or proposal is announced; and that copies of the consultation papers, and summaries of responses and, 'where appropriate', individual replies should generally be lodged with Parliament's libraries (Cabinet Office 1996c: 7–8). It is a modest stab at openness.

Ministers may – or may not – issue green or white papers in advance of legislation, and consultative documents of various kinds on issues for legislation or decision. Green papers were introduced in 1969 to consult the public more widely while proposals were in a formative stage, well in advance of possible legislation. White papers were supposed to follow green papers and other consultations between civil servants and interested parties and set out firm proposals for legislation. But there are no formal requirements or conventions governing their use. Mrs Thatcher's governments actually abandoned publishing green papers altogether after 1988 and also issued fewer white papers. By convention, governments are also supposed to establish royal commissions on policy issues of great public significance, but Mrs Thatcher took the view that they were too slow-moving and unpredictable forums for 'conviction' government; and it was left to her successor, John Major, to renew the tradition with the Royal Commission on Criminal Justice in 1991 after a series of serious miscarriages of justice. The Labour government which won power in 1997 has begun making more use of both green and white papers.

In 1991–92, a Hansard Society Commission undertook a full audit of the legislative process in the UK, and consulted widely on consultation, largely on primary and secondary legislation, as part of its inquiries. The Commission took written evidence from a wide range of bodies and individuals, and also met representatives of 23 bodies, including industry and commerce, the legal and other professions, pressure groups, statutory bodies, local government associations, government departments, MPs and academics (Hansard Society 1993). Research for its report found that government departments had issued between three and 15 green papers a year between 1976 and 1988 (when they came to an end). But this dwindling trickle of green papers was accompanied by a very large increase in the use of consultation documents from 11 in 1976 to a high of 288 in 1988 and 232 in 1991. These documents were not confined to legislative proposals, but were concerned with government decisions and policies more generally, and varied greatly in significance from 'Scallop dredging in the 12-mile inshore zone' to 'Local Government Review: the internal management of local authorities in England'. A variety of organisations welcomed the increase in consultation, including the local authority associations which complained of the unwillingness of Mrs Thatcher's governments to consult properly.

Some bodies (e.g. the Bank of England, the Institute of Directors, the National Trust) had few or no complaints about government consultation. However, the great majority of organisations and individuals who gave evidence were dissatisfied. The Consumers' Association spoke for others in agreeing that extensive consultation now took place (it was currently preparing responses to 30 consultative documents). But it was severely critical, complaining that:

> There can be much consultation, some or none; it can be general or detailed; it can be formal, with green and white papers, or it can be informal, consisting of no more than a few soundings on the telephone . . . it can be a genuine request for help or merely an attempt to legitimise proposals that the government has already made up its mind to pass into law. . . . There are inconsistencies in practice between, and even within, government departments and agencies and other statutory bodies. This results in a mixture of good and bad consultation practice and more fundamentally in a distortion of the whole consultation process.
>
> (Hansard Society 1993: 226)

The wide variation and inconsistency of practice was not simply the result of variations in circumstances, but reflected the absence of a coherent set of rules governing the role consultation should play in making the law. The Hansard Society report found that 'this central assessment is confirmed by the varying experience of other bodies involved in consultation with different departments' (*ibid*.: 18). Among these, for example, were the BMA, the local authority associations, the Scottish Consumer Council and Shelter, all of which complained about no consultation at all and insufficient consultation, even on major issues. The BMA pointed out that the major 1991 NHS changes (themselves the product of a tightly-knit group under Mrs Thatcher's direction) were based on a white paper for which there had been no green paper or any other form of consultation. Once published, the Health Secretary made it plain that he was prepared only to accept comments which would assist him in carrying out the changes (*ibid*.: 181). The Consumers' Association also complained about the absence of consultation on the NHS changes and the poll tax legislation. Both, it said, had been decided in advance by 'the government's party line' and proceeded at once to a white paper with no attempt to seek the views 'of those most affected'. While government may not wish to consult on its political objectives, it should consult on how they might best be achieved: 'There is no justification for refusing to consult *at all* on the grounds that proposals contain some party political elements and the government wishes to circumvent awkward pressure groups completely' (*ibid*.: 227).

At times, ministers were liable to make announcements, often at political conferences or rallies outside Parliament, or even simply in the press, and then legislate.

On occasions tabloid campaigns sparked off emergency legislation, as with the Dangerous Dogs Act 1991. After seeking to withstand panic about adults and children being mauled and killed by dogs from June 1989 onwards and extensive consultation, the government was suddenly galvanised into action in May 1991 after another savage mauling of a child provoked a tabloid offensive. On 22 May the then Home Secretary, Kenneth Baker, promised legislation and rushed consultations then took place. A fortnight later an unworkable bill was published; a week later, it was guillotined through its first Commons stages in a day. No use seems to have been made of the (unpublished) responses to the previous consultation document and only the Police Federation made much impact on the bill as it passed through Parliament. Britain now has an unworkable law which has failed to control dogs in public areas. The Criminal Justice and Public Order Bill was announced by a later Home Secretary, Michael Howard, at a Conservative Party conference in autumn 1993. Frances Crook, director of the Howard League for Penal Reform, said the absence of consultation obliged affected organisations to examine political speeches and tabloid reports, trying to assess what would be in the bill and what would not:

> We knew that there would be provisions for creating new prisons for 12–14 year-olds, restrictions on bail and the ending of the right to silence. But there had also been rumours of additional punishment for the parents of young people who commit offences, and possibly even the lowering of the age of criminal responsibility. Yet there had been no green paper, no white paper and no formal consultation meetings. The only 'consultation' has been through the tabloids.
>
> (*Independent*, 16 December 1993)

The local authority associations were subjected to a barrage of Acts of Parliament between 1979 and 1992, 58 of them containing major changes. They noted a 'serious decline in the extent and nature of consultations and inquiry':

> the recent pattern has seen fewer white papers, the severe compression of consultative deadlines, the dropping of formal green papers in favour of looser 'consultative documents' and the frequent exclusion of interested parties altogether from consultation, even on implementation.
>
> (Hansard Society 1993: 295)

For example, short consultative documents, hurriedly published in July and August 1987, and allowing five to 11 weeks during the summer holiday period for reply, were the only precursors of the Education Reform Act 1988 – which introduced the national curriculum, grant-maintained schools, devolved school budgets and the abolition of the Inner London Education Authority. There was no green or white paper. No analysis of responses was published. Local education authorities were at no stage consulted on these major changes, but only on the less controversial issue of school charges. The bill was published, substantially unaltered, a few weeks from the end of the consultative period. Other significant pieces of legislation on education and housing were also rushed through brief consultation periods and on one occasion a housing bill received its second reading in the Commons before the end of the four-week consultation period. The associations were no doubt viewed as 'awkward pressure groups' by a 'can-do' government, impatient to carry through its revolution in local government (see Chapter 9). Yet local authority advice would, if considered, have lessened the need for continuous amendments to local government legislation and, for example, constant changes of practice in schools, and might even have avoided the costly poll tax 'policy disaster'. The associations were also critical of the glossy and superficial consultation documents and dismissed the 1990 review of local government as a superficial exercise, with no real exchange of views and important questions left unaddressed. The BBC, Independent Television Commission and TUC were similarly critical of the absence of prior consultation and even preparation on broadcasting and industrial relations legislation.

There was considerable criticism of departments' failure to consult and of rushed consultation on secondary legislation. The CBI objected in principle to the increasing government reliance on statutory instruments, given the risk of significant laws and regulations passing unnoticed and unchecked through Parliament, where such instruments are rarely debated (**pp. 389–393**). At the very least, the CBI asked for 'full, detailed and measured consultation on statutory instruments' (Hansard Society 1993: 221–222). As statutory instruments set out important issues of law, administration, enforcement, adjudication, and so on – of particular importance to lawyers, accountants, the police, the courts, and business – and are not bound, as primary legislation is, by the pressures of the parliamentary timetable – it is hard to see why the requests of the CBI cannot be met; indeed, it would be possible to institute consultation at the draft and near-final stages, as several bodies suggest. As statutory instruments cannot be amended in the Commons – they may be only accepted or rejected whole – they must surely be got right by the time they are presented to the House.

The biggest single complaint by bodies that are regularly consulted by government departments – including the Association of Chief Police Officers, the BBC, the former British Railways Board, the Law Society, Lloyd's, the Magistrates' Association, the National Consumer Council (NCC), the National Trust and Shelter – was that consultations were often rushed and allowed insufficient time for responses. The Consumers' Association (CA) analysed 100 consultation documents issued in the first half of 1991. In its experience, six weeks was a reasonable time to allow for responses; but organisations which had to consult memberships or all affected bodies, and smaller, less well-resourced bodies, might well require longer. The Scottish Consumer Council suggested three months. Four documents in the CA sample allowed a week or less for responses; 10 per cent three weeks or less; and a further 20 per cent had a four-week deadline. The full range varied from less than a week to more than eight months. Sometimes consultation actually began too late: consultation on what information should be published in school league tables took place after the information to be required was set out in a bill (Hansard Society 1993: 21–24; 229–230).

The CA expressed concern that too much weight was given to the representations of well-established organisations in policy communities which were in regular contact with departments at all stages (see **p. 274**). Other groups and interests, including consumer organisations, were likely to be consulted much later, generally in a trawl of 'all interested parties', when policies were mostly finalised and their influence was likely to be minimal. The Law Society and NCC made similar comments. The position was worse in the EU legislative process, said the CA, for major producers had representatives in Brussels, encouraged by the UK government, while the influence of consumer interests was weak because they could not afford to put people in Brussels and anyway were often not invited to give their views. The CA added that there may not be a conspiracy to advance organised producer interests at the expense of others, but there is a need to recognise the 'dangers of bias, created by inequality of resources and access to influence' in the consultation process. This bias prevents consultation exercises from giving governments the clear and undistorted picture of the considerations which need to be taken into account. The CA additionally suggested that government and other public agencies sometimes go through the motions of consultation, but pay no attention to the results (*ibid.*: 227, 230–231). However, on occasion the views of organisations consulted do make a difference. For example, near unanimous opposition from 300 organisations and 3,000 individuals to proposals in February 1994 to privatise Britain's forests led to the proposals being abandoned; instead, the Forestry Commission became an executive agency within government (*Independent on Sunday*, 13 February 1994).

For all the good intentions expressed in the Cabinet Office's *Guidance on Guidance* (see **p. 291**), government departments do not generally publish the results of their consultation exercises, arguing implausibly that they do not have the consent of those who respond to publish their views (even though the *Guidance* paper says that respondents should be warned that their views might be made public). The Consumers' Association has argued that before consultation periods end, bodies and individuals who gave their views should be informed of the overall direction of views and the influence they have had on proposals, as well as being given feedback on their own representations. The Campaign for Freedom of Information has proposed that all the representations should be published, together with the government's own assessment of the likely impact of its proposals. The Hansard Society Commission agreed and recommended that the government's guidelines on consultation should be revised upwards, drawing on best existing practice, and then published (Hansard Society 1993: 39–40).

In New Zealand, a public body, the Legislation Advisory Committee, has drawn up guidelines for consultation as part of broader set of guidelines for the legislative process in general. These guidelines are published so that all interested parties can see what is expected of the initiating departments. Departments must also inform the cabinet's legislative committee what consultations on bills they are submitting for the legislative programme have been carried out within and outside government; how those consultations have been organised; the results of the consultations; and when the consultation will be over (Iles 1992). The Hansard Society Commission summed up the results of its own consultation as follows: 'The overwhelming impression from the evidence is that many of those most directly affected are deeply dissatisfied with the extent, nature, timing and conduct of consultation on bills as at present practised' (Hansard Society 1993: 30).

AUDIT

The general culture of informal and flexible processes in British government generally makes it easy for government and its officials to co-opt and bargain with organised interests and private companies and to blur the boundaries of the public domain and private enterprise. This culture also means that government has no systematic and open strategy nor any legal framework for consulting interest groups and the public in advance of preparing legislation, making policy or taking decisions. The framework which exists ignores the interpenetration of public and private and so provides no safeguards against the obvious dangers of undue or improper influence. These dangers range wider than the consultation process. Government can co-opt and mobilise all manner of bodies, including private companies, consultants and advisers, to carry out major tasks, such as industrial re-structuring, training and employment policies. The government itself has no direct control over such interests and processes.

For officials, issues of consultation are subordinate to the imperatives of carrying out government business as efficaciously as possible. Policy communities of departmental officials and long-established corporate and professional interests have dominated policy-making in broad areas of national policy, such as transport, agriculture, food, health, pharmaceuticals and defence, throughout the postwar period. These communities have generally been closed to other interests, the public and even Parliament and other departments, have pursued wasteful and damaging policies (road-building programmes, the Chevaline nuclear defence programme, etc.), and have created or worsened long-term and immediate 'policy disasters' (traffic pollution, heavily subsidised intensive farming, the poll tax, the salmonella, *E Coli* and BSE crises, and so on). Recently, some dominant interests, like the roads lobby and doctors within the NHS, have been challenged from within government and outside and others have been partially opened up to consumer representation. The new Food Standards Agency will represent perhaps the most significant challenge yet to a major policy community, but policy communities exert influence across the board in government policy-making, and it is very much a one-off.

Policy communities usually pre-empt the parliamentary loop in the decision-making process and may subvert the government's more general consultation exercises. Decisions negotiated by officials and interests in these closed groups often prevent changes being made to legislation in Parliament, or are implemented through the prerogative or statutory powers of ministers and as secondary legislation, thus escaping parliamentary scrutiny. All the regulations relating to BSE have to date been through statutory orders. In these circumstances, select committees and MPs can only be involved on a retrospective basis.

Formal consultation processes are unsystematic, are often rushed and may be quite arbitrary about which organisations and individuals are consulted, and which are not. On occasions, they are a token cover for decisions which have already been taken and legislation may even be introduced into Parliament before consultation periods are over. No official rules govern the conduct of consultation exercises. The responses are rarely published and when summaries are made, they often give only the barest detail. Overall, the processes are highly formal and do not encourage widespread participation outside the 'participating classes' of major corporate interest groups, trade associations, professional bodies, and so on.

This chapter has necessarily concentrated on the conduct of recent Conservative governments. It is too soon to write with any confidence about the new Labour government's willingness to consult and be ready to pay attention to the responses ministers receive. The key word here is 'willingness': a Labour government may well consult more widely, but it need not. However, the white paper on open government, published in late 1997 (Cabinet Office 1997c), may offer the prospect of a statutory regime of openness which could do a great deal to open up the world of policy communities and networks. Recent practice has shown the need also for systematic reforms and transparent rules which governments, however large or small their majorities, departments and officials are obliged to observe.

Practice in other countries can indicate reforms which might assist in bringing more open and participatory policy-making to the UK. In Australia, policy agencies not only develop policy options very openly, they are then held directly accountable for the policies they present. The New Zealand government has approved guidelines for consultations on intended legislation. These require departments to give details of all consultations which have taken place, within and outside government, and their results, to the cabinet's legislation committee, when bills are presented to it. In the United States, Capitol Hill is the home of the concepts of 'agency capture' (the capture of regulatory agencies by the industries they are supposed to supervise) and 'the iron triangle' (policy coalitions formed between government departments, the relevant Congressional committees and main producer interests). To deal with these serious pathologies, the US has introduced a package of laws giving the public access to the documents and meetings of public agencies. The most relevant of these measures seeks to place all discussions and meetings which public agencies undertake – even the most informal – on the public record. For all their failings, Congressional committees provide public structures for the kind of bargaining between government and organised interests which takes place here in policy communities deep in the bowels of departments. Such developments are possible in the UK.

DAC15: Systematic and open government consultation

Government consultation of interests and the general public is unsystematic and opaque. Much formative consultation takes place within policy communities of officials and interests which are generally closed to outside scrutiny and may subvert formal public consultation exercises and parliamentary decision and scrutiny. Even responses to the public exercises are rarely published in their totality. Overall, certain interests get preference over others, thus blocking political equality in government policy-making and, in some areas, seriously harming the public interest.

DAC7: Public access to information on government policies

Public consultation exercises should open up the way in which governments make decisions and policies. Consultation documents often do contain valuable information on the background to proposals and policy options, but they may also be bland and glossy documents which add little to public debate. Curiously, the results of consultation exercises are rarely published in full. Most policy-making in policy communities and advisory quangos takes place in secret. No rules of access or openness or process apply to their operations.

DAC11: Transparent rules governing executive behaviour

Similarly, scarcely any rules of conduct or process, transparent or otherwise, govern the activities of policy communities or consultation exercises. The culture of informality and flexible processes make it easy for officials to co-opt and bargain with organised interests as they see fit and blur the boundaries between the public domain and interest and private enterprise and its interests. On the one hand, officials may gain improper and unaccountable accretions of power; on the other, the tendency of public officials to rely on the specialist knowledge and experience of interested private parties may make them unduly dependent in negotiation. These general concerns transcend the more obvious dangers of 'capture' and corruption in the activities of policy communities (and advisory quangos).

DAC8: Ministerial control of non-elected personnel

DAC9: Parliamentary accountability and scrutiny

The sheer weight of departmental activity and its complexity makes it impossible for ministers to exercise control over their officials' negotiations with interest groups in policy communities, and the operations of advisory quangos. Similarly, the activities of policy communities and advisory committees take place largely within the realms of ministerial discretion and policy advice, and are often protected from disclosure by rules of commercial confidentiality. Thus their activities are normally kept secret from Parliament and the public and may continue to be so under the new statutory freedom of information regime which is to come. As we have seen, they subvert Parliament's role on occasions. These conclusions are not to be wondered at. To remedy this state of affairs, a re-think of the notion of ministerial accountability is necessary (see Chapter 12).

11 The Rules of the Game

Britain's informal and flexible executive

It is absolutely indispensable to the working of the whole machine that it should be in the hands of honest and trustworthy men . . . imbued with a genuine spirit of compromise and cordially in harmony with the general spirit of the Constitution. . . . If this spirit is no longer found among rulers and Parliaments and constituencies, there is no constitution which may be more easily dislocated, and which provides less means of checking excesses of bad government.

(W. E. H. Lecky, historian, in *Democracy and Liberty*, 1896)

Governments in Britain do, of course, accept limits upon their power. But these derive not from statute, but from convention, from understandings as to how it is appropriate or not appropriate to act. It is, however, becoming increasingly doubtful whether such understandings are any longer sufficient to provide good government.

(Vernon Bogdanor, *Power and the People*, 1997)

The complicated set of actors, institutions, and powers we have reviewed in Part 2 are, between them, responsible for developing top-level policies and coordinating them into some kind of coherent 'government' policy. This process is still described as 'cabinet government'. As we have seen, it is a misleading label which conceals current mechanisms under a comfort blanket, conveying the obsolete idea of collective decision-making and responsibility. The idea that we now live under 'Prime Ministerial government' is more accurate, but too simplistic. Government in Britain is a shifting set of 'private empires' which may very well be in conflict with each other (Rhodes and Dunleavy 1995: introduction). No one actor or institution dominates the whole panorama of modern government, and what actually constitutes 'government' varies from policy area to policy area. A Prime Minister, or Home Secretary, or mandarin, can often take or determine a decision alone, but no one actor or institution can count on determining every significant decision. Even a Prime Minister depends on other actors and institutions most of the time, and can be prevented from doing what he or she wants; or forced to do what he or she does not want to do; or be overthrown. The powers of government departments and individual ministers to make policy are strong, and yet not always recognised, and organised interests exercise considerable influence over government decision-making. We have used the neutral term 'core executive' to designate the mesh of actors and institutions which, with the Prime Minister, cabinet and senior civil service at the centre, governs this country, but the term hardly conveys the nature of the sinuous Hydra of modern government in Britain.

This chapter largely concentrates on the rules of conduct for the core executive and its internal checks and balances, against a background of central constitutional provisions and law. We deal in Chapter 15 with the role of the judiciary in enforcing the rule of law on the executive. Here we largely concentrate on the executive's own rules and procedures for ensuring that government uses its powers lawfully and honestly; that it is conducted in an ordered and open manner; and that it is restrained by safeguards against oppressive or arbitrary policies and decisions. The mere fact that ministers are members of an elected government does not mean that they and those officials and bodies who act in their name are right in everything they do, or are to be trusted. Indeed, it is often the case that there is no one 'right' answer to a problem for government. This assessment also has a bearing on the quality of British government. In an influential paper on foreseeable 'policy disasters' during the Thatcher era – such as the poll tax, the costly adoption of the Trident programme, the first years of the Child Support Agency, and others – the political scientist Patrick Dunleavy tentatively identified five main causes. At their centre were 'ineffective core executive checks and balances' and the 'arrogance' of Whitehall (Dunleavy 1995a: 52–69). Checks and balances, both internal and external, are especially vital in Britain's case because of the sheer scale and scope of the executive's powers in a unitary state to enact laws and introduce policies, and its ability to steam roller legislation unamended through a compliant Parliament (DA Volume No.1, 1996: Chapters 3 and 5; Hansard Society 1993; and Butler *et al.* 1994: Chapter 10). It is the executive's virtually unbound strength which, in Dunleavy's account, leaves this country especially exposed to policy disasters. Thus, our concern with rules of behaviour in the core executive bears on the poor quality of executive decision-making as well as its democratic credentials.

We apply a single Audit criterion in this chapter, 'How far is the executive subject to the rule of law and transparent rules governing the use of its powers?' (**DAC11**). In doing so, we assess the role of statute law, conventions and procedure in governing the conduct of the core executive. We touch on the accountability of ministers for 'their private interests and sources of income that may affect the performance of their public office' (**DAC10**) in passing. We look at the rules of conduct for ministers and the machinery for their enforcement. We consider the role of the civil service as a guardian of the constitution and the rules governing its role in government. We assess the role of the Queen as the ultimate protector of constitutional government. In Part 3, we examine the checks on the core executive. We describe the principles of individual and collective responsibility to Parliament and analyse how far they satisfy the basic democratic requirements of open and accountable government; and we examine the rules for open government, and the role of the Parliamentary Commissioner for Administration (the Ombudsman), the National Audit Office and the Citizen's Charter, in making the core executive open and accountable. We then assess Parliament's ability effectively to check and scrutinise government. We also follow through the analysis begun in this chapter and examine the role of the judiciary in ensuring that the core executive is subject to the rule of law.

The ambiguities of power in the British state

This audit of the core executive's internal affairs is more than usually difficult, partly because the governing elite of ministers and senior bureaucrats have long insisted that the decisive interactions between ministers, civil servants and interest groups should remain within a closely guarded domain of utter secrecy, at least for a minimum period of 30 years. Leaks, briefings, memoirs, inquiries breach the ring of secrecy, but only selectively and (in the latter two cases) usually late. Further, government policies and decisions involve multiple considerations, not all of which relate in a close or straightforward way to democratic principles. The core executive is a critical site where criteria, based simply on 'strong' or 'effective' government, keep the canons of democratic accountability at a distance; and where the governing imperative is 'Her Majesty's government must be carried on'. This tends to be the case in all liberal democracies, but especially so in the UK, given its historical legacy (see Chapter 2). Finally, the fluidity of British arrangements, the elusive nature of ministers' prerogative powers and the absence of agreed rules means that the government of the day can decide the constitutional and political rules under which it operates to suit itself (see Hennessy 1995: 6–46). Or as Sir Robin Butler, the former Cabinet Secretary, said of the unwritten constitution, 'It is something we make up as we go along' (Barnett 1997: 5).

This fluidity is the direct result of the historic evasion which still provides the over-arching framework within which the core executive in Britain operates. Formally, it is the idea of the Crown which binds government in Britain together. The electorate chooses the MPs who decide which party, or parties, will govern, but the Prime Minister and his or her ministers then rule in the name of the Queen. In strict constitutional terms, the Queen in Parliament rules on the advice of ministers of the Crown who comprise Her Majesty's government. This government is confronted in Parliament by Her Majesty's loyal opposition. Officials in the civil service are servants of the Crown, not the state or people, and central government is carried out in the name of Queen. Most of the prerogative powers of the Crown are employed by ministers and civil servants in the Queen's name. But she exercises many powers on her ministers' advice and her assent is often required to legitimise government actions, to approve most appointments and, most notably, to give parliamentary legislation the force of law.

The Queen retains a personal discretion over the use of some powers. The most important of the Queen's surviving personal prerogatives give her ambiguous powers to dissolve Parliament, formally at the request of the Prime Minister, and to appoint a Prime Minister after the resignation (often after a general election), death or illness of a serving premier. The Queen also possesses certain ill-defined 'residual' powers which we discuss later, largely in relation to her potential role as guardian of the constitution (see **p. 324**). Here, briefly, we discuss two points which have a bearing on her powers of political initiative. First, how far do these residual powers give any monarch real power to intervene politically or even to rule in a personal capacity? The authoritative answer is none at all: a monarch has no executive capacity and requires the co-operation of ministers even for the purpose of dissolving Parliament and causing a new general election to be held. Secondly, the monarch does appoint her or his private secretary personally (along with other important members of the Royal Household); and that official does play an important part in conducting communications between the monarch and ministers, and other political leaders, and in giving the monarch advice on constitutional issues (Bradley and Ewing 1993: 244–264; Jennings 1959: 412–417).

In brief, we live in a constitutional monarchy in which the Queen reigns and her government rules; in which the Crown in an ill-fitting and archaic way embodies the state; and in which the formal statement that executive power is invested in the Crown does not correspond with the realities of government. The historic refusals formally to resolve in a written constitution ultimate questions of executive power, the authority of government, the separation of powers, the rule of law, and the advent of universal suffrage, raise all manner of ambiguities which key figures in the core executive can manipulate at will. They can fashion and re-fashion the rules so that politics, usually the politics of the government of the day, is the final arbiter. The fluidity of government in the UK is celebrated by a romantic priesthood. Ferdinand Mount, with fond irony, compares the position in Britain with that in other liberal democracies: 'Our arrangements are flexible, evolving, fluid, alive; theirs are rigid, static, ossified, dead and unable to respond to change' (1992: 10).

If Britain had a written constitution, the broad principles of democratic government and the main rules of constitutional law and practice to be observed by the core executive would be contained within it. Alterations to these rules would be made by procedures laid down for amendment to the constitution – there might, for example, be a rule that any change to the constitution required a two-thirds majority in the House of Commons. Broad democratic principles would guide the courts in interpreting the constitution and applying it in cases of dispute. The Prime Minister, ministers, civil servants and other government actors would be bound by clear and publicly known rules of conduct in the exercise of their powers, responsibilities and duties. As things stand, the UK has no written constitution, though much is written down in individual Acts of Parliament, common law and case law. In strict law, Acts of Parliament establishing the framework of government, elections, and so on, merely possess the same status as any other Act, and may be repealed or replaced by any Parliament. A few historic statutes – like Magna Carta 1215 or the Bill of Rights 1689 – though in law no different from other Acts, are held to have special constitutional significance and the judiciary might be reluctant to assent to fundamental changes in their provision. Other Acts of Parliament which set down rules for the way we are governed – for example, the Parliament Acts 1911 and 1949, the Representation of the People Act 1983, and others – may be set aside or replaced.

Many of the most important rules of democratic behaviour are not contained in Acts of Parliament, the common law or judicial decisions. Instead, at the very heart of the constitution, the core executive is bound by a 'bundle of custom, precedent and procedure' (Hennessy 1995: 33). Sir Kenneth Pickthorn, MP and constitutional historian, observing that a government with a majority in the Commons 'can at any moment do anything they like, with retrospective or prospective intention', looked wryly for protection in procedure, declaring 'procedure is all the constitution the poor Briton has' (HC Deb, 8 February 1960, c70). Procedure is often defined by important non-legal rules, known as 'conventions', which are supposed to be observed by the Queen, all actors within the core executive – the Prime Minister, other ministers, civil servants – and MPs, peers, and judges. Dicey also described conventions as 'understandings, habits or practices which, though they may regulate the conduct of several members of the sovereign power . . . are not in reality laws at all since they are not enforced by the courts'. J. S. Mill and other constitutional writers have variously described them as the positive morality of the constitution, its unwritten maxims, and a 'whole system of political morality, a whole code of precepts for the guidance of public men' (Bradley and Ewing 1993: 12–25).

No-one has ever described conventions as rules of *democratic* conduct, because they are not: in the absence of a written constitution, they rather set out the rules of *constitutional* behaviour. Conventions largely belong to the pre-democratic era of parliamentary government when they formed part of a complex morality of self-regulation for men in all areas of public life – politics, the City, the professions. Though some were – and are – regarded as 'immutable', they were enforced not by the law, but by a code of self-discipline reinforced by peer group pressure. They are the rules of a now half-obsolete club culture.

In the political realm, conventions developed to cushion the growing supremacy of Parliament – inspired in part by fears that Parliament was likely to become the instrument of mass democracy – and to make up for the absence of formal rules governing its conduct, particularly rules providing for checks and balances to the powers of the core executive and maintaining a separation of powers in the older tradition of English government. Such conventions did not develop into a coherent set of rules. As we have seen, the absolute powers of the monarch – royal prerogative powers – were gradually assumed by ministers, but were left undefined to swell executive discretion, and until as late as 1985 even the courts declined to intervene in their use. Some critical questions relating to the powers and responsibilities of the executive – such as the role of the Prime Minister or the cabinet – were simply not dealt with at all. It is famously said that the office of Prime Minister and the existence of the cabinet are unknown to the constitution. Yet overall, a tradition grew up that the government of the day should employ the near absolute powers at its disposal with moderation and respect for opposition parties. In place of formal measures restraining government and making it accountable, conventions were pressed into the service of constitutional conduct and 'the rule of law' (Harden and Lewis 1986: 29). For example, in the 1950s C. S. Emden, the constitutional writer, argued:

> the most obvious and undisputed convention . . . is that Parliament does not use its unlimited sovereign power of legislation in an oppressive or tyrannical way. That is a vague but clearly accepted conventional rule resting on the principle of constitutionalism and the rule of law.
>
> (1956: 1–3)

Geoffrey Marshall, a constitutional authority, wrote just as Mrs Thatcher's conviction government was gathering force that while conventions did not always modify legal powers, 'the major purpose of the domestic conventions is to give effect to the prin-ciples of governmental accountability that constitute the structure of responsible government' (1984: 9, 18). Mrs Thatcher's governments did much to undermine the efficacy of what Marshall described, but they are not alone in that. As Ian Harden and Norman Lewis, two experts on public law, have explained, something more than conventions is required: 'British governments do periodically behave oppres-sively, and the governmental machine at large can scarcely be regarded as being systematically accountable' (Harden and Lewis 1988: 29).

It ought to be said that conventions are important ingredients of most governing systems precisely because they are capable of gradual adaptation; and that all exec-utives require a degree of discretion if they are to operate effectively. But generally conventions and discretionary powers perform the role of oil within a machinery of government ruled by a written constitution, providing a necessary degree of lubri-cation, or flexibility. The absence of a written constitution in the UK means that many significant rules have only non-legal status, and though they may carry great authority, they are also changeable – and changeable overnight if it suits the executive. In the 1930s, Prime Minister Stanley Baldwin noted:

> it would be very difficult for a living writer to tell you at any given period in all respects, and for this reason, that almost at any given moment . . . there may be one practice called 'constitutional' which is falling into desue-tude and there may be another practice which is creeping into use but is not yet constitutional.
>
> (HC Deb, 8 February 1932, c531)

Peter Hennessy, whose researches into the elusive constitution have informed this section, describes how he sought the 'reality' of the constitution in the 'very private pieces of paper its guardians circulated among themselves about what "it" was at particular times in relation to particular contingencies'. Finally, in 1994, he realised that a core archive of such 'private pieces of paper' existed in the form of a loose-leaf folder, the 'Precedent Book', in the cabinet secretary's private office. He wrote to Sir Robin Butler, the Cabinet Secretary and (in Hennessy's view) a constitutional guardian, asking him to declassify those documents which were more than 30 years old (the period after which secret documents usually are declassified). Butler refused, explaining that the documents, precedents and internal guidance notes it contained had been gathered by the Cabinet Secretary's office 'essentially for use within that office. It is in no sense a *public* record . . . much of the Precedent Book consists of precedents about the affairs of Ministers and ex-Ministers which as I am sure you will appreciate should not be released [our emphasis]' (Hennessy 1995: 32–46). Hennessy disagrees with Butler, as we do. Any official piece of paper is a public record, as it deals with public, not private, business; papers which inform current official judgments on constitutional issues, and possibly crises, are significant records which belong in the public domain. All the more so since they form the fluid material from which Butlers 'make up the constitution as they go along' (see **p. 301**).

Butler disavowed the existence of any 'significant material' in the book. However he seems to an outsider to have employed what Max Weber, the sociologist of bureaucracy, described as the bureaucrat's 'supreme power instrument' – 'the transformation of official information into classified material by means of the notorious concept of the "official secret"' (Weber 1978: 1417–1418). For the stuff of the very constitution of a democratic state to be rendered into an official secret, be it material one year or more than 30 years old, is profoundly undemocratic.

The need for explicit conventions, precedent and guidance is more urgent now than in Baldwin's era in one important respect. In 1932, Baldwin was describing the 'organic' nature of British political practice. But at least since the end of the 1950s, the morality of public life has undergone a profound change: the 'rules of the club' no longer apply uniformly in politics, in the City, or elsewhere in public life. Conventions have (in modern terms) passed their sell-by date, but they are still supposed to entrench the rules of conduct for those who run the country. The absence of explicit rules, combined with the informal and undefined nature of the core executive, gives new meaning to Asquith's famous statement that 'the office of Prime Minister is what its holder chooses and is able to make of it'. Mrs Thatcher simply ignored conventions when they did not suit her and exploited to the full the flexible nature of her post. It is open to Tony Blair or any of their successors to follow suit. As Anthony King, the political analyst, noted of Mrs Thatcher, one of the great strengths of the British premiership:

> lies in the fact that the outer limits of its authority are so ill-defined. It is open to a determined Prime Minister to take more and more decisions and to defy other members of the cabinet to say that he or she has no right to take these decisions.
>
> (King 1985: 137)

King touches on a significant aspect for us of Prime Ministerial power. Most discussion about a Prime Minister's power tends to discuss it in relation to the power of his or her ministers. But the royal prerogative power of control of the civil service is highly significant in its own right. Mrs Thatcher achieved the most radical restructuring of the civil service in her second and third terms (see Chapter 8), intervened personally in making senior appointments (see Chapter 7), and insisted on the 1984 ban on trade union membership at the Government Communications Headquarters (GCHQ). But the flexible nature of her command of the bureaucracy was continually evident in various other ways. After disbanding the Civil Service Department in 1981, for example, 'The Prime Minister treated Derek Rayner [her adviser on civil service efficiency, recruited from Marks & Spencers] as if he were a surrogate Head of the Civil Service' (Hennessy 1989: 625). Similarly, Charles Powell, a middle-ranking official who entered her service as adviser on foreign affairs, became her close adviser and fixer, often acting quite outside the rules of non-political civil service conduct (Clark 1993; Lawson 1993). Mrs Thatcher's personal chief information officer, Bernard Ingham throughout her years in office, gradually accumulated powers until, in 1989, he became head of the entire Government Information Service (GIS) on the break-up of the Central Office of Information. Ingham, who was notoriously Mrs Thatcher's creature, effectively became the government's 'information overlord', in charge of the government's propaganda machine and a £168 million publicity budget.

In Ingham's case, as on many other issues, Mrs Thatcher broke with convention. For 40 years, the convention had been that the two posts should be kept separate, precisely because the dangers of centralising government information services under a single official whose loyalty was first to the Prime Minister personally, and secondarily to the government as a whole, were too evident. In 1954 Lord Swinton, encouraging a reluctant Winston Churchill to reinstate the No. 10 press post alone, conceded that 'a centralised information agency of this character might, in the hands of an unscrupulous extremist government, prove both a powerful and dangerous weapon of propaganda'. Ingham unscrupulously manipulated his position, first and foremost in Mrs Thatcher's service – often undermining her cabinet colleagues – in a robustly partisan way (see **p. 182**). Ingham was responsible, through the head of the civil service, to Mrs Thatcher and his activities were of immense value to his Prime Minister alone (Harris 1994: 599–600; Chapter 7; 810–814).

The rules of behaviour for government ministers

Government ministers are obliged to observe few hard-and-fast rules of behaviour, save a handful of significant rules on financial probity. The major document regulating ministers' conduct is supposed to be *Questions of Procedure for Ministers (QPM)* (Cabinet Office 1992), re-titled the *Ministerial Code* by Tony Blair in July 1997. This document sets out the conventions – a mix of procedures and guidelines – which are supposed to govern the conduct of ministers. Both Hennessy and Sarah Hogg, John Major's former policy adviser, have separately quoted Pickthorn's dictum (see **pp. 301–302**) to emphasise its significance. For Hennessy, it is a central element in this country's statecraft; for Hogg, it is 'a crucial document' containing much on 'the rules of government and the handling of policy' (Hennessy 1995: 34–37).

Though a document which has supposedly set out the procedure for the proper conduct of ministers and cabinet government in the UK for half a century, *QPM* remained a state secret until John Major finally placed it in the public domain in May 1992. But this is only one of several curiosities which attach to this ambiguous rule-book. First, its contents are very mixed. Major's 1992 version (see Box C) was largely a practical and procedural list of do's and don'ts, ranging from overseas visits, ministerial pensions and private interests, and attendance at the Privy Council to 20 paragraphs on cabinet business, laying a heavy stress on collective responsibility and communication, presentation of policies (20 paragraphs) and ministers' conduct in their departmental capacity (22 paragraphs). Blair's *Ministerial Code* is essentially the same document, bringing Major's 1992 document up-to-date with developments in practice under the Major government up to 1997. Thus, it updates certain key sections (e.g. on ministers' duty of openness in Parliament), and expands others (e.g. on ministers' financial propriety), though it does also add obvious new rules (e.g. centralising the presentation of major policies).

BOX C   THE MINISTERIAL RULE-BOOK

John Major's ministerial rule-book, *Questions of Procedure for Ministers* **(1992)**

Tony Blair's ministerial rule-book, *Ministerial Code* **(1997)**

Introduction

Every new Prime Minister introduces and updates a rule-book for ministers, which is designed to protect 'the integrity of public life' (Major) or 'to reaffirm my strong personal commitment to restoring the bond of trust between the British people and their Government' (Blair). Blair's version updates rules on accountability to Parliament, open government, ministers' relations with civil servants and their financial probity to reflect changes which took place under the Major government and to reassure the public about his determination to restore trust in British government. Thus, the 1997 version is clearer and more detailed than the 1992 *QPM*, and opens with a strong statement of ministers' prime responsibilities. It also clearly states the Prime Minister's ultimate responsibility for the conduct of ministers. Otherwise, however, in its essentials it does not vary greatly from the position of the Major government in May 1997.

Attendance at the Privy Council

Both documents stress that attendance must take precedence over all other engagements. Failure to attend is discourteous to the Queen and could prejudice 'essential Government business' by leaving the Council inquorate.

Ministers and their responsibilities within the cabinet

Both set out practical rules of cabinet and cabinet committee business. Ministers should appeal infrequently from cabinet committees to cabinet; should clear proposals involving expenditure with the Treasury first, sort out their legal implications with law officers and any likely impact on the European Convention on Human Rights, cover 'presentational aspects'; and so on. Ministers are responsible for instructing their departments to act on cabinet or committee decisions. Ministers relinquishing office should hand over or destroy cabinet documents. The decisions of full cabinet or committee meetings are binding on all ministers. Both remind ministers that 'The internal process through which a decision has been made, or the level of Committee by which it was taken, should not be disclosed' (para. 17) and require them to respect the privacy of opinions expressed in debate and of documents which need 'to be protected in the national (Major)/public (Blair) interest'.

Rules for ministers

Ministers must request consent to be absent from cabinet by way of a personal minute to the Prime Minister and should not have minutes sent to them during meetings.

Ministers and law officers

Both set out the occasions on which ministers should consult the law officers, including actions which may be subject to judicial review. Where ministers become involved in legal proceedings, primarily in their personal capacities but which 'also involve their official responsibilities', they should consult the law officers before their own solicitors. The opinions or advice of law officers 'must not be disclosed outside Government without their authority' (para. 24) – a convention which ministers and civil servants broke in the Westland affair (see **pp. 317–318**). In criminal proceedings, the law officers act wholly independently of the government.

Ministers and their accountability to Parliament

Major's and Blair's codes both contain advice and rules on making statements in Parliament and releasing documents, stressing the importance of timing and giving notice. Both contain a core statement on ministers' accountability to Parliament:

> Each minister is responsible to Parliament for the conduct of his or her Department, and for the actions carried out by the Department in pursuit of Government policies or in the discharge of responsibilities laid upon him or her as a Minister. Ministers are accountable to Parliament, in the sense that they have a duty to explain in Parliament the exercise of their powers and duties and to give an account to Parliament of what is done by them in their capacity as Ministers or by their Departments. This includes the duty to give Parliament, including its Select Committees, and the public as full information as possible about the policies, decisions and actions of the Government, and not to deceive or mislead Parliament and the public.
>
> (QPM 1992: para. 27)

> 1.ii. Ministers have a duty to Parliament to account, and be held to account, for the policies, decisions and actions of their Departments and Next Steps Agencies; iii. It is of paramount importance that Ministers give accurate and truthful information to Parliament, correcting any inadvertent error at the earliest opportunity. Ministers who knowingly mislead Parliament will be expected to offer their resignation to the Prime Minister; iv. Ministers should be as open as possible with Parliament and the public, refusing to provide information only when disclosure would not be in the public interest [as defined by statute and the January 1997 edition of the code for open government].
>
> (Ministerial Code 1997: para. 1. ii–iv)

Ministers and their departments

Both contain practical rules for the discharge of ministers' departmental responsibilities, including the need to seek the Prime Minister's approval for changes in responsibilities or functions between ministers in charge of departments, or junior ministers; rules for deciding disputes between ministers; rules for delegating responsibilities to junior ministers, for absences from London, the conduct of parliamentary private secretaries, the appointment of special advisers (the 1997 rules limit minister to two); and the need to consult the Prime Minister over certain appointments and rules for all others. The 1997 rules update rules on making public appointments to include Nolan Committee procedures and principles and to ask for special attention to be given to the representation of people with disabilities, as well as women and members of ethnic minorities; add provision for unpaid advisers; and make other changes.

Ministers and civil servants

Important rules governing ministers' dealings with their civil servants are set out in both documents. The wording of the key paragraphs in both (para. 55 in the 1992 version; para. 56 in the 1997 rules) is almost exactly the same, except for one phrase:

> Ministers have a duty to give fair consideration and due weight to informed and impartial advice from civil servants, as well as to other considerations and advice, in reaching policy decisions; [see below]. . . . a duty to ensure that influence over appointments is not abused for partisan purposes; and a duty to observe the obligations of a good employer with regard to terms and conditions of those who serve them. Civil servants should not be asked to engage in activities likely to call in question their political impartiality, or to give rise to the criticism that people paid from public funds are being used for Party political purposes.

In 1992, the following phrasing filled the gap left above: *'a duty to refrain from asking or instructing civil servants to do things which they should not do'.*

The 1997 code had these words instead: *'a duty to uphold the political impartiality of the Civil Service, and not to ask civil servants to act in any way which would conflict with the Civil Service Code* [introduced in 1996]*'.*

Ministers should not ask civil servants to attend or take part in party conferences, except where it may be 'advantageous' for a civil servant to hear what is being said (and he or she is clearly identified as an observer). Civil servants may also be at party meetings to enable ministers to carry out urgent government business and may prepare political briefs to explain departmental policy.

The Blair document sets out the role of permanent secretaries as accounting officers.

Rules for ministers

Ministers and their constituencies

Both deal with the conduct of ministers when constituency matters may affect their role as ministers or members of the government or raise conflicts of interest. Both agree that, in making departmental decisions affecting their own constituencies, ministers should take care to avoid any possible conflict of interest. They agree that ministers should act as other MPs would in dealing with requests from the public to submit their complaints to the Ombudsman; and that they may take up a complaint with a fellow minister in the department concerned or investigate a case personally if it concerns their own department. But here they differ. Major's version said that ministers should not take part in public representations or deputations to other ministers, but may make their views known on constituency issues, Blair's allows them to take part in deputations. Both provide for safeguards designed to ensure they do not embarrass their colleagues.

Ministers' visits at home and abroad

Both set out prudential rules of conduct on visits abroad and in the UK, dealing with the size of deputations abroad, expenses, hospitality, entertainment, gifts, spouses' expenses, foreign decorations, etc.

Ministers and the presentation of policy

The presentation of policy and media relations generally play a prominent part in both codes. For the most part they agree on arrangements for press conferences explaining or announcing policies; rules for publishing green or white papers; rules for speeches, broadcasts, press articles and interviews (to which principles of collective responsibility apply); rules for articles in local newspapers, and on writing a book while in office; a general prohibition on writing to the press; and the need to get the Prime Minister's approval for complaints to the press or broadcasting authorities. Ministers may, however, write novels or books of an artistic, philosophical, musical, historical, etc., character.

However, New Labour's emphasis on managing the media is reflected in a new provision in the 1997 code insisting that ministers should agree 'all major interviews and media appearances, both print and broadcast' with the No. 10 press office before they are entered into and that departments should keep a record of media contacts by ministers and officials.

Both insist on a clear distinction between government publicity and advertising and party political publicity.

Ministers' financial interests

Both contain strict guidance on ministers' own financial interests, but in response to the 'sleaze' allegations and findings of the 1990s, the 1997 version gives far more prominence to avoiding conflicts 'between their public duties and their private interests', expanding the guidance given in 1992 and providing for possible conflicts in greater detail. The 1997 code also updates the 1992 rules, particularly in relation to the need for ministers to consult the Advisory Committee on Business Appointments about any paid appointments they wish to take up within two years of leaving office.

Two sets of rules in both documents may be said to have had a significant bearing on the democratic, and constitutional, conduct of ministers – the paragraphs on ministers' accountability to Parliament and on their relationship with their civil servants, enjoining them to respect and consider their 'informed and impartial advice' (see Box C). There are various injunctions which are designed to safeguard the political neutrality of the government machine. Both ask ministers to refrain from asking civil servants to perform political tasks; prohibit the use of public funds for party political publicity and the use of official machinery to distribute speeches 'made in a party political context'. Overall, however, both documents are mostly concerned with the co-ordination of government business, practical rules for its conduct and the presentation of policy, ministerial etiquette and political *nous*. The 1997 document is more conscious of the need to address issues of accountability, openness and financial probity, but this new emphasis does not lead to a full framework of clear rules and obligations for ministers.

What constitutional weight, then, does this central collection of conventions governing ministers' conduct – the 'Highway Code of government' (as Hogg described it) – actually possess? The document is first and foremost a symbol of Prime Ministerial authority. Every Prime Minister since 1945 has framed and revised *QPM* (now the *Ministerial Code*) to suit his or her needs. Ministers are not consulted in its drafting and historically at least one minister, Tony Benn, has refused to accept its authority. The code has grown in size during this period and has shown a marked degree of continuity. But does it have a *constitutional* continuity – that is, do key rules on parliamentary accountability, honesty and openness and respect for the impartiality of civil servants possess the constitutional status of conventions which all Prime Ministers are bound to safeguard?

In December 1992, Sir Robin Butler, Major's adviser on constitutional matters, declared to one of Peter Hennessy's students at Queen Mary College, London, that *QPM* had no constitutional force at all; its contents and authority were entirely subject to a Prime Minister's discretion: 'It is perfectly possible for an incoming Prime Minister to scrap the whole thing and to devise entirely new rules [and] . . . deal with the administration in the way he chooses.'

In January 1994, Hennessy asked for Butler's consent to quote this dictum in a public lecture. Butler now qualified his previous view, stating that 90 per cent of it only was discretionary (and thus that 10 per cent had the force of convention): 'The document itself has a discretionary status, though it deals with some things which are not at the discretion of a Prime Minister to change, for example, the description of accountability to Parliament in paragraph 27'.

The status of paragraph 27 on ministerial accountability to Parliament had by then been raised high by Sir Richard Scott, who had placed it at the centre of his inquiry into the export of defence equipment to Iraq. Paragraph 27 set out ministers' duty to explain and render account in Parliament for the exercise of their powers and duties and their departments' actions and policies. This included the duty to give Parliament, MPs, select committees and the public 'as full information as possible about the policies, decisions and actions of the Government and not to deceive or mislead Parliament and the public'. Scott had seized upon this paragraph as it contained the only clear statement of a duty of honesty and openness upon ministers, against which he could measure their actual conduct. In January 1995, Butler was dealing with Scott's preliminary findings and the paragraph was therefore very much on his mind.

As Butler informed the Treasury and Civil Service select committee, he was as Cabinet Secretary the principal formal authority and adviser to the Prime Minister and ministers on *QPM* and on any issues which arose in connection with its guidance: 'These *conventions* applying to Ministers *have accumulated over time* and the Cabinet Secretary advises on them and keeps a file, obviously, on the advice that is given and tries to be consistent in the advice that is given' [our emphasis] (8 March 1995).

This statement is very much in the tradition of commentary on the British constitution which hymns the way custom, practice, procedure and advice *accumulate*, like coral, to create *conventions* of the constitution – 'immutable parts which Prime Ministers cannot reach' (Hennessy 1995: 39). The idea of a file of accumulated wisdom passing on from regime to regime may well seem reassuring at first. But, as we have seen, it is *secret*. Moreover, Butler's change of view on the status of *QPM* shows how uncertain and mutable this process actually is. From being an entirely discretionary document in the view of the high priest of the constitution, parts at least of *QPM* suddenly accumulated a constitutional force. There is yet another sting in this tale. For the very paragraph which had metamorphosed into immutability was almost instantly made mutable by the Prime Minister – and made public in a letter from the Prime Minister to Giles Radice MP, first chairperson of the newly created Public Service Committee, in April 1994. Major inserted the word 'knowingly' before 'mislead' and also added that ministers could withhold information when to do so was in the public interest. We discuss the significance of this change for the principle of ministerial responsibility to Parliament later (see Chapter 12). Here it is sufficient to point out that the executive was able at a stroke to change what was agreed to be a profound principle governing ministerial behaviour without any public debate and to announce the changes almost informally by way of a personal letter to a select committee chair.

Who, then, is responsible for enforcing the ministerial code? In the 1990s, it seemed that Sir Robin Butler was not only the 'guardian' of the rule-book for ministerial conduct, but also the government's arbiter of ministers' conduct. Butler was asked by the Prime Minister to investigate complaints against a succession of ministers accused of misconduct – Neil Hamilton, Tim Smith, Michael Howard and Jonathan

Aitken. He was present even at a meeting between Hamilton and the government's chief whip, though he said that he withdrew 'before anything was decided'. Butler was inclined from the start to distrust the ministers' principal accuser, Mohamed al Fayed, and too ready to accept the word of ministers. He was thus heavily criticised for incompetence when the truth of Hamilton's, Smith's and Aitken's improper behaviour was finally revealed. But the fact is that it is not proper for the Cabinet Secretary to become involved in such investigations anyway. He or she must remain above politics – and the private lives of ministers – at all times. The danger of Butler's conduct soon became clear. First, the Prime Minister quoted Butler's first findings as proof of his ministers' innocence – incidentally, again breaking a constitutional convention (that the advice of civil servants to ministers should always be confidential) (HC Deb WA, 25 October 1994, c523–524); and then Aitken himself quoted Butler as proof of his own innocence (HC Deb WA, 27 October 1994, c992–993). Butler also wrote to the *Guardian,* saying that he did not regard Aitken as having lied to him or misled him. Thus, Butler entered into the political arena.

Butler insisted that the behaviour of Sir Burke Trend, Cabinet Secretary in the 1960s, constituted a precedent for his actions (*Mail on Sunday*, 15 January 1995). Trend had advised the then Prime Minister that Roger Hollis, the head of MI5, was not a Soviet spy and his judgement too was made public. But Hollis was not a political minister in distress; and in the more obvious parallel from the 1960s, the Profumo case, the then Cabinet Secretary maintained a proper distance from the drowning minister. Nor had Butler's immediate predecessor ever taken on a similar investigatory role. Butler suffered an uncomfortable grilling before the Treasury and Civil Service Committee on 8 March 1995, at which he insisted that his role had been advisory, and that the Cabinet Secretary was neither the guardian of the ministerial code, nor its arbiter, but purely an adviser who 'provides continuity' (with the 'Precedent Book' to hand) (TCSC 1995: para. 37).

No doubt the purely advisory role of the Cabinet Secretary will now be well entrenched in convention. Others, such as the Attorney-General and government Chief Whip, have been advanced as possible arbiters or investigators – and in previous government crises both have been involved. It has also been suggested that the role of the Parliamentary Commissioner for Standards might be expanded to cover ministerial conduct in the round, or even that a special new commissioner should be appointed. But, as of now, the financial interests of ministers must be entered into the registers held in the Commons or Lords, as the case may be, and they are subject to the same rules as other MPs or peers for the honesty of their entries. The duty of enforcing the wider responsibilities of ministers lies squarely and solely with the Prime Minister of the day. The political realities are unchanged: it is the Prime Minister who appoints and dismisses ministers and who is therefore responsible for their conduct in office. The ultimate sanction for ensuring that a Prime Minister takes this duty seriously lies with the House of Commons, dominated as it usually is by a majority of government MPs.

It is obviously quite proper for a Prime Minister to reserve the power to enforce the rules of collective responsibility and ministerial conduct on his or her ministers. But the conventions of the ministerial code bear upon the principle of ministerial responsibility to Parliament; respect for the party political independence of the civil service; and matters of financial probity. Here, a Prime Minister has divided loyalties, as John Major demonstrated on various occasions during his premiership – most notably with regard to the adverse finding of the Scott Report on the conduct of two ministers. On all these occasions, he placed the stability and political credibility of his government above any duty he might be under to uphold significant conventions governing ministerial conduct. This conclusion is hardly surprising – 'he would do that, wouldn't he?' What is surprising is that such rules should be contained in a relatively marginal – and until recently, secret – document; that they are so vulnerable to change by any Prime Minister in turn; and that the duty of enforcing those rules which affect the democratic conduct of ministers lies with the head of the core executive. The balance of power is heavily tilted towards the executive in Britain, and not least in its ability to change the rules of the game and the Prime Minister's own role as referee.

The fluidity of rule by constitutional convention

Non-legal conventions are at the heart of the celebrated flexibility of Britain's political system; and that flexibility in the conduct of the executive and in wider constitutional arrangements enhances the powers of the executive. Indeed, this flexibility is praised precisely because it does contribute to the executive's powers. Graham C. Moodie, the constitutional theorist, wrote for example of the unwritten constitution that:

> one of its strengths has been that for the most part it has permitted governments to wield the power necessary to govern effectively without allowing them to rule for long in an arbitrary and irresponsible fashion, disregarding the wishes at least of the more powerful and articulate sections of the governed. Another source of strength has been that . . . no rigid constitutional or political orthodoxy has been able to ossify the institutions of government.
> (Moodie 1964: 16)

The balance which Moodie perceived in 1964 in an era of political consensus has not always been obvious either previously or since. The absence of specific rules governing the conduct of the Prime Minister and other principal actors allows them great freedom of political manoeuvre in their own behaviour. Conventions actually developed to try and provide checks and balances on government and to maintain some separation of powers and roles. But recent experience suggests in fact that they possess too great and unchecked a freedom (see Part 3); and that the scale and scope of their governing powers has recently contributed to major policy disasters (Dunleavy 1995a: 52–69). The absence of special constitutional rules also enables them to avoid the formality, openness and publicity that would inevitably attend major changes under a written constitution. As we demonstrate in detail below, rules of convention were powerless to restrain the improper conduct of Mrs Thatcher, her Trade and Industry Secretary, and several civil servants in the Westland affair in 1986;

Peter Hennessy accurately described the affair as a 'bonfire of conventions' (1995: 96). Sir Christopher Foster, the highly experienced expert in British government, and Francis Plowden, of Coopers & Lybrand, comment that precisely because Mrs Thatcher was not bound by a written constitution, 'she was able to sweep aside many of the old conventions of government' (Foster and Plowden 1996: ix).

The fact is that the constitutional resources at the disposal of the 'poor Briton' – procedure and convention – provide poor and uncertain checks and balances against arbitrary government on the part of the core executive. Ferdinand Mount drew attention to the disjunction between the 'certainty, predictability and regularity which we aim for when we frame and administer new laws; and the fluid and slipshod quality of the arrangements for their framing' (1992: 14). Uncertainty about the internal rules which govern the conduct of the core executive is inherent in the very idea of convention. At heart, this idea relies wholly on the willingness of the Prime Minister, ministers and other major actors to subject themselves to a high degree of self-discipline; as the nineteenth century premier, W. E. Gladstone, pointed out, the British constitution 'presumes more boldly than any other the good sense and the good faith of those who work it' (1879: 245). He belonged to the era of the 'club' when self-discipline was assumed to be a feature of public life, and was reinforced by peer pressure (see **p. 303**). Neither are wholly characteristic of the conduct of ministers and politicians – or wider public life – in the late twentieth century, though the Nolan process is seeking to revive both.

The civil service as custodian of constitutional government

The civil service – and especially the higher civil service – constitutes a unifying presence and influence in government. Inherent in the prolonged debates which began in the mid-1970s about standards in Whitehall and its role in the core executive are several far-reaching assumptions: first, that Britain's mandarins can act individually as a safeguard against incautious or 'extreme' ministers; and that collectively they are custodians variously of the traditions of public service, of the conventions of the unwritten constitution, of constitutional conduct and integrity, and of 'good government', if not of the democratic process. Senior civil servants plainly exercise a great deal of power, principally within their own domain, but they also exert some influence over the ministers they advise, and as a class or group of permanent secretaries, they have a measure of collective power (Barker and Wilson 1977).

The belief that the civil service ought in some circumstances to act as a constitutional check on the government is consistent with the Platonic tradition of guardianship on which the civil service was founded in the nineteenth century (see Chapter 2). As Ferdinand Mount comments, 'The Civil Service is not ashamed of regarding itself as the unofficial brake in a constitutional system which has become so deficient in effective checks and balances' (Mount 1992: 147). In 1995, Peter Hennessy asked Lord Bancroft what the civil service was for. He replied:

> To act as a permanent piece of ballast in the Constitution on the basis
> that you have what can be a very volatile legislature and an equally volatile

The civil service as custodian

> ministerial executive. Sometimes, therefore, you need a degree of balance and permanence.
>
> (Hennessy 1995: 127)

These are old-school views in the Platonic tradition. It is unlikely that current civil servants would voice similar sentiments (not least after Bancroft's summary ejection by Mrs Thatcher). Even if they represented a more contemporary ethos, it would be limited to a broad concern with the overall direction of government, the proper balance between elected ministers and permanent officials and the value to ministers of the accumulated experience of Whitehall (see below). In no sense do they conceive of civil servants policing the boundaries between acceptable and unacceptable behaviour on the part of ministers and colleagues. Further, under existing constitutional arrangements, civil servants are directly responsible to ministers and not at all to Parliament or any other authority. Constitutionally, the Cabinet Secretary, is the Prime Minister's servant, and 'is always at hand to do the PM's bidding' (*Guardian*, 29 October 1994). The head of the civil service, like any other civil servant, is subject to the policies of the government of the day. Moreover, as we saw in Chapter 7, mandarins and ministers tend to work closely together in partnerships from which both sides gain. So it is not easy for civil servants to exert a 'watchdog' role.

Further, the convention-based nature of the British constitution, and the absence of a structured code of conduct for ministers and civil servants alike, makes it very hard for civil servants to define the boundaries between 'constitutional' and 'unconstitutional' – let alone 'democratic' and 'undemocratic' – actions which they would be obliged to police. They have no clear book of rules to enforce. The code of conduct for ministers is an ambiguous, mixed and weak document (see above). On one occasion, Sir Antony Part did inform Tony Benn that part of his duties as permanent secretary was to help Benn fulfil the requirements of *QPM* and that Benn was in breach of its rules. Benn simply brushed his objection aside as politically motivated (Benn 1989: 186). But that intervention seems to have been highly unusual in that no others like it have reached the public record.

The idea that senior officials can individually or collectively enforce proper standards on the part of their masters and mistresses is therefore inconceivable. It is not simply that the idea is at odds with Whitehall's culture and ethos and the symbiotic relationship between ministers and mandarins (see Chapter 7). As Sir Richard Scott said in evidence to MPs on the Public Service Committee (PSC), if the conduct of ministers is to be supervised, it must be by an official or authority outside government.

> SIR RICHARD SCOTT: After all, it is supervising government.
>
> JIM COUSINS MP: So the Cabinet Secretary in that sense cannot be regarded as being appropriate?
>
> SCOTT: The Cabinet Secretary is a very important figure *in government* [our emphasis].
>
> (PSC 1996c: vol. 3, 78)

Similarly, when Tony Wright MP described Butler as 'one of the guardians of the constitution' at the Public Service Committee (PSC) in June 1996, Butler interjected: 'I disclaim that. I regard myself as an adviser, not as a guardian'. He then refused to give his view on Scott's conclusion that ministers had behaved in constitutionally improper ways:

> I am afraid that is where I have to stand aside. That is a matter between ministers and Parliament, it is not for me to arbitrate on that, and Parliament did, very properly, debate that and it came to its conclusion. But it is certainly not for an official to rule on a question of that sort.
>
> (PSC 1996c: vol. 3, 138)

Scott's and Butler's views are clearly well-founded. The fact is that it is almost impossible to disentangle the interests and conduct of ministers and mandarins: both form part of the core executive, or 'government'. For example, being 'economical with the truth' is a tradition in Whitehall which long pre-dates Sir Robert Armstrong's disingenuous remark in 1986. Armstrong was simply echoing Harold Laski's academic dictum, in 1942, that Whitehall officials were 'economical of the truth' in their dealings with Parliament, a tradition which can be traced back at least as far as Edmund Burke. The Scott Report teems with examples of the corrosion of this tradition, in which civil servants colluded with ministers in giving MPs and the public misleading information and a civil servant even gave dishonest testimony in a criminal trial to protect the good name of the executive (Scott: para. G17.12–17.16). Civil servants gave evidence to Scott about the arts of dissembling involved in drafting replies to parliamentary questions (see **pp. 363–364** and **434**). How then is it supposed that they could police the honesty and openness of ministers in Parliament and the public domain?

The Westland crisis of 1985–86 may serve as the object lesson for any hopes that the Whitehall hierarchy might enforce proper standards of conduct by ministers and civil servants. The then Cabinet Secretary and head of the civil service, Sir Robert Armstrong, was asked to inquire into what was an unscrupulous and unconstitutional plot (Dunleavy 1995b: 181–217; Harris 1994: 749–776). The Prime Minister and Leon Brittan, Trade Secretary, and Mrs Thatcher's closest advisers, Charles Powell and Bernard Ingham, both of them civil servants, were involved in the plot to cause Sir Patrick Mayhew, the Solicitor-General, to write a letter criticising one of Michael Heseltine's statements, expressly so that its contents could be leaked to damage the Defence Secretary's case for the purchase of Westland by a European consortium.

Constitutionally, law officers are supposed to offer non-political professional advice and the advice they give is therefore meant to be kept strictly confidential. Mayhew's letter was marked 'Confidential' – 'unauthorised disclosure', according to the official definition of the term, 'would be prejudicial to the interests of the nation'. But when it arrived at No. 10 Powell at once made a copy and took it down to Ingham in the press office – 'an action which suggests they had already decided it was to be used publicly in some way', as Robert Harris, Ingham's unofficial biographer, put it. Powell then spoke to Brittan's private secretary (a career civil servant) who said that Brittan was keen to leak the letter, but only with No. 10's agreement. Ingham then telephoned Colette Bowe, the DTI's chief press officer. Though Ingham denies that he ordered her to leak the letter, the circumstantial evidence supports her account that she had strong reservations about leaking a classified letter and that she did so on Ingham's orders.

The law officers were outraged and immediately demanded a full inquiry from Sir Robert Armstrong. Part of his duty as Cabinet Secretary was to advise the Prime Minister on the constitutionality of her own and ministers' behaviour, and as head of the civil service, to uphold its tradition of impartial public service. Armstrong was reluctant to act and Sir Michael Havers, the Attorney-General, had to renew the demand twice more, finally telling Armstrong that he would send the police into No. 10 and the DTI. Finally, a whole week after the leak, Mrs Thatcher was obliged to agree to an inquiry, which Armstrong himself would undertake. Armstrong's inquiry consisted of personal interrogations of five officials, including Bowe and Ingham, who were both interviewed for about 45 minutes each, and several telephone conversations. Yet it took all of nine days and was originally intended to be kept confidential. The revelation in the House of Commons by Tam Dalyell MP that Bowe was the official who had leaked the letter forced Armstrong's inquiry report out into the open. Armstrong came to the formal conclusion that the leak came about because of a misunderstanding between Ingham and Downing Street and Bowe and the DTI 'as to exactly what was being sought and what was being given'. His form of words gave his mistress enough protective cover to survive in the Commons (see **pp. 410–411** further).

Armstrong went on to perform another service for Mrs Thatcher. MPs on the Defence Committee decided to inquire into the Westland affair and invited the five officials involved in the leak to testify. Armstrong flew back from a pre-summit meeting in Honolulu and offered to give evidence instead of the five officials. They had, he wrote, 'given a full account of their role in these matters to me . . . and co-operated fully in my investigation'; the Prime Minister and Industry Secretary took the view that it would be neither fair nor reasonable to expect them to submit to a second round of detailed questioning. He thus deprived the select committee of the opportunity to make an independent appraisal of the facts. In his evidence he explained that Downing Street had given 'cover', but not 'covering authority' for the leak; Powell and Ingham 'accepted, or they acquiesced in, or they did not object to – whatever phrase of that kind you like to use – that the DTI were going to make the disclosure' (Westland Report 1986: para. 1297). The committee did briefly agree to interview Ingham, but backed down (see **p. 410**). Their report concluded that the leak was 'an improper act' and described as 'extraordinary' the fact that no disciplinary action was to be taken against any of the officials concerned (*ibid.*, para. 213). Thatcher had relied upon Brittan's silent acquiescence in his role as scapegoat quite as much as on Armstrong's way with words; three years later, Brittan revealed truths of the matter which Armstrong had been unable to uncover. In a television interview, he stated that the leak was approved by both Powell and Ingham, saying that 'there would have been no question of the leaking of that document without that express approval from Number 10' (Harris 1994: 767–775).

It cannot be established with certainty quite how improperly Ingham had behaved: at best, he had turned a blind eye to the leak, at worst he had connived at smearing a cabinet minister and had bullied a reluctant official into breaking the Official Secrets Act, constitutional convention, and the rules then governing the conduct of civil servants. All the officials involved seem to have been complicit with at least one minister in activities which contravene the same constitutional authorities, including the ministerial code:

> Ministers have a duty . . . to refrain from asking or instructing civil servants to do things which they should not do . . . Civil servants should not be asked to engage in activities likely to call in question their political impartiality.
> (Cabinet Office 1992: para. 55)

It is inconceivable that Armstrong was not aware of the real facts of the case. How hard he tried to establish those facts amidst the cover-up engaged in by those involved in the leak, and how much evidence was at his disposal, cannot be known. But the circumstantial evidence suggests that his overriding wish was to smooth the whole crisis over. He was in an invidious position. It is not possible both to serve a Prime Minister or ministers loyally, according to the current culture of Whitehall, and at the same time to take formal responsibility for policing their behaviour. There is a conflict between a Cabinet Secretary's role as the Prime Minister's fixer (an experienced Whitehall figure told the *Guardian* in October 1994 that it was Butler's role 'to try and make sure that things don't come out to make matters worse') and his or her duty to maintain and personify the impartiality and honesty of the civil service. Yet Britain's informal constitutional arrangements constantly presume upon the ability of individuals to perform such conflicting roles. The experience of Armstrong and Butler, decent men both, shows that it is not always possible to keep the right balance in the face of a Prime Minister's demands.

As for ministers' duty to be frank and honest in giving information to Parliament (para. 27 of *QPM*), Armstrong frankly disavowed any responsibility on the part of officials in evidence to the former Treasury and Civil Service Committee (TCSC). He would allow no more than that it was the duty of officials to 'remind' ministers of their responsibility to Parliament. There was no question, he thought, that a civil servant's duty of responsibility to ministers was in some sense conditional upon ministers answering fully to Parliament (TCSC 1986: vol. 2: Questions 788–792), as the MOD civil servant, Clive Ponting, had believed when he leaked information on the sinking of the *Belgrano* to an MP after a misleading parliamentary statement by his minister. Armstrong states that it is for ministers, not civil servants, to decide what information should be made available to Parliament, and how and when it should be released. In later evidence to the TCSC, Butler, Armstrong's successor, said that it would be improper for ministers to instruct civil servants to mislead parliamentary committees but they could be ordered to withhold information (TCSC 1990a: question 123). This is a very fine distinction. Butler's ability to make other such fine distinctions became clear in his evidence to the PSC in the aftermath of the Scott Report. As we saw (in Chapter 7), government officials and departments were involved alongside ministers in misrepresenting the conclusions of the report by way of selective quotation. The Cabinet Office issued a background briefing paper for the media, entitled *Government Policy on the Control of Exports to Iran and Iraq, 1980–1990*. It was accurately described by Tony Wright MP as 'the facts paper' to Sir Richard Scott at a 1996 hearing of the PSC. Wright read out a statement from the paper, claiming 'Answers given to Parliamentary Questions gave an accurate description of the Government's policy on exports to Iran and Iraq'. Wright asked Scott: 'Could any reader of your Report believe that to be true?' Scott replied, 'I do not think so, no' (PSC 1996c: vol. 3, 67).

At a later PSC hearing, Wright took up the question of the Cabinet Office's 'untruthful version . . . of the [Scott] report' with Butler:

> WRIGHT: Is not that a troubling episode?
>
> BUTLER: No, because . . . in this respect Ministers disagreed with Sir Richard on his finding and the press notice to which you are referring represented the Government's view of the matter. That is perfectly proper.

Butler then informed another MP that the document did not purport to be a summary of the report, but was 'explicitly the government's account of what it believed the position was' (*ibid.*, vol. 3, 139–141). This was clearly not the case: the Cabinet Office document was presented as a factual background briefing.

Finally, it is inconsistent not simply with the constitutional role of the civil service and the role its senior officials play in government, but also with the democratic principles of popular control and political equality, for a small and relatively exclusive cadre of socially privileged meritocrats (see Barberis 1996: Chapter 6; Theakston and Fry 1989) to perform such a basic democratic function as policing the conduct of the core executive, especially if that role were to be performed out of the public gaze within the closed world of Whitehall. The virtually absolute and unconditional duty placed on civil servants to serve ministers loyally, to carry out their decisions zealously, whether they agree with them or not, and not to disclose information in breach of their obligation of confidence, reinforces this conclusion.

The rules governing civil service conduct

As we have shown (Chapter 7), civil servants may observe a formal political neutrality in their work for ministers, but they are expected and expect to act as their partial advisers. These expectations stem from the constitutional doctrine that civil servants have no identity in public other than their ministers'. Whatever they do publicly is in their minister's name; whatever they say is on his or her behalf. Over time under the prolonged period of Conservative government, this partiality fuelled fears that the civil service was being 'politicised'. Concerns about the effects of the government's civil service reforms on the public service ethic added to these fears and prompted non-partisan demands from the TCSC in the Commons and others that a statutory code should be drawn up, setting out the duties of civil servants with more clarity than then existed. After consulting the Nolan Committee, civil service unions and others, the government finally issued a new Civil Service Code in December 1995, modelled on a TCSC draft code. Roger Freeman, the minister responsible for the revised code, stated that the government was committed to 'maintaining the essential values of the Civil Service, including its integrity, political impartiality and objectivity' (Cabinet Office/OPS 1995).

The code reasserts the prime loyalty which civil servants owe to 'the duly constituted government', as promulgated in the celebrated 1985 Armstrong memorandum (see **pp. 175–176**). They should conduct themselves in such a way as to deserve and retain the confidence of ministers (and potential other ministers) and to ensure that they are sure that the civil service will conscientiously fulfil its duties to them and impartially assist, advise and carry out their policies. They should not disclose official information without authority, and should not leak documents or information in an attempt to frustrate or influence government policies, nor seek to frustrate government policies or decisions by refusing or failing to carry out actions which flow from ministers' decisions. They should comply with restrictions on their own political activities (items 1, 2 , 9, 10, 13). However, the duty of civil servants to ministers is made subject to:

- ministers' duty under the ministerial code to give Parliament and the public as full information as possible about government policies, decisions and actions, and not to deceive or 'knowingly mislead' either;
- rules for ministers prohibiting 'the use of public resources for party political purposes' and emphasising their duty to 'uphold the political impartiality of the Civil Service';
- the code's own rules of conduct for civil servants;
- their duty to obey the law and to uphold the administration of justice; and
- ethical standards governing particular professions (items 3 and 4).

It should be noted that, in emphasising the duty of officials to obey the law and uphold the administration of justice, the code deals with serious criticisms of official behaviour which were to be published in the Scott Report two months later. Scott found, for example, that a civil servant had given false evidence in the Matrix Churchill trial; that government lawyers had doctored witness statements; that Foreign and Commonwealth Office officials, at the behest of Customs, had tried to dissuade Iraqi and Jordanian embassy officials from giving evidence for the defence in another criminal trial (conduct which Scott described as 'thoroughly reprehensible'); and that the Customs prosecutors had been guilty of serious abuse of the justice process (Scott 1996: paras. G17.12–17.16; G18.36–18.106; J5.20; K4.4–4.15). Another set of criticisms that were to appear in the Scott Report are dealt with by item 5 of the code which states that civil servants 'should not deceive or knowingly mislead Ministers, Parliament or the public' (see **p. 317**).

Contemporary concerns about the quality of advice given by civil servants to ministers, which we have cited above (see **p. 180**) also surface in item 5 which sets out their duty to 'conduct themselves with integrity, impartiality and honesty. They should give honest and impartial advice to Ministers, without fear or favour, and make all information relevant to a decision available to Ministers'. The code's rules on openness have been reinforced by Cabinet Office guidance to officials on drafting answers to Parliamentary Questions. On the one hand, this guidance instructs them not to omit information merely because disclosure could lead to 'political embarrassment or administrative inconvenience'; on the other hand, it states that ministers will expect them 'to explain and present government policy and actions in a positive light'. The code doesn't seek to reconcile potential conflicts in this advice. It hardly needs to, since it also stresses that ministers should retain the final say on how they discharge their duty of openness (HC Deb WA, 11 November 1996, c53) (see Chapter 14 further). The new code also binds civil servants to deal with the affairs of the public 'sympathetically, efficiently, promptly, and without bias or maladministration' (see Chapter 10); to ensure the 'proper, effective and efficient use' of public money; and not to accept bribes or improper benefits, or to use their official position or information for their own or others' private interests (items 6–8).

Civil servants who believe that they are being required to act in a way which breaches these rules, or which is illegal or unethical, are obliged in the first instance to report to their departmental superiors; and should also report other breaches which they become aware of. If they are dissatisfied with the response, they then have a right to ask to see the head of the service and thereafter to report to the First Civil Service Commissioner, now an independent official. If an official who has complained is not satisfied with the outcome of these procedures, he or she is obliged to carry out the instructions they have challenged, or resign from the civil service (and continue to observe their duties of confidentiality) (items 11–13). The new code thus avoids any notion of a higher duty to the public or to the 'public interest', and effectively denies civil servants any more than a marginal element of judgement in their own right about the propriety of requests from ministers or superior officials to provide information or undertake activities which may contravene the narrower boundaries of the code. Above all, the code rules out any element of 'whistle-blowing' to any authority or body independent of the civil service (except in the case of outright criminal or unlawful activity).

The code may be contrasted with the equivalent US Code of Ethics which enjoins officials 'to put loyalty to the highest moral principles and to country above loyalty to persons, party or government department', and where 'whistle-blowers' who leak information revealing 'mismanagement, a gross waste of public funds, an abuse of authority, or a substantial and specific danger to public health or safety' have statutory protection. In Germany, too, civil service law tells officials that they 'serve the entire nation, not just a party' and that they have a special duty of loyalty to the constitution. Furthermore, it is evident that civil servants have no faith in the procedures laid down for complaints within the service. They are hardly ever used. Butler himself was able to cite only one case (not concerned with ethical issues) reaching him. Instead, officials use the First Division Association and other civil service unions as the channel for their complaints (see **p. 181**). The case of Michael Arnold, a computer scientist at the Ministry of Defence's Defence Evaluation Research Agency (DERA), hardly inspires confidence in the official channels for complaint. Arnold complained for eight years about waste, incompetence and alleged fraud to senior managers, the MOD police and finally – after being suspended – to the Office of Civil Service Commissioners, which is responsible for policing the code of conduct. His complaints were inadequately investigated and DERA dismissed him in October 1996 on the grounds that his repeated complaints made his continued employment unacceptable. In 1997, the Civil Service Appeal Board concluded that his dismissal was unfair, stating that 'The procedural failings and the inadequacy of the investigation were so serious as to involve a denial of natural justice'. The Police Complaints Authority has confirmed that there was 'malpractice' in one of the projects he complained about. But a DERA spokesman has stated that the MOD police found no evidence of fraud (*Guardian*, 1 October 1997).

Crucially, the civil service code also fails to deal with the central problem of the relationship between ministers and officials – the fact that officials' partial political service and loyalty to ministers damages the democratic process even when it stays the right side of the confused boundary between 'neutral and partial' and 'political and partisan'. The British civil service's processes are incompatible with any generally recognised principle of ethical public service such as those which equivalent democracies unquestioningly accept and sustain.

Permanent secretaries as accounting officers

Permanent secretaries are constitutionally bound in one respect to act entirely independently of their ministers. As accounting officers, they are personally responsible to Parliament for the legality, propriety and efficiency of departmental expenditure. A key control in the hands of a permanent secretary is to issue an accounting minute to a minister, requiring the minister to direct him or her in writing to authorise expenditure on actions or projects which seem improper, irregular, wasteful, or poor value for money. If a minister decides nevertheless to proceed, the accounting officer must ask him or her to issue written instructions and send the relevant papers to the Comptroller and Auditor General (by convention, the chairman of the Public Accounts Committee (PAC) is also immediately informed). Thus, publicity is ensured since the National Audit Office (NAO) investigates such cases and publishes a report on which the PAC holds a public hearing. This happens only rarely. In 1975, Sir Peter Carey, second permanent secretary at the DTI, wrote one of these minutes about his minister Tony Benn's proposal to provide funds for a workers' co-operative. In 1993, Sir Tim Lankester, then permanent secretary at the Overseas Development Administration, acted similarly on the Pergau Dam project, telling the NAO that it would be an uneconomical and imprudent use of aid funds and would actually harm the Malaysian economy. The courts later declared the loan to be unlawful. The whole episode was embarrassing for the government and the Public Accounts Committee rebuked Douglas Hurd, the Foreign Secretary, for going ahead with the loan. But wait for the sting. When the two departments of Education and Employment were merged in 1995, the two permanent secretaries worked in tandem for a while and one, a recent recruit to the civil service, was then preferred over the other. Until recently a permanent secretary passed over like this would have been found a place until the next relevant vacancy arose. In this case, the career official was told that he would have to compete for it, which he declined to do. This was a general, and not a specific, result of all such posts becoming liable to be advertised. Yet the official in question was Sir Tim Lankester. The process itself may very well be sensible, but there are two drawbacks, as two experienced observers from Coopers & Lybrand comment:

> The first is that it increases the power of ministers to the point where there may be the appearance, if not the fact, of political choice. [And secondly] . . . However innocent the circumstances leading to his departure may have been, it was impossible for many not to draw the moral that, however justified, a permanent secretary who writes such a minute censuring ministerial behaviour will be caught up with in the end.
>
> (Foster and Plowden 1996: 231–2)

For the most part, however, mandarins behave almost precisely in the same way as accounting officers as they do as permanent secretaries. In both roles (as a former Prisons Agency official informed us), 'a mandarin's most sacred task' remains unaltered: 'protecting the minister'. It goes without saying that the second most important task is to protect the department and deflect the blame. The official described how a Home Office accounting officer prepared for weeks for a Public Accounts Committee appearance after a critical National Audit Office (NAO) report on financial controls at the Prisons Agency, marshalling a common 'line' of defence and rehearsing all potential witnesses on their evidence to ensure that none of them contradicted it. The line agreed upon bore little relation to the actual situation. The official who headed the 'full-time defence team' had been in charge of the unit where the lapses had occurred; 'he knew where the skeletons were buried and was therefore best placed to ensure that they stayed there'. No blame was to attach, first, to ministers (though they had known perfectly well that financial controls in the agency were deficient); none to the Treasury ('it was quite against the rules for the accused to try and pass the buck to another department, least of all the most important department of all'); and none to the Home Office. Though all had been implicated, the blame was to be allocated to the agency during the period when Derek Lewis, the recently sacked director, was in charge, even though Lewis had sent the permanent secretary a memorandum two years earlier complaining about ineffective financial controls and poor year-end cash management – the focus of the NAO report.

The Queen as guardian of the constitution

The potential role of a reigning monarch and the use of her or his vestigial prerogative powers, as guardian of the constitution, is another of the mysteries concealed in the unravelled mix of conventions, precedents and procedures which makes up the constitutional background to British politics – and perhaps in the Cabinet Secretary's 'Precedent Book' (see **p. 304**). For some commentators, like Ferdinand

Mount, the Crown is not solely a symbol of national tradition, community and the state. For him, allegiance to the Crown, as owed by ministers, civil servants, the armed forces and others, constitutes a check on undemocratic or unconstitutional conduct in government and confers on the reigning monarch a 'fundamental role of guardianship' of the rule of law and the constitution itself (1992: 100). Mount's argument is not without precedent. In *The Hidden Wiring*, Peter Hennessy quotes Sir David Keir, author of *The Constitutional History of Modern Britain*, on the monarch's ultimate constitutional role:

> The [Queen's] prerogative, however circumscribed by conventions, must always retain its historic character as a residue of discretionary authority to be employed for the public good. It is the last resource provided by the Constitution to guarantee its own working.
>
> (Hennessy 1995: 27)

Hennessy himself assigns the 'reserve powers' of the Crown to the 'efficient' working side of the constitution rather than its 'dignified heritage museum' (ibid: 65). However, by definition, a monarch's intervention must be a 'last resort' solution. It is notice-able that throughout the constitutional traumas and the 'sleaze' and 'arms for Iraq' crises of the late 1980s and 1990s, there was (and properly so) no role for the Queen, who herself suffered a crisis of legitimacy.

What, then, does the monarch's 'last resort' role amount to? It seems to be agreed among constitutional writers that the monarchy has retained certain residual, and undefined, powers, and that such powers should be, and have been, exercised with tact and discretion. One of the reasons the hereditary monarchy has survived in Britain is that successive monarchs have nearly always taken care not to become involved in politics and to keep their own political views confidential. There is general agreement that a monarch's political role is confined to Bagehot's three rights: 'the right to be consulted, the right to encourage, the right to warn' a Prime Minister at regular audiences. There are, however, two principal residual powers that the Queen exercises with a limited degree of personal discretion: those of choosing a new Prime Minister in the case of resignation (often after an election), death or illness; and of granting a dissolution on request from the Prime Minister (which she is not in all circumstances bound to grant). In the exercise of a monarch's remaining powers, convention demands that the monarch should act on the advice of the Prime Minister, for refusal could precipitate a government's resignation and a constitutional crisis. In 1910, George V insisted that a general election be held on the Liberal proposal to remove the veto of the House of Lords before he would agree to create enough peers to pass the Parliament Bill through the Lords and the then premier, Henry Asquith, accepted his decision. During the 1912–14 Home Rule for Ireland crisis, opposition leaders urged George V to withhold the royal assent from the Government of Ireland Bill (on the grounds that the relationship between the Liberal government and the Irish Nationalist MPs was 'a corrupt Parliamentary bargain'). The king concluded that he should not adopt such an extreme course 'unless there is convincing evidence that it would avert a national disaster, or at least have a

Role of monarch

tranquillising effect on the distracting conditions of the time'. The same king played a positive role in 1931, actively encouraging the formation of the National government, led by Ramsay MacDonald with Conservative and Liberal support, after MacDonald's Labour cabinet had split and resigned over a financial crisis. The king was criticised for behaving unconstitutionally, but the criticisms do not seem to have been justified. George V's actions in 1931 seem to have been the last occasion on which a monarch has behaved in an overt political fashion, except perhaps in trivial matters (e.g. the present Queen's refusal to allow Tony Benn, as Paymaster General, to 'behead' UK postage stamps in 1965 (Bradley and Ewing 1993: Chapter 12; Nicolson 1952: Chapter 14; Bassett 1958; Marquand 1977: 629–643; Benn 1987: 218–300).

Precedent, then, is against the idea that a modern monarch might ever reject the advice of a Prime Minister on a major issue, or refuse to give royal assent to a bill which has passed through both Houses of Parliament. There are, however, precedents from Commonwealth practice of the Queen, or her representative, dismissing a Prime Minister on constitutional grounds (Ian Smith's declaration of independence in 1965; Gough Whitlam's refusal to hold an election to resolve a political deadlock over financial legislation in 1975). In the sense that both the Queen and a Prime Minister hold office subject to some ill-defined principles of constitutional conduct, it may be open to the Queen or a successor to dismiss a premier, or intervene to safeguard a highly significant constitutional principle. If a Prime Minister or cabinet seriously broke one of the customary rules or understandings between the parties and their leaders in Parliament, on which the political system largely depends, the Queen's use of her residual powers to intervene on constitutional grounds might seem to be justified. If a crisis developed which was not covered by those rules – as it could do, say, in the first phase of Parliaments elected under proportional representation – the Queen might be called upon to assist in resolving the impasse. On an entirely different line of hypotheses, the Prime Minister in a duly elected government might have to seek the monarch's aid to deal with the threat of mutiny from the armed forces.

In any of these cases, it is likely that the Queen would be advised by the 'golden triangle' of three officials – her own private secretary (whom she herself appoints), the Cabinet Secretary, and the Prime Minister's private secretary. The Prime Minister and other party leaders would no doubt be consulted. If there were time, other experienced officials and constitutional authorities, living and dead, would also be canvassed. We are assured by all the present Queen's biographers that she has a firm belief in consensus and would never act without the agreement of 'the sensible members of the body politic' (Pimlott 1996; Hennessy 1995: 48). It is not likely that their views have hardened into a constitutional convention, nor is it necessarily an easy task, let alone a democratic one, to determine who the 'sensible members' of the body politic might prove to be. The case for having a respected authority, with 'reserve powers' to resolve constitutional crises or deadlock and to uphold the principles of the constitution, hardly needs arguing. However, any such authority requires guidance from known principles of the constitution and these are missing in the UK. If the Cabinet Secretary's secret 'Precedent Book' contains information on the precedents and principles which have guided a monarch in the past, they ought to be published. The key decisions in a constitutional crisis ought not to be the province of three unelected, and largely unknown, men or women. If the Queen, under their guidance, really is a last-resort 'guardian' of the constitution and rule of law – and thus of British democracy and liberties – her subjects ought not to be the last to know.

AUDIT

Politicians and pundits commonly celebrate the 'fluidity surrounding the bundle of custom, precedent and procedure at the very heart of the Constitution' (Hennessy 1995: 33). In our view, this fluidity – and the secrecy which accompanies it – calls into question the ability of Britain's democratic arrangements to deliver open and accountable government. In Part 2, we have described an immensely powerful body of actors and institutions – the core executive – which operates a highly centralised political and bureaucratic system of government. This executive has at its disposal wide-ranging discretionary powers, through both statute and the royal prerogative. The use of these powers by ministers and officials is not governed by clear consti-tutional rules of conduct. Statutory powers are to a degree limited by the legislation, but tend nowadays to be very widely framed to give the executive a broad measure of discretion; prerogative powers, discretionary in their very nature and usually non-justiciable, are supposedly ruled by non-legal conventions. Thus, an untidy 'bundle' of statutory rules and non-legal precedents and conventions loosely governs a core executive with highly developed discretionary powers of decision and action. The non-legal rules of convention are in constant flux and change with political circum-stances, usually to suit the convenience of the executive. Some are a closely guarded secret. Procedure and its attendant conventions, all the constitution the 'poor Briton' has, are too much at the mercy of the core executive in our fluid system.

DAC11: Clear and transparent rules of conduct for government

The rules of conduct for ministers are framed by the Prime Minister and may be changed at his or her discretion (though now there are probably political limits to his or her ability to alter significant rules, such as those enjoining ministers to be open and honest in their dealings with Parliament and the people). The Cabinet Secretary advises the Prime Minister and ministers on how these rules should be interpreted, but the Prime Minister alone is responsible for enforcing them. The rules in respect of financial irregularities and clashes of interest have become highly developed and in the aftermath of the Hamilton, Smith and Aitken cases, are likely to be strictly enforced (**DAC10**). But the rules for ministers' conduct of government are hardly more than pious expressions of general principle. Thanks to the secrecy within which govern-ment works, these rules may be breached in minor or major ways to suit executive secrecy, and breaches can readily be covered up. The absence of internal checks and enforcement mechanisms is troubling, especially the deliberate refusal to countenance 'whistle-blowing' which can be an effective check in other polities (though the Public Interest Disclosure Act 1998 could now make 'whistle-blowing' more effective).

It is clear that, at least until the unravelling of the Aitken affair, the ethos of the gentlemen's club still influenced the way in which the rules of ministerial conduct were enforced. The *Guardian* newspaper, which had published the allegations against the guilty ministers, rightly complained about the 'dismal complacency' at the heart of a government which had already dealt feebly with a succession of revelations by various newspapers:

> As with Hamilton and Smith, the Aitken affair was treated as if it were a matter of footling consequence. It is painfully clear that Sir Robin Butler set about his inquiries into the *Guardian*'s initial allegations with all the ferocity of a spaniel. Once his case was closed, Jonathan moved on and up. Just as Tim Smith was promoted after admitting taking £25,000 from a company under investigation by the DTI, so Aitken was elevated to the cabinet.
>
> (21 June 1997)

Two journalists, commenting upon the Aitken affair in the *Sunday Telegraph*, wrote what is presumably the epitaph for the club ethic:

> In a system which works on trust, as British government still does, there is not much else that Butler could have done. Aitken's lies have destroyed that system. Who, in future, will be able to say of a minister, 'He has given me his word' and expect anyone to believe that settles the matter? Aitken has delivered poison to the civilised system in which civil servants trust ministers, and ministers are trusted by the public . . . . The destruction of government based on assuming people behave honestly will be Aitken's lasting legacy.
>
> (*Sunday Telegraph*, 22 June 1997)

The problem is, nothing very solid seems to have taken its place. The ministerial code has been strengthened under Blair, but its 'organically grown' and unplanned character remains inadequate, like the constitution at large.

It is no secret that the class of senior bureaucrats, Butler included, was wholly opposed to the proposal for a published code of practice for the civil service. But rising elite and public concern had to be assuaged. Thus, the code which has emerged is far less detailed than that which the managers' own union, the First Division Association, had drafted and it offers almost no advance on the status quo ante. It may well have given civil servants more confidence in their ability to maintain due impartiality, but the conflicts between their primary duty to ministers of the day and a still undefined idea of the public interest are not reconciled, or even admitted, in the code. These conflicts, as we have shown, reach to the very heights of the civil service.

Overall, what's required is a strategic overview to deal not only with the age-old weaknesses of Britain's governing arrangements, but also with current attempts to adapt those arrangements, as the Thatcher and Major regimes tried in their different ways, to a new age of responsive government and public–private interaction. In what will undoubtedly be another government under Blair determined both to keep a strong political impetus going, and to give a high priority to managing its image, the need to create a legal framework of accountability and openness around the core executive is overwhelming. We have largely dealt here with internal rules and procedures governing executive conduct. We now move on to examine the external political and legal checks upon the executive, beginning with the doctrine of ministerial responsibility to Parliament, collective and individual, the starting point for further discussion of the democratic accountability of the core executive.

PART 3

Checks and Balances

Introduction

We have described a very powerful, many-headed executive in Part 2. In chapter 11, we examined the internal rules governing the conduct of this executive, and the relationship between ministers and civil servants and their departments. We now go on to consider the major external mechanisms by which this executive is held to account. The body charged with the political responsibility for doing so is of course Parliament, and primarily the elected chamber, the House of Commons. Individually and collectively, ministers have a duty to account fully and frankly to Parliament for the policies, decisions and actions (and non-policies, non-decisions and non-actions) of their departments, executive agencies and other public bodies – as well as their own decisions and actions – under the doctrine of ministerial responsibility to Parliament. They therefore answer formally in Parliament for the actions and decisions of officials.

Government is becoming far more open with Parliament and the public. The voluntary Code of Practice on Access to Government Information, introduced in 1994 (Cabinet Office 1995–97), was a big step forward, in principle at least. The Labour government is introducing a statutory regime of openness. And as Lord Armstrong, the former head of the civil service, has pointed out:

> British government today makes public a torrent – a veritable Niagara – of information in one way or another: through statements and answers to questions in Parliament, speeches in parliamentary debates, written and oral evidence to parliamentary select committees, government replies to reports of such committees, Command papers presented to Parliament – White Papers, Green Papers, Blue Books, annual estimates, reports and accounts of government departments, quangos and other public boards and bodies, and so on.
>
> (Armstrong 1995: 55)

Under the Code of Practice on Access to Government Information, however, government ministers were authorised to withhold substantial amounts of official information from Parliament and the public – and naturally among the information they tended to withhold was that which could hurt or embarrass them. The 1996 Scott Report on the export of defence equipment to Iraq showed conclusively that the government was deficient in its duty of openness in various ways, including answers to Parliamentary Questions, letters to MPs and their constituents, ministerial statements in the House and evidence to select committees (Tomkins 1996: 478–483). Ministers had not only failed in their duty of frankness, they had deliberately misled the House, individual MPs and their constituents over a period of time. On other occasions, such as the Westland affair, ministers and officials are also known to have misled the Commons and frustrated its inquiries (**pp. 317–318**). Part 3 explores how far this situation may have changed and may change further under the new Labour government.

Openness is only part of the duty ministers take on under the doctrine of ministerial responsibility. Ministers are constitutionally bound to respond to failures or misconduct by putting things right, and if they are personally to blame for a serious failure or are guilty themselves of misconduct, they may be required to resign. However, the provision of information is the means by which government is best held to account. As the Treasury and Civil Service Select Committee (TCSC) argued in 1994, effective accountability depends on 'two vital elements': 'clarity about who can be held to account and held responsible when things go wrong: confidence that Parliament is able to gain the accurate information required to hold the Executive to account and to ascertain where responsibility lies' (TCSC 1994: vol. I, para. 132).

There is of course a third element – the power, ability and willingness of the House of Commons actually to hold the executive to account. As we have shown, the executive generally dominates the Commons through its control of the majority party in the House. For the most part, party political loyalty and the self-interest of individual members of the majority party ensure that the government and ministers will escape censure or demands for resignations. This is, however, more than simply a question of the survival of a government or ministers. The whole state is made politically accountable through the doctrine of collective and individual responsibility to Parliament; and if this crucial mechanism is deficient, then the goal of accountability for the executive as a whole is frustrated.

In Part 3, we first consider the efficacy of the doctrine of collective and individual responsibility to Parliament and the rules of openness which underwrite it (Chapter 12). Chapters 13 and 14 on the House of Commons are interlinked: Chapter 13 analyses the adversarial ethos of the House of Commons, the influence of party on its operations and the role of the opposition as the prime agent of scrutiny; Chapter 14 assesses the overall role of the Commons in holding the executive to account and obtaining information, and focuses in particular on select committees, which were specifically introduced to redress the balance between the executive and Parliament in 1979. Parliament is also charged with the scrutiny and amendment of legislation – nowadays almost wholly the government's legislation. The first Democratic Audit volume, *The Three Pillars of Liberty*, dealt fully with Parliament's inability to fulfil these responsibilities under the pressure of government business and in the adversarial circumstances of Parliament (Klug *et al.* 1996: Chapters 3 and 5). In Chapter 14, we briefly summarise and update this previous coverage. We also consider the contribution of the House of Lords and examine the role of two parliamentary offices – the Ombudsman service and National Audit Office.

Finally, we also audit the ability of the judiciary to ensure that the executive obeys the rule of law (Chapter 15). Judicial review is the principal channel through which the actions and policies of the executive may be challenged in the courts and since the late 1970s, the readiness of the courts to sit in judgement on the actions of ministers and government departments – and to find against them – has given the judiciary a reputation for legal, and even political, activism. The huge surge in cases of judicial review has added to this reputation. Judicial review is the closest that the law in Britain comes to having a specialised and exclusive process for handling litigation against the executive and public bodies on the grounds that they have exceeded or abused their legal powers – or propose to. Chapter 15 seeks to place the process of judicial review in perspective; to consider how far it is compatible with democracy for unelected judges to be in a position to control ministers in an elected government and public bodies under their control; and how effectively the judiciary acts in practice to check the executive and subject it to the rule of law.

12   Giving Account to Parliament

How ministerial responsibility works in practice

The success of a democracy is to be judged to the extent to which it can assure that Government is publicly accountable.
(John Griffith and Michael Ryle on parliamentary practice, 1989)

The secrecy culture of Whitehall is essentially a product of British parliamentary democracy. Economy with the truth is the essence of a professional reply to a parliamentary question.
(Sir Patrick Nairne, former permanent secretary, 1987)

The doctrine of ministerial responsibility – both collective and individual – is supposed to be the democratic 'buckle' between the executive and Parliament and the people. As we have seen, ministers from the Prime Minister down are said to be answerable in the House of Commons for practically all government activity from a decision to order the sinking of an enemy battleship or flying a ragged Union Jack upside-down in Whitehall on Remembrance Day to a health authority's policy on AIDS treatments or young people's training programmes provided by a publicly funded private company. Yet the idea that the doctrine of ministerial responsibility to Parliament is a *democratic* check on the executive belongs in the shadowy and uncertain world of constitutional convention. It may be developing in that direction, but it is far from being fully developed.

Over the past few years, the doctrine has been the subject of intense political and semantic debate, interpretation and re-interpretation, and subtle re-definitions of its terminology and terms, all sharpened up to May 1997 by political crises such as the Westland affair, the 'arms to Iraq' controversy and the Scott Report on arms sales to Iraq, the handling of the BSE saga and Gulf War Syndrome, rows between a Home Secretary and the head of the prison service over responsibility for prisons, and continuing concern over 'sleaze'. At its worst, the debate recalls the notorious medieval dispute over how many angels could dance on the head of a pin; at its best, it has reflected a new resolve in the House of Commons – and in two select committees in particular – to reduce the executive's domination of Parliament and to bring clarity to the principal means by which government is meant to be held accountable by MPs.

How far ministerial responsibility has grown into a fully-fledged democratic check upon government is the question this chapter addresses. We employ the following Democratic Audit criteria for this and the next two chapters:

DAC7. How accessible to the public is information about what the government does, and about the effects of its policies, and how independent is it of the government's own information machine?

DAC8. How effective and open to scrutiny is the control exercised by elected politicians over non-elected executive personnel, both civilian and military?

DAC9. How extensive are the powers of Parliament to oversee legislation and public expenditure, to scrutinise the executive and hold it accountable, and to secure redress when necessary; and how effectively are they exercised in practice?

DAC15. How systematic and open to public scrutiny are the procedures for government consultation of public opinion and of relevant interests in the formation and implementation of policy and legislation?

Between them, these criteria enable us to construct a democratic version of what ministerial responsibility to Parliament should consist of and requires to be effective. First, ministers should be under a duty to give account in Parliament – and so to the wider public – for their own and their departments' policies, actions and decisions (**DAC7**). They should do so, as far as practicable, in time for parliamentary and public opinion to influence at least the most significant policies and decisions, and should be under an equal duty to take note and act on the response (**DAC15**). They should be open with Parliament and the public about the government's or their own failures, mistakes and misconduct (**DAC7**), and be ready to amend policies, rectify mistakes, root out misconduct and provide remedies or redress where necessary (**DAC9**). The process must also allow for sanctions to be imposed. The major and broadest sanction is that which the voters exercise at elections; more immediate sanctions include the resignation of a government, a minister's resignation or apology, or disciplinary action against civil servants. For these sanctions to be effective, three elements of control are required:

- full and accurate information for MPs and the public about government policies, actions and decisions (**DAC7**);
- clarity about who can be held to account and held responsible when things go wrong (**DAC7** and **DAC8**). (In this country, this means above all distinguishing between the responsibility of ministers and bureaucrats.); and
- the power, ability and willingness of the House of Commons to gain the information required to hold the executive to account, to ascertain where responsibility lies, and actually to hold it to account.

The rise of the ministerial state

As we have seen, the UK lacks both a written constitution and a codified system of public law, two features which give shape and order to the state in most liberal democracies. In an illuminating essay, the political historian Alan Beattie describes how the doctrine of ministerial responsibility was invented in the pre-democratic

The ministerial state

Victorian era to overcome this absence and developed as a unifying and co-ordinating process while British government expanded from 1870 to 1920 (Beattie 1995: 158–178). As the House of Commons became dominant in Parliament, the merito-cratic civil service was established and the two-party system grew to give direction and coherence to British politics, the doctrine of ministerial responsibility developed to found government unity on a ministerial and parliamentary monopoly of policy-making (see also the Haldane Report 1918).

It was here that the idea that politics, or 'policy', could be distinguished from 'administration' was born, and the goal of insulating the new professional civil service from political pressures, except those of ministers, was established. For example, Walter Bagehot described the role of ministers in 1867 – the year in which Disraeli's Reform Act expanded the suffrage – both as bringing 'outside sense and outside animation' into the 'inside' worlds of Whitehall departments and preventing 'the incessant tyranny of Parliament over the public offices'. Through the device of minis-terial responsibility, ministers stood between their departments and officials and 'the busy-bodies and the crotchet-makers of the House and the country' (Bagehot 1867: 193). In this sense, it developed as an anti-democratic device. Further, the notion of collective responsibility, necessary earlier to achieve stable government in a less than stable House, demanded that government ministers and policies had to be judged as a whole and policy-making presented as a unified and consistent process (Cranston 1985: 269–272). It was therefore held necessary to keep secret all the traffic between ministers, and between ministers and civil servants.

The doctrine of ministerial responsibility developed, then, within the historic canons of 'strong government' and the need for secrecy. It was very much designed to protect the state, to strengthen the two-party system and to shore up Britain's flexible governing arrangements. Beattie, however, distinguishes two strands of the idea of ministerial responsibility – a more representative 'Whig' theory which, though shot through with the 'guardianship' ethic (see Chapter 2), stressed the need for political control to be paramount and for government to be held responsible for state actions; and the 'Peelite' theory which saw the doctrine as a means of limiting democratic control to ensure that the business of government could be carried forward undisturbed and the stability of the state safeguarded (Beattie 1995: 166–176). In practice, the two views have combined to elevate the role of ministers and justify the unlimited notion of parliamentary sovereignty. The Whig tradition tends to be paraded as the acceptable face of ministerial responsibility, but the Peelite view has formed a strong undercurrent in governing attitudes in at least the two larger parties to this day. It was Jim Callaghan, a Labour Prime Minister, for example, who ruled that the existence of cabinet committees should remain a closely-guarded secret on 'the underlying principle that the method adopted by Ministers for discus-sion among themselves of questions of policy is essentially a domestic matter, and is of no concern of Parliament or the public' (Hennessy 1995: 104).

The doctrine of ministerial responsibility thus remains very much the creature of its origins. From the beginning, the doctrine's more representative aspirations have been undermined by the influence of the prevailing culture of strong and secretive government on those who have shaped its actual workings – the political elite and higher echelons of the civil service. Its practical and unifying aspirations have been frustrated by the loosely federal and pluralistic nature of a vastly expanded state which a handful of individual ministers cannot realistically hope to control. From a parliamentary perspective, the executive's dominance over both Houses has prejudiced Parliament's ability to develop the doctrine as an effective instrument of scrutiny and control. This is the historic perspective within which we analyse its efficacy as the central guarantor of open and accountable government in the UK.

Ministerial responsibility has evolved since Bagehot's day through political crises, ministerial statements, internal Whitehall memoranda, unwritten, uncoded and unpublished conventions, to emerge blinking in the 1990s into the light of intense and unprecedented parliamentary scrutiny, most recently by a select committee – the Public Service Committee (PSC), consisting only of Tory and Labour MPs – following the Scott Report and the dismissal of Derek Lewis, former director-general of the Prison Service. Its modern history perhaps began in 1954 when Thomas Dugdale, an agriculture minister, announced that he was resigning over the misconduct of officials in the department – a statement that maintained the myth that ministers took personal responsibility for the serious mistakes of their officials. Dugdale actually resigned for the age-old reason that he had lost the confidence of his colleagues and Conservative backbench MPs. But the affair perpetuated the expectation that ministers would take personal responsibility for the serious mistakes of officials by resigning. Thereafter, however, ministers continued to cling to office until they knew 'the political game' was up and enough backbench colleagues (and fellow ministers) had effectively withdrawn support. The Home Secretary at that time, Sir David Maxwell-Fyfe, sought to define the circumstances in which ministers ought to resign. But his statement to the House failed to clarify the obligations upon ministers to resign (Woodhouse 1997: 268). In hindsight, the statement is actually more significant for the emphasis it gives to ministers' duties to 'defend and protect' officials (against, though unsaid, Bagehot's bogey, 'the incessant tyranny of Parliament'?); and for defining 'responsibility' in blame-free terms in much the same way as Sir Robin Butler was to 40 years later: 'According to the well-established constitutional convention, ministers are responsible to Parliament for all the actions of their departments. But that does not mean they take the consequences and resign if things go wrong' (HC Deb, 20 July 1954, c1285–1287). Here, 'responsibility' simply means to report and explain to Parliament.

Harrying ministers to resign has become part of the stuff of adversarial politics, and has contributed to a damaging culture of blame in Westminster. Ministers and officials have become defensive and secretive in response, and have over time narrowed the scope of the doctrine in order to diminish their culpability. But a 'more realistic' version than the Dugdale myth, based on the age-old division between 'policy' and 'administration', has long existed. Broadly, this version holds that ministers can only be expected to take the blame for 'policy', and not 'administrative', failures. Inevitably, this interpretation results in a blurring of responsibilities between ministers and officials since in practice the making of 'policy' and its implementation ('administration') are two interdependent parts of the same process. According to Diana Woodhouse, an authority on the doctrine of ministerial responsibility, this version has also developed in recent years so that the idea that a minister is responsible for the overall conduct of his or her department, and may be negligent in its 'administration', disappears (1997: 269).

A parallel process distinguishing between 'responsibility' and 'accountability' has also taken place. This re-definition holds that ministers are *accountable* for the policies and actions of their departments, but are not *responsible* – in the sense of being blameworthy – for actions which (to paraphrase Sir Robin Butler) 'occur as a foreseeable result of their own actions or instructions, or which they could reasonably be expected to have known about or discovered in time to have amended them' (Norton-Taylor 1995: 77–80). The Public Service Committee (PSC) sensibly commented that such distinctions were not always useful and concluded:

> It is not possible absolutely to distinguish an area in which a Minister is personally responsible and liable to take the blame, from one where he is constitutionally accountable. Ministerial responsibility is not composed of two elements, with a clear break between the two.
>
> (PSC 1996c: vol. I, para. 21)

In fact, no ministers in this century have resigned solely over their officials' mistakes or misconduct. But meanwhile the politics of blame have obscured other significant issues and soured officials' attitudes towards MPs (who seem to them to be always seeking scalps). Of course, any system of accountability requires sanctions, such as a minister's resignation, in the case of serious misconduct or failure, if only *pour encourager les autres*. And those sanctions must bite. Further, if the public are to be able to judge a government's record properly at elections, they must have accurate and full information on its mistakes and cases of misconduct as well as its successes; and if Parliament is to have any power to persuade or oblige government to rectify mistakes or root out misconduct, it first needs the powers to investigate them and their causes effectively. Equally, it is in the nature of governments and ministers to adopt practices that protect them from damaging disclosure of mistakes in general, and to do their utmost to conceal particular mistakes or misconduct. Thus, MPs on the PSC recognised, 'Proper and rigorous scrutiny and accountability may be more important to Parliament's ability to correct error than forcing resignations' (PSC 1996c: vol. I, para. 26).

Yet the emphasis given in conventional official and political debates on accountability to Parliament to a retrospective seeking out of blame and the fixation on resignation – or even 'proper and rigorous scrutiny' – is deficient. For example, in 1994, the Treasury and Civil Service Select Committee identified 'two vital elements' for making government and ministers accountable: clarity about who should be held to account when mistakes or misconduct occurs and accurate information to ascertain where responsibility lies. This is a far narrower focus than that of the Democratic Audit (see **p. 337**). Sir Richard Scott, who conducted the official inquiry into the sale of defence-related equipment to Iraq, also focused on 'responsibility or blame', but did also recognise the importance of ministers' duty to give account for the benefit of the public:

Without the provision of full information, it is not possible for Parliament, or for that matter the public, to assess what consequences, in the form of *attribution of responsibility or blame* [our emphasis], ought to follow. A denial of information to the public denies the public the ability to make an informed judgment on the Government's record. A failure by Ministers to meet the obligations of Ministerial accountability by providing information about the activities of their departments undermines, in my opinion, the democratic process.

(Scott 1996: para. K8.2–4)

The tendency after the report's findings of fault were published was naturally to concentrate upon the refusals of ministers who had misled Parliament or made personal blunders to accept blame and resign and the government's closing of ranks around them (and, to a lesser degree, upon the fate of civil servants guilty of misconduct – who also went 'unpunished').

As we have said, it is important for there to be effective sanctions when ministers and officials are guilty of misconduct. But it is equally important to remember why it mattered in the arms for Iraq affair – for ministers had misled Parliament and the public to prevent public debate on the government's policy on arms sales to Iraq. Lord Howe was quite open about this in his evidence to Scott. In September 1988 Howe, then Foreign Secretary, wished to relax the guidelines on arms sales to Iraq, but feared that to do so openly would provoke outrage in Parliament and the public over Saddam Hussein's oppression of his Kurdish subjects, and especially the gassing of some 5,000 men, women and children in an air raid on Halabja. One of his officials noted that it 'could look very cynical if, so soon after expressing outrage about the treatment of the Kurds, we adopt a more flexible approach to arms sales'. So the policy change took place in secret. Howe informed Scott that relaxing the policy – necessary to enhance Britain's commercial interests – could not be explained to the public because of 'the emotional way in which such debates are conducted in public' (Norton-Taylor 1995: 60–61). Scott suggested that he was taking a 'sort of 'Government-knows-best' approach':

HOWE: It is partly that. But it is partly, if we were to lay specifically our thought processes before you, they are laid before a world-wide range of uncomprehending or malicious commentators. This is the point. You cannot choose a well-balanced presentation to an elite parliamentary audience.

SCOTT: You can, can you not, expose your hand to people of this country?

HOWE: There are reasons for caution. Justice is exposed to emotional misunderstandings in this country.

Howe added that, 'there is nothing necessarily open to criticism in incompatibility between policy and public presentation of policy. . . . It [the government] is not necessarily to be criticised for difference between policy and public presentation of policy' (Scott 1996: para. D4.52).

Civil service evidence

For the Democratic Audit, openness and accountability ought to be part of the continuing fabric of public life and should contribute more to democracy through informed debate and public participation in policy-making than simply establishing blame when something goes wrong. Our version of accountability (see above) therefore contains an element which is missing from existing ideas of ministerial accountability and the culture of retrospective blame. In our view, ministers in a democracy should be under a duty to give an ongoing account of policies and decisions as they evolve and to take note of the responses of MPs, interested parties and the public. Howe's view runs entirely counter to this argument. He and his officials decided deliberately to exclude MPs and the public from their debates over the policy to be adopted towards Iraq. But it is typical of the political establishment of the ministers and senior civil servants who are supposed to observe a duty of frankness. His attitude, for example, is reflected in the oral evidence to Scott of Sir Robin Butler, who has been, as Cabinet Secretary, the adviser on ministerial duties to several cabinets. Butler's written evidence had reiterated the traditional formula that ministers should give as full information to Parliament as is possible. But how did he define what is possible?

> SCOTT: In your experience of government – and you have had a very great deal – do you think there is anything in the proposition that the convenience of secrecy . . . about what the Government is doing, because it allows government to proceed more smoothly without the focus of attack that might otherwise be levelled, does in practice inhibit the giving of information about what [the] Government is doing?
>
> BUTLER: You can call that a matter of convenience, if you like. I would call it a matter of being in the interests of good government.
>
> (*Ibid.*: 91)

In other words, a manipulative secrecy is the norm, at least at times when the government or ministers are in danger of being embarrassed or running into a crisis; as Butler also said, 'You have to be selective about the facts'.

The rules governing civil service evidence to Parliament

The obverse side of the doctrine that ministers are answerable to Parliament is that civil servants are not. Officials give evidence and make information available 'on behalf of their Ministers and under their directions', as the official rules (originally known as the 'Osmotherly rules' after the civil servant who first drafted them) for civil servants giving evidence to select committees state, and by the same principle, 'it is customary for Ministers to decide which official or officials should represent them' (Cabinet Office 1997). The Osmotherly rules are the standing instructions to officials appearing before select committees, and may be supplemented by specific ministerial instructions. They have never been endorsed by Parliament and have no parliamentary status whatever. In short, they remain a document for which the government has sole responsibility.

The rules broadly prohibit officials from revealing any politically sensitive or embarrassing information; offering their own views on issues of political controversy; or becoming involved in what amount to disciplinary investigations. They are bound to present government policy on behalf of their ministers and departments, and not to undermine it; as the rules say:

> officials should as far as possible confine their evidence to questions of fact and explanation relating to government policies and actions. They should be ready to explain what those policies are; the justification and objectives of those policies *as the Government sees them* [our emphasis]. . . . Officials should as far as possible avoid being drawn into discussion of the merits or alternative policies where this is politically contentious.
>
> (Cabinet Office 1997: para. 48)

Government specialists, such as economists or statisticians, are warned not to 'describe or comment on the advice which they have given to Departments, or would give if asked. They should not therefore go beyond explaining the reasoning which, in the Government's judgment, supports its policy' (*ibid.*: para. 49). In both cases, officials are advised that if they are pressed for their own views or a professional judgement, they must refer questioners to ministers.

These central principles are buttressed by detailed advice on what and how information may be provided, largely through memoranda, written replies to questions, and oral evidence, and not by giving access to internal files and correspondence; on how to handle questions which may be *sub judice*; on the confidential nature of disciplinary and employment matters; and so on. The prevailing tone is defensive. For example, officials are advised that if they become aware that one of their department's quangos or other related bodies has been asked to give evidence, 'they should consider whether it would be helpful to discuss the lines of evidence with the witnesses before the hearing' (*ibid.*: para. 88). The rules are designed to prevent any critical review of government policies, as part of the ring-fencing of 'policy' (an issue to which we return). They are also used by ministers to stop officials from giving factual evidence on what ministers have told select committees and the involvement of officials in political activities, as in the Westland affair, and to prevent named or retired officials from giving evidence (see Chapter 14). However, civil servants have also in practice been more relaxed about giving information than the restrictive rules imply, and policy issues in particular can be more widely discussed in front of select committees. Civil servants have become more visible and better known. And in 1981 the then government undertook that ministers would be prepared to attend a select committee if civil servants were unable to answer questions under the Osmotherly rules or a minister's express instructions (PSC 1996c: para. 128).

The same rules state that while select committee powers to send for papers are 'unqualified', they are nevertheless qualified in practice by 'certain long-standing conventions on the provision of information which have been observed by successive administrations on grounds of public policy' (*ibid.*: para. 60). Thus, the government's commitment to provide as much information as possible to select committees is largely met, at the discretion of ministers, through oral evidence, memoranda and written replies to committee questions: 'it does not amount to a commitment to provide access to internal files, private correspondence, including advice given on a confidential basis, or working papers' (*ibid.*: para. 49).

In 1978, the path-breaking 1978 Procedure Committee report which led to the establishment of departmental select committees recommended that they should be given the power, which formerly belonged to any backbench MP, immediately to 'move for an Address or an Order for a Return of Papers' (1978: para. 7.18) – in other words, to seek parliamentary approval for an order for government to produce documents which ministers refused to hand over. It was no surprise when the government made sure that this proposal was rejected in the debate establishing the committees (HC Deb, 25 June 1979, c245–246). In 1981, the government did agree that it would seek to provide time for the Commons to express a view 'where there is evidence of widespread general concern in the House regarding an alleged Ministerial refusal to divulge information to a Select Committee' (HC Deb, 16 January 1981, c1312).

In principle, of course, the rules contradict the central constitutional idea of parliamentary sovereignty. As the Procedure Committee, which first obtained and published the then secret rules in 1978, commented at the time: 'it would be objectionable if [they] sought to imply any restrictions on the rights of Committees to send for persons, papers and records, other than those restrictions imposed by the House or by Law of Parliament' (1978: vol. I, para. 7.13).

In 1990, a Procedure Committee review of the workings of select committees returned to the issue after several other committees had also expressed their objections:

> the only areas in which restrictions on the giving of information by officials can be justified, apart from security matters, or issues of great diplomatic or commercial sensitivity, are the contents of advice to Ministers and the need to preserve collective responsibility. Even the latter should be interpreted as liberally as possible. We doubt whether the fabric of constitutional government would suffer fatal injury if witnesses were more forthcoming about the level at which decisions are taken and the extent of the involvement of different departments.
>
> (TCSC 1990a: vol. I, para. 159)

But MPs and their committees have never dared to assert parliamentary sovereignty or to seek a review of the rules. This is simply because government's *de facto* control of the House means that any government could draft new guidelines, which 'whilst superficially less restrictive, would then be applied rigorously and to the letter' (*ibid.*: para. 157). In 1996, the PSC noted that the recent civil service code contained only passing reference to civil servants' obligations to Parliament and proposed that they should be under the same obligations as ministers themselves – a proposal which the government and Labour opposition front benches both rejected. Thus the rules remained in place even though, as Diana Woodhouse commented in her evidence to the PSC, the limitations they impose, 'are beyond those necessary for the maintenance of good government and are inconsistent with the Government's stated aim of greater openness and with the constitutional requirement of accountability' (PSC 1996: vol. I, para. 80).

However, the rules simply provide guidance to officials within the existing principle that civil servants are not directly responsible to the House. The principle itself provides a greater obstruction to the accountability of the executive. The main difficulty arises where ministers decline to accept accountability for certain actions of their civil servants. As the TCSC put it, 'If Crichel Down is dead and Ministers are not accountable to Parliament for some actions of their officials, then who is? Not to put too fine a point on it, who ought to resign or to be penalised if mistakes are made? If it is not Ministers, it can only be officials' (TCSC 1986: vol. I, para. 3.17). Moreover, the principle does not reflect the role of the modern civil servant. Originally, it was justified on the grounds that ministers were responsible for 'policy' (or politics) and so rightly open to political criticism; while civil servants were concerned only with giving advice and then carrying out policies, or 'administration' (a supposedly non-political activity), and so should be protected from political pressures or attack. But the senior civil service is now intimately involved in formulating and advising ministers on policy. As the former head of the civil service, Sir Douglas Wass, has observed, 'in the real world ministers and civil servants are inextricably mixed up with each other' (Wass 1984: 46). Recently, for example, an outstanding study found that 'ministers and officials devised the poll tax together', and the tax policy was, in this respect, 'typical of first-order policy departures in the mid and late 1980s'. They commented that 'The divide between "advising" and "deciding" is always blurred: in the case of the poll tax it is more than usually difficult to disentangle the two, because they took place so closely in tandem' (Butler *et al.* 1994: 214–215).

Civil servants now advise on the politics and public presentation of policies and undertake extensive negotiations with outside interests. Such negotiations were not allowed for in the original formula, but now they tend to be kept under the same mantle of confidentiality on the grounds that the officials involved are acting directly in place of the minister. This is formally true, but in practice officials do not, and cannot, act as political eunuchs, and they often take political initiatives.

The distinction between policy and administration, however, remains at the core of the continuing arrangement, even though it does not allow for the fact that the senior civil service is as much a part of government as ministers who sit around the cabinet table (Chapter 7). Paradoxically, this close relationship has become an additional reason in official arguments against making civil servants directly responsible or accountable to Parliament. If their policy views or advice are thus made known, it is argued, they will be identified as 'political' actors and their non-political status will be prejudiced. All this of course is formulated within the convention that the civil service is not partisan in the party political sense, and is equally willing to serve governments of any party. Reassuring though the non-party political nature of the civil service may be, civil servants do serve governments in a strongly politicised spirit; and the practical effect of the doctrine of ministerial responsibility, as it currently works, is to protect both ministers and civil servants from effective scrutiny in Parliament for what is in effect their joint policy-making. Between them, ministers and officials thus generally avoid censure or dismissal for serious mistakes or miscon-duct; and while ministers are ultimately accountable for the activities of the central state, it is far more difficult to make either responsible for policy mistakes. In brief, the doctrine generally serves as a mutual defence pact for ministers and senior civil servants alike, though as we shall see, ministers and civil servants can on occasion disagree over where responsibility lies.

Ministerial responsibility in action today

The formal responsibilities of ministers, as set out by government, remain fairly widely drawn. In 1995, as Woodhouse points out, the government's own white paper on the civil service, *Taking Forward Continuity and Change* (Cabinet Office 1995), held ministers responsible for:

- 'the policies of the Department';
- 'the framework through which these policies are delivered';
- 'the resources allocated';
- 'such implementation decisions as any agency framework document may require to be referred or agreed with the Minister'; and
- 'responding to major failures or expressions of Parliamentary or public concern'.

But as we have seen their actual realm of responsibility has been shrinking, through the 'policy–administration' divide and the shift from 'responsibility' to blame-free versions of accountability. And Woodhouse identifies omissions from the govern-ment's list, notably the idea of 'cumulative fault or mismanagement' (when a series of mistakes occurs within an area of responsibility); poor organisation which prevents a minister from knowing about matters he or she should have known about; minis-terial interventions in an agency's operations which are not provided for in the framework document; and decisions not to intervene when an issue is brought to a minister's attention (1997: 277–278).

It is at once obvious, too, that the creation of executive agencies (see Chapter 8) makes concerns about the slippery division between 'policy' and 'administration' more acute. By 1997, some 145 executive agencies and two departments operating as agencies were active on a semi-autonomous basis within government. Between them, they employed three-quarters of the home civil service and over 30,000 members of the armed forces. As they legally remain part of their original depart-ments, they are subject to control by ministers and civil servants in Whitehall within the realm of ministerial responsibility. Agencies are often substantial and politically sensitive bodies. The Prison Service, for example, is not a mere off-shoot of the Home Office; of 53,000 Home Office staff, 40,000 work in the Prison Service and others are in effect uncounted support staff (see Landers, forthcoming book). The need to ensure that such large, complex and powerful agencies are made open and accountable is correspondingly large – and obvious. But smaller agencies, like the Medicines Control Agency, perform vital functions and their operations also need to be made properly open and accountable.

The doctrine of ministerial responsibility is a slippery concept anyway. It becomes more slippery still in the case of agencies, as Michael Howard's regime at the Home Office and his dealings with Derek Lewis, the sacked prisons head illustrated (see below). An official review in 1995 found that agency status clarified the roles and functions of chief executives, agency and departmental officials and thus 'facilitated accountability'. But how far? The roles of agencies are not defined in statute nor by legal contracts. Though the roles and responsibilities of ministers and agency chief executives are defined in framework agreements, the chief executive's contract, and the like, and are therefore relatively transparent, they still rest almost wholly on the imprecise division between policy and administration which bedevils other attempts to establish exactly where responsibility lies as between ministers and officials.

As Derek Lewis, former director-general of the Prison Service, explained to a select committee, 'there is difficulty in defining precisely who takes what decisions or when the Secretary of State should be involved – in popular terms, what is "policy" and what is "operations"' (PSC 1996c: vol. III, Q637). In case Lewis appears too partial a witness, Sir John Woodcock, who held the official inquiry into escapes from Whitemoor prison in 1993, identified 'the difficulty of determining what is an operational matter and what is a policy, leading to a confusion as to where responsibility lies' (Woodcock 1994: para. 9.29). Moreover, ministers set the parameters of resources within which agencies are obliged to work, and reserve the right to intervene as they see fit, even in minute detail. Lewis told the Public Service Committee that he was surprised by 'the quantity of briefing and the level of detail in which ministers became involved', often intervening in operational decisions. The Learmont inquiry into further escapes in 1995 found that the Prison Service HQ submitted over 1,000 documents to Home Office ministers and officials, including 137 'full submissions', in just four months. Learmont recommended a review to give the agency 'the greater operational independence' its status was meant to confer (PSC 1996c: vol. I, paras. 98–99).

Obviously the Prison Service is a special case, since it is the site of intense political interest. Additionally, the Home Office bureaucracy, just as much as Howard, was reluctant to let it go. But while the 'distancing' of ministers from detail was a major objective in the Next Steps process which established agencies, ministers have also asserted a general right to interfere, justified by the doctrine of ministerial responsibility. For example, Roger Freeman, the minister responsible for the public service, argued that ministers need to retain 'the right – indeed, the responsibility – of Ministers to inquire, nay to intervene, in the activities of any agency so as to discharge their responsibility to Parliament', even if this means interfering in areas for which a chief executive is responsible (HC Deb, 12 February 1996, c680–681). The combination of 'distancing' and intervention is a recipe for confusion over the location of responsibility which gives adroit ministers room enough for manoeuvre. This room is, however, greatly expanded by ministers' refusal to countenance the idea that agency chief executives should account to select committees on their own behalf. The government has refused to free them from the constraints of the Osmotherly rules which explicitly insist that chief executives giving evidence do so 'on behalf of the Minister to whom they are accountable and are subject to that Minister's instructions' (PSC 1996c: vol. I, para. 43). Thus, while chief executives can be publicly interrogated on an agency's failures, mistakes or maladministration, they cannot in reply question government policy or reveal its defects, or raise issues of under-resourcing, or discuss how a minister's intervention or changes in policy might have affected the agency's performance. In practice, many agency chief executives already give evidence to select committees far more freely than the rules allow, and with only the most formal involvement of ministers (PSC 1996c: vol. I, para. 110). But whenever ministers' own interests demand it, they can always bring down the Osmotherly curtain.

The conflict between Michael Howard and Derek Lewis over responsibility for operational and managerial errors within the Prison Service identified by the Learmont Report illustrate the confusion and inconsistencies that now arise. For the last government, Roger Freeman said in the Commons debate on ministerial responsibility that there were occasions when a minister's interference might make a failure in the operations of an agency his or her responsibility rather than the chief executive's. Indeed, a minister might be obliged to resign because of such failures (HC Deb, 12 February 1996, c681). However, ministers are not formally held to be responsible for their interventions in the operations of agencies, nor for failures to intervene when issues are brought to their attention (see **p. 346**). And as Diana Woodhouse has pointed out, without a clear record of instances of ministerial interference, the point at which responsibility changes hands is unclear. Howard held Lewis responsible for the errors found by Learmont. Lewis argued that Howard had intervened so regularly and directly in the running of the agency that he shared responsibility for the errors. But more broadly, as Woodhouse points out, even in areas where the government has said ministers are to be held responsible, Howard:

> failed to take responsibility for policy, the framework document under which the Prison Service operated, and the performance indicators to which it worked. Yet these had also been criticised by the report, thereby indicating 'some degree of responsibility' for security problems.
>
> (1997: 270, 278)

Howard used his considerable ministerial powers to dismiss Lewis (unlawfully breaking Lewis's contract; had Lewis been a career civil servant, then his dismissal would have been lawful use of Howard's prerogative powers). Howard also managed to distance himself from responsibility before the Commons, thanks in part to the loyalty of colleagues and backbench Tory MPs, and in part too to his skilful manipulation of the *actualité* in the debate on the affair (HC Deb, 19 May 1997, c398–408; c461–467).

The idea that ministers, most of them elected, should take responsibility in public for what their government does – or equally does *not* do – to an assembly of elected representatives of the people is basic to representative democracy itself. In practice, individual responsibility does have some bite in so far as it relates to a minister's personal conduct, though more often in his or her personal life than in the minister's government role. But more generally ministers are not in practice held responsible for the failures of their own or departmental policies, nor for other areas of govern-ment and departmental work where they are formally responsible. The doctrine which is supposed to be at the heart of representative democracy in Britain was framed initially both to centralise power in the hands of the cabinet and ministers and to protect the executive from parliamentary scrutiny and attack. It largely accom-plishes those aims today.

As we have shown, the doctrine offers ministers a wide measure of flexibility: 'they can avoid culpability by nominating areas over which they have temporarily or vaguely relinquished authorial responsibility; but they are free to intervene in those areas, when necessary, by invoking their ultimate responsibility' (Beattie 1995: 174). Various Conservative ministers demonstrated that it is possible to set policy frame-works which lead to operational failure (Michael Howard), mislead the House (William Waldegrave, on arms to Iraq) or personally to commit serious blunders (Sir Nicholas Lyell, Attorney-General, over the preparations for the Matrix Churchill trial) without being forced to resign, if the Prime Minister and colleagues are prepared to back them. For a Prime Minister, indeed, it is often necessary actively to avoid resignations in order to maintain the stability of his or her government, especially if the question of collective responsibility arises, as it did after the Scott Report.

The collective aspect of ministerial responsibility was originally designed to cement cabinet unity in an unstable parliamentary environment. From 1835–68, eight of the nine governments formed came to an end as a result of defeat in the House of Commons. Since 1945, only one out of 13 governments (Callaghan's, in 1979) has done so. But still the doctrine persists in enforcing the convention that govern-ments must present a united front to the public. Individual ministers – and, indeed, Prime Ministers – and their immediate advisers do not in practice observe the convention. When it suits them, as it frequently does, they will leak information about government business unattributably to the media; and this happens quite as much in Blair's government as it has previously. Otherwise, exchanges and discussions between ministers, and between ministers and officials, must be hidden from public view and most certainly may not be revealed to Parliament or the public. Collective responsibility is therefore one of the main props of 'closed' rather than 'open' govern-ment. Further, it can obscure the real origins of policies and decisions and undermine the parallel idea of individual responsibility. The individual minister who announces a policy or defends a mistake is not necessarily the principal actor, even in respect of his or her 'own' policy. Collective secrecy can deny Parliament and the public the information necessary to identify the relative contributions of the Prime Minister, other ministers and departments, and cabinet committees.

Opening up government – now and in the future

When you start saying, 'Well, we must only reveal the minimum amount of information possible to the public', and the presumption is that the public and Parliament do not have the right to know, you lead towards totalitarianism and political dictatorship, and I think that is fundamentally different from my conception of a parliamentary democracy.

(Roger Freeman, Chancellor of the Duchy of Lancaster, 1996)

Duty of openness

The Scott Report's insistence on 'the provision of full information' is the key to real accountability. Sir Richard Scott quotes from two academic witnesses to the Treasury and Civil Service Select Committee (TCSC), both making the point that 'true' accountability requires 'some genuinely independent source of information' and 'open government and access to information' (Scott 1996: para. K8.2). The Scott Report itself catalogues numerous examples of the failure of ministers from 1988–92 to carry out their duty under their then rule-book, *Questions of Procedure for Ministers*, to give full information and not to deceive Parliament (see, for example, paras. D1.151–165, D2.111–120, D4.57, D6.49–54 and F4.59–79). How far has practice changed? In this section, we consider the rules for openness both to Parliament and the public.

For our purposes, the current version of ministers' duty to provide information to Parliament was declared in a parliamentary resolution, drafted by the government and approved on 20 March 1997, which affirmed their wider duty to account to Parliament for the policies, decisions and actions of their departments and executive agencies. The resolution followed a Commons debate on 12 February 1997 on a Public Service Committee report which urged the House to adopt a resolution on accountability and submitted a draft resolution for debate (PSC 1996c: vol. I, para. 60). The crucial passages from the government's revised version of the resolution were as follows:

> It is of paramount importance that Ministers give accurate and truthful information to the House and its Committees. Any inadvertent error should be corrected at the earliest opportunity. If Ministers knowingly mislead the House, the House will expect them to offer their resignation to the Prime Minister.
>
> Ministers should be as open as possible with this House and its Committees, refusing to provide information only when disclosure would not be in the public interest, which should be decided in accordance with relevant statute and the government's *Code of Practice on Access to Government Information*. Similarly, Ministers should require civil servants who give evidence before Select Committees on their behalf and under their directions to be as helpful as possible in providing full and accurate information in accordance with the duties and responsibilities of civil servants as set out in the Civil Service Code.
>
> (PSC 1997: Annexe 1)

The resolution is significant, at least in a symbolic way, for it shifts the locus of the duty of openness from the Prime Minister (and his rule-book) to Parliament itself. The PSC specifically recommended that Parliament should itself issue such a resolution, in the wake of the Scott Report, to confirm the constitutional duty of ministers to be frank and honest when accounting to Parliament and to assert a moral authority over the executive. However, the passage of the resolution depended upon the executive's support and its terms leave considerable opportunity for ministerial manoeuvring – e.g. as we have seen above, 'being as open as possible' is a matter of judgement (see also PSC 1996c: vol. I, para. 30).

The PSC draft resolution was changed by ministers in three significant respects. The government strongly objected to the PSC's initial proposal that civil servants giving evidence in Parliament should be directly bound, like ministers and all other witnesses, by an obligation '[not] to obstruct or impede Members or Officers of the House in the discharge of their duties'. This clause would have edged civil servants closer to being directly accountable to Parliament. The government's own final draft asserted the traditional practice that civil servants gave evidence on behalf of ministers and 'under their direction', as described above, and required them simply 'to be as helpful as possible in providing full and accurate information' (a phrase which again leaves plenty of room for manoeuvre). In thus protecting the interests both of ministers and senior bureaucrats, they had the backing of a Labour front bench already confident of soon being in office. The second notable difference was over the conduct of ministers who knowingly mislead the Commons. The PSC draft stated simply that 'The House will expect [them] to resign'; the government draft, by contrast, restored the final decision to the discretion of the Prime Minister. Thirdly, the PSC wanted the Commons resolution to accept that ministers might need to withhold information on occasions, but also to insist that they 'should only do so exceptionally'. The government removed that condition.

The government also refused to countenance the idea that the Ombudsman should rule on ministers' refusals to answer PQs, though the Table Office is now to prepare annual lists of these refusals. But a full list of incomplete or unsatisfactory answers is not possible, for the judgement involved is highly subjective and the inadequacy of the answer may not be apparent at the time. These of course are problems which the idea of employing the Ombudsman as adjudicator was designed to address. The most significant obstacles to ministerial openness, however, lie, first in the prevailing executive culture, shared by ministers and senior civil servants alike; and second, in the current state of law and practice for open government. The first shapes the second. The Commons resolution accepted the then current position, agreeing that ministers could refuse to provide information 'when disclosure would not be in the public interest, which should be decided in accordance with relevant statute and the government's *Code of Practice on Access to Government Information*'. This voluntary code, introduced in 1994, was a great advance on previous practice and was clearly a response to the public revulsion about the secrecy and lies which had surrounded the 'arms to Iraq' affair. But Britain has remained one of the few countries in western Europe which has not (yet) given its MPs and citizens a statutory or constitutional right of access to government documents.

The code of practice on access to government information

The Labour government is committed to introducing a statutory right of access to official information right across government departments, executive agencies and quangos, the armed forces, nationalised industries, the NHS, local authorities, universities, housing associations, TECs, NHS bodies, the BBC, Channel 4, and so on (Cabinet Office 1997b). Clearly, the new statutory freedom of information regime will have a profound impact on the way the principle of ministerial responsibility works in practice, as it will provide the official framework for what ministers and officials reveal in Parliament. This audit is of course of government practice as it was in May 1997. At that point, the previous government's code of openness set the rules on parliamentary and public disclosure; and, as we write, it remains the main formal instrument of open government for Parliament and the public. Labour's new statutory provisions are yet to be set down in detail and legislated for; and it is the detail which makes all the difference. In this section, therefore, we carry out our audit with an eye to the future and briefly compare and contrast the provisions of the code and the government's white paper on a statutory freedom of information (FOI) regime. But judgement on Labour's FOI regime must await the next Democratic Audit at the end of Labour's term in office.

The openness code has provided for the disclosure not of specific documents as of right, but only of edited versions at the discretion of civil servants. Under the code, MPs on select committees have also received official summaries and not original documents. Thus, MPs, citizens or organisations seeking to see particular documents have not been entitled to do so in Britain; and have therefore been unable to check that they have been given a full and accurate account. And it is open to any government department or public body which fears that full disclosure may expose it to criticism to produce a summary which slants or even conceals the truth. Most FOI regimes do disclose the actual documents, often including information held on computers, tapes, and videos.

The need for exemptions to any scheme of freedom of information is generally agreed. The right to information has to be balanced against the right to privacy and the right to govern. Thus, all FOI regimes protect sensitive information. Britain's voluntary code contains 15 broad exemptions from disclosure: defence and national security; international relations; communications with the royal household; law enforcement and legal proceedings; internal government opinion, discussion and advice; immigration and nationality; management of the economy (now greatly relaxed); tax collection; effective management and operations of the public service; public employment; public appointments and honours; personal privacy; commercial confidentiality; some research, statistics and analysis; and information given in confidence (for further detail, see below).

In addition, there are statutory bars to the release of official information. In 1993 the government identified 193 Acts of Parliament and 63 sets of statutory regulations which prohibited the disclosure of certain types of information held by government. Forty-eight of the Acts, and 25 regulations, allowed for some discretion to disclose information in the public interest. These prohibitions are generally backed by criminal sanctions and disciplinary proceedings. In 1992, the government began reviewing these laws, many of them routine, promising to amend or repeal excessive provisions, but the review finally left them all in place. Access requests for information they cover must therefore be refused. Thus, information of public interest, such as the safety of drugs or safety records of firms, has been withheld.

Further, the Official Secrets Act 1989 makes unauthorised disclosures of a range of official information a criminal offence. Security and intelligence staff are subject to a lifetime ban on disclosure of any information obtained in the course of their work. Civil servants and government contractors commit an offence if they make unauthorised disclosures 'damaging' to the security services or the armed forces; if they endanger British interests or citizens abroad; if their information facilitates criminal activities or escape from legal custody, or hinders criminal investigations. It is also an offence to release information obtained through phone taps or the security services' activities on private property, or 'relating to the obtaining of [such] information'. It is not only officials who are bound by these rules. Newspapers or other third parties are liable to be prosecuted if they publish protected information which is 'damaging' and has been leaked without authority. There is no public interest defence in any of these cases, even though the pressure to reform the Official Secrets Act 1911 was in part inspired by the absence of such a measure in cases like that of Clive Ponting, the MOD official who leaked documents relating to the sinking of the *General Belgrano* during the Falklands War to Labour MP Tam Dalyell. Ponting (who was actually acquitted by the jury in defiance of the judge's summing-up) would still be guilty under the 1989 Act; and that Act is still flanked by the Official Secrets Act 1920, which covers the retention and communication of *all* official documents. Ministers or officials may, however, disclose such information if they do so in accordance with their official duties, which are as likely to be in the government's political interest as in the public interest.

On the other hand, there is other FOI legislation on the statute book. Significant legislation with an FOI content includes the Data Protection Act 1984, the Local Government (Access to Information) Act 1985, the Access to Personal Files Act 1987, the Access to Medical Records Act 1988, the Access to Health Records Act 1989 and the Environmental Information Regulations 1992.

Information which is withheld may, if significant, be deposited in the Public Records Office and will usually be disclosed after 30 years, under the Public Records Act 1967, though it may be open for public inspection sooner or later, at the discretion of the Lord Chancellor. In June 1992, a government review decided that records should always be released after 30 years unless their release would 'harm national security, international relations, defence, or the economic interests of the UK', or distress or endanger individual people or breach confidence (Cabinet Office 1993: Chapter 9). Public records in Scotland and Northern Ireland are made available under administrative arrangements which parallel the legislation for England and Wales.

The code on access has for the first time in Britain provided citizens who have been denied information by an official or minister with the opportunity of an independent review of the refusal by the Parliamentary Ombudsman, who is of course independent of government. The Ombudsman usually has access to relevant official documents and reports to the Ombudsman select committee. The Ombudsman's role in investigating refusals of access has, however, been limited to those departments and public bodies which fall under his jurisdiction under the 1967 legislation which established his office. It is hard to see why the public should not be able to complain about maladministration in certain departments and bodies. Thus, many departments and bodies, such as the Cabinet Office, Atomic Energy Authority, Bank of England, Broadcasting Standards Council, Civil Aviation Authority, Crown

Code on openness

Prosecution Office, Monopolies and Mergers Commission, Securities and Investment Board, the police and security and intelligence services, and local quangos have been excluded from the code's access provisions.

The Ombudsman is prohibited under the 1967 Act from investigating certain government functions, including commercial and contractual matters, which have therefore also become 'no-go' under the code. The Ombudsman is also expressly denied the right to obtain information or documents relating to the proceedings of the cabinet or cabinet committees. This is an unacceptable anomaly, as cabinet and committee papers are not automatically exempted from release under the code. A harm test (see below) applies. But a department refused to supply such documents to the Ombudsman, and frustrated his review of its refusal to disclose information. In 1994, the Lord Chancellor's Department used the rule to stop the Ombudsman's review of its refusal to give the Campaign for Freedom of Information details from an interdepartmental paper on a court decision with far-reaching constitutional implications.

Enforcement of the Ombudsman's findings has relied on the convention that departments abide by them. The Ombudsman has no power to enforce compliance with his recommendations by departments or public bodies. Departments could, if they were so minded, refuse to accept them. The Ombudsman has proceeded by first publishing a recommendation on disclosure, without detailing the information requested, to give departments the first opportunity to put things right. So far departments have taken this opportunity. Generally, the Ombudsman would seek to shame a recalcitrant department into compliance through the Ombudsman Select Committee which could summons officials and ministers to give evidence on their refusal. In exceptional cases, he has indicated that he might disclose disputed information in his reports, but would first of all inform principal officers of his intention. However, ministers retain the ultimate power to prevent the Ombudsman from releasing information where it would be 'prejudicial to the safety of the state or otherwise contrary to the public interest' – a very wide discretionary power. They, in turn, remain accountable to Parliament for refusing to release information or blocking its release by the Ombudsman. The Ombudsman has himself been willing to rely on his powers of persuasion and argument. But ultimately a government or department has had the power to refuse to disclose information in cases where the political stakes are high enough for either to decide to ride out parliamentary and perhaps media pressures to do so.

The code has not caught the popular imagination. The government expected several thousand requests for information every year, but in the first year departments received a mere 41. Requests to departments and agencies in 1996 numbered some 2,000, of which about one in ten were refused. Between April 1994 and the end of 1996, the Ombudsman received a total of only 116 requests – which must come via MPs – to review refusals (a rate of less than 50 a year). In 1996, the Ombudsman Select Committee roundly blamed the government's 'meagre publicity' for the low take-up. The code allows government departments to charge fees for providing information, but there is little evidence of high fees being charged. Departments are also entitled to dismiss requests which are 'vexatious or manifestly unreasonable', or otherwise time consuming.

The Ombudsman has secured the release of information, originally refused by officials, and on several occasions his intervention has led to a change in policy. The process of request, refusal and appeal can also bring to light problems and potential injustices. But perhaps his most important function has been to build up 'case law' on access to information through his interpretation of the code and his rulings in individual cases. Further, he has made it clear that his decisions are not bound by official guidance on what officials may or may not release. The Ombudsman has overseen the development of a 'harm test' in the way the code has been applied. Rather than refusing to disclose any information which falls under the head of most exemptions – such as the protection of internal policy – civil servants have had to consider whether release of the information would do harm; and then whether the harm done by releasing particular information was outweighed by the public interest in making it available (PCA Committee 1996: para. 26). But there is as yet no working definition of the 'public interest', and as Mr Justice Scott's inquiries established, the concept of a public interest in disclosure is not familiar to civil servants and does not necessarily form part of their operating tradition (see, for example, Scott 1996: para. D2.434). The Ombudsman has, however, chalked up an advance on the disclosure of documents. He has taken the view that people who ask for actual documents should receive '*all the information*' [emphasis in original] they contain, subject to exemptions. On occasions, he has concluded that 'the most practical way to release the information' is to hand over a copy of the document (PCA 1996: para. 80).

The Ombudsman's robust pioneering work has been vital in encouraging a culture of openness within Whitehall. The fact that the Office of Public Service, within the Cabinet Office, has circulated his 'case law' among all departments and agencies has been an encouraging sign of executive willingness to co-operate. This same case law is an obvious base for advance, both under the existing code and the new FOI regime which is to succeed it. But the culture of secrecy remains strong. Resistance to change has been evident among Labour ministers and senior officials since May 1997. David Clark, the Chancellor of the Duchy of Lancaster, also had to be robust and withstood attempts to de-stabilise his position while he was preparing the *Your Right to Know* proposals, published in December 1997 (Cabinet Office 1997c) and afterwards. Indeed, the absence of government enthusiasm for Clark's white paper provided a sombre counterpoint to its broad and imaginative proposals. As *The Stakeholder*, the specialist public service magazine, noted:

> Dozens of official statements emerge daily; but those in charge of government information strategy choose to spin only a few of them – usually about new task forces and hit squads to abolish crime, illiteracy, hospital waiting lists and truancy. The official spin doctors ensured that the White Paper on Freedom of Information was greeted with a deafening silence: the open government dog was commanded not to bark.
>
> (January/February 1998)

Clark has clearly learned from the code's weaknesses. His white paper proposes, first, that British government will release actual documents and records, including disks, tapes, etc., across the board rather than edited information. Second, the code's broad categories for exemption, which have been widely criticised for their catch-all quality, will be abolished. He also criticises them for encouraging a 'class-based' approach to what may or may not be disclosed. In their place, the white paper proposes seven 'specified interests': national security, defence and international relations; law enforcement; personal privacy; commercial confidentiality; the safety of the public, individual people and the environment; information supplied in confidence; and 'the Integrity of the Decision-making and Policy Advice Processes in Government'. The test for disclosure of information under the first six of these 'specified interests' will not, as under the code, be a simple 'harm' test; instead, the test will be: 'Will the disclosure of this information cause substantial harm?' The idea of the public interest will also be defined more substantially. Documents and records will then be assessed on a 'contents basis', and may be released with deletions of protected information rather than being wholly withheld. Third, in place of the Ombudsman, a powerful new independent official, the Information Commissioner, will be established with wide powers to consider appeals and order disclosure.

But all information about the security services, special forces, police, prosecuting authorities and others will be wholly excluded from Labour's freedom of information legislation. Under the head of protecting criminal investigations and court proceedings from harmful disclosure, the work of the Department of Social Security and the Immigration Service will also be excluded. While government departments and public bodies will be encouraged to make available factual background information which has contributed to their policy-making, the 'policy domain' of government and its satellites will continue to be protected. Instead of the test of 'substantial damage', a simple harm test will be applied on policy issues; and government legal advice, 'from any source', will be entirely withheld (Cabinet Office/OPS 1997b).

Protected areas of government 'policy' and activity

> *'Policy' is secreted within the interstices of administration.*
> > (Professor Christopher Hood, specialist on British government, 1986)

> *At the heart of the freedom of information debate is a particular problem of public service management – the need (as the 1997 White Paper puts it) to protect 'the integrity of decision-making and the policy advice and the policy advice processes of government'. . . . This is right. If every word managers utter is subject to immediate riposte, they cannot manage.*
> > (Editorial in the Stakeholder magazine, February 1998)

'Policy', the central policy-making and decision-taking processes of government, must be open to influence and scrutiny by Parliament and the public if the doctrine of ministerial responsibility is to satisfy our democratic criteria. But policy in British government has been a closed and highly protected process; like Count Dracula, it shrinks from exposure to the light. The code of practice for access to official information, on which the House of Commons resolution detailing ministers' duty of openness to Parliament is founded, contains an exemption for policy, or 'internal discussion and advice', which is so broadly drafted that it shrouds almost every aspect of the way government makes policy and takes decisions, including:

> Information whose disclosure would harm the frankness and candour of internal discussion, including:
> – proceedings of Cabinet and Cabinet committees;
> – internal opinion, advice, recommendation, consultation and deliberation;
> – projections and assumptions relating to internal policy analysis; analysis of internal ['alternative' in the Labour government's 1997 update] policy options and information relating to rejected policy options;
> – confidential communications between departments, public bodies and regulatory bodies.
>
> (Cabinet Office 1995–97: Exemption 2)

Between the Major and Blair government's version of the code, there is just one change in phrasing – the word '*internal* policy options' becomes '*alternative* policy options'. But there is an advance in the definition of 'harm'. Before May 1997, the government simply said:

> References [in exemptions] to harm or prejudice include both actual harm or prejudice and risk or reasonable expectation of harm or prejudice. In such cases, it should be considered whether any harm or prejudice arising from disclosure is outweighed by the public interest in making information available.

The second edition adds to the definition a presumption that 'information should be disclosed'. Now, of course, the Blair government is poised to legislate for a broad, though limited in vital areas, re-casting of government openness (see above).

Policy remains the key to opening up government in the UK. It is first important to understand precisely what Whitehall means by the term 'policy'. Policy is not made by skilled and neutral analysis of 'objective' data and alternative policy options. It is a political process which is influenced by the values and ideologies of ministers, departmental views and the play of outside interests – which are as diverse as those of the aerospace industry, the processed food industry, Formula One, the Dunblane parents or the pensioner lobby. These interests are by definition partial, and the policy process therefore needs to be exposed to ensure that the public interest – indeed, where possible, the public itself – is clearly involved too (see Chapter 10). External interests can, of course, overwhelm a 'rational' policy (for example, the Royal College of Nursing and trade unions wrecked local pay bargaining in the NHS) or even a party's policy (e.g. Formula One's exemption from a ban on tobacco sponsorship in sport). But in Whitehall policy ideally balances these interests while satisfying ministers' wishes, and presents the outcome in a good light to the public. It is not always possible to hold the balance and in such circumstances, government can resort to subterfuge: the 'arms to Iraq' crisis came about because ministers and civil servants were unable to balance the interests of manufacturing industry, the demands of the various nations involved, and British public opinion.

Protected areas

Formally, policy includes any decision or policy taken by ministers, or involving ministers. In effect, then, for ministers policy is everything they are interested in; and for civil servants, it is everything they do for ministers, however trivial. With the advent of 'can-do' civil servants and ministers, it also involves a managerial element which blurs still more the divide between policy and 'administration' or 'operations'.

Brian Landers, who was briefly Finance Director at the Prison Department, was shocked by the looseness of the process:

> The policy senior civil servants are fixated on has no content. Policy in Whitehall-speak is a process, not an output. And the process is Whitehall politics. Senior civil servants are Westminster groupies . . . [and] . . . rather than there being a well-established policy formulation process, practice seemed to be determined overwhelmingly by the personal characteristics of the minister.
>
> (Landers, forthcoming book)

The minister in question for Landers was Michael Howard. Other ministers are less strong and more willing to be 'advised' by senior bureaucrats. But one example of the looseness of the policy process is the policy package on crime and prisons drawn up by the Home Office for Howard's 1993 'crime-busting' conference speech without informing, let alone consulting, the Prison Service at all (see **pp. 155–156**). The focus on Westminster was also, in Landers' view, very damaging for the agency's operational capacity. For example, all area managers' offices were in London, so that if a riot or escape occurred on their patch, they could be immediately available to brief ministers (Landers, forthcoming book).

Landers seeks also to describe the culture in which policy is made. For the senior civil service, he says, policy is the core of their professional being – 'the magic process which they uniquely understand and which takes priority over all else'. This sense of mystique strengthens the service's long-established guardianship ideals and their unwillingness to allow MPs or the public into the inner sanctums of policy-making. Howe's exchange with Scott (see **p. 341**) is an example of this aloof mystique in action. The Scott hearings also provided numerous examples of the precisely evasive language in which the policy process is cocooned, with its discreetly guarded formulas, at once elastic, economical, and even 'ectoplasmic' (as Howe put it). In private Alan Clark confessed that he 'could not express myself in Whitehall, convoluted phrases, double negative conditionals' (Clark 1993: 23). Yet in court, he chose to describe the terms in which he, as a minister, advised machine tool manufacturers as a 'matter of Whitehall cosmetics'.

> GEOFFREY ROBERTSON: A matter of Whitehall cosmetics, to keep the records ambiguous?
>
> CLARK: Yes, yes.
>
> (Leigh 1993a: 252)

Ian McDonald, the MOD official, said before Scott that 'Truth is a very difficult concept'. The point is to make it so.

The code of practice has reinforced the ring of secrecy around policy. It does not simply presume that the political decisions of ministers in cabinet, cabinet committees and their departments, and the advice which civil servants give them, should be protected from automatic disclosure. The terms of the exemption are phrased to hoover up all 'internal opinion, advice, recommendation, consultation and deliberation', all intra-government communications, and most of the 'objective' elements of policy-making – data, projections, policy analysis, and alternative policy options. Of course, much of this information is in fact made public, but ministers and civil servants have the discretion themselves to judge what may or may not be released. They would be less than human if they did not withhold information which might embarrass the government or department, or expose mistakes and misconduct, or even indicate policy options which might be judged superior to those adopted by ministers. As Eric Beston, a DTI official told Scott, 'the avoidance of controversy [is] not an uncommon concern in the presentation of policy, or ... the non-presentation of policy' (Norton-Taylor 1995: 85). The way in which senior civil servants assured Scott that it was acceptable to give MPs and the public only 'half a picture' suggests that this too is not uncommon (Scott 1996: para. D4.52). William Waldegrave was quite open about the way in which ministers manipulate information in his evidence to the TCSC: 'much of government activity is much more like negotiating, much more like playing poker than it is like playing chess. You do not put all the cards up all the time in the interests of the country' (TCSC 1994: 168, para. 1841).

The official line is that 'background' policy information is always available. There is, however, no official definition of 'background information'. One senior bureaucrat says the crucial distinction is between 'objective' information (the collection of evidence and data) and 'subjective' information (analysis and advice: the fit of policy with evidence). But these two elements are not distinct – they are inter-connected, and they merge. Even at the simplest level, there is room for manipulation. Take, for example, a government study tour of US prisons policies. It can be written in a purely descriptive way and qualify as a 'background' paper; or an official can insert one or more judgements and it becomes 'subjective' and thus potentially secret. Internal downsizing and de-layering within the civil service has further worked to limit the release of objective material. As, indeed, does the ethos of Whitehall itself. Much academic research is withheld or re-written if it points in a direction which is not easily reconciled with existing policy; even the Home Office's own researches were suppressed in the 1980s because they clashed with government policy. Government does not only withhold information. For the past 20 years governments have used the laws of confidence and copyright to suppress the release or publication of information, such as cabinet minister Richard Crossman's diaries and former agent Peter Wright's *Spycatcher* memoir. (See also DA Volume No. 1: Chapter 8.)

Most FOI regimes protect high-level policy advice and decision-making. But British governments have withheld low level documents and technical information, which can remain secret for 30 years. Even in the Matrix Churchill case, in which three men might wrongfully have been gaoled, officials sought to withhold whole classes of documents, many routine and quite innocuous, from release to the court under public interest immunity (PII) certificates (see DA Volume No. 1: Chapter 8). They argued that such secrecy was 'necessary for the proper functioning of the public service' in (as Sir Richard Scott described the process) 'an abundance of caution or excessive concern'. A senior government lawyer admitted to Scott that the PII certificates were often used for 'administrative convenience'. The Attorney-General argued that secrecy was necessary to prevent ill-informed criticism; as to being ill-informed, Scottt replied acidly, 'the more information there is, the less likelihood there is of it being ill-informed' (Norton-Taylor 1995: 178–179).

Whitehall outrage about the Scott Report suggests that attitudes towards openness are likely to change only very slowly. Scott's crime was not so much 'naivety' as public trespass in the sacred domain of policy. In his report for 1995, the Ombudsman complained about the tendency in some departments to erect defences, 'many of which prove to have no foundation', and to use 'at times simply obstructive' arguments, against disclosures. The case for withholding information remains essentially the same, whether it is from a criminal court or a select committee. As the Campaign for Freedom of Information (CFI) said in evidence to the PSC:

> These are essentially that disclosure of advice, however innocuous in itself, would undermine the frankness and candour of future internal deliberations; and that publicity would undermine the decision-making process, for example, by prematurely exposing preliminary ideas to criticism.
>
> (PSC 1996c: Vol. 2, 99)

Cabinet Office advice to civil servants reveals another 'harm' that officialdom fears – that of disclosed 'different or dissenting views being quoted in political argument to attack [government] policy'.

It may well be, as the CFI hoped, that officials have abandoned the practice of exempting all advice as a 'class', as Scott recommended, under the existing code and now assess material which may be withheld on a 'contents' basis only. This will become official practice under Labour's FOI legislation. However, it is too soon to know how open government is becoming across all departments and public bodies, and the Ombudsman's caseload has been too slight for us to come to a reliable judgement. But it is clear that the Ombudsman's view that a new commitment to openness requires 'a pretty immense attitude change within the public service' is entirely justified. The value of the Labour government's proposals for a statutory right of access will ultimately depend on how much the voluntary rules set out in the code, and currently being interpreted and 'codified' by the Ombudsman, fix the parameters of statutory access and how firmly and narrowly the borders around the policy process are drawn.

The Labour government may very well be set to adopt a generally traditional attitude, and it came under considerable pressure from senior civil servants and some influential ministers to do so. The white paper sets out the government view:

Now more than ever, government needs space and time in which to assess arguments and conduct its own debates with a degree of privacy. Experience from overseas suggests that the essential governmental functions of planning ahead, delivering solutions to issues of national importance and determining options on which to base policy decisions while still maintaining collective responsibility, can be damaged by random and premature disclosure of its deliberations under FOI legislation. As a result, high-level decision-making and policy advice are subject to clear protection in all countries.

(Cabinet Office 1997c: para. 3.12)

For this reason, the government proposes a 'modified, straightforward harm test', rather than a substantial harm test, which is likely to prevent disclosure of information relevant to collective responsibility. It stresses the political impartiality of officials; 'the importance of internal discussion and advice being able to take place on a free and frank basis'; and the need to consider the extent to which documents relate to publicly announced or impending decisions. Such ringing words inspire ironic reflections on the role of random 'leaks' and continual unattributable briefings in modern British government, under the last Conservative and current Labour regime, through which ministers and officials take advantage of being within the closed policy circle to achieve partisan objectives of their own. It may very well seem likely to less privileged observers that informed and broad-based public and parliamentary access to information would do a great deal less 'harm' than such processes.

The 1997 white paper states that the 'specific interest' of decision-making and policy advice is primarily designed to protect 'opinion and analytical information' and promises that the Labour government will encourage publication of raw data and factual background information. *The Stakeholder*'s comment that managers should be protected from immediate riposte is well taken, but where the line is drawn between 'analytical' and 'raw' information is going to be critical, especially if such information will then be placed under a 30-year embargo. The Campaign for Freedom of Information has already proposed that the exemption for policy advice should be drafted:

so as to distinguish between the recommendations of an individual [official] . . . and the analysis and interpretation of factual data and projections based on such data. We have also proposed that 'expert' advice in the sense of specialist professional or technical opinion, should also be excluded from the scope of any policy advice exemption.

(PSC 1996c: vol. 3, 99)

One possible adjustment to the government's plans may be for there to be an embargo on 'analytical' information up to the point at which sensitive policies or decisions are announced, after which such information may be disclosed; and in as many instances as possible, for such information to be released as part of government's routine consultation processes. In other words, Parliament and the public should be entitled to the government's best estimates of the likely effects of a new policy, and alternative options. At the moment, government's protection of policy advice is designed precisely to prevent any such public appraisal; and ministers and officials have the power to withhold the whole of the 'objective' spine of policy analysis, against which Parliament, the public, the media and interested parties could judge the final policies chosen or decisions taken.

Policy is not the only highly protected area of government activity. As we have seen, the security agencies, the police, the Immigration Service, and legal advice are no-go areas under the openness code and will remain so under Labour's statutory FOI regime. 'We are clear,' the 1997 white paper states, 'that [the security agencies] could not carry out their duties effectively in the interests of the nation if their operations and activities were subject to freedom of information legislation' (Cabinet Office 1997c: para. 2.3). These agencies are already free of almost any oversight, either within the executive or by Parliament and the courts (see **pp. 428–430** and **450**), and are not excluded from FOI laws in other liberal democracies, where sensitive information and their operations are protected by exemption rules. As Professor Patrick Birkinshaw, an academic authority, has pointed out, the CIA, Defence Intelligence Agency, National Security Agency and FBI all fall within the ambit of American FOI law, though 'much of their operational information is exempt' (PCA Committee 1996: 107). At present, there is also an absolute exemption on information on 'immigration, nationality, consular and entry clearance cases' – a total exclusion in other words, which will now apply also to the police and is unprecedented in FOI regimes around the world. The Ombudsman has criticised this ban, which bears of course on individual cases as well as policies and administration, and makes it harder for individual people to get justice. Official Cabinet Office guidance has allowed an element of discretion in enforcing this exemption, but it is clear that a generally open policy could be followed and private information could be protected by tighter exemptions, the harm (or substantial harm) test, and so on. It is not yet clear exactly where the FOI legislation will draw the boundaries of the exclusion zone.

Under the code, exemptions have been employed in such a way as to undermine a coherent regime of openness. Here we discuss briefly the two most central exemptions – those protecting 'commercial confidentiality' and 'national security'. The Scott Report was strongly critical about the way in which ministers and civil servants sheltered the government's policy on arms sales to Iraq and Iran with 'spurious' and insubstantial arguments about the need to protect 'commercial confidentiality' and references to established government and parliamentary practice. Scott concluded that the government unreasonably extended the idea of commercial confidentiality deliberately to avoid domestic criticism – 'an unacceptable reason for withholding from Parliament information about the activities of Government'. The time was ripe, he wrote, for an urgent re-think, asking:

> Is it any longer satisfactory that Parliament and the British public are not entitled to be told to which countries and in what quantities goods such as artillery shells, land mines and cluster bombs have been licensed for export?
> (Scott 1996: paras. D1.29; D2.432–434; D4.1–2; K8.10)

Commercial confidentiality is not an absolute bar on disclosure under the code, and under the proposed FOI regime, only the prospect of 'substantial harm' should prevent disclosure. But it has traditionally provided blanket coverage against disclosures which might embarrass ministers or government departments. How far departments have become readier to release commercial information under the code is not yet clear, but the evidence is not encouraging. The Ombudsman has criticised the Agriculture and Health departments for casting the web of 'commercial confidentiality' too wide. Surveys of practice up to May 1997 by the Campaign for Freedom of Information found that departments varied in their approach, but some refused to give any information at all about the costs of consultancies, head-hunting services, and so on, while others would give only aggregate figures. The Department of Health refused to release data on prescriptions for various classes of drugs. The Ombudsman persuaded the department to disclose the information in this instance, but is powerless to insist on disclosure when companies have given information in confidence or voluntarily. Such information is often clearly of public interest – for example, fatal accident reports to the Health and Safety Executive are withheld not only from the public, but also from victims' families. The DTI has even been found guilty of advising firms how to classify their information to prevent virtually all of it from disclosure.

With the movement to government by contract and the use of private consultants, there is a further danger that commercial confidentiality could be used to remove much activity on government's behalf from public inquiries and scrutiny. However, the new Labour government seems to have taken the CFI's advice to adopt the US principle that openness is part of the price of doing business with government in its FOI legislation, and the white paper specifically promises that FOI will apply to 'services provided for public authorities under contract'.

The code's exemptions for foreign and defence policies are re-constituted as 'specified interests' in the government white paper. These exemptions, or specified interests, are justified by the need to safeguard 'national security or defence' and to protect Britain's international relations. The term 'national security' has never been defined; the provisions are 'catch-all' phrases which leave government with wide discretion. The Ministry of Defence is a fortress of secrecy. So much so that loyal figures like Michael Mates MP, former Conservative chairman of the Defence Select Committee, has criticised the MOD for a culture which assumes that the less said to the committee, 'the safer the MOD will be'. Mates said that this attitude had on occasion gone beyond acceptable bounds, with officials giving evidence that 'concealed a serious state of affairs' from MPs (a specific reference to evidence on the Trident nuclear submarine programme). MPs of all parties find it more difficult to obtain reliable and comprehensive information on defence than any other policy area (Oxford Research Group 1996: 1). Sir Michael Quinlan, formerly permanent secretary at the MOD, described attitudes towards Parliamentary Questions in a frank and uncompromising memorandum to the Scott inquiry. He argued that the answers to PQs should be assessed within the 'unflaggingly adversarial context' of Parliament where the key purpose of PQs was not to bring information into the public domain, but 'to give the Government a hard time'. He explained:

the reactive purpose of the Government is to avoid having a hard time. The game is a tough one, played by determined people for high stakes; and it is humanly inevitable that each set of players will operate, within the rules, to maximise advantage or minimise disadvantage. . . . The Government . . . will be reluctant to disclose information of a kind, or in a form, which will help the Opposition [to exploit the information] . . . the fact that the competition can work to the detriment of balanced public understanding rests less with individuals than with the dynamics. . . . Other considerations may legitimately motivate Ministers to be wary about what they disclose – the sensitivities of foreign Governments; the need not to weaken the British position in nego-tiations; the need to maintain confidentiality owed to individuals, organisations or countries; the need to protect secret sources; the need not to prejudice investigations or possible legal proceedings; concern for proper loyalty to team or colleagues.

(Scott 1996: D4.61)

But answers to PQs are not simply part of an arcane game played for the benefit of ministers, bureaucrats and MPs. Quite a few MPs are primarily concerned to get at the facts. As Scott himself commented, they 'are also an important medium by which information and its activities is made available to the public'; and:

the respects in which answers to PQs about Government policy on defence exports to Iraq were inadequate and misleading were also respects in which some of the letters written in response to correspondence from members of the public were inadequate and misleading. The context described by Sir Michael's paper for the answers to PQs would have no application to those letters

(*Ibid.*: para. D4.62)

Scilla Elsworthy, of the Oxford Research Group, analysed openness on defence issues after Major's 'all-out attack on official secrecy' was announced in 1992. He published a list of previously secret cabinet committees, but failed to mention the 'MISC' sub-committees on defence and nuclear issues. The MOD's initial response to PQs from Peter Kilfoyle, a Labour MP (and now a minister), on the members of its quangos was to refuse to divulge any names at all. (The MOD finally gave names after the Speaker intervened, but still kept membership of several quango boards secret.) Annual defence white papers have become clearer and more infor-mative and annual statements on the defence estimates contain 'much genuinely useful information'. However, nowhere do MPs see what the US Congress sees, namely 'line items' which set out the research, development, testing and manufac-turing costs of weapons systems – information they require to assess the costs and check progress. A substantial proportion of the Defence Select Committee's hear-ings are secret and MOD evidence is studded with deletions. Ministers and civil servants questioned in public by the committee frequently refuse to answer questions on grounds of the 'risk to national security'. Overall, despite the code of practice, the following subjects remain secret:

- detailed budgets for weapons procurement, broken down into research, development and production stages;
- agreements with other nations on defence and nuclear issues, especially on research and development, including the texts of nuclear agreements with the US and France;
- numbers, targeting and control of British nuclear weapons; and
- a definition of what may be kept secret on defence and nuclear issues (Elsworthy 1996: 1–6).

In 1996, the MOD finally announced that it would end its blanket ban on disclosure of arms sales, but MPs' questions would be answered only as fully as four constraints allowed: the need to protect 'national security'; legitimate security concerns of importers; commercial confidentiality; and British relations with other countries. Independent observers wondered if government policy would in practice change at all (*ibid.*: 6). Such secrecy may very well safeguard national security, but it also protects the closed policy community of the MOD and defence industry, and waste, fraud and negligent financial control (see Chapter 11). The National Audit Office found that the MOD police were investigating financial malpractice amounting to £22 million in 1993–94, but evidence from whistle-blowers and other sources has convinced experts like Scilla Elsworthy that the cost of waste and malpractice in defence procurement is actually much greater (*ibid.*: 4; National Audit Office 1995; Public Concern at Work 1995). In 1996–97 the MOD's budget was £21.5 billion, of which nearly half was for research and development work.

As far as freedom of information is concerned, then, Britain is at a crossroad. In response to the Scott Report, the Conservative government placed a paper in the House of Commons Library in February 1996 asserting the traditional view that 'the inner workings of the Government machine' should not be 'exposed to the gaze of those ready to criticise without adequate knowledge of the background and perhaps with some axe to grind'. This concern is usually justified by the argument that a necessary candour between ministers and civil servants would suffer if these inner workings were exposed. Instead of recording advice and analysis on an 'audit trail' of paperwork a new official practice on 'Post-It' notes and oral advice will grow up; e-mail communications will replace the traditional files.

It seems that the Labour government might very well adopt a similar position, though more open in practice. But a certain scepticism is in order here, informed by recent government practice. Ministers often decide to make the contents of documents known, sometimes openly, sometimes not. For example, classified documents – the so-called 'Crown Jewels' – were disclosed to the judge and jury (but not the public) for the prosecution of Clive Ponting in the *Belgrano* case (see **p. 319**). The discussions in government on their disclosure were untouched by alarm about the effect on future candour within government. Similarly, the Home Office supplied the courts with the minutes of an important meeting at which officials advised Kenneth Baker, the then Home Secretary, on the deportation of the Nigerian dissident known as *M*. What, then, of cabinet documents which even the Ombudsman may not see? Lady

Thatcher's memoirs and those of her colleagues contain countless descriptions of high-level confidential papers and discussions, including those with other international leaders; see, for example, her account of her government's economic strategy in the early 1980s and nuclear defence policies (Thatcher 1993: 123–128, 239–248). These disclosures do not seem to have had shattering effects on the candour of government policy-making or the inner workings of government.

Moreover, in April 1994 the then Chancellor, Kenneth Clark, decided to publish, after six-week delays, the minutes of his monthly meetings with the Governor of the Bank of England – a disclosure of high-level analysis and advice which would still be unthinkable in any other area of the government policy-making. The decision was not taken in the interests of open government, however, but to restore the confidence of the international money markets in government's economic policies after the spectacular 'Black Wednesday' disaster, when sterling fell out of the ERM. In other words, the inner workings of government policy-making were deliberately exposed to restore international faith in them. In brief, the main arguments against opening up the policy portmanteau to public scrutiny are spurious. Civil service advice could easily be made anonymous. More information would make ill-informed criticism less rather than more likely. Governments, naturally enough, dislike political criticism, whether it is 'axe-grinding' or well informed, or both. But criticism is an inevitable and essential part of the processes of democratic government, against which British government has traditionally built its own Berlin wall of secrecy.

AUDIT

In this chapter, we have assessed the quality of democratic accountability and openness in British government, focusing on the doctrine of ministerial responsibility to Parliament and the code of practice for public and parliamentary access to government information. In doing so, we have used two main criteria – **DAC8** on democratic control of the state, and **DAC7** on government's openness.

DAC8: Ministerial control of the core executive

In principle, the doctrine of ministerial responsibility still holds that a mere two dozen or so individual ministers, powerful though some of them are, can control the whole of the core executive, government officials, departments, executive agencies and public bodies and officials of all sorts, which we described in Part 2. They are then said to be publicly accountable to Parliament for the activities of what is in effect the whole central state. In practice, their claim to such control has been abandoned. But no mechanism has been devised to ensure that the workings of the central state are under effective democratic control. Thus, the first proposition that the doctrine advances – that ministers can properly be responsible to Parliament for the actions of the state and its bureaucracy – is shown up as obsolete and ineffective. The conclusion that the doctrine fails to meet our democratic criteria is therefore inescapable, even before we assess Parliament's ability to enforce ministers' duties of accountability and openness (see Chapter 14).

The doctrine obscures the reality of dealings between ministers and their civil servants and departments and feeds the continued illusion that somehow ministers are able to run the show. Ministers can, as we have seen, enter a department and oblige civil servants to prepare and carry through particular legislative proposals or policies; they can take broad control, reject or even turn around departmental policy views, and take, say, up to 250 decisions personally a week. But they cannot be the fulcrum of policy-making and decision-making, expressly delegating responsibility to officials across the board and monitoring their performance. Departments are the motors of continuing government and they continue seamlessly in motion under successive ministers. But the officials who man the machines of government are in effect rendered invisible by the doctrine of ministerial responsibility. At the same time, these same officials are in charge of universes of discretionary decision-making which are not directly known to ministers and could never be run by them. It is for this reason that Parliament has in fact long since abandoned any idea that ministers can be held responsible for the mistakes or misconduct of officials who are not acting directly under their command or carrying out their express policies. But if neither civil servants nor ministers are to be held responsible, or often accountable either, then there is an effective vacuum in the accountability of the state in the UK.

DAC9: Parliamentary powers of scrutiny and accountability

The doctrine also pre-supposes that an assembly of some 560 non-ministerial MPs, overworked and under-resourced men and women with a conflicting variety of duties, of which scrutiny of the executive is just one, can ensure that ministers fulfil a duty of responsibility across the whole range of executive action. In fact, such scrutiny is not a priority in a modern House of Commons, which is generally the creature of a government sustained firmly in office by a disciplined party majority. Frequently, it is not even a primary objective of the opposition parties, for they know very well that they can only rarely gain any direct advantage in Parliament from their activities there. The political reality is that ministers can generally avoid giving a full account of their or their officials' actions, and can rely on the loyalty, ambition and discipline of their party majority to ensure that no sanctions are applied to them, even in cases where they are guilty of breaking major conventions, such as not lying to the House. Further, the loose nature of ministerial responsibility and accountability in action; the executive's refusal to allow civil servants to give evidence in their own right; and the limits on openness under the current code of access, all make it virtually impossible for Parliament to police, let alone enforce, the accountability of the executive to the House of Commons. Thus, the second proposition of the doctrine also falls down.

The doctrine may arguably have had some acquaintance with reality in the mid-Victorian era of the small state. But it is pure fantasy now. This is the position this country has reached: the central mechanism for ensuring democratic control of the executive is entirely deficient. The governing principle of reform in the UK is, 'If it ain't broke, don't fix it'. Ministerial responsibility requires urgent 'fixing'. Parliamentarians have recently begun to try and fix it, and the government-drafted Commons resolution, originally inspired by the Public Service Committee, is at least a marker of MPs' intent (see **p. 350**). But will it make very much difference in practice? Parliament's ability to police the resolution clearly remains limited. Diana Woodhouse has summarised the difficulties which lie ahead:

> Moving into the twenty-first century, the convention of ministerial responsibility can be defined loosely as requiring, first, information rather than resignation; secondly, ministerial 'accountability' for everything, but 'responsibility' for only some things; thirdly, civil servant 'responsibility' for some things but 'accountability' only when this suits ministerial interests. Thus, rather than being clarified and refined, the convention remains opaque and incoherent. It accords neither with traditional constitutional understandings nor with the needs of modern government, and where there have been changes in practice, these retain elements of uncertainty. It therefore fails to provide the framework necessary to hold government to account.
>
> (1997: 280)

DAC7: Public access to information about government actions and policies

There are severe limits on the provision of information which is independent of the government's own information machine. A voluntary code of practice on access to government information was introduced in 1994, marking a serious effort to open up government and reform Whitehall's culture of secrecy. The code is a real advance on past practice, but falls short of giving the public clearly defined rights of access, especially in the crucial area of government 'policy' – or in other words, the crucial decision-making processes of the central state. Moreover, it is by its nature a retrospective mechanism. In Parliament, the Commons resolution on ministers' duty of openness confines that duty to the terms of the code of practice; and the Osmotherly rules ensure that officials give evidence under the direction of ministers, and not independently, even on specialist and technical matters.

The *cordon sanitaire* around 'policy' is fatal to open and, for that matter, effective government. Along with most of the active rules of British government, the code and Labour white paper alike – and therefore the Commons resolution – specifically exempt 'policy' from disclosure or critical scrutiny, but policy is precisely what ministers and the senior civil service 'do'. Thus, the significant work of Whitehall is carefully guarded against parliamentary or public scrutiny and the mutual responsibilities of ministers and civil servants are cancelled out. In practice, the current and future disclosure rules reinforce the essential secrecy which lies at the heart of British government.

It is inevitable that any obligation on government to give information on its activities will contain exemptions in the overall public interest. No FOI regime in the world, legal or voluntary, does not have such exemptions. It is also inevitable that government will be the first judge of how such exemptions should be applied, and will (as Scott once observed) in effect be 'judge in its own cause'. But there are several ways in which misuse of exceptions can be brought under control. First, government officials must be placed under a duty to weigh the public interest in disclosure against the public interest in secrecy in any case. Such an idea is only partially in place in the UK, but will be given added force under Labour's FOI legislation. But it has also to be absorbed into official culture. Secondly, what may or may not be disclosed must be defined, preferably in law and as clearly as possible. The current voluntary code of practice fails to meet this test, but the forthcoming legislation will establish statutory freedom of information rules which make documents and records available rather than edited highlights drafted by officials. The legislation will also put an independent commissioner on government information in place. At present, the Parliamentary Ombudsman provides the element of independent scrutiny, but there are various limitations on his effectiveness. His jurisdiction is limited; his inquiries are restricted by statutory rules; and at the end of the day, governments or ministers can order the Ombudsman not to disclose certain information and can reject his findings outright. Overall, however, the code has brought about a substantial advance on previous practice and the Ombudsman has been able to create a rule-based process for the disclosure of information, though progress has been slow and crab-like, since very few and comparatively random cases have come to him for determination. Sir Richard Scott has suggested that the Ombudsman, or another officer of Parliament, should have sufficient powers and security clearance to investigate every invocation of exemptions within government and should report every two years, say, to Parliament on their use and misuse during that period (Oxford Research Group 1996: 15–16).

DAC15: Consulting the public on making and carrying out policy

An important element of democratic practice is entirely absent from cuurent ideas and comment on ministerial responsibility and accountability to Parliament and the public. Its concern is almost wholly on what has been done, rather than what is to be done; and the focus is one seeking to blame. In Chapter 10 we assessed the processes of public consultation in Britain. Governments in Britain do consult the public and interested parties, but the amount of current official thinking exposed is carefully rationed, even in consultative green papers, and the 'policy' embargo is generally enforced. The level of public participation is generally low and is essentially restricted to organised interests and active minorities. It is important for the future that any re-definition of the idea of ministerial responsibility recognises that full public consultation and participation are not merely desirable, but also essential, features of policy-making and (as far as possible) decision-taking in a modern liberal democracy.

13   A Parliament Bound

Party constraints on scrutiny and accountability

> *Parliament, unlike some of its counterparts abroad, is not meant to govern. Still less is it meant to control the executive. Its job is to check it – by scrutinising, debating and refining laws in the making. What has gone wrong is that oppositions have come to see their role almost solely as obstruction, while governments are obsessed with getting their legislation through.*
>
> (*The Economist*, 18 December 1993)

> *The moment that we distinctly perceive that the House of Commons is mainly and above all things an elective assembly, we at once perceive that party is of its essence . . . bone of its bone, breath of its breath.*
>
> (Walter Bagehot, in *The English Constitution*, 1867)

As the received wisdoms of orthodoxy quoted above show, Parliament is traditionally supposed not to govern, nor to make laws, nor even to control the executive. Its role is narrowly defined as one of scrutinising the executive, checking and improving legislation, and debating issues of government. It is within these limits that the doctrine of ministerial responsibility to Parliament of the government collectively and ministers individually operates. In the previous chapter we have assessed the practical value of the doctrine and of the code of practice for access to government information in making ministers and the core executive accountable and open to MPs. Our conclusions were that the idea of ministerial responsibility acts more as a shield for ministers and the senior bureaucracy than a mechanism for either to be made responsible to Parliament; and that the code of practice is so defined as to allow the executive discretionary powers to withhold significant information from MPs, and that in particular the critical realm of 'policy', or the central workings of government, are totally withheld. This will largely remain the case under the Labour government's proposal for a statutory freedom of information (FOI) regime.

This chapter is the first of two which centre upon Parliament's ability to make the executive accountable and open, as set out in **DAC9** (see **p. 337**), which asks how extensive are Parliament's powers to oversee legislation and public expenditure, to scrutinise the actions of ministers, departments and officials, and to hold ministers to account; and how effectively they are exercised in practice. In Chapters 13 and 14 we concentrate on the parliamentary aspects of these questions. There are three dimensions to our inquiries:

- The first is *structural*: how far do relationships within Parliament – which revolve around the structures of party government and opposition – facilitate or hinder scrutiny and control of the executive?
- The second is one of *values*: how far do the values, norms and 'ethos' of the House, and of MPs individually, engender a political climate within which effective public scrutiny can be realised?
- The third is *procedural*: do the formal structures, institutions, rules and working practices of Parliament – such as for example legislative procedures, select committees, Parliamentary Questions, debates, and so on – allow MPs to scrutinise government programmes and policies in an open, informed and accessible manner?

In practice, these dimensions are inextricably intertwined. Structure and values have a profound influence upon the rules and working practices of MPs and in effect set the perspective within which the more tangible and practical third dimension operates. This chapter deals with the first two dimensions and their repercussions on the collective performance of MPs in practice; the effects of single-party government and the party ethos on the legislative process; and considers the role of the House of Lords. Chapter 14 then concentrates upon the main instruments of parliamentary scrutiny – select committees in the House of Commons and Parliamentary Questions – and briefly examines the associated work of the National Audit Office and Ombudsman, and the official oversight of the security and intelligence agencies. We are thus obliged to leave aside other aspects of Parliament's and MPs' role – such as constituency affairs; the welfare role of MPs; lobbying and petitioning Parliament; the representativeness of MPs; rules of conduct for MPs and peers (**DAC10**); Parliament's ability to subject European legislation to scrutiny (**DAC17**); and so on. Significant though these are for the quality of parliamentary democracy in the UK, they are outside the central focus of this study.

Our conclusions on the issues considered in both Chapters 13 and 14 are set out at the end of Chapter 14.

Party government, opposition and elective dictatorship

House of Commons scrutiny of the executive is the chief focus of this and the next chapter, but it is not the primary role of the House. Its main task is to create and sustain government, and only secondarily to hold that government to account. The political executive itself mostly sits in the House, combining the leadership of the government of the day, the Commons and the majority party. It is therefore profoundly wrong to conceive of the House of Commons as a corporate body, separate from the government. As Peter Riddell, the highly experienced *Times* political columnist, has pointed out, 'It is muddled and idle to try to define Parliament separately and, in some way, as opposed to the Government' (1998: 25). No more is the House in any sense 'above party politics'. Political parties are the work-horses of democracy and MPs are elected to the Commons as representatives of their parties. Not only do they owe their own place in Parliament to their party;

Party government

their chances of forming and participating in government and realising their political goals depend on it too. And parliamentary government itself depends upon party. Parliament, therefore, has little distinct life or identity of its own, separate from government and party.

The model for party government in Britain remains that of the early postwar period, though it has irretrievably broken down. The two-party system of that era was widely regarded as 'responsible'. The winning party was bound to govern in accordance with manifesto commitments put to the electorate at an election. The losing party was consigned to opposing the government in Parliament, subjecting its policies and actions to systematic scrutiny, and acting as an alternative government in waiting. The prevailing ideological consensus ensured that governments were not unresponsive and oppositions were not irresponsible. Both parties abided by the parliamentary rules of the game: the fact that neither party expected to be permanently in government or opposition enhanced their sense of constitutional propriety (Judge 1983a).

But 'responsible' government largely worked because governments were willing to let it work. As we have seen, there is no separation of powers at the heart of British government. Political power is highly centralised and the leadership of the executive, Parliament and majority party is hierarchically conjoined in the offices of Prime Minister and cabinet. Thus, even simple scrutiny of the executive effectively stems from the self-control of governments rather than the pressures that Parliament collectively, or partially through the 'opposition' or individual MPs, can bring to bear. Democratic notions of 'opposition', scrutiny and accountability depend, at least for the time being, upon executives allowing themselves to be 'opposed', scrutinised and made accountable. This goes beyond the mere provision of procedural opportunities for debating and examining government's policies and actions, and extends to encompass the norms of genuine inquiry and the information made available for informed criticism. So it is that Peter Hennessy, the contemporary historian, estimated, perhaps over-generously, that in the 46 years from 1945 to 1991 there were only about seven years of 'truly effective, classical opposition' (1991: 5).

As has become increasingly clear since the late 1960s, a brutal truth lay behind the facade of 'responsible' government. In practice, a single-party government, backed by a parliamentary majority, can legislate as it wishes on whatever it wishes and can evade parliamentary criticism almost without compunction. Traditionally, this executive dominance, lauded as 'strong government', had the advantage at least of processing legislation expeditiously and efficiently. (Whether such legislation was effective in achieving its objectives was another matter entirely.) But as the postwar consensus evaporated during the 1970s, responsible government was transmuted into 'elective dictatorship' – Lord Hailsham's critical, and not undeserved, description of the Labour government then in power (Hailsham 1978). Ironically, it was to be the Conservative governments of Mrs Thatcher that became the embodiment of such dictatorship, but by the end of the Callaghan regime in 1979, it was already evident to parliamentarians of all colours that executive dominance of Parliament was no longer tolerable. In 1978, the Procedure Committee issued the following warning:

The balance of advantage between Parliament and the government in the day-to-day working of the constitution is now weighted in the favour of government to a degree which arouses widespread anxiety and is inimical to the proper working of our Parliamentary democracy.

(Procedure Committee 1978: 588)

At the end of the 1992–97 Parliament, three-quarters of a sample of MPs of all parties – and a majority of MPs in the three larger parties – agreed that this classic statement remained correct nearly 20 years later; and among them, more than two-thirds believed that the imbalance had grown worse (DA Paper No. 9, 1996).

The significance of party loyalty in Parliament

If it is the political executive's tripod of power in Whitehall, Westminster and party that creates the structure of its dominance over Parliament, then it is essentially party loyalty which holds it in place. Party loyalty is the key to understanding the dynamics of party government in the House of Commons. It is often forgotten that political parties in Parliament are built around an overwhelming consensus of opinion and sense of identity, which is reinforced for most MPs by their constant contact with their constituency parties. The predominant pattern is of leaders and back-benchers mutually supporting common programmes of action. While governments pursue their manifesto pledges, then majority party MPs will naturally vote for them. But continuing loyalty when governments fail to initiate agreed programmes, or deviate from, redirect, or even renege on election promises or long-established party positions, needs to be explained. Perhaps the most potent explanation is to be found in the way Prime Ministers mobilise the idea of party loyalty to ensure support for government policies which deviate from manifesto programmes or ideological expectations, by shifting the focus of representation away from party interests and concerns towards an articulation of a broader 'national interest'. In the absence of a spontaneous party consensus, governments are willing to settle for compliance on the part of their backbenchers.

If too little is made of straightforward party consensus, then too much is often made of the power of the whips and the coercive and manipulative mechanisms they employ to deliver the party vote. We examine those mechanisms here. But it is important to note at the outset that, as the political scientist Ivor Crewe has concluded, 'compliance mechanisms are the weakest influences on parliamentary voting behaviour' (Crewe 1986: 163). Compliance may be secured through both positive and negative inducements. Party leaders and whips have at their disposal the power of patronage – the allocation of positions and offices within party and within government, knighthoods, peerages and other goods. Loyalty may be encouraged through the knowledge that the whips control appointments to parliamentary positions such as ministerial appointments, places on select committees, overseas delegations, and so on. Rumours of darker arts, of blackmail and so forth, also surface from time to time. Equally 'disloyalty' may be punished, as Tory MP Nicholas Winterton found in the newly elected Parliament of 1992. Winterton had earlier incurred the displeasure of the Conservative whips for his outspoken criticism of government policy, his voting record, and the critical stance adopted by the Health Select Committee under his chairmanship. As a consequence, the Conservative whips ensured that Winterton was not re-appointed as chairman of the committee in July 1992. His response was to accuse party managers of 'heavy-handed bullying': 'They want to muzzle [independent] people who have something to say from a position of informed knowledge' (*Guardian*, 9 July 1992).

The positive and negative dimensions of patronage are even more manifest when the allocation of government posts is considered. In 1997, the incoming prime minister, Tony Blair, had at his disposal some 130 government jobs (86 ministerial positions and 44 parliamentary private secretaries, or PPSs). The holders of such posts are commonly known as the 'payroll vote' (even though PPSs are not paid). Significantly, for present purposes, promotion to these posts is frequently seen to be based upon an assessment of a backbencher's voting record and reputation for loyalty. Thus, in November 1992, when six of the new Conservative intake were made PPSs, a direct connection was made between promotion and loyalty to the government. All were rewarded for supporting the government on the Maastricht Treaty (*The Times*, 19 November 1992), as other Conservative MPs were well aware (*Guardian*, 18 November 1992). Equally, the whips warned some Maastricht rebels that they were ending their ministerial careers before they had even started. One new MP claimed that:

> he was frogmarched by a whip on to the chilly terrace for a proper dressing down. The theme, he reports, was that rebellion would bring him 'ten minutes of fame' followed by a life time in the political wilderness. He gave in.
>
> (*The Times*, 5 November 1992)

Other Conservative rebels who 'gave in' on the Maastricht vote did so variously because of pressure from constituency associations, or John Major's 'personal charm offensive', or peer group pressure exerted by other backbench loyalists. But the overwhelming reason was undoubtedly that the party chairman, Norman Fowler, and Major himself, made it clear that the vote was tantamount to a vote of confidence in the Prime Minister. Hence, the authority of formal office was used as a mechanism for bolstering internal party support for the Conservative Party leader, backed by the prospect of a general election at an inauspicious time should Major lose the vote. The inextricable interlinkage of party and personal calculation and executive convention was clearly apparent. The potency of this mix of partisan and executive concerns was vividly illustrated by the major turn-around in voting on the vote of confidence on 23 July 1993 (see **p. 379**). Only one 'Euro-rebel' failed to back the motion of confidence. The others caved in.

It is this conjunction of loyalty simultaneously to the leadership of party and government that provides the analytical key to understanding the operation of British parliamentary government. It is a complex relationship. Simple analyses revolving around sanctions, positive or negative, fail to appreciate that 'the crack of the [party] whip ... is a minor part of the story' (Crewe 1986: 180). The apparently most punitive sanction, withdrawal of the party whip is, paradoxically, the least effective.

Far more significant are the values and norms of the House which, as with any other dominant value system, reflect the interest of the most powerful actors and the existing distribution of power (Judge 1981: 10–14). The distinctive feature of the Commons in this respect is that the majority party is led by a centralised hierarchy, located in the adjacent offices of the Prime Minister and whips in Downing Street. The official opposition party reflects back the same hierarchy across the floor of the House, underpinned in its case by the hope rather than possession of political power. It is on the opposition that the main task of systematic scrutiny of the government falls; but its performance of this task is almost wholly shaped by the adversarial party nature of the House and the gross imbalance of power between government and opposition. Obviously, the main opposition party can be outvoted at most turns by a majority-party government. But that government also controls much of the information that opposition parties require to oppose effectively, and as we pointed out in Chapter 7, Whitehall is invariably mobilised on its side.

Modern governments have become partisan and aggressive. Ministers and whips have become determined to get their legislation through Parliament intact, and are far less likely to accept amendments, especially from the official opposition. The ideal of responsible opposition has similarly collapsed. Reasoned arguments and well-intentioned amendments have no force against a government determined to get its own way. Opposition leaders and MPs wrestle with government ministers and majority-party MPs in a traditional struggle over parliamentary time – seeking to wear them down, to table wrecking amendments, to filibuster, all tactics designed to deprive them of time for their legislative programme.

Legislating degenerates into a virility test – and ultimately a false one at that, since oppositions also generally collude with governments through the 'usual channels' (i.e. the whips) to allow them to get their business through. Otherwise, parliamentary life would become intolerable for both sides. The formal processes of law-making and scrutiny have become equally false, for they do not centre primarily on testing the quality of government policies and legislation. The House has rather become one site of the long-drawn-out electoral saga, in which the media images of the parties of government and opposition are at stake, and the arguments are rehearsals for the party lines at the next election.

Thus, authority in the House rests generally in the safe-keeping of the political executive and is secured by its grasp of majority party support. From the conjunction of executive and party hierarchies, ministers effectively assert executive hegemony within a system of values and norms that justifies and perpetuates their own powerful position. In doing so, they have subverted the historical assumption, institutionalised in the equality of voting rights in the House, that all MPs are equal. Within this perspective, the adversarial character of Commons proceedings reduces the policy choices for backbenchers in all parties from the potentially infinite variety associated with the Burkean idea that they act as trustees for their constituents to a basic dichotomy: either voting for or against the government. In making this choice, backbench MPs are socialised to accept a reinforcing strategy of decision-making: voting with their party. Thus, executive and party cues coalesce into an adversarial style of decision-making which simplistically reduces voting options to two mutually exclusive alternatives: voting for or against the government on partisan grounds. One observer, Nevil Johnson noted, 'adversary politics becomes more than a way of conducting political argument: it becomes a mechanism of choice too' (1977: 12).

These mechanisms affirm the primacy of party loyalty in the House and make ascent of the relatively short 'greasy pole' to ministerial office or its shadow a far more compelling career goal than mere parliamentary status, despite recent proposals to attach more recognition (and indeed remuneration) to, say, chairing select committees (see Dunleavy 1995c; Riddell 1998: 234–236). By the same token, they mean that specialisation in the Commons is undervalued. Political careers are conceived fundamentally in governmental rather than in parliamentary terms. Nowadays, too, larger governments make promotion to office a readily attainable goal, as 'the ministerial promotion pyramid is broad and rather flat' (John Biffen, *Guardian*, 2 November 1993). Thus Conservative MP Robert Rhodes-James noted that in the newly elected 1992 Parliament:

> While it is not yet the case that every backbencher hungers for office, and judges success or failure on whether he or she receives it or not, the sheer personal ambition of the majority [characterises MPs in the 1990s] . . . the professional politician has become the norm, not the exception.
>
> (*The Times*, 7 November 1992)

Backbenchers therefore subscribe to those norms which are most likely to lead to office – pre-eminent among which is loyalty to the party leadership. In turn, the former Tory minister, Lord St John of Fawsley, made the connection between ambition and the norms inculcated amongst backbenchers:

> deference has grown within the political system and deference within the House of Commons is now at a historical high, despite all the noise, despite all the appearances of rebellion, the deference to those holding office . . . has grown and is growing.
>
> (Hennessy and Smith 1992: 17)

Notably absent are those values enhancing detailed scrutiny and criticism of executive actions by Parliament as a collectivity. The dominant ethos of the Commons thus fragments MPs into either supporters or opponents of the government, into frontbenchers or backbenchers, party loyalists or dissidents, and in each case asserts the primacy of the former over the latter. The idea of 'Parliament' as a political force, or as whole, is therefore simply a myth. Parliament in this sense simply does not exist.

The 1996 Democratic Audit survey found, however, that few MPs acknowledged that their primary duty was to party – rather they subscribed to the more populist myth of the 'constituency MP', primarily representing his or her constituents (see Table 13.1). The links between MPs and constituents have grown in significance over the last 30 years, and constituency case work alone increased by nearly half between 1982 and 1989. In the 1980s, individual MPs received some 10,000 letters

Table 13.1 What is the most important duty of MPs?

	Public view %	MPs' view %
Supporting their party loyally in parliamentary votes	8	8
Representing constituency interests	39	36
Taking up individual constituents' problems and grievances	17	14
Ensuring that government does its job efficiently and honestly	31	12
Voting and acting in line with their own judgement	4	15
Don't know/none of these	–	15

Sources: NOP poll for Democratic Audit 1996; Rowntree Reform Trust 'State of the Nation' poll (ICM), 1996

a year on average, and more than half were from constituents. Nearly two-thirds of MPs believed that their mail served as an important barometer of public opinion and the great majority claimed to act on their complaints or suggestions, very often by way of writing to ministers. There is circumstantial evidence to support the claim that 'a torrent of mail' helped to change Tory MPs' minds about pit closures (*The Times*, 22 October 1992), and thus led to their ultimately abortive pressure on government to reverse its policy (see **p. 379**). But their constituency work is normally undertaken out of enlightened self-interest, as it reinforces their tenure as the local MP, and their constituency interests do not pose a real challenge to the ever-present party regime at Westminster.

No more does the myth of the independent-minded MP who votes according to his or her own judgement or conscience, even though a substantial minority of MPs say they believe in it (see Table 13.1). The reality is that the values and norms of the House prevail, and as Roy (now Lord) Hattersley has stated, 'Party government requires Members of Parliament to vote against their judgment and personal opinions time after time' (*Guardian*, 9 November 1992). The deferential 'mind set' of backbenchers proves to be a potent form of self-control and self-limitation which militates against sustained critical scrutiny of executive actions. Indeed, the poll of MPs showed that they gave scrutiny – 'ensuring that government does its job efficiently and honestly' – a remarkable low priority (see Table 13.1), and far less than the general public.

There is a dynamic at work. As considerations of party become enmeshed with parliamentary functions, so, in reverse, they also become equally ensnared in executive actions. Hence, the executive has developed its own mentality, very evident in the Major years, which equates ministerial culpability with party embarrassment, and leads to constitutional responsibilities being avoided for partisan reasons. In this mentality, the principle of ministerial accountability is inverted (see Judge 1993). Far from welcoming scrutiny, successive governments have sought to limit parliamentary powers of scrutiny to prevent ministers from being politically embarrassed. To this end there is common cause between ministers and government backbenchers, for whom ensuring that their government is re-elected is far more important than subjecting it to rigorous scrutiny. As Professor John Griffith has explained, Parliament thus works 'as a party machine, and that means that the majority party and the

Party loyalty

government have a common interest and are interdependent' (Hennessy and Smith 1992: 6). It is this interdependence which makes government 'strong', institution-alises the weakness of 'opposition' and Parliament as a whole, and sustains the formal rules and working practices which prevent MPs from subjecting governments' programmes and policies to open and informed scrutiny.

Some political analysts, most notably Philip Norton, argue that the notion of 'elective dictatorship' has been a caricature and that political realities are more complex and less centralised (Norton 1978a, 1980, 1991b, 1991c). Norton's basic argument is that 'if control is taken in the sense of providing the broad limits within which government may govern, of influencing and even restraining measures of public policy, then recent years have witnessed no decline in parliamentary control' (Norton 1991a: 153–62).

Norton's claim rests in part upon the assertions that backbench government MPs have been more 'involved in scrutinising and influencing government and were prepared to use their basic power – that of the vote – to achieve that involvement'; and that 'MPs are more independent in their voting behaviour ... and [this] has been sufficient to prevent government from assuming that it has an automatic majority for whatever it wishes to have passed (Norton 1991c: 348 and 1991b: 67). The political effect of this view, which came close to becoming academic orthodoxy, was to direct the focus of attention away from control or scrutiny exercised collectively by the House, or even by the official opposition, towards phenomena like cross-party voting on select committees (which we examine in Chapter 14) and internal dissent within the governing party.

Internal dissent is arbitrary in its impact, as became increasingly evident during the unprecedented flow of internal rebellions within the governing party from 1992–97. The split over Britain's relationship with Europe was the fundamental cause of rebellion, but former ministers and backbench MPs also voted against their government over VAT charges on fuel, the future of coal pits, hospital closures, MPs' extra earnings, and so on, in a total of 18 rebellions. Altogether, nearly two-thirds of the parliamentary Conservative Party – 202 Tory MPs in all – rebelled on at least one occasion. Labour also suffered rebellions during this period, most notably over the Prevention of Terrorism Act, income tax and Maastricht, illustrating that even a well-oiled opposition machine can be derailed if MPs feel strongly enough about a particular issue. But Norton drew attention to earlier manifestations of independence. Previously, as he pointed out:

- during the Heath government (1970–74), two-thirds of all Conservative back-bench MPs voted against the party on one or more occasions, and in one in five divisions, government MPs entered the opposition lobby;
- in 1974, the minority Labour government was defeated 17 times; and
- in the 1974–79 Parliament, Labour minority governments were defeated on 23 occasions as a result of cross-voting by their own backbenchers and 42 times in all.

Even after majority government returned in 1979, Norton and others maintained that 'the independence on the part of MPs was maintained', while accepting that cross-voting became less effective (1991c: 348). But while, for example, one or more Tory MPs voted against the government in Mrs Thatcher's last three years on 314 occasions (*The Times*, 16 August 1991), her governments suffered only three direct legislative defeats (not counting votes on MPs' own interests) – the temporary rejection of new immigration rules in 1982; the defeat of the 1986 attempt to reform Sunday trading laws (when 72 Conservatives rebelled), and the insertion of a clause on social security benefits for elderly people in private residential homes into a bill on community care (see Table 13.2). In the torrent of controversial and ideologically motivated legislation that swept through Westminster in the Thatcher years, even Norton has to concede that the backbench independence was 'less apparent' (1990a: 20). After 1992, Major's weaker administration was punctuated with 11 defeats in all, but only three were on its own non-European proposals; and five were on the House's affairs.

Over and above the actual defeat of government, there is the argument that the *threat* of defeat, or of serious defection in the lobbies, constitutes a significant means of backbench influence, especially on the government side, which can lead governments to modify their policies. Norton held that this is frequently sufficient to induce 'action by government in advance of public deliberation on the floor of the House' (1990a: 20). Apparently compelling testimony for Norton's case was provided in the last few months of 1992. The then Industry Secretary, Michael Heseltine, announced a moratorium on pit closures on 19 October, and made further concessions in the Commons debate on 21 October. It was reported that MPs had forced Heseltine to change course to 'avert a full-scale rebellion by Conservative backbenchers' (*Financial Times*, 20 October 1992). Equally, calculation of the scale of the likely rebellion over the motion on the reintroduction of the European Communities Amendment Bill on 4 November led the Prime Minister to concede that the final vote on the bill would not be held until after a second Danish referendum on the Maastricht Treaty. This 'last-minute climb-down' (*The Times*, 6 November 1992) was sufficient to ensure a 319–316 majority for the government's motion.

Yet in both instances the extent of policy concessions remained ambiguous. On pit closures, only 12 pits were finally to be 'reprieved' after a review in March 1993, and by July 1993, executives at British Coal were openly speculating that no more than 'a handful' of the 12 pits would be open at the end of the financial year. As for Maastricht, cabinet minister Malcolm Rifkind denied any 'interdependence between the Danish referendum and the Commons' third reading' within days of the vote (*Guardian*, 9 November 1992). Thereafter, a weak government experienced a bruising and nerve-wracking period over Maastricht and suffered heavy defeats over British representation on the proposed Committee of the Regions and a government motion on the Maastricht protocol on social policy (see Table 13.2). Major immediately responded by tabling a vote of confidence for the following day on the government's policy 'on the adoption of the Protocol on Social Policy'. He won the day by 339 votes to 299 and just one Conservative MP was absent from the vote. The rebellions and rumours of rebellions over Maastricht illustrated the theatrical side of ordinary MPs' influence on their governments. The cold realities are neatly captured in Gerald Kaufman's comment that Conservative rebellions on major issues are:

Table 13.2 Government defeats in the House of Commons, 1905–97

1847–1905	301 government defeats on whipped votes
1905–78	At least 84 government defeats on whipped votes, of which 50 occurred from 1972–78. Government resigned on only two occasions, both after losing votes of confidence in 1924. On only three occasions do defeats appear to have been followed by votes of confidence

From 1979

29 March 1979	Confidence motion. The Callaghan government was defeated on an opposition motion of 'no confidence' by 311–310 votes. The government resigned the following day
15 December 1979	Mrs Thatcher's government defeated by 290–270 votes on motion making changes to immigration rules
14 April 1986	Shops Bill (second reading) to reform Sunday trading laws defeated (296–282)
16 July 1986	MPs amended motion on MPs' allowances (office, secretarial and research) to increase the limit (172–128)
13 March 1990	New clause in NHS and Community Care Bill on social security benefits to elderly people in private residential homes passed against government's wishes (256–253)
14 July 1990	MPs again voted to increase allowances (for office costs) on motion on MPs' allowances on a backbench amendment (324–197)
8 March 1993	First defeat for John Major. Amendment on committee stage of the European Communities (Amendment) Bill confines UK membership of the EU Committee of the Regions to elected local council members (314–292)
22 July 1993	On government's low-key motion to note government policy on adoption of the EU Social Protocol, designed to avoid defeat, a Labour amendment was passed 318–317 on Speaker's casting vote, but was found to be a miscount (corrected result, 317–316). The government motion was itself defeated (324–316)
6 December 1994	On a Resolution on the Budget, a Labour amendment to remove VAT on fuel and power was passed (319–311)
17 July 1995	Motion on parliamentary pensions accepted without division
6 November 1995	Four Labour amendments passed on motion on standards in public life: declaring MPs' fees and benefits from consultancies (322–271); public inspection (325–202); excluding deputations from register of MPs' interests (291–266); non-participation of MPs in delegations in which they have interest (289–264)
19 December 1995	Fisheries Bill: Government defeated over departmental memorandum on allowable catches (299–297)
17–18 December 1996	Defeat on Protection from Harassment Bill (committee stage) on compulsory counselling for convicted stalkers (179–172)
27 January 1997	At report stage of Education Bill, government defeat on new clause to relax controls on grant-maintained schools (273–272). Actual result tied, but original defeat stood

Defeats in Commons standing committees, 1979–94

	Total of 16 government defeats, including three in the Scottish Grand Committee. Six defeats were on opposition amendments to government bills; four on backbench Conservative amendments

Sources: Lowell 1924: 79–80; Norton 1978b; House of Commons Library and original Democratic Audit research

a traditional, if somewhat unstately gavotte [of ministers and backbenchers] – here a step backwards, there a lurch to the side. But we all know that the dance will end with most backbenchers quickstepping through the government lobby.

(*Guaràian*, 26 October 1992)

The dance on this occasion resembled a bruising highland reel rather more than a gavotte. But once the issue became one of confidence, its conclusion was never in question. The same realities obtain under a Labour government, as the first backbench revolt in November 1997 over cuts to single parent benefits revealed.

There are other ways in which MPs are said to exercise influence over party leaders in government. Of some significance in the life of parliamentary parties are party committees (Judge 1990: 200–208). Thus Paul Silk, a senior Commons clerk, notes that 'through these committees backbenchers can force the leadership to change its mind' (1987: 49). More cautiously Philip Norton concludes that

Party Committees . . . appear to provide a structured means . . . and forums through which Members may communicate with and seek to influence their party leaders, communication which may be more uninhibited and effective than on the floor of the House, given the privacy and party exclusivity of committee meetings.

(1983: 8)

The conditional nature of this statement indicates its true importance for a democratic audit, as such influence is partial, is exercised in 'smoke-filled' rooms, away from public scrutiny, and achieves indeterminate results. All that can be said with certainty is that in 1997 the Conservative Party had 27 subject committees and subcommittees (including the 1922 Committee), and seven regional groups; whereas Labour operated 18 subject committees and nine regional groups. More informal and capricious forms of influence include 'bumping into each other' in a corridor (as the then Tory whip, David Willetts, and Sir Geoffrey Johnson Smith MP did on a now famous occasion in October 1994); buttonholing one another in the tearoom or a bar; or for Tory MPs, attending a dining club. The exact influence exerted by this unstructured 'climate setting' and 'sounding opinion' is potentially significant, but it remains unquantifiable, usually partisan, and obscured from public view. But there is no doubt that ministers in their departments constantly fear trouble in Parliament, and that they adjust their policies as a result. Therefore, the civil service does the same.

In conclusion, then, we have seen that the ability of the House of Commons to control the executive, or to keep it under effective scrutiny, is limited at its very roots. Modern governments suffer very few defeats in Parliament, even if they are minority governments. Only one government since the war has lost a vote of confidence and was obliged to go to the country; and no government this century has been forced out of office by a rebellion within its own ranks, apart from the exceptional case of May 1940 when a Tory revolt forced Neville Chamberlain's resignation

Parliamentary debates

as Prime Minister and his replacement by Winston Churchill. As Peter Riddell argues forcibly, Parliament's major role this century has been to translate the votes of the public at general elections into clear-cut decisions about which party should form a government, and then to sustain it in office. Apart from the formation of wartime coalitions in 1915, 1916 and 1940, and their break-up in 1922 and 1945, only twice this century has a change in government not been the result of a general election – in 1905 and 1931 (Riddell 1998: 26–27). Moreover party loyalty and discipline ensures that the electoral decision is usually sustained throughout a Parliament, and even party governments with very small majorities, or even minority governments, have been able to survive in office for a long time.

Within the House, as we have seen, the official opposition and other parties can only bring influence to bear on the executive if the government of the day allows them to do so, or in the case of minor parties, requires their votes. Otherwise they are generally powerless. It is argued that government backbench MPs – just one part of Parliament – have the capacity to harass and influence, though hardly to control, the executive. But such influence is essentially partisan rather than public, specific rather than general, often expedient rather than principled, and as we have seen, exaggerated too. Even John Major, a weak Prime Minister, was ultimately able to maintain a more or less even-handed, if hardening, attitude on Europe against all the pressures of his Euro-sceptic backbench and cabinet colleagues. As we write, it is clear that the complexity of the issues, rather than Labour parliamentarians, has blunted the welfare reform programme of Tony Blair and Gordon Brown.

Dealing with the government's business

There is a notion that runs around the Benches of the House . . . that the Government must have their business. The only thing that the Government should have is the finance. . . . I want hon. Members to look cautiously at every ambitious engagement of a Minister of the Crown. That is our function.

(Richard Shepherd MP, in the House of Commons, 1 February 1994)

Democracy is not only about the election of politicians; it is about setting limits to their powers.

(Select Committee on the Scrutiny of Delegated Powers, 1994)

Romantic parliamentarians and textbooks alike still proclaim the value of debate on the floor of the Commons as a means of holding the government accountable for its actions. Debates have thus variously been conceived as the 'arena for constitutional opposition' within which government must 'publicly submit its activities to appraisal' (Coxall and Robins 1991: 209); or as 'the prime means by which the Commons fulfils its "expressive" function and at times of crisis . . . can be used to express the national mood with devastating effect' and 'oblige ministers continually to rationalise and justify their conduct' (Adonis 1990: 97, 99). Around half the House's time is devoted to discussion of the government's legislation and motions in debates which may be specific and policy-oriented, or wide ranging. Government legislation comes before the whole

House for wide-ranging debate at second reading, and then for more detailed scrutiny at report stage after its committee stage, and finally at third reading.

Most substantive debates are initiated by the government or the official opposition. The opposition parties choose what to debate on 20 days out of an average parliamentary session of 160 days or more. Backbenchers may enter ballots to initiate adjournment debates lasting from half an hour to one-and-a-half hours on Wednesday mornings, or to raise an issue in a poorly-attended 30-minute adjournment debate at the end of a day's business; or can very rarely indeed spark off an emergency debate, at the Speaker's discretion. Otherwise a backbench MP may put down an early day motion which will never be debated, but he or she can argue a case on the order paper and seek to generate the backing of backbench MPs, often on a cross-party basis. MPs are broadly satisfied with this balance, which they found compares favourably to other 'Westminster-based' parliaments (Procedure Committee 1992b: III; 1992a: viii).

But how time is spent is rather more important than how much is available. An audit must attempt, therefore, to measure quality as much as quantity. Some observers insist that the quality of debate in the Commons 'is much higher than most people realise' (John Grigg, *The Times*, 18 October 1991). However, a more focused assessment is that the term 'debate' is largely inappropriate to what occurs on the floor of the chamber when legislation is being considered or motions discussed. Instead of reasoned arguments, and opinions being swayed and modified through deliberation, which is the hallmark of the traditional emphasis placed upon legislators' discussions, debates in the Commons are often simply ritual exchanges of party political propaganda. This is not to say that thoughtful and well-argued speeches do not occur. They most certainly do. But the general tendency is well summarised by Professor Philip Norton in evidence to the Procedure Committee:

> there is no real debate, speaker after speaker delivering prepared speeches which make no reference to preceding speeches and which may have no particular relationship to them. Debates on general topics, such as foreign affairs, tend to be particularly disparate. Debate may also be said to be artificial in that there are very few Members present to have a debate with.
>
> (Procedure Committee 1992b: 76)

Most debates are poorly attended, except when ministers or their shadows are on their feet, at Prime Minister's Question Time, or when a major issue is being thrashed out. Generally only about 15 or 20 MPs are present, most of them waiting to speak themselves; an adjournment debate is often attended only by the MP, a junior minister and government whip. When the House is full, members cheer their own side and jeer the spokespersons of opposing parties. Members are often shouted down, and in recent years the drowning out of speakers by backbench claques seems to have been organised, or at least implicitly encouraged, by party managers, most frequently on the Tory side. After dinner, debates are generally rowdier, and since May 1997, certain Conservative MPs have become notorious for offensive remarks and gestures towards women Labour MPs (see Shirley Williams, *Guardian* G2, 15 December 1997).

Parliament's legislative role

Curiously, the Speaker rarely intervenes, presumably because such behaviour is regarded as customary. But it detracts from the quality and seriousness of debates and encourages aggressive rather than thoughtful speeches and debate.

Even the length of debates is largely artificial, with set times for their duration irrespective of how many MPs wish to speak. This is convenient for the whips and MPs alike, as it gives them a predictable end-time at which to be present for votes. But it sometimes means that MPs with little or no interest in the subject under discussion have to be cajoled into speaking simply to keep the debate going until the specified time; or, alternatively, a ten-minute time limit is placed on backbench contributions because too many MPs wish to speak. Adjournment debates do give backbench MPs the chance to raise issues of concern and to secure a ministerial response. But government and opposition debates are conducted within an adversarial ethos and structured and dominated primarily by frontbenchers rehearsing themes and issues for the next general election; and the end results are decided by MPs who have not heard the debates at all, acting on their whips' instructions.

Most votes are a charade, even those on parliamentary bills which will become the law of the land. A farcical episode in January 1990 sums up the position. John Stradling Thomas, a Conservative MP, was denounced in the *Daily Mail* (1 February 1990) under the headline, 'Is this the laziest MP in the Commons?' Alan Clark MP explained in his diary that Stradling Thomas ('Stradders as he is known') had to break off drinking with the *Mail* journalist in Strangers Bar on the evening of 31 January to vote: 'When the unfortunate Stradders came back from voting and the reporter asked him what he had been voting "on", Stradders didn't know. Great indignation. But we seldom ever know what we are voting "on"' (Clark 1993: 279).

In fact, it has long been the case that the great majority of MPs are ignorant about the merits of any legislation or other issue on which they are voting, and few of them have heard even a portion of any debate. It was recognised before the beginning of this century that the advent of party government meant that MPs would generally be obliged to vote with their party rather than on the merits of any argument or legislation. In 1953, Herbert Morrison, Labour's deputy leader, opposed a proposal that certain divisions (votes) should not at once follow the debate, but MPs should have time to read the debate in Hansard. He warned the Select Committee on Delegated Legislation:

> You are shouting to the world that we are deliberately going to vote . . . on something which we know the bulk of us have not heard the merits of . . . while it is perfectly true that the debate may proceed, and three quarters of the Members taking part in the division may not have heard a word of it, nevertheless it is respectable on the face of it.
>
> (Minutes of Evidence, 1953: 81, HC 310)

The legislative role of the Commons

This is the perspective within which the Commons fulfils its duty to subject legislation to scrutiny and amendment. Traditionally, Parliament has never acted as a legislature, literally a maker of law, in its own right, but has instead served to restrain and inhibit the executive's legislative capacity. It is not supposed to do so in an obstructionist sense of defeating and overturning legislation, but rather positively amending, improving and authorising laws by allowing for public scrutiny and opinion to be brought to bear on their passage through Westminster. But the adversarial nature of the relationship between the governing party and the others, the aggressive debating style of the Commons, and the procedural weakness of the scrutiny processes has made nonsense of this notion. There is instead widespread and long-standing dissatisfaction with both the executive's and Parliament's legislative role. In the modern era, the Heap Report in 1970, the Stow Hill Report in 1972, a Procedure Committee Report in 1973, and the Renton Report in 1975, were all critical of the legislative process and proposed reforms.

Outside concerns rose steadily during the Thatcher era. Massive and ill-prepared bills were forced through a largely compliant Parliament by the Prime Minister and can-do ministers, often requiring last-minute amendments in their hundreds in the House of Lords, or even tidying-up legislation soon after they were passed, simply to make them workable. In 1993, the all-party Hansard Society for Parliamentary Government published *Making the Law*, an authoritative report on the legislative process by a high-powered commission (Hansard Society 1993). The commission considered evidence from at least 57 organisations and individuals, all of whom found the process wanting in some respect or another.

We have already subjected the various stages of the legislative process in the Commons and Lords to critical analysis in the first Democratic Audit volume (1996: 61–67; 83–89). Here our concern is with MPs' ability to subject legislation to effective and informed scrutiny. Philip Norton informed the Hansard Society commission that their capacity to do so was limited: 'The House is constrained by a lack of time, information, specialisation and resources from submitting bills to effective scrutiny' (Hansard Society 1993: 326).

It is not simply that Parliament fails to subject individual bills to effective scrutiny, but that it is obliged to collude with the executive in an ongoing process in which government's own role is profoundly unsatisfactory. Thus another constitutional expert, Rodney Brazier, has noted: 'It is in the process of legislation that the impotence of the opposition parties and backbenchers when faced by a cohesive majority government may be seen the most clearly' (Brazier 1988: 182).

The sheer weight of legislation is a problem in itself. Governing has recently produced ceaseless legislative activity. The Labour government pressed some 65 Acts a year through Parliament from 1974–78, plus over 2,000 statutory instruments annually; the Thatcher governments passed 348 public bills between 1985 and 1990 – an average of 58 Acts per annum – and from 1979–90 made 10,632 statutory instruments (an average of 886 annually). These bills are frequently huge and unclear, and have often been presented 'half-baked' in Parliament, leaving the detail to be worked out and inserted by way of late amendments. Mrs Thatcher's governments in the late 1980s introduced literally thousands of amendments to bills each year (DA Volume No. 1: 63). Yet it has long been a truism that government bills almost invariably become law. Broadly, some 90 per cent of government bills

Parliament's legislative role

introduced in Parliament become law by the end of the session, and those which don't normally fall for procedural reasons and most certainly not because they have been de-railed by critical appraisal. The qualitative evidence is harder to assess, but critical evidence about the inaccessible and ill-thought-out legislation from lawyers and other 'end-user' witnesses to the Hansard Society commission was damning; from a democratic viewpoint, the most pertinent comment came from Sir John Bourn, Comptroller and Auditor General: 'If Departments and the National Audit Office find it difficult to interpret legislation, what chance has the man in the street?'

The Law Society pointed out that many bills now are mainly or partly of a highly technical nature and few MPs have the necessary specialist knowledge or interest to contribute to detailed debate on or scrutiny of the issues (Hansard Society 1993: Appendix 1, 263). But, as we have seen (see Chapter 13), the ethos of the House discourages MPs from developing specialist knowledge. Further, the detailed scrutiny of bills is delegated to standing committees appointed on an ad-hoc basis which 'militates against developing any form of specialisation or corporate spirit' (Norton, *ibid.*: 326). Such committees have no powers of investigation. They simply replicate the comparative strength of the parties in the Commons, with ministers and whips on board, and their deliberations tend to continue the adversarial politics of the larger assembly. For example, the specialist authors of the study of the poll tax, which we have already quoted, described its standing committee as a 'futile marathon' of 35 sessions:

> A colossal amount of committee time was spent on the first few clauses . . . after which the government resorted to a guillotine so that most of the later clauses went through with virtually no debate. . . . The committee stage was mostly a matter of posturing. There were a few honest attempts to improve the detail of the bill. . . . For the rest, it was scrutiny by slogan and sound-bite.
>
> (Butler *et al.* 1994: 116–117)

It is widely agreed that the root of Parliament's weak capacity for scrutiny is the combination of the party ethos of the House, which we describe in Chapter 14, and the determination of postwar governments to get their 'business' – i.e. legislation – through both Houses. Governments have also been less willing to accept warnings, amendments or criticisms from the opposition, even when they are well-founded, or even from their own backbench MPs. The Tory MP Sir Brandon Rhys-Williams was foremost among members of the standing committee on the poll tax who were trying to improve its detail, but his minister brushed his proposals aside (*ibid.*: 117). But the poll tax was simply one among a variety of bills which were major disasters, like the Child Support Act 1991, or generally unworkable, like the Dangerous Dogs Act 1991 and the Football Spectators Act 1989.

The journalist Andrew Marr chose as his cautionary tale in *Ruling Britannia*, his study of the British constitution, the passage of the Social Security Act 1986, which was steered through the Commons debates and committee stage in 1986 by the then Social Services Secretary, Norman Fowler, and two able junior ministers, Tony

Newton and John Major. The bill was designed to encourage people to switch from their existing state and occupational schemes to 'portable' personal pensions and contained a 2 per cent financial incentive. Marr tells the tale vividly (1995: 143–153). The official opposition, and Labour and Tory MPs, continually warned ministers of 'key flaws in the legislation', such as likely high administrative charges and commissions, hidden by 'the opacity of the all-important information', the absence of protection against high-pressure sales, the dangers of people being misinformed and cheated. But the bill became law, was promoted by a £1.2 million advertising campaign, and at the height of the economic boom, some 6.5 million people went for private pensions. What MPs had predicted happened. Hundreds of thousands of people – an untold number of them wrongly advised or deliberately misled – made a bad bargain which ruined many of their lives. The incentives cost the government £1.3 billion, rather than the £60 million estimate, and by April 1995, the Personal Investment Authority estimated that up to £3 billion more might be needed to compensate some of the 350,000 losers. Most losers are still awaiting compensation. Yet all the flaws were both predicted and preventable:

> In some cases, the very proposals which were laughed at by ministers were later adopted by the government to limit the damage that followed. . . . The story could be repeated, with variations, in a vast range of cases, grave and trivial, narrow and broad. . . . The culture has failed.
>
> (*Ibid.*: 146–152)

The opposition's role is bound up in this culture. What governments propose, oppositions oppose. As we have seen, reasoned arguments from the opposition or back benches rarely sway governments. Instead, governments and oppositions play out a tug-of-war over parliamentary time (Chapter 13). Moreover, on occasions, oppositions do not see it as being in their own interests to oppose some government bills vigorously. For example, the Labour opposition to the poll tax legislation was ineffective, and deliberately so. Party tacticians like Peter Mandelson were fearful of being too closely associated with local Labour councils, and anyway, were delighted to leave the real opposition to Tory rebels, thus emphasising the governing party's splits over the bill. But behind the thunder of political strife, as we have seen, opposition parties co-operate with governments to deliver their legislative programmes on time to keep parliamentary life 'civilised' and free from late-night sittings, 'ambush' votes, and so on. No wonder, then, that the Hansard Society report on the legislative process was contemptuous of the opposition's scrutiny role.

Oppositions do sometimes signal their political disapproval of some pieces of legislation by obstructive tactics to which governments respond by cutting short scrutiny of a bill by means of the 'guillotine' – formally an 'allocation of time motion'. Governments have generally justified the use of the guillotine by arguing that they will otherwise lose the legislation through lack of time. But nowadays governments impatient of opposition resort to the guillotine of their own accord. In the 30 years of largely consensus politics from 1945 to 1975, the guillotine was applied 38 times. But since 1975, more adversarial politics has led to abuse. The minority Labour government of the late 1970s applied the guillotine to 12 bills, with five guillotines being introduced in a single afternoon. Labour's argument was that being in a minority made this abuse inevitable, when they may well have considered that having failed to carry the country with them, they had no right to introduce a guillotine motion at all. Even with large majorities, Mrs Thatcher's governments applied the guillotine more ferociously still, employing 58 guillotines in the 1987–88 session alone. Six bills were guillotined, the largest number ever, in a single session.

The guillotine fell to force ill-considered legislation through the House. Perhaps the most striking, and absurd, example was the Dangerous Dogs Act 1991: all its stages were guillotined through in a single day. The committee stage on the floor of the House was able to consider only the first clause. The Major government required 18 guillotines in three years and a constitutional innovation – imposing the guillotine on five occasions not to rescue a bill from obstruction by the opposition, but in advance of any debate at all. The Conservative MP Richard Shepherd protested:

> I came here, having been elected by the citizens of Aldridge-Brownhills, with the thought that, when they had cause to be anxious about something, I might be able to contribute to the process of debate – the detailed scrutiny of legislation where appropriate. This constitutional innovation . . . is an extraordinary development. . . . It reduces the House to nothing.
>
> (HC Deb, 14 December 1993, c871–873)

The depths of abuse may not yet have been plumbed. In response to a Labour campaign of non-co-operation in protest, cabinet 'hawks' pressed for a permanent regime of guillotine, or 'time-tabling', to be introduced unilaterally and across the board. In an old-fashioned legislature, in which time is the battleground, the use of the guillotine is inevitable at times of intense partisan disagreement. But it exacerbates the failings of the legislative process and wholly undermines the goal of democratic scrutiny. Further, as Paul Silk has commented, 'In a sense the guillotine is a negation of the principle of parliamentary debate, and it could be a dangerous weapon in the hands of a government determined to stifle opposition' (1987: 140).

As we went to press, the Labour government was considering a more consensual procedure for 'timetabling' government bills after second reading to avoid the capricious use of the guillotine. It is believed that such a measure might improve the quality of scrutiny of legislation (see the Procedure Committee Report 1992a: xxi). In procedural terms the case might seem fairly clearcut. But, as always, procedure cannot be abstracted from the norms and values of the House. What worries many backbenchers is the danger that timetabling would deprive oppositions of their main weapon – pressure of time on government. Such a move would thus switch 'the initiative to the government' still further, as the late Bob Cryer MP warned the Committee (*ibid.*: 109). Peter Shore MP was sure that ministers would almost inevitably, given their 'executive mentality', seek to 'take the strength out of opposition' (*ibid.*: 60).

For Tory backbencher Andrew Rowe, the then government's abuse of the guillotine simply brought home the reality of Parliament's impotence in the face of executive arrogance:

We claim we are here to control the executive, but that claim is difficult to sustain when the executive propose the business, guillotine the business, and virtually never lose their business. We claim that we call the executive to account. . . . To suggest that we here call effectively to account an executive whose patronage extends even further through British institutions is to delude ourselves.

(HC Deb, 3 November 1993, c461)

The making of 'executive law'

At least governments cannot yet secure their primary legislation out of sight of the public and MPs. But while about 2,405 pages of primary legislation are put to the Commons every year, there are also some 6,725 pages of secondary (or delegated) legislation, often just as important, but MPs examine only a fraction of them, hardly ever discuss them, and have no power to amend them. Acts of Parliament generally confer powers on ministers to make rules or regulations following on from the Act itself. These rules have the same force of law as the actual Act and are laid before Parliament by ministers, usually in the form of statutory instruments (SIs) or Orders in Council. But they may also be issued as 'quasi-legislation' – administrative orders, regulations and codes of practice, which are often of a quasi-legal nature. The undemocratic nature of secondary legislation has occasioned concern since the 1920s, but Parliaments have simply acquiesced in its growing abuse over the years and bills giving ministers more and more powers still go through by grace of majority party rule.

In effect, ministers are enacting their own 'executive law' – and some 2,000 statutory instruments and orders ghost like neutrons through the House every year (as do some thousands of EU directives and regulations). The Law Society has pointed out that this executive law is not 'secondary' in importance, but is more important in some cases than 'primary' legislation, and 'should therefore be accorded the necessary time for full and detailed scrutiny' (Hansard Society 1993: 286). The implications both for democracy and human rights in Britain are serious. The first Audit volume, *The Three Pillars of Liberty*, found that of 37 violations of the European Convention on Human Rights, no fewer than nine had their origin in secondary or 'quasi' legislation (DA Volume No. 1: 66).

The scope of secondary legislation has never been defined by Parliament or the courts, its boundaries are equally uncertain, and 'quasi' legislation in particular is inconsistent and unsystematic (Ganz 1987: 36). It is widely recognised that parliamentary scrutiny of such legislation ranges from being weak to virtually non-existent (e.g. Garrett 1992: 59–65; Riddell 1998: 217). MPs cannot amend these instruments and orders – they must accept or reject them. The vast majority, however, go through unseen, except by the two specialist committees on SIs – the Commons Select Committee on SIs and a joint Commons and Lords committee on SIs. Fewer than 20 per cent – 'affirmative' instruments – actually even require members' approval. The rest – 'negative' instruments – become law if no MP has objected within 40 days of their being laid before the House. Few objections are ever debated, fewer still achieve their objective. 'Quasi-legislation' – the dense mass of official regulations, codes of practice, and rules promulgated by government departments – is almost wholly outside parliamentary control. The quasi-judicial rule-books for prisons, the immigration service, health and safety at work, social security offices, and so on, represent the sharp end of executive practice in the most sensitive areas of social and civil life in Britain. Some, like certain ministerial instructions to immigration officers, are unpublished. The most that MPs can do when they do debate 'quasi-legislation' is to make recommendations which ministers may accept or reject as they please.

Secondary legislation has long aroused judicial and parliamentary concerns, but the volume of instruments has grown inexorably, as has the range of powers they confer on ministers and officials. Andrew Bennett MP, formerly chairman of the Commons SI Committee and a member for some 20 years, has described their growing and dangerous use: 'A major change in the nature of instruments has occurred. Provisions in the past which would have been contained in primary legislation are dealt with in delegated legislation' (Bennett 1990). A striking recent example of the dangers of backdoor executive law escaping parliamentary scrutiny was the Home Office proposal to give the police new powers to shred prosecution evidence in jury trials after only three years. These powers were contained in a code of practice attached to the Criminal Procedure and Investigations Act 1996. They were not debated in Parliament, but came to light in the aftermath of the release of the Bridgewater Three in February 1997. Two former Home Secretaries – Lord Jenkins and Lord Merlyn-Rees – joined the protests pointing out that miscarriages of justice, such as the convictions of the Bridgewater Three, the Maguire family and the Guildford Four, could never have been discovered if these powers had been in use. For in each case it was analysis of the original prosecution papers – more than 20 years old – which proved that the convictions were unsound. The Home Secretary decided finally not to introduce the powers, and laid a new order bringing an amended code of practice before Parliament for approval.

Some Acts actually create 'Henry VIII powers', named after that monarch's autocratic Statute of Proclamations of 1539, which enable ministers to amend or repeal primary legislation by statutory instruments – i.e. to evade proper parliamentary scrutiny while they make and re-make the law. For example, local government acts in the 1990s gave ministers powers to change 'capping' regimes on local authority budgets, to alter council tax bands, to reorganise and change the powers of local authorities, to extend compulsory competitive tendering for local services, and so on. The House of Lords removed the clause giving ministers this last power on the grounds that it was 'unconstitutional', but it was restored by the government's Commons majority. Social security acts gave ministers powers to adapt and change by instruments undebated in the House social security provisions and benefit levels which could affect millions of people, while far less significant tax changes might be debated for hours. These powers were so wide that Lord Donaldson, in the Court of Appeal, complained that child benefit regulations allowed the minister 'to prescribe that black is white and nothing is something. . . . This just will not do' (*Guardian*, 22 February 1991).

Under Conservative governments, indeed, social security and local government bills often took the form of 'skeleton' legislation, which set out a very general framework to which ministers could later add the vital details by way of statutory instruments – once again, in effect, enabling ministers and officials to determine crucial policy issues without reference to Parliament. Such bills, according to an authoritative parliamentary committee, 'are little more than authority for Ministers to determine the policy and to legislate to give effect to it' (Delegated Powers Scrutiny Committee 1993a: 8, para. 28).

Governments use these instruments and orders as they allow them to act with 'speed, flexibility and adaptability' (Erskine May 1989: 538). Their original purpose was to allow ministers to fine-tune and update detailed aspects of legislation, but the temptations of power have proved irresistible. Now they can put important and unsupervised powers in the hands of ministers and officials; as the Joint Committee on SIs has observed:

> Secondary legislation has increased not only in volume but in scope. Instead of simply implementing the nuts and bolts of government policy, SIs have increasingly been used to change policy, sometimes in ways which were not envisaged when the enabling primary legislation was passed.
>
> (Procedure Committee 1990a: Memo No. 11)

Often ministers do not themselves know what use they intend to make of the powers they are assuming (Procedure Committee 1987, *Minutes of Evidence*: 9); and, as authoritative observers like Sir William Wade, the public lawyer, have pointed out, they may abuse their powers by placing them 'in cold storage' – i.e. 'storing up' these powers to make executive law for the purposes of carrying out the government's longer term and less well developed policies later on (Delegated Powers Scrutiny Committee 1993a: 25). In some cases, it is obvious that rule-making powers are assumed well in advance of any serious consideration as to how they will eventually be used (Puttick 1988: 23). Further, while MPs and peers receive only a very limited retrospective chance to debate them, they are often the product of confidential negotiations in Whitehall between officials and organised interests, which contribute significantly to their final form (Hansard Society 1993: 41, 189; see also Chapter 10).

Parliament's defences against the flood of secondary legislation are limited in scope and powers. All instruments which require MPs' express approval now go to standing committee or to the House. The two specialist SI committees seek only to establish whether SIs conform to the 'parent' Act, and whether the attention of the House should be drawn to a particular instrument. They are not empowered to consider the merits of SIs, nor does the House necessarily have to follow their recommendations. Debates may also take place on SIs where there is evidence of significant opposition to them. But MPs can only vote on the motion that they have considered an instrument. Any substantive vote on whether or not to approve an instrument takes place on the floor of the House without debate. Where there is evidence of significant opposition, debates on SIs may also take place in the House anyway. But Commons debates on SIs invariably take place after 10pm; very few MPs participate;

and a time-limit of one hour and a half is imposed on 'affirmative instruments', allowing governments to circumvent criticism (see Garrett 1992: 61–63; Griffith and Ryle 1989: 345; and Procedure Committee 1987).

Academic analysis of the work of the specialist committees from 1973 to 1983 found that though they were processing significantly more SIs over these sessions, they were also constantly racing against time and often failed to produce their reports in time to influence debates (Hayhurst and Wallington 1988). In fact it often happens that governments put down motions to approve SIs while the committees are still considering them. Over the ten sessions, the committees reported 703 SIs as defective or requiring extra scrutiny out of a total of some 13,500. Of those reported, only 129 (or 18.5 per cent) were tabled for debate in either the Commons or the Lords. No reported instrument was voted down by either House; the one that was rejected, on its merits, was not reported. Further, of 16 instruments found to be *ultra vires* by the courts from 1914–86, only three of the 12 considered by the joint committee, or its predecessor, had been reported (and in these cases, the *ultra vires* question came to light only because of the litigation). The Commons SI Committee complained in 1989 that SIs of 'uncertain legality' are allowed to take effect in the absence both of any parliamentary power to amend SIs and of any formal mechanism for ensuring that 'necessary corrective measures' are taken. Further, some departments respond to the committee's points 'in a truculent manner and refuse to repair the faults in instruments. The committee finds that it is not acceptable that so little account is taken of its work' (Procedure Committee 1990a: Memo No. 11).

The Hansard Society commission concluded that the committees did valuable work in examining the legality and clarity of SIs, but like other select committees, they had to operate within the constraints of 'an unreformed Parliamentary system' in which the House ignored their reports and criticised ministers escaped censure. The 'balance of accountability' was weak and Parliament's approach to delegated legislation was 'highly unsatisfactory' (1993: 90). Gabriele Ganz, the academic expert, comments that it was surprising 'how little the [Joint] Committee has done to curb the worst excesses of delegated legislation falling within its terms of reference' (1997: 74). The need for thorough review of the Commons procedures for scrutiny of statutory instruments is clear, but the House has failed to act.

However, mounting concern about secondary legislation, especially among law lords, led the House of Lords to take the initiative in 1992 and establish its own select committee to examine and report on the powers ministers were proposing to take in draft bills, and in particular to watch out for 'Henry VIII powers' and skeleton bills. The Delegated Powers Scrutiny Committee (since re-named the Delegated Powers and Deregulation Committee) was modelled on a similar body in the Australian Senate, though with fewer powers and a narrower remit. The government ostensibly welcomed the setting up of the committee, but insisted that its scrutiny should be confined to considering 'the merits of the Government's proposed use of delegated powers . . . case by case in each specific context' rather than a structural analysis of secondary legislation as a whole. Further, it ought not to examine the procedural and timetabling aspects of affirmative and negative resolutions nor orders stating when new powers would come into force (which, for example, allow ministers to 'store' powers for future use). The committee was almost as cautious as the government, perhaps reflecting the House of Lords' habitual inhibition about fully using its formal powers (see below). Even on Henry VIII powers, the committee has been lenient to ministers, as an academic study of its first two years (1992–94) has shown; 'not all such powers have been drawn to the attention of the House, and in some cases, the Committee has been happy to have them subject to the negative procedure or subject to no parliamentary control at all' (Himsworth 1995: 41).

Where the committee has decided to draw particular abuses to the attention of Parliament, its experience has been mixed. The government has often, though not always, responded to its criticisms. But it has provided scrutiny where there would otherwise have been none, and has identified major and inappropriate attempts to create delegated powers. In 1993, its first report condemned a major part of the then Education Bill as 'skeleton' legislation and severely criticised the Secretary of State's intention to take delegated powers to interfere with students' freedom of association Delegated Powers Scrutiny Committee 1993b: 1, para. 4). Substantial changes were made to the bill (later the Education Act 1994) and the committee had, according to Lord Russell, thereupon 'won its spurs' (HL Deb, 22 March 1994, c608). Chris Himsworth was more sceptical, considering that the committee stuck too much to technical rather substantial issues (1995). Be that as it may, Parliament as a whole has significantly failed to take seriously the dangers that the mass of secondary legislation it allows through represent for the quality of democratic in the UK.

The House of Lords: an undemocratic anomaly

> And whereas it is intended to substitute for the House of Lords as it at present exists a Second Chamber constituted on a popular instead of a hereditary basis, but such substitution cannot be immediately brought into operation.
>
> (Preamble to the Parliament Act 1911)

> The House of Peers, throughout the war,
> Did nothing in particular,
> And did it very well.
>
> (Gilbert and Sullivan, *Iolanthe*, II)

Uniquely among modern representative democracies, Britain's second chamber, the House of Lords, is predominantly hereditary in composition; and none of its members are elected, either directly or indirectly (see Table 13.3). The Lords may well be the oldest legislative chamber in the world, with a history which predates Parliament itself. It has survived abolition (from 1649–60), two major Acts curtailing its powers, in 1911 and 1949, and has been on Death Row, so to speak, since 1911. Through most of its history, the Lords has been a small assembly. It was large-scale creation of peers by Prime Ministers from Pitt the Younger to Lloyd George which swelled its membership to more than 700 by 1925 (Adonis 1990). In 1958, it was rejuvenated by the Life Peerages Act, which gave Prime Ministers powers to appoint life peers as well as to create hereditary peers, and its size has swelled even further since.

Composition of Lords

Two archbishops, 24 bishops of the Church of England and 26 'law lords' (see Chapter 15), complete the House.

In brief, the chamber remains an undemocratic anachronism, in which there is no element of popular election (**DAC1**) and thus no possibility of its composition reflecting a democratic choice (**DAC4**). Yet the chamber plays an active, and increasingly busy, role in Britain's legislative and political processes, and its contribution is frequently praised, often at the expense of the elective Commons. Several claims are advanced in favour of the Lords. We are informed that the hereditary principle brings a wide cross-section of society into the House, made wider still by the presence of life peerages, which allow people of distinction who would not submit to the indignity of election to make a contribution to public life. The Lords is said to be more independent than the elected Commons and 'democratic' by default; and though hereditary peers give the Conservatives a built-in advantage, the 'working House' is less partisan, and the 'working peers' raise the quality of debate and scrutiny in Parliament and provide an informed and valuable revising chamber for legislation. We examine these claims below.

The composition of the House of Lords

At the beginning of 1998, hereditary peers made up 60 per cent of the upper House's active members (see Table 13.3). In addition, there were 461 life peers. Until 1958, women members were forbidden. Membership remains overwhelmingly male, with only 97 women (7.6 per cent) in the House, 16 of them hereditary peers. There are 12 peers from among Britain's ethnic minorities and the 26 members of the Church of England's hierarchy are uniquely privileged among the wide range of religions and sects represented in the population outside.

The creation of life and new hereditary peerages is ultimately the decision of the Prime Minister, and is but one more indication of the power of patronage highlighted in Chapter 6. From 1958–79, half the life peers appointed (194 out of 391) were Labour members in a bipartisan effort to redress the unbalanced political make-up of the Lords. Mrs Thatcher broke with convention and used her power for overtly

Table 13.3 Composition of the House of Lords, 1998*

Archbishops and bishops	26	–
Hereditary peers	759	(16)
Law lords	26	–
Life peers	461	(81)
Active membership	1,272	(97)

Source: House of Lords Information Service
Notes:
Figures in brackets indicate women members.
* 121 eligible peers do not attend the House; three hereditary peers are minors; 10 people who have inherited peerages have disclaimed them for life (including three who sit in the House by virtue of other titles).

partisan purposes. Of the 199 life peers created between 1979 and 1990, 99 were drawn from the Conservative Party and only 45 from Labour. Labour protests that she was seriously weakening their ability to fulfil their duties of opposition in the Lords were brushed aside. In 1983, Mrs Thatcher also revived the practice of creating new hereditary peerages (none had been created since 1964) and four men were duly ennobled. That the Prime Minister of the day can in effect determine the composition of an active part of the legislature, and on partisan grounds, with no effective check on this power; and that the opposition parties should depend on a political rival to keep themselves adequately supplied with recruits in the second chamber is a major and irredeemable deficiency of the Lords.

Arguments for the House of Lords

As we say, it is occasionally claimed that, through the accident of birth (and death), peers by succession represent a cross-section of society. Close examination reveals such a claim to be sentimental nonsense. The Lords remains disproportionately composed of financially well-to-do white men, privately educated at public schools (in 1981, 86 per cent of them were educated at public schools, and half at Eton alone). In the 1980s, a survey found that land and business interests dominated the hereditary peerage, relieved somewhat by experience in the armed forces (20 per cent) and public service (14 per cent). The presence of a bongo-playing cabaret artist or slipper salesman, or of a peer who owes his place in the House to being the product of a virgin birth (the most exalted qualification of all?), may add to the charm of the place, but it hardly matches the Athenian principle, of representation by lot among all citizens, and falls well short of the 'equal opportunity to stand for public office, regardless of social group' set out in **DAC1**. (Baldwin 1993: 37). It has been claimed that life peers are 'drawn from a much broader social, political and professional spectrum' (Adonis 1990). But this is to claim relatively little. Life peers are still drawn largely from people who have made their career in politics and public service, augmented by a restricted range of professional backgrounds; and their creation is frequently linked with partisan political service, especially in the lower House, and sometimes with party donations.

There is no doubt that the Conservative Party is the largest political group in the Lords, accounting for 43 per cent of peers eligible to take their place at the beginning

Table 13.4 Party strengths in the House of Lords, 1998*

Party	Life peers	Hereditary peers	Lords spiritual	Total
Conservative	173	323	–	496
Labour	141	17	–	158
Liberal Democrat	44	24	–	68
Cross Bench	119	204	–	323
Other	5	73	25	103
Total	482	641	25	1,148

Source: Shell and Beamish 1993, Table 2.12

of 1998 who acknowledged taking a party whip. The party's powerful position rests on its numerical supremacy among hereditary peers, 323 of whom took the Conservative whip. By contrast, 17 took the Labour whip and 24 the Liberal Democrat whip. Such figures are, however, said to be misleading: first, because the Tory peers are, like other peers, a notably independent-minded bunch; and second, because they do not relate to the 'working' House – the near 400 or so peers who regularly attend, speak and vote in the Lords. Let us examine these claims in turn. It is possible to find a number of witnesses to the relatively independent spirit of Conservative peers and the whole House. As an anonymous Labour peer told an academic observer:

> The whole chamber has voted many times for Labour motions and amend-
> ments, according to conscience. There is no ego, no constituency, no power
> push to persuade the Lords to vote in any way they don't want to. They
> are *very* independent.

> (Shell and Beamish 1993)

In the mid-1980s, the House of Lords even temporarily won a reputation for inde-pendence from the Conservative government, and indeed, became known as 'Her Majesty's Alternative Opposition' during Mrs Thatcher's years in office. The Conservative peer, Lord Bruce-Gardyne, declared, 'No Tory government in modern times has been so consistently savaged by the watchdog once described as "Mr Balfour's Poodle"'. A more impartial observer, Nicholas Baldwin, wrote of the 'more balanced second chamber' in the mid-1980s, and the growing 'professionalism and independence' of its members (Baldwin 1993: 56–60).

The most reliable point of departure for scrutiny of such claims is the Study of Parliament Group's exhaustive analysis of the House of Lords at work in the 1988–89 session (Shell and Beamish 1993). It is true that the peers were – and remain – less intensely party political than MPs in the lower House and peers of all parties are more independent of the party whips. Their votes are fewer and less predictable than divisions in the Commons. But party solidarity in the Lords remains remark-ably high. In 1988–89, 40 Conservative peers voted once against the government, and 40 on more than one occasion, casting in all a total of 223 dissenting votes. Place these figures against the sheer weight of 366 Conservative peers casting 17,010 pro-government votes in the divisions on government bills during the session – a 53.7 per cent majority of all the votes cast. Even this understates the Conservatives' strength. The substantial body of 'crossbench' peers, who take no party whip, tend to vote about 2:1 with the Conservatives; in 1988–89, 1,771, or 61.0 per cent, of their votes were pro-government.

As for the argument that the 'working' House is more balanced than the crude overall figures might suggest, the Study of Parliament Group analysis found that the 'crude' Conservative numerical dominance among peers who actually attended the House (48 per cent) was marginally stronger than its strength among all peers eligible to sit in the House (46.6 per cent). Additionally, on an 'average' day during that session, the Conservative presence stood at 46.6 per cent, easily outnumbering Labour

(22.1 per cent) and the then combined centre parties (11.7 per cent). Life peers, though far more active in debates and committee business, mustered only a bare majority (50.3 per cent of those attending). In brief, the Conservatives may have been less active on the floor of the House, but their level of attendance built in a commanding advantage in the divisions which followed.

The Conservative whips were sparing with three-line whips, largely because they could generally rely upon an in-built majority of voting peers at most times, especially after 5pm when 'the City vote' came in. Among this majority in 1988–89 was a substantial 'silent minority' of 127 Conservative peers who, between them, cast what amounted to a block vote without ever intervening in debate. They often belonged to the rotas of peers who were called in by the whips on certain days. For important votes in 1988–89, the government could summon up 200-plus peers with a three-line whip. By contrast, Lord Cledwyn, Labour's leader in the Lords, estimated in 1991 that, allowing for age, illness and so on, 'we would be very pleased if we got 70–75 Labour peers in the lobby' for a very heavily whipped division (*Analysis*, BBC Radio 4, 10 January 1991).

In the 1988–89 session, strong Conservative whipping pulled in 234 and 236 Tory peers on two critical days of divisions – one to reverse an amendment requiring company directors to consult shareholders before making political donations. They comfortably outvoted the rest of the House put together. On both occasions, the presence of hereditary peers and 'rare and infrequent attenders' was substantially higher than usual, as the attendance figures show:

Peers in attendance:	Tory peers	Other peers[1]	Hereditary peers	'Rare and infrequent attenders'[2]
4 May 1989	234	196	225	134
7 November 1989	236	192	207	105
Average per sitting	147	169	145	46

Source: Shell and Beamish 1993, Appendix A
Notes:
1 by political affiliation, including crossbenchers, 'others' and bishops
2 those attending up to a third of sittings or less

For the most part, then, the Conservative whips rarely needed to call out their loyal reserves of hereditary peers, disparagingly known as 'the backwoodsmen', but for votes of major political importance they could be relied on to turn out and vote as required. The most spectacular example of the Tory whips' power when it matters came in their defence of the poll tax legislation in 1988. A strict whipping operation resulted in the attendance of large numbers of 'backwoodsmen' to defeat an 'ability to pay' amendment, a serious challenge to the central principle of the bill, by 317 votes to 183.

In Mrs Thatcher's early terms in office, however, the House of Lords earned a reputation for resisting her government's legislation, thanks to significant government defeats, such as the Lords' amendment to an Education Bill to prevent local authorities from charging for school transport in rural areas in her first term. Around 40 Conservative peers voted against the government. In the next session, the peers added special status for Gibraltarians to the British Nationality Bill. After the Conservatives were returned with an even larger majority after 1983, Donald Shell, the academic authority on the Lords, observed 'a noticeably enhanced determination . . . to play the role of responsible opposition' to compensate for Labour's weakness in the Commons (Shell 1993: 328). A first sign of this resolve was the wrecking of the paving measure for the abolition of the Greater London Council and six metropolitan counties in 1983–84 on the constitutional grounds that central government should not cancel out the local electoral process. The House of Lords refused to allow the government to abolish the GLC until arrangements for the transfer of its responsibilities were in place. This was described as 'quasi-constitutional' by Butler (Butler *et al.* 1994: 121). But the Lords' new reputation also owed much to observers' surprise that the House was voting against Conservative legislation at all. However, Table 13.5 shows clearly that the Lords' willingness to vote against Conservative measures was far less strong than was popularly believed. The figures demonstrate that the Lords voted against a far lower proportion of Conservative bills under Mrs Thatcher than they had during the previous Labour governments from 1974–79 (see Table 13.5).

Table 13.5 shows the record of the House of Lords from 1970 onwards. The Conservative government of Edward Heath (1970–74) suffered 26 defeats in Lords, notably on immigration and health legislation; 'most of these defeats ministers felt it imprudent or impolitic to try to reverse' (Shell 1993). Conflict between the Lords and government intensified under the Labour governments of 1974–79, as Labour's precarious initial majority gave way from 1976 to minority government, kept in place by the limited 'Lib-Lab' pact. The Labour governments suffered over 350 defeats in the Lords, as they continued to promote controversial legislation, some of which (e.g. the Dock Work Regulation Bill, 1975–76) the government was unable to reverse in the Commons. The Lords refused to give way on three measures it had defeated, even though the measures were endorsed and returned by the Commons. These were the Trade Union and Labour Relations (Amendment) Bill 1974–75 (on 'closed shops' for journalists); the Aircraft and Shipbuilding Industries Bill 1975–76 (nationalisation of ship-repairing); and the British Transport Docks (Felixstowe) Bill 1975–76 (a private bill to nationalise the dock). (They let the bills through, amended, in the next session.) Such items were clearly controversial, but so too were many of the legislative proposals of Mrs Thatcher's government; and the Lords was evidently far less inclined to check her government's measures than they were those of the Labour governments. It may be argued that the Labour government had been returned to office on a very small minority of the popular vote and was in a minority in the Commons from April 1976 to 1979; but Mrs Thatcher received a commanding majority in the Commons after 1983, on just over 40 per cent of the vote, largely because the non-Conservative vote split almost evenly in the election.

Table 13.5 Government defeats in the House of Lords, 1970–97

	No of divisions	Govt wins	Govt defeats	Other divisions	Defeats as % of divisions
Conservative government (Heath)					
1970–71	196	–	4	–	2.04
1971–72	171	–	5	–	2.92
1972–73	73	–	13	–	23.28
1973–74	19	–	2	–	10.52
1974	17	–	2	–	11.76
Labour government (Wilson 1974–76; Callaghan 1976–79)					
1974–75	119	–	n/a	–	n/a
1975–76	146	–	125	–	85.61
1976–77	45	–	25	–	55.55
1977–78	96	–	78	–	81.25
1978–79	21	–	11	–	52.38
Conservative government (Thatcher 1979–90; Major 1990–97)					
1979–80	305	–	15	–	4.91
1980–81	184	–	18	–	9.78
1981–82	146	–	7	–	4.79
1982–83	89	–	5	–	5.61
1983–84	237	–	20	–	8.43
1984–85	145	–	17	–	11.72
1985–86	250	215	22	13	8.80
1986–87	80	75	3	2	3.75
1987–88	279	254	17	8	6.09
1988–89	189	173	12	3	6.34
1989–90	186	160	20	6	10.75
1990–91	104	87	17	0	16.34
1991–92[1]	83	73	6	4	7.22
1992–93[2]	165	140	19	6	11.51
1993–94	136	98	16	21	11.76
1994–95	106	94	7	5	6.60
1995–96	109	97	10	2	9.17
1996–97[1]	67	55	10	2	14.93
1997–98[3]	55	36	14	5	25.45

Source: Figures provided by House of Lords Library
Notes:
1 Short session terminated by general election.
2 Longer than usual session of about 18 months (following general election).
3 Figures refer to divisions up to and including 16 March 1998.

Democratic 'by default'? The modern role of the Lords

The argument that the Lords is 'democratic' by default rests on the House's role in subjecting executive policy and legislation to scrutiny, a role we have identified as being at the heart of contemporary democracy in the UK. Given the limited powers of the Commons for the effective exercise of such scrutiny, it is argued, the Lords, unrepresentative though it is, has come by default to perform a significant scrutinising and deliberative role. Basically the work of the House of Lords replicates the major functions of the Commons: it deliberates, scrutinises, and seeks to control executive actions and policies. The Lords, of course, are greatly circumscribed by the limits imposed on their powers by the 1911 and 1949 Parliament Acts. The House has no power to amend or delay a financial measure, or 'money bill', and can delay other legislation by only one year. Curiously, it has retained a power to reject secondary legislation, but under a self-denying convention it has employed this power only once since 1945.

The quality of some Lords debates is unquestioned. Thus, Shell has noted that the Lords' deliberative role is enhanced by 'the presence of a wide range of expertise and a degree of procedural flexibility unparalleled in the Commons' (Shell 1992a: 181). Andrew Adonis goes so far as to suggest that 'the capacity of the Lords to stage impressive debates across the range of policy issues is undoubted – and probably equalled by few other assemblies' (1990: 145).

The presence of the law lords during Michael Howard's tenure of office at the Home Office substantially raised the quality of debate and scrutiny of his legislation in particular, but also on other bills which raised issues of human rights and the quality of British justice. The House has in recent years confined itself to only two regular select committees, on Science and Technology and the European Union, both of which have been praised for the influence of 'well-researched apolitical inquiry on a long-term issue' (Bates 1989: 52). The EU committee has been held up as an example to the select committees in the lower chamber; and in its inquiry into scrutiny of EU legislation the Commons Procedure Committee acknowledged the 'efficiency', the 'methodical approach' and the 'many attractive features' of the Lords committee (Procedure Committee 1989: xxxi). As we saw above, it was also the Lords which established a committee on delegated powers in order to deal with the worst excesses of secondary legislation (**p. 392**). The tradition of choosing to examine subjects which the Commons does not look at thoroughly is also continued in ad-hoc committees of inquiry, such as life sentencing for murder and unemployment under Mrs Thatcher's governments (and since, under Labour, the question of cannabis).

The House has also come to perform an increasing role in the legislative process: to the extent that frequent complaints have been voiced in the Lords about the sheer quantity and scope of legislation coming before it and the lack of time to deal with it. However, it is difficult to assess how well it performs as a revising chamber. Most of its legislative work involves making what may be fairly described as minor, technical and drafting amendments to bills; and half to two-thirds of public bills, regardless of the party in government, pass through the House of Lords unamended (Brazier

1988). Its antiquated procedures, including taking bills on the floor of the House rather than in committee, gravely handicap its revising work. But it has taken on sufficient legislative scrutiny to attract the attention of lobbyists who in a recent survey ranked the Lords roughly equal with the Commons when seeking to influence policy (Baldwin 1990). Given the unrepresentative nature of the House and the social and business backgrounds of its members, this is potentially an undesirable development, especially if peers were regarded as a 'softer' option than MPs. Masses of amendments have recently been added to bills in the Lords, but these have overwhelmingly been government amendments, which may sometimes be brought forward by non-government peers. Even when the Lords assiduously seeks to improve legislation, its efforts can sometimes be set aside with contempt in the Commons. Academic observers consider that the Lords serves far more as a convenience for government than an independent forum of scrutiny. Further, ministers and whips maintain a high degree of control over the legislative process in the House and are as ruthless in pressing their bills through the Lords as they are in the Commons.

The part-time nature of the House is a major weakness which is rarely discussed. The Lords, as currently constituted, is hard-pressed to carry out its existing role in a large modern democratic state. Bills are often revised in haste and superficially. The House concentrates its committee work on only a few issues, primarily because it could not sustain more. Committee attendance is already poor. In recent years, the House has considered establishing further committees, but held back from doing so because of the lack of staff, and uncertainty about the capacity of peers to sustain a higher level of committee work. Shell acknowledged the House's modest, but useful, work in the conclusion to the Study of Parliament Group study of the Lords, but his overall conclusion was harder: 'It is foolish to pretend that a House of accidentally selected part-timers can function adequately as a second chamber in a country as large and as complex as the United Kingdom' (Shell 1993: 351).

Political and democratic limits to the role of the Lords

Government defeats in the Lords are often high-profile occasions which generate a great deal of publicity. Far less attention is given to the climbdowns which almost invariably follow. Only once since the Parliament Act 1949 has the House of Lords forced a government to use the Act's procedures to get its legislation through. This was the War Crimes Bill which the Lords rejected on second reading in 1990 and 1991. Upon the second defeat the bill went straight for Royal Assent, becoming law on 9 May 1991. Otherwise, the Lords has submitted to the will of the House of Commons, or more accurately, the government of the day. That is not to say that its actions never have any political effect. In 1969, for example, the Lords blocked a gerrymandering government bill which sought to evade boundary changes proposed by the Boundary Commissions (see **p. 51**). They did so on impeccable constitutional grounds, but the fact that it was a Labour government raised suspicions that they might also have had partisan reasons for doing so. But even when they do occupy the moral high ground, they do not use their limited powers of delay under the 1949 Act to the full. Thus, for example, the peers voted in 1990–91 to amend the Criminal Justice Bill to abolish the mandatory life sentence for murder, but the government insisted on overturning the amendment; and even though this was the principal recommendation of the Lords' own ad-hoc select committee, the Lords concurred. Similarly, they abandoned amendments to the Criminal Justice and Public Order Bill 1994, designed to protect human rights standards, when the Commons returned it after reversing all the amendments.

Formally, the House has adopted a self-imposed limitation, the 'Salisbury doctrine', under which they do not oppose a measure from the House of Commons which has been clearly put before the electorate in an election manifesto. But their self-constraint normally goes far further. The Lords will amend and (less commonly) reject parts or the whole of government legislation, but if the government insists on its legislation, the Lords almost invariably assents to a bill when it is returned from the Commons, even if all its amendments have been reversed. For their part, governments rarely give way on points of significance. After 1987, for example, Conservative governments hardened their attitude to Lords' amendments, despite considerable unease on the Conservative benches in the Commons, and reversed almost all its amendments to bills on community care, student loans and social security legislation in the 1989–90 session. Only very limited concessions were made. In the same session, the government also rejected a Lords dog registration scheme which many Tory MPs favoured.

It is not simply respect for the will of a democratically elected government which inspires this deferential attitude. The Lords are perfectly aware of the tenuous nature of the electoral mandate and often express contempt for the heavily whipped lower chamber. But they are also aware that their continued existence depends on the will of the Commons. There are numerous anguished debates in the Lords on 'consideration of Commons reasons for disagreeing to Lords amendments'. For example, in November 1993, the Lords reluctantly acquiesced in the reversal by the Commons of three key amendments to the Railways Bill. Lord Simon of Glaisdale argued that though the government committed itself to privatising the railways in its manifesto, the Salisbury doctrine could not cover every detail, especially late additions which had not come under proper scrutiny. He reminded the Lords of other measures, like the Child Support Bill, which had been forced through the House 'at very late hours and at very early hours', and which had subsequently proved to be defective. The Lords commanded 'an unexampled and unparalleled wealth of experience and knowledge' but the government treated the House 'as though it were of no consequence'. He asked, 'Are we supinely to allow your Lordships' House to be marginalised and sidelined in the constitution?' The answer was 'Yes'. As Earl Russell acknowledged, 'In dealing with another place [i.e. the Commons], which we must challenge but from which we derive our power, we must walk on a tightrope'. Russell actually advised his colleagues to 'justify their existence', but common prudence prevailed, as it usually does (HL Deb, 14 November 1993, c1163–1176).

As stated above, the Lords has retained the power to veto secondary legislation, but peers adhere to a parallel convention of self-constraint, 'conscious of their constitutional position as the unelected House' (Ganz 1997: 67). Only once has this convention been broken – in 1968, when the House in partisan mood voted against the Rhodesian sanctions order. In 1995, the government took advantage of the convention by placing a broadcasting order, which had been rejected in the Commons, in front of the Lords. The Labour opposition in the Lords, however, complied with the convention, as it did when other secondary legislation they disliked, such as the regulations withdrawing social security benefits from asylum-seekers, were tabled in the House. They were not motivated by respect for the convention, but by a simpler political calculation – the fear of what a House of Lords, with its built-in Conservative advantage, could do to the secondary legislation of a Labour government (*ibid.*: 68).

Donald Shell is in no doubt about the central flaw of the Lords position in the Commons:

> The House might speak with the authority of experience and expertise, but not with the authority of democratic persons. As a result, the legitimacy of the House has become threadbare and its effectiveness, even as a revising chamber, called into question.
>
> (Shell 1992a)

In other words, it cannot 'justify its existence'. In theory, we have a second chamber with an important constitutional purpose, to revise and reconsider. In reality, the unelected House cannot stand in the way of the Commons; and up to now, the Commons has liked it this way. As we write, a cabinet committee is considering reform of the Lords. Originally, the intention was to remove all but a few active hereditary peers from the House and leave it as a predominantly appointed chamber. It is commonly said that it would become a 'super-quango'. But those who describe the prospect in these terms fail to understand the profoundly undesirable nature of any such proposal. For the Lords is part of the legislature and cannot with constitutional propriety be put wholly under the control of the executive. A House in which appointed peers hold the majority is as democratically unacceptable as one in which a mix of hereditary and appointed members hold sway, and as likely to have no independent legitimacy on which to check the executive. The fact that such a House is intended to be temporary is not comforting, since the 1911 Act's promise to institute an elected chamber remains unfulfilled.

14 Heckling the Steamroller

The imbalance of power between government and Parliament

> *The House should no longer rest content with an incomplete and unsystematic scrutiny of the activities of the Executive merely as a result of historical accident or sporadic pressures, and it is equally desirable for the different branches of the public service to be subject to an even and regular incidence of select committee investigation into their activities.*
> (House of Commons Procedure Committee, 1978)

> *The holding of Ministers and officials to account for their policies, actions and decisions . . . is carried out by the departmentally related Committees in a far more vigorous, systematic and comprehensive scrutiny than anything which went before.*
> (House of Commons Procedure Committee, 1990a)

Since the mid-1960s, reform-minded MPs of all parties have been seeking to rescue the House of Commons from servility. The major impetus for change was a Procedure Committee report in 1978, which recommended that a new system of select committees should be established to subject the executive to more systematic scrutiny. Their existence, however, failed to check the arrogance of the executive during the 1980s and early 1990s, and the Scott Report revealed the corruptions of power and the proliferation of executive agencies and raised new alarms about Parliament's surveillance of the executive. In 1995–96, the Public Service Committee (PSC) analysed the weaknesses of the House's arrangements for scrutiny of the executive and pressed the case for clearer rights for select committees and MPs. In the dying hours of the last Parliament, the PSC persuaded the government to propose a symbolic resolution of the House clarifying the duties of ministers and officials to the House (see Chapter 12). It remains to be seen whether MPs in the current Parliament will take up the baton.

In Chapter 13, we analysed the roots of the political executive's dominance over Parliament and saw how its control of the House led to the great mass of legislation, primary and secondary, being whipped through largely unexamined and unchanged. But it is not simply the *political* executive and its legislation which benefits from Parliament's weakness. The whole unco-ordinated machine of central government, executive agencies, quangos, the intelligence services, regulators, and local quasi-public bodies, plus policy communities incorporating major industrial interests, all shelter behind the loyalty of the majority party in the Commons and escape effective scrutiny thanks to the deficient machinery of ministerial responsibility (see Chapter 12) and the weaknesses of current arrangements for scrutiny.

Individual MPs have, of course, their own rights and powers to raise issues and question ministers. As well as asking Parliamentary Questions, they can seek an adjournment debate to press ministers on the floor of the House and can write to ministers, raising questions and concerns. However, as we saw, only one in eight MPs actually believes that his or her main duty is to keep the executive under scrutiny. Fewer still are the irrepressible MPs – Richard Shepherd, Dale Campbell Savours, Chris Mullin, among them – who seek directly to challenge the Leviathan of big government; they have their successes, but for the most part, as Austin Mitchell, another of their number, strikingly described their role, they are simply 'heckling the steamroller' (Garrett 1992: 6). Therefore, in this chapter we concentrate upon select committees – the main instruments by which MPs seek collectively in practice to subject the executive to scrutiny, oversee its expenditure, and provide redress for maladministration. We look in particular at the strengths and weaknesses of departmental select committees, and examine briefly the work of the two select committees, which are linked to parliamentary agencies – the Public Accounts Committee (PAC), which relies on the National Audit Office (NAO); and the Committee on the Parliamentary Commissioner for Administration (PCA), or Ombudsman, which considers the Ombudsman's reports on his most significant cases. (In 1997, this committee was merged with the Public Services Committee to become the Public Administration Committee.) We also consider the work of the special Parliamentary Intelligence and Security Committee, and the Intelligence Services Commissioners and Tribunals, with which the committee has no formal links. Finally, we examine the efficacy of Parliamentary Questions. As in Chapter 13, our guiding criterion remains **DAC9** (see **p. 337**), though in passing we consider how readily citizens can gain access to the Ombudsman in cases of maladministration and how effective the redress he gives is to them (**DAC13**; see **p. 423**).

Scrutiny by select committees

In 1998 there were 17 select committees, shadowing government departments, in the House of Commons, and a further 21 more specialised select committees. The current system of select committees in the Commons was established in 1979 after a series of the House's Procedure Committee reports in the late 1970s had condemned its 'incomplete and unsystematic scrutiny of the activities of the executive' (Procedure Committee 1978: lii). While introducing the new departmental select committees, the then Leader of the House, Norman St John Stevas, now Lord St John of Fawsley, talked grandly about redressing 'the balance of power to enable the House of Commons to do more effectively the job it has been elected to do' (HC Deb, 25 June 1979, c36). But he failed to give them the additional powers that the Procedure Committee report had recommended they should possess in order to scrutinise the executive effectively and make an impact on the House by being able to order ministers to attend and give evidence, and to produce papers and records.

From the beginning, therefore, the new select committee system was hamstrung by the fact that the committees had to work within the same boundaries as their predecessors; and also within a House dominated by an adversarial party culture (see

Chapter 13). Yet the verdict of posterity, as represented by a host of academics, politicians and political writers, is that while they have failed to realise the quixotic aims of the 1978 report, they have over time strengthened both Parliament's ability to scrutinise and hold the executive accountable and the executive's sense of being accountable (Drewry 1989b; Procedure Committee 1990a; Adonis 1990; Judge 1990 and 1992; Garrett 1992: Chapter 4; Hawes 1993; Giddings 1994; Marr 1995; Riddell 1998: 203–214). Summarising such studies, the political columnist Peter Riddell concluded that select committees 'have gained in influence and improved scrutiny' (Riddell 1998: 205).

Select committees 'examine the expenditure, administration and policy' of the relevant departments and their 'associated public bodies'. They have powers to 'send for persons, papers and records', 'to adjourn from place to place' (i.e. travel away from Westminster), and 'to report from time to time'. The powers to compel people to give evidence and produce papers are formidable, not least because the giving of evidence is protected from legal action by parliamentary privilege and Britain's repressive libel laws do not therefore apply. Witnesses are normally willing to give evidence, but committees can issue orders to compel them to attend and give evidence, formally on pain of imprisonment. In 1992, however, the Social Security Committee ordered the late Robert Maxwell's two sons to attend a hearing in its inquiry into pension funds, and while they did so, they refused on legal advice to answer questions. The committee reported their refusal to the House, but the difficult legal issues which arose were left unresolved because the 1992 general election intervened. The committees can also insist on being shown documents – a power the Trade and Industry Committee (TISC) has twice evoked to force British Shipbuilders in 1984, and British Coal in 1993, to show the committee their corporate plans. Norman Tebbit, then Trade and Industry Secretary, had actually instructed British Shipbuilders to withhold the information from the committee and it took a formal order, served on the company by the Commons officer, the Serjeant at Arms, to make them hand over the documents.

There are, however, significant limits on these powers. First, the committees cannot compel MPs or peers to attend and since all ministers are members of one House or the other, committees cannot order the attendance of a particular minister. Though ministers normally meet their requests to give evidence, this rule means that in the last resort it is the Prime Minister who decides which minister should attend, not the committee. Their inability to compel MPs to attend meant, for example, that Sir Hal Miller MP, a key witness, was able with impunity to refuse to give evidence in the TISC's inquiry into the Supergun affair in 1991 (see below). In 1988, a former minister, Edwina Currie, came close to refusing to give evidence to the Agriculture Committee on the salmonella in eggs crisis over which she had been forced to resign; and later, in 1986, Sir Leon Brittan, a ministerial casualty in the Westland affair, refused to tell the Defence Committee inquiry what he had done and when he had done it. (He finally broke his silence three years later – on television; see **p. 318**.) Nor does the power to 'send for persons and papers' extend to particular civil servants or documents held by government departments. As we saw in Chapter 12, officials give evidence and make information available 'on behalf of their Ministers and under their directions', under standing civil service instructions, the 'Osmotherly rules'. They are broadly prohibited from revealing any politically sensitive or embarrassing information, offering their own views, or commenting on issues of political controversy (see Chapter 11).

Ministers, too, decide 'which official or officials should represent them' (Cabinet Office 1997b) and can refuse to let officials, even past officials, chosen by the committees attend hearings. The same rules assert the executive's right to withhold documents from select committees and to supply instead memoranda, written replies to committee questions, and oral evidence, at the discretion of ministers. The 1978 Procedure Committee's proposal that the new departmental select committees should be given the power to seek Commons approval for an order requiring a minister to produce withheld documents was, as we have seen, refused by the government. In sum, then, government can, whenever necessary, successfully resist select committee demands for the production of 'persons, papers and records'.

Select committees are inevitably selective about the issues they choose to examine. As two experienced parliamentary officials state, MPs are too busy to devote more than about four or five hours a week to committee work (though some committees demand more time): 'Most committees therefore meet once a week, perhaps three times a fortnight and very seldom more than twice a week. There are very few meetings during parliamentary recesses' (Silk and Walters 1995: 213).

Typically, committees appoint one or two specialist advisers, usually academics, depending on the topic under inquiry, invite evidence from representative groups and experts, make relevant visits, and hold oral evidence sessions at which ministers, civil servants and other selected witnesses give evidence and are questioned, in turn, by the committee members. Finally, the committees normally produce a report. Usually their clerk (a senior official) will write up the report, though sometimes the chairperson does, for the committee to amend and approve. In 1995–96, the 18 departmental committees, plus the PCA (Ombudsman) and Public Accounts Committee, had a total of 86 staff, and spent £1.36 million on specialist advice, taking evidence, visits, and other expenses, and £1.93 million on publishing their reports.

The committees generally proceed by consensus in contrast to the adversarial nature of most proceedings in the House, in order to avoid fragmenting on party grounds and to produce non-partisan reports. In general, they succeed in doing so, on occasions nobly so. For example, in March 1997 – on the eve of the general election – the Education and Employment Committee reported that the government's flagship nursery voucher scheme was unlikely to raise standards, increase parental choice, or even provide extra nursery places for children. Instead of a split on party lines, it was the Conservative majority which split. But, as the composition of committees reflects that of the House as a whole, the majority of MPs on every select committee are of the governing party. This matters when it comes to inquiries which have a direct bearing on the government's, or party, interests; the majority is generally reluctant to push ministers too hard on providing information. Though efforts are made to maintain a non-partisan approach, select committees usually divide on a partisan basis on sensitive issues, though not necessarily destructively so.

Effectiveness

Formally, individual committee members are chosen to serve by a Selection Committee for each parliamentary term. Certain key political players are excluded formally under the convention that government ministers, parliamentary private secretaries and front-bench opposition spokespersons are not eligible to be nominated. The new committees then choose their own chairperson from among themselves, and between them they share out the chairs between government and opposition party MPs in close consultation with the whips' offices. The chairpersons also serve on a Liaison Committee which oversees the system (its most difficult task being to allocate the travel funds fairly). The Selection Committee was designed to remove the influence of the whips in choosing members in order to make the committees less party political, but has not been able to avoid their influence. Government and opposition whips are so busy trying to ensure that their preferred candidates are in place, and their MPs are rewarded or punished for their past conduct, that they even significantly delay setting up committees after a general election: 180 days in 1983, 160 in 1987, 77 in 1992 (Cremin 1993). In 1992, the Conservative whips took a disproportionate share of committee chairs at the expense of the smaller parties. They also secured the exclusion of their rebel MP, Nicholas Winterton, from the chair of the Health Committee by inventing a new parliamentary convention, limiting membership of particular select committees to three parliamentary terms. Many Tory signatories of an anti-Maastricht early day motion also suffered for their boldness.

It is hard to estimate just how serious the problem of the whips' interference in the selection of committee members is. In 1990, the Procedure Committee certainly underestimated both its effect and extent. The committee cited in a notably critical way one example quoted by the Defence Committee chairman, who said that an MP had been offered an appointment to the committee 'on condition that he took a certain view about the forthcoming election of the Chairman of that Committee' (Procedure Committee 1990a: xliii). The committee regarded this interference as exceptional, rather than common practice. But a 1990 survey by David Judge, an academic expert on Parliament, led him to a radically different conclusion:

> If the Committee had investigated further it would have found that the 'general picture of self-denial and moderation on the part of the Whips' was tarnished not solely by the experience of the Defence Committee but by that of other committees as well.
>
> (Judge 1992)

How effective are departmental select committees?

There is a fairly high degree of consensus about the record of the still developing system of departmental committees (see, for example, Adonis 1990; Giddings 1994; Riddell 1998). On the positive side, select committees are now part of the lives of ministers, civil servants and agency chief executives and the overall policy-making process. They provide the only forums where ministers and officials are questioned relatively closely and publicly about their policies and activities, and where their replies may be openly and critically evaluated. Unfortunately, the MPs' questions are too often self-serving in purpose and amateur in method. They do, however, bring pressure groups, organised interests and specialists publicly into a broader debate on government policies and actions, and have raised the profile and reputation of the Commons in Whitehall, policy communities and the media, though perhaps not as yet among the wider informed public. Select committees have also improved the professionalism and specialist knowledge of MPs (about one in three of the MPs who don't hold a government or official opposition post serve on a select committee). Further, scrutiny of the executive can on some committees be searching and overall, though uneven, it is undoubtedly more systematic and rigorous than it was before 1979, or could be on the floor of the House. This is not necessarily saying a great deal, but the very fact of being potentially open to their scrutiny does make a difference to ministers and their officials.

Peter Riddell has praised the willingness of some committees to tackle controversial issues, such as the Pergau dam aid project, the BBC's future and the Child Support Act, though he considers that the gathering of evidence is generally more important and influential than the eventual reports. However, other committees have, like the Environment Committee under Sir Hugh Rossi, deliberately eschewed controversial matters, though committee members may well have thought that their influence on policies on the green belt and housing land, acid rain, and waste disposal justified their cautious position (Hawes 1993: 76–142). There is also, however, almost universal agreement that select committees have failed to exert influence over government policies at large and even to make a major impact on Commons opinion; and that their reports on policy disasters and scandals, such as those on the Westland affair, the sinking of the *Belgrano*, arms for Iraq, BSE and Gulf War Syndrome, have exposed some of what has gone wrong, but have not been fully satisfactory. The failure of the Defence Committee to penetrate the 'arms to Iraq' affair, as exposed by the independent Scott inquiry, was particularly – and depressingly – plain (see below).

Even so, select committees have weathered ministers' lack of regard or even contempt for their reports, which was especially obvious in the later 1980s, an example being the absurd spectacle of ministers dismissing a critical Health and Social Services Committee report in 1989 before it had even been published! But perhaps ministers have simply learned to dissemble. The more active committees, or their chairmen, frequently claim to have produced influential reports. Some academic observers, like Derek Hawes, suggest that proactive committees, such as TISC and the Energy and Social Services committees, have produced reports with a direct bearing on policy and bills which came before Parliament (Hawes 1993). But overall they have had little influence on government policies and conduct, as observers such as Andrew Adonis and Philip Norton have found (Adonis 1990: 108). Norton commented in evidence to the Commons Procedure Committee:

> In the formulation of policy the government will be influenced by its own political philosophy and, in some cases, by bodies external to the House of Commons. Select Committees are no more than proximate actors in the process.

Norton's point is given added force by the fate of notably well-argued and thoughtful reports, such as the 1984 Employment Committee report on the GCHQ trade union ban; the 1993 Defence and 1989 Public Accounts Committee reports on privatisation of the Royal Dockyards in 1987). These simply ran counter to the 'political philosophy' of the government and were ignored; and committees are, of course, impotent if the government rejects or fails to act on their recommendations.

Moreover, the House of Commons gives only cursory attention to their findings. Select committees have been remarkably industrious, publishing no fewer than 591 reports, and 231 special reports, between 1979 and June 1990. They have thus significantly increased the amount of information available to MPs and the public. But only one in four of their reports from 1979–88 (116 in all) were actually discussed in the Commons, and of these, only 13 were the subject of a substantive debate or adjournment motion. In 1995–96, only eight of the 18 select committees produced reports which were debated by the House, and another seven had a report referred to as relevant to a particular debate.

The failure of committees to get to the heart of policy disasters, or scandals, is partly due to the manner in which their inquiries are conducted (see below). Here we examine in detail the inquiries into the Westland affair and the Supergun fiasco. We have already described in Chapter 11 how Mrs Thatcher and Sir Robert Armstrong, the Cabinet Secretary, frustrated the 1986 Defence Committee inquiry into the Westland affair and the leak of the Solicitor-General's letter, against strict official rules, in order to discredit Michael Heseltine. Armstrong was the key player. He flew back from a pre-summit meeting in Honolulu to give evidence to the committee in place of the five officials involved in the leak whom MPs wanted to interrogate. Among them were Mrs Thatcher's press secretary, Bernard Ingham, and her adviser, Charles Powell.

Armstrong's gambit might, however, have been rejected had it not been for loyalist party culture of the Commons. The committee's vice-chairman, Labour MP John Gilbert, proposed that they should refuse Armstrong's offer, but he was outvoted by the Tory majority. After Armstrong's silkily evasive appearance before them, however, Tory and Labour committee members agreed a compromise – they would drop the demand to see all the officials, save only Ingham. But by then Mrs Thatcher had delivered a clearly weak statement to the House and weathered an emergency debate; Leon Brittan, the DTI minister, had resigned. Alan Clark's diaries make it clear that Brittan had for several days been singled out as the 'unhappy fall guy' in the affair; there had also been 'much talk of "too many jewboys in the Cabinet"'. On the day of her statement, the whips passed a copy around backbench MPs and Clark could not 'keep a straight face' on reading it. Clark's diaries describe the highly charged atmosphere in the Commons:

> [*The statement*] How can she say these things without faltering? But she did. Kept her nerve beautifully. I was sitting close by. . . . It was almost as if the House, half horrified, half dumb with admiration, was cowed. A few rats came out of the woodwork – mainly from the *Salon des Refusés* . . . a little later [she] came to a meeting of the '22 [the backbench Conservative organisation, the

1922 Committee]. The mood was wholly supportive of her, and the Scapegoat was duly tarred. But is that the end of it? [*The emergency debate*] . . . Every seat in the House had been booked with a prayer card and they were all up the gangways. For a few seconds Kinnock had her cornered, and you could see fear in those blue eyes. But then he . . . gave her time to recover. A brilliant performance, shameless and brave. *We* are out of the wood. [our emphasis]

(Clark 1993)

The Defence Committee was therefore obliged to consider its demand that Ingham should appear before it against the background of a Conservative majority in the House intent on remaining 'out of the wood'. Their loyalty to Mrs Thatcher and party transcended the tradition that MPs were fiercely attached to the dignity of the House and would punish those who misled it. Even Michael Heseltine, the major casualty in the affair, had agreed that Mrs Thatcher's speech should 'end the politics of the matter'. Ingham was adamant that only an order from the House would make him appear – which meant that the committee would have to seek the House's approval for an order – and that even then he would not answer any questions. Conservative MPs on the committee came under intense pressure to let the affair die. Sir Humphrey Atkins, the committee's Conservative chairman, met the Tory Chief Whip and then appealed to the committee's Tory majority not to press their demand to the vote. The ties of party loyalty won the day. They duly backed down (see Clark 1993: 132–135; Harris 1994: Chapter 8). The committee saved its face by recalling Armstrong once more and issuing an unusually assertive report (Drewry 1989a: 415). The report found fault with all the key players in the affair, but especially Armstrong, stating that it was 'to the Head of the Home Civil Service that all civil servants have to look for example. In this case that lead has not been given' (1986: para 214). The Defence Committee inquiry, and a parallel inquiry by the Trade and Industry Committee, both extracted considerably more by way of disclosures from ministers and officials than is usual. Yet most observers agree with Andrew Marr's verdict on the attempts of the committees to sit in judgement on the skulduggery which took place:

Their hearings were riveting and got further to the heart of the affair than MPs would have been able to manage in the chamber. In the end, however, the ability of the civil service and ministers to block and avoid the most difficult questions meant that the investigations were neither fully satisfactory nor conclusive.

(1995: 156)

Some observers have taken comfort in the fact that Brittan, at least, paid the price for his complicity in the affair. His resignation was seen as an assertion of Parliament's ability to extract some degree of accountability from ministers, and as belated retribution for his earlier misleading responses to questions over his attempts to put pressure on British Aerospace to withdraw from Heseltine's Euro-consortium plan. Brittan had also been forced back to the House the same day to apologise for those responses. However his explanation in apology was as misleading as the original responses, and yet he would have remained in office if there had not been a greater need for a scapegoat after Mrs Thatcher had caused the leak (Dunleavy 1995c: 186–214). And the Conservative majority in the House swallowed the larger cover-up whole.

The Trade and Industry Committee (TISC) investigation into the narrowly averted export to Iraq of parts of barrels for the Iraqi Supergun provided another opportunity to assess how far select committees could inquire into issues which go to the heart of government. Further, it allows us to make a comparison with the subsequent Scott inquiry into arms exports. The TISC investigation was also unprecedented in the history of select committees since it was (and remains) the nearest a select committee has come to probing a specific intelligence operation. Government has consistently resisted such inquiries since 1979 (e.g. the Home Affairs Committee inquiries into the Special Branch in 1984–85 and MI5 in 1993–94). Indeed, the very nature of the material under scrutiny played a large part in undermining the committee's ability to uncover the truth about Supergun.

The committee's inquiries were obstructed both by an MP and the government. As we saw above, Sir Hal Miller MP, who had alerted officials to the existence of the Supergun, refused to appear before it, yet later he gave valuable evidence to the Scott inquiry which would have 'strengthened the [TISC's] evidence establishing government knowledge of the project from June 1988' (Leigh 1993b: 637). Following established practice, ministers refused to allow intelligence officials, who knew about Iraq's attempts to obtain arms, and two retired MOD civil servants, who had been directly involved in the affair, to give evidence to TISC. Ministers also exploited the *sub judice* rule to prevent two senior DTI officials from giving evidence, on the grounds that they were prosecution witnesses in the Matrix Churchill case. These officials were Anthony Steadman, the former head of the DTI export licensing unit, who had been originally contacted by Sir Hal Miller, and his senior, Eric Beston, who was head of the DTI's export control machinery. Both were key witnesses who, as journalist David Leigh observed, could (if they had wished) 'have given startling evidence' about the Supergun and other military exports following the 1989 relaxation of the Howe guidelines (1993a: 31, 175). Steadman in particular was closely involved in the DTI's handling of the Supergun barrel exports. As it was, the DTI could not even provide a record of Steadman's conversation with Miller, claiming that it could not then record telephone conversations. Customs officers also declined to give evidence on the grounds that disclosure of the reasons for dropping the Supergun prosecution would prejudice the position of the Matrix Churchill defendants. This sleight-of-hand was uncovered at the Scott hearings when the then Attorney-General, Sir Patrick Mayhew, said any such disclosure would *not* have resulted in any prejudice.

The committee's difficulties were compounded by the fact that, as evidence which emerged at the Scott inquiry revealed, at least two of its witnesses who did appear were 'nobbled'. The managing director of Walter Somers, the firm at the heart of the affair, withheld some information after being briefed by intelligence officers, and one of the firm's executives concealed his MI6 links. Scott was himself critical of the government's lack of co-operation, stating that 'the refusal to facilitate the giving of evidence to TISC by [the two retired officials] may be regarded as a failure to comply fully with the obligations of accountability to Parliament' (1996: para. F4.66).

The result of this official obstruction was that 'the Committee were seriously misled in their conclusions' (Leigh 1993b: 636). They decided that all the ministers involved should be exonerated. They did publish some key political information, but failed to appreciate the wider significance of Supergun and what this information signified. For example, they did not follow up an FCO official's admission that the Howe guidelines on arms sales to Iraq and Iran had been revised following the 1988 ceasefire. Thus, finally, they attributed the failure to refuse a licence for the Supergun tubes simply to poor information flows between officials and from departments to ministers.

In the circumstances, it was perhaps an achievement that the committee produced a report at all, given the absence of government co-operation, the party political pressures on Tory members, and the sensitivities which surround any issues involving the intelligence services. The committee was also under time pressure from the impending 1992 general election and had to cut short its inquiries. The committee's Conservative members made it clear that there would be either a compromise report before Parliament dissolved or none at all. Thus, only Supergun – merely one element of the larger issue of arms sales to Iraq and Iran – was explored in any depth. The alternative was to postpone the inquiry until after the general election with the risk that it might never have re-emerged – an outcome some Conservative members were looking for. The final report split along party lines, weakening its authority still further. But it did highlight the lack of accountability of the intelligence services and laid some important groundwork for Scott's full inquiry; 'many of the later revelations were possible because of the earlier work of the committee, especially in amassing unglamorous evidence' (Leigh 1993b: 639). However, the committee did not realise that they were dealing with a serious abuse of executive power, and so failed in two of their key roles – scrutiny of the executive and making significant official information public. The committee's perseverance is an important consideration in terms of MPs' commitment to taking on inquiries which strike at the secret heart of British government, but most assessments of their report conclude that it was a failure. For example, Ian Leigh's final verdict was that 'The most obvious conclusion from this experience is that short-term political considerations and limitations on gathering evidence may decisively impinge on a Select Committee's work to the detriment of effective scrutiny and accurate reporting' (*ibid.*: 639).

It was left to the Scott inquiry to provide a comprehensive and thorough exposé of the whole affair. Scott's unprecedented and unqualified powers to see all the government's papers and decide how much of them to reveal greatly exceeded those of any select committee and throw into relief the constraints and obstruction that the TISC had to contend with. This audit does not seek to review postwar experience of judicial and other inquiries. However, the Scott process, deeply unpopular as it was with the executive which was not accustomed to consistent and systematic investigation, bears testimony to the obvious advantages of subjecting government to independent non-political review (see below).

The Agriculture Committee's inquiry into the BSE crisis

The Agriculture Committee inquiry into the government's handling of the BSE crisis is generally also regarded as an example of the inability of select committees to get to the bottom of policy disasters. But the failure of its inquiry was not the result of government obstruction or dissembling, but rather of its own preoccupations. The committee's report in 1990 was very supportive of government policy on BSE and dismissive of its critics. The committee found that the government's handling of the crisis 'represents *a substantial improvement*' [emphasis in original report] on its handling of the salmonella crisis, and concluded that:

> Witnesses taking a more pessimistic view seemed to do so mainly on the basis that one should prepare for the worst possible eventuality. Members of the public who share this assumption will not be easily reassured. *But we heard no evidence of any sort to constrain those taking a more balanced view of the risks from eating beef. We believe [the Government's] measures should reassure people that eating beef is safe* [emphasis as in original report].
> (Agriculture Committee 1990: extracts from conclusions (i) and (ii))

The reference to the salmonella crisis reveals the angle from which the committee was approaching the BSE crisis – its concern was primarily with the stability and commercial well-being of the farming industry rather than public safety. And thus its report got it spectacularly wrong (see **pp. 282–289**).

The report's conclusions are less surprising when we study the background of committee members. Nine of the 11 members represented rural constituencies with a strong farming component. Three had direct interests in farming or the meat industry: the Tory chairman, Jerry Wiggins (Worcestershire farmer); Christopher Gill (farmer, butcher and sausage-maker, and member of National Council of Bacon and Meat Manufacturers Association); and Paul Marland (1,000-acre Cotswold farm with pig fattening unit). Wiggins was a stalwart champion of farming interests who, for example, spoke out strongly as chairman against 'curried eggs' and 'radioactive lamb' scares; Marland was described as a 'defender of his own farming interests' and an adviser to Unigate (Waller and Criddle 1996: 367). Ann Winterton had previously opposed the import of milk in order to defend her local dairy industry in Cheshire.

Analysis of the balance of evidence the committee heard shows that out of 40 witnesses, 18 were official government sources, 16 represented farming interests, and only six were independent experts (four) or representatives of the Institute of Environmental Health Officers (two). Members of the committee tended to share both the concern of the majority of these witnesses to reassure the public about the safety of British beef, and their anxiety about the economic effects of the crisis on the farming industry – a legitimate concern, especially after the effects of the salmonella crisis. The committee also proved to be hostile towards Professor Richard Lacey, the leading critic of government policy, for mixing 'science and science fiction' and denounced those 'television producers and newspaper editors who beat a path to his door as an authority on all aspects of food safety'. In fact, their concerns, like their conclusions, exactly paralleled those of ministers, officials and the National Farmers Union, though they did acknowledge scientific concerns about the dangers in a complacent aside: 'If they [most scientists] shrank from giving cast-iron reassurances [on the threat to human health], it was mainly for the philosophical reason that nothing in life is certain' (Agriculture Committee: para. 91).

Of course, specialist experience is valuable on any select committee. And the simple fact that MPs have a constituency or personal interest in the farming, meat or any other industry, does not mean that they will automatically defend such interests. However, the membership of this committee was seriously unbalanced. It is true that Labour MP Dale Campbell-Savours, an effective parliamentary campaigner, was also a member, but there were no members with a strong background in science nor in consumer affairs. For select committees to perform their functions effectively, they must not only be impartial, but must be seen to be so. The notion of 'industry capture', familiar from the experience of US congressional committees, is rarely raised in the UK. However, as we have seen, food and farming have historically been run by closed policy communities of departmental officials and vested interests (see Chapter 10), and the select committee ought not to reflect the influence of the same interests if it is to exert an effective check on government policy-making.

The absence of political ambition and will

In 1990, the Procedure Committee published a collaborative review of the progress made by departmental select committees which found near unanimous agreement among the witnesses – from committee members to expert academics – that the committees had achieved a more systematic and rigorous scrutiny of executive actions than the pre-1979 select committees or present activity on the floor of the House (Procedure Committee 1990a). This is not a demanding yardstick, but it is typical of the insular and complacent attitude and absence of analytic rigour with which the committee carried out the review (see Judge 1992: 99). The committee relied almost wholly on assessments – 'often brief, generalised and "non-scientific" (*ibid.*: 94) – from the select committees themselves. Thus, while they did, for example, acknowledge difficulties in obtaining relevant information from ministers and civil servants, such as those we have described above, they dismissed them as exceptional (Procedure Committee 1990a: xxiv).

But did this assessment reflect political realities? Out of the political limelight, Judge for example found that the Trade and Industry Committee had to deal with repeated obstructions during the mid-1980s. Two of its inquiries were severely undermined by the department's unwillingness to co-operate, and yet they were not even mentioned in the committee's own return to the Procedure Committee. The only witnesses that even raised the restrictive Osmotherly rules for officials giving evidence to select committee (see Chapter 12) as an obstacle to effective scrutiny and open government were academic witnesses, like Gavin Drewry, Philip Giddings and Peter Hennessy. No committee chairman referred to them at all, and the outside academic concerns were dismissed by the Procedure Committee: '[the Osmotherly rules], it found, 'have no parliamentary status whatsoever . . . [and have not placed] *unaccept-able* constraints on Select Committees across the whole range of their scrutinising functions' [our emphasis] (1990a: xxix).

The key word here is 'unacceptable'. Instead of demanding the withdrawal or radical re-writing of these Whitehall rules, the deferential committee indicated that it was willing to 'accept' the strict limits they place on civil servants giving evidence, and simply reiterated the 'somewhat forlorn plea' for ministers to be as co-operative as possible (Judge 1992: 95).

The committee's unwillingness to challenge the executive is characteristic of the relationship between the House and the executive. At root, MPs and their commit-tees are fearful of making demands on the executive in case they fail to obtain what they want, and provoke reprisals instead. Another observer, Derek Hawes, has described how committees therefore seek to operate an (often fine) series of balances – challenging and criticising a department *versus* collaboration with it; tough inqui-sition of ministers *versus* accepting their right to make policy; partisan loyalty *versus* all-party consensus; overall, maintaining an equilibrium between ministers and offi-cials, different interest groups and lobbyists. The end result is, as he admits, 'the one thing which Committees have signally failed to do is overtly to restore more power to Parliament at the expense of the Executive: it is not that kind of game' (1993: 210).

That it isn't 'that kind of game' is at least in part due to the subservient balancing acts that MPs and their committees perform. In evidence to the Public Services Committee, Peter Hennessy was critical of the poverty of aspirations of select commit-tees. They were, he said, the best instruments he knew for 'getting us closer to the reality', but could be 'far, far more assertive than they are' (PSC 1996c: vol. I, lviii). Certainly, most of the restrictions which the executive imposes upon a 'sovereign' Parliament have no statutory basis.

'Poverty of aspirations' extends beyond the unwillingness to confront the execu-tive. From 1979 onwards the House of Commons has accepted the obsolete model of select committees as they have traditionally worked, with all the limitations of their chamber-bound procedures and practice. They are poorly staffed for the inquiries they take on and, as we saw above, the time of their members and of the committees themselves is severely limited. By comparison with their US and western European counterparts, they operate with minimal support staff and on a shoestring budget. In the session 1995–96, the full committee apparatus cost just under £4 million and the select committees employed only 86 staff in all. The result is that select committees remain far too reliant on the executive for their information – especially financial information – and on ad-hoc specialist advice. They actually take pride in their low-cost activities and spurn the very idea of building up their own independent research facility, as in the United States. So in giving evidence to the Procedure Committee's 1989–90 inquiry, chairmen and committees were 'not clamouring for additional staff, other than marginal increases in a small number of cases'.

The Procedure Committee was equally unenthusiastic, fearing feebly that members would not be able to cope with an inevitable increase in paperwork and quoting the Tory MP, Sir Ian Lloyd with approval: 'present staffing levels are probably about right ... and I fear that if we had more staff our enquiries might become staff-driven rather than being Member-driven as they are at present' (1990a: para. 93).

This insistence on the prerogatives of members' status, which is damaging in other contexts, such as access to the Ombudsman service (see below), makes the House more of a parliamentary museum than a modern legislature. Our first reaction is to ask why MPs are not confident of managing staffs and directing research to ensure that their work remains 'Member-driven'. The influence on policy of 'committee aides' in the US is sometimes criticised, but given political will on the part of committee members, there is no intrinsic reason why larger staffs should capture the direction of their work. More fundamentally, the fact is that most members of most committees are amateurs who are badly in need of access to detailed and expert knowledge. One of the major criticisms of select committees concerns their haphazard choice of issues to examine. But they cannot possibly maintain close and systematic scrutiny of the policies and activities of the relevant ministers, their departments, executive agencies and other public bodies within their remit, and oversee their expenditure, on shoestring budgets with the assistance of the occasional hired hand taken on for a single inquiry. They require consistent research resources which can match the complex and fast-changing modern institutions they are shadowing. As it is, they can scarcely absorb the huge mass of information that government gives them voluntarily. Kate Jenkins, former head of the Prime Minister's Efficiency Unit, told the PSC:

> One of the things, as an outsider watching what happens in some Select Committees, is that it is such a pity to see that the important issues and the important points are not pursued; quite clearly in many cases because the members ... are not sufficiently informed of what is happening.
>
> (PSC 1996c: vol. I, para. 142)

The way in which select committees conduct their business is equally old-fashioned. The hearings can be fruitful with co-operative witnesses and occasionally provide illuminating theatre, especially with non-co-operative witnesses. But they are a cumbersome and time-wasting process for seeking out information, especially as the key witnesses – ministers and officials – are well-defended, practised in giving carefully-prepared answers, and will have been thoroughly briefed in advance. Few MPs are trained or skilled in cross-examining and pressing witnesses; the convention by which every member takes a share in the questioning means that lines of inquiry are hit and miss; important questions must often be abandoned unanswered and are not followed through; and the oral hearings are generally very brief, taking only a few hours, in contrast to, say, the days which a court case or judicial inquiry like Scott's might require. It is not unknown for witnesses to play for time. The former Foreign Secretary, Lord Howe, is one of many witnesses who have criticised the inability of committees to follow issues effectively to their end – 'the point is this,' he said, 'the forensic inquiry can pursue the issue to the end of the road, the Select Committee hops around amongst you' (PSC 1996c: vol. I, para. 132).

Committees and agencies

The absence of resources and their old-fashioned proceedings require the committees themselves to 'hop around' between issues. Their scrutiny is unsystematic, and 'has a distinctly random quality about it, with major aspects of the work of departments never being investigated' (Adonis 1990: 110). There are signs in the 1996 PSC report that MPs are readier to recognise the need for additional resources. Andrew Bennett, chairman of the Environment Committee, said in evidence that the width of its remit meant that:

> however hard the Committee works, it is simply not possible to monitor in depth the full range of responsibilities of the Environment Department and its agencies . . . some parts of the Department inevitably escape scrutiny for perhaps several years at a time.
>
> (PSC 1996c: vol. I, para. 142)

Even so, the PSC itself persisted in the conventional wisdom and suggested that the extra resources need only be 'modest'.

Linked with these concerns about resources and their conduct is another associated constraint on the ability of select committees to deliver effective scrutiny: that is, members' time. The insistence on select committee inquiries being 'Member-driven' has not only inhibited demands for extra resources. In itself, the 'Member-driven' character of their work imposes a major handicap on their powers of inquiry. The Trade and Industry Committee, for example, complained that it 'sensibly restricted' its inquiry into arms to Iraq to one aspect of the issue, the Supergun, as that alone took almost half of its allotted sessions. 'The difficulty is Members' time', not resources, the TISC explained, as its members had a wider remit for scrutiny of the DTI, and other parliamentary and constituency duties too (*ibid.*: para. 131). The handicap is, however, largely of a self-imposed cultural nature. Members need to be reassured that they can employ research resources, change the old-fashioned way in which they conduct their inquiries, and still remain in charge of the process, if not as visibly so; and the House as a whole has to discuss and rationalise the conflict of duties and demands on MPs' time. As it is, select committees are able only to produce at most two major reports every parliamentary session – a rate of scrutiny which is utterly inadequate to match the scale and diversity of the executive's activities. The essential issue is one of members' self-confidence and their ability to control investigations largely conducted by experts on their behalf. They need to develop the skills necessary to organise and control their inquiries to fulfil their formal remit.

Parliamentary committees and agencies

Two select committees are directly linked to parliamentary agencies – the Public Accounts Committee (PAC), which works closely with the Comptroller and Auditor General (C&AG) and the National Audit Office (NAO); and the Committee on the Parliamentary Commissioner for Administration, or Ombudsman, which considers the Ombudsman's reports on his most significant cases. Another committee, the

Parliamentary Intelligence and Security Committee, was recently established to exercise oversight over the activities of the intelligence services, alongside already existing commissioners and tribunals. This is a government-appointed committee outside the select committee system.

In this section, we briefly consider the contribution the two committees and agencies make to parliamentary powers to scrutinise and make the executive accountable. (We do not examine the role of the Audit Commission, a parallel agency of public audit, as it is non-parliamentary.) However, we also assess how well select committees in general fulfil Parliament's duty to oversee public expenditure; and, in passing, consider how readily citizens can gain access to the Ombudsman in cases of maladministration and how effective the redress he gives is to them.

The Public Accounts Committee is generally regarded as the most effective select committee. It was actually established in 1861, but its modern history began in 1983 with the National Audit Act, a private member's bill introduced by Norman (now Lord) St John Stevas, which wrested control of public audit back from the executive to Parliament. The 1983 Act also added the duty to carry out 'value-for-money' audits to the existing duties of the C&AG and NAO, which are to conduct strict financial audits of the regularity and propriety of the spending of government departments and associated public bodies. In 1987, Labour MPs tried to ensure that the C&AG should be appointed by the House on a motion from the chairperson of the PAC, by convention a senior opposition MP. But Mrs Thatcher insisted on retaining the power of appointment (which is, by statute, discharged in consultation with the PAC chairperson). However, the NAO budget is approved by a Commons Public Accounts Commission (consisting of the chairperson of the PAC, the Leader of the House, and seven non-ministerial MPs appointed by the House); and the 1983 Act gives the C&AG 'complete discretion' in the discharge of his functions. These measures are designed to secure his independence from the executive (though the Treasury still seeks to retain some measure of control; Garrett 1992: 143).

Parliament traditionally exists to examine and authorise all government spending, but neither the House of Commons as a whole, nor the departmental select committees, examine spending programmes in detail. The House tends to concentrate far too much on minor taxation issues and far too little on spending and financial management. One of the key duties in the original mandate of departmental select committees was to remedy the House's lack of interest in public expenditure, but it is generally agreed that they neglect departmental expenditure issues, despite the production of draft model questions by the Treasury Committee (see, for example, Adonis 1990; Garrett 1992; Giddings 1994; Riddell 1998). In part, select committees suffer from having no direct links with the NAO, a state of affairs of which they are bitterly critical. But the PAC endorses the current position in order to retain its unique status. Thus, Parliament's duty to examine public spending has been left too much to the Public Accounts Committee, the C&AG and the NAO.

The NAO has a staff of about 1,000 and thus it may be said that the PAC at least has a substantial resource base. The C&AG is responsible for both financial and 'value-for-money' (VFM) audits of central government, executive agencies, 157 executive quangos, advisory committees and tribunals, and for VFM audits of universities, further education bodies and grant-maintained schools, and shares VFM duties with the Audit Commission (which has the major responsibility for both types of audit in local government and the NHS). In conducting audits, the C&AG has rights of access to all documents in a department, authority or body that he needs, and he may also require officials to give information. The central weakness of the formal arrangements is that the C&AG is prohibited under the 1983 Act from using his position to 'question the merits of the policy objectives of any department, authority or body in respect of which an examination was carried out'. Thus, the executive defence of 'policy' is unbreached (see also **p. 368**). By contrast, the Audit Commission has the right to examine the impact of policies on the efficiency and effectiveness of the public services being audited, and exercises it vigorously; these are often policies which emanate from central government.

The NAO produces up to 50 reports of uneven quality a year. Senior civil servants often assert that these reports are unimpressive and have on occasion been scornful of particular reports. The NAO reports are discussed and agreed with departments before they go to the PAC. These discussions have given rise to criticisms that they take the edge off reports, which are anyway written and presented in understated terms. But these encounters, and the accounting officers' subsequent appearance in front of the committee, cause considerable disquiet in departments and officials meet well in advance to prepare evidence, with the main purpose of presenting the department in the best possible light and avoiding public embarrassment. The PAC then considers the reports and publishes its findings. The committee takes evidence from the permanent secretaries of departments, acting as accounting officers, and other officials and witnesses, and as well as possessing the powers of other select committees, can call for actual accounts if need be.

Brian Landers, the former finance chief at the Prison Department, has vividly described how Home Office officials cleverly constructed a blind alley for the PAC to take on an inquiry into budgetary issues, thus preventing disclosure of long-standing departmental problems. PAC hearings also suffer from the same failings as those of other select committees, being cumbersome and hit-and-miss, and Landers vividly describes how members, intent on scoring points publicly, entirely missed the main issues in their hearing (Landers, forthcoming book). The PAC does, however, focus parliamentary (and on occasions media and public) attention on matters which might otherwise never come into the spotlight; and, in turn, the committee has a powerful ally. Treasury officials sit in on its hearings, and it is their presence which accounts for most of the discomfort permanent secretaries feel when they give evidence. The Treasury also often primes the NAO with weaknesses and errors around Whitehall which it has detected; and makes sure that the NAO's significant recommendations are put into effect by departments. Gavin Drewry, an expert observer, has commented: 'Remove the expertise of the C&AG and the muscle of the Treasury and the PAC would become just another investigatory committee, inevitably out of depth in a highly technical field of scrutiny' (1989b: 158).

There is an annual debate in the Commons on the PAC's reports, held to allow the PAC to draw the attention of MPs to issues that it considers to be of special importance and in effect to reinforce pressure on the Treasury to act on its findings.

Debate inevitably focuses on only a few reports and in the 1994 debate Michael Shersby, a committee member, commented wryly that he doubted whether any MP, apart from other members of the PAC, had read more than a handful of its reports. On several occasions MPs taking part have complained that the attempt to consider some 50 reports in one debate is symptomatic of the House's time problems and scarcely does justice to the work of the NAO and PAC. Committee members certainly work hard; the PAC sits weekly throughout the parliamentary session. But the time constraints of its members also constrain the auditing activities of the NAO. The agency brings most departments under its scrutiny about once in every two years, but it is hard to see why it cannot also work with departmental select committees and thus expand scrutiny of central government.

While some NAO reports are superficial, others make a major impression; still others ought to attract media and public attention, but don't, in part because of the deliberately neutral terms in which they are written and their Spartan presentation. (Here again there is a contrast with the Audit Commission, which has invested heavily in a high public profile and publishes glossy reports which skilfully use graphic design; though it is not unknown for NAO staff to tip off the media as to where they can find the 'juicy bits' in their more restrained publications.) Among reports and findings which have brought significant failures to light have been a series on the NHS from 1987–90; criticism of the costs of the government programme encouraging people to switch to personal pensions (see **pp. 386–387**); analysis of bad privatisation deals; substantial overpayments and underpayments of state benefits; poor management of housing benefits; inefficiencies in the immigration service; and the failures of the NHS computing system; an inquiry into waste on the Thatcher government's failed programme for turning public housing estates over to private ownership; and a searching look at cost and time overruns on the ambitious Eurofighter project. The PAC's greatest coup recently, however, was its 1994 report, *The Proper Conduct of Public Business*, which recycled several previous reports on financial irregularities and abuse in government departments, health authorities and quangos, and was cleverly timed to catch public disquiet about 'sleaze' in public life (PAC 1994).

Yet experts on public administration who have served within Whitehall and Westminster are highly critical of the NAO's deference to the statutory prohibition on policy. In their view, the NAO has more room for manoeuvre than its officials seem to realise. They argue that the crucial issues that need informed auditing inside the policy laager are at least partially within its reach, but that the NAO obediently stays outside. One academic insider comments:

> Civil servants laugh at the NAO. Their chaps simply aren't clever enough to exploit ways into the policy domain. And it is not only a question of high-level policy. They even respect the outer boundaries of policy, though this is territory they could move into. There is an important infrastructure of policy development which turns policy 'goals' into actual behaviour. This can be done well or badly, it may be adequately funded or under-funded. It is a vital part of the government process, which requires auditing, but it's untouched by the NAO.

Committees and agencies

The PAC is not prohibited from considering policy issues, but its chairmen have made it a firm principle not to do so. There are two reasons for this. The principle establishes a non-partisan basis for its inquiries and avoids the danger of party controversy entering into its deliberations. Secondly, it is in a real sense part of the establishment and seeks therefore to maintain good relations with departments and senior officials. Even so, as John Garrett, the former Labour MP and a management specialist, comments, some officials have complained from time to time that the PAC strays too far in a policy direction. He considers that the PAC's self-discipline is not obvious to outsiders; and that its reports often reveal where policy decisions have contributed to failures and where inadequate research has created problems. In his view, 'its members have developed an expertise and a network of contacts which have made them a very effective investigatory body' (1992: 144–145).

The PAC's semi-establishment status seems to mean that its chairman, deputy chairman and perhaps members are too ready to conceal information from Parliament and the public. In 1987, for example, the then chairman, Labour MP Robert Sheldon, denied knowledge of the Zircon spy satellite project of which he was fully aware. In 1991, the NAO carried out an investigation into the Al Yamanah agreements between the UK and the Saudi regime. Al Yamanah was the biggest arms deal in history and inspired 'an underground river of money of at least £300 million in secret commissions ... corrupting British business life' (Harding *et al.* 1997: 57–58). But the NAO report was suppressed on Sheldon's orders, on the grounds that, 'It says things which would have upset certain people and endangered the contract'. In 1992, the journalist Paul Foot interviewed Sheldon who admitted to spending 'many, many hours worrying' about his decision, but too many jobs were at stake. He promised that the report found 'no evidence of corruption, or of public money being used improperly' (*London Review of Books*, 1 January 1997). However, the suspicions of widespread corruption, reaching right into the heart of public life, remain to poison faith in government in Britain and seem to have been partially confirmed by the downfall of Jonathan Aitken, the former minister, because of his Saudi connections (Harding *et al.* 1997). In such circumstances, the watchdog ought to bark, not slink away.

The recent changes in the structure of government and public services, described in Chapters 7 and 8, have made the public audit model partially obsolete. Contracting out and privatisation mean that public funds, which would previously have been kept under scrutiny by the NAO, now fall outside its jurisdiction, even though the funds are still public and are still spent on the same public services or functions, but under new terms. Witnesses to the Nolan Committee, including the NAO, the Audit Commission and the public finance foundation, CIPFA, sought to place the question of 'sleaze' within the wider perspective of the uncertain divide in public governance between the public and private. In evidence, Sir David Cooksey, chairman of the Audit Commission, said, 'We believe that wherever public money is spent in any significant quantity, then the principles of public audit ought to apply' (Evans and Thornton 1997: 4). This basic proposition has become a theme in public debate. As we have seen, the NAO's jurisdiction over quangos and other public bodies is incomplete and fitful (see **Tables 8.2** and **9.2**); and while the list is periodically updated, there is no evident principle of selection at work. In the 1994 debate on PAC reports, Robert Maclennan MP, a committee member, drew attention to the 1994 *Proper Conduct of Government* report's proposal that the NAO should be given powers to examine and audit all executive quangos and other bodies largely funded by central government and to report back to the PAC. The Nolan Committee recommended that public audit arrangements should be reviewed.

Finally, the Conservative government ruled out proposals for a full public audit regime for all public bodies, and private companies, voluntary bodies and contractors funded by government to perform public functions. Instead, it would continue to consider the need for public audit on a 'case by case' basis and make incremental improvements spreading 'best practice' rather than introduce major structural changes. A white paper in March 1996, *Spending Public Money: Governance and Audit Issues* (Chancellor of the Duchy of Lancaster 1996), proposed that the NAO should have 'inspection rights' over all executive quangos which it does not audit, and over companies wholly or mainly owned by them, but these inspections should focus on key areas and should not be burdensome. The NAO should be given access to contractors' records, if necessary, for auditing purposes. Otherwise, it foresaw only some tinkering with the existing patchwork of external audit of public bodies and ducked the issue of combining the NAO and Audit Commission (suggesting merely an independent review of the interface between the bodies). It failed to explain the rationale behind the fact that some quangos, but not others, were audited by the NAO.

Clearly, the ministers' main preoccupation was to give quasi-government bodies, public, voluntary and private, as much freedom from external interference as possible. But in doing so they rejected the goal of a common and systematic scheme of annual audit and scrutiny for all bodies in receipt of public funding on behalf of Parliament and the public. If public audit is to be effective, it is essential that public auditors should have the right to follow public money *wherever* it goes, as they do, for example, in the United States. There is a further weakness in the powers of the NAO. The auditors of local authorities and health bodies, who are appointed by the Audit Commission, have substantial powers to obtain documents and information not only from the public authorities and bodies, but also from third parties, such as banks and contractors. The powers of NAO auditors are much narrower (Evans and Thornton 1997). There are also deficiencies in the NAO inspection rights. The NAO can inspect bodies that have received money from audited public bodies, but unless the inspection rights are specified by statute, they have to be negotiated with those bodies. This means, for example, that the NAO has no right to inspect individual housing associations, even though the Housing Corporation pours significant public funds into them.

The Ombudsman and his parliamentary links

The Ombudsman – the Parliamentary Commissioner for Administration, to give him his proper title just the once – is a another example of 'exceptionalism' in British constitutional practice. When the office was finally established in 1967, it was possible only on the basis that 'he'[1] should deal with complaints about maladministration which were 'filtered' through MPs. MPs were (and remain) very jealous of their existing prerogatives, and especially their traditional role of dealing with constituents' complaints about government. The new Ombudsman service was therefore designed to work alongside MPs and to accommodate their own constituency caseloads. But the decision also reflects the wider tradition of public administration in this country. Britain does not have a developed tradition of administrative law and civil servants are made accountable through political and parliamentary, not legal, mechanisms. The Ombudsman was thus also incorporated within the framework of ministerial responsibility. By the same token, Ombudsmen have so far usually been civil servants rather than lawyers; and their work is directly linked with the House of Commons and one of its committees.

The Ombudsman is an independent and non-partisan officer who has power to investigate complaints of maladministration against government departments, executive agencies and an assortment of quangos (see Chapter 8). He operates in an inquisitorial way and has the power to report upon individual cases and administrative procedures, to criticise and to recommend remedial actions, redress and changes in practice; but he has no power to make orders, to alter decisions or to compel financial compensation, redress or administrative reforms.

The term 'maladministration' was not defined in the Parliamentary Commissioner Act 1967 and it was never in any sense designed to constitute a substitute for a more thoroughgoing set of administrative rules. In his 1993 report, Sir William Reid, the then Ombudsman, argued with typical British pragmatism that to define the term would be to limit his powers to accept cases. Richard Crossman, the minister who introduced the Act, said that maladministration included 'bias, neglect, inattention, delay, incompetence, ineptitude, arbitrariness' (HC Deb, 18 October 1966, c51); in 1993, Reid added rudeness, refusal to answer reasonable questions, knowingly giving misleading or inadequate advice, failing to recognise the rights of people who complain, failing to inform people of rights of appeal, offering no or too meagre redress, and so on. Some of these matters of course overlap with responsibilities of the courts under judicial review (see Chapter 15).

The Ombudsman is appointed by 'Letters Patent' – that is, in practice, by the Prime Minister, who by convention has consulted the chairperson of the PCA Committee (who is, in turn by convention, a senior government backbench MP). He may only be dismissed by an address from both Houses of Parliament; and so far, in practice, PCA Committee reports have maintained due impartiality and sturdy independence from government. The Ombudsman appoints his own staff (some 100 seconded civil servants), subject to Treasury approval of his budget, the size of staff, and so on. For the time being, the PCA also acts as the Health Service Ombudsman, but is separate from the local government ombudsman service. He reports on indi-

---

[1] We accept the tradition of anglicising the term, Ombuds*man* with the plural Ombuds*men* and we use the masculine pronoun only uniquely in reference to the Ombudsman. Though Ombudswomen have been appointed in other countries, none of the seven UK Ombudsmen so far has been a woman.

vidual cases to the MP who has referred it to him; reports annually to Parliament (including significant cases); and can produce special reports to Parliament if a department's refusal to accept a finding causes injustice to someone (a power he has used twice since 1967). The small PCA Committee (now submerged within the former PSC to form the Public Administration Committee) receives his reports and issues reports of its own, having taken evidence from the PCA, his deputies, ministers and officials. There is a clear parallel with the arrangements for the NAO and PAC. The C&AG and Ombudsman are also both officers of the House of Commons, but there the resemblance ends: the C&AG is responsible for systematic financial and 'value-for-money' audits across a broad range of government, whereas the Ombudsman carries out random checks among fewer bodies (126 in all) specifically listed in a statutory schedule.

The PCA Committee's 1994 report on the Ombudsman service itself found that it was both 'bureaucratic and confusing'; that 'any obstacle to clear and transparent access to the Ombudsman is to be deplored'; and that 'the assumption must surely be that the jurisdiction of the Ombudsman runs through all areas of government, unless there are very strong reasons to the contrary' (PCA Committee 1994: xv). On this and on other occasions the committee has recommended that the Ombudsman should be able to take up issues raised by the committee itself. But the committee fudged the issue of the MP 'filter', which is clearly an obvious potential obstacle to 'clear and transparent access'. The then Ombudsman wished to abolish the filter, as had others before him. In the 1970s, for example, his predecessor argued for direct access, commenting that:

> 635 people cannot expect to operate in the same sort of way. If they cannot do that, is it fair that constituents in different parts of the country should have less access to the Parliamentary Commissioner than in other parts?
> (PCA Committee 1978: 65)

In the early years of the service, between about a third and just over half of MPs did not refer cases to the Ombudsman. But since 1993, there has been a significant increase and by 1996 some nine out of ten MPs (87 per cent) did so (Giddings 1998).

But the filter remains the most controversial aspect of the British arrangements. A comparative survey of Ombudsman services around the world has even stated that 'direct access to the Ombudsman is . . . an essential requirement of the office' (Drewry 1997: 96). While care is necessary in comparing the size of Ombudsmen's caseloads – their remits and powers vary considerably within quite different administrative and political settings – nevertheless the comparatively low level of cases dealt with by the UK Ombudsman does seem to suggest that that the filter is a real obstacle. The caseload has recently risen considerably under Reid, from 986 cases in 1993 to 1,933 in 1996, but this is less than half the total of 4,000 in Sweden, first home of the Ombudsman, from a population which is nearly seven times smaller than Britain's (Drewry 1997: 91, 96). This disparity cannot be entirely attributed to the filter: the Swedish Ombudsman, for example, is a long-established part of government in Sweden, and the service is well known within a much smaller population.

Ombudsman

The UK Ombudsman was designed to be insulated from the public at the outset and publicity for his service has been inadequate; a survey in March 1995 found that less than half the population (46 per cent) had 'heard of' the Ombudsman. As Philip Giddings notes, publicity campaigns and outreach programmes are common in other Ombudsman schemes, often with an emphasis on reaching disadvantaged citizens (Giddings 1998).

The Conservative government was reluctant to expand the Ombudsman's jurisdiction, though urged to do so by the PCA Committee and the Ombudsman himself. The Ombudsman was especially concerned by the grey area between public and private provision of public services, recently created by governments through contracting out, market testing, and the use of private contractors, private companies and voluntary bodies, all performing public functions and thus falling within the realm of public administration. In 1992 he argued strongly that departments and executive agencies should retain responsibility for the standards of services that they contracted out, but the government assured MPs that changes of this kind would not diminish the Ombudsman's jurisdiction. In fact, it has and the PCA Committee argued strongly in 1994 for the principle that the Ombudsman should be able to go wherever public administration took him. But, as with audit (see above), the government wanted to protect the private colonies in its empire from the burdens over-zealous officials might impose on their activities. There are other specific 'no-go' areas of public administration which restrict the Ombudsman's jurisdiction.

But the most troubling 'no-go' area is that of policy. The Ombudsman is prohibited from inquiries which bear upon policy and may not, for example, gain access to cabinet papers. But he can review decisions taken by officials, and even ministers, which are 'administrative' in character; and he has reviewed decisions in which ministers were involved on three occasions:

- In the Sachenhausen case, in 1967, the Ombudsman criticised Foreign Secretary George Brown's use of rigid and unsatisfactory departmental criteria for awarding compensation to British prisoners of war held in an inhumane German prison camp. Brown heatedly rejected his criticisms, but grudgingly gave the men improved compensation.
- In the mid-1970s, the Ombudsman criticised misleadingly reassuring statements made by Peter Shore, the Trade and Industry Secretary, about the soundness of a travel company which then went bankrupt. Again, his criticisms were rejected, but many people who had lost money and holidays were finally compensated under the Air Travel Reserve Fund Act 1975.
- In 1992, the Ombudsman found the DTI guilty on five counts of maladministration in its regulation of a fraudulent investment company, Barlow Clowes, which collapsed, causing serious losses to thousands of investors. The Ombudsman encouraged MPs to refer complaints to him and some 159 MPs of all parties did so. The government disputed his findings, but his intervention in this high-profile case forced a government U-turn and a remarkably generous compensation scheme was introduced (Drewry 1997: 100–101).

More recently, the Ombudsman took on the Department of Transport over complaints passed on by three Tory MPs in Kent about the department's unwillingness to make *ex gratia* awards to people suffering exceptional hardship from blight on the value of their homes caused by uncertainties over the Channel Tunnel rail link. The Permanent Secretary at the department refused to accept the Ombudsman's findings. The Ombudsman laid a report before Parliament about the injustice the refusal was bringing about. The department finally gave in and agreed to consider establishing a compensation scheme for people suffering from exceptional hardship; but at the same time, the department refused to admit maladministration, fault or liability. The Ombudsman's inquiries into the Child Support Agency in the mid-1990s made a real contribution to reform of the agency after its disastrous first year. But while ministers refused to accept suggestions of responsibility for its failures and the chief executive was obliged to resign, it was clear from the Ombudsman's reports that maladministration within the agency 'could not be divorced', in the words of the PCA Committee, 'from the responsibility of Ministers for the framework' the CSA worked under (PCA Committee 1995: para. 27). These cases demonstrate the authority the Ombudsman can summon up when he has to confront recalcitrant ministers and officials and the influence he can exercise on significant official and ministerial decisions. At times he does touch upon policy; but though policy and administration (and so maladministration) are often inextricably linked, he cannot investigate policy matters which are relevant to his inquiries.

As the political scientist Gavin Drewry reminds us, however, the efficacy of the Ombudsman must also be measured by the hundreds of less notorious cases in which, from the point of view of redress at least, his 'cumulative effectiveness ... in dealing with [familiar bureaucratic delinquencies] and winning apologies and small *ex gratia* payments by way of compensation is every bit as important a measure of "efficacy" as are his relatively few headline-hitting successes' (Drewry 1997: 104). Continuous criticisms of the delays involved in investigating complaints and writing up meticulous reports do take some shine off Drewry's implied praise. Admittedly against a background of a rising caseload, it took the Ombudsman 88 weeks in 1996 to investigate and report upon the average case, considerably longer than the target of 39 weeks set in 1992; and in 1994 the Ombudsman actually had to refuse fresh cases against the CSA.

The Ombudsman's links with Parliament are, as we have seen above, a strength and a weakness. MPs often fail to appreciate what is being done. The PCA Committee wanted to claim an annual debate for the Ombudsman's and its reports, as with the NAO/PAC, but the government rejected the proposal on the grounds that there was no demand for such a debate. Rising use of the service by MPs suggests that its reputation has increased considerably since a 1990 survey found that two-thirds of MPs felt that the PCA was 'only slightly useful to them' (Harlow and Drewry 1990). But Richard Crossman's original dream that the Ombudsman would act as 'the "cutting edge" of the backbenchers' complaints service' is far from being realised (*ibid.*: 764).

Overall, the consensus among informed observers seems to be that the Ombudsman service has made a positive and original contribution to improving public administration in this country, but that its profile remains too low and that its original potential remains unrealised (see, for example, Bradley 1995; Drewry 1997). The Ombudsman's jurisdiction, powers and scope remain restricted and so the service's scrutiny of the executive is limited, especially with the dispersal of public functions since the mid-1980s onwards. There is concern that Ombudsmen drawn from the civil service have established a civil service tradition for the service, functioning as an investigatory branch of the civil service inquiring into ad-hoc complaints, preparing scrupulous but long-drawn-out reports in neutral language, and not working within the rhythms of parliamentary and political life nor to the needs of MPs and the constituents who complain to them. Some MPs in the Harlow–Drewry survey wanted a tougher body – with 'greater scepticism about Westminster's ability to defend the indefensible' and a 'tougher approach' (Harlow and Drewry 1990: 768). The reports have been a source of practical reform and due process; and there is evidence of the effect that the investigations have had in the booklet of guidance published in 1995 by the Cabinet Office for civil servants, *The Ombudsman in Your File*. The nebulous notion of maladministration does give the Ombudsman's work a dynamic quality and allows his remit to grow and strengthen. But his work is too contained to develop into a set of general principles of good administration. The ad-hoc nature of the Ombudsman's role and the growing uncertainties about the boundaries of public administration make the absence of a developed corpus of administrative law and a written constitution all the more alarming. But who would trust the executive to draft the limits of their own powers, no doubt with a view to preventing any advances by the Ombudsman and the judiciary?

Parliamentary control of the security services

As we saw in Chapter 7, a series of alleged scandals and rulings by the European Court of Human Rights finally obliged the government to place the intelligence agencies, MI5, MI6 and GCHQ, onto a statutory footing, and to establish appeals procedures. The Security Service Act 1989 created a Security Service Commissioner and tribunal to monitor MI5's activities and hear complaints. In 1994, MI6, the foreign intelligence agency, and GCHQ, the government's electronic information-gathering agency, followed MI5 onto the statute book with a parallel Intelligence Services Commissioner and tribunal to consider complaints. MI6 and GCHQ inherited the same judge as MI5, Lord Justice Stuart-Smith, as their Commissioner.

The MI5 tribunal has received 242 complaints since 1990 and has not yet upheld one. In addition, none of the 95 complaints regarding 'property warrants' (i.e. warrants for 'bugging and burglaring') referred to the Security Service Commissioner by the tribunal have been upheld. Were all these complaints really unjustified? In the light of what is known and alleged about the activities of the service, it is hard to believe that they were, and impossible to check. Up to 1994 the Commissioner had also refused to reveal how many warrants had been issued to sanction bugging, surveillance or burglary, simply expressing instead his satisfaction with the way warrants were issued and the conduct of the security and intelligence services. The tribunal's proceedings are secret. The people who complain do not know what information is being assessed and get no opportunity to make further representations on its decisions. The tribunal cannot even question the grounds for the agency's actions if they belong to a group or category of people regarded as requiring investigation. Its final decisions provide no indication of what the tribunal discovered and cannot be challenged in the courts. These provisions fall well short of the standards laid down by international human rights instruments, which require states to adopt clear rules on surveillance and adequate and effective safeguards against abuse (DA Volume No. 1: 229).

In its first two years, the 1994 tribunal has failed to uphold any of the 24 complaints it has investigated and the Commissioner has dismissed 92 'property complaints'. However, the Commissioner's 1996 report does note that the tribunal members feel that their investigative powers are limited and they recommend that they should adopt adversarial hearing with legal representation for complainants rather than the inquisitorial review process they now employ.

The 1994 Act also allowed for the creation for the first time of a Parliamentary Intelligence and Security Committee to subject the activities of the intelligence and security services to scrutiny. Like the departmental select committees, it is empowered to examine the expenditure, administration and policy of the three agencies, but there the similarity ends. The Prime Minister appoints committee members from the Commons and Lords – and he can veto opposition nominations. The committee meets and takes evidence in secret in the Cabinet Office; has no powers to call for papers and persons or to require that evidence be given on oath; is serviced by Cabinet Office officials rather than parliamentary clerks; and reports directly to the Prime Minister who can censor its reports before they are laid before Parliament. So the government and agency chiefs retain full control over the information the committee receives and imparts to Parliament. Its members are subject to an absolute, life-long duty of confidentiality under the Official Secrets Act. This is no parliamentary watchdog, but rather the executive's poodle, performing tricks in a 'ring of secrecy' (as its first report lamely complained).

The committee reports so far suggest that committee members have confined themselves largely to routine managerial and administrative inquiries, drawing witnesses entirely from within the system (the Home and Foreign Secretary, agency and departmental officials, the police, etc.), while acknowledging the importance of also obtaining information from informed outsiders who can 'challenge accepted opinions'. The first two reports also consider issues ranging from the changing nature of the security agencies after the end of the Cold War, the implications of a 1987 spying case and organised crime. It is to be hoped that what was left out is at least of more interest than what remains in these reports. The 1996 report is particularly vague. For example, it gives only a single grand total for the annual expenditure and budgets of the three agencies up to 1999–2000, as John Major refused to let Parliament know the size of the agencies' spending and budgets separately. Interestingly, although the expenditure has been falling up to this year, it will rise over the next two years, but we are not allowed to know why (though we are informed that the 'funding arrangements for ✱✱✱' attracted the committee's attention!). Also missing are the committee's views on the agencies' attempts to protect the UK's economic well-being and three of its ten conclusions.

Control of security services

The committee has failed to meet at least two fundamental challenges. Its starkest failure has been the refusal to investigate the past activities of the intelligence agencies, accepting the advice of Lord Howe, former Foreign Secretary and a committee member, not to get involved in 'political archaeology' despite protests from the Labour minority. Thus, a fully catalogued body of MI5's human rights abuse and undemocratic activity – from surveillance of people lawfully engaged in civil liberties and trade union work to smears on leading political and trade union figures, a dirty tricks campaign against the miners' union, and the alleged attempt to de-stabilise the Wilson government – was left unexamined (see Wright 1987; Leigh 1988; Dorril 1993; Lustgarten and Leigh 1994; Milne 1994). By contrast, equivalent bodies in the United States, Canada and Australia – similarly set up in the wake of intelligence scandals – investigated them fully as a first priority to see what lessons could be learned from them. Such an inquiry might also have thought through the intelligence agencies' failure to warn government of the two most serious crises this country has faced internationally – the Falklands and Kuwait invasions – and their bungled role in Iraq's astoundingly successful defence procurement activities.

Secondly, the ending of the Cold War might well have led the committee to question the value of the secret intelligence services, as currently constituted. The docile reviews which have taken place so far have been a cosmetic exercise. For its part, MI5 has been given new roles, especially in the ill-defined area of 'serious crime', and its powers were extended by the 1996 Security Service Act to allow it to tackle such crime in co-operation with the police and Customs. Only the Liberal Democrats in Parliament warned of the dangers to civil liberties inherent in the deficiencies in MI5's democratic accountability, in which the government's committee of carefully selected parliamentarians is almost wholly complicit.

Finally, the executive has traditionally strongly discouraged any scrutiny of the activities of the intelligence and security forces within the House as a whole. For example, shortly after the SAS shot dead three unarmed IRA members in Gibraltar in 1988, the then Prime Minister, Mrs Thatcher, told the Commons, 'We do not discuss matters relating to the SAS, and no-one would want to unless he wished to undermine the security of the country'. The British government was the only government in western Europe not to admit to the existence of the undercover Gladio network after it was exposed during a parliamentary inquiry in 1990 into terrorist activities in Italy which were designed to discredit the left. This network, involving security and intelligence services, including MI5, MI6 and the SAS, and paramilitary groups, saw its task as subverting left governments, trade unions and legitimate protest groups in western Europe. Whitehall stuck to the official practice of 'not commenting on such matters'. In January 1992, Paul Flynn MP asked about reports that the SAS had trained Gladio undercover groups in Italy, Germany and other European countries. The Defence Minister replied, 'Training is provided in a variety of military subjects for personnel of foreign armed forces. Details are generally confidential between Her Majesty's Government and the overseas government concerned' (HC Deb WA, 21 January 1992, c187).

The democratic value of Parliamentary Questions

There is no more valuable safeguard against maladministration, no more effective method of bringing the searchlight of criticism to bear on the action or inaction of the executive government and its subordinates. A minister has to be constantly asking himself . . . what kind of answer he can give if questioned about [these actions] in the House and how that answer will be received.

(Sir Ilbert Courtney, Clerk of the Commons, 1911)

Question Time is an extremely important mechanism by which Ministers are held account-able to Parliament. It also allows Members to represent their constituency interests and Ministers to explain and clarify their policies. . . . Overall . . . I believe that Question Time works well and efficiently and I am not aware of widespread abuse.

(Malcolm Rifkind, cabinet minister, 1991)

Belief in the democratic credentials of the Parliamentary Question (PQ) is long-lived. Eighty years separate the words quoted above, but nothing separates the continuing belief in the efficacy of PQs as an instrument of parliamentary scrutiny of the executive. Questions are quantitatively far more important today than in Courtney's day. Even in the postwar era, the volume of written questions tabled has increased from 3,525 in 1946–47 to 34,612 in 1995–96 and 18,439 in 1996–97, though perhaps largely at the expense of oral questions which have actually decreased from 13,785 to 2,622 over the same period. But Rifkind's view that they 'work well and effi-ciently' is rather more contentious. The Procedure Committee had sufficient misgivings about the procedure of PQs to issue two reports in successive sessions in 1990 and 1991. Both inquiries were driven by 'repeated expressions of concern [from members] about the quality of Question Time as a proceeding'. Both revealed a variety of ways in which the objectives of raising individual and popular grievances, obtaining information, and scrutinising executive actions were subverted.

Oral questions are now devoted largely to partisan point-scoring in the adver-sarial 'hot-house' atmosphere of the chamber. In 1990, stringent rules were introduced to outlaw the 'syndication' of oral questions – the practice adopted by ministers' parliamentary private secretaries (PPSs) and by whips of farming out pre-arranged groups of favourable PQs or vague texts to backbench MPs to increase the chances of 'desirable' subjects dominating Question Time. Fewer oral PQs were tabled for a time, but within a year the Principal Clerk responsible for questions reported that 'syndication is alive and well' (Procedure Committee 1990b: vi; and 1991b: 16). The grip of the 'executive mentality' upon the House has also been evident recently in the growth of questions asking the Prime Minister or ministers to list the government's or departmental achievements. Not to be outdone, opposition MPs retaliate by asking for lists of failures. This has resulted in 'inordinately long' answers, which were argumentative rather than informative, and which the Procedure Committee viewed 'unequivocally' as an abuse (1991b: xxiv–xxv). Similarly, 'open questions', asking ministers simply to list their engagements for the day, have increased dramatically since the 1970s. Such questions can make Question Time

more topical and open, but the supplementary questions and replies generally degenerate into long and partisan examples of 'party warfare' rather than a genuine seeking
and giving of information. As the Procedure Committee concluded, very few MPs
now table an oral question unless they already know the likely answer (1991b: xi).

The fact that the Prime Minister is questioned weekly in the House – now for a
half-hour session – is sometimes held to be one of the distinguishing qualities of
British democracy. In what other country, it is asked, is the head of government
publicly quizzed in the legislature? The Prime Minister's Questions is disfigured by
precisely the same defects as other ministerial question times. Analysis by the *Sunday
Times* of the first 21 'reformed' Prime Minister's question times found that they were
well primed by 'planted' questions. Blair's standard reply to such questions – 'My
honourable friend is absolutely right' – was used 35 times (*Sunday Times*, 1 February
1998).

Written questions are another matter. Here, MPs are really seeking information,
usually – and naturally – for political purposes, but the process is not in the gladi-
atorial arena and government is more open. Skilled MPs can fashion questions which
pull information together in an analytical framework of their choosing to reveal, for
example, trends in policies or provision, economic projections, and so on. For
example, under the Major government, Labour MPs Hugh Bayley, Tony Wright
and Margaret Hodge used written PQs to investigate the Citizen's Charter, the
accountability of quangos, and the incidence of cases of judicial review across departments. Thus, the pages of answers to written PQs in Hansard, the parliamentary
report, are invaluable seams of information, which academics, professional organisations, pressure groups and others outside government mine assiduously. But it is
possible for the executive or individual departments to extinguish Courtney's 'searchlight' of critical scrutiny. Some departments, like the MOD, are notably less open
to PQs than others. Quite a few departments use catch-all replies, such as that the
PQs cannot be answered, except at 'disproportionate cost' (i.e. an average £450 per
question in 1997), or that the information is not held in an appropriate form, while
others give full replies. The officials who draft answers have always been economical
with the truth, as the Scott Report confirmed, in an attempt to head off potential
criticism or embarrassment for the government, minister or department.

The Scott Report also focused attention on the wide range of issues upon which
ministers refuse to answer PQs. Erskine May, the Bible of parliamentary practice,
lists a variety of grounds upon which governments of both parties refuse to answer
PQs, including those which touch, however remotely, on discussions between ministers, official advice to ministers, the cabinet process, national security, commercial
confidentiality and the like; or those asking for information available in published
documents, on past policies of the last government (if of a different party), on 'matters
about which successive administrations have refused to answer Questions', or simply
on past history going back 30 years or more (Erskine May 1989: 292). These embar-
goes can be changed over time, but in practice only at the discretion of the executive.
In December 1991, for example, previously 'blocked' questions on MI5 could at
least be tabled, if not necessarily answered. Much of this up to May 1997 was in
line with the code of practice on access to official information, but the code's criteria

could be used to withhold information which ought to have been publicly available. Scott found that 'commercial confidentiality' was used to justify refusals to answer PQs on defence sales to Iran and Iraq in 1986–87, and on details of the exposure of the Export Credits Guarantee Department to individual countries in 1989–90 (Scott 1996: paras. D2.117–118, 432). In Scott's view, the information should have been given. The real reason for the refusals was to protect controversial government policies from criticism (*ibid.*: para. D2.434).

In the 1995–96 session, the Public Services Committee (PSC) took up the issue of answers to PQs. Roger Freeman MP, the relevant minister, indicated that the then government gave a low priority to reform and found current practice acceptable. Of 250 PQs which ministers refused to answer in the session, he told the PSC that it was fairly plain why answers could not be provided for the vast majority: 'either it was commercially confidential or it was covered by well-established practice in relation to military sales abroad in terms of their value and customer, or indeed for other reasons'. Here Freeman was directly at odds with Sir Richard Scott who found that the refusal to answer PQs on defence sales to Iraq and Iran was not justified on the grounds of 'commercial confidentiality' and did not comply with the terms of the current *Questions of Procedure for Ministers* (Cabinet Office 1992), nor with the principles suggested in evidence to him by Sir Robin Butler, the then Cabinet Secretary. Scott recognised the need to balance the public interest in full disclosure against the public interests which might be adversely affected, but added: 'In circumstances where disclosure might be politically or administratively inconvenient, the balance struck by the Government comes down, time and time again, against full disclosure' (Scott 1996: para. D1.165).

We, too, recognise that a balance must be held; that information must at times be withheld in the public interest; and that in certain critical cases, incomplete answers must be given to protect vital interests. Yet the House of Commons has been very weak on asserting its right to information. MPs have not only accepted that ministers might have reasonable grounds for refusing to answer particular PQs, but they have also accepted the whole Erskine May portmanteau of classes of PQs which are never answered, simply on grounds of past practice. Moreover, they have accepted that a minister's refusal to answer a PQ is not to be regarded as a contempt of the House; and until recently, acceded to the Table Office's practice of 'blocking' – that is, not allowing PQs which governments habitually refused to answer, or which were 'of their nature secret', to be placed on the order paper at all (PSC 1996c, vol. I, para. 38). In effect, 'blocking' kept secret the fact that classes of PQs were simply not answered. Thus, MPs are poor guardians even of their own right to know. For their part, the Table Office clerks have insisted that they are only following the House's own instructions in preventing any PQ being tabled.

In November 1996, the Cabinet Office issued guidance to officials on drafting answers to PQs. Officials are instructed to have regard to their ministers' obligation of openness; to take care not to draft answers 'which are literally true but likely to give rise to misleading inferences'; not to 'omit information sought merely because disclosure could lead to political embarrassment or administrative inconvenience'; and to draw ministers' attention to answers might be either too open or too closed

(HC Deb WA, 11 November 1996, WA, c53). It is clear that the culture of Whitehall, and ministers, has to undergo a profound shift to live up to this guidance, if it is not to be simply a pious screen behind which the Quinlan ethic (see **p. 363**) flourishes – and the more so in those departments, like the MOD and DTI, which have over time had more reason to withhold information and remain most reluctant to disclose it. Of course, the promised government Freedom of Information Act could be expected gradually to bring about a greater acceptance of openness. However, an official in the First Division Association of senior civil servants informed the PSC that:

> there is a commonly accepted culture that the function of the answer to a PQ is to give no more information than the Minister thinks will be helpful to him or her, the Minister, *in the process of political debate* in the House. Individual officials are aware of that assumption and in preparing a draft answer will act accordingly.
>
> (PSC 1996c: vol. I, para. 46; [our emphasis])

In other words, civil servants frame replies designed to protect ministers in the adversarial arena of the House. Sir Michael Quinlan, author of the frank memorandum quoted earlier, informed the PSC that brevity was not the point: 'any answer is necessarily selective . . . if you are not going to write an encyclopaedia, you are selecting something and you are inevitably motivated by some presentational desires' [our emphasis] (*ibid.*: para. 46). On that 'inevitably' much turns and will turn in the future. How far and fast will the engrained culture of economy with the truth shift to a fully open attitude? And will the most secretive departments change at all?

The Labour Freedom of Information (FOI) Act, as set out in the 1997 white paper (Cabinet Office 1997c), does not touch on answers to PQs and so has nothing to say on the question of auditing ministers' refusals to answer PQs, or the accuracy and honesty of their answers. The position in 1997 was that the Ombudsman, who was responsible for examining complaints from the public about refusals to give information, was not empowered to act on complaints from MPs about the way their questions were handled. The Public Service Committee's proposal in 1996 that MPs should be able to ask the Ombudsman directly to investigate ministers' refusals to answer PQs was refused by the then government, which did however agree that the Table Office should maintain a list of ministers' refusals to answer PQs. Sir Richard Scott has similarly proposed that an officer of Parliament should be appointed to fulfil this role (Oxford Research Group 1996: 15). It is to be hoped that the new independent Information Commissioner, to be appointed to police the Labour government's intended FOI regime, will be empowered to provide a satisfactory check on decisions by ministers to withhold information from MPs. Even then, incomplete, or misleading, answers would not necessarily come to light. But partial independent scrutiny of ministers' decisions is preferable to no scrutiny at all.

The chief executives of agencies also answer PQs on issues within their areas of responsibility. Since 1992 their answers have been on the record in Hansard. But the fact that the chief executives formally answer the PQs does not mean that ministers have no hand in the replies. Some agencies, like the Benefits Agency, send their ministers copies of their answers at the same time as they send the originals to the MPs who have asked the PQs. But the answers in other agencies – the Prison Service Agency has been a notable example – go to ministers' private offices for approval and may very well be changed there by or on behalf of a minister. This compounds the confusion over responsibility between chief executives and ministers to which we have already drawn attention; and there remains a need for the government to clarify practice and inform Parliament and the public.

AUDIT

The Labour government's new select committee on 'modernisation' of the House of Commons was set an ambitious target by Ann Taylor, its chair and (then) Leader of the House, who promised significant changes to create a 'vital and effective' House of Commons that would revive public confidence in politics and public life (Press Statement, 24 June 1997). But its first report was confined largely to procedural changes, like more use of special standing committees to scrutinise legislation, timetabling of the legislative process to avoid over-use of the guillotine, and relaxing the strict rules against carrying bills over from one parliamentary session to the next. Such changes are capable of bringing more order to legislative processes and relieving the relentless time pressures on government 'business', and the special standing committees at least will take more time and may lead to re-drafting of less contentious bills. Overall, however, the measures are executive-friendly. They do not come close to solving the profound problems, identified in this and the previous two chapters, which prevent the House from fulfilling its role of holding the executive to account and subjecting its legislation and activities to effective scrutiny.

DAC9: Making government accountable

The ethos of the House is determined above all by party. Both governing and opposition parties are driven by the adversarial politics and loyalties this ethos reasserts daily during parliamentary sessions. The House of Commons does occasionally unite, usually on an issue of MPs' pay and privileges, or when members' dignity is at stake, but the idea of the House, or MPs, acting as a whole to assert its rights as the democratic heart of British politics, or to make its scrutiny of the executive effective, belongs in the realm of mythology. The task of systematic scrutiny therefore falls primarily to the opposition parties. But they are denied information they require; must take on the combined weight of the government and civil service; and can ultimately be outvoted. It is within this perspective that we must consider how extensive Parliament's powers to oversee legislation and public expenditure, to scrutinise the executive and hold it accountable, really are; and how effectively they are exercised in practice.

Holding the executive accountable

From the outset, as we showed in Chapters 12 and 13, the party ethos in the House of Commons, the dominant role of the majority party in government, and the House's primary role of sustaining party government in power place pre-determined limits on all the formal processes of scrutiny and accountability, and how effectively they can be exercised in practice. We concluded in Chapter 12 that the main mechanism for making the core executive and central state accountable to Parliament – the doctrine of ministerial responsibility, collective and individual – is obsolete and ineffective; that ministers cannot possibly direct and control the vast apparatus of government for which they are nominally accountable; and that there is therefore 'an effective vacuum in the accountability of the state in the UK'. Further, the realities of parliamentary life, ministerial control of information and official evidence to Parliament, the limits of openness under the current code of access, and the loose and incoherent nature of the principle of ministerial responsibility make it virtually impossible for Parliament to make a reality of accountability of the executive to the House of Commons through this political mechanism.

Holding governments accountable depends on access to information about government actions and policy. Such access for MPs, as for the public at large, is still governed as we write by the code of practice which falls far short of providing information on government 'policy' – the crucial decision-making processes of the central state. The chastity belt around 'policy' is fatal to any open and, for that matter, effective government; and it remains to be seen how far the Labour government's proposals for a statutory freedom of information regime will unlock it. But full and accurate information is only one part of the accountability equation. Much depends on MPs' determination to hold governments and ministers accountable for the misuse of their powers, or misleading the House, when they have the information to hand. This chapter makes it clear that on various occasions, such as Westland, majority party MPs were aware that they were being given untruthful and inadequate information by ministers and officials, but nevertheless voted in the interests of sustaining their party's government in power rather than holding a Prime Minister, ministers and officials to account.

Scrutiny of the executive

In this chapter, we have reviewed the ability and willingness of select committees to subject the executive to scrutiny. We have reviewed the weakness of their powers to secure evidence and information from ministers and officials who give evidence under instruction from ministers. There is past evidence of government's willingness to obstruct their inquiries, and even contempt for their findings. Select committees are industrious, carry out worthwhile inquiries, and are prepared to take on politically difficult investigations. But though MPs have tried very hard to create a non-partisan spirit on select committees, they are ultimately under the control of majority party MPs; and when push comes to shove on a major government or party question, party loyalties seem ultimately to determine their findings.

Select committees are also hampered by their own adherence to an old-fashioned framework for their activities; their members' lack of specialist knowledge, generally poor inquisitorial skills and lack of co-ordination; and the apparently general desire for their proceedings to be 'member-driven'. This desire means that they can deal only with a few issues each session, as MPs' own time is limited, and thus rules out any possibility of the more wide-ranging scrutiny of departments, agencies and other public bodies which larger staffs and permanent specialist advice could bring nearer to reality. Further, they rarely make an impact on Parliament, the media or the general public, and the House debates only a fraction of their reports.

The Scott Report revealed serious executive abuses in the way Parliamentary Questions were answered up to the early 1990s. The code of practice for access to government information, fewer restrictions on which questions may be answered, new rules for civil servants drafting answers, and greater emphasis on ministers' duty to give full and honest information to Parliament presage reforms in the system. How far good intentions will prevail over the previous 'game-playing' culture of economy with the truth is unclear – and likely to remain so since there is no independent scrutiny of refusals to answer PQs, nor any check on the veracity of those answers which are given.

Parliament's oversight of legislation and public spending

There is universal agreement outside Whitehall that Parliament's scrutiny of primary legislation is seriously flawed by governments' determination to get their legislation through unchanged, with the backing of the majority parliamentary party; the weakness of opposition parties; and the insubstantial nature of checks and balances from a second chamber which lacks the democratic legitimacy to challenge an elected government. At the same time, secondary legislation has increased in volume and significance and cannot in general be amended or scrutinised effectively in Parliament, often even in terms of its legality. One constitutional innovation, the Delegated Powers Committee in the Lords, has temporarily tempered government enthusiasm for taking 'Henry VIII' powers to change the law by way of statutory instruments, and for the time being, ministers have been conciliatory in their use of de-regulation powers. But the executive's powers in both areas remain undiminished and unchecked by due process in Parliament. Every Act which passes through Parliament confers additional, and on occasion unknowable, powers to make executive law upon ministers and their officials.

The Public Accounts Committee is by common consent the most effective Commons committee and it gives a parliamentary and public profile to the work of the Comptroller and Auditor General and National Audit Office. However, even though there is an annual Commons debate on its reports, the body of its work is generally neglected by MPs. We have not audited the work of the NAO as such, but it certainly provides a sound basis for effective public audit. To some extent, its work is limited by the ability of the PAC to keep up with its activities, and the PAC suffers from the same sort of deficiencies as other committees, even though it can recruit able and knowledgeable members. The NAO also suffers from the prohibition on inquiring into 'policy' and the growing confusions over the public–private divide prejudice public audit generally. The departmental select committees do not systematically scrutinise the expenditure of their departments and have no links with the NAO to enable them to do so. Thus the overall arrangements for audit even of government departments is deplorably unsystematic.

The Ombudsman and the intelligence services

The Parliamentary Commissioner for Administration is potentially a significant instrument of scrutiny and accountability. He is generally regarded as an effective and independent officer of Parliament and his scrupulous investigations of mal-administration in government have gained widespread respect. But take-up of the Ombudsman's service is low, in part probably because it is still regarded as a supplement to the constituency work of MPs rather than a public service in its own right. Thus the Ombudsman can only take on cases which come through MPs – the MP 'filter' – and the public do not normally have direct access to his service. The Ombudsman's jurisdiction over quasi-government bodies is limited and patchy, and confused further still by the uncertainties of the public–private divide. Further, the prohibition on inquiries into policy issues extends even to his work, though he can and has issued critical reports on government decisions involving ministers. The Ombudsman, too, has a low parliamentary and public profile. In general, the Ombudsman service has an inbuilt dynamism which is valuable, but there is also a need for a developed system of administrative law.

From the point of view of redress, as set out in **DAC13** (see **p. 13**), these factors also devalue the Ombudsman's detailed work of satisfying the legitimate complaints of ordinary citizens. Variations in the attitudes of MPs make access uncertain and uneven across the country and the MP filter is an unnecessary obstacle to public access. The Ombudsman service should not be a supplement to the MP's surgery, but an alternative and, where possible, an addition to what an individual MP can do.

Commissioners and tribunals have been established to provide official oversight of the intelligence and security services, and to allow people to have their activities inquired into on their behalf. The secrecy in which these scrutineers work makes it hard to judge how effective they are, but so far they have not identified a single cause for complaint in the activities of the agencies. A new Parliamentary Intelligence and Security Committee was recently established to exercise political oversight of their activities, but its work is vitiated by its carefully neutered status.

Enforcing scrutiny and accountability

In lectures after his report was published, Sir Richard Scott suggested that MPs could institute contempt proceedings against ministers who refused to provide information or who prevented serving or former civil servants from giving evidence to select committees (Oxford Research Group 1996). The former Public Service Committee addressed the issue of enforcement seriously in the 1996–97 session of Parliament and designed its draft for a resolution to be passed by the House in terms of a contempt of Parliament (the highest court in the land). The version that the government substituted for the House finally to approve simply set out 'general principles' governing ministers' conduct in relation to Parliament.

But even if a refusal to provide information to MPs, or the provision of misleading information, were considered to be a contempt of Parliament, the PSC acknowledged that the procedures for dealing with a contempt or breach of parliamentary privilege are 'cumbersome, and are not used for the purpose of ensuring that Ministers are properly accountable to Parliament' (1997: xxxi). An MP would have to complain to the Speaker who would allow a debate if she decided there were a case to answer. If an adverse motion were passed, then the case would go to the Select Committee on Standards and Privileges; and any action the committee recommended would again be debated on the floor of the House. It is impossible to test a minister's claim that a refusal to provide information was justified in the public interest because a select committee cannot enforce its powers to obtain either policy or administrative papers against any government department. Finally, a complaint would be subject at two stages to a government's whipped vote and thus, as the Clerk of the House wrote in his memorandum to the PSC, 'party politics may stand in the way of a traditional assertion of the House's rights' (*ibid.*).

On any refusal by a minister to supply information, or suspicion that a reply or information is misleading, MPs would require an effective power to obtain government papers. The PSC finally suggested that MPs who were not satisfied with a minister's reply to a Parliamentary Question should be able to complain directly to the Ombudsman for a ruling (the Ombudsman is already the adjudicator on refusals to provide information under the Code of Practice on Access to Government Information). But the Conservative majority on the committee drew back from a more radical proposal put forward by the Labour MP, Tony Wright:

> We believe that the absence of effective mechanisms whereby Ministerial accountability can be made a reality rather than a fiction in an age of party government is central to the contemporary difficulties of the traditional doctrine. The Ombudsman already exists as a servant of Parliament, with full access to papers, and it would seem sensible to utilise this mechanism further. *We therefore recommend that the Ombudsman should have the power, upon request from an MP or a Select Committee, to investigate refusals by the Government to make information available, and to make a Report.*
>
> (PSC 1996c: xc)

The committee divided six to four, on party lines, against the proposal. It went on to recommend that the Table Office, the Commons office which handles PQs, should provide a list of all ministerial refusals to answer them for each session of Parliament; and that ministers withholding information in answers to PQs should explain why. Finally, then, after seeking hard to find means of enforcing higher standards of responsibility, the committee left Parliament to rely largely on ministerial integrity, adversarial political pressures and media vigilance to ensure that ministers observed the resolution – the mixture as before.

The fact remains that the House of Commons, supposedly the sovereign body in British democracy under the rubric of 'The Crown in Parliament', is too subordinate, as we have shown, to the 'Crown' in its midst – the monarchical executive. None of the limitations on the House's, or MPs', powers to call the executive to account are statutory. They are imposed on Parliament by the executive and are kept in place by loyal government majorities.

15 The Rule of Law

The limited role of the judiciary

Ultimately, this country's checks and balances are no longer here. They are in our courts and are called judicial review.

(Richard Shepherd MP, in the House of Commons, 14 December 1993)

I am quite worried about the pronouncements of some of the judges who appear to think that there is a policy role to be adopted by some of the judiciary.

(Ann Widdecombe, then Home Office Minister, in *The Times*, 3 November 1995)

Judicial review is the principal channel through which the actions and policies of the executive may be challenged in the courts.[1] Since the late 1970s, the readiness of the courts to sit in judgment on the actions of ministers and government departments and to find against them has given the judiciary a reputation for legal, and even political, activism. The huge surge in cases of judicial review has added to this reputation. There has undoubtedly been a sea-change in judicial attitudes since the mid-1960s. Previously it was fair to say that the judiciary was about as executive-minded as the executive. The modern judiciary is now prepared to take a critical look at the legality of the acts and policies of the executive and has made major inroads into the executive's legal immunity.

It is important, however, to place the process of judicial review in perspective. Though applications for judicial review have increased dramatically to more than 3,000 a year, the courts refuse to hear more than half of the applicants, and less than a third of those who are heard obtain the remedy they seek. Further, the vast majority of these cases have little to do with the exercise of power by ministers, their departments and major public bodies. Most cases are brought by desperate people seeking to avoid deportation or to secure a decent roof over their heads from local authorities. Judicial review is also available – and is employed – against a wide variety of other public bodies, including many which are not elected, such as quangos

[1] There are three legal systems in the UK, those of England and Wales, Scotland and Northern Ireland. Many of the points with which we are concerned arise equally in each of these jurisdictions, and the substantive law of judicial review is largely similar (though the Scottish system is particularly distinctive). For the sake of simplicity, we use the term 'British' in our scrutiny of judicial review. For consideration of the different systems in Northern Ireland and Scotland, see further Hadfield 1995 (especially Chapters 10, 11 and the Appendix).

of all kinds, executive agencies, the police, hospital trusts, training and enterprise councils, the Law Society, professional bodies, and so on.

In short, judicial review is the closest that the law in Britain comes to having a specialised and exclusive process for handling litigation against the executive and public bodies on the grounds that they have exceeded or abused their legal powers – or propose to. In a series of high-profile cases, the courts have, for example, found senior ministers' actions and decisions unlawful – like the then Foreign Secretary, Douglas Hurd's expenditure of £234 million on the Pergau dam project in Malaysia in 1995; Home Secretary Michael Howard's use of prerogative powers to reduce compensation payable under the Criminal Injuries Compensation Board Scheme in 1995; and the use of secondary legislation by Peter Lilley, Social Service Secretary, to deny welfare benefits to asylum-seekers who had not declared themselves as such immediately on arriving in the UK in 1996. In 1994, the House of Lords, acting in its judicial capacity, even held the Home Secretary in contempt for deporting a Zairean political refugee to Nigeria, despite having been ordered by a judge not to do so.

These cases aroused considerable controversy and the judiciary was accused, furiously in some newspapers and by some Conservative MPs, of interfering in politics – Tony Marlow MP, for example, demanding after the Lilley decision: 'Have I missed something? Do the judiciary now have a democratic mandate to decide which laws are acceptable?' (HC Deb, 24 June 1996, c42). In November 1995, Mr Justice Sedley provoked a typical storm of outrage when he overturned the Home Secretary's decision to exclude the Rev. Moon from the UK because he had not first given the American cult leader the opportunity to make representations about the decision. *The Times* castigated Sedley's judgment on the ground that Moon was thoroughly undesirable in a leader headed, 'Judicial Moonshine' (3 November 1995), the *Daily Express* denounced 'the sickness sweeping through the senior judiciary – galloping arrogance' (4 November 1995), and the *Daily Mail*'s front-page headline got to the bottom of the sense of outrage felt on the government's side – 'Does this judge think he's above democracy?'

Such reactions emphasise the political importance of judicial review. They raise important questions about the nature of the judicial role when reviewing the actions of elected ministers and show how politically controversial that review can become. Is it, for example, compatible with democracy for unelected judges to be in a position to control ministers in an elected government and public bodies under their control? If their role is justifiable in democratic terms, as we argue it is, how effectively does the judiciary act in practice as a check on the executive and public bodies? How far do the rules the judges apply satisfy our democratic criteria? Our main criteria are set out in **DAC11**:

How far is the executive subject to the rule of law and transparent rules governing the use of its powers? How far are the courts able to ensure that the executive obeys the rule of law; and how effective are their procedures for ensuring that all public institutions and officials are subject to the rule of law in the performance of their public functions?

Rule of law

We also examine the conduct of the judiciary under other criteria:

DAC12. How independent is the judiciary from the executive? How far is the administration of law subject to effective public scrutiny?

DAC13. How readily can a citizen gain access to the courts; and how effective are the means of redress available?

Democracy, politics and the rule of law

The contrast between 'elected' ministers and 'unelected' judges is often made in discussion of the democratic role of the judges. In fact, both ministers and judges are appointed by the Crown, and neither are elected; some ministers are peers, not MPs; ministers need not belong to either House, and in recent history two ministers at least (Patrick Gordon Walker and Frank Cousins) held ministerial office when they were neither peer nor MP. Moreover, the mere fact of being elected as MPs does not mean that ministers will not misbehave and act unlawfully; and, as we have seen (Chapter 7), ministers' actions and decisions are most frequently in fact taken by civil servants, who are also appointed and not elected. In any democracy, ministers, their departments and public bodies, even if democratically accountable, are also fallible. There is, therefore, a general need to ensure that the executive in all its forms is subject to the rule of law, and that government is conducted in accordance with laws and procedures that provide safeguards against arbitrary and oppressive rule. This is especially the case in the special circumstances of government in a country, like the UK, in which the conduct of the executive is governed by non-legal conventions rather than a written constitution or legally binding rules. Ministers – and by extension, their officials and agencies – have vast powers at their disposal: executive powers under the royal prerogative and statute and delegated powers to legislate by proxy. The need for constant scrutiny, by Parliament, to ensure that policy and practice conform with Parliament's remit and wishes, and by the courts, to ensure that they conform with the law, is equally vast. The weakness of Parliament, and of existing political mechanisms of accountability, such as ministerial responsibility to Parliament, means that ministers, government departments and associated public bodies are outside effective political control, making the case for 'auxiliary precautions', such as legal scrutiny and control, all the more important. As we have seen, it is possible, even usual, for ministers to avoid responsibility in various ways.

It is also important to point out that the fact that 'the people', or a majority of the people, endorse what government does or wishes to do does not mean that that action is necessarily right, or even 'democratic'. Democracy does not mean majority rule or rule by the representatives of the majority of voters in Parliament. (The argument for 'majority rule' via Parliament in the UK is further weakened by the fact that the majority in Parliament represents only the largest minority of voters.) Democracy relies on open political processes in which freedom of speech and association flourish, the dignity and autonomy of individuals is respected and the liberties of all, and most especially minorities, are protected. All these goods are vital to the political equality on which democracy itself rests (see DA Volume No. 1, Introduction). And to the extent that political decisions interfere with the rights of individuals, political accountability cannot be sufficiently independent and objective to provide the necessary safeguards for individuals and minorities. It is through the rule of law as well as through political mechanisms that these democratic freedoms are protected; ministers and public bodies must be held legally accountable through the courts as well as politically accountable through Parliament.

The rule of law, as it is applied to the executive, is embodied in the process of judicial review. Judicial review has no democratic basis in this country; its rules and processes are not set out in a written constitution, nor are they established by statute law. Rather, judicial rule is a process which the judges have taken upon themselves and which has been tolerated by Parliament. It has developed from pre-democratic and late Victorian origins, according to Lord Diplock, the late law lord, as a reactive process by which judges in this century, and especially since 1945, have moved to 'preserve the integrity of the rule of law' in the face of the changing and growing activities of modern government (Sedley 1997). Constitutionally speaking, judges and others justify judicial review as a process by which both the common and statute law is applied to executive actions to ensure that they are fair and lawful; that they conform with Parliament's intentions in passing legislation; that they do not exceed the executive's legal powers; that they do not breach citizens' basic common-law protections; and most recently, that their actions and parliamentary legislation alike are compatible with European law. They stress that it is a democratic process because the judiciary's main concern is to secure that Parliament's will is obeyed and government does not exceed or abuse the powers granted to it by Parliament; thus, judicial review does not enhance the supremacy of the judges, but of Parliament itself (Loveland 1997). And as for rivalry with the executive, Lord Nolan, then a member of the Court of Appeal, said in 1992:

> The proper constitutional relationship of the executive with the courts is that the courts will respect all acts of the executive within its lawful province, and that the executive will respect all decisions of the courts as to what its lawful province is.
>
> (*M v Home Office*, 1992)

There is, however, a major systemic deficiency in defining the role of the judiciary and the purpose of judicial review so far as democratic criteria are concerned. The absence of a written constitution or statutory authority means that the judiciary possesses no fundamental set of constitutional, or democratic, principles on which to act as a constitutional watchdog. Since Parliament has never set them out, judges have had to deduce constitutional principles, or invent them, and through some form of constitutional telepathy give effect to 'Parliament's unexpressed intentions ... [and] passive intent' (Sedley 1997). In particular, they have to make choices between the traditional British emphasis on strong government, and the need for lawful and accountable government. If the UK had a written constitution, its under-lying values and priorities would give the judges more explicit and approved standards of conduct for decision-makers. This is what happens in France, for example, where the Declaration of the Rights of Man and the Preamble to the 1946 Constitution set out the country's basic values; and in the USA and other countries whose consti-tutions include a Bill of Rights or statements of state policy.

Thus, judicial review cannot be wholly justified as a democratic process, even though (as we shall see) it enjoins rules of 'natural justice', fairness and proper process which are important to democratic conduct of government. Nor is it true that there no conflict in practice between ideas of democratic legitimacy and the rule of law. The most obvious cases are those in which local authorities have claimed a 'mandate' from the electorate to take actions which the courts have found to be unlawful, such as the 'Fares Fair' case (see **p. 453**). The House of Lords held in this case that the mere fact that a policy has been set out in a manifesto cannot make that policy lawful, if for other reasons it is unlawful. Moreover, judges like ministers are fallible. Yet judicial review is at least a limited democratic procedure in so far as it does give effect to certain principles of democracy and constitutional behaviour. What is important for our purposes here, then, is whether and how far the substantive rules applied in judicial review conform with and promote democratic values.

How accessible is judicial review?

The growth in judicial review gives the impression that it gives ordinary people an accessible, cheap and flexible legal remedy – a significant issue for the Audit (**DAC13**). In 1988, for example, a Justice–All Souls review of administrative law remarked that 'the flexibility of the new procedure has made it very much easier to use and hence more attractive to litigants' (Justice–All Souls 1988: 147). In 1989, Lord Justice Woolf claimed that the 'simplified procedure and the length of hearings' normally kept the cost of judicial review within reasonable bounds; 'there is therefore little risk of those who are moderately well off not being able to afford the costs of an application for judicial review' (Woolf 1990). But analysis of the process and data suggests that access may well be more problematical than is generally believed (Sunkin 1995).

First, back to basics. Judicial review is generally a procedure of last resort. In other words, people can normally only apply for judicial review when they have exhausted other legal remedies – such as an appeal to an employment tribunal. In the absence of a right of appeal, judicial review may be the only form of legal recourse available and may be used immediately, provided it can be argued that the public body has abused or exceeded its powers. Judicial review now has a fear-some reputation, but is in fact a relatively narrow process – in principle, it is simply supervisory. The court is not concerned whether the policy or action under challenge is right or wrong; just whether it is properly made or carried out. If there is, or will be, an abuse in the actual process of decision-making, the courts may declare an action to be unlawful or quash a decision – but they cannot replace the original decision with their own. Usually they just refer the issue back to the minister or public body, at which point the decision may be retaken, but properly. Thus, even after successfully applying for judicial review, applicants may find themselves confronted by the same effective decision as the one which they challenged.

Judicial review is pre-democratic in origin and despite extensive reforms in the 1930s, and further reforms in the mid-1970s and early 1980s, the procedure remains far from ideal. Procedural limits remain which can create huge obstacles for applicants. Its mere location can cause problems, for it is a highly centralised High Court procedure which is available only in London. The main obstacle is the 'leave requirement'. Aggrieved people have a general right to take any case to court as long as they satisfy certain rules on time limits and can afford the costs. But to instigate judicial review proceedings, they must first obtain the 'leave' – i.e. the permission – of the court. They must have a 'sufficient interest' in the issue at stake and must apply 'promptly' and, in any case, within three months of the action being challenged. This time limit is considerably shorter than those in most private law cases, where six years is the norm (and three years where personal injuries are involved). Finally, the court must be satisfied that the case is 'arguable'.

The 'leave' requirement – which is unique to judicial review – creates considerable obstacles to wider access. Arguably, it breaches the general principle that people ought to possess rights of access to the courts for the resolution of legal grievances. Some commentators, including the Justice–All Souls review, have argued that it is wrong in principle to require people to obtain judicial permission to proceed against the state or other public bodies and that the requirement should be abolished (1988: 153). However, in 1994, the Law Commission held that it is in the public interest for the judges to be able to filter out 'hopeless applications' (Law Commission 1994: para. 5.6). There is clearly a case for removing such cases which could otherwise jam the court machinery and delay cases with merit. It is also important to protect ministers and public bodies from unreasonable challenges and unnecessary delays or costs. The risk is that the 'leave' test can make accountability and redress subordinate to the needs of the administration; it certainly makes it potentially more difficult to obtain justice against public bodies than against other bodies.

However, the main problem is that the 'leave' requirement empowers judges summarily to deny applicants for judicial review 'without any testing of the evidence or the legal submissions of the body alleged to have acted unlawfully' (Le Sueur and Sunkin 1992). Judges reject a substantial number of applications at the 'leave' stage. From 1987–89, for example, between 39 and 44 per cent of all applications annually were refused leave. Most of these (85 per cent) were handled by both solicitors and barristers and so were backed by qualified professional advice. The high failure rate, therefore, suggests that the courts are rejecting more than simply hopeless cases and are being over-protective of public bodies. Cases are being prematurely rejected without the applicant having the benefit of full argument in court. In recent years, too, the stringency of the test used seems to have increased. One of the main problems is the uncertainty of the criteria applied by the judges. To take one example, the key test is said to be whether the case is 'arguable'. But judges apply quite different criteria in determining whether a case is 'arguable', some indicating that even arguable cases should be refused leave unless the applications are in some way exceptional (Le Sueur and Sunkin 1992). This uncertainty makes for inconsistent decisions. Analysis of the 'leave' decisions of the judges most frequently involved in 1987, 1988 and early 1991 found very wide variations in the rates of leave granted in each of the years (Bridges *et al.* 1995: 164–170). For example, the most 'liberal' judge in 1987 granted leave in some four out of five applications, the least 'liberal' in less than one in five (18 per cent). In 1988, the rates of leave granted by each judge varied between 22 and 69 per cent; in 1991 (first quarter) between 33 and 70 per cent. The judges themselves were consistent, particularly those at either end of the scale, but the system was not. Obtaining leave to apply for judicial review is something of a lottery.

Who uses judicial review ? No-one really knows. There is a chronic shortage of data about who uses judicial review, how often, and in respect of which government activities or bodies. In 1993, the Public Law Project (PLP) filled in some of the gaps in our knowledge in a major report, *Judicial Review in Perspective* (PLP 1993) and a second edition was published in 1995 (Bridges *et al.* 1995). But there remains an urgent need for information on the use of judicial review and its influence on ministers' and government decisions (Richardson and Sunkin 1996). If basic information of this kind is not available, then we cannot answer the basic questions we have set ourselves: how readily can citizens gain access to the courts for redress of their grievances against government decisions (**DAC13**)? How effectively are the courts able to ensure that government ministers, public bodies and officials obey the rule of law in carrying out their public functions (**DAC11**)? And how far is the performance of the courts open to 'effective public scrutiny' (**DAC12**)?

Yet this essential democratic information is not available in any official format. The annual *Judicial Statistics*, the main official source of information on the way the courts are used, give only snapshots of the overall scale of litigation in the courts. They are too general to provide a sound basis upon which to assess, for example, how accessible the courts are, or whether they are effective vehicles for the control of government. Even on the judicial process itself, the data on the way the courts are used and how they function are patchy. Thus we rely heavily here on the PLP report (Bridges *et al.* 1995). The official statistics reveal that between 1981 and 1994, applications for leave to apply for judicial review rose over six-fold, from 558 to 3,208. In 1995 there were 3,604 applications for leave. These figures are often used as evidence of the growing importance of judicial review over the past decade or so. But they tell only part of the story. They do not record how many potential cases do not reach the courts. This means that we cannot, for example, accurately tell what proportion of actual problems involving conflicts between citizens and government or other public bodies the courts are dealing with. We do not know how many aggrieved people are being blocked by lack of adequate legal advice or funding. We know very little about the subject areas in which judicial reviews are sought and types of public bodies being challenged.

We also need to set these figures against the vast scale of decision-making by governmental bodies and the caseloads of the Ombudsman service and tribunals which also give redress to aggrieved citizens. It is obvious enough that some 3,600 applications for judicial review annually are infinitesimal when compared with the millions of decisions taken every year by public bodies. Even in areas where judicial review is used relatively often, the 'volume of judicial review litigation is tiny by contrast to the scale of administrative decision-making' (Bridges *et al.* 1995: 11). To take some comparisons:

- During 1993, social security tribunals received 161,208 cases, immigration adjudicators 25,244 cases, and the Immigration Appeal Tribunal 6,559 cases; there were 2,886 applications for judicial review.
- In 1994, 170,000 homeless or potentially homeless families who applied for assistance from local housing authorities were rejected and constituted a potential pool for judicial review. In the same year, 447 aggrieved people applied for judicial review of decisions involving homelessness.

Three areas – crime, immigration and housing – dominate the judicial review caseload. The PLP report found that during the periods they studied (1987–1989 and the first quarter of 1991) these areas accounted for between 57 and 68 per cent of all leave applications. In other areas, very few people applied for judicial review. For example, in 1989, there were only 26 family cases, 16 prisoner cases, 34 health cases, and 29 benefits cases. The PLP research also found that much of the recent growth in judicial review tended to be at the expense of local, rather than central, government, and most challenges to local authorities involved homelessness. Some three-quarters of the cases involving central government were against the Home Office (mostly immigration, but also prisons and certain criminal cases) over the period of study. Cases against the Department of the Environment – mostly planning – came next (7 per cent), then tax cases against the Inland Revenue (4 per cent). Only three other departments received 10 or more challenges during any one year – the (then) Department of Health and Social Security, the Department of Transport and the Welsh Office. For most central government departments, judicial review challenges were very infrequent, happening at most only once or twice a year.

Government departments themselves do not necessarily keep proper records of legal challenges to their actions. In June 1996, Margaret Hodge MP asked government departments how many of their actions or policies had been challenged through judicial review since 1991–92. Five departments gave no information on the grounds that they did not keep records – one of these was the Home Office! – or that the cost of assembling the information would be 'disproportionate'. After the change of government, the Home Office replied to a further PQ from Mrs Hodge in July 1997 that it had been involved in 'several thousand' cases since 1991–92, of which some 1,029 were immigration cases (1991–96). The Home Office estimates that its decisions were upheld in more than 90 per cent of the applications (HC Deb WA, 16 July 1997). Table 15.1 broadly confirms the pattern of challenges found earlier by the PLP research team, at least for the 12 departments which were able to answer Mrs Hodge's question. In more than half the cases (54 per cent), the department's decisions were upheld; in a third, the courts found for the applicants. There were nine appeals, of which six succeeded.

These figures are too limited to provide the basis for judging the value and importance of judicial review. However, they seriously qualify the general impression

Table 15.1 Judicial review challenges to government departments, 1991–97

Department	From:	Total	Annual average	Department's decision upheld	Challenge upheld
Agriculture (MAFF)	1991*	11	2.0	8	3
Defence	Information 'not held centrally'				
Education and Employment	1992	20	4.0	11	9
Environment	'Disproportionate cost'				
Foreign Office	1991*	6	1.2	4	2
Health	1994	23	11.5	11	4
Home Office	Detailed information 'is not readily available'				
Lord Chancellor's Department	1991	6	1.2	5	0
National Heritage	1993	4	1.0	4	0
Northern Ireland	'This information is not available'				
Scottish Office	'Disproportionate cost'				
Social Security	1994	22	11.0	15	7
Trade and Industry	1991	27	5.4	12	4
Transport	1993[1]	36	9.0	15	0
Treasury	1991	2	0.5	–	–
Welsh Office	1991*	17	3.6	9	8

Source: These statistics are assembled from the replies to Parliamentary Questions tabled by Margaret Hodge MP on 19–20 June 1996 and 10 July 1997. As cases were withdrawn, held over pending other hearings, and so on, the totals given in the decision columns do not necessarily match the total number of challenges by way of judicial review.

Notes:

* No central records.

1 Calendar years.

conveyed by recitals of the overall figures for judicial review, let alone tabloid images of a judicial juggernaut towering above hapless ministers of an elected government. They also make it clear that judicial review is used very frequently to challenge local authorities and comparatively rarely against ministers and their departments. The PLP report suggests, 'it has been used more often as a weapon to further limit the autonomy of local government rather than as a constraint on the power of the central state' (Bridges *et al.* 1995: 194).

But why is the expansion of judicial review confined to a few significant areas of government activity and almost entirely absent in many others? Most explanations – such as, for example, the existence of alternative remedies in some areas – seem marginal by comparison with the infinitesimal scale of litigation across so broad and various a range of potential use. It is most likely that major structural obstacles stand in most people's way. In evidence to the Law Commission, the Public Law Project suggested that the low levels of litigation reflected 'a range of problems of access', beginning with widespread ignorance of public law and judicial review among advice networks and lawyers (Bridges *et al.* 1995). For example, in the 1980s Citizens' Advice

Bureau advisers often overlooked potential judicial review challenges in housing cases. Further research shows that very few private solicitors have any experience of handling cases of judicial review, and those who do handle only one or two such cases a year (Bridges et al. 1995: Chapter 4).

Funding is also likely to restrict challenges from potential applicants. Unless they litigate in person (without a lawyer), judicial review can be extremely costly. To apply for leave in open court (as opposed to doing so in writing) could easily cost £5,000, except in a very basic case. Legal aid is available, but the test for obtaining it works against aggrieved people in judicial review. It may, for example, be refused where the authorities consider that an applicant would not gain sufficient personal benefit from the proceedings to justify the expenditure of public funds. This rule has excluded poor people on state benefits who stand to gain sums of money which seem relatively small to a professional lawyer, though not to themselves and other state beneficiaries. It has also blocked cases raising a non-material point at issue: for example, a right to a fair hearing. Another obstacle is the absence of legal aid for voluntary organisations wishing to pursue actions, for example, on behalf of the poor and the disadvantaged. The prospect of having to pay the costs of the public body (as well as their own) is a major deterrent for many aggrieved people (Bridges *et al.* 1995: Chapter 7).

But if more people did make use of judicial review, there is room for doubt whether the courts could actually handle the larger caseload. In the past, the growing caseload has not been matched by the additional resources needed to cope with it. In the early 1990s, it took between 21 months and two years for non-urgent judicial review cases to be heard, once leave had been granted; and for every case disposed of, two more entered the lists. In a lecture to the Administrative Law Bar Association, Lord Woolf compared judicial review to a motorway on which 'the tailback, or backlogs, are becoming more and more disturbing. The use of judicial review has grown and is continuing to grow at a pace with which the present structure cannot cope' (4 November 1991). In a High Court hearing in 1992 Mr Justice Popplewell described the delays as a 'public scandal'. In the House of Lords, the Lord Chief Justice said the overload amounted to 'a state of near crisis' and 'a national disgrace'; and the former Master of the Rolls, Lord Donaldson, said, 'It means that we have no effective administrative court in this country' (HL Deb, 22 October 1992, c875). An infusion of additional judge time, including the employment of part-time QCs as deputy judges to clear homelessness cases, did ease the crisis. By July 1994, waiting times for non-urgent cases had been reduced to 12 months and by the end of 1995 they were down to approximately nine months (Bridges *et al.* 1995: 128). Yet, as on the motorway, the judicial review caseload is susceptible to surges of unpredictable traffic which can quickly create delays.

This raises a further, perhaps more profound problem: namely, to what extent should judges be concerned with managing the caseload? Is it, for example, justifiable for judges to adopt a more stringent attitude towards granting 'leave', simply to reduce the flow of cases entering the system – rather than solely to ensure that the cases are legally arguable? Judges disagree on this question, but the Law Commission has endorsed the 'managerial' approach (Law Commission 1994: para. 5.6; and Gordon 1995).

The rules and procedures of judicial review

The rules and procedures of judicial review clearly determine whether it is an effective means for ensuring that the executive is subject to the rule of law – our main concern in this chapter (**DAC11**). Judicial review is essentially an adversarial process, designed to handle conflicts of law rather than fact. The two parties define the nature and parameters of each case. The courts rely almost totally on the arguments and evidence they present. This is true of most court cases; but unlike these cases, which are primarily concerned with private disputes, judicial review cases often raise wider issues of public interest and accountability. However, again unlike in ordinary civil proceedings, people applying for judicial review have no automatic right to see documentary evidence that may be in the hands of a minister or public body. Evidence is normally given in the form of affidavits (or sworn statements) and witnesses are rarely cross-examined. In other words, ministers under challenge generally have no need to sign public interest immunity certificates, or judges to consider them, in judicial review proceedings. This is because judicial review is designed to deal with legal rather than factual disputes. Finally, the judges reserve to themselves considerable discretionary power in judicial review proceedings and may decide to deny applicants remedies, even where they accept that the government body has abused its powers. They might, for example, decide that quashing a department's decision might create too many administrative problems.

The passive role of the courts, their dependence on the parties, their inability to control the range of issues and the variable worth of the evidence available to them all have important implications for the quality of judicial scrutiny of the executive and the ability of the courts to make the executive and public bodies generally accountable. Professor John Griffith, an eminent legal analyst, has argued that:

> judges are being increasingly required to make decisions on policy matters, but . . . the[ir] traditional practices and procedures frequently preclude them from acquiring the relevant information without which such decisions are inevitably less good than they should be.
>
> (Griffith 1985)

The courts are well aware of these limitations. Judges often use them as partial explanations for their refusal to allow themselves to be drawn into sensitive areas of decision-making, such as national security, the intelligence services, and similar issues. In the case of the government ban on trade union membership at the Government Communications Headquarters (GCHQ) in 1984, for example, Lord Diplock said that the judicial process was 'totally inept to deal with the sort of problems' which national security involves (*CSSU v Minister for the Civil Service*, 1984).

The courts prefer not to coerce public bodies but to rely on their willingness to co-operate. Thus, though they have discretionary powers to allow cross-examination and the disclosure of documents, they very rarely exercise these powers, even where, for example, the documents have been quoted in affidavits. The result is that it may be far more difficult for applicants to obtain documentary evidence from public bodies in judicial review cases than it is in other types of proceedings. Unless a public authority is prepared to be open and to disclose relevant documentary material, an aggrieved applicant may be seriously disadvantaged by his or her inability to establish the facts or to challenge the public body's factual assertions. Moreover, the courts will also be deprived of potentially important evidence.

The GCHQ case provides an example of these limitations. Here the government argued before the Court of Appeal and the House of Lords that it did not consult the unions before imposing the ban on their presence at GCHQ because consultation was likely to lead to disruption that would have threatened national security. The law lords accepted that they could not decide what was in the interests of national security. But they expressed unwillingness to accept without question a statement by ministers that the interests of national security outweighed other considerations, such as the duty to act fairly. Two of them, Lords Fraser and Roskill, both stated that the government was under an obligation to produce evidence, 'and not mere asser-tion' (Roskill), that the decision was based on grounds of national security. Despite these strong words, however, the only 'evidence' the government was obliged to give was the mere assertion of the threat to national security contained in the affidavit of the Cabinet Secretary, Sir Robert Armstrong. As Griffith commented:

> Had the courts . . . wished to discover the truth . . . two people knew the real reason why the government did not consult the unions. They were the Prime Minister and the Foreign Secretary. Is it not a commentary on the system itself that neither was able to be required at any stage to give evidence either orally or by affidavit and to be subject to cross-examination?
>
> (Griffith 1985)

The ease with which the new Labour government lifted the ban on coming into office in 1997, and the paucity of evidence since to suggest that national security has been endangered, suggests that neither witness would have provided convincing evidence of a real threat to national security, and certainly not enough to justify a breach of international human rights standards and the dismissals of responsible GCHQ staff which followed (DA Volume No. 1: 95–96, 221–222, 300).

Applicants for judicial review may also be denied access to documents which are protected by public interest immunity (PII). Government ministers may claim PII to prevent disclosure of documents which are otherwise relevant to legal proceedings on the grounds that their release would prejudice the public interest. As their much-criticised use in the Matrix Churchill prosecutions in 1993 revealed, government lawyers have required ministers to apply for immunity for documents which are not sensitive in their own right, but belong to a class of documents which the authorities withhold to safeguard the 'proper functioning of the public service'. These 'class claims' cannot be justified on principle; and, in practice, government departments were not disturbed by being obliged by the trial judge to disclose such documents in the Matrix Churchill case (see the Scott Report 1996: paras. G.10.1–18.43; J.6.1–94; K – Chapter 6). The courts have the power to inspect documents covered by a PII certificate to determine whether they should be disclosed, but they will not even inspect such documents unless applicants for disclosure satisfy the judge that they are very likely to contain material which would give substantial support to their case. Under judicial review, the courts' reluctance to consider disclosure means that applicants are potentially at a double disadvantage against the executive. Certainly, this reluctance to order disclosure limits the power of the courts to exercise effective legal oversight of the executive (**DAC11**) and to provide redress for aggrieved citizens (**DAC13**). When the UK has a Bill of Rights and a Freedom of Information Act, the position ought to be much clearer. Ministers would be obliged to justify non-disclosure rather than, as now, being able to pass the buck to the courts.

Judicial remedies and the impact of judicial control

It is a broad principle of English law that it is more important that remedies should be available for wrongs than that 'rights' should be available to individual people. However, the courts have no authority to award damages to those adversely affected by an abuse of power by ministers or public bodies, unless an action or decision gives rise to a claim in tort (for example, where a body is negligent or guilty of trespass), constitutes a breach of contract, or infringes rights provided by European Community law. In judicial review proceedings, the court can normally only order the body in question not to act unlawfully, or require it through court orders to act lawfully, quash unlawful decisions, or declare what the law is. The courts cannot decide for themselves what a minister or other public official ought to have done and order accordingly. In civil law systems such as France, by contrast, the court – the *Conseil d'État* – can award compensation, or decide for itself whether the decision that is being challenged is right or wrong, as opposed to being legal or illegal.

Again for historical reasons, the remedies in judicial review are discretionary. Even if the court finds that a minister or public body has acted unlawfully, with procedural impropriety, or irrationally, it may refuse to grant a remedy. Reasons for refusing might include the fact that the applicant delayed too long before bringing the case, or, more worrying for people who are adversely affected by abuse or misuse of power, because to grant a remedy would cause administrative disruption. So where, for example, regulations for the payment of benefits are found to be invalid, a remedy might be refused because of the administrative difficulties this would cause the government. Again, we find clashes between our democratic values and the need for 'strong' government being potentially resolved against the individual and in favour of the state.

Finally, although contempt proceedings or further litigation may be used if a public body flagrantly fails to comply with a judicial order, judicial review remedies are not designed to provide judges with a means of policing future government action to ensure that judgments are generally complied with. In the United States, by contrast, the courts have a much wider range of remedies at their disposal, enabling them to order agencies to change their processes, enforce performance standards, or order specific action to be taken. For the purpose of giving effect to these orders the courts can appoint monitors or masters directly to oversee compliance (Cooper 1988; Wood 1990).

The grounds of challenge to the executive

In the absence of a written constitution and a codified set of grounds on which public decisions can be questioned, three important democratic questions must be asked. What criteria do the judges apply in reviewing the acts of government and public bodies? Are these effective instruments of judicial control? Are they compatible with principles of democracy?

The courts claim that they seek to establish whether ministers and public bodies have kept 'within the four corners' of the legal powers they have been granted, usually by Parliament, and whether basic legal rules have been adhered to, such as the common law principles of procedural fairness and European Union law. In the GCHQ case in 1984, Lord Diplock enumerated three broad grounds for judicial review: *illegality*, *procedural impropriety* and *irrationality* on the part of the minister or body under review. Let us consider what each of these grounds involves and measure them against our democratic criteria.

First, *legality*: has the decision-maker acted unlawfully in the technical sense that he or she has exceeded legal powers? This is central to ensuring that ministers and public bodies perform their functions within the rule of law and on the face of it is a straightforward and uncontroversial ground for review. In reviewing the exercise of a power which has been granted in a statute, for example, the courts are surely seeking to give effect to the intentions of Parliament in accordance with democratic principles? However, the statute in question may be ambiguous. In their interpretation, the courts may import their own views and values. In this way, this ground for judicial review can bring the judges into political controversy. For example, in the high-profile 'Fares Fair' case, taken by Bromley Council against the Labour Greater London Council in 1983, the House of Lords found that the GLC's cheap fares policy was unlawful, partly because it was not 'economic'. The Transport (London) Act 1969 required that the GLC's policies must 'promote the provision of integrated, efficient and economic transport facilities and services'. The Lords took the view that the word 'economic' meant making a minimal possible loss and ruled that it rendered unlawful the GLC's decision to subsidise fares in order to encourage use of public transport for environmental, social and wider *economic* reasons. The GLC claimed that 'economic' meant 'not wasteful', arguing that it was well established when the Act was passed that subsidies to public transport were inevitable, and that larger than necessary subsidies were often acceptable and beneficial. The judges were criticised for making a narrowly conceived decision in a case where they had no knowledge or understanding of transport policies or the use of the word 'economic' in public transport, local government and government circles.

The *illegality* ground for judicial review is not, therefore, as simple as may appear at first sight. Part of the problem in the case was to do with procedures – judicial procedures focus on narrow legal issues and are not designed to allow judges to consider the more general economic, environmental and political aspects of cases, unless such evidence is presented by one of the parties. If such evidence were permitted, for example through the introduction of a new public official responsible for ensuring that the courts were fully informed of the public interests involved in any case, the judiciary might be able to come to better-informed judgments. In France's special administrative court, the *Conseil d'État*, such wider issues are fully ventilated before a tribunal which includes experienced public servants in its membership.

The second broad ground for judicial review is also uncontroversial in principle. Decision-makers – ministers, local authorities, quangos, etc. – should act with *procedural propriety* before making a decision that affects the rights or vital interests of a person or body. Broadly speaking, two forms of procedural propriety may arise. Decision-makers are obliged to follow procedures laid out in the legislation – for example, an Act may require a minister to consult with certain individuals or groups before taking action. If he or she fails to consult, it is the duty of the courts to ensure that Parliament's intentions are followed. Second, the courts also require public bodies to comply with common law principles of procedural fairness, often referred to as 'the rules of natural justice'. These principles, for example, seek to ensure that ministers or public bodies are not unfairly prejudiced against individuals affected by their decisions, and require ministers and public bodies to give people who may be adversely affected a chance to put their case. It was on this ground, for example, that Mr Justice Sedley ruled in 1995 that the Home Office's refusal to allow the Rev. Moon to enter Britain was unlawful – and set off a huge, and ill-informed, media controversy.

Such grounds are consistent with some of our democratic criteria. For example, the courts may ensure that information is available to those affected by decisions (**DAC7**) and can require a degree of consultation with them (**DAC15**). In a modest way, they can buttress civil and political rights, especially in certain areas such as discrimination. However, in the absence of statutory guidance or publicly agreed criteria, much depends on the way judges exercise their discretion, and particularly on how they perceive and reconcile the competing interests in a case (as with the other grounds of judicial review). Take, for example, the amount of information that government or the authorities should supply to people who are affected by their decisions. Clearly, there are cases in which decision-makers – and the courts – must hold a balance between the right of such people to be fully informed and the interests of good administration or the need to protect the privacy or interests of other involved people. There can therefore be a legitimate conflict between democratic principles and effective, or 'good', government.

However, the courts could at least begin from the presumption that adequate information should be given to people who are affected by a decision or who are being consulted by government – and then allow specific exceptions to protect people's privacy, and so on. But they don't. Rather, they tend to put the interests of ministers and public bodies first. They are also generally hostile to attempts to broaden the provision of public information and allow governments to use private-law rights of copyright and confidentiality to prevent the release of public information, as, for example, in the case of Sarah Tisdall who passed on information of public interest about the activities of the security forces (*Guardian Newspapers Ltd v Secretary of State for Defence*, 1984). In 1981, Lord Justice Wilberforce ordered Granada TV to name a BSC 'mole' who had passed on information to *World in Action*, stating that 'the legitimate interest of the public in knowing about [BSC's] affairs is given effect to through information which there is a statutory duty to publish and through reports to the Secretary of State who is responsible to Parliament' (*BSC v Granada TV*, 1982).

There is also an all-important omission in the way the principle of fairness is applied. The courts do not impose a general duty upon ministers and public bodies to give reasons for their decisions. Sir Louis Blom-Cooper QC recently argued that people affected by government decisions should know the reasons for arriving at such decisions, 'except possibly where the giving of reasons would reveal some aspect of national security, or unintentionally disclose confidential information or invade privacy' (*R v London Borough of Lambeth*, 1994). But Lord Justice Neill specifically rejected this argument in 1996: 'There may come a time when English law does impose a general obligation on administrative authorities to give reasons for their decisions. But there is no such requirement at present' (*R v Kensington and Chelsea Council*, 1996).

This is the orthodox position, on which even 'liberal' judges reluctantly agree, though it was qualified by an Appeal Court ruling in 1994 that 'such a duty may in appropriate circumstances be implied'. In some cases, therefore, judges do insist on reasons being given, but the presumption is still strongly against reasons being given rather than the other way round. And the 'appropriate circumstances' are more likely to reflect the perceptions of the judiciary, a privileged, largely male body of people, and to arise, say, in a planning case involving questions of property rather than in a social security case.

In 1971, a Justice report argued that, 'No single factor has inhibited the development of English administrative law as seriously as the absence of any general obligation upon public authorities to give reasons for their decisions' (1971: 23). It is an omission which seriously handicaps the very principle of fairness, for how can anyone know whether a minister or public body has decided in accordance with this – or any other – principle if they are not required to explain how they came to their decision? The people affected cannot know whether the decision-maker has been, for example, influenced by irrelevant or inaccurate material, has taken a mistaken view of the law, or has acted in bad faith, and so on. Evidently, too, the absence of a duty to give reasons for a decision limits the accountability of ministers and their officials, public bodies, local authorities, the police, Customs and Excise Officers and other officials. The reluctance of the courts to develop this aspect of judicial review tends also to justify the government's own traditional dislike of being obliged to explain itself. The giving of reasons would also improve the quality of decision-making, as well as checking arbitrary government, by obliging decision-makers to focus their minds clearly on the pros and cons of any decision.

Another handicap from a democratic perspective is that ministers and officials are not required to demonstrate that their decisions are fair and rational. For example, objectors at an inquiry into the route of the M42 (Bromsgrove) and the M40 (Warwick) in 1973 were allowed to give evidence on the government's forecasting methods, but were not allowed to cross-examine the government's forecasters. After the inquiry the government changed its forecasting methods, but the inquiry was not reopened. The courts held that there had been no breach of natural justice because the methodology was not a fit subject for debate in the inquiry (even though, in fact, the accuracy of the government's forecasts was central to its case). Further, the Environment Secretary was prepared to hear further representations on 'any of the department's proposals' – though he would, of course, be considering them in private. Thus, the courts were willing to accept that the department did not need openly to receive criticisms and show how it reassessed policy and it could therefore, if it so wished, carry out purely token consultations (Harden and Lewis 1988: 208–209).

The third, and most controversial, ground for judicial review is that a decision-maker should act *rationally*. The 'irrationality' test perfectly illustrates the judiciary's dilemma in holding the executive to account without being accused of interfering in politics. Judges can justify their interference on ground of *legality* and *fair process* by reference to the rule of law. Governments are not voted into power to behave unlawfully or to disregard due process. They invented the principle of 'irrationality' as a safeguard against arbitrary government. It may seem self-evident that decisions should be rational, but applying such a principle in practice inevitably means entering onto territory where the judiciary has traditionally feared to tread – that of executive policy. The trouble is that there is no fixed idea, and certainly no political or legal consensus, about what constitutes arbitrary, or 'irrational', executive conduct to guide them in this sensitive domain. The judiciary's solution has been to adopt uncertain criteria and to set the threshold for interference very high. In the leading case, the Master of the Rolls said that the courts could interfere if a decision was so unreasonable that no reasonable person would decide it that way (*Associated Provincial Picture Houses v Wednesbury Corporation*, 1948). In the GCHQ case, Lord Diplock said the principle would apply to a decision 'which is so outrageous in its defiance of logic or of accepted moral standards that no sensible person who had applied his mind to the question to be decided could have arrived at it'. The problem with such criteria is that they have no relation whatever to democratic or constitutional principle and are so vague that it may appear that the courts find a decision to be irrational if they do not like it and rational if they do. They can even be used as a cover for the judges second-guessing or substituting their own view of the right decision to be taken for the decision-maker's view – a process which is not consistent with our democratic criteria.

This discussion highlights a major problem with public law in this country – the absence both of clear principles and of developed priorities between principles and values. The law reports are full of judges declaring that political and civil freedoms are fundamentally important, but they also find that national security, law and order, and administrative efficiency are very important. Their own guiding criteria give no lead as to how these often conflicting values can be balanced. On one view, the judges could be blamed for not developing such priorities further themselves. However, judges seeking to develop their own priorities inevitably lay themselves open to charges of acting undemocratically, of meddling in politics, of subverting parliamentary sovereignty, and so on. The true culprits perhaps are our politicians who have not legislated as to how these conflicts should be legally resolved, what the grounds for judicial review should be, which matters ought not to be subject to judicial review at all, and which are better suited to other ways of redressing grievances, through the Ombudsman services, the Citizen's Charter, and so on. But single-party governments in the UK, elected as they invariably are on a minority of the popular vote, do not possess the democratic or moral legitimacy to settle such sensitive decisions on the borders between political and judicial authority, especially given their natural partiality for 'strong' government and 'flexible' (i.e. as far as is practicable, unexamined and ungoverned) discretionary powers.

Judicial review and the executive

Judicial review of the executive has, as we have seen, been properly inhibited by concern not to trespass into the political domain. Judges are mindful still of the profound conflicts of the seventeenth century and wish to avoid damaging schisms in modern times. It is for this reason that judges stress that their concern in judicial review is to assert the rule of law and seek to avoid, wherever possible, straying into the domain of executive 'policy'. The courts have also traditionally been reluctant to adjudicate upon the use by ministers of the pre-democratic discretionary powers they have inherited under the royal prerogative. Until recently, the royal prerogative was a virtual 'no-go' area for the courts. These powers are very vaguely defined and are generally also not capable of being challenged by Parliament. There was – and remains – an archaic deference to the presumption of infallibility of the monarch in the judiciary's reluctance to intervene in cases where ministers (or their officials) had employed royal prerogative rather than statutory powers. But there is also of course a recognition that certain executive actions and central government activities are 'non-justiciable' in the sense that they are too complex and politically sensitive for the courts. This will certainly be true for many prerogative decisions and a similar rule in US law protects 'political questions' from judicial review.

The judiciary has moved on from the tradition of judicial passivism followed by judges like Lord Simonds who, in 1962, refused to be led 'by an undiscerning zeal for some abstract kind of justice to ignore our first duty which is to administer justice according to the law, the law which is established for us by Act of Parliament or the binding authority of precedent' (*Scruttons v Midland Silicones*, 1962). Yet there are obvious limits to the courts' ability to intervene in 'policy' issues. It is possible to distinguish between two separate aspects of limits on their role. The first is practical. Judges are not qualified, for example, to assess the economic arguments for and against closing coal pits, or the social, environmental and economic case for and against the location of a new London airport; nor is it constitutionally proper for them to intervene on the substance of such decisions.

On other policy issues, the courts may have constitutional competence to intervene, but the question of whether they are best left to the executive and Parliament is open – for example, questions such as whether a local authority's spending is 'excessive', or whether hospitals should provide expensive treatment for suffering children where the long-term prognosis is poor. Judges decided not to adjudicate in several such cases in the 1980s and 1990s (Jowell 1997). In some cases, the deference of the courts to Parliament has attracted criticism. In 1986, for example, Nottinghamshire County Council, a Labour-run authority, felt that the Environment

Secretary's decision on its 'grant-related expenditure' and his guidance for calculating that expenditure unfairly limited its spending capacity. His decision and the
guidance in a Rate Support Grant Report was laid before the House of Commons
and approved by an affirmative resolution (and was thus not debated or voted upon).
Labour authorities generally felt that the Conservative government's expenditure
allocations were biased against them and the county council sought to have
the Secretary of State's decision quashed and the guidance declared invalid on the
ground, among others, that the guidance was unreasonable, or 'irrational'. The
House of Lords decided that they should not interfere. Lord Scarman said:

> I cannot accept that it is constitutionally appropriate, save in very exceptional
> circumstances, for the courts to intervene on the ground of 'unreasonable-
> ness' to quash guidance framed by the Secretary of State and by necessary
> implication approved by the House of Commons ... these are matters of
> political judgment for him and for the House of Commons. They are not
> for the judges or your Lordships' House in its judicial capacity.
>
> (*R v Secretary of State for the Environment, ex parte Nottinghamshire County Council*,
> 1986)

The unwillingness of the courts to interfere in executive decision-making has also
been very partial. For example, they have decided that it is not appropriate for them
to review the host of cases in which homeless people challenge the facts on which
the housing authorities have based their decisions, 'save in a case where it is obvious
that the public body, consciously or unconsciously, are acting perversely' (*R v
Hillingdon LBC, ex parte Puhlhofer*, 1986). In immigration and asylum cases the courts
take a similar view; even in 'genuine visitor' cases, they will only grant judicial review
in exceptional circumstances. In other areas, however, the courts have been more
willing to interfere in findings of fact by officials. So access to the courts in some
subject areas is more restricted in practice than in others. The courts are also far
more consistently deferential towards 'Parliament' – i.e. in effect, the executive –
than to other public bodies, and especially local authorities. In other 'Westminster
model' constitutions, the courts consider whether constitutional procedures for
passing Acts have been complied with. British courts will not interfere to regulate
the legislative processes of Westminster because its legislative procedures are not
governed by a written constitution or any other higher law. The Westminster
Parliament's procedures are self-governing, mainly through the party whips' 'usual
channels', and the executive's dominance generally ensures that they reflect its convenience.

Deference to Parliament reflects the constitutional reality that the courts are subordinate to Westminster. In the absence of a written constitution or modern Bill of
Rights, the courts have no power to review the constitutionality of Acts of Parliament
and strike them down as being incompatible with either. Generally, therefore, the
courts cannot hold legislation to be invalid, for example, on the grounds that it is
unjust, interferes with the civil and political rights of individuals, contravenes international law (other than European law), and so on. From the perspective of the

Audit, it would be difficult to justify the courts striking down statutes on such grounds, since they have no democratically agreed criteria against which to measure them. Occasionally, the courts have decided to frustrate Parliament's intent, usually to get round statutory clauses (known as 'ouster clauses') which seek to 'oust' the jurisdiction of the courts, or to prevent retrospective legislation which affects individual people. For example, the Foreign Compensation (Egypt) (Determination and Registration of Claims) Order 1962, made under the Foreign Compensation Act 1950, gave the Foreign Compensation Commission the power to award compensation to owners of property which had been expropriated when the Suez Canal was nationalised. The legislation provided that the Commission's decisions 'shall not be called in question in any court of law'. The House of Lords found that it could hear a challenge if a decision was tainted by a legal error (*Anisminic v Foreign Compensation Commission*, 1969). Such cases may seem to be examples of conflict between democratic and judicial decision-making. On the one hand, they may be regarded as anti-democratic because the courts appear to frustrate the will of Parliament. On the other hand, the courts are asserting the need to make the executive and its creatures subject to the rule of law and to give people aggrieved by executive decisions access to the courts; and the rule of law is essential to fully democratic practice. In general, however, the executive in effect exercises legislative powers through its command of a party majority in Parliament. Opposition parties are not able to provide an effective political check on the executive's legislative supremacy. Nor can the courts exercise effective legal control because one of their two guiding principles is to ensure that the will of Parliament, as expressed in legislation, is upheld. It is for this reason that governments in postwar Britain have been able to legislate as they will, without regard, for example, for some citizens' political and civil rights and their international obligations to protect such rights (see DA Volume No. 1).

Subjecting the executive to legal scrutiny

However, judges have been increasingly willing to use the common law – another realm of flexibility – creatively in the 1980s and 1990s to subject the executive's discretionary powers to legal scrutiny and to breach executive immunity. Paradoxically, the GCHQ case, in which the courts ultimately upheld the government ban on trade union membership, was a landmark among such advances. In the UK, workers possess no legal right to belong to a trade union, but in the GCHQ case the unions argued that since governments had always consulted staff at the intelligence-gathering centre previously when their terms and conditions of employment were changed, they had a legitimate expectation to a fair hearing before a ban on union membership was imposed. An one legal observer comments, 'They would have no rights under private law, but public law required a focus on the way the state should act towards an individual' (Jowell 1997). The government's lawyers argued that the power to organise the civil service stemmed from the royal prerogative which the courts had always accepted as non-justiciable. Though the House of Lords found for the government on a point of national security (see **p. 450**), it threw aside its self-imposed refusal to review any decision taken under prerogative power. While certain decisions taken under the prerogative would remain non-justiciable, the law lords now recognised that not all prerogative decisions fell into this category. They decided that, in future, they would review the exercise of executive powers, whether they were prerogative or statute, or even *de facto*, as long as they were 'justiciable'. Unfortunately for the unions, the judges held that while prerogative decisions about the civil service were justiciable, prerogative decisions on national security concerns were not; though even here, as we saw above, some (though slight) evidence of danger to national security had to be provided.

The GCHQ case is an example of the courts effectively changing the law, something which in principle seems to be undemocratic. But the content of the principle that they developed is consistent with our democratic criteria, enhancing the access of citizens to the courts for redress. It is vital to ensuring that the courts can subject public authorities to the rule of law in the use of their executive powers as they affect ordinary citizens.

Until 1990, the courts could not even grant injunctions against the Crown – i.e. ministers. Nor could ministers be found in contempt of court if they disobeyed court orders. (Injunctions could, however, be granted against other bodies subject to judicial review – local authorities, for example.) But in 1990, the House of Lords issued an injunction against the government to uphold the rule of European law, and in 1993, it finally reversed this rule in a domestic case involving M, the Zairean refugee mentioned briefly above (**p. 443**). M was deported to Nigeria, where he feared for his life, contrary to the order of a High Court judge (*M v Home Office*, 1993). The law lords decided that injunctions could be granted against ministers of the Crown; and that ministers, acting in their official capacities, could be found guilty of contempt of court. Kenneth Baker, the Home Secretary, was duly found in contempt for having gone ahead with the deportation on his officials' advice. Again, the judges were in effect using a legislative power to remove a historical impediment and to enhance the idea of accountability. Further, the new powers allow the courts to impose the rule of law on government in circumstances where political mechanisms cannot be relied upon to protect individuals from oppression. The House of Commons, for example, dominated as it was by members of the minister's own party, had no intention of calling Baker to account on such an issue. The decision is of particular importance, since the Lords rejected the argument of government lawyers that Baker was not liable to contempt proceedings because ministers obey court orders only as a matter of grace rather than duty. (Unfortunately, they were too late to save M who had at once disappeared after being deported to Nigeria.)

Recent cases we cited earlier are further evidence of the dynamism of judicial review and the courts' willingness to subject significant ministerial policies and decisions to scrutiny. In the case of asylum-seekers, the courts lowered the 'irrationality' threshold in judicial review in cases where an individual's right to life was at stake to impose 'anxious' or 'heightened' scrutiny of a minister's decision. Observers argue that the courts are gradually making the principle of irrationality broader and less obscure and developing a duty on government to provide reasons. If the government does, as promised, incorporate the European Convention on Human Rights, then there will be a fourth ground of judicial review. The courts have also broken with a previous rule that applicants must have a 'sufficient interest' – or 'standing' – to take up an issue and have opened the doors wider to organisations which wish to resolve an issue of broad public interest. Recently, for example, Greenpeace and the World Development Movement have been granted standing, even though they were not directly affected by the government's actions. This more liberal approach opens the way for judicial review to be used by campaigning groups as an alternative, or in addition, to more overtly political action.

But other recent court decisions reveal a continuing inhibition on the courts when it comes to sensitive policy decisions. In the case of the 'broadcasting ban' on spokespersons for organisations proscribed in Northern Ireland, for example, the courts upheld this use of the broad discretionary powers given to the Home Secretary by Parliament, in spite of the damage done to freedom of expression in the UK; and with greater reluctance, also refused to rule against the government's ban on homosexuals in the armed forces, 'outrageous' though the continuing ban is by international human rights standards (DA Volume No. 1: 97–98, 121, 193–194). In both cases, the courts feared to intervene in high-profile political issues, especially where the judiciary probably assumed that public opinion was likely to be on the ministers' side. Ultimately, too, the doctrine of parliamentary sovereignty, which gives single-party governments in Britain formidable legislative and broad executive powers, prevents the judiciary from protecting this country from arbitrary, and even oppressive, government.

The independence of the judiciary

It may be too great a temptation to human frailty, apt to grasp at power, for the same persons who have the power of making laws to have also in their hands the power to execute them.

(John Locke in *Second Treatise of Civil Government*, 1690)

The late Lord Diplock, a lifelong friend of mine, said in a recent case that it could not be too often emphasised that the constitution of the country is based upon the separation of powers and that the independence of the judiciary is the weakest and most vulnerable of the three parts.

(Lord Hailsham in the House of Lords, 7 April 1989)

It is one of the principles of British justice that 'judges who are appointed to administer the law should be permitted to administer it under the protection of the law independently and freely, without favour and without fear' (*Scott v Stansfield*, 1868). Further, the principle of a separation between the courts and both legislature and executive was established in the seventeenth century. However, the head of the judiciary, the Lord Chancellor, is also a senior cabinet minister and Speaker of the House of Lords. His presence in the cabinet is often not merely a formality, and recent Lord Chancellors like Lord Hailsham and Lord Mackay – and now, it seems, the Labour government's Lord Irvine – have been very active politicians. The law lords, judges in the highest court of appeal in the land, are also members of the

House of Lords in its legislative role. So the separation is not complete and the potential for political interference with the independence and impartiality of the judges is clear.

Judicial appointments are formally a matter for the executive. The Prime Minister and Lord Chancellor 'advise' the Queen on judicial appointments to the House of Lords and the most senior judicial posts in England; in Scotland, she takes the advice of the Secretary of State who, by convention, forwards the names submitted to him by the Lord Advocate (who is also a member of the government). There is no formal independent commission to insulate judicial appointments from executive control or partisan influences. Nor is there, as in the United States, any machinery for subjecting the executive's nominees to scrutiny and confirmation by the legislature. It is partly by statute, but largely by convention, that the impartiality of the process is maintained. Only senior barristers and solicitors may be appointed judges. In practice, the Lord Chancellor's Department is responsible for senior judicial appointments. In order to make a 'fair and informed judgment about every appointment', officials collect data about every candidate, interview candidates, and consult the judicial and professional community very widely. The formal criteria are set out in the department's *Judicial Appointments* – professional ability, experience, standing and integrity.

The Lord Chancellor occupies another point of influence; he also appoints QCs, an important staging post for senior practitioners and potential judges. Barristers and solicitors may well take care not to offend him or other ministers for fear of damaging their prospects of appointment. The whole process is carried out in secrecy, and the informal and unsystematic nature of the 'sounding out' of opinion provides no guarantee that considerations other than those published do not influence the final decisions made. By contrast, lists of candidates for appointment to the European Court of Human Rights are made public, along with detailed résumés of their legal careers and achievements.

There is no evidence to suggest that recent judicial appointments have been made on party political grounds. However, prominent lawyers have expressed strong concern about a perceived bias towards candidates of a conservative rather than radical inclination – including, for example, those who have represented the Crown or official prosecution service in court. The argument is that this has affected the general character of the judiciary and made it more sympathetic to the needs of the executive. Perhaps in reaction to such criticism, a number of very 'liberal' judges have been appointed in recent years. It may not be accurate to suggest that the current informal process inevitably favours conservative, or illiberal, candidates; but it certainly allows for such biases to affect the composition of the judiciary. No more are there any formal safeguards against politically inspired appointments, overt or covert. Given the erosion of conventional safeguards in other areas of public life, such as Parliament and the City, a respected authority on constitutional and administrative law has concluded, 'it is not beyond the bounds of possibility that senior appointments could be influenced by political considerations' (Wade and Bradley 1993: 337). For the Audit's criteria (**DAC12**) to be met, the executive should play no part in appointments and the procedures would have to be made accountable and transparent.

The independence of the judiciary is protected by various means – by the security of tenure of judges, their legal immunity from civil action in their capacity as judges, the law of contempt, the ethos of the legal profession and conventional rules governing criticism of the judiciary by members of the executive, whether ministers or civil servants. Senior judges hold office during 'good behaviour' and they may only be dismissed on an address of both Houses of Parliament. No dismissal has taken place for centuries. Their pay is high to protect them from the temptation to engage in incompatible activities and to attract into the judiciary the best practitioners. Their salaries are charged on the Consolidated Fund to protect them from parliamentary or executive interference. While the conduct of the judiciary and individual judges may properly be criticised in Parliament (as elsewhere), there are parliamentary procedures designed to prevent MPs or ministers bringing undue pressure to bear on judges for possibly party or partisan purposes. The *sub judice* rule prevents reference to most matters awaiting or under adjudication (though it is also open to abuse by denying debate on matters of general public concern).

Finally, the judges are appointed from legal professions which have a tenacious tradition of independence. However, this element of judicial independence is not an unqualified good. Members of the judiciary are often warm, courteous and considerate human beings. But their high and protected standards of living, closed and privileged careers, and introverted gentlemen's club culture – all of which they justify in terms of 'independence' and 'integrity' – have tended to produce a self-appointing and relatively isolated caste, more powerful in their own sphere than politicians or senior civil servants, too jealous of their dignity, often too intolerant of outside criticisms and advice, and often contemptuous of the civil servants with whom they are obliged to work. In *Murmuring Judges*, David Hare's theatrical satire on the judiciary, a young barrister catches something of the subtle damage such an environment can bring about:

> All this behaviour, the honours, the huge sums of money, the buildings, the absurd dressing-up – they do have a purpose. It's anaesthetic. It's to render you incapable of imagining life the other way round.

At their worst, such attitudes can engender the near systemic complacency which the judiciary demonstrated as the Birmingham Six and other notorious miscarriages of justice exposed the corruptions and legal failings of an incompetent and destructive criminal justice system. Britain's most eminent judges, including the then Lord Chief Justice, closed ranks, refusing at appeals to countenance the 'appalling vistas' that would open up should they recognise that they had been mistaken, and then angrily repudiating public criticisms of their own failures. The fact that judges are not accountable to the public through election does not justify the view that they are in no sense publicly accountable. Plainly, if civil liberties and individual rights are to be paramount in our legal system, then there will be cases where the judges must not be swayed, for example, by a 'moral panic' in public and media opinion. But the present highly insulated judicial lifestyle has not been a conspicuous success in preventing recent miscarriages of justice where political expediency and public outrage have been a factor.

Independence of judiciary

All this said, the judiciary does not, of course, see itself as separate from the state. Judges are clearly 'public' officers, and part of their role is to protect the stability of the system – a conservative with a small 'c' role. Professor John Griffith has argued vigorously that they are therefore 'politically parasitic', bound by their position to support the authority of the state and status quo against individual liberties (Griffith 1997). Several law lords have rejected Griffith's views as 'nonsense', arguing as Lord Ackner has from his own experience, that they do not come to the House of Lords 'with a bias towards the government – you don't owe the government any allegiance' (*Guardian*, 11 October 1991). However, one law lord, Lord Templeman, has implicitly conceded some of Griffith's case: 'After all, any judge is appointed by society to see that the rules are kept, and I have always seen it as a contradiction to have a revolutionary judge, because a judge is really there to *keep* the system' (*Guardian*, 11 October 1991).

He insisted, however, that judges do not exhibit 'political' bias, plainly in the sense of *party* political or pro-government bias. Yet judges are inevitably obliged to give judgments in cases in a wider 'political' domain and here their adherence to stability inevitably has political consequences. For example, during the miners' strike of 1984–85, the judges upheld police powers to control the movement of people heading for demonstrations in order to protect public order, thus denying them basic human rights of freedom of movement and assembly.

Judges have been ready to define the relationship of the judiciary to the state themselves. Making due allowances for the diversity of judicial opinion, it is possible to identify some broad strands of thought. There is a strong tradition among judges which regards their role as 'enforcing the will of Parliament', or 'upholding the legitimacy of public power'. In 1986, Lord Donaldson, then Master of the Rolls, added a gloss to this tradition, explaining that judicial review had 'created a new relationship between the courts and those who derive their authority from the public law, one of partnership based on a common aim, namely the maintenance of the highest standards of public administration' (*R v Lancashire County Council, ex parte Huddleston*, 1986). Another – apparently opposed – judicial conception of their role is that they form a bulwark between the citizen and the state, or as Lord Hailsham described it, 'The judiciary remains the guardian of the liberties of the people' (HL Deb, 7 April 1989, c1333). This became an increasingly common view from the mid-1980s onwards. In 1992, the newly-appointed Lord Chief Justice, Lord Taylor said:

> Independent judges form the only line of defence between the citizen and what has been in recent years an increasingly authoritarian government. . . . Although the public may not realise it at the moment because of the publicity, the judiciary really does stand between citizens and abuse of power.
>
> (*Independent*, 2 June 1992)

The fact is that the judiciary seeks to hold a balance between the two broad roles. How well they hold that balance is a matter of judgement for others as well as for them.

The Lord Chancellor and his department are traditionally regarded as buffers which protect the judiciary from political pressure rather than as channels for such pressure. But this is not always the case. At the height of the industrial troubles of the Heath government, Lord Denning, Master of the Rolls, was subjected to undesirable visits from the then Lord Chancellor, Lord Hailsham (*Guardian*, 30 April 1992). The self-same Lord Hailsham later explained that the Lord Chancellor had to belong to the executive and Parliament to defend the independence and integrity of the judiciary:

> [He] is the judges' friend at court, whether he is acting as their public defender in Parliament or as their private representative in Whitehall. For this purpose he is to be regarded as the representative of the judicial body and not simply as a member of the executive.
>
> (Hailsham 1989: 314)

In the 1980s, the judiciary became hostile towards Lord Mackay, the then Lord Chancellor, for being too executive-minded. Judges complained that he and his department were willing accomplices in damaging Treasury 'value-for-money' disciplines; pushed through 'divide-and-rule' reforms in the legal professions which weakened the professional infrastructure on which judicial independence rests; and reduced the independence and quality of judges by lowering the age of retirement to 70 in the Judicial Pensions and Retirement Act 1993. Judges were strongly critical of Lord Mackay for failing to consult them in advance of such changes, and resented the Lord Chancellor's Department's more active role – especially its plan to create an executive agency to run the courts service (which they saw as an 'executive-centred' model for the administration of justice). The strong element of 'special pleading' in these complaints and fears is clear enough. Lord Mackay's reforms, for example, were meant to weaken the monopoly of the bar in court – an indefensible restrictive practice – not to strike at the 'infrastructure' of judicial independence. Departmental officials are bound to play a role in the administration of justice. But the complaints do raise important issues for the independence of the judiciary and the quality of justice. The judges argue that they must at least be 'senior partners' in all issues which concern the facilities and resources of the courts, and cannot be confined to taking charge only of the trial of cases and their listing.

Public scrutiny of the courts

There are major built-in mechanisms of accountability in the courts (**DAC12**). Court hearings, especially those involving the liberty of the individual, are almost invariably open to the public and the press are permitted to report them. Unlike administrators and politicians, judges generally have to give full reasons for their decisions; there are extensive rights of appeal; and, ultimately, Parliament has the power to change any law or even reverse a decision of the courts. But judicial decisions have a 'political' dimension which cannot be confined to the formal courts system. Judges cannot be insulated from public debate, criticism and scrutiny, and the need to respond and explain, in the name of judicial 'independence'; indeed, the high degree of independence that they possess makes it possible for them to be responsive to public opinion and open to public scrutiny. Lord Taylor, while Lord Chief Justice, recognised the need to make the judiciary more accessible, stating on the day of his appointment that 'the judiciary ought to be open to criticism' (*Guardian*, 30 April 1992). Indeed, the judiciary have recently gone further, intervening for example in 1994 in debates in the House of Lords and in public over the possible consequences for the quality of justice of the Criminal Justice and Public Order and Police and Magistrates' Courts bills.

It may seem obvious that the judges have a proper role to play in political debate in a wider sense. Yet the Kilmuir Rules for judges, set down by the then Lord Chancellor in 1955, placed prime importance on 'keeping the Judiciary in this country isolated from the controversies of the day'. The judges do, however, clearly have a public role to play in a complex, and interdependent, political and bureaucratic world, where Westminster, Whitehall, the media and the public have legitimate interests in the relationship between the various arms of our governing arrangements and judicial conduct itself. In practice, judges are not expected to be entirely independent in fulfilling this public role in the sense of being indifferent to the state. In the final event, judges in Britain are expected to protect the stability of the state as well as the legal interests of individual citizens.

AUDIT

At the beginning of this chapter we set out three Democratic Audit criteria – **DACs 11–13** about the rule of law, the independence of the judiciary and access to the courts – on which we would assess the role of the judiciary. We took the view that, in principle, judicial review is not only compatible with the Audit's criteria, but is essential to give redress to individuals aggrieved by executive action and to control ministers and public bodies. However, its use is concentrated largely in the areas of crime, immigration and homelessness. Local authorities (homelessness) and the Home Office (immigration) are most likely to be challenged. Otherwise ministers and the public realm are only sporadically required to answer to the courts. As judicial review is activated only by litigation, broad areas of government activity remain free from challenge and many important issues are never reviewed by the courts. By its nature, too, judicial review is backward-looking. Judicial attention is focused on what has happened in a particular case rather than on what should happen in general in the future.

We are concerned about the absence of higher laws governing constitutional, or democratic, conduct in government and protecting human rights. Their absence obliges the courts to devise their own criteria for review. The grounds for review have developed in a dynamic fashion in the past 30 years to improve and widen judicial scrutiny of executive action. This process may very well continue, but its legitimacy is open to argument and doubt and the grounds are subject to change in the light of judicial experience. General principles of 'fairness' and 'reasonableness' may be fairly criticised as being vague and uncertain. They may be accurately applied by judges in particular cases, but they offer little concrete guidance to government on its future conduct. It is also difficult for both potential applicants and public bodies to predict how judges will react to issues – especially in cases determined on grounds of 'irrationality'. The grounds of review are incomplete and even on their own terms suffer from important gaps – notably, for example, the failure to require the giving of reasons for all decisions.

In 1995, the liberal judge, Lord Justice Woolf, argued that the common law 'enables the courts to vary the extent of their intervention to reflect current needs, and by this means it helps to maintain the delicate balance of a democratic society' (Rozenberg 1997: 87). This claim is politically naïve and democratically unsound. Throughout this chapter, we have stressed the need for the grounds of judicial review to be focused more widely on a set of clearer principles than now, and not simply on procedural questions, important though they are to democracy. We have shown how the absence of agreed, legitimising principles has weakened the willingness and capacity of the courts to subject the executive to effective scrutiny. This is a failing which cannot be met alone by members of an unrepresentative section of society, interpreting and stretching the common law as they see fit. Legal principles of equality, rationality, certainty and proportionality (a major pillar of European law) are important to strengthening judicial review. But a broader-backed vision of the judiciary's role is also necessary. The courts ought to be readier to sustain the idea of the public interest than they are, enforcing democratic standards of accountability, openness and consultation in the use of public power. Such power, after all, derives from the people and ought to be exercised in accordance with their participation and consent.

If a broad set of principles were adopted to insist upon a clearly defined and transparent process of public decision-making, if interests and the public were openly consulted, and if the authorities were required to give reasons for the decisions they take, then judicial scrutiny of the executive, and intervention in 'policy' issues, would be justifiable on democratic grounds. It would also become more effective if the courts did seek to establish the facts of cases more certainly and were prepared to sanction cross-examination of ministers and public officials. The role of the courts would then be to ensure that executive decisions matched both the evidence and reasons given for decisions and the principles of public decision-making. This should be sufficient to legitimise the judiciary's intervention in 'policy decisions' and the high, vague and somewhat arbitrary threshold for the 'irrationality' test of such decisions could be lowered.

DAC11: The rule of law

The impact of judicial review on government may perhaps best be judged at two levels. At the level of *actualité*, expert studies describe the impact of judicial review on government actions as 'only a sporadic, peripheral and temporary impact on government policy' (Sunkin and Le Sueur 1991). This is hardly surprising. The judiciary in Britain is constitutionally subordinate to a Parliament which is dominated by a political executive which therefore in practice combines supreme law-making as well as executive powers. Effectively, the courts can exert only marginal controls over its legislative decisions while gradually expanding their powers to subject executive action to legal scrutiny. In turn, the executive can overcome or circumvent judicial decisions that it dislikes through its command of Parliament by way of primary or secondary legislation. There are many examples of this political power being employed. One of the most extreme is the provision in the Social Security Act 1990 (Schedule 6, para. 7(2)), which in effect states that the Department of Social Security need not in future treat judicial decisions as binding, other than in the particular case where they are made. This tiny sub-paragraph, buried deep in the schedules of the Act, was effectively telling the courts to get lost.

It is government's democratic prerogative to decide that judicial decisions may not be allowed to obstruct its policies. But in present circumstances that democratic prerogative must be severely qualified. As we have seen, a partisan single-party government in Britain may employ its parliamentary majority, obtained on a minority of the popular vote, to push a mass of ill-prepared legislation through Parliament with utterly inadequate scrutiny and to reject the great majority of amendments, however well-intentioned (Chapter 13). When judicial decisions are liable to be overturned or evaded by techniques that are adopted in order to minimise parliamentary scrutiny and accountability still further – when, for example, the relevant provisions are buried in a detailed schedule or relegated to complex regulations – there can be little, if any, democratic justification. The existing parliamentary system in effect allows government to escape the decisions of the courts and to undermine the rule of law.

It has been argued that the importance of judicial review ought not to be measured by the direct influence of judicial rulings on government policy, but by a wider and less visible impact on public administration – for example, in the effects of litigation on the internal and informal working practices of departments, their management systems and decision-making culture. There are no empirical data to substantiate this statement of faith. Indeed, what is known suggests that the effects of judicial review are likely to be a great deal more mixed. It has certainly generated pressure to improve levels of legal awareness within government and to develop systems designed to reduce the risks of legal challenge. Ministers preparing proposals for cabinet or cabinet committee have been required in *Questions of Procedure for Ministers* (Cabinet Office 1992) to examine issues which might give rise to judicial review. Yet the advent of 'can-do' ministers and civil servants in the 1980s led to a culture in Whitehall in which the advice of government lawyers diminished in significance and departments followed 'a policy of doing what is thought best and leaving any legal challenges to the courts' (Sedley 1997). In the Pergau dam case, for example, ministers did not consult the Foreign Office's lawyers before deciding unlawfully to fund the project from aid funds. At a more general level, ignorance of basic legal principles is endemic in most government departments and public bodies. Administrators, driven by the desire to implement government policy as efficiently as possible, rarely think in terms of legal powers and principles of legality, as Mr Justice Scott's inquiries revealed. Even officials working in areas of administration which are heavily regulated by statute do not necessarily look at the Act of

Parliament establishing the scheme they are administering or the case law. When administrators do take account of judicial review, they are liable to direct their attention to saving costs and avoiding bad publicity rather than seeking to comply with principles of legality and standards of fairness (Loveland 1995).

Yet at the widest level, there is no doubt that the expansion of judicial review has created the idea among ministers and government officials that they are under the broad scrutiny of the courts in a way that they were not a generation ago. The cumulative effect is likely to be positive, not least because it has inspired public debate about the previously near unquestioned use of executive powers.

DAC11: How effective are the procedures of judicial review?

The exercise of judicial review raises troubling questions, quite apart from general questions of accountability and the criteria judges employ. There are doubts, for example, as to whether the courts, as presently constituted, are fit forums for making decisions that have public policy implications. Judges are often ill-equipped to reach decisions on the issues which arise and do not have an adequate range of expertise and information at their disposal to resolve them. Judicial review is not designed to get at the facts, or to oblige ministers and public bodies to account for their actions and to explain themselves. Thus, aggrieved people challenging public bodies in the courts often cannot obtain the information and evidence that is necessary to support their case; and the scrutiny of public decision-making is so much the poorer.

DAC11: Ensuring compliance with judicial decisions

The judicial review process does not enable judges to monitor and enforce executive or administrative compliance with judicial decisions. Compliance may only rarely be a problem, but we know very little about the way government adapts its policies, procedures and culture to adverse findings. Thus judges in this country have no way – short of further litigation or possibly contempt proceedings – to ensure that their decisions are complied with in day-to-day administration. In the US, by contrast, the federal courts have assumed an active role in ensuring that decrees ordering institutional changes are complied with.

DAC12: The independence of the judges

In most respects, the level of judicial independence in Britain scores highly. At the heart of their independence is the guarantee that judges are absolutely irremovable from the bench, short of mental decline or serious misconduct. Respect for the idea of judicial independence is axiomatic in politics and the law. But the role of the executive in judicial and career appointments is a dangerous anomaly and appointments procedures are insufficiently independent, open and accountable. The judiciary could no longer be described as more executive-minded than the executive, but judges are frequently prone to show themselves more sensitive to the needs of the administration than to those of the individual. They are also confined within an undesirably narrow class and social milieu. But overall, the spirit and quality of judicial independence in Britain is alive and well – and certain recent judgments against senior ministers in the courts and the judiciary's willingness to cross swords with Michael Howard over penal policies in the mid-1990s offer breathtaking proof of that sense of independence.

DAC13: Redress in the courts

We simply do not have sufficient data to judge whether judicial review allows citizens to make effective claims against government departments and public bodies. Yet there clearly are weaknesses in the process. Applicants may well have problems in obtaining documentary evidence from public bodies. Cross-examination of witnesses is rarely permitted. Such weaknesses reduce both the range of evidence available to applicants and the capacity of the courts to assess the issues raised in any case and its wider public interest implications. Further, judicial review remedies are discretionary. They do not provide a right to compensation for unlawful governmental action.

DAC13: Access to the courts

Judicial review is not as accessible and cheap as it ought to be. Procedural rules, like the drastically short limitation period, and the operation of the 'leave' requirement unduly restrict access. Judicial inconsistency in granting or refusing 'leave' is particularly worrying and the procedure is too liable to be used as a rationing device. Judicial review is not cheap, bearing in mind that applicants will be confronted by often relatively well-funded public bodies. Most individuals depend on the legal aid scheme which does not fund public-interest cases brought by groups like Greenpeace. There are also unanswered questions about access to judicial review, such as who uses it and why many significant areas of public action go unchallenged. Large numbers of cases are withdrawn: why? Are they settled and, if so, on what terms? Are settlements in public law cases in the public interest? These are important questions to ask in view of the unequal negotiating strengths of the executive and public bodies and the applicants who challenge them.

PART 4

The Balance Sheet

Findings: Good in Parts

Measuring British democracy against Democratic Criteria

In this section, we summarise the findings for each of the Democratic Audit Criteria used throughout this book to measure the health of British democracy. They are divided into two broad sections: *Free and fair elections*, covering the issues addressed in Part 1, and *Open, accountable and responsive government*, covering Parts 2 and 3.

FREE AND FAIR ELECTIONS

DAC1. How far is appointment to legislative and governmental office determined by popular election, on the basis of open competition, universal suffrage and secret ballot; and how far is there equal effective opportunity to stand for public office, regardless of which social group a person belongs to?

- Parliamentary elections to the popular chamber are determined on the basis of universal suffrage popular vote, but the second chamber, the House of Lords, is not elected. Membership is determined by the hereditary principle, appointed public office, and executive patronage. Men are privileged over women, people of white European descent over all other ethnic groups, and landed, business and professional people over other classes (**pp. 75–76**).
- The return of 101 women Labour MPs at the 1997 election represented a dramatic advance for women in Parliament, but Britain still compares badly with other nations and is far from equal in representation of the genders. The law on positive discrimination in Britain may mean that the key to the adoption of more Labour women in winnable seats – all-women shortlists – may no longer be possible (**p. 76**).
- Ethnic minorities are poorly represented in the House of Commons (**p. 76**).
- The ballot is secret at the point of voting, but the authorities and intelligence agencies can check how individual people have voted from their ballot papers, which are kept in storage. There is some evidence that the intelligence services have made use of this facility (**p. 97**).
- Some 4,500 local quangos under self-appointing or appointed boards now run a wide range of public services at local level, many of which have been removed from the control of elected local authorities. This 'new magistracy' is not subject to popular recall; its members are not broadly representative; and they are not accountable to local communities or users (**p. 269**).

Free and fair elections

DAC2. How independent of government and party control and external influences are elections and procedures of voter registration, how accessible are they to voters, and how free are they from all kinds of abuse?

- Election procedures and voter registration broadly meet international standards, but the processes of voter registration leave a significant number of people disenfranchised, most notably inner-city dwellers and members of ethnic minorities. Arrangements for postal and proxy voting are deficient (**p. 41**).
- Elections are formally free of government and party control, but the Prime Minister's effective power to call an election at the time of his or her own choosing within the five years of a Parliament gives the governing party an undue advantage which could – and should – be removed (**p. 81**).
- The Prime Minister is able to determine the length of a campaign period, again to his or her advantage (**p. 82**).
- Through their powers to vary the structures and boundaries of local authorities, ministers have an indirect influence over the critical fixing of parliamentary boundaries (**p. 97**).
- Big corporations, often run by powerful and wealthy proprietors, control undesirably large concentrations of newspapers and frequently dictate their editorial positions. Up until 1997, the press has been heavily biased towards the Conservative Party and groups of newspapers have campaigned in strongly partisan spirit against the Labour Party at election time. The influence of the press over the outcome of elections is a complex and unresolved question (**pp. 97–98**).
- The switch in allegiance of the Murdoch press from its extremely partisan support of the Conservatives since 1979 to less strident backing for Labour in 1997 has raised additional questions of press influence over policies and conduct of government (**p. 98**).
- The donations of businesses, wealthy individuals and trade unions to the two larger parties gives them a major advantage over other parties, which has a significant, though unquantifiable, influence on the results of elections. These contributions raise the question of the influence of these interests on the policies of the parties. The fact that individual donations can be made secretly to parties is an additional cause for concern, raising as it does the possibility of improper influence (**p. 98**).

DAC3. How effective a range of choice and information does the electoral and party system allow the voters, and how far is there fair and equal access for all parties and candidates to the media and other means of communication with them?

- Voter choice in the UK is relatively restricted by comparison with other European democracies, largely as the result of an electoral system which favours the two major parties and tends to squeeze out rival parties. The electoral system also greatly reduces the chances of candidates from third parties from being elected. This effect is less marked in Scotland, Wales and (in 1997) the south-west of England, where nationalist parties and the Liberal Democrats have strong national or regional support (**p. 77**).

- Though people who vote for the Liberal Democrats are most uniformly denied a fair chance of representation in Parliament, voters for the two larger parties also suffer disadvantage and sometimes effective disenfranchisement in Scotland, Wales and some English regions (**p. 77**).
- The political parties are given 'fair and equal' access to the broadcast media which are also legally bound to report their policies, arguments and activities in an even-handed and impartial way. The public service ethos of the BBC has also had a strong influence on the conduct and coverage of commercial television (and to a lesser degree) radio (**p. 98**).
- Election rules which allow candidates in local constituencies to veto full television or radio reports on local campaigns reduce the quality of their coverage of elections and should be repealed (**p. 98**).
- People have access to a wide diversity of information and comment in magazines, journals and books of all kinds. This healthy state of affairs is offset by the partisan conduct of the press; and the political parties do not enjoy 'fair and equal' access to the tabloid press in particular. The broadsheet press is generally fair and balanced in its reporting, but certain titles have been strikingly partisan in their editorial stances (**p. 98**).

DAC4. To what extent do the votes of all electors carry equal weight, and how closely does the composition of Parliament and the programme of government reflect the choices actually made by the electorate?

- The current 'plurality-rule' elections for Westminster are valued in political circles for producing decisive election results, in which a clear winner gains more than 50 per cent of the seats in the House of Commons, though usually on a substantially smaller share of the popular vote, and the runner-up is usually also privileged against third parties. This outcome is believed to produce 'strong' government, though the single-party governments which dominate Parliament are not by the same token necessarily 'effective' (**p. 75**).
- In consequence, elections in Britain breach the basic democratic principle that everyone's vote should be of equal value. The value of an individual vote varies according to the party a voter chooses to support, the region and local area in which he or she lives and the political circumstances in the actual constituency (**pp. 58, 63, 75–76**).
- Thus elections to the House of Commons reflect the choice of the electorate arbitrarily and imperfectly, and the outcomes for particular parties can be most perverse. The level of distortion in British elections is markedly higher than in other European democracies, most of which employ proportional electoral systems (**p. 76**).

- Another consequence of the current electoral system is that the results of most elections are decided in about 100 'marginal' seats. The parties naturally concentrate their efforts in such seats and seek to tailor their policies to appeal to the half a million voters in these constituencies, and to the most undecided of them. They are therefore likely to have a disproportionate influence on party policies (**p. 64**).
- The composition of the House of Lords is not affected by the electorate's choices (**p. 76**).
- The idea of the electoral mandate is a valuable, but imperfect, component of the democratic process in the UK. The idea seems to be taken seriously by the parties, public and media, although manifestos are inevitably framed in loose terms. At the least the idea pays lip-service to the principle of popular control and provides a yardstick by which governments may be judged (**p. 115**).
- There is academic evidence that the contents of manifestos do influence future government policies, but governments are liable to be 'blown off course'. Mandates may be abused by parties to justify policies which are incidental to the main themes of election campaigns, or they may conceal their real intentions (**pp. 106–109**).
- The idea that only single-party governments can properly offer electorates a clear choice of post-election accountability is central to the defence of the current electoral system. The trouble with this argument is, first, that single-party governments can satisfy only the wishes of the largest minority of voters. They have no duty to meet the wishes of the majority left over. Further, academic research has found that coalition governments in European democracies employing proportional electoral systems are as good, if not better, at keeping pre-election manifesto pledges (**pp. 114–115**).

DAC5. What proportion of the electorate actually votes, and how far are the election results accepted by the main political forces in the country?

- Broadly, between 20 and 30 per cent of the registered electorate fail to vote in British elections and a further 5 to 9 per cent of people eligible to vote are not registered, including 24 per cent of the black population, 15 per cent of the Indian, Pakistani and Bangladeshi community and 23 per cent of other minority groups. In a global league of turnout since 1945, the UK is placed at No. 48; and in western Europe during the 1990s, at No. 14 (out of 25) (**p. 77**).
- In 1997, electoral turnout fell to 71.5 per cent, the lowest level since 1935. So only 30.9 per cent of citizens eligible to vote actually voted for Labour (**p. 77**).
- Political parties and other major institutions and forces in the country accept the results of elections, and opposition to the policies of elected governments follows democratic channels and is generally peaceful. There are and have been significant exceptions – most notably, mass action and paramilitary violence in Northern Ireland, inner-city riots in 1981, and the 1990 poll tax riots. The armed forces have always remained loyal to the government of the day.

There are, however, allegations that elements in the security forces conspired against the Wilson government and otherwise interfered in the democratic process (**pp. 77–78**).

DAC6. How far is there systematic opportunity for the electorate to vote directly on measures of basic constitutional change?

- There is a clear trend towards placing constitutional proposals directly in front of the public through referendums. This tendency is far from hardening into convention and has no constitutional nor statutory basis. A referendum is not binding on government, although it would be very hard for a government to proceed against a clear verdict in a referendum (**pp. 111–113**).
- The absence of legal rules or even non-legal guidance for the conduct of referendums leaves important questions to the discretion of governments. They can decide which proposals should be made subject to a referendum and which should not as suits their own political purposes and convenience. Thus governments cannot be said to be governed by the rule of law in their decisions to hold referendums and in the way they organise them (**p. 115**).

OPEN, ACCOUNTABLE AND RESPONSIVE GOVERNMENT

DAC7. How accessible to the public is information about what the government does, and about the effects of its policies, and how independent is it of the government's own information machine?

- From 1994 onwards, a major voluntary effort to open up routine government information to the public was adopted through the code of access to official information. But it does not give the public clearly defined rights of access, especially in the crucial area of government policy. Thus the significant work of Whitehall remains carefully guarded against parliamentary or public scrutiny (**pp. 349–366**).
- Proposals for a statutory regime, giving people a right of access policed by an independent commissioner, were published by the Labour government in December 1997. They will open up government across the board, but how deep they will penetrate into the policy domain and other sensitive areas (e.g. commercial confidentiality) will not be known until the detailed proposals are revealed (**pp. 351–352**).
- However, up to the beginning of 1998, the policy-making processes have remained wholly closed to public view, except for the unprecedented access given to Sir Richard Scott for his inquiry into the 'arms for Iraq' affair (**pp. 368–369**).
- Key executive decisions are taken by cabinet committees, and less accessible ad-hoc committees and processes, and even MPs may not know the source of such decisions, let alone the arguments and information attached to them. Certain corporate interests, however, may be privy to decisions taken within these structures, at the executive's discretion (**p. 149**).

- Citizens generally receive undoctored official information and far more information is now available. But information on subjects which touch upon government policies is increasingly likely to be manipulated in the government's interests. Ministers and their officials routinely control the timing and extent of any release of politically significant information and often withhold or censor information which does not comply with their policy intentions or which is politically embarrassing. Even research findings and official statistics are liable to be manipulated, and inconvenient statistics series may be terminated or substituted by more congenial series (**pp. 175, 190**).

- Government information officers are expected by Conservative and Labour governments to be more partial in their work than other civil servants who operate under rules of impartiality. Modern public relations techniques now practised by government are not appropriate for handling public information and are inimical to democracy (**p. 190**).

- There are no consistent rules for consulting the public. Too many consultation exercises are for the benefit of interested parties and vary considerably in their openness. Consultation documents often contain valuable information on the background to proposals and policy options, but they may also be bland and glossy public relations documents. The results of consultation exercises are rarely published in full (**pp. 297–298**).

- Most policy-making in policy communities of officials and organised interests takes place in secret. Advisory quangos which determine decisions on the safety of drugs, food, environmental hazards, etc., which have a significant importance for people's everyday lives, do not explain their findings publicly, and generally keep their data and debates secret. No rules of public access or due process apply to their operations (**p. 298**).

DAC8. How effective and open to scrutiny is the control exercised by elected politicians over non-elected executive officials, both military and civilian?

- Government departments and their associated public bodies are the main organs of policy-making, even under conviction governments and 'can-do' ministers. Ministers can exercise control over their senior officials and departments, but largely only in the limited areas where they take a direct interest. Even in these areas their control is broad-brush only. Departments have strong 'departmental views' and deal with organised interests which prevail unless ministers take a contrary view, and most departmental decisions take place out of sight of ministers (**p. 189**).

- Ministerial direction or influence over significant policy decisions remains secret under the official prohibitions on policy advice and information being made public (**p. 189**). This secrecy is reinforced by official rules ensuring that officials give evidence to select committees in Parliament under the direction of ministers and do not reveal information on policy matters (**pp. 342–343**).

- Ministers are responsible to Parliament for the conduct of officials as well as departmental policies and decisions, but their close relations with officials create an identity of interest between them and a shared vision of the interests of the state. The fusion of interests detracts from the idea of ministers taking responsibility for their officials' conduct (**p. 187**). Further, civil servants act as a partisan arm of the executive, thus greatly strengthening the government of the day and reducing the ability of Parliament to subject it to effective scrutiny (**pp. 187–188**).

- Civil servants have no formal identity, separate from their ministers. As in theory they act only through and with ministers, they possess no separate locus for a wider democratic responsibility. But in practice they do act in a political sense, and their invisibility makes it hard for them to be held accountable (**p. 189**).

- Executive quangos can be valuable and flexible bodies in any modern democracy. However, the Cabinet Office has admitted that neither ministers nor Parliament has the information required to judge how they are performing, noting weak departmental controls and ministerial neglect (**p. 206**).

- Executive quangos at national and local level are a means by which government can remove important issues from the democratic agenda (**p. 205**).

- Paradoxically, 'arm's-length' quangos are under ministerial and departmental control to such an extent that the idea of their semi-independent status can easily be compromised. Bodies such as National Consumer Council, Equal Opportunities Commission and others are in need of formal arrangements which allow for government's ultimate responsibility, but also protect their semi-independence (**p. 231**).

- The security and intelligence services report to a high-level committee in the Cabinet Office, but political and official control of their activities is weak (**pp. 161–163**).

- The central determination of local government budgets and many policies does not allow for adequate scrutiny and control by elected local politicians and publics (**p. 269**).

- The sheer weight of departmental activity and its complexity makes it impossible for ministers to exercise control over their officials' negotiations with interest groups in policy communities, and the operations of quangos (**pp. 189, 231**).

- The principle of individual ministerial responsibility to Parliament – which advances the claim that ministers can properly be responsible to Parliament for the actions of the state and its bureaucracy – is obsolete and ineffective. The doctrine obscures the reality of dealings between ministers, civil servants and departments and feeds the comforting idea that the state is subject to political and democratic control (**pp. 366–367**).

- The principle of collective ministerial responsibility to Parliament – enshrining the ideal of 'cabinet government' – is important for the stability of governments in the UK. But the implicit promise of balanced and collegiate government which it holds out is false (**p. 148**). Modern cabinets rarely take significant decisions; historically, Prime Ministers have avoided taking big decisions to cabinet unless they are already pre-determined, or they require to bind all ministers to a particularly controversial policy (**pp. 127–130**). Prime Ministers can use their flexible powers to remove decisions to cabinet committees of their own choosing, or even create hand-picked committees or forums to advance their policies (**pp. 144–146**).

- But ministers themselves possess strong and flexible powers of action and have at their disposal the resources of their departments. Ministers and departments are often able to pursue policies or take decisions which a Prime Minister or the cabinet cannot control (**pp. 152–156**).
- There is a 'core executive' in modern British government within which most significant decisions are taken. The Treasury, Cabinet Office, No. 10 Downing Street and the whips' office are at the centre of the core. The Prime Minister is the most powerful figure, but there are major limitations on his or her power of command. If any one institution is in overall charge of government it is the Treasury, but in the loose federation that is Whitehall no one person or institution could possibly be responsible for the universes of discretionary decision-making which take place (**pp. 159, 299**).
- The principle of ministerial responsibility, individual and collective, has created an illusion of political control over an effective vacuum in the accountability of the state in the UK, allowing neither civil servants nor ministers to be held responsible or often accountable (**p. 367**).

DAC9. How extensive are the powers of Parliament to oversee legislation and public expenditure, to scrutinise the executive and hold it accountable, and to secure redress when necessary; and how effectively are they exercised in practice?

- The complexity of policy-making within the core executive, divided as it is between formal and informal 'partial governments', and the secrecy within which policies are prepared, severely constrains the ability of cabinet, let alone Parliament, its members, select committees and agencies charged with scrutiny, like the National Audit Office, to scrutinise and hold the executive accountable (**p. 149**).
- The rules governing the relationship between ministers and mandarins almost wholly removes them from any wider duty of accountability to Parliament or the public for their conduct at the heart of government. Their obligation to be open and honest in their dealings with both is ill-defined and ultimately unenforceable (**p. 189**).
- These rules, especially those relating to political activity by officials, have been broken by Prime Ministers, ministers and officials in recent governments. Constitutional practice and the culture of Whitehall, focused as they are on loyalty to the government of the day and its ministers, does not provide civil servants with a firm base for a public service ethic and a more independent and impartial relationship with ministers (**p. 187**).
- The fusion of interests between ministers and mandarins, the flexibility within which they work, and the secrecy which surrounds their dealings, undermines the very idea of applying transparent rules of conduct to the core executive's decision-taking and policy-making process (**pp. 189–190**).
- Officials and organised interests negotiate and make policies, often in closed policy communities, and their activities are hidden from sight within the realms

of ministerial discretion and policy advice, and are often additionally protected from disclosure by rules of commercial confidentiality. On occasions, policies determined in these negotiations are in effect fixed and cannot be unpicked by Parliament (**p. 296**).

- The conventional idea that the House of Commons is an agent of scrutiny and accountability is entirely subverted by the realities of the party ethos among MPs and their party loyalties. The House is divided by party and party loyalties determine most votes. The main task of the majority party is to sustain the government – a task which almost wholly frustrates the House's other functions (**pp. 376, 382**).

- In such circumstances, the opposition parties are unable to fulfil these roles either, and in effect can do so only to the extent that governments allow them space to do so. The result is that Parliament becomes the creature of government, which now combines the main executive and legislative role in Britain (**pp. 372, 435**).

- In recent years majority party MPs have failed to hold governments and ministers accountable for the misuse of their powers, or for misleading the House, despite the fact that they were aware that they were being given untruthful and inadequate information (**pp. 411–412**).

- The loose nature of ministerial responsibility and accountability; the executive's refusal to allow civil servants to give evidence in their own right; and limits on government openness make it virtually impossible for Parliament to police, let alone enforce, the accountability of the executive to the House of Commons (**p. 367**).

- Select committees, established in 1979 to improve parliamentary scrutiny of the executive, are industrious, carry out worthwhile inquiries, and are prepared to take on politically difficult investigations. However, although MPs have tried very hard to create a non-partisan spirit, they are liable to split along party lines on issues of political controversy and the writ of the majority party rules (**p. 436**).

- Select committees are hampered by the old-fashioned framework within which they work; and their members' lack of specialist knowledge, generally poor inquisitorial skills and on occasion lack of coordination (**p. 436**).

- Select committees are further limited by the low level of resources at their command, a weakness which is partly due to their wish to ensure that their inquiries are 'member-driven' (**p. 436**).

- Select committees rarely make an impact on Parliament, the media or the general public and the House debates only a fraction of their reports (**p. 437**).

- The Scott Report revealed a culture of evasive and partial answers to Parliamentary Questions in Whitehall up to the early 1990s, and it is impossible to determine whether this culture is still pervasive (**p. 437**).

- There is universal agreement outside Whitehall that Parliament's scrutiny of primary legislation is seriously flawed by governments' growing determination to get their legislation through unchanged; the party ethos of the House of Commons which turns scrutiny of draft legislation into a trial of strength rather than an endeavour to improve legislation; and the sheer weight of legislation which passes through Parliament (**p. 437**).

- The undemocratic composition of the House of Lords prejudices its role as an effective revising chamber, since its lack of legitimacy and dependence on the goodwill of the lower House means that it is unwilling even to use its limited delaying powers under the Parliament Acts; and that valuable amendments can be reversed by governments determined to get their bills through intact (**pp. 402–403**).

- The House of Lords is now more a convenient forum for adding government amendments to their own bills than a revising chamber, and these amendments are often introduced in large numbers too late to be properly considered by a House which often has considerable experience and knowledge of the subjects of legislation (**p. 401**).

- Secondary legislation has increased in volume and is often as significant as primary legislation; on occasions, secondary legislation has violated the human rights of British citizens. Yet it cannot be amended, is rarely debated and often escapes detailed scrutiny for legality in Parliament. Parliament has been remarkably indifferent to this unsatisfactory state of affairs (**p. 389**).

- Some forms of secondary legislation give ministers the power to make and change the law by executive orders ('Henry VIII powers'). These now come under scrutiny by a special committee in the Lords, but such provisions can be introduced to draft bills after they have been looked at by the committee and they are likely therefore to pass through Parliament unchecked (**p. 390**).

- 'Quasi-legislation', the host of regulations, codes, etc., which set out official rules for official use of discretionary powers, may be debated by Parliament, but MPs cannot reject it, and can only ask ministers to think again (**pp. 389–390**).

- The National Audit Office (NAO) has become a parliamentary agency and its powers have been expanded to embrace value-for-money audits as well as strict auditing of government expenditure. The NAO provides a sound basis for effective public audit, but its work is limited by the ability of the Public Accounts Committee (PAC) in the Commons to deal with NAO reports; it is not allowed to inquire into 'policy' and is perhaps too mindful of this prohibition; and the proliferation of quangos, contracting out and other measures means that much public activity escapes its grasp. There is a need to free the NAO to follow 'public money' wherever it goes (**pp. 419–423**).

- The PAC is by common consent the most effective Commons committee and it gives a parliamentary and public profile to the work of the NAO. Yet it also suffers from the old-fashioned procedures and assumptions which hamper the work of other select committees and its members are often too bound by the prohibition on trespassing on policy ground (**pp. 420, 437**).

- There is an annual Commons debate on the PAC's reports, but the body of its work is generally neglected by MPs (**pp. 420–421**).

- Parliamentary scrutiny of government expenditure could be greatly improved if departmental select committees forged links with the NAO and took on responsibility for systematic monitoring of their departments' spending. But the PAC is jealous of its exclusive links with the NAO and so far departmental select committees have been unable to establish links of their own (**p. 437**).

- The Parliamentary Commissioner for Administration (or Ombudsman) is potentially a significant instrument of scrutiny and accountability. He is generally regarded as an effective and independent officer of Parliament and his scrupulous investigations of maladministration in government have gained widespread respect. However, low take-up of his services, limited and confused jurisdiction over quasi-governmental bodies, the prohibition on inquiries into policy issues and a low parliamentary and public profile have all diminished his effectiveness (**p. 438**).

- The loosely defined nature of his jurisdiction allows the Ombudsman to develop his areas of inquiry and gives his work a valuable dynamic quality. But the idea of maladministration has not grown into a developed system of administrative law which could be a significant parallel process of scrutiny and redress to his and Parliament's oversight of the state bureaucracy (**p. 438**).

- Commissioners and tribunals have been established to provide official oversight of the security and intelligence services, but the secrecy within which they assess complaints does not inspire confidence. So far they have not upheld any complaints against the agencies. The recently established Parliamentary Intelligence and Security Committee is the creature of the Prime Minister. Its inquiries are limited by the exaggerated secrecy which surrounds the agencies and its reports are censored (**p. 438**).

- Even if a refusal to provide information to MPs, or the provision of misleading information, by ministers, were considered to be a contempt of Parliament, it has been acknowledged by Parliament that the procedures are 'cumbersome, and are not used for the purpose of ensuring that Ministers are properly accountable to Parliament' (Public Services Committee 1997: xxxi) (**pp. 438–439**).

- Parliamentary sovereignty is the central principle of the British state, but in practice it becomes executive supremacy. Parliament is too subordinate to 'The Crown' in its midst – the monarchical executive. The limitations on the power of the House of Commons to call the executive to account are not statutory, but are imposed on Parliament by the executive. The Commons acquiesces in them for fear of worse (**p. 438**).

DAC10. How publicly accountable are political parties and elected representatives for party and private interests, including sources of income that might affect the conduct of government and public duties and the process of election to public office?

- The funding of political parties remains opaque, unequal and unregulated. As matters stand, the political parties are not obliged in law to disclose the sources of their income. The room for improper influence is large (**p. 98**).

- The Labour government's decision in 1997 to refer the issue of party funding to the Committee on Standards in Public Life is welcome, removing recommendations for the future to a politically balanced forum which can consider the issues in a practical way (**p. 99**).

Open and accountable government

- Both Houses of Parliament have adopted rules of disclosure and conduct for the financial interests of their members, following the first report of the Nolan Committee. A Parliamentary Commissioner has been appointed to oversee compliance and investigate potential abuse and the Commons disciplinary mechanisms have been tightened (**p. 19**). The major doubt is whether the investigatory arrangements are robust enough to deal with a complex case.

DAC11. How far is the executive subject to the rule of law and transparent rules governing the use of its powers? How far are the courts able to ensure that the executive obeys the rule of law; and how effective are their procedures for ensuring that all public institutions and officials are subject to the rule of law in the performance of their functions?

- Constitutional arrangements in the UK are based on the premise that the executive is held accountable for its actions primarily by political means. But the political constraints on arbitrary use of their powers by a Prime Minister, or ministers, are not strong. As we have seen, cabinet government is a myth and the principle of collective responsibility to Parliament is not an enforceable instrument of discipline. Such rules of conduct which exist are non-legal conventions and codes which change over time and may be reinterpreted to suit the government or ministers of the day (**pp. 150, 327**). Thus the executive is not subject to effective and transparent internal rules of conduct.

- The rules governing the conduct of ministers towards civil servants, and the civil service code, are framed in generalities and have only a modicum of influence on the actual relations between ministers and senior officials. Although they prohibit ministers from asking officials to undertake party political tasks and officials are similarly bound, civil servants are under a duty to serve and support ministers in the political domain and undertake political activities on their behalf. Thus the ban on *party* political activity is of limited practical import (**p. 345**).

- Relations between ministers and officials are generally concealed within the closed policy-making channels of government. The culture of informal and flexible process allows much room for manoeuvre and makes it hard to determine whether ministers or officials have behaved improperly (**p. 345**).

- The rules for ministers' conduct are few and loosely framed. The rules are set by the Prime Minister and may be changed at his or her discretion. There are probably political limits now to his or her ability to alter significant rules, such as those enjoining ministers to be open and honest in their dealings with Parliament and the people (**p. 327**).

- The Prime Minister is ultimately responsible for enforcing the rules governing ministers' conduct, but the interests of the government naturally take precedence over questions of misconduct. Severe crises are normally resolved through the political process, and often become tests of political strength between the majority and opposition parties (**p. 314**).

- The absence of effective internal checks and enforcement mechanisms within the executive is a serious weakness, especially given the contingent nature of political checks. The refusal to adopt procedures allowing for responsible 'whistle-blowing', which is a feature in other democratic polities, further weakens the defence of propriety in government (**p. 327**) (though the Public Interest Disclosure Act 1988 may change this).

- Quangos are not governed by a regime of constitutional or public law sufficient to render them accountable and open, and to give the public access to their business. Initiatives such as the Nolan Committee's principles for public life, the new appointments process and the spread of codes of conduct are bringing about a significant, but piecemeal advance in their governance (**p. 232**).

- The impact of judicial review on both government actions and public administration is mixed. The expansion of judicial review has created a climate in which ministers, officials and public bodies are aware that their decisions may come under the scrutiny of the courts and they are thus more conscious of the need to observe due process. But only a few cases are heard and fewer still impact directly on executive conduct at the highest levels (**p. 467**).

- Judicial review is fairly narrowly confined to the way decisions are taken: their legality, procedural propriety and rationality. The courts rely almost wholly on the court papers and arguments and rarely inquire into the facts; and access to the courts is costly and leave to take a case to court is determined in an arbitrary fashion. The greatest weakness is that they do not yet enforce a duty on the executive to give reasons for their decisions, though they are nearing such an eventuality (**pp. 450ff., 455**).

- The courts have traditionally been reluctant to interfere in certain areas of executive discretion, like national security. But they have ended the self-imposed exclusion zone around government use of royal prerogative powers (**p. 460**).

- The rules of natural justice which they enforce are consistent with the Democratic Audit's criteria as far as they go, but they stop short of requiring a developed procedure for public decision-making which would ensure that proper consultation takes place and that the public have due access to decision-making bodies. Judicial review is no substitute for a properly developed scheme of public law governing the conduct of the executive and all public bodies (**p. 467**).

- Judicial review is an incomplete process in that it does not enable judges to monitor and enforce executive or administrative compliance with judicial decisions (**pp. 468–469**).

DAC12. How independent is the judiciary from the executive, and from all forms of interference; and how far is the administration of law subject to effective public scrutiny?

- The judiciary is in most practical respects independent of the executive and there is a strongly developed culture of independence. But the role of the executive in judicial and career appointments is a dangerous anomaly; and although governed by conventions which are clearly observed, appointments procedures are insufficiently independent, open and accountable (**pp. 469–470**).

DAC13. How readily can a citizen gain access to the courts, Ombudsman or tribunals for redress in the event of maladministration or the failure of government or public bodies to meet their legal responsibilities; and how effective are the means of redress available?

- The factors which inhibit the work of the Parliamentary Commissioner for Administration (see **DAC9** above) also devalue the detailed work of redress which the Ombudsman service supplies for ordinary citizens. Variations in the attitudes of MPs make access uncertain and uneven across the country and the 'MP filter' – the general rule that citizens must lodge their complaints via an MP – is an unnecessary obstacle to public access (**pp. 425–426**).

- Government departments and public bodies are not formally obliged to accept the recommendations of the Ombudsman, and he cannot order changes in policy or specific measures of redress. In practice, his recommendations are generally accepted (**p. 424**).

- There is not sufficient data to judge whether judicial review allows citizens to make effective claims against government departments and public bodies. Yet there are clearly weaknesses in the process – the fact that public bodies need not give reasons for their decisions; the difficulties for applicants in obtaining documentary evidence from public bodies; the near bar on cross-examination of witnesses. Such weaknesses reduce access, the range of evidence available and the capacity of the courts to assess the issues raised (**p. 469**).

- The discretionary nature of judicial review remedies means that they do not provide a right to compensation for unlawful government action (**p. 470**).

- Judicial review is not as accessible and cheap as it ought to be. Procedural rules unduly restrict access while the legal aid scheme does not fund public interest cases. Important questions concerning the use of judicial review need to be answered in view of the unequal negotiating strengths of the executive and public bodies and the applicants who challenge them (**p. 470**).

DAC14. How far are appointments and promotions within public institutions subject to equal opportunities procedures, and how far do conditions of service protect employees' civil rights?

- Of the institutions examined the processes of appointment to the judiciary and quangos give cause for concern.

DAC15. How systematic and open to public scrutiny are the procedures for government consultation of public opinion and of relevant interests in the formation and implementation of policy and legislation?

- Government policy-making through closed negotiations with certain organised interests means that other interests and the general public may be disadvantaged and may result in decisions which cannot be altered even in Parliament (**p. 150**).

- Major business interests are represented on significant advisory bodies which may often also contain professional and academic experts who have interests in the industries affected. These bodies then come to their conclusions in secret. There is an urgent need to bring balance to the composition of such bodies and to open up their proceedings to peer review and the public gaze (**pp. 219–230**).
- Government consultation of interests and the general public is unsystematic and opaque. Consultation papers vary considerably in their value. Consultation exercises may leave out some interests; give too much weight to organised interests; and may give those being consulted too little time to organise their evidence. The results of these exercises are not necessarily published in full. Overall, the absence of firm rules for consultation gives rise to concern (**p. 297**).
- The level of public participation in government policy-making is low and unduly restricted by the rules of secrecy which surround it (**p. 369**).

DAC16. How accessible are elected politicians to approach by their electors, and how effectively do they represent constituents' interests?

- National governments and hierarchies of quangos effectively take, usurp or limit decisions of local authorities and are not accessible to local communities, undermining the principle of representation by local politicians (**p. 269**).
- The effective representation of constituents' interests by MPs is very much dependent on their individual ability and time, and MPs are cross-pressured and lack adequate resources (**pp. 69–70**).

DAC17. How far do the arrangements for government both above and below the level of the central state meet the above criteria of openness, accountability and responsiveness?

DAC18. To what extent does government below the centre have the powers to carry out its responsibilities in accordance with the wishes of regional or local electorates, and without interference from the centre?

- Local government in the UK is not protected by constitutional guarantees, but only by a convention which has been unable to constrain the undue interference of recent Conservative governments. Generally the arrangements fail to satisfy the main criteria of the Council of Europe Charter for Local Self-Government. There is some hope in that the Labour government has signed the Charter (**pp. 243–245**). But the need to place local government on a constitutional footing and define and limit central government's powers to interfere is as yet unmet.
- Central government's controls over the current and capital spending of local authorities, and powers to cap rate-fixing, do not allow local authorities sufficient autonomy to respond to local needs and wishes and to develop services, and confuse accountability at local level (**pp. 268–269**).

Open and accountable government

- Hierarchies of national, regional and local quangos have been erected to remove public functions and services from local government. The national bodies are not directly accountable to local communities for the policies they lay down and the resources they make available locally (**p. 232**).

- The proliferation of local quangos, or spending bodies, often taking over local authority services and functions; the appointed and self-appointing nature of their governing boards; and the fragmented nature of the local quango state, is a serious inroad into local democracy and accountability. These bodies are typically accountable upwards, and not locally to local authorities and communities; and they are generally closed bodies which allow little effective public access (**pp. 232, 269**).

- Conservative reforms introducing rules of openness in local government, giving citizens access to local authority documents and meetings, and enforcing the publication of comparative statistics are potentially valuable advances (**p. 248**).

- The cumulative effect of Conservative government policies has been to diminish local government and frustrate local accountability (**p. 269**).

- Elected government at regional level in England does not exist at all. The new Labour government is committed to a new structure of nine powerful regional development agencies in England, while postponing plans for regional assemblies which could make them democratically accountable at an appropriate level (**p. 268**).

- The new Scottish Parliament and Welsh Assembly represent significant advances in self-government for Scotland and Wales and plans for both incorporate genuine democratic features (such as proportional electoral systems). The Scottish Parliament has legislative powers over a wide area of domestic affairs, but not over social security, nuclear power, and other important issues. The Welsh Assembly's legislative powers are far more circumscribed, amounting only to ministerial powers to make orders under the legislation of the Westminster Parliament.

- The Scottish Parliament and Welsh Assembly are creatures of statute and their independence and powers are not protected by constitutional safeguards (**p. 268**). However, at least in the case of Scotland, the creation of a Scottish Parliament and its existing powers are likely to remain protected by powerful national sentiment which cannot be set aside from Westminster.

Conclusions: Tying Down Gulliver

The absence of a written constitution

> *It is not for the benefit of those who exercise the powers of government that constitutions, and the governments issuing from them, are established. . . . A constitution is the property of a nation, and not of those who exercise the government. . . . In England, it is not difficult to perceive that everything has a constitution, except the nation.*
>
> (Thomas Paine, *The Rights of Man*, 1790–92)

We have carried out a systematic audit of the political process and central institutions of government in Britain, according to the democratic criteria set out and explained in Chapter 1. These take their starting point from the two basic principles of popular control and political equality, which we have refined to produce workable criteria for assessing the state of democracy in practice in each area of a country's political life. In the first Audit volume, *The Three Pillars of Liberty*, the three authors developed from these criteria an index of international human rights standards to assess the condition of political rights and freedoms in the UK. Here we have used the criteria to audit the conduct of elections in the UK; the internal rules by which Britain's strong and centralised core executive regulates its behaviour; and the principles and practical means by which Parliament, the judiciary and other agencies subject that executive to scrutiny and make it accountable. We shall summarise our conclusions about each of these in turn. This audit is as of May 1997.

Fair and free elections

First, then, the electoral process. In so far as the major legislative and executive offices are subject to popular election by universal suffrage under conditions that are in the main procedurally fair, then the UK clearly qualifies as democratic. Citizens are free to campaign for electoral office without hindrance, and can turn a government out of office when it has lost their confidence. Such an outcome is accepted by the losers, whatever the degree of public humiliation it may entail. A major advantage of democratic arrangements – that they allow for political and generational renewal without upheaval or violence – is thus clearly met, at least in Great Britain, though not in Northern Ireland (where it may at last be possible).

However, our criteria have also helped us identify serious failings in Britain's electoral arrangements, which could be regarded as systemic rather than merely occasional or accidental. Many public offices exercising political functions are not given popular authority through elections; the office holders, therefore, are not accountable directly to the public and nor are they subject to popular recall – the ultimate means of securing accountability in any democracy. Membership of the second chamber of Parliament is dependent on inheritance, on holding other (unelected) public office, or on executive appointment, rather than election. Unelected executive quangos, often hierarchies of national, regional and local bodies, perform political as well as administrative functions at various levels of public life. Local quangos, normally unrepresentative of local communities, have taken over many such functions from local authorities. In mid-1997 there was no regional level of elected government in England, and one is only now being put in place for Scotland and Wales. Northern Ireland had had no elected assembly since 1972; and since the major UK parties do not contest parliamentary elections in the province, its citizens were denied the right to vote for a governing party at Westminster. Elected local authorities remain in place, but there is a substantial case for arguing that local government is now so dominated by central government that it amounts in practice to little more than local administration. These are substantial gaps in the structure of democratic authorisation and accountability.

The plurality-rule (or 'first-past-the-post') electoral system denies citizens the basic democratic right of votes of equal value. There are systemic inequalities between citizens in the value of their vote, according to which party they vote for, and which region and constituency they happen to live in. The way in which votes in local constituencies are translated into parliamentary seats is entirely arbitrary, depending as it does on the number and relative strength of the different political parties which contest each constituency. The overall results at national level are severely disproportional in terms of the voters' party choices, and usually exaggerate the parliamentary strength of the two leading parties at the expense of third parties. Thus plurality-rule elections, as they operate in the UK, also cause a systematic narrowing of electoral choice to those political parties and programmes which have a realistic chance of representation in Parliament, and lead to the distortion of voters' real preferences involved in 'tactical voting'. It has also become apparent that the parties are encouraged by the way elections work in practice to concentrate their campaigning attention very narrowly on the views of swing voters in a small number of marginal constituencies. These voters are not representative of the electorate as a whole. No electoral system works perfectly. But it would be difficult to find one that deviates in practice so markedly from the democratic principles of political equality and popular control.

A third systemic deficiency is the way the government is able to control aspects of the electoral agenda to its own advantage. The Prime Minister can determine the timing and campaign length of national elections at any point within the five-year term of a Parliament. Ministers can alter the structure and boundaries of local government at will, and through these exercise indirect influence over parliamentary boundaries, and if they so wish, may even delay the implementation of recommendations by the independent Boundary Commission for their own political advantage. The government can determine whether and when to hold a referendum on constitutional issues, and the wording of any referendum. These deviations from impartiality are symptomatic of the lack of separation between the powers and prerogatives of the government of the day, and the constitutional rules that are supposedly independent of party. Any such clear separation is impossible in a system where sovereignty resides in Parliament rather than in the people, and the executive operates within loose and flexible constitutional rules which are largely ungrounded in law and which the public has never been asked to approve.

Another concern in electoral politics in the UK is the way in which social and economic inequalities are reproduced politically in differential access to the suffrage, to candidature for public office and to influence over the electoral process itself. Among the disproportionately influential are those wealthy individuals and corporations who own newspapers, help finance political parties, or advise politicians who are running for office. Women and members of ethnic minorities are greatly disadvantaged in the political processes for choosing candidates for office, and are therefore poorly represented in Parliament (as in public life generally). The rules and procedures of voter registration tend to discourage, if not actually prevent, inner-city inhabitants, young people, unemployed and homeless people, and those in temporary accommodation or institutional homes, from access to the suffrage. Although such differential advantages and disadvantages are common to most European countries, one test of the quality of democratic life is the seriousness with which attempts are made to reduce their impact.

Thus, there are significant gaps in electoral reach, inequalities and limitations in electoral choice, partialities in electoral administration, and differential access to the electoral process and influence over it for different social groups: these four deficiencies seriously damage and neutralise what is at heart a recognisably democratic system of electoral accountability.

Open, accountable and responsive government

If we turn now to our second area of democratic life – what we call open, accountable and responsive government – then the balance sheet in respect of central government in the UK shows many obviously democratic features. Government is required to explain and justify its policies to Parliament and the wider public, and it does so in the face of tough questioning and criticism. It provides an enormous amount of information about its policies; and civil society and the media are rich in channels of expertise which are capable of independently assessing their effects. Government is subject to the principle of the rule of law, and the judiciary is in practice independent of the executive. The state bureaucracy is accountable to elected ministers, and the armed forces are subject to civilian control. In general, public officials maintain high standards of probity, and the appointment of the independent Committee on Standards in Public Life will serve to reinforce these. The government remains responsive to public opinion through the discipline of the electoral process, through processes of public consultation, and through the attentions of the independent media. These are all clearly democratic features of our political arrangements.

However, our criteria have helped to identify a number of serious deficiencies from a democratic point of view. These, again, are systemic rather than accidental.

Open accountable government

We itemise them in turn. First, Britain has a remarkably strong and highly centralised executive, in which the interests of the government of the day and the permanent civil service tend to fuse. The central idea of British constitutional arrangements that this executive is responsible to Parliament in any other than a formal sense is a profoundly misleading myth. Thanks to the agency of party, which until recently was not formally recognised anywhere in these arrangements, the executive dominates Parliament; and the House of Commons acts only very rarely as a unified political or corporate body. What is left in the vacuum is the political party which is for the time being in control of the House of Commons. By virtue of that control, this party's government has nearly unlimited executive and law-making power at its disposal.

As we have shown, the capacity of Parliament to scrutinise the executive is hampered by the adversarial and partisan character of the House of Commons. On the one side, government backbenchers have a much greater interest in supporting the government and its programme than in exposing it to rigorous scrutiny. On the other, the official main opposition party is largely powerless, except as a potential alternative government-in-waiting; and the chief aim of the governing party is to prolong its waiting for as long as possible. In this adversarial relationship, the civil service owes exclusive loyalty to the government of the day, to assist it in managing information and policy presentation, and owes no independent loyalty to Parliament or the public, as the Scott Report amply demonstrated. The supposed sovereignty of Parliament thus means in effect the sovereignty of the executive in Parliament, which is all the more absolute, the tighter the control the governing party exercises over its backbench MPs (as Labour has done since May 1997).

The inability of Parliament to make the executive accountable is compounded by the near total absence of effective accountability within what we have called the core executive itself. The system of policy-making within a closed and secretive world of cabinet committees hampers effective scrutiny of government policy by the cabinet itself, let alone by Parliament, and renders policy vulnerable to serious errors of judgement, whether of policy design or of public acceptability. The system is open to manipulation by a determined Prime Minister, who can set up carefully selected ad-hoc committees which will take decisions which become binding on the whole government, or simply bypass the cabinet and committees through various stratagems. The cabinet can no longer control or keep sight of the policies of the ministers who make up its membership, and they, their departments and public bodies are significant political actors in their own right. In turn, ministers themselves are unable to oversee more than a small fraction of the work of their departments or the public bodies for which they are formally answerable, yet in practice government departments and their satellites are responsible for the great bulk of executive policy-making and decision-taking, even under dynamic political regimes, such as Mrs Thatcher's. At the core of government, too, the secret security and intelligence agencies have an operational autonomy to a degree which is not compatible with democratic practice. Thus, the idea of cabinet government, supposedly the lynch-pin of balanced and collective government in this country, is nothing more than a reassuring myth.

Executive powers and the rule of law

The activities of the core executive are also largely ungoverned by the 'rule of law'. In the absence of a written constitution, and with it a developed body of constitutional and public law, substantial areas of government activity are left to wide executive discretion, governed only by the operation of conventions, informal guidelines which can be varied at will. This 'flexibility' is prized by those who defend the constitutional status quo. But it represents yet another systemic weakness in British democracy, and in our view, has severely compromised the quality of government policy-making. Among the areas of discretion that bear most directly on democratic accountability is the government's ability to determine what information should be made publicly available, and how it should be presented. Policy-making itself is a highly protected area of discretionary activity by ministers and officials; normally only raw information is made available and all policy analysis is withheld. Specialist agencies, such as the National Audit Office and Ombudsman service, which are charged with examining the executive's conduct, are prohibited from access to or scrutiny of 'policy' matters, and other bodies, such as the Committee on Standards in Public Life, are also routinely excluded. The pervasive habit of secrecy extends to the informal rules of conduct for ministers and civil servants, which may be varied or broken with impunity; and to their relationships with advisory bodies and outside interests.

In addition, the increased practice of bypassing parliamentary scrutiny by means of secondary, or delegated, legislation gives ministers a further substantial arena for discretion. Secondary legislation was first introduced as a means of allowing governments to fine-tune and update primary legislation, but has now developed into a parallel legislative process through which governments can change or abolish statute law, or initiate major policy programmes, simply by way of executive orders which are virtually uncheckable in Parliament. Such secondary legislation, often characterised as 'executive law', has been responsible for breaches of Britain's international human rights obligations. There has been mounting concern about this practice since the late 1920s, but the House of Commons still neglects to tackle what has become a major democratic loophole, and it was left to law lords and other peers to establish in 1992 the small, part-time committee of the House of Lords which seeks to check the worst excesses of such legislation.

The executive is supposed to be checked politically by Parliament and legally by the judiciary. The judiciary has responded to growing alarm about the unaccountable nature of modern government since the 1960s by developing the practice of judicial review. The courts have undoubtedly begun to rein in executive discretion. They have decided, for example, that executive claims of public immunity for official papers relevant to court proceedings cannot be absolute and that ministers' use of royal prerogative powers should at last be made justiciable. But judicial review serves to curtail executive discretion only at the margin, and is itself limited in scope. Though its basic principles correspond broadly with democratic norms, they fall short of modern democratic standards and do not, for example, insist on transparency, public consultation and the giving of reasons in executive decision-making and policy-making. The practice also raises two serious questions. Are the courts the right instrument on their own to remedy gaps in *political* accountability? Is it right that the tests of natural justice, due process and reasonableness, which the courts apply to government and public decisions, should be judge-made, and not derive from the wider agenda which a publicly approved written constitution would supply?

The weakness of Parliament

Since the late 1970s, members of the House of Commons have also become increasingly concerned to make up the gap in political accountability. In 1978, they complained that the imbalance in power between the executive and Parliament was damaging parliamentary democracy. A year later, departmental select committees were introduced in the House to enable it to subject the executive to more systematic and effective parliamentary scrutiny. These committees have increased its ability to examine the policies and practice of government, and their inquiries have become part of the working life of ministers and civil servants. But they do not have effective powers to insist that ministers, MPs or named officials attend their hearings; they cannot demand government documents as of right, and are usually given official summaries; and officials give evidence under the direction of ministers. Their operations are generally amateur in nature and they are not backed up by adequate research resources. In the final event, they split over their findings on politically sensitive issues on party lines, and as the government invariably has a majority of members on each committee, the government party's views usually prevail.

There have also been attempts to improve the way in which the principle of collective and individual ministerial responsibility to Parliament works in practice. There have been parallel efforts to make civil servants more directly responsible to Parliament. The Scott Report's dissection of actual executive practice and the culture of the 'half-truth' which characterised the dealings of ministers and officials with Parliament over the arms to Iraq affair added impetus to this trend. But little has been achieved. Lord Nolan recently described the attempt as 'Lilliputians trying to tie down Gulliver'. A symbolic House of Commons resolution has re-affirmed the duty of ministers to be open and honest in their dealings with Parliament, but this pious hope is not enforceable, as MPs generally have no means of knowing whether ministers have misled the House. The principle of ministerial responsibility remains too confused and loose to serve as a practical mechanism for achieving genuine accountability; and given that ministers must, by definition, command a majority in the House, the accountability it provides is never likely to be strong, except in exceptional circumstances. Further, the distinction between 'policy' (for which ministers are formally responsible) and 'operations' (for which they are not) is so flexible that it can be used to evade responsibility when serious failures come to public notice.

There are anyway significant weaknesses in the traditional idea of ministerial responsibility. First, the very idea focuses the accountability of the executive on a very narrow point – two dozen secretaries of state are made answerable to an assembly of some 650 men and women for all the activities of a vigorous and many-headed executive. This is wrong in principle, mistaken in design, and impossible in practice. Second, parliamentarians have become obsessed with the ultimate sanction – that of ministerial resignation – at the expense of rectifying and learning from the mistakes which have inspired any particular crisis. This obsession turns an inquiry into any crisis into the stuff of party political warfare and encourages ministers and officials to be even more secretive and obstructive than they might otherwise have been. Episodes such as the Westland crisis and the debate on the Scott Report are trials of political strength which generate far more heat than light. Even the most senior officials may be suborned into misconduct. Ministers frequently resign over failings in their private lives, but almost never over some failing in their public duties. In sum, the supposedly reassuring concept of ministerial responsibility, like that of cabinet government, is substantially unworkable in practice.

Our audit has also exposed a House of Commons which is reluctant to assert its own rights against the executive, preferring to accept the executive's views of the conventions which govern their relationship rather than provoke it to insist on something worse. In part, this is the product of political realism since in the last resort the executive will get its way. But the House of Commons' acquiescence in what is universally acknowledged to be a highly deficient system for the scrutiny of legislation; its unwillingness to tackle the evil of wide-ranging secondary legislation; the absence of any challenge to executive supremacy over its own rules: all these manifestations of impotence suggest a deeper malaise of the spirit.

There is yet another systemic weakness in our democratic arrangements. Public consultation is notoriously unbalanced and unsystematic in many areas of policy-making. Much formative consultation takes place within narrow policy communities of government officials and selective organised interests which are generally closed to outside scrutiny, and tend to pre-empt more formal public consultation exercises where these take place. Certain powerful interests enjoy preferential access to ministers and their officials, and in some cases can be said to have 'captured' the department concerned. This may result in a serious loss of public confidence, as has happened in areas of food policy, environmental protection and public health, and in major 'policy disasters' causing death, illness and economic damage. The effect is particularly damaging when the same interests are involved directly in the funding of political parties. Such practices not only undermine public confidence in government. They also infringe the democratic principles of equality of consideration due to all citizens in the formulation of policy, and the openness of government to a wide range of opinion within society.

The extensive use of quangos, which we mention above, also diminishes the ability of ordinary citizens to contribute to debate over public policy, as well as the role and authority of Parliament and the more obvious erosion of local government. In practice, the quango state removes layers and areas of policy-making and action from the parliamentary – and public – gaze. The absence of a constitutional framework and the informal and secretive nature of its policy processes blocks scrutiny and leaves government free to co-opt and mobilise all manner of bodies, including private companies, consultants and advisers within the domain of quasi-government to carry out major tasks, such as industrial re-structuring, training and employment policies. Parliament has no oversight over the government's creatures, their inter-ests and processes, as they operate under cover of ministerial discretion. Indeed, government itself often has no direct control over them.

In this audit we have not assessed the effect of Britain's membership of the European Union on the workings of central government; but all the evidence we have suggests that the deficiencies in the democratic accountability of government policy reviewed here have been intensified by our membership. This only consti-tutes a further argument for treating them seriously. It is often argued in mitigation that each of these deficiencies from a democratic point of view – the dominant exec-utive, protected by secrecy and operating in a context of informal guidelines and discretionary powers – contributes to Britain's tradition of strong and effective govern-ment. In other words we are invited to choose between the virtues of effectiveness and democratic accountability. As we have argued, this is a false choice. Policy outcomes are both more coherent and more publicly acceptable if they are publicly tested against alternatives and a wide range of points of view. Moreover, once enough citizens expect openness and accountability from their governments, then secrecy proves a hindrance rather than a help to effective policy-making, since a culture of leaks, erratic though also predictable, becomes the inevitable counterpart to the culture of secrecy.

The overall conclusion, then, of our audit of the electoral and governmental process in the UK is that it is a process operating within democratic norms and procedures, but that systemic features are at work which substantially limit their reach and impact in practice.

The impact of Labour's reforms

This audit and its overall judgement applies to the situation at the end of the long period of Conservative rule, as of April 1997. Since then, the Labour Party under Tony Blair has won a landslide electoral victory, in terms of parliamentary seats at least, with a mandate for substantial constitutional reform. As we write, legislation is proposed or under way on freedom of information, on devolved government for Scotland and Wales, on a referendum for electoral reform for elections to Parliament, on elections by proportional representation to the Scottish Parliament, Welsh Assembly, European Parliament and London assembly, on reform of the House of Lords, and on the partial incorporation of the European Convention on Human Rights into domestic law, to mention only the most important. There are also signs of a cautious approach to liberating local government from the recent regime of strict central controls. Overall, this is a significant set of measures, which will address a number of the democratic deficiencies identified in this audit. These measures demonstrate the capacity of the political process for self-renewal, even if that renewal is being advanced under the slogan of modernisation rather than of democracy as such. They may very well also encourage a more dynamic sense of democratic self-confidence in much of the country.

Will these reforms make the conclusions of our audit redundant? By no means, for two reasons. First, even on an optimistic assumption about their effects, they will only address some of the deficiencies identified here. In particular, though they reveal a willingness to share power, especially in the devolution proposals, and to open up the broad spectrum of government to the public gaze, they do not directly do much to alter the executive dominance over Parliament or the way the core executive itself functions. The proposals for statutory freedom of information will have a direct impact on the conduct of the executive, but that impact is for the moment at least questionable in the critical areas of executive policy-making, the conduct of the security services and police, immigration control and others; and there are signs that the powers of the Information Commission will be diminished in the government's actual legislative proposals. Thus, there is a danger that the unhealthy concentration of power within the central executive will continue and perhaps intensify under the New Labour government. There are signs that ministers wish to reinforce government's dominance over the parliamentary party, and thus indirectly over the House of Commons; and that the presentation of government policies is being made more manipulative than previously. Of course these are early days. But the traditions of strong central government are very powerful and have a place within Labour's own culture, be it Old or New. Tony Blair's electoral appeals were founded in part on the promise of 'strong' government. Thus, it remains possible that the more the process of democratisation encroaches from the periphery of British government (both geographically and institutionally), the more the old imperial core will prove its ability to resist its force and impose its time-old will on the future.

The main concern, as we take stock, is that executive dominance, not only over Parliament but over all the institutions of the state, including local government, and over all but the most powerful corporations and organised interests in civil society, will remain unchecked at the heart of Britain's democratic deficits. Since 1979, the weight of the central executive and its wide and often coercive powers has increasingly born down directly on the lives of ordinary citizens and local affairs throughout the land. There are scarcely any institutions which can act as checks on the executive and its creatures or as constitutional or political counterweights. The writ of single-party government at the centre runs almost everywhere. Executive dominance, masked as it is by the doctrine of Parliamentary sovereignty, was also identified in the conclusions of the first Democratic Audit volume as the fundamental cause of the state's inability properly to protect the political and civil rights of British citizens. The three authors wrote, 'There is an urgent need for restraint of government-in-Parliament and its much-vaunted flexibility which too often degenerates into a licence for misrule' (DA Volume No. 1: 315). But deference to the idea of parliamentary sovereignty remains strong within the Labour cabinet. The government is now passing a Human Rights Bill through Parliament to incorporate the European Convention on Human Rights into British law, but not fully. The bill is specifically designed to protect the principle of Parliamentary sovereignty, and remove existing UK law from its remit. To accomplish this, the bill also omits the Convention's guarantee of an effective remedy to anyone whose rights and freedoms have been violated.

The practical effects of this doctoring are likely to be small in relation to the substantial rights and freedoms which the Convention protects. It may very well be that the Labour cabinet is simply asserting a traditional reluctance to give primacy to the judiciary. But it is equally likely that Labour ministers are determined to maintain executive and legislative supremacy in the name of parliamentary sovereignty, and ultimately even over the political freedoms of British citizens. By the same token, the government's constitutional changes do not include introducing a written constitution or a new constitutional framework of rules for the conduct of government in this country. Further, the first proposals for its modernisation programme in Parliament will not significantly strengthen the legislature against the overweening power at the government's disposal. Nor is there any sign that the government will take lessons in democratic practice from the US, where measures of open government are linked to public access laws which open policy consultations with all outside interests and policy-making by federal departments and quangos to the public gaze. We do not doubt Blair's commitment to more open and honest government. But legal rules of conduct are a far more reliable guarantee of democratic rule than a simple plea to 'trust in me', or in a media-friendly annual report to the electors on election pledges fulfilled. There is, in fact, much that Labour can properly take pride in, apart from its major reforms, which does not make the headlines. For example, the government has passed a Public Interest Disclosure Act, which will authorise 'whistle-blowing' in the public services; it is experimenting with draft bills which are examined by a select committee in advance of going through the formal legislative processes. The critical Freedom of Information bill will be one of these.

A choice between two futures

But, broadly speaking, it seems as though there are two possible lines of evolution for this government, based on what we already know of Labour's reform programme and the attitudes of the Prime Minister, ministers and advisers to the contents of that programme. As we have warned in the Foreword, there is a danger that the Blair government will adopt the 'strong', flexible and informal executive practice which is borne in the bone of British governance and major party politics – and which is the biggest enemy of democratic practice in the UK. The emphasis on discipline within the Parliamentary party, and the moves to take charge of the party nationally, to stifle dissent and to tighten control over the selection of candidates for election all belong within this tradition. The apparent indifference of most ministers to their government's democratic reform programme, the hostility of some influential ministers towards the FOI proposals, and the absence of any joined-up democratic strategy further suggest that the government may well ultimately stick to the status quo. Instead of having a constitution or framework of rules which sets out the respective powers of the executive and other organs of state, which defines the limits of those powers and establishes rules of conduct, and which substitutes popular sovereignty for executive supremacy, the citizens of this country would continue to be governed under a 'magically flexible constitution' which allows their political masters and mistresses to make up the rules as they go along.

Yet the proposals for a Scottish Parliament and Welsh Assembly, and especially now for the imaginative constitutional settlement in Northern Ireland, envisage a quite different form of democratic politics from the established model of Westminster and Whitehall. It is one based on multiple identities rather than a single focus of political loyalty. It gives priority to consensus-building and legislative and executive decision-making by coalition rather than single-party domination and winner-takes-all politics. The legislative process itself is strictly subject to a court-adjudicated Bill of Rights rather than superior to it. All these features are, for obvious reasons, more explicitly encoded in the Northern Ireland legislation, with its guarantee of multiple citizenship, the power-sharing executive, cross-community voting and the emphasis on wide-ranging human rights. Yet these features represent a common thread running through all the proposals for devolution, which promises a very different form of democratic politics from the adversarial traditions of the House of Commons and its hard-edged party politics.

Not only that: the proposals also offer the peoples of Northern Ireland, Scotland and Wales the framework for pursuing a political future that is distinctively theirs. In Northern Ireland, this involves a process of reconstruction, based on broad agreement among the people, and finding a new way in which communities of very different and opposed traditions can live together and govern themselves across old divides. In Scotland, it involves establishing a form of economic and social settlement, appropriate to political traditions that are different from England's. In Wales, the Assembly offers the opportunity of a national focus and public arena which the country has long lacked. It is the combination of these distinctive projects, with a new form of self-governing democratic politics, which opens up progressive possibilities for the future, especially for new generations of citizens.

What impact will these developments have on Westminster? Much will depend, first, on the government's resolve to fulfil its more representative ambitions to become a 'people's government'. Further, there are welcome signs of change in ministers' new approaches to consultation and the more consensual government style in Parliament, away from the snarling confrontations at Prime Minister's Questions. The agreement with the Liberal Democrats on the reform agenda, which has been honoured thus far despite the initial scepticism in Westminster and Whitehall, reveals a new openness to cooperative party politics. The way the Prime Minister jumps on the choice the Jenkins Commission offers the public at a referendum between a 'broadly proportional' electoral system and the existing 'first-past-the-post' system for elections to Westminster will be crucial. If he decides to take the lead on advocating change, he could bring about a historic culture change in Westminster, substituting coalition for adversarial party politics – even if he does so purely for the long-term strategic motive of reuniting the centre-left. If he does not, the imperatives of winner-takes-all politics are likely to assert themselves, and the chances of a genuinely more pluralist and open form of government will be significantly lessened.

But there are other separate, though related, issues here. It is possible that a more pluralist and open style of politics and governing may be transmitted from the peripheries of the United Kingdom to its centre. The new self-governing parts of the UK may very well insist on it, and even on re-balancing their subordinate position vis-à-vis Westminster. And the settlement in Northern Ireland has laid the foundation not only for Northern Ireland's relationship with the Irish state, but for the totality of relations in these islands. Moreover, Scotland's political classes are determined to make their new Parliament a model for popular access and involvement and are likely to introduce proportional elections into local government as well. If they succeed in establishing a democratic and effective form of governing throughout Scotland, it is hard to see how Westminster and England could resist pressures to follow suit. England is of course by far the largest component part of the United Kingdom, and how what might be called the 'problem of Englishness' is resolved will be very significant for the future of British politics. What will it mean to be English in a context in which the other peoples of the UK are likely to be pre-occupied with their own specific political destinies? Is there a distinctive English identity, and how might its redefinition relate to a specific political project for England and the reformulation of its relationship with the rest of the UK?

It may be argued that English identity is primarily bound up with the quality of its civil society rather than with its politics as such. Yet the meaning of what it is to be English is evidently now in part at least a matter of political choice, about the definition of the relationships within the UK, the nature of our political represen-tation, and the way we are governed. Is the distinctiveness of the people who live in the United Kingdom to be found in their historical diversity, both in the commu-nities within England and their relationship to the other peoples of these islands; and is this diversity to be reflected in a more pluralistic form of politics, with a genuinely representative Parliament, a more open and less monopolistic executive, and an acknowledged place for multiple political identities, local, regional, national and European? Or will a new-found self-confidence on the part of the other nations of the UK, on the one side, and a more powerful European Union on the other, provoke a response in England that is inward- and backward-looking, exclusive in its definition of identity, and defensively self-enclosed and manipulative at the heart of its government?

Which of these possible futures, or what combination of them, will emerge only time will tell. The precise character and impact of the New Labour government have yet to reveal themselves fully, and to work their way through; and the new politics of London, Northern Ireland, Scotland and Wales are waiting to be born. We could see a dynamic process of wider democratic renewal, or the resilient tradi-tions of strong government could assert themselves over the reform agenda. This is why a future audit, using the findings we set out here as a benchmark, will be necessary in due course. However, it will not be only a matter of specific criteria and indices, but of a larger picture in which issues of political identities and relation-ships combine with the everyday patterns of politics and governance to give a distinctive character to the governing arrangements in this country and to the life of its citizens.

Appendix

The Democratic Audit, at the University of Essex, was founded in 1992 to inquire into the quality of democracy and political freedoms in the United Kingdom. Its main task is to research and publish major 'landmark' studies, against which both democracy and political freedom in the United Kingdom can be measured over time; and thus to enable the public to judge whether the country is becoming more or less democratic and free.

Political Power and Democratic Control in Britain is the second of the Democratic Audit's landmark volumes. In November 1996, the Audit published its first major report, *The Three Pillars of Liberty* (by Francesca Klug, Keir Starmer and Stuart Weir; Routledge), on the protection of political and civil rights in the United Kingdom. The current report deals with accountability and openness in Britain's constitutional arrangements. Negotiations are under way to produce two further volumes: one on popular participation in politics, and the other on social, economic and cultural rights in the UK.

The Democratic Audit will also publish a major 'follow-up' study of *The Three Pillars* and *Political Power and Democratic Control* at the end of the Labour government's first term in office. The government's huge programme of democratic reform has profound implications for the quality of Britain's governing arrangements and citizens' rights, but is also riven by contradictions and cross-pressures which will compromise the apparent drive to modernise and open up democracy in the United Kingdom. It is also the intention to publish an annual *Democratic Charter* monitoring the progress of democracy and political freedom.

The Democratic Audit publishes regular reports on issues of democratic interest. The Audit's most influential publications have been on the quango state (*EGO-TRIP*, *Behind Closed Doors* and *The Untouchables*) and on electoral change (*Making Votes Count*, *Devolution Votes*, *Making Votes Count 2* and *Stability and Choice*). *Behind Closed Doors* was published jointly with Channel 4 Television in conjunction with a *Dispatches* documentary based on Audit research. The Audit has just completed a new study on the Labour government's task forces and is preparing an international almanac on elections and voting for the forthcoming referendum on electoral systems in the United Kingdom.

The Democratic Audit also undertakes international consultancy and educational work. The Audit runs regular international courses on consolidating democracy at the University of Essex, and has facilitated major programmes of parliamentary reform in Namibia and Zimbabwe, organised a major Indo-British seminar on democracy and human rights in India, and participated in a wide-ranging conference on regional democracy in central and east Europe. Democratic Audit packs – teaching aids for education and democracy and freedom – are being developed for use both in international seminars for practitioners and secondary schools in the UK.

The proceedings of a conference on issues arising from *The Three Pillars* (with contributions from Baroness Kennedy QC, Professor Richard Falk, Alun Michael MP, the Home Office minister, and Professor Philip Alston, chairperson of the UN Committee on Economic, Social and Cultural Rights) are published in a special human rights issue of *Political Quarterly* (vol. 68, No. 2, April–June 1997).

The Audit is sponsored by the Joseph Rowntree Charitable Trust and is based at the Human Rights Centre, University of Esssex. But scholars and specialists from other universities and institutions are co-operating as 'auditors' and advisers on the project. The director of the Audit is Stuart Weir, a Senior Research Fellow at Essex. Professor Kevin Boyle, director of the Human Rights Centre at Essex, is overall academic editor of Audit publications. Scholars in the departments of law and government at Essex naturally play a role in the Audit's work, but several external scholars have also made important contributions, most notably Professor David Beetham, Department of Politics, Leeds University; Professor Patrick Dunleavy, of the London School of Economics; and Dr Helen Margetts of Birkbeck College, London.

Please send any comments you may have on this or any other Democratic Audit publication to:

Professor Kevin Boyle
Human Rights Centre
University of Essex
Wivenhoe Park
Colchester
Essex CO4 3SQ

The Democratic Audit's website can be accessed at the following address: http://www.fhit.org/democratic_audit/
The site contains details and summaries of Audit publications as well as case studies concentrating on the themes of political freedom and democracy.

Table of Cases

Bibliography and Sources

The bibliography is divided into a section for published books and articles, and a section for government and other official publications. Except where explicitly stated, the place of publication of books cited is London. In cases where we have followed up references to books, government publications or law cases in secondary sources, we have checked the original source and cited that rather than the secondary source, which we also cite generally. For government papers, we have tried to operate as follows: first, we cite the place of origin of departmental and agency reports (e.g. the Cabinet Office) rather than the title; second, select committee and parliamentary reports are identified first in simplified form by the committee or agency (e.g. Procedure Committee for the Select Committee on Procedure); third, other official reports either take the name of the committee or body making the report, or the name of the chairperson when that committee or body is most commonly identified by that name (e.g. we cite the reports of the Committee on Standards in Public Life under the name of its first chairman, Lord Nolan).

Parliamentary and committee stage debates, statements and Parliamentary Questions and Answers are all referenced in the text and are not repeated in the Bibliography. HC Deb and HL Deb are references to the Hansard for the date shown, and the Hansard column number then follows; 'WA' indicates entries in the relevant Written Answer section of Hansard. Newspaper articles and reports, and television news, current affairs and other programmes are also directly referenced in the text. Quotations from politicians which are not referenced to media reports have been obtained from or verified with the press office of the relevant party or government department, or with the politician himself or herself.

Much information has been obtained on confidential and Chatham House terms. We have not specifically referenced this information, though where relevant we have broadly identified sources.

Books and articles

Adam Smith Institute (1989) *Wiser Counsels* (Adam Smith Institute)

Adonis, A. (1990) *Parliament Today* (Manchester University Press, Manchester)

Alexander, A. (1982) *The Politics of Local Government in the UK* (Longman)

Anderson, P. (1987) 'The Figures of Descent', *New Left Review* 161

Armstrong, Lord (1995) 'Argument: the Case for Confidentiality in Government', in Miller, W.L. (ed.) *Alternatives to Freedom: Arguments and Opinions* (Longman)

Armstrong, Sir W. (May 1970) 'The Civil Service and its Tasks', *O and M Bulletin* 25(2) (HMSO)

Ashford, D. (1981) *Policy and Politics in Britain* (Blackwell, Oxford)

Association of County Councils (1991) *The Constitutional Role of Local Government* (ACC)

Association of Metropolitan Authorities (1992) *Policy and Financial Prospects, 1993–94* (unpublished)

Austin, R. (1989) 'Freedom of Information: the Constitutional Impact', in Jowell, J. and Oliver, D. (eds) *The Changing Constitution* (Clarendon Press, Oxford)

Bagehot, W. (1993 [1867]) *The English Constitution* (with introduction by Richard Crossman) (Fontana)

Baine, S., Benington, J. and Russell, J. (1992) *Changing Europe: Challenges Facing the Voluntary and Community Sectors in the 1990s* (National Council of Voluntary Organisations)

Baldwin, N. (1990) 'The House of Lords', in Rush, M. (ed.) *Parliament and Pressure Politics* (Clarendon Press, Oxford)

Baldwin, N. (1993) 'The Membership of the House', in Shell, D. and Beamish, D. (eds) *The House of Lords at Work* (Clarendon Press, Oxford)

Baldwin, Sir P. (1998) 'A National Service in Quangoland', in Flinders, M. and Smith, M. J. (eds) *Quangos, Accountability and Reform: the Politics of Quasi-Government* (Macmillan)

Banks, J.C. (1971) *Federal Britain?* (Harrap)

Barberis, P. (1996) *The Elite of the Elites: Permanent Secretaries in the British Higher Civil Service* (Dartmouth, Aldershot)

Barker, A. (ed.) (1982) *Quangos in Britain* (Macmillan)

Barker, A. (1982) 'Government Bodies and the Networks of Mutual Accountability', in Barker, A. (ed.) *Quangos in Britain* (Macmillan)

Barker, A. and Wilson, G.K. (1977) 'Whitehall's Disobedient Servant', *British Journal of Political Science* 27

Barnett, A. (1997) *This Time* (Vintage Original)

Barnett, S. and Curry, A. (1994) *The Battle for the BBC* (Aurum Press)

Barron, J., Crawley, G. and Wood, T. (1991) *Councillors in Crisis* (Macmillan)

Bassett, R.G. (1958) *1931: Political Crisis* (Macmillan)

Bates, St J.N. (1989) 'Select Committees in the House of Lords', in Drewry, G. (ed.) *The New Select Committees: A Study of the 1979 Reforms* (Clarendon Press, Oxford)

Batley, R. (1991) 'Comparisons and Lessons', in Batley, R. and Stoker, G. (eds) *Local Government in Europe* (Macmillan)

Batley, R. and Stoker, G. (eds) (1991) *Local Government in Europe* (Macmillan)

Beattie, A. (ed.) (1970) *English Party Politics* (Weidenfeld and Nicolson)

Beattie, A. (1995) 'Ministerial Responsibility and the Theory of the British State', in Rhodes, R.A.W. and Dunleavy, P. (eds) *The Prime Minister, Cabinet and Core Executive* (Macmillan)

Beer, S.H. (1969) *Modern British Politics* (Faber and Faber)

Beetham, D. (1993) *Auditing Democracy in Britain* Democratic Audit Paper No. 1 (Human Rights Centre, University of Essex and Charter 88 Trust)

Beetham, D. (ed.) (1994) *Defining and Measuring Democracy* (Sage, London)

Benn, T. (1990) *Conflicts of Interest: Diaries 1977–1980* (edited by Winstone, R.) (Hutchinson)

Benn, T. (1987) *Out of the Wilderness: Diaries 1963–67* (Hutchinson)

Benn, T. (1989) *Against the Tide: Diaries 1963–67* (Hutchinson)

Bennett, A.F. (1990) 'Uses and Abuses of Delegated Legislation', *Statute Law Review* 11: 1

Bennett, S. and Resnick, D. (1988) 'Political Participation Reconsidered: Old Ideas and New Data', paper presented to the annual conference of the Midwest Political Science Association, Chicago, April

Bentham, J. (1843) *Works* Bowring, J. (ed.) (William Tait, Edinburgh)

Berrill, K. (1985) 'Strength at the Centre – The Case for a Prime Minister's Department', in King, A. (ed.) *The British Prime Minister* (Macmillan)

Bevan, A. (1978) *In Place of Fear* (Quartet Books)

Bibby, J.F. (1992) *Governing by Consent: An Introduction to American Politics* (CQ Press, Washington, D.C.)

Birch, A.H. (1964) *Representative and Responsible Government: An Essay on the British Constitution* (Allen & Unwin)

Birch, A.H. (1972) *Representation* (Macmillan)

Birch, A. (1984) 'Overload, Ungovernability and Delegitimation: the Theories and the British Case', *British Journal of Political Science* 14, part 2

Blackburn, R. (1995) *The Electoral System in Britain* (Macmillan)

Blackstone, T. and Plowden, W. (1988) *Inside the Think Tank; Advising the Cabinet* (Heinemann, London)

Blair, P. (1991) 'Trends in Local Autonomy and Democracy: Reflections from a European Perspective', in Batley, R. and Stoker, G. (eds) *Local Government in Europe* (Macmillan)

Bloch, A. and John, P. (1991) *Attitudes to Local Government: a Survey of Electors* (Joseph Rowntree Foundation, York)

Body, R. (1984) *Farming in the Clouds* (Maurice Temple Smith)

Bogdanor, V. (1981) *The People and the Party System: The Referendum in British Politics* (Cambridge University Press, Cambridge)

Bogdanor, V. (1986a) *Electoral Systems in Local Government* (Institute of Local Government Studies, Birmingham)

Bogdanor, V. (ed.) (1986b) *Representatives of the People?* (Gower, Aldershot)

Bogdanor, V. (1987) 'Electoral Reform and British Politics', *Electoral Studies* 6 (2)

Bogdanor, V. (1993) 'Internationalism Begins at Home', *Local Government Chronicle*, 19 March

Bogdanor, V. (1997) *Power and the People* (Gollancz)

Bogdanor, V. and Butler, D. (eds) (1983) *Democracy and Elections: Electoral Systems and their Political Consequences* (Cambridge University Press, Cambridge)

Bollen, K.A. (1991) 'Political Democracy: Conceptual and Measurement Traps', in Inkeles, A. (ed.) *On Measuring Democracy* (Transaction Publishers, Newhaven and London)

Bradley, A.W. (1995) 'The Parliamentary Ombudsman Again – a Positive Report', *Public Law*, Autumn

Bradley, A.W. and Ewing, K.D. (1993) *Constitutional and Administrative Law (Wade and Bradley)* (11th edn) (Longman)

Brand, J. (1992) *British Parliamentary Parties* (Clarendon Press, Oxford)

Brazier, R. (1988) *Constitutional Practice* (Oxford University Press, Oxford)

Brazier, R. (1997) *Ministers of the Crown* (Clarendon Press, Oxford)

Bridges, L., Meszaros, G. and Sunkin, M. (1995) *Judicial Review in Perspective* (2nd edn) (Cavendish)

Budge, I. (1987) 'The Internal Analysis of Election Programmes', in Budge, I., Robertson, D. and Hearl, D. (eds) *Ideology, Strategy and Party Change: Spatial Analyses of Post-War Election Programmes in 19 Democracies* (Cambridge University Press, Cambridge)

Budge, I. (1998) *Stability and Choice*, DA Paper No. 15 (Human Rights Centre, University of Essex, in association with the Department of Government, University of Essex and Scarman Trust Enterprises)

Budge, I. and Hofferbert, R.I. (1990) 'Mandates and Policy Outputs: US Party Platforms and Federal Expenditures', *American Political Science Review* 84: 111–131

Budge, I. and Keman, H. (1993) *Parties and Democracy: Coalition Formation and Government Functioning in 20 States* (Oxford University Press, Oxford)

Budge, I., Robertson, D. and Hearl, D. (eds) (1987) *Ideology, Strategy and Party Change: Spatial Analyses of Post-War Election Programmes in 19 Democracies* (Cambridge University Press, Cambridge)

Bulpitt, J. (1983) *Territory and Power in the UK* (Manchester University Press, Manchester)

Burch, M. and Moran, M. (1985) *A Reader in British Politics* (Manchester University Press, Manchester)

Burke, E. (1790) *Reflections on the Revolution in France* (Doubleday Anchor edition, 1973)

Butler, D. (1952) *The British General Election of 1951* (Macmillan)

Butler, D. and Kavanagh, D. (1979) *The British General Election of 1979* (Macmillan)

Butler, D. and Kavanagh, D. (1983) *The British General Election of 1983* (Macmillan)

Butler, D. and Kavanagh, D. (1987) *The British General Election of 1987* (Macmillan)

Butler, D. and Kavanagh, D. (1992) *The British General Election of 1992* (Macmillan)

Butler, D. and Kavanagh, D. (1997) *The British General Election of 1997* (Macmillan)

Butler, D., Adonis, A. and Travers, T. (1994) *Failure in British Government: The Politics of the Poll Tax* (Oxford University Press, Oxford)

Butler, D., Penniman, H., and Ranney, A. (eds) (1981) *Democracy at the Polls: A Comparative Study of Competitive National Elections* (American Enterprise Institute, Washington, D.C.)

Butler, D. and Ranney, A. (eds) (1978) *Referendums: A Comparative Study of Practice and Theory* (American Enterprise Institute, Washington, D.C.)

Bynoe, I. (1996) *Beyond the Citizen's Charter* (Institute for Public Policy Research)

Byrne, I. (1997) *Quangos on the Internet: a Democratic Critique of http://www.open.gov.uk/pau/paupoint.htm*, DA Paper No. 13 (University of Essex/Scarman Trust Enterprises Ltd)

Byrne, I. (1998) *What Price Party Politics? Proposals for the Regulation of Party Funding* (Charter 88, Reinventing Series Paper No. 4)

Byrne, T. (1992) *Local Government in Britain* (5th edn) (Penguin, Harmondsworth)

Campbell, C. (1993) Paper to the American Political Science Association Conference, Hilton Hotel, Washington, D.C. 2 September

Campbell, J. (1987) *Nye Bevan and the Mirage of British Socialism* (Weidenfeld & Nicolson)

Cannon, G. (1988) *The Politics of Food* (Century)

Cannon, J. (1972) *Parliamentary Reform 1640–1832* (Cambridge University Press, Cambridge)

Castle, B. (1980) *The Castle Diaries, 1974–76* (Weidenfeld & Nicolson)

Castle, B. (1984) *The Castle Diaries, 1964–70* (Weidenfeld & Nicolson)

Castles, F. (ed.) (1989) *The Comparative History of Public Policy* (Polity Press, Cambridge)

Caterall, P. (ed.) (1993) *Contemporary Britain: An Annual Overview* (Blackwell, Oxford)

Catt, H. (1990) *The Intelligent Person's Guide to Electoral Reform* (Common Voice and New Statesman and Society)

Cawson, A. (1986) *Corporatism and Political Theory* (Blackwell, Oxford)

Channel 4 Television (March 1994) *Poll on Democracy* (ICM)

Childs, D. (1992) *Britain Since 1945. A Political History* (3rd edn) (Routledge)

Clark, A. (1993) *Diaries* (Weidenfeld & Nicolson)

Clarke, H.D., Jenson, J., Leduc, L. and
Pammett, J.H. (1984) *Absent Mandate:
The Politics of Discontent in Canada* (Gage,
Toronto)

Clarke, M. and Stewart, J. (1988) *The Enabling
Council* (Local Government Training Board,
Luton)

Colley, L. (1982) *In Defiance of Oligarchy: the Tory
Party 1714–60* (Cambridge University Press,
Cambridge)

Commission for Local Democracy (CLD) (1995)
Taking Charge: The Rebirth of Local Democracy
(Municipal Journal Books)

Constitution Unit (1996a) *Regional Government in
England* (Constitution Unit)

Constitution Unit (1996b) *Scotland's Parliament:
Fundamentals for a New Scotland Act* (Constitution
Unit)

Constitution Unit (1996c) *An Assembly for
Wales/Senedd I Cymru* (Constitution Unit)

Constitution Unit (1996d) *Report of the Commission
on the Conduct of Referendums*, joint report by a
commission formed by the Constitution Unit
and the Electoral Reform Society
(Constitution Unit)

Consumers' Association (1992) 'The Role of
Consultation in the Legislative Process', in
Hansard Society *Making the Law: The Report of
the Hansard Society Commission on the Legislative
Process* (Hansard Society)

Cooper, P.J. (1988) *Hard Judicial Choices* (Oxford
University Press, New York)

Coulson, A. (1990) *Devolving Power – the Case for
Regional Government*, Fabian Tract 537 (Fabian
Society)

Cowling, M. (1978a) 'The Present Position',
in Cowling, M. (ed.) *Conservative Essays*
(Macmillan)

Cowling, M. (ed.) (1978b) *Conservative Essays*
(Macmillan)

Coxall, B. and Robins, L. (1991) *Contemporary
British Politics* (Macmillan)

Cranston, F. (1985) *Legal Foundations of the Welfare
State* (Weidenfeld & Nicolson)

Cremin, M. (1993) 'The Setting up of the
Departmental Select Committees after the
1992 Election', *Parliamentary Affairs* 46 (3)
(Hansard Society)

Crewe, I. (1986) 'MPs and their Constituents in
Britain' in Bogdanor, V. (ed.) *Representatives of
the People?* (Gower, Aldershot)

Crick, B. (1980) *Orwell: A Life* (Penguin,
Harmondsworth)

Crick, B. (1989) 'Beyond Parliamentary Reform',
Political Quarterly 60 (4)

Criddle, B. (1992) 'MPs and Candidates', in
Butler, D. and Kavanagh, D. *The British
General Election of 1992* (Macmillan)

Crossman, R. (1964) Introduction to Bagehot, W.
(1867) *The English Constitution* (Fontana)

Crossman, R. (1975) *The Diaries of a Cabinet
Minister; Vol. 1, Minister of Housing 1964–66*
(Hamilton)

Crouch, C. and Marquand, D. (1989) 'How
Worried Should We Be?', *Political Quarterly* 60

Crouch, C. and Marquand, D. (eds) (1989) *The
New Centralism* (Blackwell, Oxford)

Crowe, E. (1986) 'The Web of Authority: Party
Loyalty and Social Control in the British House
of Commons' *Legislative Studies Quarterly* 11: 2

Curtice, J. (1990) 'What Might Labour Gain from
Electoral Reform?', *Samizdat*, Issue 12

Curtice, J. (1997) *New Labour, New Tactical Voting*,
Paper for the EPOP General Election
Conference, CREST (Centre for Research
into Elections and Social Trends) (SCPR,
London/Nuffield College, Oxford)

Curtice, J. and Steed, M. (1997) 'The Results
Analysed', in Butler, D. and Kavanagh, D.
The British General Election of 1997 (Macmillan)

DA Papers, *See under* Democratic Audit

DA Volume No. 1. *See under* Democratic Audit

Dahl, R.A. (1971) *Polyarchy: Participation and
Opposition* (Yale University Press, New Haven
and London)

Dahl, R.A. (1985) *Controlling Nuclear Weapons:
Democracy versus Guardianship* (Syracuse
University Press, Syracuse)

Davis, D. (1997) *A Guide to Parliament*
(BBC/Penguin)

Davis, H. (ed.) (1996) *Quangos and Local Government:
a Changing World* (Frank Cass)

Davis, H. and Skelcher, C. (eds) (1995) *Briefing
Papers for the Nolan Committee* (School of Public
Policy, University of Birmingham)

Day, P. and Klein, R. (1990) *Inspecting the
Inspectorates* (Centre for the Analysis of Social
Policy, University of Bath)

Day, P. and Klein, R. (1992) 'Constitutional and
Distributional Conflicts in British Medical
Practice, 1911–1991', *Political Studies* 40 (3)

Deacon, D., Golding, P. and Billig, M. (1997)
'Between Fear and Loathing: National Press
Coverage of the 1997 General Election',
paper delivered at the conference of the
Specialist Group on Elections, Public Opinion
and Parties (EPOP), Political Studies
Association, on 'Assessing the 1997 Election',
at the University of Essex, September 1997

Dealler, S. (1996) *Lethal Legacy: BSE – the Search for
the Truth* (Bloomsbury)

Dearlove, J. and Saunders, P. (1991) *Introduction to
British Politics* (2nd edn) (Polity, Cambridge)

Democratic Audit Papers published by the
Human Rights Centre, University of
Essex/Scarman Trust Enterprises:
DA Paper No. 1 (1993) *Auditing Democracy in
Britain*, Beetham, D.
DA Paper No. 2 (1994) *EGO-TRIP*, Weir, S.
and Hall, W. (eds)

DA Paper No. 3 (1994) *British Democracy in the Balance*, Weir, S.

DA Paper No. 4 (1995) *Behind Closed Doors*, Weir S.

DA Paper No. 5 (1995) *In Place of Fear*, Livingstone, S. and Morison, J.

DA Paper No. 7 (1996) *The Other National Lottery*, Dunleavy, P., Margetts, H. and Weir, S.

DA Paper No. 8 (1996) *The Untouchables: Power and Accountability in the Quango State*, Hall, W. and Weir, S.

DA Paper No. 9 (1996) *Power to the Back Benches? Restoring the Balance between Government and Parliament (a Report on a Poll of Backbench MPs)*, Weir, S. and Wright, T.

DA Paper No. 10 (1997) *Liberties in the Balance (a Report on a Poll of Backbench MPs)*, Weir, S. and Byrne, I.

DA Paper No. 11 (1997) *Making Votes Count*, Dunleavy, P., Margetts, H., O'Duffy, B. and Weir, S.

DA Paper No. 12 (1997) *Devolution Votes*, Dunleavy, P., Margetts, H. and Weir, S.

DA Paper No. 13 (1997) *Quangos on the Internet: a Democratic Critique of http://www.open.gov. uk/pau/paupoint.htm*, Byrne, I.

DA Paper No. 14 (1998) *Making Votes Count 2*, Dunleavy, P., Margetts, H. and Weir, S.

DA Paper No. 15 (1998) *Stability and Choice*, Budge, I.

DA Volume No. 1 (1996) *The Three Pillars of Liberty: Political Rights and Freedoms in the UK*, Klug, F., Starmer, K. and Weir, S. (Routledge)

Denver, D. and Hands, G. (eds) (1991) *Issues and Controversies in British Electoral Behaviour* (Harvester Wheatsheaf, Brighton)

Dicey, A.V. (1886) *England's Case against Home Rule* (John Murray)

Dicey, A.V. (1885) *Introduction to the Study of the Constitution* (8th edn 1915) (Macmillan)

Dickinson, H.T. (1977) *Liberty and Property: Political Ideology in Eighteenth Century Britain* (Weidenfeld & Nicholson)

Doig, A. (1991) 'The Ethics of Lobbying' in Jordan, A.G. (ed.) *The Commercial Lobbyists* (Aberdeen University Press, Aberdeen)

Donoughue, B. (1987) *Prime Minister: The Conduct of Policy under Harold Wilson and James Callaghan* (Cape)

Dorril, S. (1993) *The Silent Conspiracy: Inside the Intelligence Services in the 1990s* (Heinemann)

Dowding, K. (1995a) *The Civil Service* (Routledge)

Dowding, K. (1995b) 'Model or Metaphor? A Critical Review of the Policy Network Approach', *Political Studies* 43 (1)

Downs, A. (1957) *An Economic Theory of Democracy* (Harper & Row, New York)

Dozier, R.R. (1983) *For King, Constitution and Country; the English Loyalists and the French Revolution* (University Press of Kentucky, Lexington)

Drewry, G. (ed.) (1989a) *The New Select Committees: A Study of the 1979 Reforms* (Clarendon Press, Oxford)

Drewry, G. (1989b) 'Select Committees and Back-bench Power', in Jowell, J. and Oliver, D. (eds) *The Changing Constitution* (Clarendon, Oxford)

Drewry, G. (1997) 'The Ombudsman: Parochial Stopgap or Global Panacea?', in Leyland, P. and Woods, T. (eds) *Administrative Law: Facing the Future* (Blackstone Press)

Druce, C. (1988) *Chicken and Egg: Who Pays the Price?* (Green Print)

Dudley, G.F., and Richardson, J.J. (1996) 'Why does Policy Change over Time? Adversarial Policy Communities, Alternative Policy Arenas and British Trunk Roads Policy 1945–95', *Journal of Public Policy* 3

Dunleavy, P. (1981) *The Politics of Mass Housing in Britain, 1945–75: A Study of Corporate Power and Professional Influence in the Welfare State* (Clarendon Press, Oxford)

Dunleavy, P. (1989) 'The UK: Paradoxes of an Ungrounded Statism', in Castles, F.(ed.) *The Comparative History of Public Policy* (Polity Press, Cambridge)

Dunleavy, P. (1991) *Democracy in Britain: A Health Check for the 1990s* (inaugural professorial lecture at the London School of Economics) (LSE Public Policy Group Paper No. 1)

Dunleavy, P. (1995a) 'Estimating the Distribution of Positional Influence in Cabinet Committees under Major', in Rhodes, R.A.W. and Dunleavy, P. (eds) *The Prime Minister, Cabinet and Core Executive* (Macmillan)

Dunleavy, P. (1995b) 'Policy Disasters: Explaining the UK's Record', *Public Policy and Administration* 10(2)

Dunleavy, P. (1995c) *Re-inventing Parliament: Making the Commons More Effective* (Charter 88 and Democratic Audit)

Dunleavy, P. and Margetts, H. (1993a) *Auditing Democracy: The Case for Experiential Measures*, Paper to the European Consortium for Political Research (ECPR) Workshop on Indices of Democracy (University of Leiden)

Dunleavy, P. and Margetts, H. (1993b) *Disaggregating Indices of Democracy: Deviation from Proportionality and Relative Reduction in Parties*, ECPR Workshop Paper (University of Leiden)

Dunleavy, P. and Margetts, H. (1994) 'The Experiential Approach to Auditing Democracy', in Beetham, D. (ed.) *Defining and Measuring Democracy* (Sage, London)

Dunleavy, P. and Margetts, H. (1997) 'The Electoral System', *Parliamentary Affairs* (special 'Britain votes 1997' issue) 50 (4)

Dunleavy, P., Margetts, H., O'Duffy, B. and Weir, S. (1997) *Making Votes Count: Replaying the 1990s General Elections under Alternative Electoral Systems*, Democratic Audit Paper No. 11 (Scarman Trust Enterprises Ltd in association with the LSE Public Policy Group)

Dunleavy, P., Margetts, H. and Weir, S. (1992a) 'The Making of a Euro-Brit', *The Guardian*, 19 June 1991

Dunleavy, P., Margetts, H. and Weir, S. (1992b) *Replaying the 1992 General Election: How Britain would have Voted under Alternative Electoral Systems*, LSE Public Policy Group Paper No. 3 (Joseph Rowntree Reform Trust and LSE)

Dunleavy, P., Margetts, H. and Weir, S. (1996) *The Other National Lottery*, Democratic Audit Paper No. 7 (Human Rights Centre, University of Essex and Scarman Trust Enterprises)

Dunleavy, P., Margetts, H. and Weir, S. (1997) *Devolution Votes*, Democratic Audit Paper No. 12 (Human Rights Centre, University of Essex and Scarman Trust Enterprises)

Dunleavy, P., Margetts, H. and Weir, S. (1998) *Making Votes Count 2*, Democratic Audit Paper No. 14 (Human Rights Centre, University of Essex, in association with the LSE Public Policy Group, Department of Politics and Sociology, Birkbeck College, and Scarman Trust Enterprises)

Dunleavy, P., Gamble, A., Holliday, I. and Peele, G. (eds) (1993) *Developments in British Politics 4* (Macmillan)

Elliott, M. (1989) 'The Control of Public Expenditure', in Jowell, J. and Oliver, D. (eds) *The Changing Constitution* (Clarendon, Oxford)

Ellis, J. and Johnson, R.W. (1974) *Members from the Unions* (Fabian Society)

Elsworthy, S. (1996) 'Introduction' to Oxford Research Group, *Weapons Decisions: Proposals for an Informed Parliament* (Oxford Research Centre, Oxford)

Emden, C.S. (1956) *The People and the Constitution* (2nd edn) (Clarendon Press, Oxford)

Ennals, D. and O'Brien, J. (1990) *The Enabling Role of Local Authorities* (Public Finance Foundation)

Englefield, D. (ed.) (1984) *Commons Select Committees: Catalysts for Progress* (Longman)

Erskine May (1989) *The Law, Privileges, Proceedings and Usage of Parliament* (21st edn) (Butterworths)

Evans, M. and Thornton, S. (1997) *What is the Proper Scope of Public Audit? A Framework for Policy* (CIPFA/ Public Finance Foundation)

Ewing, K. (1987) *The Funding of Political Parties in Britain* (Cambridge University Press, Cambridge)

Falkender, M. (1983) *Downing Street in Perspective* (Weidenfeld & Nicolson)

Farrell, D.M. (1997) *Comparing Electoral Systems* (Prentice Hall/Harvester Wheatsheaf, Hertfordshire)

Fiorina, M.P. (1981) *Retrospective Voting in American National Elections* (Yale University Press, New Haven)

Flinders, M., Harden, I. and Marquand, D. (1997) *How to Make Quangos Democratic* (Political Economy Research Centre, University of Sheffield, and Charter 88)

Flinders, M. and McConnel, H. (1998) 'Maybe Minister: Quangos and Accountablity' in Flinders, M. and Smith, M.J. (eds) *Quangos, Accountability and Reform: The Politics of Quasi-Government* (Macmillan)

Flinders, M. and Smith, M.J. (eds) (1998) *Quangos, Accountability and Reform: The Politics of Quasi-Government* (Macmillan)

Foot, M. (1973) *Aneurin Bevan: 1945–1960* (Davis-Poynter)

Forrester, A., Lansley, S. and Pauley, R. (1985) *Beyond our Ken* (Fourth Estate)

Foster, C.D. (1997) *A Stronger Centre of Government* (paper) (University College London)

Foster, C.D. and Plowden, F.J. (1996) *The State under Stress: Can the Hollow State be Good Government?* (Open University Press, Buckingham)

Fry, G.K. (1985) *The Changing Civil Service* (Allen & Unwin)

Game, C. (1987) 'Public Attitudes Towards the Abolition of the Mets', *Local Government Studies* 13, Sept/Oct

Game, C. (1991) 'Local Elections', in Stewart, J. and Game, C. (eds) *Local Democracy: Representation and Elections*, Belgrave Paper No. 1 (Local Government Management Board, Luton)

Ganz, G. (1987) *Quasi-legislation* (Sweet & Maxwell)

Ganz, G. (1997) 'Delegated Legislation: a Necessary Evil or a Constitutional Outrage', in Leyland, P. and Woods, T. (eds) *Administrative Law: Facing the Future* (Blackstone Press)

Gardner, D. (1995) *The Making of the New Electoral Map*, paper for conference on Boundary Determination in the UK Parliament (Nuffield College, Oxford)

Garrett, J. (1992) *Westminster: Does Parliament Work?* (Victor Gollancz)

Gibson, J. and Stewart, J. (1992) 'Poll Tax, Rates and Local Elections', *Political Studies* 40: 3

Giddings, P. (1994) 'Select Committees and Parliamentary Scrutiny: Plus Ça Change', *Parliamentary Affairs* 47: 4

Giddings, P. (1998) 'The Parliamentary Ombudsman: a Successful Alternative', in Oliver, D. and Drewry, G. (eds) *The Law and Parliament*, Study of Parliament Group (Butterworths)

Gilmour, I. (1978) *Inside Right* (Quartet)

Gilmour, I. (1992) *Dancing with Dogma* (Simon & Schuster)

Gladstone, W.E. (1879) *Gleamings of Past Years* (Vol. 1) (John Murray)

Glanville, M.P. (1993) *Councils, Committees and Boards* (8th edn) (CBD Research, Beckenham, Kent)

Gordon, R. QC (1995) 'The Law Commission and Judicial Review: Managing the Tensions between Caseload Management and Public Interest Challenges', *Public Law* Spring

Gowland, D.H. and James, S. (eds) (1991) *Economic Policy after 1992* (Dartmouth, Aldershot)

Graham, A. (1998) 'The Accountability of Training and Enterprise Councils' in Flinders, M. and Smith, M.J. (eds) *Quangos, Accountability and Reform: The Politics of Quasi-Government* (Macmillan)

Grant, W. (1989) *Pressure Groups, Politics and Democracy* (Phillip Allen)

Grant, W. (1995) 'The Limits of Common Agricultural Policy Reform and the Option of Denationalisation', *Journal of European Public Policy* 2 (1)

Grantham, C. (1989) 'Parliament and Political Consultants', *Parliamentary Affairs* 42: 4

Grantham, C. and Seymour Ure, C. (1990) 'Political Consultants', in Rush, M. (ed.) *Parliament and Pressure Politics* (Clarendon Press, Oxford)

Greger, M. (1994) 'Mad Cow Disease: Much More Serious than AIDS', *Animal Life*, Spring

Griffith, J.A.G. (1982) 'The Constitution and the Commons', in *Parliament and the Executive* (Royal Institute of Public Administration)

Griffith, J.A.G. (1985) 'Judicial Decision-Making in Public Law', *Public Law* Winter

Griffith, J.A.G. (1997) *The Politics of the Judiciary* (3rd edn) (Fontana)

Griffith, J.A.G. and Ryle, M. (1989) *Parliament* (Sweet & Maxwell)

Gyford, J., Leach, S. and Game, C. (1989) *The Changing Politics of Local Government* (Unwin Hyman)

Gyford, J. (1991) *Citizens, Consumers and Councils* (Macmillan)

Gyford, J. (1992) *Does Place Matter? Locality and Local Democracy*, Belgrave Paper No. 3 (Local Government Management Board, Luton)

Hadenius, A. (1992) *Democracy and Development* (Cambridge University Press, Cambridge)

Hadfield, B. (ed.) (1995) *Judicial Review: A Thematic Approach* (Gill and Macmillan, Dublin)

Hailsham, Lord (1978) *The Dilemma of Democracy* (Collins, Glasgow)

Hailsham, Lord (1989) 'The Office of Lord Chancellor and the Separation of Powers', *Civil Justice Quarterly* 8

Haines, J. (1977) *The Politics of Power* (Jonathan Cape)

Hall, W. and Weir, S. (1996) *The Untouchables: Power and Accountability in the Quango State*, Democratic Audit Paper No. 8 (Human Rights Centre, University of Essex, and the Scarman Trust)

Hall, W. and Weir, S. (1997) *The Citizen's Charter*, working draft paper, Democratic Audit (unpublished), Human Rights Centre, University of Essex

Halpern, D., Wood, S., White, S. and Cameron, G. (eds) (1996) *Options for Britain* (Dartmouth, Aldershot)

Hamilton, N. (1986) *Monty: The Field Marshal 1944–1976* (Hamilton, London)

Hansard Society (1976) *The Report of the Hansard Society Commission on Electoral Reform* (The Hansard Society for Parliamentary Government)

Hansard Society (1991) *Agenda for Change* (report of the Commission on Election Campaigns) (The Hansard Society)

Hansard Society (1993) *Making the Law: The Report of the Hansard Society Commission on the Legislative Process* (Hansard Society)

Harden, I. and Lewis, N. (1988) *The Noble Lie: The British Constitution and the Rule of Law* (Hutchinson)

Harding, L., Leigh, D. and Pallister, D. (1997) *The Liar: the Fall of Jonathan Aitken* (Penguin, Harmondsworth)

Harlow, C. and Drewry, G. (1990) 'A "Cutting Edge": The Parliamentary Commissioner and MPs', in *Modern Law Review*, 53

Harris, R. (1990) *Good and Faithful Servant* (Faber and Faber)

Harris, R. (1994) *The Media Trilogy* (Faber and Faber) (originally Harris, R. (1990) *Good and Faithful Servant* (Faber and Faber))

Harrop, M. and Miller, W.L. (1987) *Elections and Voters: a Comparative Introduction* (Macmillan)

Hart, J. (1992) *Proportional Representation: Critics of the British Electoral System, 1820–1945* (Clarendon Press, Oxford)

Harvey, J. and Bather, L. (1972) *The British Constitution* (3rd edn) (Macmillan)

Haviland, J. (ed.) (1988) *Take Care, Mr Baker!* (Fourth Estate)

Hawes, D. (1993) *Power on the Back Benches?* (School for Advanced Urban Studies, University of Bristol)

Hayhurst, J.D. and Wallington, P. (1988) 'The Parliamentary Scrutiny of Delegated Legislation', *Public Law* Winter

Heath, A., Jowell, R. and Curtice, J. (1985) *How Britain Votes* (Pergamon, Oxford)

Heath, A., Jowell, R. and Curtice, J. (eds) (1994) *Labour's Last Chance? The 1992 Election and Beyond* (Dartmouth, Aldershot)

Held, D. (ed.) (1991) *Political Theory Today* (Polity, Cambridge)

Heclo, H. and Wildavsky, A. (1974) *The Private Government of Public Money* (Macmillan)

Henkel, M. (1991) *Government, Evaluation and Change* (Jessica Kingsley)

Hennessy, P. (1986) *Cabinet* (Blackwell, Oxford)

Hennessy, P. (1989) *Whitehall* (Fontana)

Hennessy, P. (1991) *The Hidden Wiring*, Fabian Society Discussion Document 2 (Fabian Society)

Hennessy, P. (1995) *The Hidden Wiring, Unearthing the British Constitution* (Gollancz)

Hennessy, P. (1997) *Beyond Any Mortal* (Hull University Press, Hull)

Hennessy, P. and Arends, A. (1983) 'Mr Attlee's Engine Room: Cabinet Committee Structure and the Labour Governments 1945–51', Strathclyde Papers on Government and Politics No. 26 (University of Strathclyde, Glasgow)

Hennessy, P. and Smith, F. (1992) *Teething the Watchdogs*, Strathclyde Analysis Papers, 7 (University of Strathclyde, Glasgow)

Himsworth, C.M.G. (1995) 'The Delegated Powers Scrutiny Committee', *Public Law* Spring

Hirst, P.Q. (1990) *Representative Democracy and its Limits* (Polity, Cambridge)

Hirst, P. and Khilnani, S. (eds) (1996) *Reinventing Democracy* (Political Quarterly Publishing/Blackwells, Oxford)

Hofferbert, R.I. and Budge, I. (1992) 'The Party Mandate Model and the Westminster Model: Election Programmes and Government Spending in Britain, 1948–85', *British Journal of Political Science* 22

Hofferbert, R.I. and Klingemann, H.-D. (1990) 'The Policy Impact of Party Programmes and Government Declarations in the Federal Republic of Germany', *European Journal of Political Research* 18 (3)

Hogg, S. and Hill, J. (1995) *Too Close to Call: Power and Politics – John Major in No. 10* (Warner)

Hogwood, B.W. (1993) 'The New Administrative Regionalism', paper given at the ESRC funded Research Seminar on Regionalism and Devolution (University of Strathclyde, Glasgow)

Hogwood, B.W. and Keating, M. (eds) (1982) *Regional Government in England* (Clarendon Press, Oxford)

Hood, C., Dunsire, A. and Thompson, K.S. (1978) 'Departments are . . .?' in *Public Administration Bulletin*, No. 27

Hood, C. (1986) Administrative Analysis – An Introduction to Rules, Enforcement and Organizations (Wheatsheaf, Brighton)

Horne, A. (1990) *Macmillan: 1894–1956* (vol. 1) (rev. edn) (Macmillan)

Hoskyns, Sir J. (1983) 'Whitehall and Westminster: An Outsider's View', *Parliamentary Affairs*, 36

Hughes, C. (1949) *The Civil Strangers* (Phoenix House)

Iles, W. (1992) 'The Responsibilities of the New Zealand Legislative Advisory Committee' in *Statute Law Review* 13 (1)

Inkeles, A. (ed.) *On Measuring Democracy* (Transaction Publishers, New Brunswick and London)

Jacobson, G. (1980) *Money in Congressional Elections* (Yale University Press, New Haven, Connecticut)

Jenkins, S. (1995) *Accountable to None: the Tory Nationalisation of Britain* (Hamish Hamilton)

Jenkins, T.A. (1996) *Disraeli and Victorian Conservatism* (Macmillan)

Jenks, E. (1923) *The Government of the British Empire* (3rd edn) (John Murray)

Jennings, Sir W.I. (1933) *The Law and the Constitution* (Cambridge University Press, Cambridge)

Jennings, Sir W.I. (1936) *Cabinet Government* (Cambridge University Press, Cambridge)

Jennings, Sir W.I. (1939) *Parliament* (Cambridge University Press, Cambridge)

Jennings, Sir W.I. (1959) *Cabinet Government* (3rd edn) (Cambridge University Press, Cambridge)

Jogerst, M. (1993) *Reform in the House of Commons: Select Committee System* (University Press, Kentucky)

Johnson, N. (1977) *In Search of the Constitution* (Methuen)

Johnson, R.W. and Schlemmer, L. (1996) *Launching Democracy in South Africa: the First Open Election, April 1994* (Yale University Press, New Haven and London)

Johnston, R.J. (1985) 'People, Places and Parliament: A Geographical Perspective on Electoral Reform in Great Britain', *The Geographical Journal* 151 (3)

Johnston, R.J. (1987) *Money and Votes: Constituency Campaign Spending and Election Results* (Croom Helm, New York)

Johnston, R.J. (1995) *Possible Reforms*, paper for conference on Boundary Determination in the UK Parliament (Nuffield College, Oxford)

Johnston, R.J., Pattie, C.J. and Allsopp, J.G. (1988) *A Nation Dividing?* (Longman, Essex)

Johnston, R.J., Rossiter, D.J. and Pattie, C.J. (1996) 'How Well Did They Do? The Boundary Commissions at the Third and Fourth Periodic Reviews', in McLean, I, and Butler, D. (eds) *Fixing the Boundaries: Defining and Redefining Single-Member Electorial Districts* (Dartmouth, Aldershot)

Jones, B. (1990) 'Party Committees and All-Party Committees' in Rush, M. (ed.) *Parliament and Pressure Politics* (Clarendon Press, Oxford)

Jones, B., Gray, A., Kavanagh, D., Moran, M., Norton, P. and Seldon, A. (eds) (1991) *Politics UK* (Philip Allan)

Jones, B. and Robins, L. (eds) (1992) *Two Decades in British Politics* (Manchester University Press, Manchester)

Jones, G. and Stewart, J. (1992a) 'Selected not Elected', *Local Government Chronicle*, 13 November

Jones, G. and Stewart, J. (1992b) 'Party Discipline', *Local Government Chronicle*, 30 October

Jones, G. and Stewart, J. (1993) 'When the Numbers Don't Add Up to Democracy', *Local Government Chronicle*, 8 January

Jordan, A.G. (ed.) (1991) *The Commercial Lobbyists* (Aberdeen University Press, Aberdeen)

Jordan, A.G. (1994) *The British Administrative System: Principles versus Practice* (Routledge)

Jordan, A.G. and Richardson, J.J. (1987) *British Politics and the Policy Process* (Allen & Unwin)

Jordan, A.G., Maloney, W.A. and McLaughlin, A.M. (1992) 'Policy-Making in Agriculture', British Interest Group Project Working Paper No. 5 (Aberdeen University)

Jowell, J. (1997) 'Restraining the State: Politics, Principle and Judicial Review', lecture given in the Current Legal Problems series 'Law and Opinion at the End of the Twentieth Century'

Jowell, J. and Oliver, D. (eds) (1989) *The Changing Constitution* (Clarendon Press, Oxford)

Judge, D. (1978) 'Public Petitions and the House of Commons', *Parliamentary Affairs* 31: 4

Judge, D. (1981) *Backbench Specialisation in the House of Commons* (Heinemann)

Judge, D. (1983a) 'Why Reform? Parliamentary Reform since 1832: An Interpretation', in Judge, D. (ed.) *The Politics of Parliamentary Reform* (Heinemann)

Judge, D. (ed.) (1983b) *The Politics of Parliamentary Reform* (Heinemann)

Judge, D. (1989) 'Parliament in the 1980s', *Political Quarterly* 60: 3

Judge, D. (1990) *Parliament and Industry* (Dartmouth, Aldershot)

Judge, D. (1992) 'The Effectiveness of the post-1979 Select Committee System : the Verdict of the 1990 Procedure Committee', *Political Quarterly*, 63

Judge, D. (1993) *The Parliamentary State* (Sage)

Justice (1971) *Administration under Law: A Report by JUSTICE* (Stevens)

Justice–All Souls (1988) *Administrative Justice: Some Necessary Reforms* (Oxford University Press, Oxford)

Kavanagh, D. (1981) 'The Politics of Manifestos', *Parliamentary Affairs* 34: 7–27

Keating, M. (1985) 'Whatever Happened to Regional Government?' *Local Government Studies* 11(6)

Keating, M. (1988a) 'Does Regional Governance Work? The Experience of Italy, France and Spain', *Governance* 1(2)

Keating, M. (1988b) *State and Regional Nationalism* (Harvester Wheatsheaf, London)

Kellas, J.G. (1989) *The Scottish Political System* (4th edn) (Cambridge University Press, Cambridge)

Kellner, P. and Crowther-Hunt, Lord (1980) *The Civil Servants: an Inquiry into Britain's Ruling Class* (Raven Books)

King, A. (ed.) (1985) *The British Prime Minister* (Macmillan)

King, A. (1981) 'What Do Elections Decide?', in Butler, D., Penniman, H., and Ranney, A. (eds) *Democracy at the Polls: a Comparative Study of Competitive National Elections* (American Enterprise Institute, Washington, D.C.)

King, D. (1993) 'Government beyond Whitehall', in Dunleavy, P., Gamble, A., Holliday, I. and Peele, G. (eds) *Developments in British Politics 4* (Macmillan)

King, G. and Laver, M. (1993) 'Party Platforms, Mandates and Government Spending', *American Political Science Review* 87(3)

King, M. and May, C. (1985) *Black Magistrates: A Study of Selection and Appointment* (Cobden Trust)

Kirk, R. (ed.) (1982) *The Portable Conservative Reader* (Penguin, Harmondsworth)

Klein, R. (1989) *The Politics of the NHS* (Longman)

Klingemann, H-D., Hofferbert, R.I. and Budge, I. (1994) *Parties, Policies and Democracy* (Westview Press, Boulder, Colorado)

Klug, F., Starmer, K. and Weir, S. (1996) *The Three Pillars of Liberty: Political Rights and Freedoms in the UK*, Democratic Audit Volume No. 1 (Routledge)

Labour Party (1993) *Streets Ahead. A Survey of Local Government Initiatives on the Citizen's Charter* (Labour Party)

Lacey, R. (1994) *Mad Cow Disease* (Cypsela, St. Helier)

Lakeman, E. (1974) *How Democracies Vote* (4th edn) (Faber)

Lakeman, E. (1991) *Twelve Democracies: Electoral Systems in the European Community* (Arthur McDougall Fund)

Lancet (1988) 'Salmonella Enteritidis Phage Type 4: Chicken and Egg', 11, 8613, 24 September

Laver, M. and Hunt, W.B. (1992) *Policy and Party Competition* (Routledge)

Lawson, N. (1993) *The View from No. 11, Memoirs of a Tory Radical* (Corgi)

Lawson, N. and Armstrong, R. (1994) 'Cabinet Government in the Thatcher Years', in *Contemporary Record* 8 (3)

Le Sueur, A.P. (1996) 'The Judicial Review Debate: from Partnership to Friction', *Government and Opposition* 31

Le Sueur, A.P. and Sunkin, M. (1992) 'Applications for Judicial Review: the Requirements', *Public Law* Spring

Leach, S. (1992) 'The Disintegration of an Initiative' in Leach, S., Stewart, J., Spencer, K., Walsh, K. and Gibson, J. (eds) *The Heseltine Review of Local Government: A New Vision or Opportunities Missed?* (Institute of Local Government Studies, Birmingham)

Leach, S. and Stewart, J. (1992) *The Politics of Hung Authorities* (Macmillan)

Leach, S., Stewart, J., Spencer, K., Walsh, K. and Gibson, J. (eds.) (1992) *The Heseltine Review of Local Government: A New Vision or Opportunities Missed?* (Institute of Local Government Studies, Birmingham)

Leadbeater, D. and Mulcahy, L. (1996) *Putting it Right for Consumers* (National Consumer Council)

Leapman, M. (1983) *Barefaced Cheek: Rupert Murdoch* (Hodder & Stoughton) (Coronet edition)

Lecky, W.E.H. (1899) *The Map of Life: Conduct and Character* (Longman, London)

Leigh, D. (1988) *The Wilson Plot* (Heinemann)

Leigh, D. (1993a) *Betrayed* (Bloomsbury)

Leigh, I. (1993b) 'Matrix Churchill, Supergun and the Scott Inquiry', *Public Law* Winter

Leonard, D. (1991) *Elections in Britain Today* (Macmillan)

Lewis, D. (1997) *Hidden Agendas: Politics, Law and Disorder* (Hamish Hamilton)

Lewis, N. (1992) *Inner City Regeneration: The Demise of Regional and Local Government* (Open University Press, Milton Keynes)

Lewis, N. and Birkinshaw, P. (1993) *When Citizens Complain: Reforming Justice and Administration* (Open University Press, Buckingham)

Lewis, N. and Longley, D. (1996) 'Ministerial Responsibility' in *Public Law* ('The Scott Report') Autumn

Leyland, P. and Woods, T. (eds) (1997) *Administrative Law: Facing the Future* (Blackstone Press)

Leys, C. (1955) 'Petitioning in the 19th and 20th Centuries', *Political Studies* 3: 1

Liberty/Electoral Reform ociety (1997) *Ballot Secrecy* (Liberty/ERS)

Likierman, A. and Taylor, A. (1992) *Government Departmental Reports: Pointers from the Future*, Research Report 29 (Chartered Association of Certified Accountants)

Lindsay Keir, Sir D. (1946) *Constitutional History of Modern Britain 1485–1937* (Adam & Charles Black)

Linton, M. (1994) *Money and Votes* (Institute for Public Policy Research)

Lijphart, A. and Grofman, B. (1984) *Choosing an Electoral System* (Praeger Publishers, New York)

Lijphart, A. (1994) 'Democracies: Forms, Performance and Constitutional Engineering', *European Journal of Political Research* 25(1)

Livingstone, S. and Morison, J. (1995) *In Place of Fear*, Democratic Audit Paper No. 5 (Human Rights Centre, University of Essex and Scarman Trust Enterprises)

Local Government Management Board (1993) *Local Government and Community Leadership* (Luton)

Loughlin, M., Gelfand, M. and Young, K. (1985) *Half a Century of Municipal Decline, 1935–1985* (Allen & Unwin)

Loughlin, M. (1990) *Administrative Accountability in Local Government* (Joseph Rowntree Foundation, York)

Loveland, I. (1995) *Housing the Homeless: Administrative Law and Process* (Clarendon Press, Oxford)

Loveland, I. (1997) 'The War Against the Judges' in Weir, S. and Boyle, K. (eds) *Political Quarterly* (Special Human Rights Issue) 68(2)

Lowe, P., Cox, G., MacEwan, M., O'Riordan, T. and Winter, M. (1984) *Countryside Conflicts* (Temple Smith/Gower)

Lowe, P. and Goyder, J. (1983) *Environmental Groups in Politics* (Allen & Unwin)

Lowell, L.A. (1924) *The Government of England*, vol. 2 (Macmillan, New York)

Lowndes, V. (1992) 'Decentralisation: the Potential and the Pitfalls', *Local Government Policy Making* 18(4)

Lustgarten, L. and Leigh, D. (1994) *In From the Cold: National Security and Parliamentary Democracy* (Oxford University Press, Oxford)

Mackenzie, W.J.M. and Grove, J. (1957) *Central Administration in Britain* (Longman)

Mackie, T. and Rose, R. (1991) *The International Almanac of Electoral History* (3rd edn) (Macmillan)

Mackintosh, J.P. (1962) *The British Cabinet* (Methuen)

McAuslan, P. (1988) 'The Constitution: Does the Bill Offend It?', in Haviland, J. (ed.) *Take Care, Mr Baker!* (Fourth Estate)

McCallum, R.B. and Readman, A. (1947) *The British General Election of 1945* (Oxford University Press)

McKenzie, R.T. (1963) *British Political Parties* (Heinemann)

McKie, D. (ed.) (1992) *The Election* (The Guardian)

McLean, I. (1991) 'Forms of Representation and Systems of Voting' in Held, D. (ed.) *Political Theory Today* (Polity, Cambridge)

McLean, I. and Butler, D. (eds) (1996) *Fixing the Boundaries: Defining and Redefining Single-Member Electoral Districts* (Dartmouth, Aldershot)

McLean, I. and Mortimore, R. (1992) 'Apportionment and the Boundary Commission in England', *Electoral Studies* 11(4)

McLean, I. and Smith, J. (1994) 'The Poll Tax and the Electoral Register' in Heath, A., Jowell, R. and Curtice, J. (eds) *Labour's Last Chance? The 1992 Election and Beyond* (Dartmouth, Aldershot)

Margetts, H. and Smyth, G. (eds.) (1994) *Turning Japanese? Britain with a Permanent Party of Government* (Lawrence & Wishart)

Marquand, D. (1977) *Ramsay MacDonald* (Jonathan Cape)

Marr, A. (1995) *Ruling Britannia* (Penguin, Harmondsworth)

Marsh, D. (ed.) (1983) *Pressure Politics* (Longman)

Marsh, D. (1991) 'Privatisation under Mrs Thatcher', *Public Administration* 69

Marsh, D. (1993) 'The Media and Politics', in Dunleavy, P., Gamble, A., Holliday, I. and Peele, G. (eds) *Developments in British Politics 4* (Macmillan)

Marsh, D. and Read, M. (1988) *Private Members' Bills* (Cambridge University Press, Cambridge)

Marsh, D. and Rhodes, R.A.W. (eds) (1992) *Policy Networks in British Government* (Oxford University Press, Oxford)

Marsh, I. (1986) *Policy Making in a Three Party System* (Methuen)

Marshall, G. (1984) *Constitutional Conventions* (Clarendon Press, Oxford)

Marshall, G. (1997) 'The Referendum: What, When and How?', *Parliamentary Affairs*, 50(2)

Medawar, C. (1992) *Power and Dependence: Social Audit on the Safety of Medicines* (Social Audit)

Middlemas, K. (1979) *Politics in Industrial Society* (Deutsch)

Miliband, R. (1982) *Capitalist Democracy in Britain* (Oxford University Press, Oxford)

Mill, J.S. (1861) *Representative Government*, published as Mill, J.S. *Utilitarianism, On Liberty and Representative Government* (Dent)

Miller, W. (1988) *Irrelevant Elections?* (Clarendon Press, Oxford)

Miller, W. (1989) *Electoral Representation: How Fair?*, paper to The Future of Scottish Local Government Conference (University of Strathclyde, Glasgow)

Miller, W.L. (ed.) (1995) *Alternatives to Freedom: Arguments and Opinions* (Longman)

Mills, M. (1993) *The Politics of Dietary Health* (Dartmouth, Aldershot)

Milne, S. (1994) *The Enemy Within – MI5, Maxwell and the Scargill Affair* (Verso)

Minkin, L. (1978) *The Labour Party Conference: a Study in the Politics of Intra-Party Democracy* (Allen Lane)

Minkin, L. (1991) *The Contentious Alliance: Trade Unions and the Labour Party* (Edinburgh University Press, Edinburgh)

Minogue, K. (1978) 'Hyperactivism in British Politics', in Cowling, M. (ed.) *Conservative Essays* (Macmillan)

Mitchell, A. (1991) 'The View from the Lobbied: a Consumer's Guide', in Jordan, A.G. (ed.) *The Commercial Lobbyists* (Aberdeen University Press, Aberdeen)

Mitchell, J. (1996) *Strategies for Self-Government* (Polygon, Edinburgh)

Moodie, G.C. (1964) *The Government of Great Britain* (Thomas Crowell, New York)

Morgan, K. and Osmond, J. (1995) 'The Welsh Quango State' in Davis, H. and Skelcher, C. (eds) *Briefing Papers for the Nolan Committee* (School of Public Policy, University of Birmingham)

Morley, J. (1889) *Walpole* (1922 edn) (Macmillan)

Morrison, H. (1954) *Government and Parliament: A Survey from the Inside* (Oxford)

Mount, F. (1992) *The British Constitution Now* (Heinemann)

Muguan, A. and Patterson, S.C. (eds) (1991) *Political Leadership in Democratic Society* (Nelson Hall, Chicago)

Namier, L. (1957) *The Structure of Politics at the Accession of George III* (2nd edn) (Macmillan)

Newton, K. (1976) *Second City Politics* (Oxford University Press, Oxford)

Nicholas, H.G. (1951) *The British General Election of 1950* (Macmillan)

Nicolson, H. (1952) *King George the Fifth* (Constable & Co.)

Norris, P. (1991) 'Electoral Systems and Women in Legislative Elites', in Muguan, A. and Patterson, S.C. (eds) *Political Leadership in Democratic Society* (Nelson Hall, Chicago)

Norris, P. and Lovenduski, J. (1989) 'Women Candidates for Parliament: Transforming the Agenda?', *British Journal of Political Science*, 19

Norris, P. and Lovenduski, J. (1995) *Political Recruitment Gender, Race and Class in the British Parliament* (Cambridge University Press, Cambridge)

Norton, P. (1978a) *Conservative Dissidents* (Temple Smith)

Norton, P. (1978b) 'Government Defeats in the House of Commons: Myth and Reality', *Public Law* Winter

Norton, P. (1980) *Dissension in the House of Commons 1974–79* (Oxford University Press, Oxford)

Norton, P. (1981) *The Commons in Perspective* (Martin Robertson, Oxford)

Norton, P. (1982) 'Dear Minister: The Importance of MP to Minister Correspondence', *Parliamentary Affairs* 35: 1

Norton, P. (1983) 'Party Committees in the House of Commons', *Parliamentary Affairs* 36: 1

Norton, P. (1985) (ed.) *Parliament in the 1980s* (Blackwell, Oxford)

Norton, P. (1990a) 'Parliament in the UK', *West European Politics* 13: 3

Norton, P. (1990b) 'Choosing a Leader: Mrs Thatcher and the Parliamentary Conservative Party 1989–90', *Parliamentary Affairs* 43: 3

Norton, P. (1991a) 'In Defence of the Constitution: A Riposte to the Radicals', in Norton, P. (ed.) *New Directions in British Politics?* (Edward Elgar, Aldershot)

Norton, P. (1991b) 'The Changing Face of Parliament', in Norton, P. (ed.) *New Directions in British Politics?* (Edward Elgar, Aldershot)

Norton, P. (1991c) 'Parliament – The House of Commons' in Jones, B., Gray, A., Kavanagh, D., Moran, M., Norton, P. and Seldon, A. (eds) *Politics UK* (Philip Allan)

Norton, P. (1991d) (ed.) *New Directions in British Politics?* (Edward Elgar, Aldershot)

Norton, P. and Wood, D. (1990) 'MPs Constituency Service and the Personal Vote', *Parliamentary Affairs* 43: 2

Norton-Taylor, R. with Lloyd, M. (1995) *Truth is a Difficult Concept: Inside the Scott Inquiry* (Fourth Estate)

Norton-Taylor, R., Lloyd, M. and Cook, S. (1996) *Knee Deep in Dishonour: The Scott Report and its Aftermath* (Gollancz)

Oliver, D. (1989) 'The Parties and Parliament: Representative or Intra-Party Democracy', in Jowell, J. and Oliver, D. (eds) *The Changing Constitution* (Clarendon Press, Oxford)

Oliver, D. (1991) *Government in the UK: the Search for Accountability, Effectiveness and Citizenship* (Open University Press, Milton Keynes)

Oliver, D. and Drewry, G. (eds) (1998) *The Law and Parliament*, Study of Parliament Group (Butterworths)

Ostrogorski, M. (1902) *Democracy and the Organisation of Political Parties* vol. 1, (1964 edn) (Quadrangle, Chicago)

Oxford Research Group (1996) *Weapons Decisions: Proposals for an Informed Parliament* (Oxford Research Centre, Oxford)

Padfield, C.F. and Byrne, A. (1992) *British Constitution* (Butterworth-Heinemann, Oxford)

Page, E. and Midwinter, A. (1979) *Remote Bureaucracy or Administrative Efficiency: Scotland's New Local Government System* (University of Strathclyde, Glasgow)

Page, E. and Goldsmith, M. (1987) (eds) *Central and Local Government Relations: a Comparative Analysis of Western European States* (Sage/ECPR)

Paine, T. (1791) *The Rights of Man* (Philp, M. ed. (1995)) (Oxford University Press, Oxford)

Panebianco, A. (1988) *Political Parties: Organisation and Power* (Cambridge University Press, Cambridge)

Parry, G., Moyser, G. and Day, N. (1992) *Political Participation and Democracy in Britain* (Cambridge University Press, Cambridge)

Patten, J. (1991) *Political Culture, Conservatism and Rolling Constitutional Change* (Conservative Political Centre)

Peck, J.A. (1992) 'TECs and the Local Politics of Training', *Political Geography* 11(4)

Peet, A. (1998) 'Quango Watch – a Local Authority in Perspective', in Flinders, M. and Smith, M.J. (eds) *Quangos, Accountability and Reform: The Politics of Quasi-Government* (Macmillan)

Phillips, A. (1994) *Local Democracy: the Terms of the Debate*, Report No. 2, Commission for Local Democracy

Pinto-Duschinsky, M. (1981) *British Political Finance 1830–1980* (American Enterprise Institute for Public Policy Research, Washington D.C.)

Piper, J.R. (1991) 'British Backbench Rebellion and Government Appointments, 1945–87', *Legislative Studies Quarterly* 26: 2

Pitkin, H.F. (1974) *The Concept of Representation* (California University Press, Berkeley)

Plant Report 1991, *Democracy, Representation and Elections* (Labour Party)

Pliatsky, L. (1989) *The Treasury under Mrs Thatcher* (Blackwell, Oxford)

Pocock, J.G.A. (1987) *The Ancient Constitution and the Feudal Law – a Study of English Historical Thought in the Seventeenth Century* (2nd edn) (Cambridge University Press, Cambridge)

Polsby, N.W. and Wildavsky, A. (1988) *Presidential Elections: Contemporary Strategies of American Electoral Politics* (The Free Press, New York)

Pomper, G.M. and Lederman, S.S. (1980) *Elections in America. Control and Influence in Democratic Politics* (2nd edn) (Longman, New York)

Ponting, C. (1986) *Whitehall: Tragedy and Farce* (Hamish Hamilton)

Powell, C. (1997) 'What was New in 97', paper delivered at the conference of the Specialist Group on Elections, Public Opinion and Parties (EPOP), Political Studies Association, on 'Assessing the 1997 Election', at the University of Essex, September 1997

Power, A. (1987) *Property Before People* (Allen & Unwin)

Prentice, S. (1996) 'Health Policy and Care' in Halpern, D., Wood, S., White, S. and Cameron, G. (eds) *Options for Britain* (Dartmouth, Aldershot)

Prior, D., Stewart, J. and Walsh, K. (1993) *Is the Citizen's Charter a Charter for Citizens?* (Local Government Management Board, Luton)

Pritt, D.N. (1963) *The Labour Government 1945–51* (Lawrence & Wishart)

Public Concern at Work (1995) *Blowing the Whistle on Defence Procurement* (Public Concern at Work)

Public Law Project (1993) *Judicial Review in Perspective*, by Sunkin, M., Bridges, L. and Meszaros, G. (Public Law Project)

Public Law Project (1995) *The Applicant's Guide to Judicial Review* (Sweet & Maxwell)

Pulzer, P.G.J. (1975) *Political Representation and Elections in Britain* (George Allen & Unwin)

Puttick, K. (1988) *Challenging Delegated Legislation* (Waterlow)

Radford, T. (1996) 'Twists and Turns on the Trail of a Killer', *Guardian*, 21 March

Rallings, C. (1987) 'The Influence of Election Programmes: Britain and Canada 1956–79', in Budge, I., Robertson, D., and Hearl, D. (eds)

Ideology, Strategy and Party Change: Spatial Analyses of Post-War Election Programmes in 19 Democracies (Cambridge University Press, Cambridge)

Rallings, C. and Thrasher, M. (1991) *Electoral Reform for Local Government* (Electoral Reform Society)

Rallings, C., Thrasher, M. and Denver, D. (1996) 'The Electoral Impact of the New Parliamentary Constituency Boundaries', in McLean, I. and Butler, D. (eds) *Fixing the Boundaries: Defining and Redefining Single-Member Electoral Districts* (Dartmouth, Aldershot)

Rawlings, H. F. (1988) *Law and the Electoral Process* (Sweet & Maxwell)

Reeve, A. and Ware, A. (1991) *Electoral Systems: a Comparative and Theoretical Introduction* (Routledge)

Reynolds, A. and Reilly, B. (1997) *The International IDEA Handbook of Electoral System Design* (International Idea, Stockholm)

Rhodes, R.A.W. (1994) 'The Hollowing Out of the State', *Political Quarterly* 65

Rhodes, R.A.W. and Dunleavy, P. (eds) (1995) *The Prime Minister, Cabinet and Core Executive* (Macmillan)

Richardson, J. (ed.) (1982) *Policy Styles in Western Europe* (Allen & Unwin)

Richardson, G and Sunkin, M. (1996) 'Judicial Review: Questions of Impact', *Public Law*, Spring

Riddell, P. (1991) *The Thatcher Era and Its Legacy* (2nd edn) (Blackwell, Oxford)

Riddell, P. (1998) *Parliament under Pressure* (Gollancz)

Ridley, N. (1988) *The New Right* (Conservative Political Centre)

Riley, K. (1993) *Education – A Major Local Authority Service: Themes and Issues: Conference Report* (Local Government Management Board, Luton)

Rippon, Lord (1990) 'Constitutional Anarchy', *Statute Law Review* 11: 1

Robertson, D. (1976) *A Theory of Party Competition* (John Wiley & Sons)

Robinson, A. (1988) 'The House of Commons and Public Money', in Ryle, M. and Richards, P.G. (eds) *The Commons under Scrutiny* (Routledge)

Roper, J. (1989) *Democracy and its Critics: Anglo-American Democratic Thought in the Nineteenth Century* (Unwin Hyman)

Rose, R. (1974) *The Problem of Party Government* (Macmillan)

Rose, R. (1980) *Do Parties Make a Difference?* (Macmillan)

Rose, R. (1983) 'Elections and Electoral Systems: Choices and Alternatives', in Bogdanor, V. and Butler, D. (eds) *Democracy and Elections: Electoral Systems and their Political Consequences* (Cambridge University Press, Cambridge)

Rose, R. (1984) *Do Parties Make a Difference?* (Macmillan)

Rowntree (Joseph) Reform Trust (1991–96) *State of the Nation* series of opinion polls: conducted by MORI (March 1991); MORI (May 1995) and ICM (September 1996)

Rowntree (Joseph) Reform Trust (August 1991) *Alternative Ballots and Electability* poll (MORI)

Rowntree (Joseph) Reform Trust (1992) *The 1992 General Elections: How People would have Voted under Different Electoral Systems* (ICM)

Rowntree (Joseph) Reform Trust (February 1996) *The Scott Inquiry Poll* (ICM)

Royal Institute of Public Administration (1987) *Top Jobs in Whitehall* (RIPA)

Royed, T.J. (1996) 'Testing the Mandate Model in Britain and the United States: Evidence from the Reagan and Thatcher Eras', *British Journal of Political Science* 26, part 1

Rozenberg, J. (1997) *Trial of Strength: The Battle between the Government and the Judiciary over Who Makes the Laws of Britain* (Richard Cohen)

Rush, M. (1988) 'The Members of Parliament', in Ryle, M. and Richards, P.G. (eds) *The Commons under Scrutiny* (Routledge)

Rush, M. (ed.) (1990) *Parliament and Pressure Politics* (Clarendon Press, Oxford)

Ryan, M. (1983) 'The Penal Lobby: Influencing Ideology', in Marsh, D. (ed.) *Pressure Politics* (Longman)

Ryle, M. and Richards, P.G. (eds) (1988) *The Commons Under Scrutiny* (Routledge)

Saward, M. (1992) 'The Nuclear Power Network', in Marsh, D. and Rhodes, R.A.W. (eds) *Policy Networks in British Government* (Oxford University Press, Oxford)

Scruton, R. (1980) *The Meaning of Conservatism* (Macmillan)

Sedley, S. (1997) 'The Common Law and the Constitution', *London Review of Books*, 8 May

Seldon, A. (1995) 'The Cabinet Office and Co-ordination' in Rhodes, R.A.W. and Dunleavy, P. (eds) *The Prime Minister, Cabinet and Core Executive* (Macmillan)

Shaw, K. (1990) 'The Lost World of Local Politics Revisited: In Search of the Non-Elected Local State', *Regional Studies* 24(2)

Shell, D. (1992a) *The House of Lords* (2nd edn) (Harvester Wheatsheaf)

Shell, D. (1992b) 'The House of Lords: The Best Second Chamber We Have Got?', in Jones, B. and Robins, L. (eds) *Two Decades in British Politics* (Manchester University Press, Manchester)

Shell, D. (1993) 'Conclusion', in Shell, D. and Beamish, D. (eds) *The House of Lords at Work* (Study of Parliament Group Study) (Clarendon Press, Oxford)

Shell, D. and Beamish, D. (eds) (1993) *The House of Lords at Work* (Study of Parliament Group Study) (Clarendon Press, Oxford)

Silk, P. (1987) *Parliament at Work* (Longman)

Silk, P. and Walters, R. (1995) *How Parliament Works* (Longman)

Sked, A. and Cook, C. (1993) *Postwar Britain: A Political History* (4th edn) (Penguin)

Skelcher, C. and Davis, H. (1995) *Opening the Boardroom Door: the Membership of Local Appointed Bodies* (Joseph Rowntree Foundation, York)

Skelcher, C. and Davis, H. (1996) 'Understanding the New Magistracy', in Davis, H. (ed.) *Quangos and Local Government: a Changing World* (Frank Cass)

Smith, B. (1976) *Policy-making in British government: an Analysis of Power and Rationality in British Government* (Martin Robertson)

Smith, J. and McLean, I. (1992) *The UK Poll Tax and the Declining Electoral Roll: Unintended Consequences* (Warwick University)

Smith, M. (1993) *Pressure, Power and Policy* (Harvester Wheatsheaf)

Smith, M.J. (1990) *The Politics of Agricultural Support in Britain; the Development of the Agricultural Policy Community* (Dartmouth, Aldershot)

Smith, M.J., Marsh, D. and Richrads, D. (1995) 'Central Government Departments and the Policy Process', in Rhodes, R.A.W. and Dunleavy, P. (eds) *The Prime Minister, Cabinet and Core Executive* (Macmillan)

Stedman-Jones, G. (1983) *Languages of Class: Studies in English Working Class History* (Cambridge University Press)

Stephens, P. (1996) *Politics and the Pound: The Conservatives' Struggle with Sterling* (Macmillan)

Stewart, J. (1995) 'A Future for Local Authorities as Community Guardians', in Stewart, J. and Stoker, G. (eds) *The Future of Local Government* (Macmillan)

Stewart, J. (1989) 'A Future for Local Authorities as Community Government', in Stewart, J. and Stoker, G. (eds) *The Future of Local Government* (Macmillan)

Stewart, J. (1990) 'The Enabling Authority', *Management Education and Development* 21: 5

Stewart, J. (1991) 'The Councillor as Elected Representative', in Stewart, J. and Game, C. (eds) *Local Democracy: Representation and Elections*, Belgrave Paper No. 1 (Local Government Management Board, Luton)

Stewart, J. and Game, C. (eds) (1991) *Local Democracy: Representation and Elections*, Belgrave Paper No. 1 (Local Government Management Board, Luton)

Stewart, J., Lewis, N. and Longley, D. (1992) *Accountability to the Public* (European Policy Forum)

Stewart, J. and Stoker, G. (eds) (1989) *The Future of Local Government* (Macmillan)

Stewart, J. and Stoker, G. (eds) (1995) *Local Government in the 1990s* (Macmillan)

Stoker, G. (1991) *The Politics of Local Government* (2nd edn) (Macmillan)

Stoker, G. (1996) *The Reform of the Institutions of Local Representative Democracy: Is There a Role for the Mayor-Council Model?* (Municipal Journal Books)

Stoker, G. (1998) 'Quangos and Local Democracy', in Flinders, M. and Smith, M.J. (eds) *Quangos, Accountability and Reform: The Politics of Quasi-Government* (Macmillan)

Stokes, E. (1959) *The English Utilitarians and India* (Oxford University Press, Oxford)

Stratton, C.N. (1990) 'TECs and PICs – the Key Issues which Lie Ahead', *Regional Studies* 24(1)

Sunkin, M. (1995) 'The Problematical State of Access to Judicial Review', in Hadfield, B. (ed.) *Judicial Review: A Thematic Approach* (Gill and Macmillan, Dublin)

Sunkin, M. and Le Sueur, A.P. (1991) 'Can Government Control Judicial Review?', *Current Legal Problems* 44: 161

Sutherland, J. (1990) *Mrs Humphrey Ward: Eminent Victorian, Pre-eminent Edwardian* (Clarendon Press, Oxford)

Taagepera, R. and Shugart, M.S. (1989) *Seats and Votes* (Yale University Press, New Haven and London)

Taylor, P. and Johnston, R. (1979) *The Geography of Elections* (Penguin, Harmondsworth)

Thain, C. and Wright, M. (1995) *The Treasury and Whitehall: The Planning and Control of Public Expenditure, 1976–93* (Clarendon Press, Oxford)

Thatcher, M. (1993) *The Downing Street Years* (Harper Collins)

Theakston, K. (1987) *Junior Ministers in British Government* (Blackwell, Oxford)

Theakston, K. (1992) *The Labour Party and Whitehall* (Routledge)

Theakston, K. (1995) *The Civil Service since 1945* (Blackwell, Oxford)

Theakston, K. and Fry, G. (1989) 'Britain's Administrative Elite: Permanent Secretaries, 1900–1986', *Public Administration* 67(2)

Thompson, H. (1994) 'Joining the Exchange Rate Mechanism: The Core Executive and Macro-Economic Policy-making in Britain' (PhD thesis) (London School of Economics)

Tomkins, A. (1996) 'Government Information and Parliament: Misleading by Design or by Default?', *Public Law*, Autumn

Topf, R. (1994) 'Party Manifesto', in Heath, A., Jowell, R. and Curtice, J. (eds) *Labour's Last Chance? The 1992 Election and Beyond* (Dartmouth, Aldershot)

Wade, E.S.C. and Bradley, A.W. (1993) *Constitutional and Administrative Law* (11th edn by Bradley, A.W. and Ewing, K.D.) (Longman)

Waldegrave, W. (1993) Speech to the Public Finance Foundation, 5 July, issued by the Office of Public Service and Science

Walkland, S.A. and Ryle, M. (eds) (1981) *The Commons Today*, The Study of Parliament Group (revised edn) (Fontana)

Waller, R. (1994) 'Polling Evidence and Conservative Ascendancy', in Margetts, H. and Smyth, G. (eds) *Turning Japanese? Britain with a Permanent Party of Government* (Lawrence & Wishart)

Waller, R. and Criddle, B. (1996) *The Almanac of British Politics* (5th edn) (Routledge)

Walsh, K. (1993) 'Local Government', in Caterall, P. (ed.) *Contemporary Britain: An Annual Overview* (Blackwell, Oxford)

Waniek, R.W. (1993) 'A New Approach towards Decentralization in North-Rhine Westphalia', *Regional Studies* 27(5)

Ware, A. (1987) *Citizens, Parties and the State* (Blackwell, Oxford)

Wass, Sir D. (1984) *Government and the Governed* (Routledge & Kegan Paul)

Wass, Sir D. (1996) 'Scott and Whitehall', *Public Law* ('The Scott Report'), Autumn

Weber, M. (1978) *Economy and Society* (vol. 2) edited by Roth, G. and Wittich, C. (University of California Press, Berkeley)

Weir, S. (1992) 'Waiting for Change: Public Opinion and Electoral Reform', *Political Quarterly* 63(2)

Weir, S. (1994) *British Democracy in the Balance* Democratic Audit Paper No. 3 (Human Rights Centre, University of Essex and Scarman Trust Enterprises)

Weir, S. (1995) 'Quangos: Questions of Democratic Accountability', in 'The Quango Debate', *Parliamentary Affairs* 48(2)

Weir, S. (1996) 'From Strong Government and Quasi-Government to Strong Democracy', in Hirst, P. and Khilnani, S. (eds) *Reinventing Democracy* (Political Quarterly Publishing/Blackwells, Oxford)

Weir, S. and Byrne, I. (1997) *Liberties in the Balance (a Report on a Poll of Backbench MPs)*, Democratic Audit Paper No. 10 (Human Rights Centre, University of Essex and Scarman Trust Enterprises)

Weir, S. and Hall, W. (eds) (1994) *EGO TRIP: Extra-governmental Organisations in the UK and their Accountability*, Democratic Audit Paper No. 2 (Human Rights Centre, University of Essex and Scarman Trust Enterprises)

Weir, S. and Hall, W. (1995a) 'National Executive Quangos', in Davis, H. and Skelcher, C. (eds) *Briefing Papers for the Nolan Committee* (School of Public Policy, University of Birmingham)

Weir, S. and Hall, W. (1995b) *Comments on the Government's Evidence to the [Nolan] Committee: Supplementary Working Brief for the Committee on Standards in Public Life* (Democratic Audit, Human Rights Centre, University of Essex)

Weir, S. and Hall, W. (1995c) *Behind Closed Doors*, Democratic Audit Paper No. 4 (Human Rights Centre, University of Essex/Dispatches, Channel 4)

Weir, S. and Wright, T. (1996) *Power to the Back Benches? Restoring the Balance between Government and Parliament (a Report on a Poll of Backbench MPs)*, Democratic Audit Paper No. 9 (Human Rights Centre, University of Essex and Scarman Trust Enterprises)

Wells, J. (1997) *The House of Lords: From Saxon Wargods to a Modern Senate* (Hodder)

Wertheimer, E.F.R. (1929) *Portrait of the Labour Party* (translated by P. Kirwan) (G.P. Putnam & Sons)

Whiteley, P., Clarke, H. and Stewart, M. (1998) 'The Economics and Politics of Satisfaction with Democracy in Britain, 1992–97', paper presented to ESRC seminar on democracy and participation (University of Sheffield), January

Winter, G. (1981) *Inside BOSS* (Allen Lane)

Winter, M. (1996) *Rural Politics: Policies for Agriculture, Forestry and the Environment* (Routlege)

Wood, B. (1976) *The Process of Local Government Reform 1966–74* (Allen & Unwin)

Wood, R. (ed.) (1990) *Remedial Law: When Courts become Administrators* (University of Massachusetts, Amherst)

Woodhouse, D. (1997) 'Ministerial Responsibility: Something Old, Something New', in *Public Law*, Summer

Woolf, Lord Justice (1990) *Protection of the Public: A New Challenge*, Hamlyn Lectures 41st Series (Stevens & Sons)

Wright, P. (1987) *Spycatcher* (Viking, New York)

Wright, T. (1998) 'Reforming the Patronage State', in Flinders, M. and Smith, M.J. (eds) *Quangos, Accountability and Reform: The Politics of Quasi-Government* (Macmillan)

Wynne, B. (1996) 'Patronising Joe Public', *Times Higher Education Supplement*, 12 April

Young, H. (1990) *One of Us* (2nd edn) (Pan Books)

Young, K. and Rao, N. (1994) *Coming to Terms with Change?* (Joseph Rowntree Foundation)

Young, S. (1994) 'The Environment', in Allan, P. et al. (eds) *Focus on Britain 1994 – Review of 1993* (Perrenial, Oxford)

Government and official publications

Agriculture Committee (1989) *Salmonella in eggs: Minutes of Evidence*, Session 1988–89, HC 108-II (HMSO)

Agriculture Committee (1990) *Bovine Spongiform Encephalopathy*, Session 1989–90, HC 449 (HMSO)

Audit Commission (1993) *Passing the Bucks: The Impact of Standard Spending Assessments on Economy, Efficiency and Effectiveness* (HMSO)

Audit Commission (1995) *Updated Code of Audit Practice for Local Authorities and the NHS in England and Wales*

Audit Commission (1996) *By Accident or Design: Improving A and E Services in England and Wales* (HMSO)

Birmingham City Council (1992) *City Strategy Report 1991–2* (Strategic Policy and Planning Unit, Birmingham)

Bozdan, P. (1991) *The House of Commons and EC Legislation*, Factsheet 56, Public Information (Office of the House of Commons, London)

Cabinet Office (1988) *Improving Management in Local Government: The Next Steps*, A Report to the Prime Minister (overseen by Sir Robin Ibbs) (Efficiency Unit, Cabinet Office)

Cabinet Office (1992) *Questions of Procedure for Ministers*, May 1992 (HMSO)

Cabinet Office (1993) *Open Government*, Cm 2290 (HMSO)

Cabinet Office (1995) *Taking Forward Continuity and Change*, Cm 2748 (HMSO)

Cabinet Office (1995–97) 'Citizen's Charter' *Open Government: Code of Practice on Access to Government Information* (Cabinet Office)

Cabinet Office (1996a) *Objective Setting and Monitoring in Executive Non-Departmental Public Bodies*, Efficiency Unit, Cabinet Office (HMSO)

Cabinet Office (1996b) *The Citizen's Charter – Five Years On*, Cm 3370 (HMSO)

Cabinet Office (1996c) *Guidance on Guidance* (Cabinet Office)

Cabinet Office (1997) *Ministerial Code: A Code of Conduct and Guidance on Proceedings of Ministers* (Cabinet Office)

Cabinet Office/OPS (1993) *Public Bodies 1993* (HMSO)

Cabinet Office/OPS (1995), 'New Civil Service Code Comes into Force', News release OPS 316, 28 December 1995 (Cabinet Office)

Cabinet Office/OPS (1996) *Public Bodies 1996* (HMSO)

Cabinet Office/OPS (1997) *Guidance on Interpretation of the Code of Access to Government Information*, OPS 2nd edn (Cabinet Office)

Cabinet Office/OPS (1996) *Model Code for Staff of Executive NDPBs* (HMSO)

Cabinet Office/OPS (1997a) *Next Steps Agencies in Government: Review 1996*, Cm 3579 (HMSO)

Cabinet Office/OPS (1997b) *Departmental Evidence and Response to Select Committees* (Machinery of Government and Standards Group)

Cabinet Office/OPS (1997c) *Your Right to Know: The Government's Proposals for a Freedom of Information Act*, Cm 3818 (HMSO)

Cabinet Office/Treasury (1992) *Non-Departmental Public Bodies: A Guide for Departments* (HMSO)

Cabinet Office/Treasury (1997) *The Governance of Public Bodies: A Progress Report*, Cm 3557 (HMSO)

Chancellor of the Duchy of Lancaster and the Financial Secretary to the Treasury (1996) *Spending Public Money: Governance and Audit Issues*, Cm 3179 (HMSO)

CIDP (1989) *Chronicle of Parliamentary Elections and Developments 1 July 1988–30 June 1989* (Inter-Parliamentary Union, Geneva)

CIDP (1990) *Chronicle of Parliamentary Elections and Developments 1 July 1989–30 June 1990* (Inter-Parliamentary Union, Geneva)

CIDP (1991) *Chronicle of Parliamentary Elections and Developments 1 July 1990–30 June 1991* (Inter-Parliamentary Union, Geneva)

CIDP (1992) *Chronicle of Parliamentary Elections and Developments 1 July 1991–30 June 1992* (Inter-Parliamentary Union, Geneva)

Citizen's Charter (1995) *Open Government: Code of Practice on Access to Government Information* (Cabinet Office)

Civil Service Yearbook 1997 (1997) (HMSO)

Committee of Inquiry into Local Government Finance (chaired by Frank Layfield QC) (1976) Cm 6453 (HMSO)

Committee on Standards in Public Life (chaired by Lord Nolan) (May 1995) Cm 2850-I (HMSO)

Committee on Standards in Public Life – Local Public Spending Bodies (chaired by Lord Nolan) (May 1996) Cm 3270-I (HMSO)

Committee on Standards in Public Life – Local Government in England, Scotland and Wales (chaired by Lord Nolan) (July 1997) Cm 3702-I (HMSO)

Committee on Standards in Public Life – Review of Standards of Conduct in Executive NDPBS, NHS Trusts and Local Public Spending Bodies (chaired by Lord Nolan) (November 1997)

Council of Europe (1985) *European Charter of Local Self-Government*, Treaty Series No. 122 (Council of Europe, Strasbourg)

Council of Tribunals (1994) *Annual Report*, Session 1993–94, HC 22 (HMSO)

Crowther-Hunt and Peacock Royal Commission on the Constitution 1969–73 (1973) Vol. II – *Memorandum of Dissent*, Cm 5460-I (HMSO)

Defence Committee (1986) *Fourth Report, Westland plc: The Government's Decision Making*, Session 1985–86, HC 519 (HMSO)

Defence Committee (1993) *Seventh Report, The Royal Dockyard*, Session 1992–93, HC 637 (HMSO)

Delegated Powers Scrutiny Committee, (1993a) House of Lords *First Report 1992–93*, HL 57 (HMSO)

Delegated Powers Scrutiny Committee, (1993b) *The Education Bill*, HL 79 (HMSO)

Department of Health (1996) *CJD and Children* Press Release 96/92

Department of Health/MAFF (1989) *Report of the Working Party on Bovine Spongiform Encephalopathy (the Southwood Report)* (Department of Health)

Department of Prices and Consumer Protection (1978) *A Review of Monopolies and Mergers Policy*, CM 7198 (HMSO)

Departmental Committee on Section 2 of the Official Secrets Act (1972) *Report of the Committee*, Session 1971–72 Cm 5104 (HMSO)

Employment Committee (1984) *Trade Union Legislation, Unions and the Government Communications Headquarters*, Session 1983–84, HC 238 (HMSO)

Energy Committee (1988) *The Structure, Regulation and Economic Consequences of Electricity Supply in the Private Sector*, Session 1987–88, HC 307 (HMSO)

Franks, Lord (1983) *Falkland Islands Review (South Atlantic) Report of a Committee of Privy Councillors* (Chaired by Lord Franks), Cm 8787 (HMSO)

Fulton, Lord (1968) *The Civil Service: Report of the Committee 1966–68* (the Fulton Report), Cm 3638 (HMSO)

Haldane, Lord (1918) *Report on the Machinery of Government*, Cm 9230 (HMSO)

Heap Report (1970) *Statute Law Deficiencies* (Statute Law Society, Sweet & Maxwell)

Home Affairs Committee (1983) *Representation of the People Acts*, Session 1982–83, HC 32I and II (HMSO)

Home Affairs Committee (1993a) *Funding of Political Parties*, Session 1992–93, HC 301 (HMSO)

Home Affairs Committee (1993b) *Funding of Political Parties: Minutes of Evidence*, Session 1992–93, HC 726 (HMSO)

House of Commons (1991) Sessional Returns 1989–90, HC 218 (HMSO)

House of Commons (1992a) Sessional Returns 1990–91, HC 271 (HMSO)

House of Commons (1992b) Sessional Returns 1991–92, HC 204 (HMSO)

House of Commons (1993–94) Minutes of Evidence to TCSC's Fifth Report on 'The Role of the Civil Service', HC 27II (HMSO)

House of Commons (1997) Sessional Returns 1995–96, HC 164 (HMSO)

Ibbs Report (1988), *Improving Management in Government: The Next Steps* (overseen by Sir Robin Ibbs), A Report to the Prime Minister (Efficiency Unit, Cabinet Office)

Lacey, R. and Dealler, S. (1990) 'Memorandum submitted by R. Lacey and S. Dealler' in Agriculture Committee Report *Bovine Spongiform Encephalopathy*, Session 1989–90, HC 449 (HMSO)

Law Commission No. 226 (1994) Administrative Law: *Judicial Review and Statutory Appeal*, Session 1993–94, HC 669 (HMSO)

Layfield, F. (1976) *Report of the Committee of Enquiry into Local Government Finance* (chaired by F. Layfield QC), Cm 6453 (HMSO)

Massey, A. (1995) *After Next Steps: an Examination of the Implications for Policy-making of the Developments in Executive Agencies* (Office of Public Service, Cabinet Office)

Members' Interests Committee (1988) *Parliamentary Lobbying*, Session 1987–88, HC 518 (HMSO)

Members' Interests Committee (1990a) *Minutes of Evidence*, Session 1989–90, HC 283 (HMSO)

Members' Interests Committee (1990b) *Second Report*, Session 1989–90, HC 506 (HMSO)

Members' Interests Committee (1990c) *Third Report*, Session 1989–90, HC 561 (HMSO)

Members' Interests Committee (1991) *Parliamentary Lobbying*, Session 1990–91, HC 586 (HMSO)

Modernisation Committee Report (1997) *The Legislative Process*, Session 1997–98, HC 190 (HMSO)

National Audit Office (1995) *MoD: The Risk of Fraud*, Session 1994–95, HC 258 (HMSO)

NHS Executive (1993) *Guidance to Staff on Relations with the Public and the Media*, HSG(93)51

Nolan Report (1995) *First Report of the Committee on Standards in Public Life*, Cm 2850-I (HMSO)

Nolan Report (1996) *Second Report of the Committee on Standards in Public Life*, Cm 3270-I, (HMSO)

Nolan Report (July 1997) *Third Report of the Committee on Standards in Public Life*, Cm 3702-I (HMSO)

Nolan Report (November 1997) *Fourth Report of the Committee on Standards in Public Life*

North, R. (1990) 'Memorandum submitted by Richard North' in HC 108-II

Office of the Commissioner for Public Appointments (OCPA) (1996a) *Guidance for Departments on Appointments to ENDPBs and NHS Bodies* (OCPA)

OCPA (1996b) *Commissioner for Public Appointments: First Report 1995–1996* (OCPA)

OCPA (1996c) *Code of Practice for Public Appointments Procedures* (OCPA)

OCPA (1997) *Commissioner for Public Appointments: Second Report 1996–1997* (OCPA)

Office of Public Service – see Cabinet Office

Parliamentary Commissioner for Administration (PCA) (1994–97) *PCA Annual Reports* (HMSO)

PCA (1994) *Access to Official Information: The First Eight Months*, Second Report, Session 1994–95, HC 91 (HMSO)

PCA (1995) *Investigation of Complaints against the Child Support Agency*, Third Report, Session 1994–95, HC 135 (HMSO)

PCA Committee (Select Committee for the Parliamentary Commissioner for Administration) (1978) *PCA (Review of Access and Jurisdiction)*, Fourth Report, Session 1977–78, HC 615 (HMSO)

PCA Committee (1994) *The Powers, Work and Jurisdiction of the Ombudsman*, First Report, Session 1993–94, HC 33 (HMSO)

PCA Committee (1995) *The Child Support Agency*, Third Report, Session 1994–95, HC 199 (HMSO)

PCA Committee (1996) *Open Government*, Second Report, Session 1994–95, HC 84 (inc 290-i-iii of Session 1994–95) (HMSO)

Pliatzky, Sir L (1980) *Report on Non-Departmental Bodies* Cm 7797 (HMSO)

Procedure Committee (1971) *Second Report from the Select Committee on Procedure*, Session 1970–71, HC 538 (HMSO)

Procedure Committee (1978) *First Report*, Session 1977–78, HC 588

Procedure Committee (1985) *Public Bill Procedure*, Session 1984–85, HC 49 (HMSO)

Procedure Committee (1986) *Allocation of Time*, Session 1985–86, HC 324 (HMSO)

Procedure Committee (1987) *Use of Time on the Floor of the House*, Session 1986–87 HC 350 (HMSO)

Procedure Committee (1989) *The Scrutiny of European Legislation*, Session 1988–89, HC 622 (HMSO)

Procedure Committee (1990a) *The Working of the Select Committee*, Session 1989–90, HC 19 (HMSO)

Procedure Committee (1990b) *Oral Questions*, Session 1989–90, HC 379 (HMSO)

Procedure Committee (1991a) *Review of European Standing Committees*, Session 1991–2, HC 31 (HMSO)

Procedure Committee (1991b) *Parliamentary Questions*, Session 1990–91, HC 178 (HMSO)

Procedure Committee (1992a) *Select Committee on the Sittings of the House* Volume 1, Report and Proceedings, Session 1991–92, HC 20-I (HMSO)

Procedure Committee (1992b) *Select Committee on the Sittings of the House* Volume 2, Minutes of evidence and appendices, Session 1991–92, HC 20-II (HMSO)

Procedure Committee (1992c) *Fourth Report: Public Petitions*, Session 1991–92, HC 286 (HMSO)

Public Accounts Committee (PAC) (1994) *The Proper Conduct of Public Business*, Eighth Report, Session 1993–94, HC 154 (HMSO)

Public Service Committee (PSC) (1996a) *The Code of Practice for Public Appointments*, PSC First Report, Session 1995–96, HC 168 (HMSO)

PSC (1996b) *Role and Responsibilities of the Deputy Prime Minister*, Michael Heseltine's evidence to PSC, 28 February 1996, HC 265 (HMSO)

PSC (1996c), *Ministerial Accountability and Responsibility*, Session 1995–96, HC 313 (HMSO)

PSC (1997) *The Work of the Commissioner for Public Appointments*, PSC Second Report, Session 1996–97 HC 141 (HMSO)

Redcliffe-Maud, Lord, Chairperson (1969) *Royal Commission on Local Government, vol. 1 Report*, Cm 4040 (HMSO)

Register of Members' Interests (1991) *Register of Member's Interests on 14 January 1991*, HC 140 (HMSO)

Register of Members' Interests (1992) *Register of Member's Interests on 13 January 1992*, HC 170 (HMSO)

Register of Members' Interests (1992) *Register of Members' Interests on 1 December 1992*, HC 320 (HMSO)

Renton Report (1975) *Report of the Committee on the Preparation of Legislation*, Cm 6053 (HMSO)

Royal Commission on the Electoral System of New Zealand (1986) *Towards a Better Democracy* (Royal Commission)

Scott Report (1996) *Report of the Inquiry into the Export of Defence Equipment and Dual-Use Goods to Iraq and Related Prosecutions* (conducted by Sir Richard Scott), HC 115 (HMSO)

Senior, D. (1969) *Royal Commission on Local Government in England and Wales 1966–69* – Vol. II Memorandum of Dissent, Cm 4040 (HMSO)

Senior, D. (1972) *Royal Commission on the Constitution* Written Evidence – Volume 8 – England (HMSO)

Sittings of the House Committee (1992) Session 1991–92, HC 20 (HMSO)

Southwood Report (1989) *Report of the Working Party on Bovine Spongiform Encephalopathy* (Department of Health)

Statute Law Society (1972) *The Key to Clarity*, Report of the Stow Hill Committee (Sweet and Maxwell)

Stow Hill Report (1972) *The Key to Clarity* on behalf of the Statute Law Society (Sweet and Maxwell)

Trade and Industry Committee (1986) *The Tin Crisis*, Session 1985–86, HC 305 (HMSO)

Trade and Industry Committee (1992) *Second Report: Exports to Iraq: Project Babylon and Long Range Guns*, Session 1991–92, HC 86 (HMSO)

Trade and Industry Committee (1993) *First Report: British Energy Policy and the Market for Coal*, Session 1992–93, HC 237 (HMSO)

Treasury and Civil Service Committee (TCSC) (1986) *Civil Servants and Ministers: Duties and Responsibilities*, Session 1985–86, HC 92 (HMSO)

TCSC (1990a) *The Civil Service Pay and Conditions of Service Code*, Session 1989–90, HC 260 (HMSO)

TCSC (1990b) *Progress in the Next Steps Initiative*, Session 1989–90, HC 481(HMSO)

TCSC (1991) *The Next Steps Initiative*, Seventh Report 1990–91, HC 496 (HMSO)

TCSC (1993) *The Role of the Civil Service* Session 1992–93, HC 390 (HMSO)

TCSC (1994) *The Role of the Civil Service* Session 1993–94, HC 27 (HMSO)

TCSC (1995) 'The Dual Role of Secretary to the Cabinet and Head of the Home Civil Service', *Minutes of Evidence* (Sir Robin Butler), 8 March 1995, HC 300-i (HMSO)

Waldegrave, W. (1993) Speech to the Public Finance Foundation, 5 July (OPS, Cabinet Office)

Westland Report (1986), *Westland Plc: The Government's Decision Making,* Fourth Report of the Defence Committee, Session 1985–86, HC 519 (HMSO)

Widdicombe (1986a) *The Conduct of Local Authority Business,* Report of the Inquiry into the Conduct of Local Authority Business (chaired by David Widdicombe QC), Cm 9797 (HMSO)

Widdicombe (1986b) *Research Volumes I: The Political Organisation of Local Authorities;* (1986c) *II: The Local Government Councillor;* (1986d) *III: The Local Government Elector;* and (1986e) *IV: Aspects of Local Democracy,* Cms 9798–9801 (HMSO)

Woodcock, Sir J. (1994) *The Escape from Whitemoor Prison,* Cm 2741 (HMSO)

Index

Figures and tables appear in *italic*.

Neill Committee *see* Committee on Standards in
 Public Life
Neuropathogenesis Group, Edinburgh 284
New Britain, The 108
News of the World, The 84
newspapers 84
Newton, Tony 386–7
Next Steps *see* civil service
Nicholl, Duncan 181–2
1922 Committee 109, 381, 410
Nirex 224
Nissan UK 93
Nolan Committee *see* Committee on Standards in
 Public Life
non-departmental public bodies *see* quangos
*Non-Departmental Public Bodies: A Guide for
 Departments* (1992) 221
Norman Conquest 27
Northam, Gerry 285
Northcote-Trevelyan reforms *see* civil service
Northern Ireland 21; 'Bloody Sunday' 161;
 elections 489; paramilitary violence 476; peace
 process 19, 78, 234; proscribed organisations
 461; public records 353; quangos 197, 201,
 202, 221; 'right to silence' 228; 'shoot-to-kill'
 policy 160; Stormont 234; voting rights 24
Northern Ireland Health and Social Services
 Department 241
Northern Ireland Housing Executive *210*
Northern Ireland Office 240, 268
Northern Ireland Standing Advisory Commission
 on Human Rights 228
Northmore, David 80–1
Norton, Philip 378, 381, 383, 385, 409–10
Norton-Taylor, Richard 160, 183–4
Nottinghamshire County Council 457–8
nuclear industry 219, 224
Nuclear Powered Warships Safety Committee
 221, *229*
nuclear weapons 36, 128, 221, *229*, 296
Nuclear Weapons Safety Committee 221, *229*
Nuffield study (1997) 88, 89
No. 10 Downing Street 151, 159, 186, 480

Observer 67, 250, 283–4
Occupational Pensions Board 203
OFFER 202, 203
Office of the Civil Service Commissioners 323
Office of the Data Protection Registrar 202
Office of Fair Trading 202, 218
Office of Passenger Rail Franchising 163, 202
Office of the Rail Regulator 202, 203
Office of Water Services 202, 203
Official Secrets Acts 319, 429; (1911) 353; (1920)
 353; (1989) 352–3
OFGAS 202
OFLOT 202
OFSTED 202
OFTEL 202, 203
Ombudsman 423–8; access to information 353,

360, 362; accountability and 10, 192, 207, 256;
 agencies 196; caseload 425, 446; 'commercial
 confidentiality' 363; departments 163;
 established 423; exceptionalism 423; 'filtering'
 417, 424, 425, 438, 486; Information
 Commissioner and 356; jurisdiction 428;
 limitations 354–5, 365, 369; local government
 260; maladministration and 157, 419; ministers
 and 310, 313, 351; NHS 424–5; policy and
 494; quangos 209–10, 227, 228, 259, 260, 262;
 redress and 13, 19, 207, 262, 419, 457, 486;
 Scott and 369; Select Committee 354, 405,
 407, 418, 424, 425, 426, 427
Ombudsman in Your File, The (1995), 428
OPB 226
OPD 142, 144
openness 17, 18–20, 27, 149, 157, 192, 200, 201,
 207–8, *210*, 211, 212, 334, 342, 477–8, 491–2;
 local government 233, 488; New Labour and
 37; quangos 221, 227–30, 231, 232, 256–60,
 261; regional government 233
opinion polls 43, 81, 83, 85, 90, 102
opposition 371–3, 387
Orders in Council 389
organised interests 120, 121, 151, 271–98, 409
Orwell, George 34
Osmotherly rules *see* civil service
'ouster clauses' 459
Overseas Development Administration 226, 323
Overseas Policy and Defence Committee 36
Overseas Projects Board 220, 225
Owen, Lord 178
Oxford Research Group 364

Paine, Thomas 31
Panorama 95, 285, 286, 287
Parliament Act: (1911) 112, 302, 393, 400, 403,
 482; (1949) 112, 302, 393, 400, 401, 402,
 482
Parliamentary Commissioner Act (1967) 424
Parliamentary Commissioner for Administration
 see Ombudsman
Parliamentary Commissions 82
Parliamentary Intelligence and Security
 Committee 419, 429–30, 438, 483
parliamentary private secretaries 374, 431
parliamentary privilege 406
Parliamentary Questions 320, 322, 333, 336,
 363–4, 371, 405, 431–5, 437, 439, 481
Part, Sir Anthony 168–9, 316
'partial governments' 141, 158, 231, 480
parties: committees 381; development 31; election
 expenditure 88–91; funding 79, 88, 91–6, 98,
 113, 198, 204, 213, 214, 225–6, 397, 474, 483;
 loyalty in Parliament 373–82; party culture
 410; party election broadcasts 86–7; party
 ethos 481; party government 371–3; whips 26,
 86, 134, 135, 159, 313, 373–83, 384, 397, 398,
 401, 402, 404, 408, 410, 431; *see also*
 manifestos

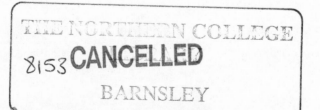

The Three Pillars of Liberty

The companion volume, *The Three Pillars of Liberty*, by Francesca Klug, Keir Starmer and Stuart Weir, provides a thorough audit of British compliance with international human rights standards. The book is the first-ever analysis of both the political and legal systems for securing political freedom in the UK as a whole and provides a detailed description of law and practice with respect to freedom of information; freedom of expression; freedom of assembly and public protest; freedom of association and trade unionism; state surveillance; the right to life and liberty; and the right to vote and stand in elections.

The study measures political freedom and the protection of civil and political rights against a unique Human Rights Index, specially constructed from international human rights instruments, laws and jurisprudence. Its rigorous and systematic review finds both the political and legal systems for protecting citizens' rights wanting and identifies an alarming catalogue of violations and near-violations of international human rights standards.

The Three Pillars of Liberty has been widely praised:

> '*The Three Pillars of Liberty* is vital reading for all people who want an authoritative evaluation of the state of civil liberties and political rights in Britain today. The analysis is lucid, balanced and scholarly'
>
> *Baroness Helena Kennedy QC*

> 'A truly great book'
>
> *Lord Scarman*

> 'This book is of the first importance. Britain was once the leader in recognising and enforcing human and civil rights. It has now fallen behind other nations, but the culture of liberty is still lively here, and what is most needed, to engage it, is thorough information and clear, calm analysis. *The Three Pillars of Liberty* is exactly that. It may turn out to be one of those few documents that makes a difference ...'
>
> *Ronald Dworkin, Professor of Jurisprudence, Oxford University*

> 'The book is a model of clarity ... It seamlessly ties together accessible accounts on leading cases with accounts of the experience of individuals and groups which rarely make it into standard textbooks or the Law Reports. *The Three Pillars* deserves to be read from cover to cover, but works admirably as a reference book ... [it] is a sign that the domestic approach to civil liberties has finally come of age'
>
> *Review in 'Public Law', Winter 1997, by David Taube,*
> *Queen Mary and Westfield College, London*